DisneyAnimation

THE ILLUSION OF LIFE

Disney

THE

ABBEVILLE PRESS • PUBLISHERS • NEW YORK

ANIMATION

ILLUSION OF LIFE

Frank Thomas and Ollie Johnston

This book is dedicated to

Walt Disney

and the staff of artists

who brought the magical quality of life

to character animation

Editor: Walton Rawls
Designer: Nai Y. Chang
Production Director: Howard Morris

LIBRARY OF CONGRESS CATALOGING IN PUBLICATION DATA

Thomas, Frank, 1912–
Disney animation.

Includes index.
1. Walt Disney Productions. 2. Moving-picture cartoons—United States. I. Johnston, Ollie, 1912– II. Title.
NC1766.U52D58 741.5'8'0979494 81-12699
AACR2

ISBN 0-89659-232-4
ISBN 0-89659-233-3 (deluxe ed.)

First edition.

Printed and bound in the United States of America.

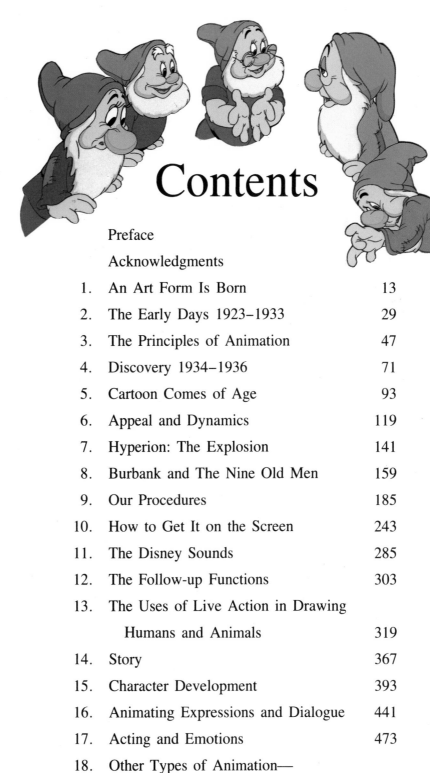

Contents

Preface

This book is about Disney character animation, an art form that created such world-famous cartoon figures as Mickey Mouse and Donald Duck. Disney animation makes audiences really believe in those characters, whose adventures and misfortunes make people laugh—and even cry. There is a special ingredient in our type of animation that produces drawings that appear to think and make decisions and act of their own volition; it is what creates the illusion of life.

No other studio has been able to duplicate this most important (but least understood) element in our films. It cannot be produced by money alone. When a producer says he is going to make a ''Disney-type'' film, he may think that full animation, nice color, and a large budget are all that is needed. But Disney animation is more than drawing, or animating, or storytelling, or painting—it is what this book is all about.

In tracing the development of character animation rather than the studio or the men in it, inevitably we will leave out the names of many fine artists. We regret slighting anyone, but we regret even more having overlooked a key scene in animation history or a special sequence in a picture that would have helped explain and clarify our meaning. It is, perhaps, misleading to credit specific artists with the drawings we show in the book, since this might imply that both the idea and the style came from one person; for this was seldom the case. So much of our own work appears here simply because it was all that was available after so many years. Animators usually do not save the thumbnail sketches, character drawings, and experimental plans that reveal the most important stages in developing a personality or piece of business. In any case, the emphasis here is on the research rather than the people who did the drawings.

One of the most rewarding parts of this project has been the interviews with old friends and colleagues, enabling us to gain perspective and insight on events that had gone whizzing by back when we were too busy to notice or appraise. Occasionally one individual disagreed with another over interpretation and even recollections, but, then, arguments were always daily occurrences when we were making the pictures. That was an important part of the team effort.

Many will look to this book to teach them the secrets of Disney animation so that they can become instant successes. Unfortunately, this craft cannot be learned by just reading a book, and not overnight under any circumstances. Our original intention had been to write a book on how to animate, hoping we could offer inspiration rather than something to copy, but as we did our research it became obvious that there was a greater need to record just how this special kind of animation had developed. Those times were unique and will never be duplicated; yet much of what was learned had been valid in the theater for several hundred years and continues to be valuable wherever there is communication with an audience. We felt that this wealth of knowledge in animation should be preserved.

Ron Miller, executive head of all production at the Disney Studios, hoped to double the staff of animators by 1981, but he found, even after an intensive search, that ''. . . there just aren't that many people capable of doing animation in the Disney style.'' What is the Disney style? Can it be explained? We hope so. This book is written for the student who wants to know how Disney animation was done; for the historian who wants to know why it was done that way; for the artist who has never realized the potential of animation as a profession; for the general public who still wonders, ''What really makes them move?''

We hope that some readers will be stimulated to carry on these traditions and elevate this art form to an ever-higher level.

Acknowledgments

This book belongs to the people, past and present, of Walt Disney Productions, whose cooperation and assistance made it all possible. Special thanks must go to the executives E. Cardon Walker, Ron Miller, and Vince Jefferds, for without their continued support over the four long years we spent putting it together, this book would never have been written.

We wish to thank the many departments who were more helpful than their jobs required. In alphabetical order, they are: the Animation Research Team, under Leroy Anderson, who stored the artwork from each picture in the basement "catacombs"; in Archives, Dave Smith and Paula Sigman, who tracked down information, checked names and dates and spellings and titles and locations; Art Props, whose skills and knowledge in salvaging and presenting materials were invaluable; the ladies in Ink and Paint who furnished us with incredible work on the cels; the dedicated staff in the Library; the crew in Merchandising and Publications, and Don MacLaughlin in particular; the cooperative men in Still Camera and their indomitable leader Dave Spencer. We are indebted to them all. We also are grateful for the encouragement received, in November 1979, from Diane Disney Miller's warm response to our manuscript in its first complete form.

We were very fortunate to have for our editor the patient and scholarly Walton Rawls. His sensitive contributions showed a remarkable understanding of our purposes that was both reassuring and appreciated. Our thanks also go to our sympathetic publisher Robert E. Abrams, whose personal interest in the project and determination to make a quality book of our writings and sketches inspired us to an even more critical approach to our work.

The day after Walt died, Woolie Reitherman said, "From this day on it will never be like it was, but only as each person remembers it." We want to express our appreciation to the following people who helped us remember the way it was:

Ed Aardal
James N. Algar
Ken Anderson
William Anderson
Xavier Atencio
Art Babbitt
Ted Berman
Al Bertino
Carleton (Jack) Boyd
Roger Broggie
Bob Broughton
Les Clark
Ron Clements
Larry Clemmons
Claude Coats
Evelyn Coats
Ed Cook
Bill Cottrell
Art Cruickshank
Jack Cutting
Marc F. Davis
Lou Debney
Al Dempster
Don Duckwall
Becky Fallberg
Vance Gerry
Blaine Gibson
George Goepper
Floyd Gottfredson
Joe Grant
Don Griffith
Betty Ann Guenther
Dave Hand
Ed Hanson
T. Hee
John Hench
Dick Huemer
Wilfred Jackson

Bill Justice
Glen Keane
Richmond (Dick) Kelsey
Katherine Kerwin
Betty Kimball
Ward Kimball
Eric Larson
Fini Littlejohn
Ann Lloyd
Mrs. Ham (Frankie) Luske
Eustace Lycett
Jim Macdonald
Bob McCrea
Bill McFadden
Bob McIntosh
Dave Michener
Clarence Nash
Grim Natwick
Maurice Noble
Cliff Nordberg
Ken O'Brien
Ken O'Connor
Dale Oliver
Bill Peet
Ken Peterson
Elmer Plummer
Martin Provensen
Wolfgang Reitherman
Leo Salkin
Milt Schaffer
Ben Sharpsteen
Mel Shaw
Art Stevens
Sandy Strother
Herb Taylor
Mary Tebb
Ruthie Tompson
Tom Wilhite

1. An Art Form Is Born

Stromboli's ferocious outburst of temper was animated by Vladimir (Bill) Tytla, first animator to achieve strong emotions and convincing acting with the human figure.
FLIP FROM BACK TO FRONT STARTS ON PAGE 53

"Animation can explain whatever the mind of man can conceive." Walt Disney

Man always has had a compelling urge to make representations of the things he sees in the world around him. As he looks at the creatures that share his daily activities, he first tries to draw or sculpt or mold their forms in recognizable fashion. Then, when he becomes more skillful, he attempts to capture something of a creature's movements—a look, a leap, a struggle. And ultimately, he seeks to portray the very spirit of his subject. For some presumptuous reason, man feels the need to create something of his own that appears to be living, that has an inner strength, a vitality, a separate identity—something that speaks out with authority—a creation that gives the illusion of life.

Twenty-five thousand years ago, in the caves of southwestern Europe, Cro-Magnon man made astounding drawings of the animals he hunted. His representations are not only accurate and beautifully drawn, but many seem to have an inner life combined with a suggestion of movement. Since that time, we have been inundated with artists' attempts to shape something in clay or stone or paint that has a life of its own.

Certain artists have achieved marvelous results: sculptures that are bursting with energy, paintings that speak with strong inner forces, carvings and drawings and prints that have captured a living moment in time. But none can do more than suggest what happened just before, or what will happen after that particular moment has passed. Yet, through all the centuries, artists continued to search for a medium of expression that would permit them to capture that elusive spark of life, and in the late 1800s new inventions seemed at last to make this possible. Along with improvements in the motion picture camera and the development of a roll film capable of surviving the harsh mechanisms for projecting its images, a new art form was born: animation. By making sequential drawings of a continuing action

From the earliest days, man has tried to capture in drawings the living quality of the creatures around him.

◁ Pinocchio

ANIMATORS: *John Sewell, Eric Larson*—Bambi.

In animation, powerful movement comes from the drawings in series more than the skillful handling of any single figure.

and projecting their photographs onto a screen at a constant rate, an artist now could create all of the movement and inner life he was capable of.

An artist could represent the actual figure, if he chose, meticulously capturing its movements and actions. Or he could caricature it, satirize it, ridicule it. And he was not limited to mere actions; he could show emotions, feelings, even innermost fears. He could give reality to the dreams of the visionary. He could create a character on the screen that not only appeared to be living but thinking and making decisions all by himself. Most of all, to everyone's surprise, this new art of animation had the power to make the audience actually feel the emotions of a cartoon figure.

What an amazing art form! It is astonishing that so few professionals have investigated its possibilities, for where else does the artist have such opportunities for self expression? There is a new excitement to the familiar elements of drawing and design when they are shown heroic size on a large screen, but, more than that, the addition of movement opens the way to almost unlimited new relationships in all areas. And the wonders continue on into color.

Even the brightest pigments on a painting can reflect back to the viewer only a limited amount of light. Their apparent brightness is relative to itself, a range from dark to light of about 20 to 1. But with the light intensity of the projection lamp and a highly reflective screen, this brightness factor increases to an exciting 200 to 1—ten times as great! Just as the stained glass window had brought dazzling brilliance after centuries of relatively dull frescoes, the introduction of light behind the film made whole new ranges of color available to the artist. Add to this the potential for building color relationships in sequence for stronger emotional response, and the artist has before him an incredible medium for self expression. But rewarding as anima-

tion is, it is also extremely difficult. Still, once an artist sees his drawings come to life on the screen, he will never again be quite satisfied with any other type of expression.

The unique challenge of this art form was aptly described by Vladimir (Bill) Tytla, first animator to bring true emotions to the cartoon screen.[1] "It was mentioned that the possibilities of animation are infinite. It is all that, and yet very simple—but try and do it! There isn't a thing you can't do in it as far as composition is concerned. There isn't a caricaturist in this country who has as much liberty as an animator here of twisting and weaving his lines in and out. . . . But I can't tell you how to do it—I wish I could."

Bill was speaking to a group of young animators who had been asking how he achieved his wonderful results on the screen. He answered simply, "To me it's just as much a mystery as ever before—sometimes I get it—sometimes I don't. I wish I knew, then I'd do it more often.

"The problem is not a single track one. Animation is not just timing, or just a well-drawn character, it is the sum of all the factors named. No matter what the devil one talks about—whether force or form, or well-drawn characters, timing, or spacing—animation is all these things—not any one. What you as an animator are interested in is conveying a certain feeling you happen to have at that particular time. You do all sorts of things in order to get it. Whether you have to rub out a thousand times in order to get it is immaterial."

Conveying a certain feeling is the essence of communication in any art form. The response of the viewer is an emotional one, because art speaks to the heart. This gives animation an almost magical ability to reach inside any audience and communicate with all peoples everywhere, regardless of language barriers. It is one of animation's greatest strengths and certainly one of

◁ Snow White

15

the most important aspects of this art for the young animator to study and master. As artists, we now have new responsibilities in addition to those of draftsman and designer: we have added the disciplines of the actor and the theater. Our tools of communication are the symbols that all men understand because they go back before man developed speech.

Scientist and author Jane Goodall reports that even lesser primates, such as the chimpanzee, have a whole "complex nonverbal communication based on touch, posture, and gesture. . . ." These actions vary from an exchange of greetings when meeting to acts of submission, often with the arm extended and the palm turned down. When a top-ranking male arrives in any

The act of touching is an important part of communication in the chimpanzee world. It has special meaning in our society, too.

From "My Friends the Wild Chimpanzees," by Baroness Jane van Lawick-Goodall. National Geographic

16

group, "the other chimps invariably hurry to pay their respects, touching him with outstretched hands or bowing, just as courtiers once bowed before their king." Miss Goodall describes how a lone male passing a mother and her family responded to her greeting with a touch, "as chimp etiquette demands, then greeted her infant, patting it gently on the head while it looked up at him with big staring eyes."[2]

Some two hundred more signs that clearly display chimpanzee emotions include preening, embracing, charging, kissing, and pounding. Chimps are apt to fling their arms around each other for reassurance, throw things in anger, steal objects furtively, and scream wildly with excitement.[3] Most of these ex-

© 1965 Time, Inc. Photo by John Dominis

Animals in the wild clearly communicate their feelings in body attitudes.

From The Cats of Africa, *Time/Life Publications*

pressions of feelings and language symbols are well known to man, whether they are buried deep in his subconscious or still actively used in his own communicative behavior.

Dogs, too, have a whole pattern of actions not only clearly understood by other dogs but by man as well. Even without using sounds, dogs can convey all of the broad spectrum of emotions and feelings. There is no doubt when a dog is ashamed, or proud, or playful, or sad (or belligerent, sleepy, disgusted, indignant). He speaks with his whole body in both attitude and movement.

The actor is trained to know these symbols of communication because they are his tools in trade. Basically, the animator is the actor in animated films. He is many other things as well; however, in his efforts to communicate his ideas, acting becomes his most important device. But the animator has a special problem. On the stage, all of the foregoing symbols are accompanied by some kind of personal magnetism that can communicate the feelings and attitudes equally as well as the action itself. There is a spirit in this kind of communication that is extremely alive and vital. However, wonderful as the world of animation is, it is too crude to capture completely that kind of subtlety.

If in animation we are trying to show that a character is sad, we droop the shoulders, slump the body, drop the head, add a long face, and drag the feet. Yet those same symbols also can mean that the character is tired, or discouraged, or even listless. We can add a tear and pinpoint our attitude a little better, but that is the extent of our capabilities.

The live actor has another advantage in that he can interrelate with others in the cast. In fact, the producer relies heavily on this. When he begins a live action picture, he starts with two actors of proven ability who will generate something special just by being together. There will be a chemistry at work that will create charisma, a special excitement that will elicit an immediate response from the audience. The actors will each project a unique energy simply because they are real people.

By contrast, in animation we start with a blank piece of paper! Out of nowhere we have to come up with characters that are real, that live, that interrelate. We have to work up the chemistry between them (if any is to exist), find ways to create the counterpart of charisma, have the characters move in a believable manner, and do it all with mere pencil drawings. That is enough challenge for anybody.

These problems would seem to create considerable difficulties for achieving the communication claimed for animation. How can it work so wonderfully? It does it in a very simple way through what we call ''audience involvement.'' In our own lives, we find that as we get to know people we share their experiences—we sympathize, we empathize, we enjoy. If we love them, we become deeply concerned about their welfare. We become involved in their lives.

We involve the audiences in our films the same way. We start with something they know and like. This can be either an idea or a character, as long as it is familiar and appealing. It can be a situation everyone has experienced, an emotional reaction universally shared, a facet of someone's personality easily recognized, or any combination of these. But there must be something that is known and understood if the film is to achieve audience involvement.

In the great days of radio, there were many programs presented in such a special, intimate way that they drew the listening audience into their stories completely. The mystery programs were particularly good at this, using voices that reached out to you—and good sound effects: heavy breathing up close to the microphone, echoing footsteps, a creaky. door; you were held spellbound. The broadcasts were projected through symbols into your imagination, and *you* made the situation real. It was not just what you heard, it was what the sounds made you believe and feel. It was not the actor's emotions you were sensing anymore. They were *your* emotions.

Fortunately, animation works in the same way. It is capable of getting inside the heads of its audiences, into their imaginations. The *audiences* will make our little cartoon character sad—actually, far sadder than we could ever draw him—because in their minds that character is *real*. He lives in their imaginations. Once the audience has become involved with your characters and your story, almost anything is possible.

For a character to be that real, he must have a per-

Dumbo

TIME CHART   1923 to 1933

1923 ───

Walt makes *Alice's Wonderland* in Kansas City. In August, Walt comes to Hollywood.
Contract for Alice series. Forms company with brother Roy.

1924 ───

Joined by Ub Iwerks and friends from Kansas City. Turn out one picture a month.

Series successful,
staff grows to 12.

1925 ───

New contract for one picture every three weeks. Buy property on Hyperion Ave. Start building.

1926 ───

Move to new studio on Hyperion.

1927 ───

Complete last *Alice* film, start new series with *Oswald the Lucky Rabbit*.

1928 ───

After 26 pictures, Walt loses rights to Oswald. Starts new series with Mickey Mouse.

SOUND COMES IN ── ── ── ── ── ── ── ── ── ── ── ── ── ── ── ── ── ── ──

Nov. 18, *Steamboat Willie* opens in New York.

1929 ───

More space needed,
building expanded.

Use of sound makes Disney's foremost cartoon studio. Animators from New York begin arriving.
First Silly Symphony—*Skeleton Dance*. *Mickey's Choo Choo*, animated train engine.

1930 ───

Staff increases to 30.

Chain Gang, has dog that later became Pluto.

New buildings added for
animators, plus sound
stage.

1931 ───

Ugly Duckling, example of stronger stories. First layout man hired.

1932 ───

Flowers and Trees, first cartoon in color. Start of art school at night.

Personnel passes 100!

1933 ───

Three Little Pigs. Astounding success finances expansion and more study. Bottom of Depression.

sonality, and, preferably, an interesting one. He must be as comfortable as an old shoe, yet as exciting as a new spring outfit. Spectators can laugh at a gag, be dazzled by a new effect, and be intrigued by something completely fresh, but all of this will hold their attention for barely ten minutes. As Charlie Chaplin said of his own beginnings in the movie business, "Little as I knew about movies, I knew that nothing transcended personality."[4] In addition to gags and effects, there must be a point of entry through which audiences can identify with the story situation, and the best way is through a character who is like someone they have known. He can be more heroic, or bigger than life, or "meaner than sin," but basically he has to be human enough for the audience to understand him and identify with the problems he faces in the story.

The great American mime and artist Angna Enters[5] used to give her class the assignment of writing a postcard under imagined circumstances, because it is an action devoid of any interest whatsoever without the addition of personality. But once a strong personality is introduced great possibilities suddenly become apparent.

To begin with, it helps to develop a situation in which your imagined personality can function. Say that you are starting out on a tour; it is morning and the bus is ready to leave. You have been urged to hurry up, but just then you remember that you forgot to put the cat out before leaving home! You must write a quick note to your neighbor who has the key, asking her to take care of things. Now, how would you write the card? If you have chosen a nervous, insecure, and disorganized personality in the first place, you will have almost unlimited bits of business to show all facets of the character—the confusion, the panic, the fear of being left behind, the inability to phrase words so that they make any sense, the flutter of imminent chaos, the desperation.

Or suppose the person writing the card is highly indignant because a computer insists that he has not paid a certain bill and has just sent him his last notice. Now the words must be chosen with care. The computer and the company that has been stupid enough to own it must be told off in no uncertain terms. There will be no recourse from the incisive accusations you

are setting down. You could be gleeful, enjoying each cruel word. Or you could be triumphant as you think of better, stronger, more biting words. Or you could be trembling with rage at the whole idea of the terrible effrontery of this mechanical age.

Suppose the writer were lovesick and writing to his dream girl—probably the third such note that morning. A silly smile might become fixed on his face as he reveled in each sugary word. With half-closed eyes and heavy sighs, he would gaze into space seeing a momentary vision of her precious face. There would be kissing of the card when he was finished, even a reluctance to drop it into the mailbox until he had sighed one last time and kissed the beloved name just once more.

It is easy to see how the development of an individual personality in a story situation can make even the dullest action become entertaining. In addition to the personality, however, there should be a change in the initial action that will enable an animator to show more than one side of this personality. The most interesting character in the world is not very exciting when sitting and listening to a symphony concert. Our true personalities are best revealed by our reactions to a change we did not expect.

Take a simple example of a golfer getting ready to make a crucial shot. He shows concentration and deter-

ANIMATOR: *Fred Spencer*— Donald's Golf Game.

Adversity brings out the true personality of the cartoon character.

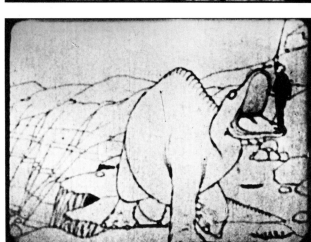

mination as he prepares for the important swing. Then, suppose he misses the ball entirely. His true character will be revealed at once! If he is Donald Duck, he will fly into a rage and blame the ball. If he is insecure and nervous, he will blame the club and promptly break it over his knee. Or, if he is a popular amateur who has been off his game but has a sympathetic gallery trying to encourage him, his response will be bitter dejection, and you will have pathos in your story.

Our goal in these studies is to make the audience *feel* the emotions of the characters, rather than appreciate them intellectually. We want our viewers not merely to enjoy the situation with a murmured, "Isn't he cu-ute?" but really to feel something of what the character is feeling. If we succeed in this, the audience will now care about the character and about what happens to him, and that is audience involvement. Without it, a cartoon feature will never hold the attention of its viewers.

The various aspects of what animation is, what it could do, and how it worked were learned slowly over the years. They were certainly not evident when the art form was first discovered, except in the epic works of Winsor McCay, the *New York Herald*'s skillful cartoonist. Working essentially alone, he turned out several astounding films between 1911 and 1921, with some cartoon figures so convincing that he was accused of tracing them from photographs. In response, McCay drew a dinosaur for his next film, and, incidentally, discovered the importance of a cartoon character's personality in establishing rapport with the audience. Today his films are historic classics, but in their time they were not commercially successful, and that forced McCay to return to newspaper work. His creations were virtually forgotten for fifty years.

Others entering the animation field lacked McCay's awesome talents, and few attempted anything more than what was commercially acceptable. After all, in those early days, movies were still a novelty and cartoons were added to the program only for amusement. They were not an important part of the show, and very little money came back to the studios that made them. Audiences responded to the gags and preposterous situations, so creative energies went into a search for different approaches, fresh angles, new tricks, rather than into making better pictures. When the men in a

studio found a gimmick that was successful, they hung onto it tenaciously. Max Fleischer had his "Out of the Inkwell" series, and Pat Sullivan's studio produced Otto Messmer's films of "Felix the Cat." Animated comic strips, illustrated jokes, live action retimed and combined with drawings, and a variety of other efforts were made to assure contract renewal for a struggling studio.

Of all the early pictures, only the films about Felix suggested the idea of giving a character personality, but his creators had failed to develop this past rudimentary beginnings, relying instead on visual tricks that got audience response. Nothing then gave a clue to what animation might someday become, and no promising artists were attracted to the studios. Most people felt that by 1923 just about everything had been done that was possible, and the exhibitors were looking in other directions for something new to keep their audiences laughing.

This was the situation when Walt Disney entered the field, and he was not an immediate success. In fact, it is even surprising that he was able to get a toehold in this tough business of limited contracts and tight money. But Walt was a fighter and had great determination; he was no aesthetic artist living in a dream world. As he said, "I have been up against tough competition all my life. I wouldn't know how to get along without it." Any man with Walt's talents but without his spirit and tenacity would never have made it.

There were constant battles, many defeats, endless disappointments: he lost the rights to his cartoon character, his staff, his contracts. And then when he finally began to achieve a bit of success, his studio became a prize to be taken over one way or another, or run out of business! Union jurisdictional problems plagued him as he developed new techniques, new equipment, and new ideas in entertainment. Yet through it all he never lost his love for people or his faith in their judgment. "I am interested in entertaining people, in bringing pleasure, particularly laughter, to others, rather than being concerned with 'expressing' myself with obscure creative impressions."

Through those first years, Walt and his brother Roy[6] struggled alone against the people who controlled the movie industry. In later decades when Walt's back

was to the wall he had the strong support of his staff, whose loyalty and dedication to both their boss and their work kept them making sacrifices through days of uncertainty. When it came right down to it, most of us were more interested in keeping animation alive than we were in making money. We were beginning to sense the magnitude of the art form that we were discovering, and its potential held us like a magnet.

Walt was basically a communicator, and in the animated film he found astounding potential for expressing his ideas. The cartoon drawing always had been a very simple and direct graphic form, and whether it was for social comment or just amusement it had to present a unified, single idea with nothing complicated, extraneous, or contradictory in its makeup. When the cartoon was transferred to film these elements still applied, and nothing was drawn that was not part of the idea. Background, costume, character, and expression were all designed for a succinct statement. Behind the character there was only a horizon, or a house, or a rock to run into, but that was all.

To include only objects that were needed for the idea became the basis for a language of drawings on film. Walt took to this naturally, and if any of his staff introduced something wrong or confusing or vague, he was quick to notice and to educate the offender. Walt gradually added the more sophisticated graphic symbols of acting, presenting complicated ideas that had to be understood very quickly. We used to indicate how successfully drawings communicated these thoughts by saying that they either "read" or "didn't read." John Hench,[7] one of the studio's most gifted artists, said "We don't really know how much we learned here about using images to communicate—to develop a kind of visual literacy." At the time, none of us thought in those terms or stopped long enough to gain perspective on what was happening. The language of imagery was emerging as a separate art form of its own, requiring skills and disciplines different from those of related crafts. Not every artist could master the demands, and most failed to realize that they were involved in something quite different and exacting.

"I think this is a little hard for people to understand," John continued, "the fact that you are developing a kind of language, and a very precise one. They figure that graphics are not precise at all—they're

TIME CHART   1934 to 1943

1934

Another building for animation.

Personnel passes 200.

New wave of artists starts coming. Action analysis, classes, lectures. *Playful Pluto*, a character *thinks*! *Flying Mouse*. *Goddess of Spring*. *Wise Little Hen* introduces Donald Duck.

Snow White
story

1935

Building for Ink & Paint.

Personnel passes 400.

Band Concert, first Mickey in color.
Cookie Carnival. *Broken Toys*.
Golden Touch. *Who Killed Cock Robin?*

experimental animation

1936

Mickey's Grand Opera. *Elmer Elephant*.
Three Little Wolves. *Thru the Mirror*.
Alpine Climbers. *Country Cousin*.

full crew

Pinocchio
story

1937

Another animation building.

Personnel passes 800.

Hawaiian Holiday.
Clock Cleaners.
The Old Mill.
Animation on *Brave Little Tailor*.

Sorcerer's Apprentice grows into

animation

December 1937

1938

Walt decides to make one feature a year.

Animation on *Practical Pig*,
The Pointer, *Goofy & Wilbur*,
Ugly Duckling.

Fantasia
story

animation stopped

more story work
animation started

Personnel passes 1000.

Bambi
story

animation

1939

Burbank Studio finished; staff moves as work is completed on *Fantasia*.

Dumbo
story

experimental animation

full crew

1940

February 1940

animation

November 1940

1941

War in Europe takes foreign market. Staff cut to 700.

October 1941

1942

Pinocchio, Fantasia, Bambi all lose money at box office. Golden Age is over.

August 1942

1943

just sort of decorative, they're pleasant to look at, they're aesthetic—instead of understanding what the basic thing is about 'image.' I don't know how else anyone could get this except in motion pictures, and, particularly, in cartoons—you sure don't get it in an art school.''

It is impossible to judge the films that were made, or the animation that was done, or even what is worth preserving in the methods that were used, without an understanding of this language of imagery that spoke so clearly from the screen—not drawings by themselves or paintings or isolated antics, but the visual symbols of communication. When the outstanding violinist Isaac Stern was asked the difference between the great and the truly great, he replied, ''The ability to communicate.'' It is the key ingredient in every art form and certainly the great strength of Walt Disney's genius.

Walt was also a gambler when it mattered most. If he believed in an idea, he would risk absolutely everything to get it before the public. But he was also practical enough to work with what he had, rather than wait for what he wished he had. He would say, ''I don't know if it's art, but I know I like it,'' and he felt intuitively that if he liked it the rest of the world would like it, too—if only he could find the right way to present it.

Walt had a restless nature and never liked to do the same things twice. As he said of himself, ''I can never stand still. I must explore and experiment. I am never satisfied with my work. I resent the limitations of my own imagination.'' Where others felt lucky if they could hang on to what they had, Walt was constantly searching for new ways, better ways, and, especially, ways that his small group of artists could handle. As many of them agreed in later years, ''One of Walt's greatest gifts was his ability to get you to come up with things you didn't know were in you and that you'd have sworn you couldn't possibly do!''[8]

As the audience response verified Walt's convictions about entertainment, he was able to fight for better contracts that brought in a little more money. Now he could begin to add to his staff men who had been better trained and artists who had a greater variety of talents. The Depression had begun, and young artists were faced with a bleak future, if any at all, in the commercial fields. The only two places for employ-

ment were the government-financed WPA and Disney's. In ten years the studio went from the raw vitality and crude, clumsy actions of *Steamboat Willie* to the surprising sophistication and glowing beauty of *Snow White*. Together we at the Disney Studio had discovered many things about communicating with an audience. We were still to learn much more.

We continued to experiment with many approaches to filmmaking and different uses of animation, from ''stop motion'' with cut outs, limited movement, stylized design, puppets, and 3-D, to the full cel animation. Whatever the method, the pictures that got the biggest response in the theaters were always the ones that achieved audience involvement by telling definite stories through rich personalities.

It had begun with Mickey and Pluto, a cartoon boy and his dog, who appeared to think and suggested the spirit of life. Then, the ''Silly Symphonies'' portrayed emotions in their characters, and there had been a feeling of life. Finally, in the telling of feature-length tales about specific characters who were convincingly real, the full illusion of life was achieved.

The illusion of life is a rare accomplishment in animation, and it was never really mastered anywhere except at the Disney Studio. Of all the characters and stories and exciting dimensions of entertainment to come from that incubator of ideas, this is the truly unique achievement. This is what must be examined and explained, understood and appreciated, taught to others and passed on to the animators of the future.

It came from new ways of thinking, ways of making a drawing, ways of relating drawings to each other—all

1928 to 1937, the decade that brought a spectacular advance in the cartoon—from novelty to art form.

the refinements in this language of imagery. But it also came from new ways of looking at stories. Ours were not written down in the usual way; they were drawn, because a few stimulating pictures could suggest far more about the potential entertainment in an episode than any page of words. More than that, our stories were kept flexible until long after the first animation had been done. Often a whole new character would appear from nowhere and take over the story. When we started *Snow White*, there was no Dopey in the cast, *Pinocchio* had no Jiminy Cricket, and *Bambi* had no Thumper. All of these characters evolved as the pictures developed. As Walt said, ''The best things in many of our pictures have come after we thought the story was thoroughly prepared. Sometimes we don't really get close to our personalities until the story is in animation.''

It was never too late to make a change; nothing was ever set as long as the possibility existed that it could be made to relate better to the overall picture or communicate more strongly with the audience. We struggled to build interesting, appealing characters, but most of all we worked to find ways to make the audience *feel* the emotions of the animated figures—emotions the audience could ''relate to, identify with, and become involved in.''

All of this took study and desire and knowledge and inspiration and months of selection and building, but that is true of any great artistic accomplishment. Fine works have never been achieved easily nor without the exercise of constant critical judgment. That is why the world's greatest mime, Marcel Marceau, says of his own work, ''It takes years of study. You can't just walk out on the stage and do it.''

Marcel Marceau also said that his teacher, Etienne Decroux, had told him that the principles of communication with an audience were the same ones in use 2,000 years ago; they had been handed down from teacher to student ever since. The entertainer's ''symbols'' that bring audience identification and arouse sympathetic feelings, as well as techniques used to portray emotions, to please, to excite, to captivate, and to entertain, have always been known by some. At Disney's we learned them painfully and slowly by trial and error. Although we had the greatest of leaders, he was not strictly a teacher. Still, by learning the rules this way we learned them thoroughly, and sometimes we think we may have added a few footnotes of our own to the historic lore of the theater.

Most of our work has been in only one small part of the vast field of animation. There are so many areas to be explored, drawings to be tried, emotions to be captured, effects to be created, new wonders to be seen. It is an exciting prospect. With electronic aids being perfected and new tools and materials being used, who can possibly foresee what lies ahead? It probably will not be another Walt Disney who will lead the way, but someone or some group of artists will surely discover new dimensions to delight and entertain the world. Hopefully, this book will be their springboard.

From the left, Dopey, Jiminy, and Thumper: three favorite characters that were not in the original scripts. Each was added to the cast after animation already had begun.

ARTIST: *Ollie Johnston.*

ARTIST: *Ward Kimball.*

ARTIST: *Frank Thomas*

27

◁ Peter Pan

ALICE'S SPOOKY ADVENTURE

A WALT DISNEY COMIC

M.J. WINKLER
DISTRIBUTOR, N.Y.
WINKLER PICTURES

2. The Early Days 1923–1933

"At first the cartoon medium was just a novelty, but it never really began to hit until we had more than tricks . . . until we developed personalities. We had to get beyond getting a laugh. They may roll in the aisles, but that doesn't mean you have a great picture. You have to have pathos in the thing."
Walt Disney

When Walt Disney first came to Hollywood he had no intention of continuing to make animated cartoons. He had done that kind of work in Kansas City, achieving only meager success with his Laugh-O-Grams and none at all with his first film, *Alice's Wonderland*. Now he wanted to try something that offered a greater outlet for his continuous stream of creative ideas: Walt intended to be a movie director in one of the big studios. It was only after his money ran out and he was yet to be appreciated by the major producers that he was forced to return to the one thing that previously had paid his bills. Disappointing as this must have been for Walt, it was extremely fortunate for everyone else. Although he was interested in many different aspects of the entertainment world—as he demonstrated in later life—animation was truly the perfect outlet for his special imagination and sense of fantasy. Still, the year 1923 was a particularly bleak one to be entering that field.

As a showcase of his work, Walt had one completed film, *Alice's Wonderland*, and when he sent it off to a cartoon distributor he was surprised to receive, in return, a contract for twelve more films. This was a startling beginning, and if one planned films carefully, watched expenses, and cut every conceivable corner, it was possible to make a profit. But Walt was not interested in cutting corners. It was typical of him that anything he went into had to be the best, and not just the best of what was currently being done, but the best it was possible to do. This always made the job of pleasing him very difficult, since the drawing that had been praised on Tuesday was regarded as only a stepping-stone to something better on Wednesday.

All his money went into films and the development of a studio, as Walt began collecting a staff likely to

Walt Disney's first contract was for a series of films featuring a live girl working with cartoon animals. Walt's partner and key animator, Ub Iwerks, drew the advertising posters.

29

◁ Alice *series poster*

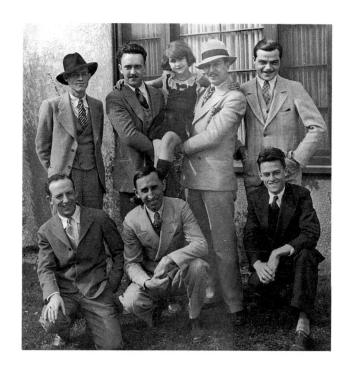

The staff in 1927. Front row from left, Friz Freleng, Roy Disney, Hugh Harman. Back row, Walker Harman, Ub Iwerks, Margie Gay, Walt Disney, Rudy Ising.

grow along with him. Ben Sharpsteen,[1] first of the animators to come out from New York, said, "I needed a job with a future, and I did not see a promising future at these other studios. But Walt was different. His high regard for the animation medium and his determination to produce a superior product greatly appealed to me." Walt had no idea then what those superior pictures might be or how he would go about making them; he had no plans and no specific stories, just the conviction that they were going to be the best cartoons anyone had ever seen.

Of course, this was not a new or unique aim. Many of the men in New York had tried constantly to improve the quality of animation. Art classes in the evenings were furnished by Raoul Barré at his studio to help improve the drawing ability of his artists. Occasionally, an animator would have an opportunity to study a specific action carefully, and everybody would be awed by the animation that followed. Still, it was difficult

for the average cartoonist really to know how to improve his work. The fun of animating, of doing gags, of thinking up funny business took precedence over the long-term, seemingly distant rewards of self-improvement. In many cases, the aspiring artist whose curiosity kept him seeking more and more knowledge often found himself the subject of ridicule from his co-workers. Bill Tytla was asked, "What the hell do you want to go to art school for—you're animating, aren't you?"

They could not know it at the time, but actually there was little chance for these cartoonists to improve, given the type of material they were animating. The spot gags, stereotyped figures, absence of personality in the characters, and slipshod method of working gave the artists little opportunity to use any new-found knowledge. Even the greatest of animators would have withered under such limited demands. This is as true today as it was then: there must be story business that calls for good animation or there will be no well-animated scenes.

In 1923, the animated figure was moved as little as possible in a cartoon, and then only to reach the location for the next gag. If his feet went up and down, he was walking. If they went up and down fast, he was running. As often as possible, the animators cut to a scene with the characters in place to "pull the gag," and then cut away afterward to the next set-up. How the gag was staged was very important and given careful thought, but the movement was considered more a chore than an opportunity for entertainment. There was no attempt either to imitate real action or to caricature it. Better work had been done earlier, especially by Winsor McCay, but no one knew how it had been done. A few wished to improve, but where could they study? Who could teach?

It was even more difficult for beginners to learn what tricks already had been discovered. The lead

Before the days of realism, Oswald's arms merely grew until he could reach his objective.

animators guarded their secrets carefully, never revealing their private devices to anyone. What you learned you had to learn by yourself as best you could.

At Walt's studio it was different. He insisted on an open atmosphere where each artist shared his views and discoveries. If one man made a drawing Walt liked, he called everyone together to point it out. Or if an action seemed clumsy or poorly staged, he would direct the artist immediately to get help from a stronger man. All the desks were in one large room at the time (which encouraged discussions of one type or another anyway), so the animators talked about their art and their problems and what the future of the studio might be. Even in those days, Walt was moving so fast into uncharted areas that his men were hard put to keep up with him. No one could deny that Walt was exceedingly stimulating and exciting to be around.

There was another factor besides talent and ability that was to play a major part in Walt's success. It was his background as a farmboy living close to the soil and working with animals, which had given him a philosophy and approach to entertainment with a universal appeal. He never put on airs, was always sincere and honest, and these basic values permeated his work. Although his tastes have been called mundane by some, he always sought quality and style. Walt said that he wanted his pictures to reflect the "feeling of happy excitement I had when I was a kid." And that spirit flowed through all the projects he touched.

There was one last custom that enabled the Disney animators to forge far ahead, and this seems to have been quite accidental. They used pegs at the bottom of their drawing boards to hold their work in place, while in the East top pegs always had been the rule. It had seemed logical to put the pegs at the top of the board, out of the way of the artist's hand, and no one recalls why Walt started to use bottom pegs back in Kansas City. No one knows why Ub Iwerks[2] and the other early animators continued to put up with the little obstructions that continually nicked their wrists and hands, but without this chance procedure animation might never have developed into a vital, forceful, and varied art form.

The reason for this is more subjective than literal. Drawings can be made almost as easily with either top or bottom pegs, and, while relationships in the action

A new team of animators is trained by Ub Iwerks. From the left, Johnny Cannon, Jack Cutting, Wilfred Jackson, Ub, and Les Clark.

Los Angeles artist Dick Lundy, in far left corner, is surrounded by the first group of animators from New York. Beside him are Norm Ferguson and Jack King. Behind him are Bert Gillett, Merle Gilson, and, in front, Ben Sharpsteen.

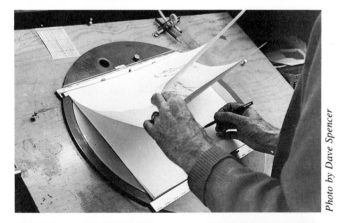

Photo by Dave Spencer

It is impossible to flip more than one drawing at a time when the paper is held by pegs at the top of the board.

Photo by Dave Spencer

When bottom pegs are used, five papers can be "rolled" at a time, enabling the animator to correct the relationships and strengthen action as he makes the drawings.

are more difficult to see when the paper is held at the top, much of the action can be portrayed almost as well. But there comes a time when the drawings are near completion that it is necessary to "feel" the life supposed to be in them. This can be done only by "rolling" the drawings back and forth, with one finger between each of any five drawings. The action is checked forward and backward in minute detail or in broad relationships. Drawings 12 frames apart can be checked against each other to see whether they really give the illusion of the action wanted, and then all the subtler secondary actions can be studied frame by frame.

A whole stack of drawings can be lifted off the pegs and flipped in sequence to give a good check on the overall scene, but the only way an animator can tell if his character is acting as the scene was conceived is to roll the drawings while feeling the action in his own body. Usually the animator tries to feel the action as he makes the initial drawings, and many a night he goes home with a stiff neck or a wrenched back after animating a dog in a quizzical look or a startled duck whirling about in astonishment. It is possible to do a very nice scene simply through careful planning and hard thinking, but without being able to roll through the drawings it is impossible to get that extra juice that produces the illusion of life.

This "rolling" action became so important during the mid-thirties that many an artist tried to enlarge his capabilities of handling more than a mere five drawings at a time. Many tried to involve both hands in the procedure, but that lost them the possibility of making pencil corrections or additions at the same time, unless they had been trained to draw with their teeth. Even that was attempted. Those were days of invention and

enthusiasm—nothing was impossible.

Walt had grown up watching the great vaudeville acts of the time, acts that had taken years to perfect before an audience, among them "Willie, West and McGinty" and "Joe Jackson and his bicycle," and also the work of the great clowns like Emmett Kelley. Walt admired Chaplin and the other film comedians, Keaton, Lloyd, and Langdon, and he quickly understood a basic truth of comedy: the personality of the victim of a gag determines just how funny the whole incident will be. For instance, falling into an open manhole is not funny in itself. A little old lady trying to sell her last bunch of violets would get a very concerned response to such a tumble. An eager Boy Scout who fell while demonstrating courtesy to his troop by helping a little girl across the street might draw some chuckles, as long as he was not hurt by the fall. But an arrogant construction boss who had just ridiculed some worker for not watching what he was doing would be certain to get a laugh. Marcel Marceau used a simpler example: if a dignified man slips on a banana peel, it is funny. If it happens to a man who is down and out, it is not.

Walt also realized that it was better to build on a gag and let the situation develop than to move quickly to another gag. And most important of all, the thing that really got to an audience was their knowing how the character on stage felt about what was happening to him: the "looks" at the camera, the "burn," the rage, the helpless stare, the bleak expression. Laurel and Hardy used these reactions extensively, and Edgar Kennedy was well known for his burn of mounting anger. Years later, Jack Benny became famous for his ability to provoke sustained laughter by merely looking blankly out at the audience. Of course, the situation

Mickey jumps with joy—but without effort, thrust, or weight.

SHORTEN ACTION

Mickey's acting shows Walt's great interest in personality and the challenges he gave to his animators. Ub Iwerks made the layout and Walt described the embarrassed attitude wanted in the scene.

had to be built very carefully and cleverly for this business to be effective, but the humor of the situation lay in the look on Benny's face and the knowledge of how he felt.

Other comedians knew the value of this device. Walter Kerr in his book, *The Silent Clowns*,[3] points out that Chaplin took care to establish himself as one of us, as belonging to the world of the audience rather than the characters on the screen. He shared everything with us—from delight to distress—and this is the

In the twenties, emotions were shown in a very elemental way. Mickey expresses anger and disgust in Steamboat Willie.

33

quality that Walt intuitively reached for even before the days of Mickey Mouse.

In his first films, the characters look at the camera and shrug, or have an embarrassed, toothy smile, or register consternation with worried brows and sweat pouring off their faces in a stream of droplets. To those of us who knew Walt, it was obvious that he had acted out each situation and, crude as that early animation was, we could visualize him up there showing how it ought to be done.

Walt's gags were intrinsically no better than any other studio's, but they were staged better, with more care taken to establish the situation. There was more concern for detail, for building comedy, for making the gag pay off, but, most important, for understanding the feelings of the characters involved in the gags. The desolation when things went wrong, the happy, bouncy walk when things went right, annoyance with indignities, determination, scheming, fear, panic, compassion —these were things that could be animated! This was acting, and it gave the animator a chance to use his medium effectively—in timing, in caricature, and in action. Animation began to come alive, and when the audiences recognized familiar situations they began to identify with the characters' predicaments. They laughed harder and remembered.

When *Reader's Digest* wanted a biographical sketch written on Walt, the magazine hired Richard Collier, who already had two successful credits in this field, one on Mussolini and the other on Captain Booth of the Salvation Army. While at the studio, Collier was asked if there was anything at all that these three men had in common. His answer was a quick and definite affirmative. "All of them had the ability to get other people to work for them, and not just a few friends but many people of diverse interests and backgrounds, very unlikely people, all working with each other for this one man!" Years later when Walt was asked what he considered his greatest achievement, he replied simply, "Building an organization and holding it." It was a real accomplishment.

Walt had started with the amazingly talented Ub Iwerks and a few friends from Kansas City, but none of them really knew anything about animation or how to make a film. He had picked up one or two young fellows working around Hollywood, but it was not until he was able to bring out men from the New York studios that he finally had some professionals to help improve the product. Typical of Walt, he told them what to do right from the start.

Wilfred Jackson,[4] who had come to the studio in 1928, recalled their reaction, "Some of them felt he was a little rough with them at times. Walt could make you feel real bad when he wanted to. I don't remember them rebelling when he told them to do it different, or asked for better animation. . . . Walt was a very persuasive individual and a very inspiring person and he had the ability to make you want to do what he wanted you to do."

These early animators were not artists as much as they were entertainers. But the field of entertainment is wide, and any thought that it refers only to humor is very limiting. Walt's ideas of entertainment went far beyond gags: he sought the new, the novel, the unexpected, the beautiful, and the colorful situation with warmth. Instead of thinking of cartoon material as being "entertaining," one might find a better concept in the word "captivating." Audiences have to be

impressed, absorbed, involved, taken out of themselves, made to forget their own worlds and lose themselves in ours for cartoons to succeed. Walt had to find actions that were funny in themselves yet easily recognized as something familiar, gags that were plausible even though very imaginative, situations that were based on everyone's experience, and characters that had interesting personalities. These were the things that could hold an audience, and to Walt they added up to one simple approach—a caricature of realism. He could be endlessly innovative, exploring all facets of the entertainment world, as long as he remembered always to captivate the audience by making it all believable—by making it real.

"As far back as I can remember," Wilfred Jackson said, "Walt wanted his drawings that were animated to seem to be real things that had feelings and emotions and thoughts, and the main thing was that the audience would believe them and that they would care what happened to them . . . and he used to stress that!" Ben Sharpsteen expressed it this way: "I think that Walt was initially inspired by animation that stressed personality. The strong impression that it made on him led to his desire to plus it in subsequent pictures. This was one of the biggest factors in the success of our early pictures; Walt recognized the value of personality animation and he stressed it in story development."

As animation, the work done in the twenties was undeniably crude, but the animators never failed to present the point of the scene clearly, and they chose the right symbols to show the attitudes of their figures. Nevertheless, there was no weight, no attempt at anatomy, no shoulders or spines or bones or muscles. The story points called for no analysis of anything beyond the staging of the business. It is small wonder that Walt started asking for realism. If an arm had to encircle a large object, it merely was stretched until long enough to do the job. If Mickey was supposed to beckon to Minnie, the shortness of his arm made the hand look as if it were scratching his nose, so the animator simply drew the arm long enough to get the hand clear of the head, out where the gesture could be seen.

One day, almost by accident, someone made a series of drawings that looked far better than anything done before. Each drawing had so close a relationship to the one preceding that "one line would follow through to the next." Les Clark,[5] who had come to the studio in 1927, told of how amazed everyone was that just making the lines flow through each drawing in a series could make such a difference. Instead of the staccato action produced by a group of poorly related drawings, suddenly there was a pleasing smoothness that led the eye from drawing to drawing. "This was really an exciting thing that we discovered!"

Many problems could not then be solved. Everyone knew that it was necessary to get a feeling of weight in the characters and their props if ever they were to be convincing, but just drawing a figure large has nothing to do with how heavy he is. A weather balloon is quite large. The animators sensed that the key to the illusion of weight lay in the timing and how far a character moved and how fluid the action was, but it was not until they were able to study live action films that the solution finally was found. Once the secrets were discovered, the animators wondered why the problem had been so difficult, but in those days the answers had eluded them.

ANIMATOR: *Ub Iwerks—* Steamboat Willie.

1928— *Mickey picks up a whole family of weightless pigs. The animator had no knowledge—or concern— about bones and muscles; his job was to create sprightly movement that put over the gag.*

If an animator's drawings finally reflected a more natural way of moving, Walt would be likely to say, "Your guy just moves in and he's there. . . . I don't see him do anything. Y'know, a guy can be funny the way he does things. Look at your comedians and clowns, they've all got funny ways they walk or funny timing—there's something there. We oughta be looking for entertaining ways of doing things. We don't want to get straight, y'know—we're not copying nature!"

"Caricature" and "exaggeration" were two favorite words to stimulate the animator's approach to his scene. These words could be misinterpreted as a request for wild, uncontrolled action, but that course always ended up with, "Look, you're not getting the idea of what we're after here!" The action had to be based on realism, had to fit the story situation, put over the point of the scene, and be in character with other things being done in different scenes. And when the animator felt he was getting close to handling that correctly, he encountered another admonition. "You're trying to do too much in the scene. Nothing comes off strong because the character is all over the place."

An animator had to choose the best action for the spot in the picture, refine it to the simplest statement, do it the best he could, make the drawing work for everything he was trying to say, keep the personality in the movement, use enough anatomy to be convincing, and do it all in an entertaining way. That really is not asking too much if one appreciates what any good actor or mime has to consider constantly. But those early animators were just beginners. As one recalled without malice, "It didn't matter how many times you did it over, Walt had to get what he wanted."[6]

Signs were made to help animators remember what they had learned:

"Don't confuse them. Keep it simple."
"Too much action spoils the acting."
"Mushy action makes a mushy statement."
"Say something. Be brave."

One man had a sign, "Why would anyone want to look at that?" which was a constant reminder that he should be sure he was putting something up on the screen that was worth another person's time or money to watch. Whenever he thought he had a great idea, that sign seemed to ask, "Really now, would anyone other than your mother like it?"

Many authors have reported that animation was the one thing that Walt could not do. As he himself realized quite early, plenty of other artists could draw better than he, but none of them seemed to have his wealth of ideas or the knowledge of how a piece of business should be presented. This gradually caused him to give up his own drawing board to concentrate on the areas of his greatest talents. At one point, he set up a table in the middle of the animators' room and had them bring their scenes to him when they were done. Studying the action, Walt called for new drawings where necessary and timed the scenes so they would be most effective. He corrected staging and expressions and was quick to educate those working with him. Years later, he admitted, "The fellows who work near me catch a lot of hell!"

As a matter of fact, Walt could animate as well as any of the men he had working on the *Alice* series, with the exception of Ub Iwerks who was in a class by himself. For five frustrating years, from the "Alices" to the more successful "Oswalds," Walt sharpened his own thinking while trying to educate his staff, but he got minimal results. Then in 1928, Charlie Mintz, the distributor of Walt's popular Oswald the Lucky

ANIMATOR: *Ollie Johnston* —Peter Pan.

1953— *The nearsighted Mr. Smee tries to pick up Capt. Hook's head. Since the humor is based on Smee's fumbling personality, the action had to be convincing and believable —not only a feeling of weight and of effort, but action conceived in an entertaining way.*

◁ Peter Pan

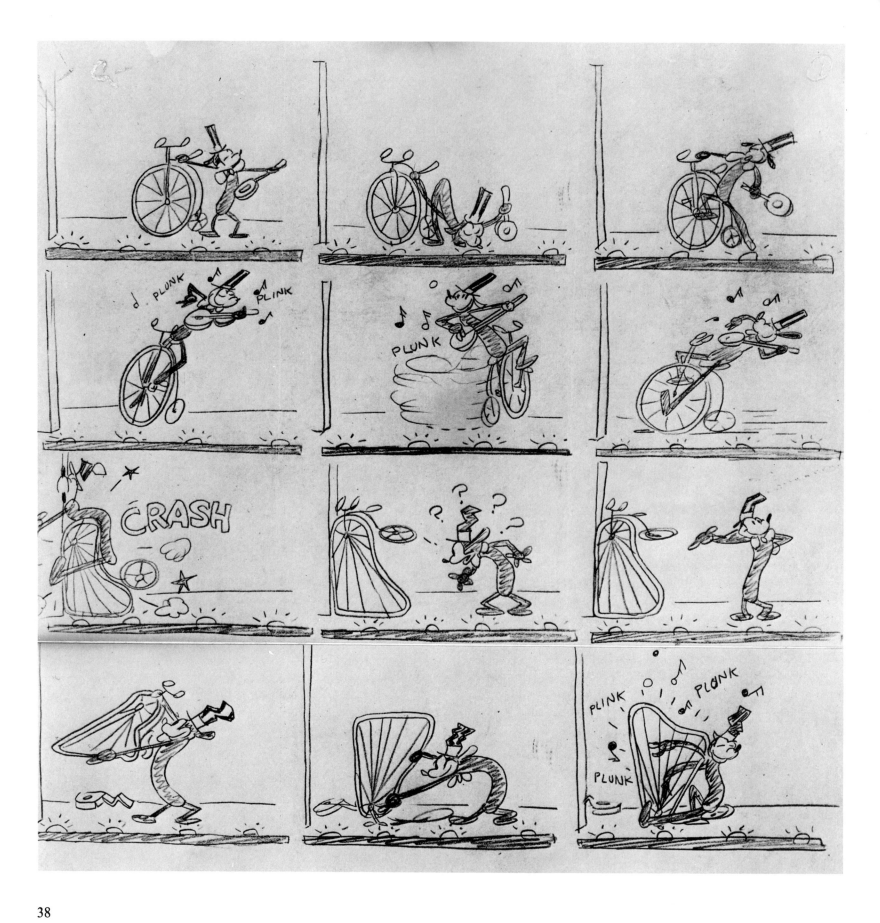

Rabbit cartoons, took over the rights to the main character and hired away all but four members of Walt's animation staff. It seemed like a disaster at the time, but actually it opened the way for a new group of animators who would soon help animation grow into a surprising art form. Les Clark commented about the men who had gone with Mintz: "These animators left the studio when Oswald left and they were *not* the group who later animated on Mickey. I think the development of animation started with the Mickey animators, inspired by Walt's interest and enthusiasm."

At this point, Walt's understanding of the mechanics of animation began to fall behind. Some felt that he merely lacked the patience ever to master the art of relating drawings to each other. Probably he lacked the particular talent to see the movement in drawings as he flipped them. It is a special ability, and many of the artists simply did not have it. Whatever the reason, as the techniques of animation progressed, Walt understood less and less of how it all worked. He knew the ingredients a scene should have and what the acting should be and what could be done with a scene that was not quite working, but he could not sit down at a desk and make the drawings that would demonstrate his ideas. It was an increasing mystery to him and, in some ways, an area of annoyance, since it was something he could not control or shape into something new. He was forced to rely on others.

This led Ben Sharpsteen to claim that, "Animation was developed far more by the animators themselves than by Walt." This is true of the specific techniques that advanced the art, but this advancement would never have occurred without Walt. As Les Clark said, "Animation developed because of Walt's insistence and supervision." The animator had to wrestle with the problem of how to make the drawings work properly, but without Walt's drive it is doubtful that any of them would have tried so hard or learned what to do.

Walt introduced two procedures that enabled the animators to begin improving. First, they could freely shoot tests of their drawings and quickly see film of what they had drawn, and, second, they each had an assistant learning the business who was expected to finish off the detail in each drawing. Walt was quick to recognize that there was more vitality and imagination and strength in scenes animated in a rough fashion, and he asked all animators to work more loosely. The assistant would "clean up" these drawings that looked so sloppy, refining them to a single line that could be traced by the inkers onto celluloid. The assistants became known as "clean-up men," and the animators developed one innovation after the other, achieving effects on the screen that no one had thought possible. In some cases, the drawings were so rough it was difficult to find any cartoon figure inside the tangled swirl of lines, and the men who made a duck or a dog out of smudges and scratches had to have a very special type of knowledge.

Shooting tests of scenes while they were still in the rough enabled the animators to check what they had done before showing it to anyone. Any part that was way off could be corrected quickly and shot again. This encouraged experimentation, exploration, and imagination, quickly promoting a closer bond among the animators. This probably began when one man wanted to show off the surprising results of his test, but the animators soon learned that there was great value in sharing ideas. And the sharing of judgment did not end with just viewing the test. An animator could take his drawings to any of the other men and they would happily make suggestions, showing what had worked for them in a similar situation or excitedly considering something completely new.

"Each generation of animators benefited from what the previous had learned by trial and error," said Ben Sharpsteen, "and consequently were more flexible in what they could accomplish, and they could reach greater heights." But it seems that the generations he

ARTIST: *Norm Ferguson.*

Walt encouraged his animators to work in a rough, free style because of the added vitality it gave to their work.

ANIMATOR: Bill Tytla
—Snow White

was referring to lasted less than a year apiece. Wilfred Jackson adds, ". . . there was always something new going on. We were all learning so fast."

The standard by which the studio's efforts were judged was undeniably the way Walt initially portrayed characters for the animators. As Dick Huemer[7] said, "Walt would take stories and act them out at a meeting; kill you laughing they were so funny. And not just because he was the boss either. And there it would be. You'd have the feeling of the whole thing. You'd know exactly what he wanted. We often wondered if Walt could have been a great actor or comedian."[8]

Walt always could show you exactly how the business should be done, but the animator was expected to go further with the idea, to come up with something of his own, some touch or bit of timing or an expression that would make it not only personal but special.

It did not take long to answer any questions or settle disagreements as to how a piece of business should be handled. Fortunately, there was a way of settling disputes while adding to our education. As soon as the answer print of a new cartoon was received, the whole staff rushed over to the Alex Theater in Glendale to see how it would go with an audience. The men never stayed for the feature film but immediately convened outside for an impromptu meeting on what went over and why, and what had missed the mark.

Each director remembers at least one dismal evening out there under the streetlights, because these meetings made them face implacable reality. It was no longer the excitement of what might be but the undeniable harshness of what was. Wilfred Jackson never forgot the sidewalk post mortem after his first picture, *The Castaway*. "Walt had his hat way down and his coat up around his ears," he recalled. "He looked like a wet bird. I walked by and on the way I heard Roy saying, 'Walt, I don't know if we should release this; it doesn't look like a Disney picture.'" They released it, of course, but Jackson had learned his lesson; he never made another film that could be called un-Disney.

It was a harsh way to learn a new profession, out there on the street at night, but it was positive and it was definite. The audience reaction was always clear and strong and undeniable. There was not so much talk about what should be done next time as there was a dissection of what had been done wrong on the current film, and Walt's comments on that were as valuable as his stimulation had been in those first story meetings.

By 1933, the animators had learned their basic lessons well, and they produced a film that would be loved around the world: *The Three Little Pigs*. It started a new era at the Disney Studio.

Rough drawings open the way to stronger action. As the animator feels the moves in his own body, he transfers that intensity to his character. This type of action could never be achieved with "clean" drawings, but once the roughs have been made refinements can follow.

ANIMATOR: *Fred Moore*
—Snow White

Types of Action Widely Used in Early Days

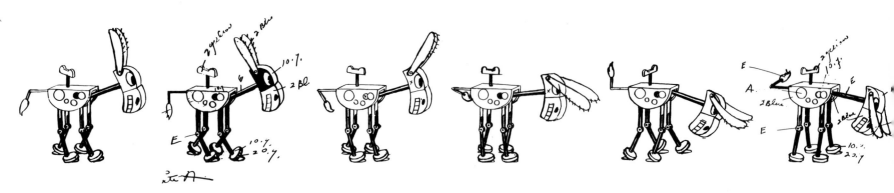

ANIMATOR: *Jack Kinney —Santa's Workshop.*

Continuous action was created by the walk cycle. This one was done by Jack Kinney, who later directed the great "How to . . ." series of Goofy films: How to Play Baseball, How to Ride a Horse, *etc.*

ANIMATOR: *Dick Huemer— Lullaby Land.*

A trio made from two figures. Crosses at the drawing's top and bottom guided the inkers in tracing a figure in a new position.

The audience was fascinated with animation that repeated the same action over and over, and, since this was quite a savings for the studio, several devices were developed to give this result:

The Cycle. This was a series of drawings that animated back into itself by having the last drawing work into the first one, creating a continuous action that never stopped. It was ideal for walks, dances, and certain "scramble actions" as a character tried to get away from something.

Repeat Action. Sometimes an action could be repeated just as it was in a second scene, but more often a new beginning or a different ending were called for. In these cases, the animator could repeat part of the action by borrowing drawings from the earlier scene. In other cases, there would be an action that could be repeated intact in the same scenes—a character climbing a slippery pole, or sliding down an incline, or being knocked down by a mechanical device. Between

times, the character would do something different in his attempts to avoid or to conquer, but when he came again to the same spot on the paper, the action of the climb, slide, or hit could be repeated.

The Cross-over. Even better than having the action repeated in a cycle was to have two or more characters doing the same action. A system called "cross-overs" took care of that problem by having the inkers trace one drawing in two different places on the same cel, matching it to sets of small crosses on the drawing. By animating a lone figure going to the left in a simple dance step, the animator could get these drawings traced over and over to make a whole line of dancers. At the appropriate time, the drawings could be flipped over and traced from the back, causing the line of dancers to sashay to the right. If everyone liked this, it was even simpler to shoot the cels a second time, making the line of dancers go through the whole procedure again. The audience was enthralled and could not

To the audience, it was magic.

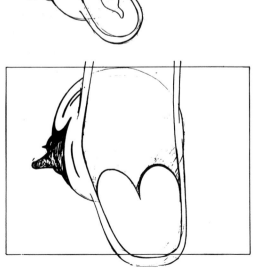

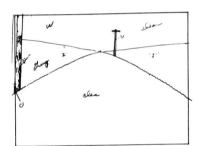

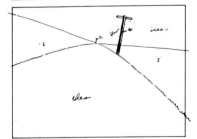

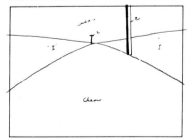

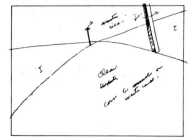

A cycle of telephone poles coming toward the camera creates the illusion of moving into the scene. These drawings from Plane Crazy *also show the road tilting as seen from a homemade airplane.*

understand how we could get all the figures to act exactly the same.

Another popular routine was to have the cartoon figure come up toward the camera, usually until his mouth filled the screen, and then retreat to his original position, using the same drawings shot in reverse. Also popular was the series of drawings run in a cycle that animated the road as a character ran or drove straight into the camera. This consisted of a row of telephone poles in perspective, a bush or two, and possibly some fence posts lining the road. By putting in a

ANIMATOR: *Woolie Reitherman* — Funny Little Bunnies.

Five separate cycles were used in making the bunnies fill Easter baskets. The top fellow lifted and closed the gate. Eggs rolled down the chute, guided by the rabbit at the left, and two bunnies pulled the baskets through in a continuous line, catching the eggs. Two playful rabbits at the right tossed little candied eggs on top. These scenes usually went to eager young animators wanting a chance to show what they can do. This one was done by Wolfgang "Woolie" Reitherman, who became a supervising animator, director, and finally, producer of cartoon features.

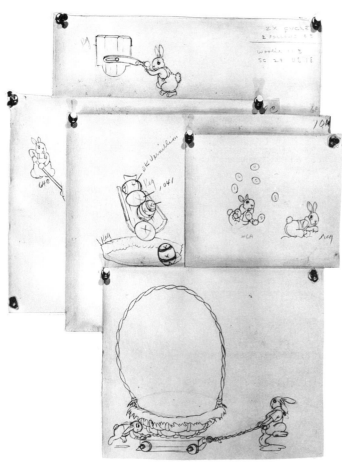

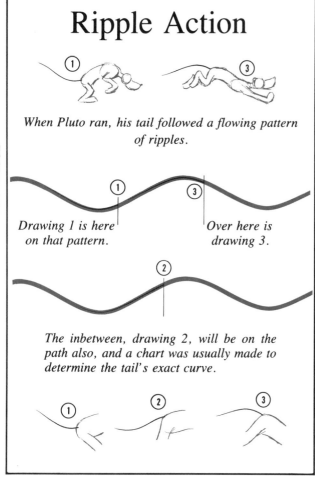

Ripple Action

When Pluto ran, his tail followed a flowing pattern of ripples.

Drawing 1 is here on that pattern.

Over here is drawing 3.

The inbetween, drawing 2, will be on the path also, and a chart was usually made to determine the tail's exact curve.

few simple inbetweens, the first pole animated back to the second and the second to the third, while one bush was moving back to become another.

The public also liked to see elaborate production lines for fanciful factories that made toys or Easter eggs or imaginative products. These scenes were tedious to animate because of all the moving parts, but there was an advantage in everything being in a cycle that could be run over and over and over—and usually was. The same was true of the great crowd shots used to start so many pictures. Such a scene was often the only contribution that particular animator could make to the whole picture, but if the scene was effective it certainly set the mood and the locale for the whole film. That alone made it worth all the work, but it was not a favorite assignment. Just slightly better were the long parades of marching flowers or cookies or toys that were made up of cycles on long pan paper that could be pulled through the scene.

There was no movement in the figures in early animation besides a simple progression across the paper. No one knew how to get any change of shape or flow of action from one drawing to another. There was no relationship of forms, just the same little cartoon figure in a new position on the next piece of paper. One solution to this stiffness of action was to conceive of a figure's appendages as sections of a garden hose. Since no one knew anyhow where bones and muscles might be on a cartoon figure, this worked well—giving great looseness and a fluid movement. There was no suggestion of realism because the concept of the character was not one of realism. This type of movement fit the design perfectly and brought about some funny action with great charm.

However, it was not the type of action Walt wanted, and he was quick to criticize. We can imagine his reaction to the cartoon camel that Oswald has just kicked into action:

"Do his legs have to be so limp like that? They don't look like they could hold up anything.

"Get some straight lines in there, like you've got in Oswald. Doesn't that camel have a knee or an ankle? And you've got the body the same all the time—he can bend back or forward, y'know. And get rid of those limp noodles; get some drawing in it!"

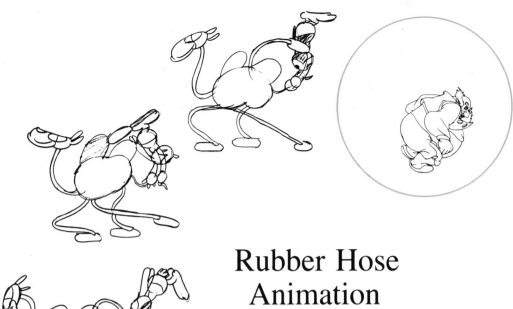

Rubber Hose Animation

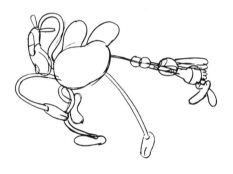

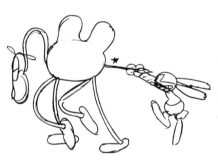

3. The Principles of Animation

"When we consider a new project, we really study it . . . not just the surface idea, but everything about it."
Walt Disney

A new jargon was heard around the studio. Words like "aiming" and "overlapping" and "pose to pose" suggested that certain animation procedures gradually had been isolated and named. Verbs turned into nouns overnight, as, for example, when the suggestion, "Why don't you stretch him out more?" became "Get more stretch on him." "Wow! Look at the squash on that drawing!" did not mean that a vegetable had splattered the artwork; it indicated that some animator had successfully shown a character in a flattened posture.

Some of this terminology was just assigning new meanings to familiar and convenient words. "Doing" a scene could mean acting out the intended movements, making exploratory drawings, or actually animating it; and once it was "done," the scene moved on to the next department. Layouts were done, backgrounds were done, recording was done, and, eventually, the whole picture had been done. Mixed in with these terms were the new names and phrases with more obscure meanings.

The animators continued to search for better methods of relating drawings to each other and had found a few ways that seemed to produce a predictable result. They could not expect success every time, but these special techniques of drawing a character in motion did offer some security. As each of these processes acquired a name, it was analyzed and perfected and talked about, and when new artists joined the staff

they were taught these practices as if they were the rules of the trade. To everyone's surprise, they became the fundamental principles of animation:

1. Squash and Stretch
2. Anticipation
3. Staging
4. Straight Ahead Action and Pose to Pose
5. Follow Through and Overlapping Action
6. Slow In and Slow Out
7. Arcs
8. Secondary Action
9. Timing
10. Exaggeration
11. Solid Drawing
12. Appeal

By far the most important discovery was what we call Squash and Stretch. When a fixed shape is moved about on the paper from one drawing to the next, there is a marked rigidity that is emphasized by the movement. In real life, this occurs only with the most rigid shapes, such as chairs and dishes and pans. Anything composed of living flesh, no matter how bony, will

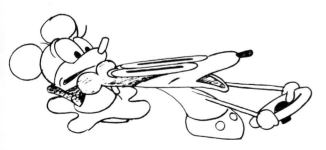

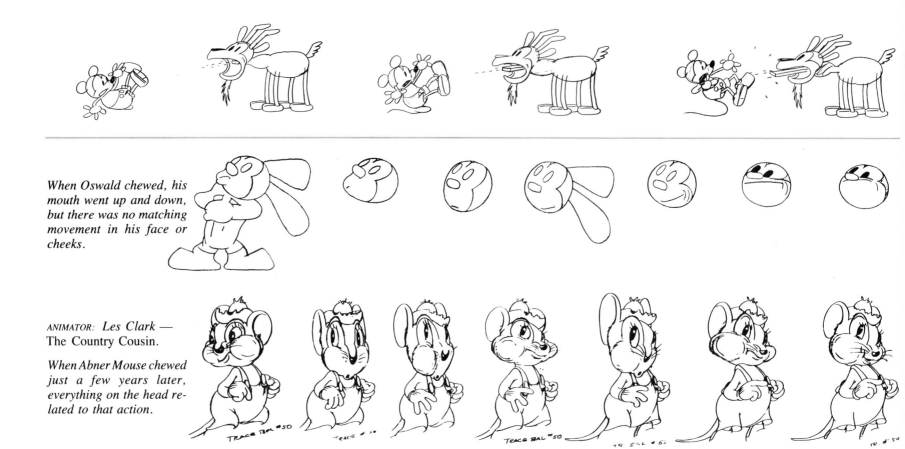

When Oswald chewed, his mouth went up and down, but there was no matching movement in his face or cheeks.

ANIMATOR: *Les Clark —* The Country Cousin.

When Abner Mouse chewed just a few years later, everything on the head related to that action.

The inhale before a heavy sigh is portrayed in broad, simple terms by simply inflating Mickey. The resulting increase in volume lost credibility, but in 1928 that did not matter.

show considerable movement within its shape in progressing through an action. A good example of this is the bent arm with swelling bicep straightened out so that only the long sinews are apparent. The figure crouched is obviously contracted into itself, in contrast to the figure in an extreme stretch or leap. The face, whether chewing, smiling, talking, or just showing a change of expression, is alive with changing shapes in the cheeks, the lips, the eyes—only the wax figure in the museum is rigid.

The squashed position can depict the form either flattened out by great pressure or bunched up and pushed together. The stretched position always shows the same form in a very extended condition. The movement from one drawing to the next became the very essence of animation. A smile was no longer a simple line spread across a face; it now defined the lips and their relation to the cheeks. Legs were no longer bent pipes or rubber hoses; they swelled as they bent and stretched to long flexible shapes.

Immediately the animators tried to outdo each other in making drawings with more and more squash and stretch, pushing those principles to the very limits of solid draftsmanship: eyes squinted shut and eyes popped open; the sunken cheeks of an ''inhale'' were radically different from the ballooned cheeks of a blowing action; a mouth chewing on a straw was first shown far below the nose, and then it actually was compressed up beyond the nose (which changed shape as well) in showing the chewing action. Through the mid-thirties, everyone was making two drawings for every conceivable action, and by working back and forth between the squash position and the stretch we found we could make each position stronger in both action and drawing.

In this early animation, the action is well staged but very rigid and stiff. There is no squash and stretch, follow through, or feeling of weight. These actions had a charm and a vitality, but they could not support more than a six-minute short.

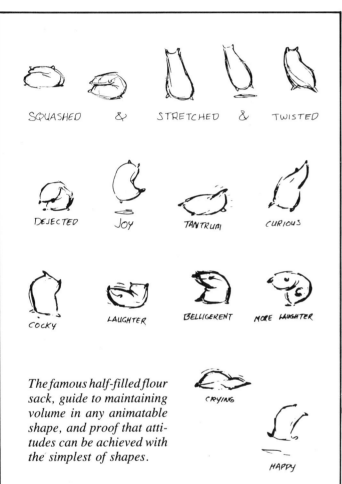

SQUASHED & STRETCHED & TWISTED

DEJECTED JOY TANTRUM CURIOUS

COCKY LAUGHTER BELLIGERENT MORE LAUGHTER

CRYING

HAPPY

The famous half-filled flour sack, guide to maintaining volume in any animatable shape, and proof that attitudes can be achieved with the simplest of shapes.

The best advice for keeping the distended drawings from looking bloated or bulbous, and the stretched positions from appearing stringy or withered, was to consider that the shape or volume was like a half-filled flour sack. If dropped on the floor, it will squash out to its fullest shape, and if picked up by the top corners, it will stretch out to its longest shape; yet it will never change volume. We even made drawings of the flour sack in different attitudes—erect, twisted, doubled-over—suggesting emotions as well as actions. That forced us to find the most direct way, the simplest statement, for if we added any extra lines to amplify an expression it was no longer a flour sack. We found that many little interior lines were not necessary since the whole shape, conceived properly, did it all. These lessons were applied to Mickey's body, or his cheeks, to Pluto's legs, or his muzzle, or even to Donald's head.

On the sports page of the daily newspapers we found

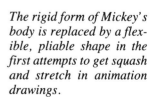

The rigid form of Mickey's body is replaced by a flexible, pliable shape in the first attempts to get squash and stretch in animation drawings.

49

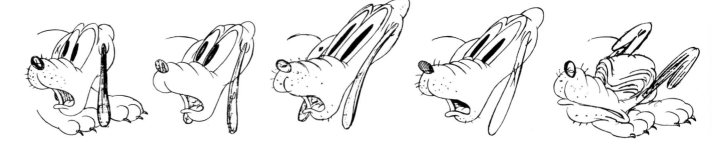

ANIMATOR: *Norm Ferguson*
—Mickey's Elephant.

Principles of squash and stretch when applied to Pluto's head give strength to the action and a feeling of moving flesh.

a gold mine that had been overlooked. Here were great photos showing the elasticity of the human body in every kind of reach and stretch and violent action. Our animation principles were clearly evident in the bulges and bumps that contrasted to long, straight thrusts. Mixed in with these contortions were examples of the whole figure communicating joy, frustration, concentration, and all the other intense emotions of the sports world. These examples opened our eyes and started us observing in a new way.

The standard animation test for all beginning artists

was to draw a bouncing ball. It was quickly rendered, easily changed, and surprisingly rewarding in terms of what could be learned. The assignment was merely to represent the ball by a simple circle, and then, on successive drawings, have it drop, hit the ground, and bounce back into the air, ready to repeat the whole process. We could have either a forward movement progressing the ball across the paper, or have all the action take place in one spot, allowing us, through a cycle of the drawings, to make the ball bounce continuously. It seemed like simplicity itself, but through

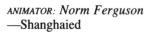

1928— Oswald shows determination by lifting his chest with one hand in front and one in back. While the gesture is easily recognizable, it is little more than a diagram of the action.

ANIMATOR: *Norm Ferguson*
—Shanghaied

1934— Peg Leg Pete does the same gesture, only now there is more belly than chest involved. This broader action gave the impression of a round solid character with a combination of life and spirit—and fat.

ANIMATOR: *Jack Campbell*
—The Riveter.

1940— The gesture has been done so often by this time that it is almost a gag in itself. An action this broad loses realism, but gains a type of comedy.

the test we learned the mechanics of animating a scene while also being introduced to Timing and Squash and Stretch.

We were encouraged to change the shape of the ball in the faster segments of the bounce, making an elongated circle that would be easier to see, then quickly to flatten it as it hit the ground, giving a solid contact as well as the squashed shape of a rubber ball in action. This change at the bottom also gave the feeling of thrust for the spring back into the air, but if we made an extra drawing or two at that point to get the most out of this action, the ball stayed on the ground too long, creating weird effects of hopping instead of bouncing. (Some tests looked more like a jumping bean from Mexico than any kind of ball.) If we misjudged our arrangement of the drawings or the distance between them, we created apparitions reminiscent of an injured rabbit, or an angry grasshopper, or, most often, a sleepy frog. However, many of the circular forms just seemed to take off as if they had a life of their own.

The beginning artists were an inventive group, and all manner of variations were tried, each revealing something about the man who had done the animation and what he considered important in the scene. Some men added distinction by starting with a big bounce, followed by shorter and shorter ones as the ball gradually lost its spring. Some put the action in perspective to show how well they could figure a complicated assignment, or they added a stripe around the ball to show how much it turned during the whole action. These men were grabbed quickly by the Effects Department, which specialized in a mechanical type of animation. Those more interested in a livelier type of entertainment preferred surprise endings: the ball exploding on contact, or crashing like a broken egg on the second bounce, or sprouting wings and flying off.

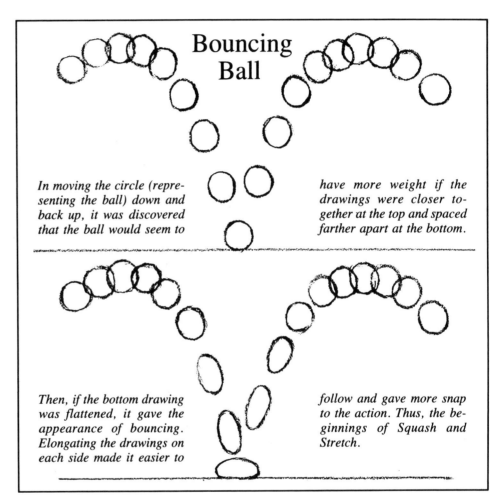

Bouncing Ball

In moving the circle (representing the ball) down and back up, it was discovered that the ball would seem to *have more weight if the drawings were closer together at the top and spaced farther apart at the bottom.*

Then, if the bottom drawing was flattened, it gave the appearance of bouncing. Elongating the drawings on each side made it easier to *follow and gave more snap to the action. Thus, the beginnings of Squash and Stretch.*

Anticipation

People in the audience watching an animated scene will not be able to understand the events on the screen unless there is a planned sequence of actions that leads them clearly from one activity to the next. They must be prepared for the next movement and expect it before it actually occurs. This is achieved by preceding each major action with a specific move that anticipates for the audience what is about to happen. This anticipa-

Donald draws back with raised leg in anticipation of the dash he will make out of the scene.

tion can be as small as a change of expression or as big as the broadest physical action. Before a man runs, he crouches low, gathering himself like a spring, or, the reverse, he draws back in the opposite direction, raising his shoulders and one leg, as he aims himself at the place of the next activity. Before Mickey reaches to grab an object, he first raises his arms as he stares at the article, broadcasting the fact that he is going to do something with that particular object.

This is the oldest device of the theater, for without it, the audience becomes nervous and restless and whispers, "What's he doing?" The anticipatory moves

may not show *why* he is doing something, but there is no question about *what* he is doing—or what he is going to do next. Expecting that, the audience can now enjoy the *way* it is done.

The opposite of this is the "surprise gag," which only works when the audience is expecting one thing to happen, and suddenly, without warning, something entirely different happens. The surprise gag cannot work if a different action has not been anticipated by the audience. Similarly, no action on the stage can be anything but a series of meaningless surprises without anticipation.

The movements in early animation were abrupt and unexpected; too often the audience was not properly alerted and missed a gag when it came. This was one of the first things Walt started to correct. He called his remedy "aiming" and acted out just how an action or gesture could be made clear so that everyone would see it. If Oswald the Lucky Rabbit is to put his hand in his pocket to get a sandwich for lunch, the whole body must relate to that hand and to the pocket. When the hand is aimed, it must be "out in the clear" so everyone can see it and anticipate what is going to happen.

Oswald lifts his foot high as he sights on his target.

In the early days, Walt referred to anticipation as "aiming." Here Oswald aims his hand at the sandwich in his pocket. No one in the audience failed to see the gesture or the action.

The head cannot be looking off somewhere else—the important action is Oswald's reaching into his pocket. It is not a gag, it is not a laugh, but it must be seen. No one should need to ask, ''Now where did he ever get that sandwich?'' As Walt demonstrated how it should be done, he exaggerated the action and made it far more interesting than the animator was ever able to capture. As Les Clark said years later, ''Today it may look simple to us; at the time it wasn't. It was something that hadn't been tried before or proved.''

Few movements in real life occur without some kind of anticipation. It seems to be the natural way for creatures to move, and without it there would be little power in any action. To the golfer, it is the backswing; to the baseball pitcher, it is his windup. The batter prepares himself with a whole series of anticipatory actions, but the one that gives the clout is the final twist and the step forward as the ball approaches the plate. Without that move the mightiest swing is no more than a bunt.

Staging

''Staging'' is the most general of the principles because it covers so many areas and goes back so far in the theater. Its meaning, however, is very precise: it is the presentation of any idea so that it is completely and unmistakably clear. An action is staged so that it is understood, a personality so that it is recognizable, an expression so that it can be seen, a mood so that it will affect the audience. Each is communicating to the fullest extent with the viewers when it is properly staged.

The most important consideration is always the ''story point.'' It has been decided, for example, that a certain piece of business will advance the story; now, how should it be staged? Is it funnier in a long shot where everything can be seen or in a close-up featuring the personality? Is it better in a master shot with the camera moving in, or a series of short cuts to different objects? Each scene will have to fit the plan, and every frame of the film must help to make this point of the story.

If a ''spooky'' feeling is desired, the scene is filled with the symbols of a spooky situation. An old house, wind howling, leaves or papers rustling through the

Clear staging keeps Minnie feminine even in broad reactions. There is no attempt at realism, but considerable caricature of the attitudes.

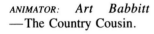

ANIMATOR: *Art Babbitt —The Country Cousin.*

Only do one thing at a time: one of the most important rules of the theater. The country mouse, tipsy from fancy food and drink, is standing on a slice of toast and tries to act nonchalant. He flips his umbrella in the air, places it in position before leaning on it, and even holds the position briefly before the umbrella breaks through the toast.

ANIMATOR: *Fred Moore —Snow White.*

Dopey uses his foot to temporarily stifle the sneeze of the dwarf beneath him. This complicated situation easily could become difficult to understand if not properly staged.

yard, clouds floating across the moon, threatening sky, maybe bare branches rattling or scraping against a window, or a shadow moving back and forth—all of these say "spooks." A bright flower bed would be out of place.

If you are staging an action, you must be sure that only one action is seen; it must not be confused by drapery or by a poor choice of angle or upstaged by something else that might be going on. You do not make drawings just because they are cute or look funny. You make the drawings that will stage each idea in the strongest and the simplest way before going on to the next action. You are saying in effect, "Look at this—now look at this—and now this." You make sure the camera is the right distance from the character to show what he is doing. If he is kicking, you do not have the camera in close on a waist shot. If you are displaying your character's expression, you do not do it in a long shot where the figure is lost in the background.

Magicians say they prefer to work close to the people they are fooling because it is so much easier to direct attention to any desired spot. When an individual works alone on a big stage it is too easy for the audience to watch his feet, what is behind him, his clothes, any unnatural movement; the spectators might be looking at everything except what the magician is trying to show them. As a director, Dave Hand emphasized the value of the close-up shot: "By its use we are able to eliminate from the mind of the audience anything that is less important than the particular point we are putting over at the time."

The animators had a special problem of their own. The characters were black and white, with no shades of gray to soften the contrast or delineate a form. Mickey's body was black, his arms and his hands—all black. There was no way to stage an action except in silhouette. How else could there be any clarity? A hand in front of the chest would simply disappear; black shoulders lifted against the black part of the head would negate a shrug, and the big, black ears kept getting tangled up with the rest of the action just when other drawing problems seemed to be solved.

Actually, this limitation was more helpful than we realized: we learned that it is always better to show the action in silhouette. Chaplin maintained that if an actor knew his emotion thoroughly, he could show it in silhouette. Walt was more direct: "Work in silhouette so that everything can be seen clearly. Don't have a hand come over a face so that you can't see what's happening. Put it away from the face and make it clear." Constant redrawing, planning, and experimenting were required to make the action look natural and realistic while keeping a clear silhouette image. We had to find a pose that read with both definition and appeal.

Straight Ahead Action and Pose to Pose[1]

There are two main approaches to animation. The first is known as Straight Ahead Action because the animator literally works straight ahead from his first drawing in the scene. He simply takes off, doing one drawing after the other, getting new ideas as he goes along, until he reaches the end of the scene. He knows the story point of the scene and the business that is to be included, but he has little plan of how it will all be done at the time he starts. Both the drawings and the action have a fresh, slightly zany look, as the animator keeps the whole process very creative.

The second is called Pose to Pose. Here, the animator plans his action, figures out just which drawings will be needed to animate the business, makes the drawings, relating them to each other in size and action, and gives the scene to his assistant to draw the inbetweens. Such a scene is always easy to follow and works well because the relationships have been carefully considered before the animator gets too far into the drawings. More time is spent improving the key

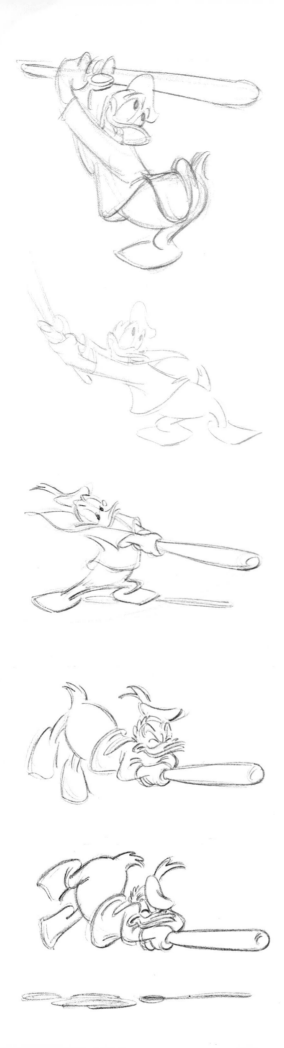

drawings and exercising greater control over the movement. With Pose to Pose, there is clarity and strength. In Straight Ahead Action, there is spontaneity.

Both methods are still in use because they each offer certain advantages for different types of action. Usually they are combined in a way that keeps the Straight Ahead Action from getting out of hand. The scene is planned with a path of action laid out, and rough drawings are made depicting the character's probable progress; although none of these will be used later in actual animation, they still serve as a guide for size, position, attitude, and relationship to the background. They offer as much control as might be needed, even though some animators feel that the very lack of control is the element that gives the spontaneity. They say: "The animator should be as surprised as anyone at the way it comes out." Most wild, scrambling actions are probably more effective with this method than with too much careful pre-planning.

Straight Ahead Animation will seldom work if there is strong perspective in the layout or a background that must be matched. One man animated a dog jumping excitedly and turning around, trying to attract attention. While he achieved a funny action with much spirit, it could not be used because he had failed to match the action to the limitations of the layout. There was no way to tell how high the dog was jumping since he never really contacted the ground, and the relationship of the drawings was thrown off by the perspective he had failed to consider. With a flat background and a clear arena in all directions, there would have been no problem.

However, many pieces of acting require a different approach. If Mickey Mouse is discouraged, he turns away, jams his hands far down into his pockets, looks back over his shoulder one last time, kicks a stone out of his path, and walks off. This must be done with Pose to Pose because each of the positions must be handled carefully for maximum clarity, appeal, and communication. They should be worked over separately and together, until they do their job as efficiently as possible. Once these poses relate well to each other, it is a simple matter to time the intervening drawings and to break down the action.

Another element that should be considered in choosing the method of animation is "texture." A series of

DONALD DUCK

ANIMATOR: *Dick Lundy—* Mickey's Grand Opera.

Donald Duck's operatic role is interrupted when he swallows a frog. STARTS ON PAGE 89

ANIMATOR: *Fred Moore—* The Three Caballeros.

Example of "Pose to Pose" animation. Once the key poses have been worked over, related properly, and refined, only in-betweens are needed to complete the scene. This method gives complete control over the staging of the scene.

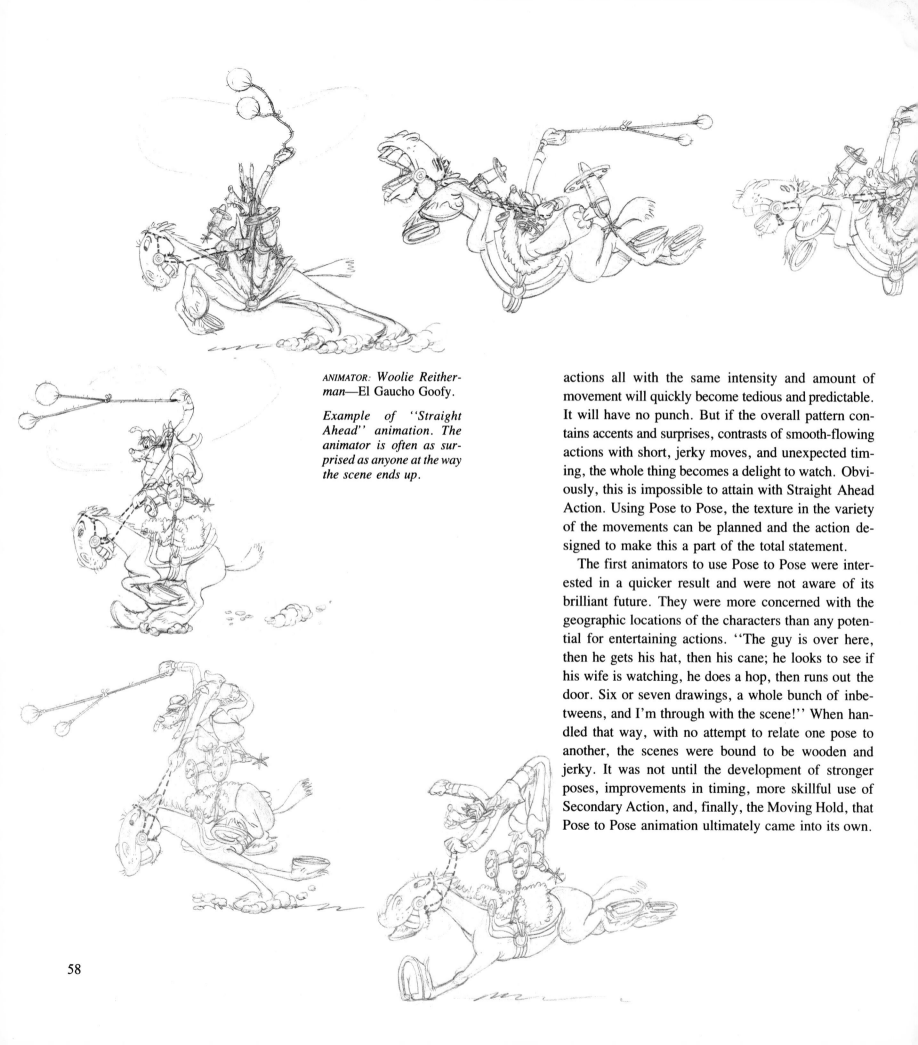

Example of "Straight Ahead" animation. The animator is often as surprised as anyone at the way the scene ends up.

actions all with the same intensity and amount of movement will quickly become tedious and predictable. It will have no punch. But if the overall pattern contains accents and surprises, contrasts of smooth-flowing actions with short, jerky moves, and unexpected timing, the whole thing becomes a delight to watch. Obviously, this is impossible to attain with Straight Ahead Action. Using Pose to Pose, the texture in the variety of the movements can be planned and the action designed to make this a part of the total statement.

The first animators to use Pose to Pose were interested in a quicker result and were not aware of its brilliant future. They were more concerned with the geographic locations of the characters than any potential for entertaining actions. "The guy is over here, then he gets his hat, then his cane; he looks to see if his wife is watching, he does a hop, then runs out the door. Six or seven drawings, a whole bunch of inbetweens, and I'm through with the scene!" When handled that way, with no attempt to relate one pose to another, the scenes were bound to be wooden and jerky. It was not until the development of stronger poses, improvements in timing, more skillful use of Secondary Action, and, finally, the Moving Hold, that Pose to Pose animation ultimately came into its own.

ANIMATOR: *Les Clark—* Mickey's Grand Opera.

Squash and stretch have now been combined with follow through and overlapping action on the feather and other parts to give a feeling of weight and living form.

Follow Through and Overlapping Action

When a character entering a scene reached the spot for his next action, he often came to a sudden and complete stop. This was stiff and did not look natural, but nobody knew what to do about it. Walt was concerned. ''Things don't come to a stop all at once, guys; first there's one part and then another.'' Several different ways were eventually found to correct these conditions; they were called either ''Follow Through'' or ''Overlapping Action'' and no one really knew where one ended and the other began. There seemed to be five main categories.

1. If the character has any appendages, such as long ears or a tail or a big coat, these parts continue to move after the rest of the figure has stopped. This is easy to see in real life. The movement of each must be timed carefully so it will have the correct feeling of weight, and it must continue to follow through in the pattern of action in a believable way, no matter how broadly it is cartooned.

2. The body itself does not move all at once, but instead it stretches, catches up, twists, turns, and contracts as the forms work against each other. As one part arrives at the stopping point, others may still be in movement; an arm or hand may continue its action even after the body is in its pose. (Peg Leg Pete's belly continued to bounce and sag interminably.) In order to put over the attitude clearly, the head, chest, and shoulders might all stop together,

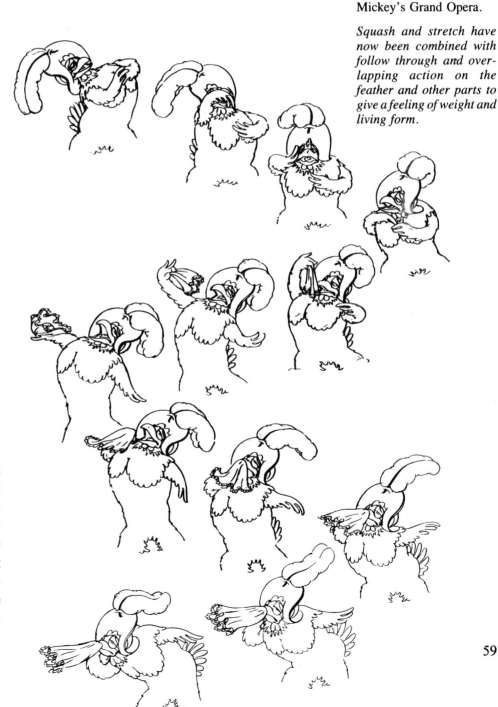

59

Jillie blows out candles on cake.

|← — *she sees cake* — →|← *inhale* — *anticipation* — →|← *blows* ——————————————| *"Moving Hold"* |
little "take" – head up – | *chest swells – up on toes –* | *leans out – arms back –* | *tail higher – chin out more* |
bigger smile – hands down. | *shoulders up* | *fanny up – head thrust –* | *arms up – lips out – hair ribbon comes up.* |

since this is the part the audience should see (the part that registers how the character is feeling). Then a few frames later, the rest of the parts would settle into their final position, possibly not all at the same time. When the whole figure has come to a stop in a definite attitude, this is called a "held" drawing.

Some of the animators thought we were getting too fussy, but that was only the beginning as Walt saw new possibilities in the work his men were doing. Les Clark said with a chuckle, ". . . we couldn't understand sometimes why he was giving us hell for something we thought was acceptable. Then later on we knew what he was talking about."

3. The loose flesh on a figure, such as its cheeks or Donald Duck's body or almost all of Goofy, will move at a slower speed than the skeletal parts. This

trailing behind in an action is sometimes called "drag," and it gives a looseness and a solidity to the figure that is vital to the feeling of life. When done well, this technique is scarcely detectable as the film is projected. In effect, the animator is drawing in the fourth dimension, for he is depicting a figure the way it would be at only that precise moment. The drawings are not designed to be viewed by themselves, but only in a series projected at an established speed.

Many comic actions have been based on this principle, as the fat on a running character drags farther and farther behind, until the ultimate occurs: the skeleton runs off, leaving the flesh to fend for itself. This type of exaggeration will bring laughs in the shorter films, but the chief value of this kind of Follow Through lies in its more subtle uses.

4. The way in which an action is completed often tells us more about the person than the drawings of the movement itself. A golfer takes a mighty swing, which covers only a few frames, but what happens to him afterward can easily take five feet of film and is much more revealing, whether he is graceful and slick in his follow through, or wraps himself up in a knot. The anticipation sets up the action we expect (or is it the action the character expects?), the action whizzes past, and now we come to the "punch line"

more entertaining the action itself could be, or what it could tell us about the character's personality.

5. Finally, there was the Moving Hold, which employed parts of all the other elements of Overlapping Action and Follow Through to achieve a new feeling of life and clarity. When a careful drawing had been made of a pose, it was held without movement on the screen for a few frames—at least eight, maybe as many as sixteen. This was to allow the audience

of the gag, the follow through, which tells us what happened—how it all turned out. Obviously, the ending should be considered part of the entire action before any drawings are made, but, amazingly, the ending was hardly ever developed in early animation. It was enough just to do the reach, the throw, the kick, and no thought was given to how much

time to absorb the attitude. That amounted to less than a second, but it was enough. However, when a drawing was held for that long, the flow of action was broken, the illusion of dimension was lost, and the drawing began to look flat. A way had to be found to "hold" the drawing and still keep it moving!

ANIMATOR: *Ham Luske*— Elmer Elephant.

The other animal kids have made fun of Elmer's trunk. He tearfully looks at his reflection and kicks at his trunk, hoping to get rid of it. This poignant scene is full of strong poses, clear staging, anticipation, follow through, squash and stretch, exaggeration, and appeal.

ANIMATOR: *Ham Luske*— Elmer Elephant.

The Moving Hold: the pose is strengthened in a second drawing as all the parts drift or coast to a final position. This keeps the character alive yet allows the audience to see the attitude clearly.

The answer was to make two drawings, one more extreme than the other, yet both containing all the elements of the pose. It was explained this way: ''You hit the pose, then drift on beyond to an even stronger pose—everything goes further, the cheeks go up, the ears fly out, the hands rise; he goes on his toes, his eyes open wider, but essentially he's still in his pose.'' Now we could use the Follow Through on the fleshy parts to give us the solidity and dimension, we could drag the parts to give the added feeling of weight and reality, and we could strengthen our poses for more vitality. It all added up to more life in the scene. The magic was beginning to appear.

Slow In and Slow Out

Once an animator had worked over his poses (the ''extremes'') and redrawn them until they were the best he could do, he naturally wanted the audience to see them. He timed these key drawings to move quickly from one to the next, so that the bulk of the footage of the scene would be either on or close to those ''extremes.'' By putting the inbetweens close to each extreme and only one fleeting drawing halfway between, the animator achieved a very spirited result, with the character zipping from one attitude to the next. This was called Slow In and Slow Out, since that is the way the inbetweens were timed. Too much of this gave a mechanical feel to the action, robbing the scene of the very life that was being sought, but it was still an important discovery that became the basis of later refinements in timing and staging.

Walt continued to ask us to analyze the actions more carefully, and to understand how the body worked, since that was the only way to get the caricature of realism he wanted. ''Our work must have a foundation of fact in order to have sincerity. The most hilarious comedy is always based on things actual.''

One animator from outside the studio was ''amazed that anyone would be that interested in the mechanics of motion,'' but this unique approach was the very heart of our work. Marc Davis[2] summed it up, ''Disney animation is just very different. Nobody, I don't care who he is, can come from the outside and draw a Disney character without a full understanding of what it's all about.''

Arcs

Very few living organisms are capable of moves that have a mechanical in and out or up and down precision. The action of a woodpecker might be an exception, and, because of the restrictions of an external skeleton, there are undoubtedly some examples in the insect world, but the movements of most living creatures will follow a slightly circular path. The head seldom thrusts straight out, then back again; it lifts slightly, or drops as it returns. Perhaps this has to do with weight or maybe with the inner structure of the higher forms of life, but, whatever the reason, most movements will describe an arc of some kind.

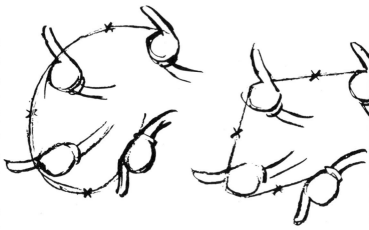

The action of a hand gesture with a pointing finger follows a circular path. The animator charts the position of his drawings along this arc. He makes his key drawings, indicating where inbetweens should be placed to keep the line of action on this arc. Inbetweens done without following this arc change the action radically.

This discovery made a major change in the type of movements animators designed for their characters, breaking with the rigid and stiff actions that had gone before. In a walk, the characters had popped up and down like mechanical gadgets on an engine; now they ''arced'' over at the top of their steps and ''arced'' under at the bottom position. A hit or a throw could be on a completely straight line, but the beginning of the action came sweeping in on an arc and the Follow Through started a corkscrew action.

As this principle was better understood, scenes were plotted out with charts and dots, as well as rough poses, to determine just how high and how low the character should go in any action. Arcs were sketched in, as the key actions were planned, to guide the eventual drawings along this curved path. When the final drawings were being made, more ways would become apparent for the character to go even farther in the action, especially using Squash and Stretch and Overlapping Action to good advantage.

One of the major problems for the inbetweeners is that it is much more difficult to make a drawing on an arc than one halfway between two other drawings. Even when the position has been indicated, or a stern warning written on the extremes, "Watch arcs!" there is a strong inclination to pull back toward a more normal inbetween. It is only as a series of drawings is "rolled" on the pegs that the proper location for the drawing becomes evident. No one has ever found a way of insuring that the drawings will all be placed accurately on the arcs, even when experienced people are inbetweening the action, and it is one of the most basic requirements for the scene. Drawings made as straight inbetweens completely kill the essence of the action.

Secondary Action

Often, the one idea being put over in a scene can be fortified by subsidiary actions within the body. A sad figure wipes a tear as he turns away. Someone stunned

SECONDARY ACTION
ANIMATOR. Bill Tytla —
Snow White.

Doc is flustered as he tells the other dwarfs to put Grumpy in the washtub. The primary action is the body jumping up and down, but Doc's confusion is shown by having his arms follow a different pattern from his body; the head bobbing with dialogue is still another action. These secondary actions add excitement without conflicting with the basic movement.

ANIMATOR: Eric Larson—
Pinocchio.

As the kitten Figaro slips into bed, his shoulders, arms, legs, and the blanket all have independent actions that support and enrich the main idea of the scene without conflicting.

63

shakes his head as he gets to his feet. A flustered person puts on his glasses as he regains his composure. When this extra business supports the main action, it is called a Secondary Action and is always kept subordinate to the primary action. If it conflicts or becomes more interesting or dominating in any way, it is either the wrong choice or is staged improperly.

The chief difficulty lies in making a unified statement through the drawing and timing of separate, but related, parts. If the sad figure has an expression on his face that should be seen, the hand wiping the tear must be carefully planned to support that look. A broad, overwhelming gesture with a fist covering half the face would hardly be acceptable. Still, if the action is too subdued, it will be mushy, restricted, and inconsequential; if it is too strong, the face will never be seen. Should this Secondary Action be made to work with the features so that the expression is actually emphasized, the scene will be outstanding.

Sometimes the Secondary Action will be the expression itself. Suppose there was to be a change from a painful hurt to a helpless, bleak look as the character turns away, before he wipes the tear. The danger now is not that the expression will dominate the scene but that it never will be seen. The change must come before the move, or after, and must be staged so that it is obvious, even though of secondary importance. A change in the middle of a major move will go unnoticed, and any value intended will be lost.

One animator found the proper relationships among all these parts through a "building block" technique.[3] First he animated the most important move, making sure that it worked the way he wanted, communicating his thought in the strongest way. Then he went through the scene a second time animating the Secondary Action, and even once more if necessary, to make the rest of the drawing relate to those two actions. He continued to change and adjust until all parts of the drawing worked together in a very natural way.

It is advisable in any case to try it all in thumbnails—little exploratory sketches—before doing anything else, to make sure that everything will stage well and will look as convincing as the animator had hoped. When used correctly, Secondary Actions will add richness to the scene, naturalness to the action, and a fuller dimension to the personality of the character.

Timing

The number of drawings used in any move determines the amount of time that action will take on the screen. If the drawings are simple, clear, and expressive, the story point can be put over quickly, and this was all that concerned the animators during the early period. Timing in those cartoons was limited mainly to fast moves and slow moves, with accents and thrusts calling for special handling. But the personalities that were developing were defined more by their movements than their appearance, and the varying speed of those movements determined whether the character was lethargic, excited, nervous, relaxed. Neither acting nor attitude could be portrayed without paying very close attention to Timing.

The complicated relationships that came with Secondary Actions and Overlapping Movements called for extensive refinements, but even the most basic moves showed the importance of Timing and the constant need for more study. Just two drawings of a head, the first showing it leaning toward the right shoulder and the second with it over on the left and its chin slightly raised, can be made to communicate a multitude of ideas, depending entirely on the Timing used. Each inbetween drawing added between these two "extremes" gives a new meaning to the action.

EXAGGERATION

ANIMATOR. Dick Lundy— Orphan's Benefit.

Donald Duck is hit in the face with a scoop of ice cream as he tries to recite a poem. Exaggeration was the key element in finding the most entertaining way to do this scene. The duck is staged clearly; there is strong impact in the timing and a funny concept to the whole action.

No inbetweens	THE CHARACTER has been hit by a tremendous force. His head is nearly snapped off.
One inbetween	. . . has been hit by a brick, rolling pin, frying pan.
Two inbetweens	. . . has a nervous tic, a muscle spasm, an uncontrollable twitch.
Three inbetweens	. . . is dodging the brick, rolling pin, frying pan.
Four inbetweens	. . . is giving a crisp order, "Get going!" "Move it!"
Five inbetweens	. . . is more friendly, "Over here." "Come on—hurry!"
Six inbetweens	. . . sees a good-looking girl, or the sports car he has always wanted.
Seven inbetweens	. . . tries to get a better look at something.
Eight inbetweens	. . . searches for the peanut butter on the kitchen shelf.
Nine inbetweens	. . . appraises, considering thoughtfully.
Ten inbetweens	. . . stretches a sore muscle.

The persistent question, especially from the New York men was, "When do you use 'ones' and when do you use 'twos'?" This referred to the number of frames of film to be shot of a single drawing. One exposure was called "ones," two exposures "twos." It had long been known that for most normal action there was no need to make a new drawing for every frame of the film. Each drawing could occupy two of the precious frames, and the audience would never detect it at 24 frames a second. This saved immense amounts of work and in the slower movements gave a smoother appearance to the action. More than that, a fast action on "twos" had more sparkle and spirit than the same action with inbetweens, which tended to make the Timing too even and removed the vitality.

Any time there was a pan move in which the character's feet or a point of contact with the background were shown, the action had to be on "ones" to match the moves on the pan, or there would be slippage which looked peculiar. Similarly, if the camera were moving in any direction (which must be on "ones"), there would be a strange jittering unless the character's actions were on "ones" also.

When more elaborate actions were called for and more delicate changes had to be seen, the animators resorted to the use of "ones"—sometimes throughout the scene and otherwise only in certain places. A scramble action or speed gag, a sharp accent or flurry of activity, the pay-off after a big anticipation, all needed "ones." But the choice was still difficult to make if the animator had not gone through a period of experimenting and trying and failing and trying again. Only then did he build up a backlog of experience that would guide him through these perpetual decisions.

Exaggeration

There was some confusion among the animators when Walt first asked for more realism and then criticized the result because it was not exaggerated enough. In Walt's mind, there was probably no difference. He believed in going to the heart of anything and developing the essence of what he found. If a character was to be sad, make him sadder; bright, make him brighter; worried, more worried; wild, make him wilder. Some of the artists had felt that "exaggeration" meant a more distorted drawing, or an action so violent it was disturbing. They found they had missed the point.

When Walt asked for realism, he wanted a carica-

ture of realism. One artist analyzed it correctly when he said, ''I don't think he meant 'realism.' I think he meant something that was more convincing, that made a bigger contact with people, and he just said 'realism' because 'real' things do. . . . Every so often [in the animation] the character would do something unconvincing, or to show how clever the animator was, and it wasn't real, it was phony.''[4] Walt would not accept anything that destroyed believability, but he seldom asked an animator to tame down an action if the idea was right for the scene.

Dave Hand told of a test he had done of Mickey riding along in his taxicab, whistling, with everything on the car rattling and bouncing. When they came to the corner, the car skidded and blew out a tire, at which point the car sagged, the license plate twirled over and landed with its numbers upside down and spelling, ''Oh, heck.'' Dave was sure that was a laugh, and he was careful to stage it so that it could not be missed. Evidently he had not considered the whole car as carefully, for Walt complained of the lack of action and asked him to do it over. The next test received the same reaction. ''It's not broad enough; it's not funny!'' Six times Dave corrected the action, erasing and redrawing until he was nearly through the paper, and still Walt did not feel the action was spirited enough for what he wanted.

At that point Dave got fed up. ''The only thing I knew to do was to do something he wouldn't take—to make it so extreme that he would say, 'I didn't mean *that* much!' So I went back and did something horribly distorted. I was kind of proud of myself and couldn't

wait for the film to come back. I put it on the Moviola, Walt came and ran it a few times, then stepped back and looked at me. I thought he was going to tell me to leave the studio, but he said, 'There, Dave, that's just what I wanted!'

''It taught me what to do at the Disney studio. From then on I never had any trouble with exaggeration. When I was directing I used to say to the animators, 'Will you do something for me? Will you make it so extreme that you make me mad?' ''

Solid Drawing

The old-timers were hard pressed to keep up with the demands of the new type of animation. More than one top man counseled the beginners, ''You should learn to draw as well as possible before starting to animate.'' Grim Natwick,[5] whose animation career started in New York in 1924, pointed out, ''The better you can draw, the easier it'll be for you. You'll have to draw the character in all positions and from every angle; and if you can't do it, and have to stage it from some other angle, it's very restrictive and takes longer.'' Marc Davis was more philosophic a few years later: ''Drawing is giving a performance; an artist is an actor who is not limited by his body, only by his ability and, perhaps, experience.'' Too many of the men, old and

Texture in a drawing is made up of open spaces, busy areas, richness of design, and a pleasing, sparkling appearance. These qualities are seen in both the rough drawing and the clean-up of Happy, each by Fred Moore.

THIS IS WHAT'S CALLED A "WOODEN" CHARACTER.

EACH EYE, EAR, HAND, FINGER, LEG, COLLAR, SHOE, etc. LOOKS THE SAME AS ITS COUNTER-PART. THE RESULT IS A VERY STIFF LOOKING POSE.

PAF!

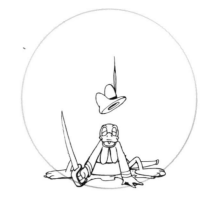

PAGE 3

...THIS CHARACTER LOOKS MORE NATURAL SIMPLY BECAUSE EACH PART OF THE BODY VARIES IN SOME WAY FROM THE CORRESPONDING OP-POSITE PART.

EYES IN PERSPECTIVE

FINGERS THAT VARY GIVE THE HANDS A MORE DYNAMIC LOOK.

No matter how hard young animators try to avoid them, "twins" creep into their work. Carson Van Osten of the Comic Strip Department reminds young artists everywhere to beware of this hazard.

Young animator Ron Clements discusses his drawing problems with Frank Thomas.

new, were full of tricks and techniques that had looked great in cartooning school but did nothing for them at the Disney studio. The little shadows under the toes of the shoes, the slick line, the flashy verve of clothing reacting to violent exertion—all these devices that had impressed us in high school were of little use anymore.

Signs were hung on many walls where the young trainees would be sure to see them, and the one we remember best was this: "Does your drawing have weight, depth and balance?"—a casual reminder of the basics of solid, three-dimensional drawing. Men had devoted their whole lives to the mastery of these elusive principles, and here was this sign about as pretentious as one that said, "Buy Savings Bonds," or pointed to the nearest exit.

Another sign admonished us to watch out for "twins" in our drawings. This is the unfortunate situation where both arms or both legs are not only parallel but doing exactly the same thing. No one draws this way on purpose, and usually the artist is not even aware that he has done it. This affliction was not limited to the thirties, for again in the seventies young animator Ron Clements was annoyed to find "twins" in his drawings no matter how hard he worked to keep them out. "It was one of the first drawing principles that I heard of at the studio. If you get into acting, you would never think of expressing an emotion with twins anywhere, but, somehow, in a drawing, if you're not thinking, it creeps in time and again."

Our main search was for an "animatable" shape, one that had volume but was still flexible, possessed strength without rigidity, and gave us opportunities for the movements that put over our ideas. We needed a shape that was a living form, ready to move—in contrast with the static form. We used the term ''plastic,'' and just the definition of the word seemed to convey the feeling of potential activity in the drawing: ''Capable of being shaped or formed, pliable.''

Appeal

Appeal was very important from the start. The word is often misinterpreted to suggest cuddly bunnies and soft kittens. To us, it meant anything that a person likes to see, a quality of charm, pleasing design, simplicity, communication, and magnetism. Your eye is drawn to the figure that has appeal, and, once there, it is held while you appreciate what you are seeing. A striking, heroic figure can have appeal. A villainess, even though chilling and dramatic, should have appeal; otherwise, you will not want to watch what she is doing. The ugly and repulsive may capture your gaze, but there will be neither the building of character nor identification with the situation that will be needed. There is shock value, but no story strength.

ARTIST: *Marc Davis*—Sleeping Beauty.

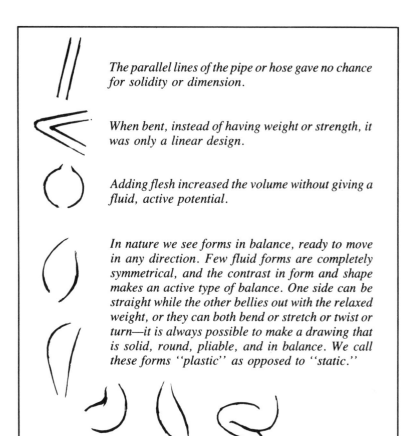

The parallel lines of the pipe or hose gave no chance for solidity or dimension.

When bent, instead of having weight or strength, it was only a linear design.

Adding flesh increased the volume without giving a fluid, active potential.

In nature we see forms in balance, ready to move in any direction. Few fluid forms are completely symmetrical, and the contrast in form and shape makes an active type of balance. One side can be straight while the other bellies out with the relaxed weight, or they can both bend or stretch or twist or turn—it is always possible to make a drawing that is solid, round, pliable, and in balance. We call these forms ''plastic'' as opposed to ''static.''

ANIMATOR: *John Lounsbery*—Lady and the Tramp.

A weak drawing lacks appeal. A drawing that is complicated or hard to read lacks appeal. Poor design, clumsy shapes, awkward moves, all are low on appeal. Spectators enjoy watching something that is appealing to them, whether an expression, a character, a movement, or a whole story situation. While the live actor has charisma, the animated drawing has appeal.

Young people, excited about the great successes achieved with line drawing, are always perplexed to hear that delicate refinements are not possible in this medium. They recall scenes of great beauty and pictures with strong emotions and cannot see that there is any problem in communication. But the problem is there, in every scene and every day. Since the medium lacks the subtle shadow patterns on the face that can reveal the shades of character in a person, we must concentrate on the acting or the story structure. Delicate expressions can be misinterpreted, to everyone's confusion, and attempting too much refinement can make the drawing so restrained or involved that no communication is possible. Only simple and direct attitudes make good drawings, and without good drawings we have little appeal.

The whole idea of trying to communicate feelings with mere lines does seem ridiculous at times. There is always the temptation to get in close so the audience can really see how the character is reacting, but the close-up presents the greatest problems. Dave Hand said, in 1938, when questioned about the advisability of using extreme close-ups: ''The face begins to flat-ten out when you get too close on it. We are attempting to overcome that now, with a new dye process, but it will be some time before it's perfected.'' (It never was.)

Many great effects are possible, but too often they cost more than the average production can afford. The constant battle is to find the elements that will look best in this medium and still allow the strongest communication of the idea presented. A drawing must be made in line, duplicated on cels, painted in flat colors, photographed over a background, and projected onto a giant screen. Tiny, sensitive lines on the drawings are now enlarged until they are more than a foot wide, and very, very black. In the mid-thirties, we wished for shading, for textures, for areas with no outlines, but they were not practical. We had to find other ways of putting over the points in the scenes, and in so doing developed character animation into a communicative art that astounded the world. But at the time there was neither glory nor pride in our efforts, only the nagging limitations. As we passed each other in the hall, we shook our heads and shared the thought, ''It's a crude medium.''

ANIMATOR: *Jack Campbell*— Pinocchio.

Extreme close-ups tend to go flat because there is so little to draw that can be related to other parts of the head. The large expanse of flat color creates a problem as well. The Blue Fairy in Pinocchio *received careful additions from the Ink and Paint Department to make this close-up believable.*

69

Peter Pan

4. Discovery 1934–1936

"I definitely feel that we cannot do the fantastic things based on the real, unless we first know the real."

Walt Disney

The mid-thirties was easily the most thrilling period for the Disney animators. It was a time of explosive growth for the whole studio, but the exploring and experimenting and discovery created an excitement never quite matched again.

Just because we had named one of the new principles of animation did not mean that we understood it or grasped the extent of its possibilities. Constant study and searching had brought us that far, and more study was the only way to keep advancing. Walt secured movies from other companies for us to see at the studio after hours, and he told us of the great vaudeville acts to see whenever they were in town. Everywhere we went and everything we did became something to study: for timing, staging, humor, personality traits, movements, action. One animator bought a 16mm camera when they first came on the market, to photograph his own resource material and study it frame by frame. It put him ahead of the others immediately, since he was able to create new actions beyond our understanding.

Don Graham,[1] top instructor at Chouinard's Art Institute, was brought out one evening a week to improve the drawing talents of the staff. At first it was just regular life drawing, but it was not long before Don came under Walt's intensive drive always to get something better. He wanted Don to become the outstanding authority on line drawing in the country. He wanted his men taught things you could not find in any existing

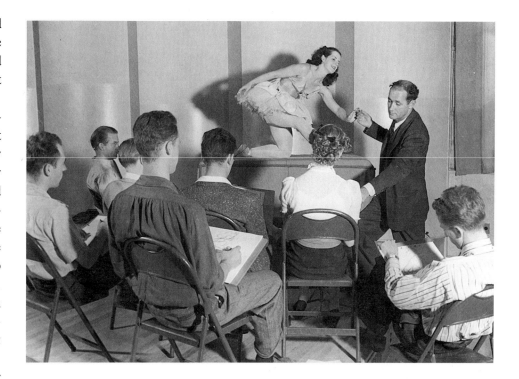

art school. Life drawing was useful, but it did not go nearly far enough or fast enough. Don soon was spending more time studying than teaching, as he tried to keep up with Walt's enthusiasm.

Walt realized that the animators teaching the art were the ones who shared his desire to achieve higher standards, and in 1936 he put out this memo: "We plan on installing night classes on action analysis immediately. I intend to have some of the best anima-

Art instructor Don Graham was hired to raise the level of the animators' drawings.

How does the animator make the character appear to think?

71

tors talk to these men and discuss with them Timing, [and] means of obtaining certain effects. . . . in this way I hope to stir up in this group of men an enthusiasm and a knowledge of how to achieve results that will advance them rapidly.'' Now we were coming back two and three nights every week either to talk or to listen. There were also guest speakers from outside the studio, but, while they were stimulating and enriched our general background, we did not get as much from them in a practical way as we did from our own ''experts.'' As Les Clark said, ''I learned more from working with the fellas, and from Walt.''

The memo continued: ''I also intend to have Don Graham study our better animation, so that he will be able to analyze things for the younger animators.'' More work for Don, and this in addition to the classes he was conducting on action analysis from live-action film clips. He selected single actions on short pieces of film and ran these backward and forward endlessly while discussing every observation he had been able to make. Our eyes flickered in sync with the slow shutter speed on the projector, but we were fascinated.

One piece of film showed a horse in a slow canter turning a half circle to his left. Don went to elaborate lengths to prepare us for this film, explaining how the horse had to lead with his left foot to keep his balance. ''If he led with his right, the support would come too late for his weight, and he would fall over.'' Then he ran the film, and to everyone's surprise—and Don's horror—the horse was running in a left turn with a right lead. Ken Anderson[2] burst out impetuously, ''Hey, Don! The horse is wrong!'' Too many nights with too many classes were getting to Don, but he stoically kept on. Actually, he made a better point in our minds than he would have otherwise, for any horseman knows that a horse can lead with either foot on a turn. However, his rhythm and balance will be better using the one that matches the direction he is turning, and we had to know that also.

Our most startling observation from films of people in motion was that almost all actions start with the hips; and, ordinarily, there is a drop—as if gravity were being used to get things going. From this move, there is usually a turn or tilt or a wind up, followed by a whiplash type of action as the rest of the body starts to follow through. This was evident first in sports films showing baseball pitchers and golfers, but soon we could see it in more general activities. Any person starting to move from a still, standing position, whether to start walking or pick something up, always began the move with the hips.

Don Graham eventually did become the leading authority on line drawing, but only a man of his patience, intellect, and calm determination could have lasted through those classes. He would shake his head in disbelief at the comments from all sides as he tried to educate masses of imaginative, enthusiastic artists. Don always had a cigarette in his hand, but it was hard to recall his lighting one. In our memories, his cigarettes were never over three-quarters of an inch long (getting shorter by the minute), and the smoke clung to his hand and went up his sleeve. There were no ashtrays up on the model stand where he generally talked, so he never seemed to have a place to put out the smoldering tip, moving it adroitly from one set of pinched fingernails to another. We found ourselves engrossed in these amazing displays of agility instead of Don's carefully chosen words.

When some of the animators were pressuring Walt to let them change Mickey's eyes so that more delicate expressions could be handled, Walt asked Don to bring it up in his class to see what all of the fellows thought. It was a difficult night for Don, since he had never pretended to inject himself into the actual work of animation, and he found himself trying to control a spirited discussion between authorities of varied opinions and even more varied personalities. Some felt the audience would never accept the new design and would wonder what was wrong. Others claimed that people would never notice. Some felt it would be all right to try it for just one picture and see what happened. As the talk became more heated, one man quipped, ''Why don't we just change one eye at a time?''[3]

Many of the animators resented the constant push toward more realism in every action. To them, putting over the gag, the business, the strong pose, was all that was needed to be entertaining. The rest was just frills. But the new types of pictures called for actions that had to be analyzed carefully if they were to come off. There was a famous scene in *The China Shop* that was talked about for years. The story was simple: an old man has a china shop, and when he leaves at night the figurines come to life. But the scene of the kindly old shopkeeper taking a last look around, then opening the door, walking through it, and closing it behind him was quite a change from the broad gags and actions in the earlier films. The action not only had to be convincing, it had to have character. The old man had little personality, but he had to be old and kindly and somewhat reminiscent of someone out of a Dickens novel.

The animator was determined to get a shuffling walk, a bent posture, and a feeling of age in the movements. He did not want this man to reach far, take big steps, or in any way appear to be athletic or strong. The layout man had drawn a door on a wall that had a true storybook feeling, but, unfortunately, the doorknob was on the far side of the door, a long distance from the elderly shopkeeper. He had to walk over close enough to reach out easily and grasp it. But this left him standing directly in the path of the door, which for some reason opened inward!

Two years after this, the animator would have run back to the Music Room and screamed about the restricting layout. "Why does it have to be at this angle?" "Why does the door open in instead of out?" "How am I supposed to get him through this door?" But this option had not been considered at the time of *The China Shop*. That animator, with great determination, attacked the problem from an action standpoint, probably hoping secretly that he would show everyone how well he could analyze the situation. The door opened four inches and hit the gentleman's foot. He stepped back in a casual, shuffling manner. He opened the door another four inches only to find that it had bumped against his other foot. Again he stepped back— another four inches. Now the door was against the first foot once more. There was no way he could step back far enough into the scene to clear this door, and the farther he backed up the more problem there would be in walking around the obstruction to get outside, where he had to be by the end of the scene. So as the film rolled by, the poor old man shuffled about endlessly as the door gradually opened enough for him to reverse his steps and struggle into the night. It was a comedy of errors on everyone's part, but the animator bore the brunt of the kidding more than the director or the layout man. There was much to be learned.

Through those days, the pictures we made reflected the wide range of concepts Walt was exploring. One film concentrated on dances and the geometric patterns dancers made when seen from above. This had become a popular camera angle because of the musicals live-action studios were making; it was felt we might do it better, but the audiences did not agree with us. We dealt with fantasies, gags, musicals, dreams, adventures, personalities; the titles alone suggest the variety of subject matter: *The Flying Mouse, Lullaby Land, Mickey's Pal Pluto, The Pied Piper, Thru The Mirror, The Klondike Kid*. Many of these were not successful, but Walt analyzed the reactions and tried something else. There seemed no end to his ideas, but the best response from both his staff and the audience was to his talent for developing personalities. It permeated his thinking on almost every venture.

Walt had always loved trains, with their almost human engines, and as early as 1929 he had one of them featured in the film *Mickey's Choo-Choo*. Ben Sharpsteen had the assignment of animating the new character. "Walt was not content to have a small engine as a prop; he wanted to give it personality. In the story, the engine came to a grade where it was having great difficulty making headway, and with much puffing and steaming it squatted down to the ground in fatigue. Mickey Mouse, the engineer, tried to prod it into action, and the engine tried to put forth a final effort. The pistons were animated to represent arms

We did many trains, all with personality. This is a British design for The Adventures of Ichabod and Mr. Toad.

ANIMATOR: *Dick Lundy—* Thru the Mirror.

Inanimate characters have proved to be popular over the years, especially when their personalities matched their appearance. More than their novelty, it was the feeling Walt had for an entertaining situation that made them successful.

73

ANIMATOR: *Leonard Sebring*
—Lullaby Land.

Even safety pins are brought to life and made into characters.

and hands; they reached out and grabbed the rails as a person might grab a rope to pull himself along.'' This was more than just a matter of personality, it was the whole idea built on character relationships that could be animated. Mickey had a clear attitude, there was something he was trying to do, and the engine offered all kinds of opportunity to the imaginative animator.

A character was never placed in a scene unless he had a definite reason for being there. He had funny business, gag material, dialogue, something to make him interesting, and, usually, something that showed who he was and how he felt. Otherwise, he was not shown. Walt never left a scene at the continuity level; he made something out of it or reworked the story at that point. As these ideas became stronger, the cutting and staging of the scenes became more important. Decisions as to where to have the camera, how far back to be, who to have the camera on, when to be on someone else—all the facets of filmmaking became important to the little cartoon. From a novelty, we were coming of age in the picture business.

The use of real personalities for the characters had come about slowly as the better type of comedy and gags developed. At first there were just general types with the traditional connotations from the comic strips: big and tough, small and quick, fat and jolly, thin and miserly. The gags called for attitudes, expressions, a certain amount of thought or consideration here and there, but no need was felt for personality as expressed in walks, reactions, motivations, or thinking. The audience was drawn into the picture through the types of gags and sprightly business; there was no necessity for anything more. People were delighted by cycles and other tricks to make the impossible look plausible.

Prior to 1930, none of the characters showed any real thought process. Although Mickey had replaced Oswald he was doing the same things, and the only thinking done was in reaction to something that had happened. Mickey would see it, react, realize that he

had to get a counter idea in a hurry, look around and see his answer, quickly convert it into something that fit his predicament, then pull the gag by using it successfully.

Of course, the potential for having a character really appear to think had always been there in the routines that Walt had envisioned, but no one knew how to accomplish such an effect. It was not even realized how much such an addition would increase the audience's enjoyment and involvement in the pictures. That all changed in one day when a scene was animated of a dog who looked into the camera and snorted. Miraculously, he had come to life! Walt was quick to appreciate the difference and so was the audience. The year was 1930 and the animator Norm Ferguson.[4]

With the gradual advancements in our skills, the way was open for Walt to explore a whole new concept: that of telling a complete story. The earlier films were made up of gags and had followed a situation or predicament through to the end, but there was never an attempt to capture an audience's interest through the story itself. Now Walt wanted to see if his staff's ability to present a simple but complete story could hold up, for that would open great new fields to us. It was a step forward for story, but a huge leap for animation. Could we sustain a character, keeping him consistent and believable for seven minutes?

Even more suprising to everyone at the time was Walt's desire to build pictures around the ideas of tenderness, the lullaby, someone in trouble, sympathy and sacrifice, the fairy story. These were concepts that none of his storymen would ever have thought of doing, and most certainly none of his competitors, but once again Walt's intuition was right. Stories with heart and warmth brought the greatest audience involvement, a response far beyond that for pictures built only on gags.

The biggest difference—and the gamble—was that these films would have to be taken seriously. Cartoons

ANIMATOR: *Dick Lundy*—
The Ugly Duckling.

The audience had to take the story seriously, and feel sorry for this little character—which seemed like asking a lot.

heretofore always were intended to be funny. Would the theater patrons accept this new genre, or would they laugh at our crude, presumptive efforts? How far could we expect them to follow us?

Fortunately, the audience was more than ready for Walt's type of entertainment. Even in the grim days of the Depression, when anything like a fairy tale would seem completely out of place, he had one success after another—not every picture, nor really even half of them, but enough to show us the way to go and encourage Walt in his ideas on communication.

It was apparent that more than mere continuity was needed in presenting a full story. An old favorite like *Babes in the Woods*, using the Hansel and Gretel stories, needed quite a bit more to make it entertaining in this new form. We quickly learned that a drab retelling of any story or an emphasis on continuity and exposition was the wrong way to go. Nothing is more

deadly in animation than explanations of who the characters are and what they are doing there, followed by more discussion of what they are going to do about it! We searched for the entertaining situations inherent in the story or in the personalities that could be developed.

One perfect example was the first Mickey cartoon in color, *The Band Concert*. It introduced the amateur barnyard musicians giving an open-air concert to an appreciative audience. The story was built around the music being played and the heckling of Donald Duck, an ice cream salesman who wanted to play the flute. There is no explanation of who anyone is or how Mickey acquired a band, so there is no need for lengthy continuity scenes. It is not the type of picture that needs a strong personality build-up, so it takes right off with entertaining business, and each and every scene is packed with entertainment.

The Pointer has very little actual story and few gags

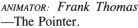

ANIMATOR: *Frank Thomas* —The Pointer.

The audience feels the suspense in this classic situation as Mickey thinks it is Pluto behind him.

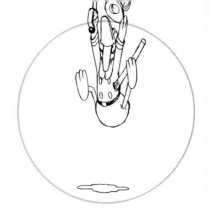

but is built almost entirely on personality. In fact, it represents the peak of Walt's feeling for Mickey and has dialogue development that is so specific for this character that it never would fit Donald or Goofy or anyone but Mickey. One simple scene of Mickey reading to Pluto from a book on how to train hunting dogs, a longer shot of their camp in the woods, and that is all anyone needs to know about the situation. There is little continuity, once again, and each scene is in the picture because of its entertainment potential.

Mickey's reaction to seeing a bear right before him is pure "Disney," unique, spontaneous, fresh, and funny. No one but Walt would have thought of that dialogue, or stretched out the situation to so much footage, or expected the animator to sustain the predicament with nothing but personality. But what personality! This is no ordinary, "Oh, Hi, Mr. Bear." Right from the first nervous gasp of recognition, while he is struggling to gain his composure, he is the Missouri farm boy living out a fantasy. "Oh. . . . It's you . . . that is, it *is* you—ain't it? I mean, isn't it? Uh, I thought you were Pluto, but you're not Pluto. . . . You're *you*, aren't cha? Uh . . . well, I'm Mickey Mouse. . . . Y'know? Mickey Mouse? I hope you've heard of me—I hope? . . ." This gave the animator strong changes of attitude and texture in the acting that are seldom found in normal dialogue.

Walt had been so funny in the story meetings acting out Mickey's confusion that we asked if we could shoot a film of him as he recorded the lines. Mickey's voice was always done by Walt, and he felt the lines and the situation so completely that he could not keep from acting out the gestures and even the body attitudes as he said the dialogue. This was before he had worked in front of a camera, and he was reticent. Doing a good job of recording the voice with all the shading and timing and expression that were required was enough creative effort for anyone, especially when restricted to an unnatural falsetto voice for Mickey.

Walt was skeptical of live action at that time and not too sure of how we would use it, but our enthusiasm won him over. Reluctantly he agreed, but with restrictions: "Well . . . if you keep the camera in the booth—not out on the stage, mind you—and if I don't know when you're doing it; and. . . ." On that day, he wore his baggiest clothes and his favorite old felt hat, which did not give him a crisp appearance but did make him feel comfortable and relaxed. The camera was set up so far away from Walt that our image on the film was very tiny, but still it captured the essence of his acting. While the animator nearly went blind trying to chart the timing and to sketch from the action, it paid off in a memorable little sequence that reflects Walt's thinking completely.

At the point in the recording where he said, "I'm Mickey Mouse. . . . Y'know? Mickey Mouse?" Walt instinctively reached out with his hand to denote the height of a little kid. It was the only time we ever knew just how big Walt considered Mickey to be. In spite of the help it gave us, he never let us put a camera on him again; and years later, when we wanted to look at that film once more, it had disappeared. No one knows what happened to it.

The use of design and color and beauty in our films was beginning to change their appearance dramatically, bringing the artwork closer to storybook illustration. The arrival of artists who were better draftsmen meant that the studio could dispense with the tricks and techniques that had brought the films this far and embark on a more ambitious course. Mood began to play an important part. Well-designed long shots are exciting to see, and if they can establish a special locale and build a mood at the same time they are invaluable. They reach immediately into the viewers' imagination, involving them in your pictures before you have barely begun.

We were helped in this by what we could do with both sound effects and music. Sound makes you think of your own experiences, which opens up a whole new range of symbols for communication. Night sounds, crickets and frogs, eerie wind, blustery wind, rain on a window or on the roof of a car—all work in our memories and immediately establish a mood. Music can do even more to arouse our emotions; and, while in the early films sound was spotty and reminiscent of a small band in an orchestra pit, music quickly found its way to a more artistic use through stirring themes that literally transported the audience into our make-believe worlds.

The Layout Department had been slow to develop, probably because there had been little call for the artistry later brought to the films, and possibly because

Before the time of individual personalities, the villain was simply big and tough, like the Captain in Steamboat Willie, *by Ub Iwerks.*

FACING PAGE:
ARTIST: Claude Coats— Pinocchio.

Skillful painting enables the viewer to see all the details of Geppetto's shop without losing the overall impact of the picture.

Walt was not aware at the time what good layouts could do. There had been no dramatic settings and not even a layout that matched the scope of ideas seen in the action. There was a lack of character in the drawing, with one house looking like another, all trees looking alike, and the final painting so gently tinted that it hardly could be seen. No one knew yet how to support the personality of an actor through the handling of his surroundings. The actor had to make his way alone.

By the time of the *Three Little Pigs*, Walt was beginning to look for entertaining ideas in a character's locale, and he loved to tell how the artists had drawn pictures of boxers and sports figures on the walls of one foolish pig's house, and pictures of girls in the next, while the practical pig had photos of Momma and Papa. This was a beginning, but few people saw that touch in the background while watching all the interesting action in front of it. Six short but busy years later, the audience was seeing the unforget-

table figures in Geppetto's house and detail after memorable detail throughout the whole picture. A way had been found to do it.

By 1936, a new type of picture was becoming possible. Technical skills were advancing and a new camera was being built that promised wonderful illusions; animation of rain and clouds and lightning had improved to the point that they were quite convincing; cartoon colors were beginning to glow; and new styling coordinated all of a film's parts into one unified concept. When these achievements were combined with the ability to portray mood on the screen, a true milestone in the development of the animated cartoon resulted: *The Old Mill*, Academy Award winner for 1937. With no story other than the reaction of various animals to one stormy night in a broken down mill, the film showed that an audience could be swept up by sheer artistry and become deeply involved in an animated film.

Walt had not been so successful in his attempts to

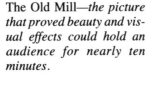

The Old Mill—*the picture that proved beauty and visual effects could hold an audience for nearly ten minutes.*

establish new frontiers in other areas, notably in the animation of human figures. He called for cartoons about Persephone in the *Goddess of Spring*, a charming sugar cookie girl in *The Cookie Carnival*, a winsome stuffed doll in *Broken Toys*, and an excitable, greedy monarch, King Midas, in *The Golden Touch*. The cookie and the doll were acceptably feminine, but the whole world is highly critical of a less than perfect representation of a pretty girl. The animator's drawings and the movement they depicted were admittedly far from perfect.

King Midas proved to be unacceptable as well, although there was at least one moment when his feelings came across to the audience so strongly that a momentary sensation of empathy was created. The trouble here was not so much with the animation as with the story, which had not been worked out with nearly the care that was customary. It made Walt realize that "Story . . . must be considered the heart of the business." He continued, "Good animators can make a good story a knockout. There is not much that the best animators can do with bad stories."

Walt's feeling about stories generally always had been to get the entertainment first and then find ways to tie it all together. Chaplin had gone even further in this direction, making extensive use of printed cards to set up his predicaments: "Seasick," "That night," "He finds a friend," "Lost"—and then he had gone right to the heart of what was funny in the situation. Walt felt the same way; he was not interested in getting from "here" to "there," only in what happened to the character once he was there.

Another frontier giving trouble was that of voices. Walt's original feeling seemed to be that cartoon characters should have cartoon voices, something different and as far from a natural voice as the drawings were from real animals or people. He had found a duck's voice in a radio comic,[5] a singing chicken in an ex-opera songstress, and his staff volunteered more unexpected sounds. Animator Fred Spencer could talk through a gargle that seemed appropriate for a fish—or at least some underwater character—and Ollie Johnston could talk with the bleating of a sheep, but no use was ever found for that particular talent.

As the stories became more sincere, the casting for voices took a new direction. Now the search was for

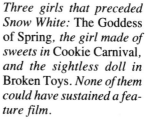

ANIMATOR: *Grim Natwick*
—Cookie Carnival.

ANIMATOR: *Grim Natwick*
—Broken Toys.

Three girls that preceded Snow White: *The Goddess* of Spring, *the girl made of sweets in* Cookie Carnival, *and the sightless doll in* Broken Toys. *None of them could have sustained a feature film.*

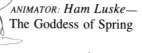

ANIMATOR: *Ham Luske*—
The Goddess of Spring

ANIMATOR: *Norm Ferguson*
—The Golden Touch.

Walt had hoped that just animation showing a range of emotions in the greedy King Midas would carry an eight-minute film.

Clarence Nash, the voice of Donald Duck.

The staff in 1932. KNEELING: *Floyd Gottfredson, Les Clark, and Johnny Cannon.* FRONT ROW: *Bert Gillett, Jack King, Ted Sears Roy Disney, Walt, Norm Ferguson, Dick Lundy, Emile Flohri (background painter).* 2ND ROW: *Clyde "Gerry" Geronimi, Bert Lewis, Frank Churchill, Ben Sharpsteen, and Albert Hurter.* 3RD ROW: *Wilfred Jackson (wearing Tom Palmer's glasses as a gag), Tom Palmer, Webb Smith (behind Churchill), Gilles "Frenchy" de Trémaudan.* BACK ROW: *Hugh Hennesy, Dave Hand, Charlie Philippi.*

sincere voices, real voices, not the trained voice of the stage but the completely natural voice of the boy and girl next door. In *Cookie Carnival* and *Broken Toys*, the voices were so commonplace that the animators could find no gestures or attitudes to caricature. Straight voices demand straight action, and the artists simply could not make the characters come alive. But Walt was not worried. He felt sure they would get it on the next picture!

There were changes in audience tastes, too, which became more sophisticated, more accustomed to better animation and more realistic presentations. People were expecting higher quality now and looked to us for extremely convincing characters. One historian, as he tried to trace the growth in Walt's thinking, asked, "Would it have been possible to create another character as broad as Donald Duck by the end of the thirties?" The answer was unanimous: "No one wanted another Donald Duck at that time." We had grown up.

Christopher Finch in his book, *The Art Of Walt Disney*, told a story about Dick Huemer meeting Ben Sharpsteen on the street after Ben had gone to work at the newly successful Disney Studio. Dick asked him, "What's the secret over at Disney's? What do you guys do that's different?" Ben answered simply, "We analyze." Dick responded that his people analyzed,

too; everyone did. There had to be more to it than that. As he thought about it, Ben decided that the key ingredient must be "realism." In his own experience, he had found that much of the material in cartoon films was lost on the viewers; they could not understand it or relate to it. Walt had bridged that gap with realism, or a caricature of it. His situations were understandable, clear, and funny. His personalities were based on someone you knew.

As the studio grew, Walt had increasing trouble keeping track of everything that was being done, so he placed more of the burden on his two directors. Happily, he found that he could turn out more product this way while still exercising just as much control. At first he had called them "storymen," because their job was to see that the story elements were preserved. They just grew into their jobs rather than being appointed with any ceremony, because of the need for making all the action sync to the beat. First it was Wilfred Jackson, who never even really was hired. (He had asked if he could come in just to learn.) Then Walt added Bert Gillett, who had come out from New York with some reputation and experience.

Eventually, when Bert moved on to other work, Walt moved up the forthright and ambitious Dave Hand, who had a talent for getting things done. By this time, the responsibilities of the director were beginning to expand. He became the hub from which all other functions radiated. He had to follow every last detail through every department, to make sure that the finished film would faithfully reflect the ideas that had originated in the Story Department. To do this, he had to have imagination, patience, drive, diplomacy, and endless creative ideas.

The director's office was called the Music Room in the early days of sound because the musician had his desk and piano there. Later, when music acquired a broader role and the musician got a room of his own, the name not only persisted but came to suggest the whole function of preparing the work for animation—even after there were more directors and "Music Rooms" than there were musicians.

The easiest times for the director were when he was told exactly what he was supposed to do. His most difficult moments came when his instructions had been vague or he had misinterpreted Walt's remarks at a

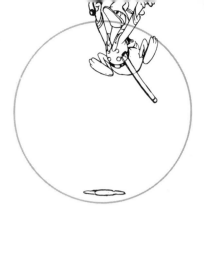

meeting. The latter was easy to do, since Walt had a way of avoiding a positive commitment when he was not quite sure in his own mind. His usual method at such times was to bolster the director's confidence, sell him on the glories of the sequence, fill the air with exciting generalities, then duck out while everyone was still elated. It was not until hours later that anyone would realize there had been no real resolution. The stronger directors, such as Dave Hand and Wilfred Jackson, would not let Walt leave the room that way, but they would push him to the point of annoyance until they were positive that Walt knew and approved of exactly what they were going to do. Another director might simply work ahead stoically, hoping that Walt would drop in later with clearer instructions, but realizing all the time that his position was precarious and his responsibilities enormous.

The animator received his scenes from the director in a special session called "the handout" (or "pickup"). This meeting could stretch out over several days as the director explained how he wanted the scene done, ideally in a way that captured the animator's imagination and excited him about the scene's potential—while keeping him on the right track. In the days when scenes were only gags, a description of the action typed on the bottom of a story sketch was all that was needed, and the handout consisted of dealing these out like playing cards to whichever animator was free to work. But when the scenes were expected to build character and utilize personalities to tell the story, printed instructions failed to convey the message. Without wide-ranging discussions with the director and per-

sonal involvement, the animator would only illustrate another person's ideas, and that is as barren an assignment as anyone ever had. Walt had been most explicit about the necessity for "getting the animators into the spirit of the picture, and not making them feel outsiders just executing something worked out by someone else."

Dave Hand explained the whole business of the handout this way: "Our entire medium is transference of thought. The thought is created first in the mind of the storyman . . . then transferred to the director, who attempts to transfer it to the animator. This is where the big problem of transference comes, because the animator then attempts to transfer it pictorially. He takes it out of the intangible, and places it in tangible form, in picture, for transference back to the mind of the audience . . . and picture presentation is clearer than any other means of transferring thought from one person to another."

At another time, Dave was not so poetic. "We can talk until we are blue in the face in the Music Room, but the animator thinks entirely a different picture." No one really knows what another person's understanding is, and the difference in conception can be unbelievably wide. A director on a live-action picture can work with the actor and see what he is going to do. The actions can be altered, refined, changed, or questioned, and the results judged on the spot. In animation, there is no way of knowing ahead of time how the scene will look. Perhaps the animator has a clear picture, but he can be fooled, too.

As more and more animators were added to the staff, there was an increased need for training on one hand and control on the other. Many systems were tried, and for a while there was a category of "junior animator" to denote someone making a contribution but limited in what he could do. The problem was how to go about teaching those who still had much to learn. With several sequence directors on the same picture it was already difficult to maintain either the quality or the characterization that Walt was seeking. The answer seemed to lie in giving more responsibility to the stronger animators, and the job of Directing or Supervising Animator was invented. Walt never liked titles, so these men were never sure of what they were, only what they had to do. (Continued on page 84)

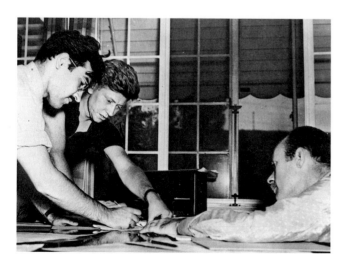

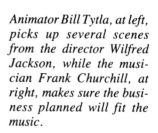

Animator Bill Tytla, at left, picks up several scenes from the director Wilfred Jackson, while the musician Frank Churchill, at right, makes sure the business planned will fit the music.

81

SWEATBOX

The first Moviola with film flapping and clacking as it goes under the viewing lens. Walt studies a test as the animators try to see over his shoulder.

Walt had to have a way to see the animation before it went into his pictures. He could flip the scenes and study the drawings on the pegs, but the only way he really could tell how they would look was to have the drawings filmed. This was known as a "pencil test," and it gave both Walt and the animator a chance to study the action and make corrections before the scene was inked and painted.

Ub Iwerks had devised a way to look inside an old projector while the film was running, eliminating the need for a screen and viewing room, and the men stood in line to see the effect of their drawings on film. It was not long before this innovation was contributing

so much to the making of the films that a standard film-cutter's viewer made by the Moviola Company was purchased. This had an enlarging lens, and two people with their heads pushed close together could watch at the same time.

When the new addition was made to the studio in 1931, the space under the stairwell was saved for a place to see the pencil tests. Prior to that, the men had shielded the lens from the light by their coats or their hands, or by placing the machine in a corner and hanging a curtain from the ceiling. This kept the area dark enough, but made very cramped quarters for the two or three people squeezed inside. That was nothing

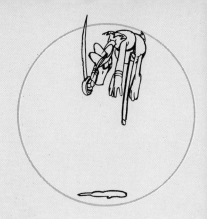

compared to the new little closet under the stairs.

By this time, as many as five or six people would check the scenes together, as Walt showed what he liked about the work in a scene; or, more often, what he did not like. It was inevitable that someone would refer to the enclosure as a ''sweatbox.'' Then as more men were hired more machines were needed, and these were placed where they could do the most to speed up production—the space under the stairs was no longer convenient enough. The old term prevailed, however, and as scenes were cut together into whole reels of pencil tests, the animator went to ''sweatbox'' when he saw his scenes with the director. From there, it was a small step for the term to become a verb. Even though by 1934 there were two full-fledged projection rooms with air conditioning and comfortable chairs, animators asked, ''Have your scenes been sweatboxed yet?'' or sometimes said, ''I better not have a beer for lunch, they're sweatboxing my stuff today.''

In these sessions, the purpose is to be sure that everything is working, whether it is the acting, the action, or the stage directions. If the scenes are good, more business may be added to make them even better; if they are wrong, changes are called for, but always with an eye to saving as much as possible of what has been done. Animation is expensive, and the morale of the animator is critical to a good result. Still, Ham Luske,[6] the first supervising animator, always cautioned the young artists, ''Never make a small change. When they ask for a change, they're thinking of a big one . . . something that will really make a difference; otherwise they wouldn't mention it.''

Walt knew what made a scene play and could explain it to the animator so that he would understand. There were many times when Walt was undecided on what direction to go, but once he saw a scene of animation he could quickly analyze why the action was not as entertaining as it should have been. The following excerpt from sweatbox notes dated March 25, 1937, show how minutely he went into each scene. This was Fred Moore's animation of Doc and Grumpy arguing about whether Snow White should be a guest in their house:

Sc 24B Shoot a corr. ruff
Punch Doc's poking Grumpy more.

Get a nervous head on Doc to ''WHO'S A . . .'' he is mad at the start and you have him calm down too much.

As Grumpy says ''AW SHUT UP'' have Doc jump back (just a little) in a fighting pose, dropping his fanny and getting a stretch in the legs. . . . get a spring in his legs and fanny wiggle (as Walt demonstrated) while in the fighting pose.

Sweatbox notes such as these were taken down by the Music Room secretary, and it was no easy job. Explicit as they sound, the discussions that led up to the final decisions were full of alternate possibilities and attempts to find corrections that the animator understood and liked. No one talked slowly enough for complete notes to be recorded, and much of the terminology was in words no one new to the business would use. While the secretary was trying to rephrase the thoughts so her notes would be clear, she would hear Walt saying, ''Yeah, I think that's your best bet . . . y'know? . . . like we talked it there . . . do it like that and we'll see how it looks . . . whaddya think?'' and she would know that one of the ways had been agreed upon. Which one?

To anyone not in the meeting, the sweatbox notes made no sense whatsoever; and to those of us who had been there it was still a mystery most of the time, since the unfortunate secretary had gone through her notes and tried to use her own memory for the parts she thought she understood, to make it all mean something. If she was questioned about some of these rather personal decisions on her part, the normal response was, ''Well, *you* were there, weren't you?'' said in a thin, piercing, and slightly threatening voice.

Walt gradually turned over the ''nuts and bolts'' of making everything work properly to the directors, and devoted his own time to the bigger ideas. This did not mean that he let things slip by or did not notice what each man was doing. Not at all! He merely realized that if he told a supervising animator or the director how he thought a particular thing should be, they should be able to see that it was done that way. After all, he had trained us carefully over the years by going over every last frame in each scene—not once, but maybe fifty times—until we had all seen clearly what was to be done.

ITS AN ANIMATORS CHANGE!

T. HEE

The three directors in 1934: Left, Wilfred Jackson, by caricaturist T. Hee; center, Dave Hand, artist unknown; and, right, Ben Sharpsteen, by T. Hee.

The animators saw Walt at the story meetings where he acted out everything as it should be, and then again in "sweatbox," when they showed him the scene as they had animated it. In between times, the directors discussed with them what actions would be used, argued about how to stage them, how long the scenes should be, and how best to do the business. The animators learned from each of the directors, and animation flourished.

In 1934, when the big expansion began, there were three directors. There had been more work than Wilfred Jackson and Dave Hand could handle, and someone was needed who could develop the talents of the younger men being hired at that time, men with ability but no practical experience in cartooning or commercial art. Ben Sharpsteen was chosen for this assignment because he was always worried and concerned and dedicated to the studio. He projected a father image and tried to raise his fledglings like his own children, counseling them on everything, from which car to buy to which comedian to study.

Ben was conservative and made us work on fundamentals until we were on firm ground before we could go ahead. He gave drawing problems to all the assis-

tants and inbetweeners, not so much as a competition but so they could learn to talk over the difficulties and observe the variety of solutions. One favorite assignment was a tug-of-war between Goofy on one side and Mickey and Donald on the other. Ben wanted to see the rope taut, the feet planted squarely on the ground, hands and arms that carried the strain of the pulling right into the bodies, heads that reflected the effort, and an overall arrangement that showed clearly what they were doing. In addition, he suggested that it would be good if the whole thing could be made entertaining, with some fresh slant on the staging or the way each of them was participating in the action.

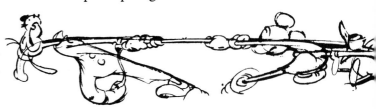

Many animators were still doing straight ahead animation at this time, and it had a greater appeal to the young and eager than the more thoughtful, disciplined "pose to pose" method. The danger, of course, was that no one stopped to make a solid drawing that had

everything in it. The animator kept thinking, "The next drawing will have it—all the character and the action and the funnies and the straights and the good drawing. You'll be able to see what he's doing in this very next drawing. . . ."

The next drawing was just as weak, as was the one after that, because a good drawing is not made casually, especially while the artist is thinking about something else—in this case, how to get the figure from one place on the paper to another. Ben Sharpsteen knew this all too well, and he knew the only cure for the mushy, indecisive action that inevitably resulted was for us to work over each drawing, strengthening and clarifying, until the drawing problems had been solved, before we went ahead with anything.

Wilfred Jackson (Dave Hand called him Willie but wrote his name "Jaxon" once, and it stuck as a nickname with the rest of us) taught us thoroughness and the importance of detail. He had an immensely creative grasp of his whole picture and what he wanted it to do, but his big strength was in the astounding attention he gave to every last detail. Every frame of each scene was carefully considered and made into something valuable; the animator was never at a loss to know what should be done in the footage he had been handed. If you had a better idea, Jaxon was all for it, but until you did he provided you with some very good material to animate. Jaxon was easily the most creative of the directors, but he was also the most "picky" and took a lot of kidding about his thoroughness.

Dave Hand's major contribution was in keeping up the quality of the work while organizing the procedures, forcing decisions, and keeping it all moving in the direction Walt said he wanted. He took on the job of making Walt's dreams and vague feelings tangible, and to do this he constantly had to try to pin Walt down to specifics. But Walt often changed his mind, and this led to some heated arguments. He confided once that Dave would storm into his office "white with rage. He'd grip the edge of my desk until his knuckles turned white. . . . I'd keep the desk between us." Then Walt would get a twinkle in his eye, and we knew that he enjoyed seeing Dave this concerned about the product and was not being unsympathetic. As Dave had admitted to him earlier, "I can't function until I get mad!" It was an interesting situation.

But Dave knew enough to recognize quality, and if Walt said, "Let's get *that* into the picture," Dave would make sure that it got in and just that way. If Walt said, "We can save money here; let's keep the cost down," Dave would use every shortcut in the book. He never confused his own views or ambitions with Walt's, and he never questioned Walt's authority. He tried to protect Walt from getting swamped with details, and he tried equally to protect the animators from too many interruptions. He liked to see things working in a productive fashion, and he was not afraid to do anything that might be needed to achieve that. These qualities made him a very good director for Walt, and later an excellent Production Manager. From Dave we learned courage and integrity and an aggressive approach to our work.

When Walt was deep in thought he would lower one brow, squint his eyes, let his jaw drop, and stare fixedly at some point in space, often holding the attitude for several moments. Unfortunately, he did the same thing when he appraised you prior to explaining a new assignment or admonishing you for not getting the idea he was presenting—or worse, when he had just noticed some quirk or mannerism in the way you did things, something he could exploit at a later date if he chose to. It was unnerving to be caught in that intense stare, and we never knew whether the scrutinization was because he was thinking of some new way to get us to do something he wanted, or if we were merely accidentally in the path of a preoccupied gaze. Many times we would look up casually during a

Walt's most typical expression, caught by one of the staff who preferred to remain anonymous.

Dave Hand, left, provided strong direction as the supervising director on Snow White; *storyman Perce Pearce used his great ability with character development to make the seven dwarfs into distinctive individuals.*

meeting to find to our surprise that we were being studied intently. No words could break the spell, and being unsure of the meaning of the look it was inadvisable to say anything anyway. So we squirmed, smiled weakly, looked thoughtful, stared back, pretended not to notice, or nodded wisely as if in tentative agreement, until Walt suddenly burst out with something like "Why don't we have Pluto get mixed up in this skating business, too?"

He expected everyone to work as hard as he did, and to be as interested and excited about what we were doing. He never spared feelings, because his interest was in the product and not in who had the best idea or who had made a poor suggestion or expected applause. We were all in it together, and the fellow who went off on his own, developing an idea that Walt had not approved, was asking for trouble, and received it.

Almost any comment about the material being considered was acceptable as long as it was offered in good faith, but it was a different story if anyone tried to get in a personal dig about either the product or Walt's methods. Sometimes an individual would feel

a little confident after a successful meeting and would try making a few kidding remarks about Walt. This rash decision was quickly regretted as Walt, with lightning response, made the culprit look utterly ridiculous —in a matter of seconds and in a very funny way. Suddenly the tables had been turned, and everyone was laughing at Walt's comments delivered at the expense of the man who had started it all. Ward Kimball[7] said, "No one ever got the best of Walt in any exchange, kidding or serious. Those who tried were cut to ribbons."

Through all these days, Walt was constantly plagued by money problems and by distributors who took the lion's share of the tiny profit from his creative efforts. He always felt that the way to win in this type of battle was to "beat them with product," to make films so good that the world would beat a path to his door. Ben Sharpsteen told of a 1929 conversation with Walt: "He was determined that he would no longer be dependent on a distributor or a victim of his chicanery."

The important thing was to improve the product, because audiences would respond to a better film. He did not believe in cutting corners to save money if it hurt the quality nor would he turn out a cheap product just to make money. Instead of looking for the maximum profit, he was looking for the maximum audience response.

Even so, he was watching his pennies very carefully. Anyone not working at the studio found this hard to believe, since it was obvious that doing a scene over three and four times was more expensive than doing it once. Reaching for new achievements, trying things that had never been done before, asking more of his staff than they knew how to do—all this cost money. And Walt knew it, but he chose to spend what money he had in those very areas, figuring that he could save someplace else. For example, simplifying the concept for a whole picture would make it less expensive: eliminating costly scenes, extra characters, crowd shots, anything that took more time or more work for the same result. Too many characters in a story not only runs up the cost but divides the audience's interest. It takes away time needed to get the most out of the main characters, who are supposed to be the most interesting anyway.

Changing his procedures, using his men differently,

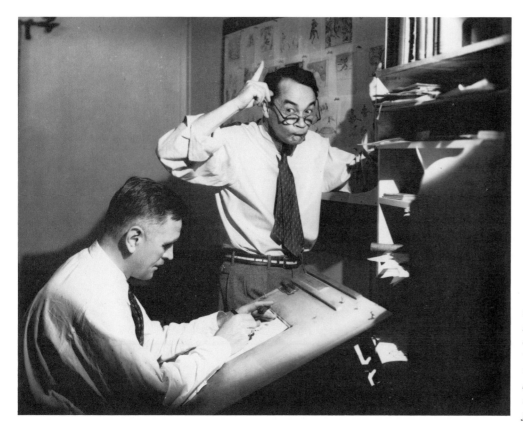

Gagman and voice talent Pinto Colvig performs for artist Albert Hurter. Pinto was the voice of Pluto, Goofy, Grumpy, and Sleepy, as well as miscellaneous crickets, bugs, and fish.

using more cycles, more repeat action, careful use of staging and cutting and field sizes to emphasize the entertainment and eliminate everything else—these were the areas in which he saved. The new ideas, the better pictures, the things that paid off with an audience, and even the training of his staff—this is where he spent every nickel he could get. We were asked many times to find more economical ways of working, but never to compromise the quality of the product.

Walt was not making works of art to hang in a gallery. He was striving purely for entertainment, and there were many ways of doing that: it could be in the story, the personalities, the visual excitement, innovations, situations, unexpected twists, beauty, mood, a spirit of fun, or just comic movements. If one part became too expensive, perhaps it could be balanced somewhere else with something that cost less but was just as effective.

The biggest saving proved to be one that started in the Story Department. If the work was carefully prepared there, it would flow through the plant at record speed. Too often a storyboard would be approved just because no one quite knew what else to do with the

material; it was felt that any weakness would show up farther down the line, or new ideas for strengthening and building would become obvious once the first animation was done. Walt was as guilty of this as anyone, but he still put out a memo stating, ''Very thorough preparation of the story in the Story Department plus the follow through of the storyman with the director . . . in the handing out and in the planning of

(Continued on page 90)

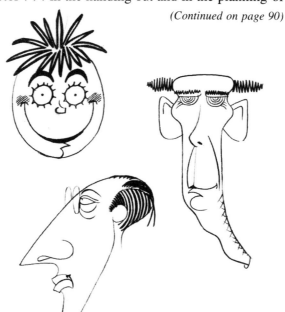

Caricaturist T. Hee captures something personal in each individual. Hugh Hennesy, right, and Charlie Philippi, bottom, the two top layout men, and a young and enthusiastic Ken Anderson, above.

87

The First Inspirational Sketches For *Snow White*

Albert Hurter depicts situations that later developed into full sequences, largely because of the stimulation that came from seeing characters in attitudes and relationships.

F. Horvath suggests a different kind of forest gnome for the dwarfs.

the action in the Music Room . . . will do a lot to eliminate lost motion on the part of the animators caused by animating a scene two or three times because the action was not planned out properly in the first place.'' And again, ''. . . . we would find that doing the preparatory work in the beginning is a very small expense in comparison to having to do it when the picture is in animation.''

His brother Roy kept cautioning Walt about spending more than they were getting for the films, but Walt's attitude was, ''Roy, *you* get the money, and *we'll* make the films!'' However, the time came when there simply was not any more money to be had for a cartoon short. Roy pleaded with the rest of the staff, ''Hey, look, fellas, you've got to work on Walt! He's got to stop spending so much money!'' (Years later Walt was making *The Magnificent Mr. Toad* and suggested a line of dialogue for McBadger: ''Somethin's got to be done about Toad! He's spending to-oo much money!'')[8]

Walt had a different answer to this predicament, according to Dave Hand: ''If we put 10 of these 700 foot shorts together, we've got us a feature—7000 feet. Now they won't pay us but 15 thousand for a short, but for 10 of these, that would be 150,000, and surely we can get more than that for a feature!'' Dave does not remember if Roy fainted at that bit of financial wizardry or not. But he does remember his own feelings: ''There was no other way he [Walt] could stay in the business. He would not sit still and make cartoons at 15 thousand dollars.''

Whatever his reasons, it seems now that it was inevitable that Walt eventually would attempt a feature-length animated film. His cartoons had become popular in the theaters (Mickey Mouse was known around the world), and he was gaining confidence in his staff. In the mid-thirties he wrote a memo, ''The animation has made a very definite advance forward which, in my estimation, is close to 100% over what it was a year and a half ago. I know that eventually we are going to attain a degree of perfection never before thought possible. It proves to me that the time we have spent studying, trying to analyze our problems, and systematizing ourselves, is bearing fruit. The hit-and-miss is going.''

He knew he had the strength in the Story Department because he was carefully adding new people,

experienced writers, to his regular staff, and he was also discovering great talents within the ranks. Perce Pearce, who had once ghosted the comic strip *The Captain and the Kids*, had been moved out of Inbetween after contributing one gag after another to the Story Department. Once there, he showed an exceptional feeling for personality coupled with the ability to act out the traits that would work best for animation.

Perce was one of the first storymen to add the little unexpected touches of character and business that enriched the films and made them so memorable. One section of the picture might tell its idea well and fit into the story nicely, but it could still be barren and cold. Perce would immediately start weaving his touches of warmth through the actions and the personalities— nothing big or important, just little things that added charm and appeal. It might be a bit of acting or perhaps a colloquial phrase in the dialogue, or it even could be a few additions to the background that would make the locale more decorative, more special, more imaginative.

There was also Pinto Colvig, ex-circus clown, entertainer, clarinet player, who had joined the staff a few years earlier contributing story ideas, voices, and funny ways of doing things. Stimulating visual suggestions would be needed for the feature film Walt had in mind: *Snow White*. In production management, there was Dave Hand with his great ability to organize and manage, along with his creative ideas. The directors had proven their capabilities, and in layout there were the outstanding artists Hugh Hennesy and Charlie Philippi, followed by Tom Codrick.

Walt would need the best action he could get for Snow White herself, and this meant careful planning and analysis in addition to talent. A feature film would have to have tender moments, sincere moments, quiet moments. There would be a need for drawings with great appeal, characters with life and believability, and personalities that could hold an audience for well over an hour. Gags, funny actions, and visual tricks would not do it. If the audience were to be drawn into this film, this world of fantasy would have to be a real world with real people doing real things. This would not be a cartoon. It would be ''theater,'' and Walt would have to have men leading the way who could make it all come true.

Instead of making separate drawings of each character, Hurter placed more emphasis on the characters interacting, which is always a more productive way to arrive at the design of the characters. It all starts with the inspirational sketch.

Pinocchio

5. Cartoon Comes of Age

NORM FERGUSON AND HAM LUSKE

"In most instances, the driving force behind the action is the mood, the personality, the attitude of the character—or all three. Therefore, the mind is the pilot. We think of things before the body does them."

Walt Disney

ANIMATOR: *Frank Thomas* —The Pointer.

This was the high point in the development of Mickey's personality and Walt's finest portrayal of Mickey's voice. This scene was based on film taken of Walt during the recording session.

STARTS ON PAGE 123

Disney storyman Dick Kelsey once said, "There is no perfect window for a house; there is something wrong with all of them. They warp, corrode, rust, swell, twist, and need constant painting. It's a matter of what you like and what you're willing to put up with." And the same applies to animation. There is no best way to animate any more than there is one "greatest animator"—or greatest painter or writer or actor. Each brings his own personal message and interpretation to his craft, and if he has something to say that audiences want to hear, and if in addition he can effectively communicate that message, he may be considered great. His work may grow and become timeless, or changing tastes may outdate him in his own time.

In late 1935, Walt picked four men from his talented group of animators to supervise the animation on *Snow White*. These men were Norman (Fergy) Ferguson, with a mastery of broad staging; Hamilton (Ham) Luske, with great ability to analyze and develop procedures that others could follow; Fred Moore, with superb appeal in his drawings; and Vladimir (Bill or T-bone) Tytla, with an ability to portray great emotions and inner feelings in his characters. We have to believe that Walt, with his uncanny intuition, must have realized that he had found a magic combination in this group.

Their rise had been rapid and their contributions tremendous. But their careers, whether due to changing tastes or personal problems, were to be fairly short-lived by Disney studio standards, where many animators have produced successfully for periods of over

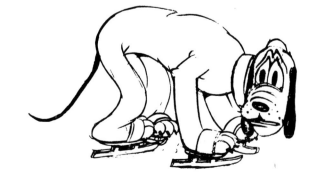

Animator Norm Ferguson searches for the right expression to draw on Pluto.

93

Walt relied on the ability of Hamilton Luske to prepare work for the younger animators.

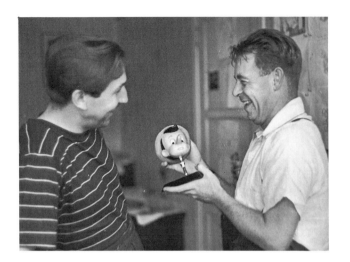

forty years. Their work, beginning with shorts in the early thirties, reached its height in *Snow White, Pinocchio, Fantasia,* and *Dumbo.* During this time they more than justified Walt's confidence in them. But continued success eluded them, and, somehow, when their time had passed, they were never again to find the same opportunities to express their particular talents. Animation took a direction that demanded a refinement no longer compatible with their styles.

These men were fine craftsmen who had helped to break away from the rigid traditions of the past. Their scenes were identified with the new, important uses of fundamentals—the broad Squash and Stretch and the

ANIMATOR: *Ham Luske*— Tortoise and the Hare.

strong Anticipation. Their work was easy to under-stand, to recognize, and to study. But as new men with formal art training came along, and Walt's think-ing turned toward an increasingly sophisticated type of animation, a more subtle kind of action with more complex acting and more meaningful expressions de-veloped. The animation became so sophisticated that it was almost impossible to recognize the basic princi-ples. The medium had developed into an art form.

Perhaps it was fate that brought these four anima-tors together with Walt at this time. Their styles were as diverse as any four could be; rough or clean, intui-tive or analytical, it did not matter. It was the combi-

Audiences instinctively re-sponded to the pleasing quality of Fred Moore's drawings.

Pinocchio

95

Of all the animators, Bill Tytla projected the strongest emotional feelings into his characters.

nation of these four men that helped Walt set a course that would take Disney films to heights never dreamed of: the creation of characters that reached out to audiences in a way only a few live-action pictures ever achieved.

However, it is conjecture to say that the big development in Disney animation came just from the chance combination of Walt, Fergy, Ham, Fred, and Bill. But because these men *were* put in positions of authority, they automatically had certain responsibilities thrust upon them that opened opportunities others may not have had. Their chances for greatness certainly were increased.

Dave Hand believes that Walt would have come up with basically the same type of picture no matter which top animators he had chosen to lead off. Wilfred Jackson felt the same way: ''It is my opinion that if Walt had started at some different place at the same time with a different bunch of guys, the result would have been more or less along the same lines, because I think Walt had a real firm hand on the tiller. There may be some things that some of the guys brought out which showed possibilities to Walt that he took advantage of that spread the gospel and the rest of us picked up, but really talented guys in other directions could have given him a similar thing I believe, because he really set the course. He was always out there and we were trying to catch up.''

Walt gave inspiration with his acting and storytelling, and his animators came up with the elements that brought about the Golden Age of animation. It is doubtful whether the warmth and the tenderness and the heart would have appeared in the pictures without this combination. Without these men it would have been a different *Snow White*—if the picture would have been made at all. But Walt drew out of each man what he could, and then continued to build on that contribution, always asking for more. He was opportunistic, in a way, in his ability to use what a man had to offer,

Pinocchio

Norm Ferguson, inscrutable expression and pale blue eyes, as seen by caricaturist, T. Hee.

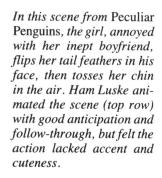

In this scene from Peculiar Penguins, *the girl, annoyed with her inept boyfriend, flips her tail feathers in his face, then tosses her chin in the air. Ham Luske animated the scene (top row) with good anticipation and follow-through, but felt the action lacked accent and cuteness.*

On his second test, he made the tail go farther and added a slide backward to accentuate the flip (vertical row). This gave unexpected emphasis and pertness to the whole action.

and then to make the fellow produce far beyond his normal capabilities.

Fergy

Norm Ferguson (or, as we always called him, Fergy) used to like to tell of the lonely night when he switched from cameraman to animator. He was staying late to finish shooting a scene when he discovered that some of the drawings were missing. There was no one else around to complete the animation and no one to call, so as Fergy put it, "I had to fill in." The scenes were so successful that he was offered a job drawing. And he reasoned, "If this is all there is to animation, I guess I'll switch over—it beats being on camera."

Fergy, who came to the studio in 1929, had an

intelligent, creative mind, and he listened and observed more than he talked. What he did say came out with a slight Brooklyn accent, and it was usually punctuated by, ''Yeah, yeah, you know, you know.'' He would laugh about events that were going wrong, so it was difficult to tell just how deeply he felt about things. Most of the time during a conversation he would be fooling with a little curl of hair on his forehead that always seemed to separate from the rest. Jack Cutting[1] said that Fergy's wide-open pale-blue eyes and fixed smile looked guileless and friendly, but every so often you got the feeling that his smile was a mask and that behind it he was observing and noting everything you were doing.

Fergy's tastes did not run to the intellectual. He loved the old vaudeville comedians, and this was probably his chief form of entertainment while growing up. He saw everything as if it were on stage, rather than in terms of the involved movements some animators were able to do after studying live action. A big part of a comedian's act was often the way he looked at his audience in response to some action or line of dialogue—sharing his reaction broadly with the spectators. Fergy adapted this very same routine for his cartoon dog who would become Pluto, having him look into the camera to show his inner feelings. No one doubted that this dog was thinking, too.

In one of his first pictures, *Frolicking Fish*, Fergy animated a girls' trio as fishes singing and doing an old-time soft-shoe dance. But Fergy's vaudeville touch was not the most memorable thing about this piece of animation. Wilfred Jackson pinpoints this as a big step forward: ''In that scene there was a fluid type of action where they didn't hit a hold and move out of it. But when one part would hold something else would move. So there was never a complete stop. And this was a scene Walt made us all look at, because he said that is the worst thing about the kind of animation you guys

are doing. Your character goes dead and it looks like a drawing.''

Ben Sharpsteen, who had come from New York only a few months before Fergy, recalls that Walt then assigned Fergy to the bloodhound in *Chain Gang:* ''Fergy was successful in getting a looseness into the bloodhound that exaggerated its ability to sniff (a wrinkling of the nose) and to think (facial expressions, such as a quizzical look or a sudden smile directed at the audience). Fergy succeeded in getting a feeling of flesh into his animation. No one realized what Fergy had done, however, until after the preview.'' No one realized, either, that this dog would develop into the famous Pluto. And Don Graham adds, ''The dogs were alive, real. They seemed to breathe. They moved like dogs, not like drawings of dogs. The drawings explained not so much what a real dog looked like, but what a real dog did.''

Walt did not tell Fergy to do a different dog or one that added a new dimension to cartoons. He did not say, ''Let's see if we can make a dog *think* this time.'' He did not tell him, ''I want you to do a dog that will act like this and do these things because I think the audience will go for it.'' That was not Walt's way—not when developing a new character. He would be apt to start talking about different dogs and the funny way they had of sniffing when they were on the trail of something. Before he knew it he would be acting it out, and the fellows in the meeting would start laughing because this was funny, the way Walt did it. And more than likely, Walt would remember a specific dog he had seen—maybe an old hunting dog that lived near the Disney farm: ''Y'know this old guy would come snuffin' along like a vacuum cleaner, his muzzle spread all over the ground. You know this loose skin they have up here; well, it would be spread out flat he was tryin' so hard to get his nose down next to the smell, and he had all these wrinkles bunched up over

ANIMATOR: *Norman "Fergy" Ferguson*—Playful Pluto

The famous flypaper sequence from Playful Pluto, *a milestone in personality animation. From the time he accidentally sits on a sheet of the sticky flypaper, Pluto's problems seem to become ever worse as he tries to extricate himself. Through it all, his reaction to his predicament and his thoughts of what to try next are shared with the audience. It was the first time a character seemed to be thinking on the screen, and, though it lasted only 65 seconds, it opened the way for animation of real characters with real problems.*

his nose and down over his eyes. But he was serious about it, y'know; he wasn't a goof ball—this was serious business to him.''

And then Walt would remember how the dog would suddenly stop and look up, as if he was thinking—you hardly knew what. Maybe he was sorting things out, maybe he was listening for something, or maybe he was trying to remember when he had last smelled that particular smell, or maybe it was just something that crazy dog did. And as Walt acted it out, it became funnier and funnier; encouraged by the response, Walt would know he was onto something that was good entertainment. He would imitate the expressions of the dog, and look from one side to the other, and raise first one brow and then the other as he tried to figure things out. Walt's eyebrows were particularly facile, and the piercing look with the one brow down and the other up was his most common expression when he was thinking. Fergy was watching all this as well as laughing at the thought of the old dog with all his wrinkles and the sniffing and trying to figure things out, and in his mind he was seeing the way it should look on the screen. He was visualizing drawings, attitudes, expressions, but they were not drawings of Walt himself; they were drawings of a dog with a personality who was thinking. Even though the animator would get his sole inspiration from the way Walt acted out a character, there was never a temptation to draw Walt.

Somehow he had the ability to make you see what was funny about the character itself, and it was the character's expressions that you saw and later tried to draw; but, still, that dog's eyebrows could only have come from Walt.

When Fergy projected the first tests of his new character sniffing and snorting and then stopping to think, everybody was enthusiastic. No one remembers what Walt said, but very probably his comment went like this: "Yeah . . . y'know, he ought to have a big snort, right into the camera, after he's thought things over— they do that, those dogs—it's to clear their noses or something. But y'know, he's looking around, side to side, and then suddenly he looks right at the camera and gives a big snort—not really disgusted, you don't know why he does it, but it's funny, and then he goes back to sniffing some more.'' Walt never stopped to praise; having seen something he liked, he started building on it immediately, making it better and funnier. Once he had seen what Fergy could do, he asked for more of the same type of thing, but always something new and something stronger. Usually the animator barely had been able to achieve the original result, and anything more seemed to be beyond his capabilities. But, once again, Walt would "talk it" and "act it out," and you had to admit that it was funny business and the sequence would be better with these new ideas; so, once again, you would strain and struggle trying to

(Continued on page 104)

Inspirational Sketches
by Gustaf Tenggren
For *Pinocchio*

Caricature of Ted Sears, outstanding storyman of the thirties and forties. Artist unknown.

capture an elusive expression or movement or attitude.

Working in this way, how could anyone claim credit for doing a certain scene or even an outstanding action? Fergy knew that he had made the drawings and timed them. They were immensely successful because he had been able to capture certain dog characteristics and to present them with enough understanding of entertainment and enough grasp of showmanship to make a funny scene. Yet, without Walt there would have been no Pluto. Fergy, on his own, would never have conceived of these scenes or this personality, and no storyman would have considered that such business and actions would ever get across in a cartoon. But first of all, no producer would have risked a nickel on such a new departure as the idea of a cartoon character having a personality. Without Walt, who had the great insight to see how an animator used his ideas, plus the great ability to adapt this to his own purposes, there would have been very little improvement in the quality of the films, and Fergy would never have had the opportunity to create a world famous cartoon character.

In his analysis of Pluto, Ted Sears, a top storyman, said, ''The flypaper sequence in *Playful Pluto* is always mentioned as the best example of his pantomime. This is because it illustrated clearly all of Pluto's characteristics from dumb curiosity to panic. It is timed in such a way that the audience feels all of Pluto's sensations—each 'hold expression' after a surprise action was carefully planned, and expressed some definite attitude causing the audience to laugh. Each small climax builds up into a better surprise.'' Wilfred Jackson also commented on Fergy's flypaper sequence: ''You can take that same gag without running over the dog's thoughts or emotions, just mechanically doing the thing, and it wouldn't be funny.''

Fergy accepted the innovations in his work as the natural course of events, and he never cared for making rules about how to do something or being tied down too much on the character. In one scene he had animated a particularly funny look on Pluto, shifting his eyes from side to side, the brows working like Walt's—one side up and the other down. The young animators dashed to his room to copy the timing on the exposure sheet and paw through his drawings. Fergy was puzzled, and he commented: ''Why do you want to memorize how I did that action? I might do it different next time.'' But this shows some of the excitement of that period—everyone rushing around to see how someone else did something. It also shows something about Fergy's approach; he would not stop trying to find a new and better way to do this same action next time. It was all well and good to learn how someone did a good piece of animation, but to copy it was very limiting and something Fergy would never understand.

Fergy had had no formal art training, so he was not inhibited by anatomy and drawing rules. Fred Moore used to laugh and say, ''He doesn't know that you can't raise the eyebrows above the head circle, so he goes ahead and does it and it gives a great effect.'' And that was but one of the many things Fergy initiated to give his work that extra life and vitality. Marc Davis says, ''Norm Ferguson wasn't the artist, but he was a sharp performer and a showman—hard to know if his drawing was there or wasn't there—he had his own kind of symbol.''

Fergy's drawing during this period in the development of animation actually was quite good and had a solid sculptured look. His feeling for stretches and tension right down to the toes and his handling of the flesh and getting meat on bones—without losing the sausage body and stuffed legs—were outstanding.

He worked very rough for first tests—usually just a circle and two lines for the body. This kept the staging simple and gave him a guide that was easy to change. With a quick test on his first rough drawings, he could see whether he had something to build on. He could keep making fast changes, never feeling that he had invested so much time in a scene that he could not discard it and try a new idea if something was not working. This style suited Fergy because he always had something he was trying out. Most animators who employed this very rough method seemed to be cast on work in which they experimented with fast action and gags—all scenes with broad movements.

Maybe there was a certain amount of impatience in Fergy's wanting to see right away what he was getting, or maybe as Jack Cutting says, "Fergy was nervous." In either case, it was this abundance of nervous energy that led Wilfred Jackson to recall affectionately the following incident. Someone asked if Fergy, after arriving from New York, had fit in rapidly and made his presence felt. "Jaxon" replied, "Fergy made his presence felt real fast with me. They had to get another row of animation desks at that time, so his desk was right back of mine. He used to shake his foot all the time, and it would wiggle my desk and I couldn't draw—so he made his presence felt right away with me."

Fergy's witch in *Snow White* was the first of the great Disney villains. Her impact on the audience

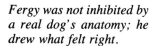

Fergy was not inhibited by a real dog's anatomy; he drew what felt right.

exceeded all expectations; in fact, to many, she was excessively terrifying. She, like Tytla's devil in "Night On Bald Mountain," was menacingly ugly, which was not a characteristic of Walt's later villains. The witch seemed to have an Arthur Rackham[2] quality and was reminiscent of his evil old woman in *Hansel and Gretel*. Fergy's handling of her face was less of a typical formula than most Disney designs, with shapes that did not relate as well as they should for animation because of the witch's illustrative quality. The mouth to cheek to eye and brow relationship, which is so important in animating expression changes, suffered from his concept in design.

By 1953, Fergy had found it extremely difficult to keep up with the new refinements in acting and drawing, and he had left Disney's to work in other studios. He had suffered much of his life from diabetes, and that, combined with other health problems, brought on his death in 1957.

Fergy's style of animating influenced younger animators and is still in use, particularly the quick test to

Fergy's witch in Snow White *was simple, direct— and frightening.*

check a proposed pattern and maintain flexibility in any plan. It suited the way he thought. If it works for you, do more.

What he did with Pluto was probably his biggest contribution. He showed the way for other animators in the use of symbols such as takes, frowns, smiles, and a whole range of expressions. Fergy's was the ultimate of the old style—a broad, loose feeling, in concept as well as drawing—a way that kept the door open for incorporating new ideas right up to the last moment.

Ham

Hamilton Luske was opening the door to a new, more refined approach in which everything one has is put into the first test. This requires an uninterrupted continuity of thought. It may take days to do the scene, but you must not lose the thread, change your mind, or lose your confidence—you must be sure!

Ham had an absolute fascination with how things moved. Eric Larson, who was Ham's assistant in the early thirties, says, "Ham was studying animation all the time—it was his whole life." One weekend Eric and Ham were on the deck of the Catalina steamer with their wives, enjoying the sea breeze and apparently trying to forget the cares of the day. But not Ham! All of a sudden he pulled off his tie and held it out in the wind. "Look, Eric! Look at the overlap. See how the end keeps going down after the center part starts up." Every time they would play golf it was the same thing. "Now watch close. See the follow-through on my putter." But this was actually Ham's way of relaxing; and if a friend was going to relax with him, he had better be ready to do some analyzing and observing, too.

Of the four animators in this group, Ham was the only one with a college education. He was graduated from the University of California at Berkeley, where he majored in business. His wife Frankie laughs about this, because she says that Ham would not even look at the bills or the bank book. Like Fergy and Fred Moore, his only formal art training came primarily from the classes that Walt initiated at the studio.

Ham had to struggle with his drawing, but he had a natural feeling for animation, story, and for what was entertaining. So despite his lack of an artistic background, he had many things going for him. Perhaps it was his college training, or maybe it was just inherent in him to have a well-organized analytical mind.

Eric Larson said, "Ham played a lot of tennis, so when he was given the chance to animate Max Hare in the tennis sequence of *The Tortoise and the Hare*, he knew precisely what he wanted to do." The important thing was his knowledge and feeling for the game, and Ham had the imagination and the vision to dream beyond what he himself could do on the court. He knew the exact poses he wanted to use in his held

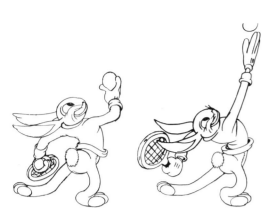

ANIMATOR: *Ham Luske—Tortoise and the Hare.*

Ham animated Max Hare performing on the tennis court the way all players wish they could play. He moved so fast that the special effect of a blue streak was used. Ham also drew elaborate after-images of the arm and racket, imitating the familiar blur on live action film when a figure moves faster than the shutter. We called these effects "speed lines."

positions and just how much overlap he needed to keep the poses alive. This was a picture in which timing was more important to the personalities than anything done so far. The cocky Hare zipped from pose to pose, with emphasis on the moving holds, and to follow the speedy action between these holds, Ham and Wilfred Jackson, the director, devised the blue streak technique. Jaxon says, "That's the first time I remember shooting a color test for a picture to find out if the blue streak was going to work out all right, and it's a good thing we did. The first two or three times we did it didn't suit Walt at all."

Everybody credited Ham with analyzing the essence of the cute pose. Fred Moore had found the same type of thing intuitively. While Ham did not have the same flair or natural feeling in his drawings, they may have been easier for most others to understand. Everything was placed exactly where he wanted it, more crudely than in Fred's drawings, but with great clarity, definition, and caricature.

He acted out the characters, finding the elements in a pose that really pinpointed the position of the feet and body, the right place for the hands, the arch of the back, the tilt of the head, right down to his famous "oooh" mouth. We came to think of Ham in these terms, a grown man acting out this cute stuff—little animals, dwarfs, or Pinocchio—and everyone caricatured him that way, and always with the "oooh" mouth at the bottom of the long upper lip like Sneezy's. No one ever caricatured Fergy acting like Pluto, but Ham

The typical Ham Luske pose with the "Ooooh mouth," as caricatured by Ward Kimball.

Caricature of Les Clark, a top Mickey Mouse animator, whose career at Disney spanned nearly 50 years. Artist unknown.

108

had become a symbol for this type of acting.

When Walt asked Ham and Les Clark to draw a believable, pretty girl for *The Goddess of Spring*, both animators were stumped. Eric Larson acted out the scenes to help Ham capture the movements, but Walt was not pleased with the animation, feeling it was too rubbery and flexible. Les fared no better, even with a real girl for a model. "I used my sister, Marceil, for certain poses," he said. "I had to get some sort of human anatomy, you know, but it came off miserable, I thought. And I apologized to Walt, and he kind of sloughed it off and said, 'I guess we could do better next time. . . .' And I think the reason it didn't come off, the character wasn't designed to be animated. To me, the key to character animation is the design quality of the figure that you can use. I had a hard time with the figure, not that I didn't know how to draw it, but to animate it."

The animators were all wrestling with their first attempt to draw the human figure in action, and they often went behind closed doors to practice their moves without the comments of their co-workers. "I'm sure Walt was thinking ahead to *Snow White*," Les Clark concludes. "Although he didn't tell me that, I assumed later because Snow White herself was designed so that she *could* be animated."

The animators occasionally got the grace, the rhythm, the relationship that distinguished the leading lady of *The Goddess of Spring* as a lady; they even got the weight and balance and perspective accurate enough so that in some scenes she moved convincingly. But, exhausted by the effort, they relied on a "pretty girl" formula for the face that not only looked as if she were wearing a mask, but defeated the total effect by giving her a zombie look. She certainly was not alive and was totally devoid of personality or feelings.

Ham's principles were followed in this action of the exhausted, panting wolf from Sword in the Stone. *Done by John Lounsbery, it has strong inhale and exhale with the head lifting and dropping and the tongue dragging, but it was not as funny as the animator wanted it.*

By adding one more extreme drawing that went further (in this case, the sides of the mouth and the eyebrows), he was able to capture the pain and tension of the gasping wolf, which gave real meaning to the scene.

109

After Ham had the experience of animating Tillie Tiger in *Elmer Elephant*, he realized that a cartoon character only lived when the whole drawing, as well as all the parts, reflected the attitude, the personality, the acting, and the feeling of the character. His analytical mind and care for detail equipped him for the job of finding a way of creating an appealing heroine who could survive the growing pains of budding artists who were eager, but still not able, to draw an attractive girl in more than one position. When they started on the heroine in *Snow White*, Ham concentrated on her eyes and mouth and getting as much relative movement in her face as in her body. Crude as many scenes were, they began to live.

Like Fergy, Ham had a strong feeling for what was entertaining, but there the similarity ended. In contrast to Fergy's natural ability to improvise while animating, Ham always seemed to follow a procedure with a step-by-step approach. However, his animation was not mechanical in any way. On the contrary, it was full of life and the feeling of the character; his ability to move the audience with his pathos was second only to Bill Tytla's. Ham could not start a scene until he had the whole thing visualized. He would sit with his arms folded staring at a blank piece of paper—thinking and planning. He felt that if he could spend half his time planning, he would animate his scene better and faster. Eric said Ham would be hunched over his board, fussing with his drawings and saying, "There must be some way to exaggerate this pose." He would choose the precise thing to do and then push it further.

Ham could make that extra drawing in the action to give more than the director asked for, always going stronger. If the animator does just what is on the story sketch, the scene will not have enough zip. And that is what Ham was best at: that, and designing the character-action relationship for an appealing, interesting result on the screen. Not everyone has the mental discipline or ability to think these problems through.

As Ham began a scene, he made careful, neat drawings that showed all the actions, expressions, and details of timing. This done, he flipped the drawings, and when he found an action that seemed weak he reached in and crudely made a big, bold correction on four or five drawings, as he held the whole batch in his hands. It looked as if two people had animated the scene, one a Dr. Jekyll and the other a Mr. Hyde, but it kept the scene strong and alive with infallable staging, clear action, and strong accents.

Ham was always probing around; that was the key feeling in those days. The animators were always trying to come up with a new way of handling an action. Ham kept experimenting, trying to find a different walk; so he kept varying the timing and relationships until he finally went so far that he no longer had a walk. He had shifted the relative timing of the arms to the legs to the body until it was now a peculiar twisting movement.

If he saw an unusual type of animation or visual effect that some other studio was using, he would get a kind of puzzled, annoyed look and say, "I wonder why we aren't doing that. We should be able to figure out how to do it, maybe even better." And he would think about it till he had a better way. And the things Ham thought about—how he could do something new, go further and make it more entertaining, give it more personality—these were all things he was beginning to understand in a way that he could define them for somebody else. This was one of the great things about Ham. He realized that this type of knowledge must be

ANIMATOR: *Ham Luske—* Who Killed Cock Robin?

The animator captured the spirit of Mae West's personality through drawing and movement.

passed on to the young animators or the studio would not progress. And Ham's knowledge was not limited to animation; his philosophy of story concepts may have equalled any other contribution he made.

When we were talking over a scene or a story point, he used to say, "I'm thinking out loud." What he meant was, "Don't take what I'm going to say too seriously yet. I'm not even sure myself." And sometimes he would say, "I'm being wishy-washy on purpose," which was also to let you know that he wanted to keep the thought alive, and to consider everything before nailing it down.

As an animator, Ham probably never had his sights set on being a director or a supervising animator. In 1935, he was only beginning to reach his great potential in animation. He had just animated the character of Jenny Wren in *Who Killed Cock Robin?* Ham's Jenny was a caricature of Mae West, and through careful study he had pinpointed what actually made her Mae West: the provocative swaying walk with the slow shifting of weight, the characteristic way she rolled her eyes and talked out of the side of her mouth. He succeeded in getting excellent dialogue sync, but in a more subtle way than ever done before. And that is one of the things that made her come off so well. Ham could tell if something was even one frame out of sync. Jenny had the slow-moving, cool, confident manner that Mae had—no quick moves or big anticipations. She, like the real Mae, seemed to have appraised the situation, sized up the opposition, and was in complete control. The material Ham had to work with was excellent, but still no animator had ever done anything like it before. Everyone said, "That's even more like Mae West than Mae herself!" In fact, Mae wrote a letter to Walt complimenting him on the outstanding

caricature. And Walt responded warmly, thanking her for being the inspiration for Jenny Wren. Ham's ability to combine analysis, subtlety, and strength had made Jenny an outstanding character.

Ham had reminded the young animators, "Our first job is to tell a story that isn't known to the audience. Then we have to tell a story that may cover several days, or several years, in a little over an hour; so consequently we have to tell things faster than they happen in life. Also we want to make things more interesting than ordinary life. Our actors are more rehearsed than everyday people; if somebody gets on a horse or opens a door or sits in a chair, we want to do it as simply and professionally as possible. Our actors must be more interesting and more unusual than you

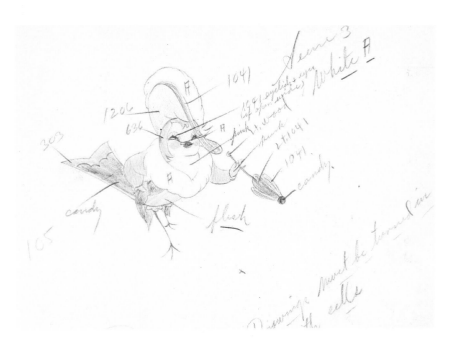

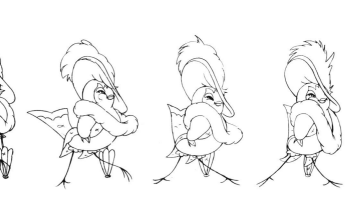

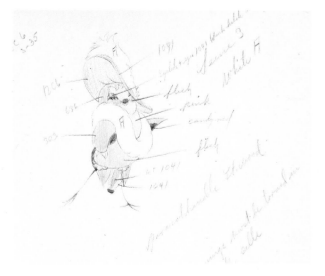

and I. Their thought process must be quicker than ours, their uninteresting progressions from one situation to another must be skipped.'' In these few sentences Ham had summed up much that is important about picture-making: the entertainment, the time element, the acting, and the elimination of unnecessary action. Similar principles have long been known in the field of literature, for as one distinguished professor has said, ''Great fiction is art and invention, not duplicated reality. Most lifetimes do not possess the crises you find in novels.''[3] Is that not what drama is anyway, life with the dull spots cut out?

Walt probably wondered many times, is this the right time to start *Snow White*? Have we got the manpower and, most of all, are they capable of doing the job? Who should be the first animator to lead off on the picture? The answer to these questions came in a casting memo put out in late 1935: ''From now on *Ham Luske* is definitely assigned to *Snow White*!'' Usually a casting memo is just a routine piece of information, but this one fairly tingled with excitement as Walt announced the first man to be cast on this daring new project. This shows the importance that Walt attached to casting and especially his great dependence on Ham at this time.

''Ham Luske moved up quite fast,'' recalls Wilfred Jackson. ''He was one of the first guys I remember who had more than just an assistant—promising young guys he would hand out little scenes to. One of the first guys who had a crew to supervise. Then on *Snow White* he took complete charge—the girls . . . the animals. If you were directing the sequence[4] with the girl, you didn't have to direct the girl because Ham did it. He knew the way it was supposed to be. He shot most of the live action on it too. He came up very fast and he showed his ability to organize and put things together.''

Ham Luske felt that the rabbits we were drawing were thin and bony instead of soft and furry. The more artists tried to draw a rabbit's anatomy, the less the drawings looked like soft fur. Ham realized that an absence of lines and fullness of shape would make the drawings look soft.

This . . . is softer than . . . this.

We were told by Ham to think of "Dr. Dentons," the sleep suits young kids wore that hid the anatomy under a thick, soft flannel covering. This is Michael from Peter Pan, *animated by Hal King.*

Out of this thinking came the rabbits in Snow White *—this one drawn by Milt Kahl while working with Ham.*

ANIMATOR: *Ollie Johnston—Bambi.*

We used the same principle when we drew Thumper, two pictures later.

Often when Ham and Fred Moore would be disturbed about something on the picture they would run up to Walt's office, full of enthusiasm, hoping to sell him their idea of how to correct it. But somehow Walt could always sense if it was something he did not want to hear about at that time. And besides, he did not want anyone in the position of telling him, or selling him, or confronting him. Walt had a great curiosity, but he preferred to find things out in his own way, asking the questions he wanted answers to; and his opening remarks were usually designed to put you on the defensive. On one occasion, before Ham and Fred could get a word out, Walt said, "Gee, Ham, I didn't know you ever wore a tie to work," which got them off balance and off the subject. They had a nice chat, and he sent them on their way. When they got halfway down the hall, they stopped and looked at each other; Fred said, "Hey, wait a minute! Do you realize we didn't get a word in?"

Ham sighed and said, "Yeah, he did it again."

It was often difficult to know precisely what Walt saw in a piece of business, and after each meeting there would be some disagreement over what he had said, and even more confusion over what he had meant. During those *Snow White* days, Ham was usually the best at knowing just what Walt wanted. As one man put it, "Someone would say that Walt said he wants it like this. Ham would say, 'No, that's not what he means. This is what he means.'" But no one hit it right all the time with Walt, and Ham's first try at the Snow White model missed as far as Walt and most of the fellows were concerned. Ham had an interesting idea, however. His drawing suggested an awkward, gangly teenager with a winsome charm, who could very well have been animated without live action. But the story had started to go a different way by this time, so Ham's girl was turned down. If a story sketch man had made the drawing it would not have attracted as much criticism, but when an animator suggests a way to draw the character, everyone figures that is the way it is going to be. Since he is the one to put the character on the screen, the animator finds himself in a very vulnerable position, and often he winds up with a wounded ego.

Some of Ham's best thoughts came out in a talk given in 1938: "Our actors are drawings. We cannot

Ham Luske's suggestion for a younger Snow White more easily animated.

work on the inspiration of the moment as an actor does, but must present our characterizations through a combination of art, technique, and mechanics that takes months from the conception to the finished product. And we have to make the audience forget that these are drawings. We cannot risk ruining a sequence or a good characterization with some mechanical imperfection or jitter that reminds the audience that we are

113

This photostat from the film shot for animators to study shows Margie Bell and Lewis Hightower as Snow White and the prince about to ride off to their castle.

ANIMATOR: *Ham Luske—* Snow White.

Subtle drawing and realistic shapes show the improvement in drawing that had taken place since The Goddess of Spring, *made just two years earlier.*

keys to her acceptance by the audience. This cannot be done arbitrarily. The live action must be studied and understood or, with a character like the girl, it could become comical. At the time, it was just thought of as a help to get the picture out, or a crutch for animators who could not draw too well, or a way of keeping the character consistent even though several animators were handling her. But looking back on it now, without Ham's control and imagination, taste and inventiveness, Snow White would not have had the conviction and appeal that really sold the character.

Walt felt that Ham had been successful in steering the fellows in the right direction on *Snow White*, and for the most part he had achieved the results wanted; so Walt rewarded him with the very difficult task of shooting live action for the Blue Fairy in *Pinocchio*. In a talk given by Ham to a group of animators and directors, it became obvious that he was especially valuable as a communications aid between these two groups:

Let's say the character of the Blue Fairy now is perfectly conceived and perfectly cast. Then I have to go over to the sound stage and shoot live action on her that will appear flawless and life-like as animation later on; and to do that, I have to invent movements again—enough movements to be able to be inbetweened. And the only movements we can find for her to do are to have her lean forward and back. So consequently, in every scene, we told Margie Bell to lean forward for one phrase and back for the next, until it got funny. We did conceive several walks and one scene of her bending confidentially into a closeup with the Cricket—and that will be our best scene of her. . . .

You should tell the actor what to do, not how to do it. I think the trouble with most of our live action has been in not giving the actor enough business to do, and then meddling with the way he does it when the scene looks stilted. If the movement seems inadequate, invent some business, such as poking the fire or scratching the head.

An example of inventing business for a character occurred in the scene where Snow White folds her arms as Grumpy would, while she is watching him. It

dealing with drawings instead of real beings. The success of *Snow White* was due to the public accepting our characters as living beings, and the lack of success of the Prince and the Huntsman [as characters] was due to their unprofessional result.''

Margie Bell, who did the live action of the girl in *Snow White*, tells of a funny incident during the shooting. So that the girl's head size would have better cartoon proportions and relate more to the rather large-headed dwarfs, someone suggested, ''Why don't we put a football helmet on Margie to make her head bigger? That oughta do it.'' That did it all right. Margie, who later achieved fame on TV as Marge Champion, said that within minutes, under those hot lights, she was perspiring more than a 260-pound tackle. She added, ''We gave that up in a hurry!''

Ham made an enormous contribution to Snow White by the way he directed Margie for the live action. Ham's choices in handling the girl, keeping her innocent, feminine, appealing, and sincere, were the real

was a very good choice of action for her, because it showed her gentle way of teasing Grumpy. And if Ham had not used an action of this type, he would have been stuck with having to move her either slightly back or slightly forward. Ham continues with his approach:

When we pick our live action takes, a person that hasn't animated is very apt to pick them for facial expressions, and not for action. And we can't afford to do that.

Ham's capacity to analyze and to work out a procedure that could be written in outline form as a guide for others made him "too valuable" to be confined to his board. Even though he did some animation on the girl in *Snow White*, Ham was really a director on the picture. Walt felt that Ham's value lay in the influence he could have on the younger animators. So, much of the animation handouts on the Prince, Snow White, the Huntsman, and the animals was turned over to Ham. Somehow Walt always seemed to load Ham up with more work than anyone else. Fred and Bill shared the supervision of the dwarfs, and Fergy took over on the witch. Any one of these jobs was a handful, but Ham's would have been insurmountable for most people. However, he had a way of spreading himself around while still being effective.

Ham's analysis of the best approach to designing a character that everyone could handle is still in use today. Certainly the execution is more sophisticated, but the principles are the same—as are the problems. It is amazing to see in Ham's 1938 outline (in the Appendix) on his approach to character handling how it all applies today. As the French say, "The more things change, the more they stay the same."

Ham had a knack for being creative in helping to develop areas of animation that needed strengthening. He was great with the younger men, and, along with Fred Moore, was probably the best teacher among the animators. The supervising position that Ham held on *Snow White* was ideally suited to his abilities. He was at his peak when he was working closely with the young animators and still had some time at the board himself. He was usually gentle and easy going with his criticism, but he could be quite blunt and forceful if the situation demanded it. For one thing, he could not tolerate anything that was not clear and definite. "If you are going to show something, be sure you don't do it halfway!" When he drew for you he would continually work his mouth and his brows, and he seemed to be urging his pencil on and willing it to do what he was visualizing.

Every time Ham would do or say something he thought was really funny, he would laugh so hard his face would turn red and tears would roll down his cheeks. His favorite jokes were puns—the visual kind, and the more farfetched, the better. Once in a meeting someone mentioned Bell & Howell projectors. In an instant Ham was on his feet ringing an imaginary bell and then just as quickly pantomiming a long, silent howl. After that he would start laughing, usually in little short bursts, and our disapproval only made him laugh harder until finally he would go into convulsions—particularly if he was really proud of his effort. When he would eventually regain control, he would look back and forth among us with this half-hurt expression and wonder why we could not see the humor in his joke. Actually he had such an infectious laugh that it was hard to resist getting into the spirit of his gags.

It is doubtful that Ham or anyone else could have realized the far-reaching impact his procedures would have on the future of Disney animation. Walt liked the refinements that these procedures brought, and it was obvious from the popularity of the pictures at the box office that the audience wholeheartedly accepted these advancements. The direction for the further development of animation had been set, and much credit could go to Ham, whose ability to analyze, organize, and plan had helped open the way.

Ham was a top director on both *Pinocchio* and *Fantasia*, a position that he enjoyed, feeling it gave him the type of control he needed to be most effective. But as time passed his interests drew him further away from animation, and as the new group of supervising animators added their contributions to the rapidly developing craft Ham had less and less influence on the art form he had done so much to advance. He continued to direct memorable sequences, notably the cartoon section of *Mary Poppins*, but, increasingly, more of his time was spent on live-action problems for the weekly TV shows, until his death in 1968.

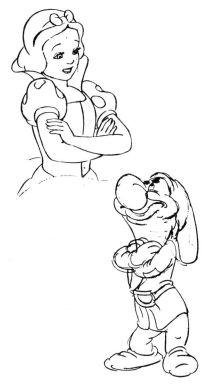

Snow White mimics Grumpy in a playful way that helps build and define both personalities.

Speed Lines, Staggers, and Vibrations

The short films of the early thirties were full of fast action, skids, and crashes. Each animator searched for a better or funnier way to draw the effect needed to fortify his action.

ANIMATOR: *Hugh Fraser*—
Adventures of Mr. Toad.

In this effect, the weasel is in position shaking Toad's hand while his trailing speed line image is still catching up to him.

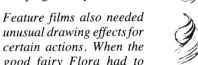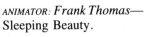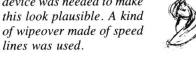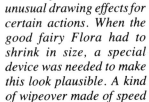

ANIMATOR: *Frank Thomas*—
Sleeping Beauty.

Feature films also needed unusual drawing effects for certain actions. When the good fairy Flora had to shrink in size, a special device was needed to make this look plausible. A kind of wipeover made of speed lines was used.

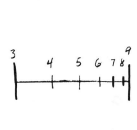

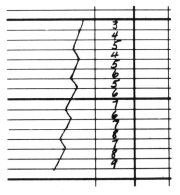

The most common stagger is the 345456567678789 timing for tension when some progression is desired. It is useful in pulls and pushes and on the end of a very strong take, adding extra life to the action. This stagger is done entirely with the mechanics of exposing the drawings under the camera. Inbetweens are made slowing into drawing No. 9 and the rest is left up to the cameraman.

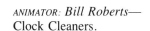

ANIMATOR: Bill Roberts—
Clock Cleaners.

This vibration effect is achieved by animating multiple images out from a single image. No special pattern has to be followed, and the particular needs of the scene will determine how it is handled. No two images should be in the same place on two successive drawings, or the eye will sense a stop in the action.

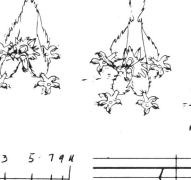

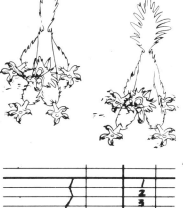

ANIMATOR: Ward Kimball—Peter and the Wolf. The cat has just come face to face with the wolf. The resulting take was made from two extremes, each progressing upward about half an inch. One set used odd numbers, the other even numbers. The odd numbers have wide eyes, brows up, ears up, tail smooth, and legs closer together. The even numbers have round eyes, brows lowered, ears pointing out to the side, tail flaired out, and legs farther out with a small trailing image. Mixing the two sets of drawings gives an animated stagger that vibrates from the odd numbers to the even, giving a shimmering effect.

117

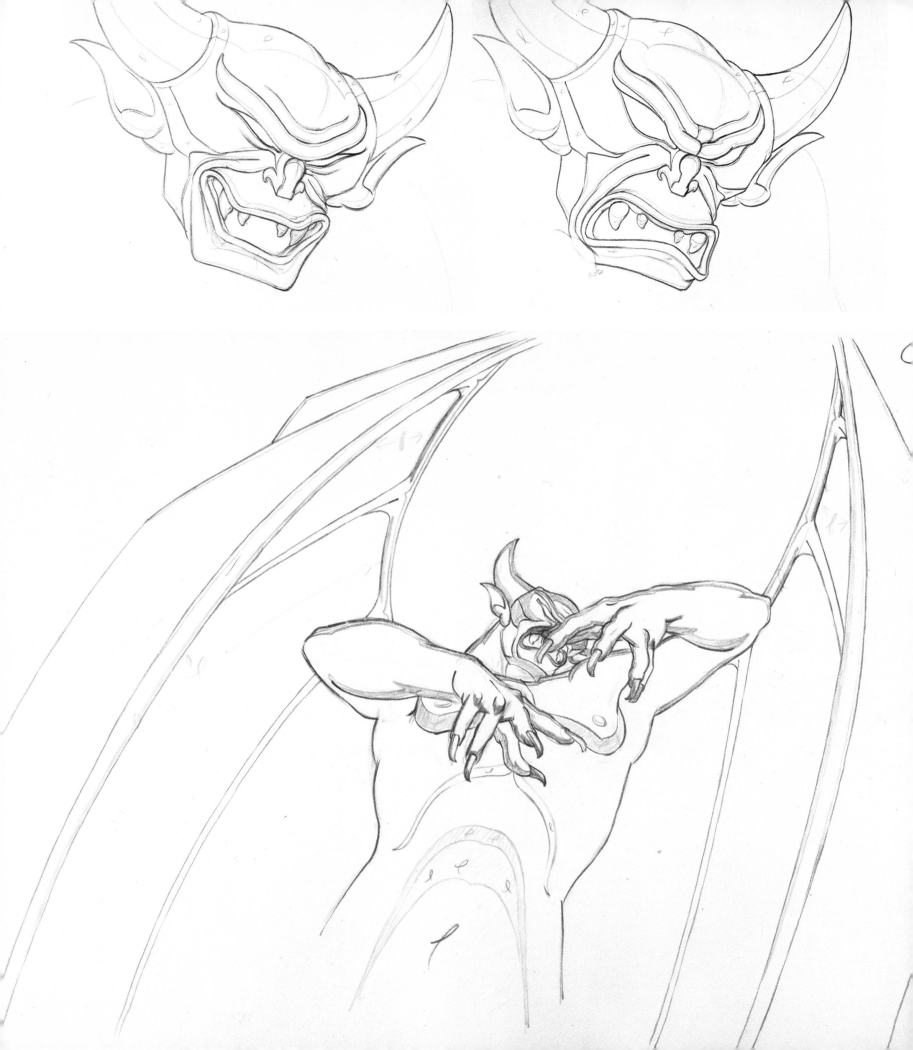

6. Appeal and Dynamics

FRED MOORE AND BILL TYTLA

"We seem to know when to 'tap the heart.' Others have hit the intellect. We can hit them in an emotional way. Those who appeal to the intellect only appeal to a very limited group. The real thing behind this is: we are in the motion picture business, only we are drawing them instead of photographing them."   Walt Disney

Fred

Fred Moore never did get to be a big guy, and when he was young he was much smaller than his brothers. They would all play baseball together, and, of course, they always made Fred play in the outfield and never gave him a chance at bat. Finally, his mother made the brothers let the little guy bat. But the first ball went over his head, and the second one came along the ground; each time they would yell, "Strike!" The third pitch was thrown behind him. "Strike three, you're out!" Fred would get so mad he could eat dirt.

However, his brothers did not know what they were missing, because Fred really was a good athlete. Ten years later, when Fred was at Disney's, he was known as "the most coordinated guy in the studio." According to Wilfred Jackson, "He used to do all these gymnastics. Fred could knock the ball clear out of the field where we were playing." But he took a lot of kidding about his size. Ham Luske was just enough bigger than Fred to call him "squirt." He liked to get Fred to stand back to back with him so they could measure. Even when Fred wore his thickest shoes, he was still looking up at the other fellows.

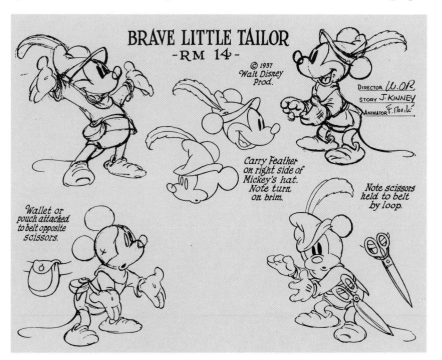

ARTIST: Fred Moore —
Brave Little Tailor.

On each picture Fred kept improving Mickey's appearance. These were perhaps his finest for proportions, appeal, and personality.

119

◁ *ARTIST: Bill Tytla*—Fantasia

He really was a funny little guy, but it was not that he was trying to be funny. It was just that his proportions were cute, like his drawings, and it kind of tickled you to watch him move around imitating someone like Fred Astaire or Chaplin, or trying some fancy juggling act. Even if the stuff dropped on the floor, Fred would always end up in a good pose—just like his drawings. He could not seem to do anything awkward.

The thing that firmly established him as the top athlete among the artists was the way he could throw pushpins and make them stick in the wooden doors at the old Hyperion Studio. He got so good that he could throw two with each hand at the same time and make all four stick. This was an incredible display of timing and natural ability, because the average fellow cannot even be sure of sticking one at a time. But everyone was trying to do it, and with all these pins banging against the doors there was an awful racket up and down the hall. The noise got so loud that it carried upstairs where Walt could hear it, and he could not figure out what was going on. Gradually the competition tapered off because Fred had mastered every way he could think of to throw them; so he lost interest except for an occasional toss behind his back or over his shoulder.

Another thing about Fred—you would have to call it a personality trait—he could not laugh at or really enjoy something by himself. He would keep the humor all bottled up inside until the right people were around to enjoy it with him. One night he was working overtime alone on *Snow White* and discovered how funny the dwarfs' voices sounded when he ran the film backward to rewind it. He probably stayed awake half the night thinking how funny it would be to run the sound backward for us in the morning.

The next day he was there ahead of any of us, waiting out in the hall and about to burst with anticipation. He pulled us into the room where he had the Moviola all warmed up and waiting. "Wait till you guys hear this!" He stepped on the pedal and immediately these crazy sounds started coming out: "Yah, yah, yah, osker baby. (Forward this is, "He never tried, hah, hah, hah.") Then, "manik de middem," which is, "I'm agin' 'em." The laughter that Fred had pent up from the previous evening came out like a dam breaking, and we all doubled up laughing with him.

"I knew you guys would think it was funny," he gasped. And the weird language continued to pour out of the speaker.

Fred was only eighteen at the time he was hired. His art training had been limited to a few night classes he got in exchange for janitorial work at Chouinard's Art Institute. He was given a seat next to Jack Cutting, who was one of the younger animators. Jack said, "Fred would sit there with his arms folded for a minute, then start drawing. He hadn't been there more than 24 hours, and he was making these great drawings. I couldn't believe it. By the end of a couple of days he was starting to animate something. Everything came easy to him."

"Yes, Fred was just right for the time," Ward Kimball says. "He was the first one to escape from the mold of the rubber hose, round circle school. He began getting counter movements, counter thrusts, in the way he drew. He decided to make Mickey's cheeks move with his mouth, which they had never done before because you drew everything inside the circle. He squashed and stretched him more and was right at the time, but Fred was a high school trained animator . . . and he more or less emerged drawing that way. Nobody seemed to remember any development. The rest of us came into this place—it was a strange place—we adapted to it, and we kept trying to improve and change, and we became students of it. Fred never thought of that, he wasn't a student of animation, he was just a natural, gifted animator, whose style and development was perfect, timing-wise, for that point in time."[1]

Even the old-hand Mickey experts such as Les Clark were amazed at what Fred could do. "Fred was a natural. He had a natural flow to his work. He couldn't make a bad drawing, really." This was because Fred was an intuitive draftsman, and it is questionable whether more formal art training would have advanced him. He just was not as oriented to classrooms and lectures as some of the men were. He would say, "Don Graham can give you the rule; I just say it looks better."

This is probably the biggest thing Fred had going for him: he had the ability to tell when something was better one way than another. It is difficult to recall a "Freddie drawing" that did not have everything in the

Everyone at the Studio wanted a Fred Moore drawing, especially a sketch of one of his girls—a charming little breed of females strictly Fred's creations, sexy in an innocent way, and often humorous because of his choice of poses. Fred's fan club put him on a pedestal and to them he was a true star.

121

Dick Lundy, a top animator of the thirties, had a bold, strong approach to animation that Fred Moore admired.

ANIMATOR: *Dick Lundy—Orphan's Benefit.*

This well-known action on Donald Duck typified his whole belligerent attitude. It was first used by Dick Lundy in 1933.

just did it.'' Fred could communicate his ideas through drawings better than anyone around, and that is one of the main reasons Walt made him a supervisor on *Snow White*. It was not that Fred had any special leadership qualities; it was because he had such great charm and appeal in his drawings. When someone was doing something well, Walt wanted everyone to benefit from it.

Walt kept prodding Fred to make drawings for the experienced animators as well as the young ones, so that all the dwarfs would look like his. This was a very difficult assignment for Fred. He would say, ''Gee, I can't go into some guy's room and say let me sit down and make a drawing for you. Walt keeps telling me to, but I just can't do it unless the guy asks me to.''

It is hard to believe that a man with Fred's talent would ever have any real difficulty with drawing, but about every four months he would have his troubles. For two months he would be happy; then, in the third month, he would be restless and start searching for something to stimulate him, looking at magazines and at drawings by animators whose techniques were different from his. But he was not really studying as much as looking. After that he would spend a miserable six weeks or so trying to incorporate what he had learned. He would have no end of trouble mastering the new ideas that he was trying to get into his work. Sometimes it was hard to tell, during this period, what Fred was talking about or what he was trying to accomplish. But finally he would come out on top and have another period of a couple of months in which he really was happy again.

At times Fred felt that a different pencil would give him a new slant on things. When he could not draw what he wanted, he was inclined to suspect the paper, the color of the lead, or the weight of the pencil. ''I

right place. The arms were always related to the rest of the drawing, and even if he put them where they would not be normally, they still looked right. The head seemed to have the right tilt for the shoulders, and when he stretched something out he could make that look correct, too. If Fred drew it, it was pleasing to look at, and it was this pleasing quality that carried his work more than the acting.

Fred could not express himself in words very well, but he had a feeling for what a drawing ought to be. As Larry Clemmons says, ''He was such a help to other guys. Guys would come in his room and say, 'Fred, how would you do this?' Fred would say, 'Well here!'—and he'd show them—he didn't lecture, he

don't know what's wrong with this pencil; it just doesn't seem to work anymore!'' This prompted George Stallings[2] to say, ''You guys are like baseball players; they have their slumps and their superstitions. They think they have to have a special bat — their 'lucky' bat — and you have to have your special pencil. . . .''

It was important that Fred be completely sold on his scene and have nothing undermine his confidence while he was working on it, because he could not work until he felt right. The story business had to be right, the layout, the staging, and the footage for his scene. These were all the responsibilities of others, he figured. Then he had to feel right about himself. He had to approach the scene with confidence, get his ego up. He would say, ''Tell me how good I am, fellows.'' We always overdid it and told him that Walt needed only one animator as long as Fred was around, and he would say, ''I don't need to be *that* good, it's only a little scene!'' But laughter and the spirit of fun had to be the atmosphere or he could not work.

When he was all square with the world and himself, he would perch on his chair and zip, zip, zip—he would go through a ten-foot scene in an afternoon, and then have time to stand around and joke about how true all those things we said about him were. He hated to make corrections, believing that all one's creative energies should go into the first exciting, complete effort. What came out sparkled and lived and appealed, and if you are an emotional type this is the only way to go! Obviously, this procedure is based on *confidence*. The drawings reflected it, and his speed and concentration showed it.

Fred's great facility with his drawing fascinated everyone. It was uncanny the way he could put his line down with such accuracy—short lines or long flowing lines, it made no difference. He could control them

ARTIST: Fred Moore — Snow White.

Drawing of Sneezy displays Fred's extraordinary control over his line.

Fred Moore bowed to Publicity's request for a silly photo. He was not too sure about the stork.

The Model Sheet Department had the responsibility for distributing drawings that showed the approved appearance of a new character. Ward Kimball was quick to kid them by featuring himself in this facsimile model sheet, which has better drawings than many on the regular ones, showing plastic shapes, animatable forms, and broad attitudes.

ANIMATOR: Fred Moore— Pluto's Judgment Day.

Pluto appears to think as the expression changes.

I.O.U-2 PDQ-6 "REVISED KIMBALL MODEL"   C.I.O.-4 P.H.A. 3

PEACE

HONESTY

PERSERVERANCE

RESPECT

KINDLINESS

VALOR

STICKTOITIVENESS

VIRTUE

TEMPERANCE

PIETY

PERSPICACITY

FIDELITY

CHARACTER MODEL DEP'T.
CK by JG DATE 10-20-39
NUMBER OM1187-AX
MODEL SHEETS SUBJECT TO RECALL
WITHOUT NOTICE
© Walt Disney Productions

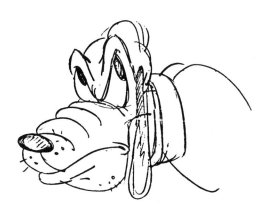

all. His line was beautiful; it almost had a quality of shading. When he naturally made the line thicker at the bottom of the dwarfs' jowls, it gave them an extra feeling of weight and dimension.

Walt was very aware of the charm and pleasing quality of Fred's drawings and usually brought the important visitors into his room. Fred found that the visitors were particularly entranced with seeing two drawings that could be flipped to show a change of expression, such as going from a frown to a "take," or a shift of the eyes that showed the brows and the face moving, the shapes animating. Fred commented over and over, "They love to see the drawings move and the characters think! Remember that! It's what they like to see in our scenes. It's what they liked with Fergy's Pluto, you know. We should always let them see the characters think!"

It was during this phase that the animators discovered the true importance of seeing the characters think by a change of expression. They were concerned with the principles of acting when they stumbled upon that idea.

It was just the best use of the medium in showing audiences what you wanted them to see. Over the years we have experimented continually, trying to make the most extreme statement of the change between two expressions on the drawings. Ward Kimball seemed to go further in this exercise than anyone else, but Fred's drawings moved just as well. Fred did not think in terms of extreme movement himself, but he was very impressed when he would see it in someone else's drawings. Albert Hurter did a drawing of Sleepy with his mouth *wide* open in a yawn, and once Fred had seen something like that he could incorporate it into his own drawings, making it look even better with his natural sense of appeal.

The more Fred worked with Mickey, the more he struggled with overcoming the restrictions of a character whose circular head and body the animators had traced from quarters or half dollars. He kept puzzling about why he was not able to make the drawings that would give him the acting he wanted. "Suppose I want Mickey to be cocky, well then I have to make

Mickey's head and body had been traced from quarters (or from dimes in the longer shots), which gave a static shape and a rigidity.

ANIMATOR: *Fred Moore—* Pluto's Judgment Day.

Fred's pear-shaped Mickey offered a far greater range of attitudes for animators and removed the necessity for them to carry loose change to work.

ANIMATOR: *Fred Moore—*
Three Little Wolves.

No other animator could portray chubby little pigs with the solidity found in the drawings of Fred Moore.

him chesty—and that means arching his back. To do that I have to push some of the mass of the lower body up into the chest, and I can't do it with that rigid body." As Les Clark also observed, "Using dimes and quarters for Mickey's head was like moving a cut-out across the screen. We found out that if we pulled something out and then brought it back to its normal volume, why it would look good." The animators realized that they would have to be able to shift that mass around, to drop it, raise it, squash it and stretch it for whatever the attitude needed.

The natural evolution for Fred was to a pear-shaped body, replacing the hard circle. Now he could get the flow and rhythm and flexibility. With these new shape relationships, he began to get a very appealing Mickey with stronger attitudes, better acting, and more personality. Mickey could be anything now—sad with sloping shoulders, chesty, or angry with shoulders up. The head and body could stretch out, and the ears, too, for a take or an accent in dialogue. Now the animators could forget about coming to work with all that loose change for the different-sized Mickeys.

Bob McCrea, who was an assistant at the time, remembers that when Fred made some of his changes in Mickey's appearance he was nervous about showing the results to Walt. Fred could not bring himself to tell Walt before sweatbox what he had done, so he was

perspiring as he waited to see if Walt would notice. When the scene came on the screen, Walt called to stop the projector! Then he had the scene run back and forth several times while Fred sat there and died. Not a word was exchanged; then Walt turned to Fred, one eyebrow down, and said, "Now that's the way I want Mickey to be drawn from now on!"

The squash and stretch of the walks that Freddie animated had more life, felt better, looked better, and probably seemed more real just because of his ability to change the shapes. He had such a simple, clear way of showing the straight leg, the bent leg, the shove off, and the highs and lows of the walk. He did not experiment with a walk in the same way Ham did, varying the timing and the relationships to get something unique, because Freddie's was all feeling. He always thought in terms of a nice, pleasing drawing. He came up with new things, but they were based on what looked right to him rather than an analysis. He had a way of hooking his forms together that gave a nice solid look. No one drew the three little pigs the way Fred did, nor had the freedom that he felt with Mickey. Mickey was not a design based on logic, there were too many cheats. But that kind of problem did not inhibit Fred because he only would pick a view that looked pleasing to him.

If a drawing looks clumsy, or lacks appeal, or no

ARTIST: *Fred Moore.*

Walt wanted all the animators to follow Fred's model of the dwarfs.

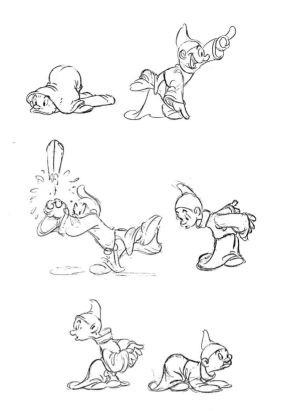

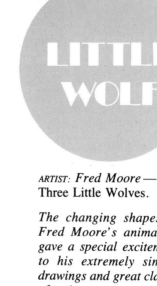
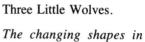
longer looks like the model, perhaps the animator is trying to show something that should not be shown. When Fred was giving a talk on drawing Mickey, he was asked, "How do you draw him looking right down on top of his head?" Fred responded, "Why would you?" If the appeal in the design of the character was based on the balance of the ears to the nose, and the relationship of the cheeks to the eyes and the head shape, Fred wondered why you would deliberately throw all that away? Why would you show a view that did not have as much going for it as possible?

Walt personally sweatboxed all of Fred's early animation on the dwarfs, and this included acting and drawing to the point where he even picked on the size of a finger in one scene. For some reason Fred kept putting off fixing the finger; it just did not seem important enough to do right away. So every week in sweatbox, Walt would mention it again. He would look at the scene in question, and then as the projectionist would run again to the next scene Walt would turn to Fred and say, "That's it, Fred, the finger is too big." Now the next scene was one that Fred was very proud of and wanted Walt to see, but while it was running by Walt would be looking at Fred and holding his own finger up and saying, "Yes, that's it; the finger is too big." Then he would turn around and look at the screen and ask to see the next scene. In order to do this

ARTIST: Fred Moore— Three Little Wolves.

The changing shapes in Fred Moore's animation gave a special excitement to his extremely simple drawings and great clarity of action.
STARTS ON PAGE 169

ANIMATOR: Fred Moore— Snow White.

The first scene Fred animated on Snow White *was with this early model of Dopey. Later scenes refined his appearance, adding charm and appeal.*

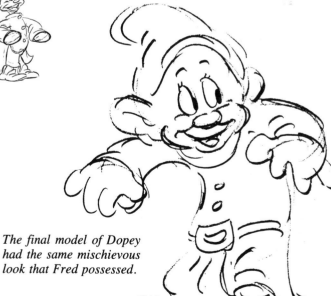

The final model of Dopey had the same mischievous look that Fred possessed.

127

Fred liked new styles in clothes. In his self-caricature, he presents himself as a natty dresser.

the projectionist would have to run back again for a fresh start and he would overlap into the scene with the big finger again. Then they would be off on another round of "the finger is too big." Fred would cringe and wonder why he did not just sit down and correct that dumb finger. Week after week the sweatbox note would be like this one from October 25, 1936:

Scene 26. O.K. for cleanup with changes:
Make Dopey, Happy and Sneezy smaller.
Grumpy's arm and finger get quite large when he says, "SHE'S AN OLD WITCH". The action is okay, just cut down on the size of the finger and the length of the arm.
The three characters in the right f.g. could be silhouetted a little bit.

It is sometimes hard on the ego to take all the criticism that goes with sweatboxing, but Fred must have realized that he was one of the few that Walt was using to set a standard of excellence for his first feature.

Everytime Fred got back a test with a mistake on it or an action that did not please him, it would be because he had forgotten something basic, something he had actually known for years. He would look disgusted and say, "Heck, everybody knows that. I shouldn't make a mistake like that. It's just because you always

forget something! I oughta make a sign and stick it up in front of me on the desk so I never make that mistake again. But there are about a dozen things you never should forget. Instead of a sign, they ought to be on a wheel; and every day when you come in, you just give that ol' wheel a turn and that way it would keep reminding you!" So he started a list of the fundamental things an animator should always remember, and he discovered that he had 14 basic points.

FRED'S 14 POINTS OF ANIMATION

1. Appeal in drawing
2. Staging
3. Most interesting way?
   [Would anyone other than your mother like to see it?]
4. Is it the most entertaining way?
5. Are you in character?
6. Are you advancing the character?
7. Is this the simplest statement of the main idea of the scene?
8. Is the story point clear?
9. Are the secondary actions working with the main action?
10. Is the presentation best for the medium?
11. Does it have 2 dimensional clarity?
12. Does it have 3 dimensional solidity?
13. Does it have 4 dimensional drawing?
    [Drag and follow through]
14. Are you trying to do something that shouldn't be attempted?
    [Like trying to show the top of Mickey's head]

The relaxed, unsophisticated manner that made his drawings so great also made it difficult for Fred to adjust to Walt's constant pressure for new things. One day Fred came back from a meeting and asked, "Why does Walt always try to get us to do things we can't do? Why doesn't he just let us do the things we *can do*?"

In the public's mind there have been no more memorable characters than the dwarfs, and Dopey in particular. Dopey seemed to reflect or contain so much of Fred himself—innocent, but with a touch of mischief; naive, but with just enough

worldliness. There was nothing hidden or mysterious about Fred. His personality was on the outside for everyone to see. What he lacked in sophistication he made up in charm. He had honesty, integrity, and was always willing to help the young animators. As Dick Huemer said, "He was the sweetest guy you would want to know."

"My God," Marc Davis says, "Fred Moore *was* Disney drawing! We've all done things on our own, but that was the basis of what Disney stood for. It was certainly the springboard for everything that came after. He had to be as close to a boy genius as. . . . He never grew up, and this is what he animated. He animated what he knew, and he died that way—never growing up."

The last ten years of his life Fred experienced disappointments and frustrations. He had burst onto the scene in full bloom and, like some others whose talents flowered early, he found that he had achieved all his goals in a relatively short time. He was quoted as saying, "I have reached everything I want, and I'm only twenty-four. Now what do I do?"

He could not have realized that the very thing that made him great was now the thing that held him back; this childlike quality that prevented him from growing with the changing standards. "Two animators whom I have always thought of as tragic victims of this development in animation," said Ben Sharpsteen, "were Freddie Moore and Norm Ferguson. They simply did not have the background, the training, and the intuitive ability to measure up to the best men we later had on our staff. What is sad is the fact that they were not secondary men; they both had been top men, and I'm sure it was a crushing blow to their pride."

On November 23, 1952, Fred Moore died as a result of an auto accident at the age of forty-two.

All the characters were drawn by Fred Moore in this publicity illustration.

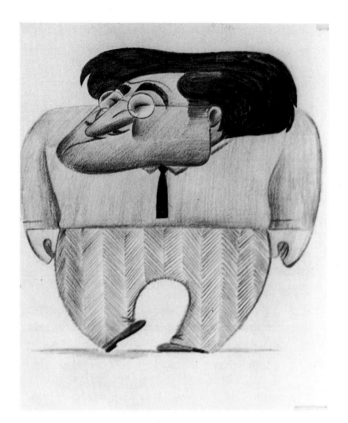

CARICATURIST: *T. Hee.*

Easterner Bill Tytla loved the image of the Western cowboy.

Bill

Bill Tytla was the last of the four supervising animators on *Snow White* to come to Disney's. Part of the great strength of these men was their dissimilarity, and many would say that Tytla was the least similar of the four. Dick Huemer said, ''Bill Tytla was the brooding type. He was the greatest.'' Physically Bill was very striking with his swarthy complexion and broad shoulders. He had a big mop of coal black hair, heavy black brows, and very piercing dark eyes. But more than that it was what was under the surface that made him stand out. He had great feelings churning around inside of him and tremendous nervous energy.

Bill was a very intense person, often moody and more often very emotional. In spite of these volatile traits, he was a very shy, gentle, and sensitive man. When he had something to say that he felt strongly about, it would come out in spite of any shyness. The words would literally pour out of him, his mind working faster than he could talk. If someone else was talking he would be too

polite to interrupt; so while he was waiting for his opening he would unconsciously start making funny little half-whimpering, humming noises, as if he were tuning up to be ready when his opportunity came, a kind of anticipatory sound.

Bill loved and believed in the characters he was creating, but he was concerned about whether he would animate them as well as he should. He need not have worried, for he had the sensitivity

to understand his characters' motivation in terms of acting, and the ability to interpret that into drawings and staging. He could portray the darkest evil and the most frightening terror. His powerful drawing of the devil in the "Bald Mountain" sequence of *Fantasia* was the most awesome piece of animation ever to reach the screen, and his Stromboli was probably the most terrifying and truly evil personality of all the Disney villains. It is true that the basis for these characters is found in the story, but to capture Stromboli's mercurial moods, his lightning changes, and to show the emotions that came from the inner feelings of his characters was one of Tytla's greatest achievements.

His comments in *Snow White* story meetings, where personality was discussed, all show that he was looking for that inner feeling and mood to

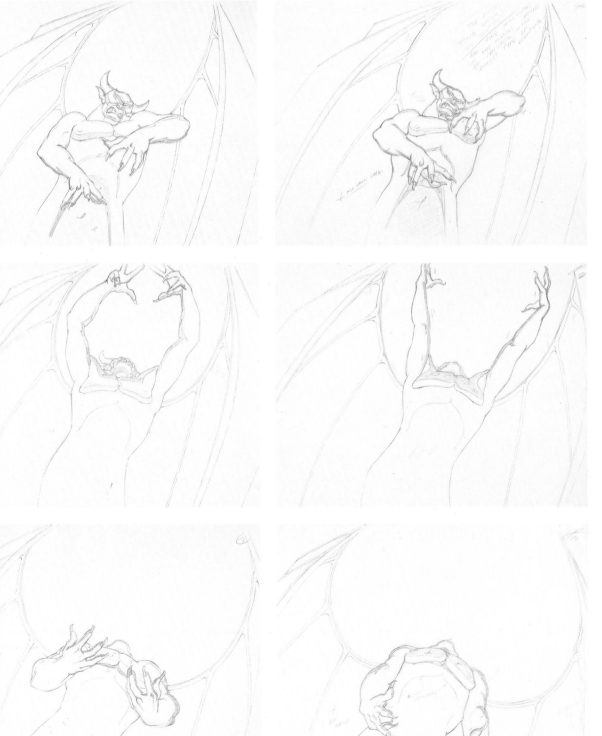

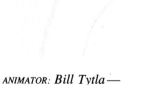

ANIMATOR: *Bill Tytla —* Night on Bald Mountain.

Powerful action, solid drawing, and dramatic staging helped to create a character never even attempted previously in animation, but it was the feeling of an inner spirit, evil and primitive, that really made him live on the screen.

131

help him determine how the character would react. Amid constant suggestions by others that there should be a special attitude in the drawing on each dwarf, Bill stubbornly came back to the same argument: the way to get a difference in the appearance and attitude is by knowing the mood and the personality. In a meeting on November 17, 1936, director and storyman Perce Pearce picked Bill's brains on this subject:

Perce: Let's take Doc, get him from scratch, and say, nobody knows him. First his most obvious feature is his pompous attitude. He shows this pompous attitude with his chest. For instance, how do you see him, Bill, when he is pompous?

Bill: His pose is a reaction to something. It is only a reaction of what he is going to do, otherwise you are just making a drawing. Since it is up to Doc to

Dumbo

132

ANIMATOR: *Bill Tytla*—
Snow White.

This pompous attitude on Doc came from the animator's knowledge of what the character was thinking.

explain to the group what is going on, he sort of takes the leadership whether he is entitled to it or not. He immediately strikes that attitude. He gets flustered, and doesn't know what he says, tries to make out—sort of a French Provincial Mayor's attitude. Grumpy throws him off balance. Doc recomposes himself and tries to regain lost ground. So far we have had no opportunity to really try to do anything as far as mannerism or gestures are concerned —in so far as gestures react in dialogue. There has been no opportunity to use any scratching or Doc fooling around with his beard. We have only had dialogue so far.

While Bill's work stood out with all its power and strength, its emotions and inner feelings, its pathos and deeply touching moments, it is reassuring to the rest of us to know that he sometimes made mistakes. In the preceding quote he explained very lucidly how he felt Doc should act in this type of situation, but in the following sweatbox note from Walt it is evident that he missed on the timing of the flustered feeling and its relation to the dialogue. Doc seemed to be anticipating his own mistake, and that was Bill's mistake, too.

March 5, 1937   Walt sweatboxing with Bill Tytla
Tytla   Scene 8   Seq. 4D   Original
Make Doc's "come on" gesture a broader one— not a point at himself on "follow me."
The feeling now is that Doc knows he is going to say HEN instead of MEN. He should say COME ON, HEN with a broad gesture, seeming to complete it, acting as if he were saying the right thing,

then do a quick half gesture on the mistake, and follow with a broad gesture on the—MEN, FOLLOW ME. The half gesture is not too definite, but just a nervous feeling.
Have Doc turn on the FOLLOW ME in anticipation of walking out.

The range of Bill's characters was phenomenal. His ability to get inside the innermost reaches of their personalities enabled him to develop great scope in his work. He seemed to understand the problems that his characters faced as well as their feelings about what was happening to them. Could anyone's thoughts be portrayed in a better way than Grumpy's after Snow White kissed him? The audience literally could feel the warmth that surged through him as he finally released his bottled-up feelings.

But, Bill's most poignant scenes were of the little elephant in *Dumbo*. Bill's inspiration for the sequence of Dumbo bathing came while watching his own son playing in the tub, and his great perception enabled him to adapt to animation the spirit of what he saw in real life. His draftsmanship is at its best in this section, and there is excellent analysis of what to exaggerate in the action as the baby scampers playfully around his mother. But through all this, the big overriding theme is the elusive quality of love and affection that Bill's animation captures so beautifully.

Many of Bill's characters were muscular like himself, and when they came on the screen it was like a charge of electricity. He made everything work for him, because he drew so well and felt the personality so strongly. He wanted his characters to move in a special way, to really live! He animated the head, body, hands, and drapery all in different colors. It was not until he had each part working, communicating, and moving properly that he would make one complete drawing in black. The eyes, the mouth, the gestures, and the secondary actions are are all brilliantly there in Stromboli. This character has been criticized for moving too much, making it hard to follow on the screen at times, yet no cartoon character has put over any better a rich, volatile, and complete personality. This character is extremely powerful and frightening.

Bill felt all these things through his whole body when he animated, always trying to transfer his tre-

Stromboli
ANIMATOR: *Bill Tytla*— Pinocchio

133

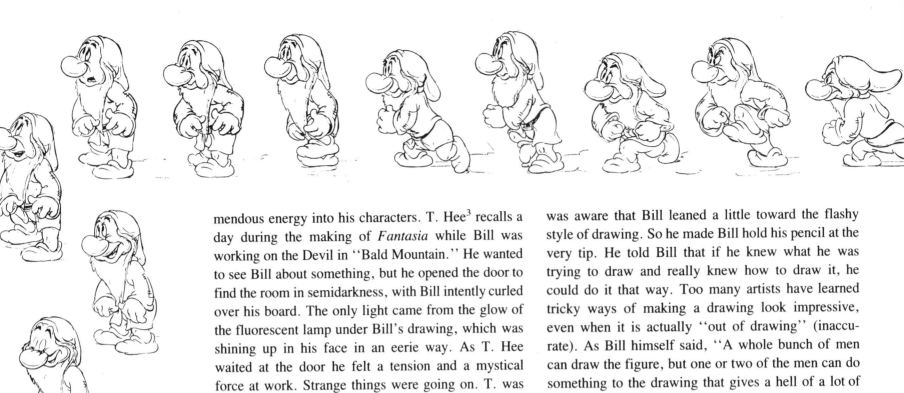

mendous energy into his characters. T. Hee[3] recalls a day during the making of *Fantasia* while Bill was working on the Devil in "Bald Mountain." He wanted to see Bill about something, but he opened the door to find the room in semidarkness, with Bill intently curled over his board. The only light came from the glow of the fluorescent lamp under Bill's drawing, which was shining up in his face in an eerie way. As T. Hee waited at the door he felt a tension and a mystical force at work. Strange things were going on. T. was so unnerved by this sight that he quietly backed out into the hall without ever saying anything to Bill.

Tytla had studied at the Art Students League in New York with Boardman Robinson, whom he regarded very highly both as a man and a teacher. Robinson was aware that Bill leaned a little toward the flashy style of drawing. So he made Bill hold his pencil at the very tip. He told Bill that if he knew what he was trying to draw and really knew how to draw it, he could do it that way. Too many artists have learned tricky ways of making a drawing look impressive, even when it is actually "out of drawing" (inaccurate). As Bill himself said, "A whole bunch of men can draw the figure, but one or two of the men can do something to the drawing that gives a hell of a lot of meaning to it, whereas others in the group can impress you, for the time, with flashy stuff."

Later he studied sculpture in Paris, which accounts in part for the solidity and weight and excellent relationship of forms in his work. Because of this art

Bill Tytla

134

ANIMATOR: *Bill Tytla* —
Snow White.

*Grumpy made a great show
of indignation when Snow
White kissed him good-bye,
but as he stomped away his
mood began to soften, until
the audience could feel the
warm glow permeating his
whole body.*

background, Bill thought of his scenes more in terms of composition than most animators. He wanted depth, not only in the drawing of the character, but also in the way it moved through the layout; so the total design of the scene had to be right. Ken Anderson says that it was difficult to make a layout that would please Bill; he always had some adjustment that would make the scene more interesting, have better staging, and be more dynamic.

Bill was one of the few animators at that time who had any art training. He was deeply appreciative that the studio was looking for more quality and better drawing from the animators, that Walt would go so far as to set up his own art school under an expert like Don Graham.[4] Bill and Don grew to have great respect for each other. It is obvious from Bill's remarks in a lecture to the young animators that this art school atmosphere was like a breath of fresh air to him:

When I first came out here about two and a half years ago, they started having action analysis classes and I fell for them like a ton of bricks. I was in a period between the old and the new stage of animation. Running stuff in slow motion was like lifting a curtain for me. Then sweatbox sessions were another revelation. After all, if you do a piece of animation and run it over enough times, you must see what is wrong with it. Formerly, I never saw what I animated. We would catch a movie every two weeks to see a scene we had experimented on for drawing, or spacing or timing, but we couldn't get much benefit from one viewing. In the theatre they would only run the picture twice—the whole thing whizzed by and you forgot all about what you tried to do. And unless you did go to the movie, you would never see what you had done. Furthermore, I never saw a thing run in reverse except once in New York when they ran a scene backwards of a fellow diving off a board. . . .

My boss in New York never knew about a moviola—he probably still doesn't. When he got a letter from one of the boys here telling about the tests—roughs, semi-roughs, semi-cleanups, cleanups and finals—then the whole thing is done over again, he wouldn't believe it. My boss thought it was funny as hell—a bunch of fellows running around in hallways with pieces of black and white film in their hands looking for moviolas. He said, "When I hire a man to animate, I want him to know how."

The things done here now, I would consider sensational, and I know the fellows back east consider them sensational when they hear descriptions of the training and opportunities here. But here at the studio those things are considered commonplace. The average fellow here doesn't even realize what is being shoved on him. He is being coaxed and encouraged to better work, and he probably thinks it is a pain in the neck. I really can't compliment Walt and the organization enough for handing out the stuff. There is no other fellow who will do it.

Besides telling a lot about Bill, this material gives an insight into why the studio rose above all other places, and it gives a graphic picture of Walt's philosophy and why there was such a thing as the "Golden Age."

Bill could not stand the ordinary. If you were interested in your work, then you should take the pains to observe and study and make your characters different and unique. No two scenes should ever be alike and no two characters should ever do something the same way. Bill put it this way:

Stock methods of doing things are careless animation; very often, moreover, they are based on no observation at all. Frequently, some animator will animate not something he has observed, but something he has memorized that some other animator

135

has done. In such cases, it is a matter of one animator copying another, memorizing a lot of stock stuff. This is evident in cartoons where all the characters, regardless of personality, walk, run and move the same way. The animator has not given even a thought to the personalities involved, to delineating character and personality through variations in reactions and actions.

ANIMATOR: *Bill Tytla* — Snow White.

Drawings show that Bill Tytla was always thinking of the individual character of each dwarf.

Bill was intolerant of any animator sloughing off on a scene just because it did not interest him. His advice on an animator's responsibility has become a classic:

Another thing in animation. When you start you will probably wish that you could get a lot of stuff that is already funny to start with. You may get a very dry piece of business to do, and no matter how you work at it, you will feel you can't make it funny. If you can make it *interesting*, you will have done a very good job. But if you can take a piece of business that is dry and uninteresting and if you can animate it so that it will be alive and vital, then as an animator, I think you have fulfilled your duty.

Not every aspect of Bill's animation can be properly analyzed, for his thinking was complicated and involved. However, it is interesting and enlightening to list the components that are found in Bill's work. In his best animation they are *all there*. It takes steady concentration to have this knowledge and skill at your

ANIMATOR: *Bill Tytla* — Snow White.

Bill's strength in movement is evident in the rough extremes for Grumpy's defiant walk.

136

fingertips and be able to use it right. Like a baseball pitcher who has that momentary lapse and gives up a home run, the animator can get himself into a hopeless situation through lack of concentration. This list of components in good animation is quite an imposing group to combine in any scene; any one element on the list is a challenge to the best of animators:

Inner feelings and emotion
Acting with clear and definite action
Character and personality
Thought process through expression changes
Ability to analyze
Clear staging
Good composition

Timing
Solidity in drawing
Power in drawing
Strength in movement
Imagination

Bill had done a scene on *Pinocchio* that he and the other animators thought was great. ''Well, it's good,'' was Walt's comment, ''but it's not what I'd expect from Bill Tytla.'' Bill was crushed. For a time, like many highly emotional, sensitive, and creative people, he found it impossible to work. A week, maybe two weeks, passed before he gradually started to search around and explore other possibilities. In the end he *did* find a better way, and Walt liked it. This had been

Pinocchio

137

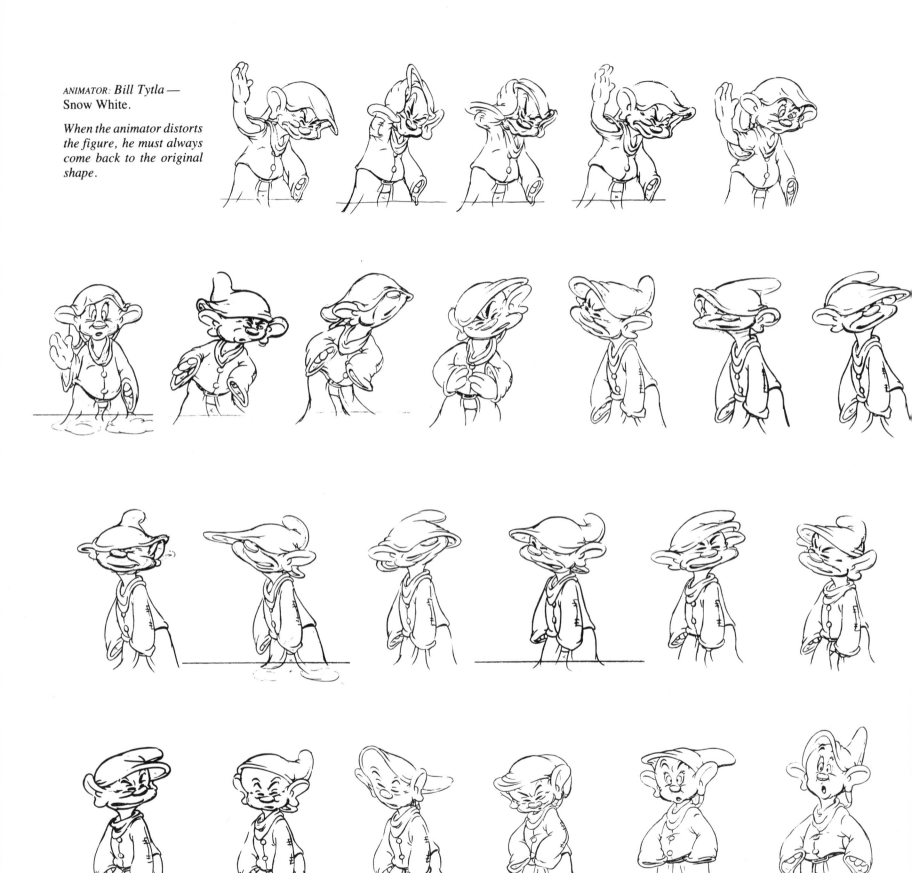

ANIMATOR: *Bill Tytla* — Snow White.

When the animator distorts the figure, he must always come back to the original shape.

terribly hard on Bill, but he had been shown something about his own great capabilities, that he had more to offer than he realized, and that was why he loved the studio.

According to Ben Sharpsteen, "Tytla somehow got pegged as an animator of heavies. After *Snow White* he was cast on Stromboli in *Pinocchio* and the devil in the 'Night On Bald Mountain' sequence of *Fantasia*. Walt made quite a point of Tytla and his abilities on the latter character. He built it up as a special feature." Wilfred Jackson, who directed the "Night On Bald Mountain" sequence, describes how he and Bill Tytla worked together on it:

I was told by somebody, maybe Walt, I was supposed to get [Bela] Lugosi and shoot live action. So we got him and he looked upon it as an actor's job, but this was not what Bill wanted. He was interested in the movement. Lugosi started showing him how he could unwrap his wings like that and we were getting along great, but Bill was having an awful time—he was telling Lugosi how he should do it. Finally Bill gave up and went over in the corner and sulked, so I got the best stuff I could out of it and after it was over Bill said, "Jack, I don't like what he's done. I like the way you do it; won't you take your shirt off and get in front of the camera?" So I took my shirt off and he ran the music and we used that stuff. Yeah, the photostats of skinny me. We never told Walt. Bill and I made it up in the music room before Lugosi ever came, then I just went through what I had been doing with Bill. Each time we'd do it he'd say fine, I even did the hocus pocus thing with the little guys on my hands.

I'm not sure Walt intended to have such a powerful character, but when you have a piece of animation like that you're not going to turn it down.

Someone once asked, "Who replaced Bill Tytla when he left?" The answer was, of course, no one—although someone may have taken over his assignment. Bill Tytla, like Fred Moore, Ham Luske, and Norm Ferguson, brought his special magic to the screen, and when he left that particular way of doing something disappeared with him. It would not be possible for anyone else to duplicate Bill's way of animating the

powerful devil or the tenderness in his handling of the poignant Dumbo scenes. What others do must be different, for as both Fergy and Bill said, "It is too limiting to copy someone else." But it is not out of reach for those who feel as deeply as Bill did, to do something equally great in their own way.

No one thing seems to explain the reason for Bill's departure from Disney's in 1943, though changing studio policies and the feeling that his family would be more secure during wartime on his Connecticut farm were certainly strong considerations. In the East, Bill continued in the animation business as both animator and director, but he was never again to find the self-fulfillment and personal gratification that he had found in his work during those great days at Disney's. Bill died in 1966.

Inspirational sketch
ARTIST: Kay Nielsen—
"Night on Bald Mountain,"
Fantasia

Pinocchio

7. Hyperion: The Explosion

"My greatest reward is that I have been able to build this wonderful organization."   Walt Disney

Many a philosopher has observed that a person's physical environment greatly determines how he will behave and what he is apt to do. One historian of animation has claimed that the old studio on Hyperion Avenue at the far eastern edge of Hollywood was largely responsible for the innovative and imaginative thinking of the artists who worked inside. The studio was indeed unique, but then it would not have been fitting for Walt's studio to be like any other place of business. From an insignificant beginning, the studio seemed gradually to take on a life of its own and grow like the magical world it was creating. The original building, first occupied in 1926, was a mere 1,600 square feet and was hardly noticed on a quiet street that meandered down a small valley. Next to it was a pipe organ factory, but there was space behind and a vacant lot on the other side that gave plenty of privacy. That first building could hold some twenty men at most, so it was not long before an addition was needed. The organ factory was purchased and combined with the Disney Studio.

Within months still more space was needed; the carpenters returned, and soon the little building was bulging and protruding in unexpected places. In 1931, Walt decided to put an end to this makeshift arrangement and to build an edifice especially designed for animation, with an office for each animator and his assistant, and two rooms for directors. Hours and hours of planning went into the design of this "perfect" building, but it was outdated before the paint dried.

First, there was only a small addition to it, then there was a connection to another building, then something out in back, and then suddenly a whole new, immense two-story structure. Soon the studio flowed clear out to the side street, then back the other way,

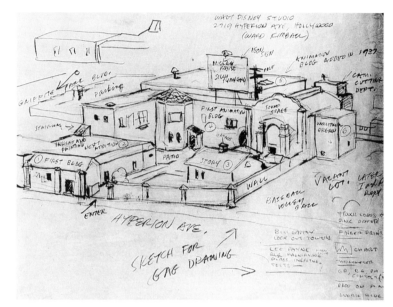

The Studio on Hyperion Avenue, 1934. Walt's office was at upper right behind balcony.

with added bungalows and things on top of things, including, finally, a special Ink and Paint building that used all the property up to the street on the east. The studio was spilling out in all directions.

141

There was also a building across the street that had been built complete with a skylight facing the north for the art classrooms, offices for Don Graham and visiting artists, and endless cubicles for young hopefuls learning the craft. The shape of the peaked roof immediately reminded Walt of the chicken sheds he used to know as a boy, so he dubbed the building "The Incubator." Before long, he added to the back of that, then installed pens beside it for the animals needed for study and drawing. Like the cooking pot in the fairy tale that continued to produce oatmeal because someone forgot the magic words, the studio continued to sprawl and spread and cover the whole area in a slow-motion eruption. There were tunnels and passageways and bridges and little doors, and partitions were put up and taken down, and walls were moved, and projection booths were made out of conference rooms and offices and even closets. As Parkinson's Law states, "During a period of exciting discovery or progress there is no time to plan the perfect headquarters."[1]

When every inch of open space had been filled, neighboring buildings were purchased and converted—apartment houses, bungalows, offices, any structure that was near and could house artists and storymen. In speaking of his own experience in those strange accommodations, Mel Shaw[2] said, "John Hench? Oh, yes, he had the kitchen of my apartment. . . . I had the bedroom and bath." The artists who were not on the main lot felt left out and isolated. All their hopes were based on "stepping up" someday to the main building across the street. In the main building the rooms were so small and everyone was so jammed in together that if one guy wanted to get out, all the others had to move their chairs to let him through. With everyone that close, there was an exchange of ideas as well as a lot of funny incidents and gags that would not have happened otherwise. Walt kept trying to shield his animators from distractions and annoyances that would drain their creative energies, but, actually, more growth was achieved through this arrangement than if we had been spread out in neat rows.

Exciting new things were happening all around us, and this close personal contact and the crazy associations kept us stimulated. We were all trying to outdo each other in thinking of screwy actions, deliberately trying to be different, to be funnier, to come up with an unexpected gag in everything we did—away from the studio as well as at work. One of the early animators, Art Babbitt, said, "Each test you did, you tried to be as inventive as possible so the other guys would comment."

Unless a gagman is thinking "funny" every day, he might find it hard to think of an unusual gag when he needs one, and we were determined always to see the unusual in the world around us. All a man had to do was stumble over a chair, or knock something off a desk, or just make a chance remark, and immediately he would be inundated with gag drawings, building the situation to outlandish proportions. It looked like a waste of valuable time, but, actually, we were all learning our most important lessons in staging and communication. If the gag was too obscure, if the drawing was not funny, if it was not something that could be understood instantly, no one laughed. This amusement actually was better training than developing business in the pictures, where it would be weeks before we would know if the gag was funny, or the right thing, or whether it even had been understood.

Gags were also a very good way to relieve tension. Ward Kimball says, "It was this close exacting work we had to do. . . . You had to let it out, so all of a sudden you'd stop and let off steam. We'd all sit down and draw gags." The drawings became broader and more preposterous by the day, yet there was always an element of believability in them, because at the core they were based on some quirk in a particular fellow's

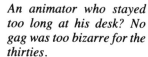

ARTIST: *Frank Thomas.*
Someone suggested that sun lamps be installed so animators could look more healthy. Immediately, the gags began pouring in. Here, Frank Thomas, Milt Kahl, and Ollie Johnston are depicted as needing far more than a tan.

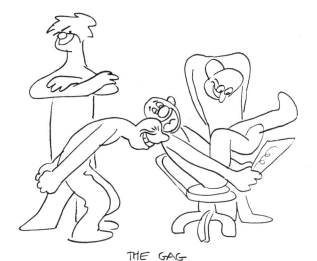

THE GAG

While Vip Partch was an assistant animator, his drawings showed the staging and insight that later made him famous as a commercial cartoonist. Above, "The Gag" catches the precise attitudes and expressions of the fellows looking at a new gag. Below, Vip's version of Ollie Johnston's animation unit. When told he had to get an inbetweener to move the work faster, Vip caricatured the only type of personality he felt he could control. Left, animators Ollie Johnston and Ken O'Brien.

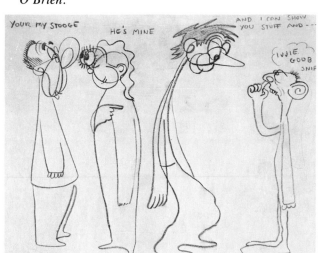

An animator who stayed too long at his desk? No gag was too bizarre for the thirties.

personality. This incisive understanding of personality brought on elaborate practical jokes as well. We had to have some idea of an intended victim's reaction to the gag, or it would be hard to see the possibilities in it. This same approach was used daily in working out the gags and situations for our cartoon characters. If you had a Donald Duck short, immediately everyone knew what type of gags to use, what situations would be funny. It was easy to find business for Donald because we all understood his personality.

The butt of the studio's most elaborate practical joke was an Englishman, Ted Thwaites. The men who worked with him had sized him up as being rather square and had planned the "business" in their little scenario accordingly. Floyd Gottfredson, then head of the comic strip department, relates the story as follows:

The whole thing happened in the comic strip department and the principal characters were Ted Thwaites and Al Taliaferro. We all worked in the back room of the annex at Hyperion. Ted carried his lunch in a brown bag and every day brought in a

143

Al Taliaferro, originator of the Studio's most famous practical joke, and Ted Thwaites, his victim.

small can of fruit cocktail and he loved it so much and he smacked his lips over it and he'd tell Al, "I just couldn't eat a lunch without this."

So this started Al's brain to working and one day he brought in a can the same size, a can of mixed vegetables. When Ted went out of the room he would always tell Al where he was going. So the minute he got out of sight, Al would jump up and take the label off, and put rubber cement on the thing and wait til it almost dries—and just switch the labels from the mixed vegetable can to the fruit cocktail.

So Ted came back the first time and he opened this thing and he actually took a spoonful of the stuff before he noticed it was not his fruit cocktail. Al, of course, was watching him. Ted stopped—then he took another spoonful of the stuff and he looked at it and he says, "I can't believe this." He was still very British and very gullible. He says, "Something's wrong here." So he shows it to Al and Al peers at it and says, "What's wrong? What is that— vegetables?"

Ted says, "Yeah! Look at the label—this is fruit cocktail."

Al says, "That's strange."

So between the two of them they decided that some way the labels had gotten mixed up at the canning factory. There wasn't anymore said about it except Ted went around and told everybody in the department. He couldn't get over it. So Al let it go for three or four days and then he switched labels again, and Ted said, "The only way I can explain this is that they must have mixed up a whole lot shipment—just imagine! These things are on the shelves of markets all over the country."

Al did it just far enough apart to keep Ted intrigued. He'd have peas or carrots and even hominy one time—and Ted had never seen hominy before. To put a little variety in the act, Al reversed the procedure and put a vegetable label on the fruit cocktail can.

"That's crazy!" Ted says, "I know I bought fruit cocktail this morning—Al, look at this."

Al says, "What's wrong with it?"

Ted says, "That's mixed vegetables!"

Al says, "That's funny. You must have picked

it up by mistake.'' So, he opens the can and it has fruit cocktail in it.

Finally it was Ted himself who said, ''Well I really think this is an item for Robert Ripley's *Believe It Or Not*. I think I should write it in to him and maybe I'll get some money out of it.''

So we all agreed and by this time everybody knew about it, and he actually wrote Ripley. After he had written to Ripley, we knew we had to do something to pay this whole thing off. We wondered for two or three days what we could do. We figured it would take eight days before he would expect an answer.

The plan called for this last can to be mailed to Thwaites, with appropriate King Features[3] labels made up by the comic strip men and was to contain a rather potent message from Mr. Ripley. But Al couldn't leave it alone. He had to switch one more can and Ted came back too soon and Al had to rush it.

When Ted came in and ate his lunch right after that and he picked up this can and the label slipped off the can and here was this wet rubber cement. He stopped and looked at it for a minute, then he says in his British accent, ''You so and so's. Suddenly everything is clear to me. I know what's been going on here!''

Walt was keenly aware of the creative process and did not criticize anyone for taking time off to do gags. He seemed to be aware that we were sharpening our skills. The only thing he used to say was, ''Why don't you get some of that in the pictures?''

The place was expanding so fast it seemed as if it would burst at the seams; it was teeming with new people everywhere, and there were new artists coming in almost every day. We were all squeezed into little nooks and crannies and so busy and excited that we could not keep up with what our friends were doing. We were always in too much of a hurry to wander around the studio and say, ''What do you do?'' Then, one day, a newly finished picture we had never heard of would be shown for the staff—such as *The Old Mill*. Where did it come from? Who had worked on it? And more important, *how had they done it?*

Our eyes popped out when we saw all of *The Old Mill*'s magnificent innovations—things we had not even

ARTIST: *Ward Kimball.*

In 1936 Walt asked Don Graham to conduct a country-wide search for new talent needed to complete Snow White *and to meet future demands. Drawing shows Graham and George Drake, then head of the inbetween department, heading east to set up a recruiting center in New York.*

dreamed of and did not understand. We did not know how any of the effects were achieved or who had done what and how it was painted. Even the inked cels and backgrounds did not look like anything we had ever seen before. Unknown to us, Walt had hired color experts and engineers and had been experimenting with new ways of lighting and a multiplane camera and all sorts of things. And when we talked with fellows like Claude Coats,[4] who had been working on the picture, we could tell they were almost as surprised and bewildered as we were. ''Oh, I don't know. Well, it was just like any other picture. We tried to do what was needed; we had our problems and our battles; we had our troubles. . . .''

Each new picture contained breathtaking improvements; the effects were better, the animation had more life, and the whole studio had an upward momentum. It was like being a player on a winning team! To us, all this was pure magic. Our own efforts to stage a bit of business or get a character to come to life in an interesting way—while keeping our footage up and

145

Mary Tebb started with Walt in 1927 as an inker. Here, in 1962, she is head of the color model department.

not getting bogged down—at times would get us so involved that we would lose sight of where the studio was headed. Everyone was working hard but few complained. If there was not always exhilaration in the work from day to day, the employees would be filled with awe and overwhelmed with disbelief when a new picture was projected for them. Where were we going? What was to happen with this cartoon medium?

There were not enough hours in a day for one person to keep up with all the new ideas and inventions and procedures, let alone deal with the imaginative concepts and ideas for future productions. But one man did! And he miraculously rode herd over hundreds of enthusiastic employees. As someone said, "If Walt had done nothing else, he would be remembered for bringing together 1000 artists and storymen and controlling their work. No one in history has ever done that."

Mary Tebb, who started with Walt as an inker in 1927, explained her feelings this way: "That dedication was the greatest thing in the world—our dedication to Walt and the product, our unquestioning attitude. No one ever said to Walt, 'Aw that's too much work, I don't want to do it.' Oh no, you'd take it home and spend all night if you had to. Walt had something, that power. It was just his personality, his genius, I guess."

"It wasn't that you *had* to do these things," Marc Davis said. "You *wanted* to do them. You were so proud. Every write-up the studio got, everybody went out and got it. Very few people have ever, as a group, experienced that type of excitement. What we were in

on, really, was the invention of animation. Animation had been done before, but stories were never told."[5]

Milt Schaffer remembers a meeting in Ben Sharpsteen's office of all the young artists. Ben told them this was going to become a great artistic medium, and they were all really going to work—that they had not even begun to learn animation yet. In the course of his talk he said, "It will be with you like it was with Michelangelo. When you guys are about sixty-five, you'll be ready to hang out your shingle." Milt says they were all impressed, even when told they were not going to be any good until they were sixty-five—even that was encouraging! All of this determined the quality of animation that would be done. It grew as an art form because everyone *cared*—and not just in the animation department but throughout the whole studio.

Out of this creative cauldron came the exciting discovery of *life* in the drawing, and with it came a new way of looking at animation. Now the animator could do more than entertain the audience with funny little movements in sync to sound; through this important revelation he could make the audience believe in his characters.

To bring a character to life, it is necessary to imbue each single extreme drawing of the figure with an attitude that reflects what he is feeling or thinking or trying to do. No scene is any better than the sum total of all its drawings. *Life* must be in *every* drawing. There should be no drawings that merely move the character from one spot to the next. In other words, the life and vitality comes not from movement or timing alone—as it did in the early Mickeys—but from that ability to make the single drawings come alive. The animator must incorporate into his work some of the power and artistry of men like Honoré Daumier. As Daumier himself said, "If my drawing does not convey anything to you, it must be bad, and no caption can remedy that. If the drawing is good you will be able to understand it."[6] There was hardly a gesture, mood, or human relationship that Daumier did not illustrate.

Animation was beginning to mean something different to each of us, and everyone was surprised at the definition one employee found in the dictionary. "Most people think the word 'animation' means movement," he said, "but it doesn't. It comes from 'animus' which

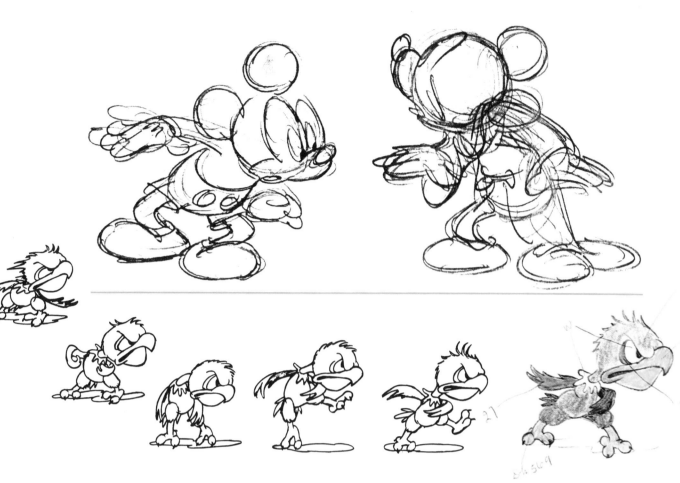

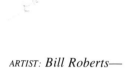

means 'life or to live.' Making it move is not animation, but just the mechanics of it.''[7]

In the early pictures there were indeed glimpses of this ''life,'' but since no animator really knew, then, what he had done, it was impossible for it to be sustained over a series of drawings. In 1934, *The Flying Mouse*, with its pathos, turned the corner—more than any other early film—from stock gags to emphasis on personality, and it was immediately apparent that this communicated better with the audience. Later, the great animation on Figaro in *Pinocchio*, the dwarfs, and the little ugly duckling were all exciting steps ahead in this new development. People responded to these characters through their feelings—something rarely achieved in a cartoon before.

The concept of instilling life in cartoon figures changed the role of the animator from a kind of creator who sat back and watched in a detached way as he put his character through amusing antics to someone who now found himself living inside that little person on his drawing board. If it was a terrified Pinocchio locked in Stromboli's cage or a shy Bambi at his first meeting with Faline, the animator had to live every minute of it or it would not be in his drawings.

Andrew Wyeth had comparable feelings about a painting he was working on and expressed them beautifully in these words: ''And then finally when you get far enough along in a thing, you feel as though you're living there—not just working at a painting, but actually working in that valley. You're there.''[8]

This is possibly what saved the animated cartoon! The whole conception of a scene became different. A new type of business was demanded from the story department, planning that would involve showing a wide range of emotions through the feelings of the characters. Storymen now had to think up situations that would draw an audience into the picture, situations that required acting that derived humor from the characters rather than just gags. And if there was a gag, it would now be a real personality that was participating in it rather than a stock cartoon character. Truly the age of the animator arrived with the first crude evidence of *life* in the single drawing.

The arrival of the latest test film was the high point of the day for animators. Some wag likened it to a maternity hospital when the babies are brought to their mothers. But there was so much discussion before a scene was done and such high interest in what new

The animator was stimulated by the strong attitudes in the drawings of Honoré Daumier.

147

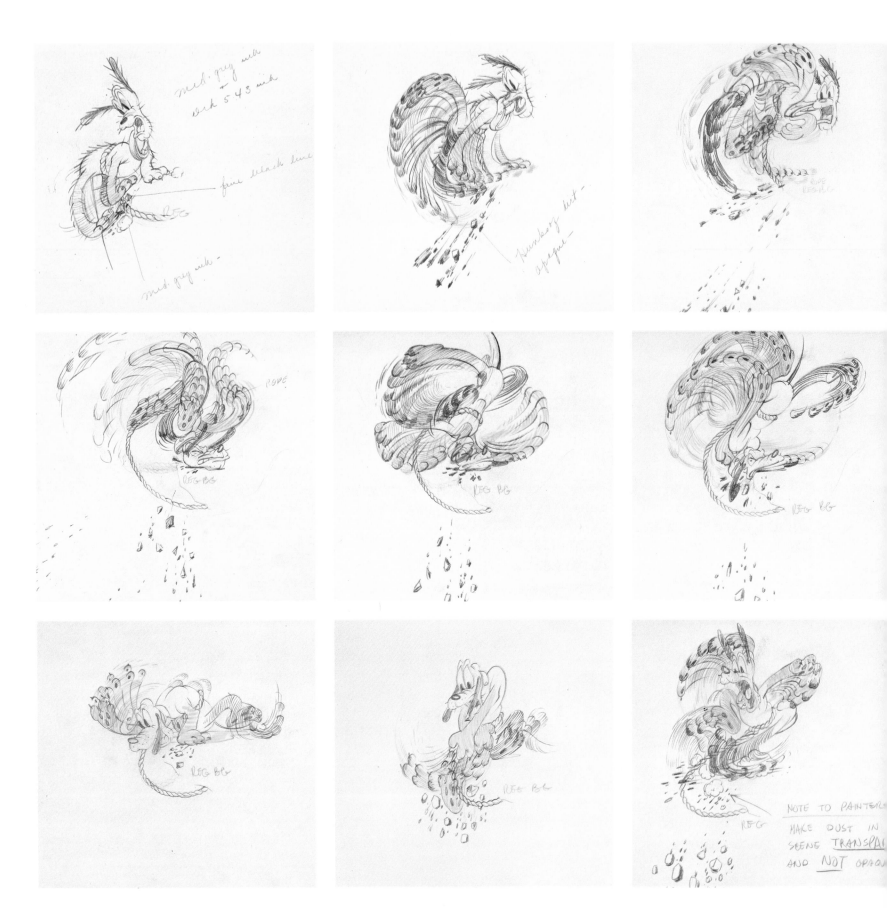

148

ARTIST: *Bill Roberts—*
Alpine Climbers.

Pluto knows he is hanging on a ledge but not how high up. Reaching about with his fanny he fails to locate solid ground, so he takes an apprehensive look. Difficult to stage and animate, yet this was the type of scene Bill Roberts liked to do. His maxim: never lose the personality of the character in either a long shot or a wild action.

149

experiments might be in each other's scenes, that we could hardly wait to see the film of what had been tried. The halls echoed with the clattering of film in the Moviolas and, soon after, the sound of feet running through the halls. "Hey, have you seen Lundy's test? It'll kill ya!"

One day Bob Carlson was trying to complete a scene of his own while this activity was going on outside his door. One room in particular down the hall had attracted quite a crowd, as the film was repeated over and over. A film could be run through the Moviola as many times as you wished without stopping, because it was always fastened together in one continuous loop. Often, if it was a long scene, some of the film would drag on the floor as it made its round trip through the machine.

As Bob listened he could hear the pattern of hushed expectancy, the clatter of the film, the explosion of hilarity, the buzz of voices discussing, congratulating, suggesting—then the hush as the action came around again. Finally Bob's curiosity got the best of him and he had to go down to the room and see what was on the film. The room was packed and it was hard to crowd in where he could get a view of the Moviola screen. Just as he got a clear view between one fellow's ear and another's shirt collar, the film ripped. There was a groan of disappointment, and all eyes angrily followed the limp film down from the Moviola, across the floor, between all the feet, and over to one big shoe that had stepped squarely on the film—Bob's!

Walt liked to have people around him who could make things, build things, create with tools. If he had an idea for a better use of some space in the building, he wanted to be able to call a capable man immediately and ask him, "Can't we do something here to move this out and get a thing here? . . ." Or if he wanted the camera to operate in a different way, "Can't we put something on here that will make this thing go around this way and . . . ?" His respect for the men who had these skills was shown by the fact that while everyone else in the studio was on a first-name basis, the carpenter who was retained full-time was always "Mr. Rogers." The only other man to have this mark of respect was Mr. Keener, who was the paymaster. The other craftsman who could do a little of everything was Jim Verity, but he did not quite merit the addition of "Mr." to his name. Still, he deserved too much respect to be called simply, "Jim," so somehow a compromise was reached whereby his name was run together like one word: "Jimverity."

In the late thirties, specialists in other fields were being added to the staff, mechanics and engineers whose salaries could not be assigned to any specific job. Walt did not know where he was going to use these men—some experts from machine shops, others graduates from Caltech—but he knew he could not pursue his dreams without them. When he wondered, "Can't we find a way to . . . ?" he wanted a man at his elbow who could say, "Well, let me work on it."

Eventually the studio had eighteen highly skilled engineers, headed by Bill Garity,[9] designing, building, creating, experimenting, extending the capabilities of the animated cartoon to reach new heights, new achievements. Walt personally directed their efforts and chose the areas for experimentation, but someone else had to find the category on the production chart where their talents and salaries seemed to fit.

In 1935, most of the country was still wallowing in the Depression, and few companies were hiring, so a job was a very precious thing. Where once Walt had worried that he was getting into the business too late, actually it seemed that the timing was perfect for him, and he was able to pick and choose from the creative talent of that period.

But there were tensions and anxieties for those seeking the jobs, since competition was very keen and only the most outstanding were hired. All manner of hardships were endured to get and keep a job. Some of the uncertainty of the times is reflected in the recollections of Betty Ann Guenther about the apprehension that characterized tryouts in the inking department: "Every Friday was Elimination Day, and we all shook in our boots, for fear we would be let go. Everyone was so scared and worried they could hardly relax enough to do their work."

Ann Lloyd added, "It's a wonder we learned to ink, we were so nervous, and it really takes a loose arm and relaxation to get this technique, and we were nervous wrecks all the time." They needed the jobs desperately, but it was more than that; it was the innocence of that period, young people hoping they would be good enough and that they would be liked.

On Fridays, their ranks were thinned down. There were many tears and hysterics. But those who survived had real dedication and the sense of accomplishment that would go with weathering such an ordeal. The supervisors still ruled them with a firm hand even after they were taken on, being stern and demanding in their criticism and exerting extreme pressure on everyone to do it faster and better.

"I came here right out of high school," says Katherine Kerwin, "and in those days you worked or else. Nobody had cars. . . . it was really difficult." Many of the young people traveled as much as two hours each way by bus and streetcar to get to work, and they often worked till 10:00 at night on *Snow White*. Katherine was asked to work all night on occasions, and she said she was pleased that someone would ask her. "The people were all so young and had so much energy, and what they could give, they gave it." The girls were all eager to learn and went to night classes, too. They loved to go to the theater when the pictures came out and excitedly pick out the scenes they had inked or painted.

"It was always a thrill when Walt came by," Ann Lloyd says. "He didn't come often, but he always came around at Christmas with all these gifts. He felt the girls had been working very hard so he brought a present for each of us." And one Christmas when there was no work he gave the girls a week's vacation instead of laying them off. "Walt was shy and uncomfortable around girls," Katherine adds affectionately, "so they didn't see that much of him, but they loved him, and he appreciated how they helped him."

With so much intensity in the air, and Walt's managing everything, and the staff passing the thousand mark, there were the inevitable inequities and some disgruntled employees. Mainly, the problem came from an individual's feeling left out or passed over. This produced a kind of bitterness and a sullen attitude, but the really explosive reactions came only as the result of an individual's work being cut out of a picture. The art of animating is very, very difficult: first, becoming committed to your way of doing the scene; then, once committed, combining all the elements that give it life—the drawing, acting, staging, timing—while being sure that it all adds up to entertainment for someone besides yourself. This may take days or even weeks of

Walt did not often see his "girls in Ink and Paint" since they were in a separate building, but he greatly appreciated the work they did and valued their opinions.

The "Ink and Paint girls" celebrate the first Christmas in their new building in Burbank.

strenuous effort. And when you finally have it on paper, you have stated, just as clearly as if it were written, your inner feelings about how this thing should be done. Then to have your own personal statement challenged or criticized or cut from the picture—for whatever reason—is a staggering assault on the ego.

At times it was terribly hard to deal with Walt's exacting demands, and often a proud young artist found himself becoming belligerent over some fault found in his work. It was not always criticism either; sometimes it was just the lack of a compliment that hurt the most. The majority of us had become accustomed to having our work criticized, but we had never been in a situation where we *cared* so much. Love and hate are closely allied. You hate only if you are deeply involved in something.

Volatile storyman Bill Peet once became so angry over Walt's criticism that he threw ink all over his wall after the story meeting was over—and left it there in defiance. Walt pretended not to notice for a long time; then, one day, when things were calm, he turned to Bill and said, "What the hell's all that stuff?" and told him to "clean up" his room. Walt understood the intensity of commitment that Bill and the rest of us had for the work, and he never wasted an opportunity to take advantage of this commitment.

In an early screening of *Snow White* someone had written on an unsigned questionnaire the startling reaction, "Stick to Shorts," little knowing at the time that he had touched Walt in a most sensitive spot. That remark would haunt us for the next three decades. It indicated to Walt that there was a rotten apple in the barrel, and since no one knew who it was he seized upon this incident as a permanent device to keep us on the defensive. Through the years, the term "Stick to Shorts" became synonymous with poor judgment. If you were trying to sell an idea that did not jell or go over in a meeting, suddenly there would be this loud, "*Ah haaa!*" and Walt's finger would come shooting out toward you; in a triumphant voice he would explain, "*You* must be the guy who said 'Stick to Shorts!'" And for that day you *were* the guy, and everyone else would keep looking at you and wondering. The best thing you could do was to become as inconspicuous as possible. Some of the men insisted they knew who the real culprit was and thought that Walt knew, too. But if he did, he was too smart to let on, and he never relented in his continuing search.

Walt felt that every idea had been thought of, every gag and even every story—the key was how you used the material to express your own work. So he was never concerned about where an idea came from. One day he stopped a young artist in the hall and complimented him on his drawings of Pinocchio.[10] When the animator started to say that he was just trying to draw like the other fellows did, Walt interrupted to say, "I

Pinocchio

don't give a damn where you get it. Just keep doing it.''

Walt tried to make best use of what talents his employees had. Obviously, not everyone cared. As Milt Schaffer says, ''There were all varieties, some more worldly wise than others, some cynical, some eager beavers.'' The practical-minded adopted the view that it was just a job. Walt was continually searching for incentives to get this group more involved, to get the maximum effort from everyone. He had used the bonus system of balancing salary against footage output as early as 1933, and, in spite of repeated failures, he continued to believe that it held the answer. But the system had an inherent weakness: the largest rewards went to the swiftest rather than to the best. Certain men took a very pragmatic view of this opportunity and spent most of their time looking for shortcuts, often giving their lesser-paid assistants much of the work to do.

This left the burden of responsibility for quality to the conscientious animators who felt that the picture came first. They could not stand by and watch inferior quality make inroads; so they took time from their own work to do whatever was necessary throughout the picture to patch up, repair, or re-animate work that lacked the illusion of life. In the long run, this ruined their own appearance on the ''time charts,'' and with it a chance for any sizable bonus. The bonus system did not produce better pictures—or even good ones. Few regulations do. Efficiency is better built through dedication rather than speed for its own sake.

Surprisingly often, confusion arose from not knowing what was expected of you. It was even hard to find out whom to ask, and this caused uncertainty and created uneasiness about one's position. There were simply too many people after a while to notify about everything. Anxiety over this lack of communication sent many people scrambling around looking for ways to protect themselves—to shore up their jobs. To do this, some began forming walls of people around them, secretaries and assistants or whatever. These ''Empire Builders,'' as Parkinson might have called them, ''wanted to multiply subordinates, not rivals.''[11]

However, if anyone started taking himself too seriously, he was certain to become a target sooner or later. One new employee in management was quite officious and tried to reorganize the workings of the studio overnight with a flood of memos and orders, all

intimating that they were Walt's wishes. He was very busy and very stuffy and very gullible. One day as storymen Ted Sears and Webb Smith got in the elevator they were joined by this bustling young executive. Casually a conversation started as Ted asked, "Hey, Webb, been meaning to ask you—did Walt send you your elevator pass yet?" Webb, kind of mumbling, "My elevator pass—let's see . . ." feeling around in his pockets. "It's here somewhere." Their companion was drinking it all in. They could see he had taken the bait already. Webb continued as he got off the elevator, "Yeah, it came yesterday; maybe the day before."

The indignant executive made a beeline for Walt's secretary, "Where's my elevator pass? How come you didn't send me one?"

What could the secretary say? She did not know what he was talking about. And neither did Walt!

We gradually developed so many separate units of directors and layout personnel on the features and shorts programs and transition sequences and special effects sequences that there was a constant traffic jam on the recording stage, in inkers, in camera, and even in inbetweening. Some way had to be found to schedule and simplify so that the best use could be made of all the facilities. It was in this atmosphere, with so many people around, that the Unit Manager was born.

These men started each day with a meeting in which they presented the work schedule of their individual units and the projected needs in all related departments. Then a little chart was made up saying that Wilfred Jackson's unit could record from 10:00 to 11:00 Tuesday, have two extra layout men for five days on Wednesday, and get top priority in camera for two weeks starting a week from Friday. Jack King's unit would record from 11:00 to 2:00, give up his two layout men on Wednesday, wait to shoot his tests for two weeks—and so it went, until each department was accounted for. As work loads shifted, or a sequence

failed to get approval, or Walt changed his mind, everything was adjusted in the morning meeting.

Supposedly, each unit manager was responsible to his unit director, who told him each day *exactly* what he needed and when he had to have it. But often the unit's representative would return to his home base to report that they could not have any of the things the director wanted. After hearing his job redefined by the irate director, the unit manager would then come down the stairs to vent his pent-up feelings on people who could not fight back. The normal procedure would be to come over to the artist's desk, without a cheery greeting, check the number of the drawing on his board and match it to the exposure sheet with an insinuating mumble: "Hmm-mm, we're still on this part, eh? Didn't get over onto the second page like we thought, did we? Can we count on this scene by 4:00 o'clock this afternoon? We're up next in Ink and Paint, you know."

All in all, the unit managers slowed the work down, yet on paper they looked like the perfect solution to our chaotic cross-purposes. It was interesting to discover that when the studio cut our personnel in half (and this type of job was no longer necessary), we still turned out as much work. Another Parkinson law confirms this point: The fact is that the *number* of officials and the *quantity* of the work are not related to each other at all.

All through the thirties and forties, Walt was bringing in one group of efficiency experts after another in an attempt to find *the* way to run the studio most efficiently. He knew there was a better way than the current one, but he never seemed to realize that his own flow of ideas foredoomed each plan to failure before it had begun. An organizational plan presupposes that all employees will stay in their own spots doing just what they are supposed to do in the way that has been selected for them to do it. This was utterly

ANIMATOR: *Les Clark—* *"Sorcerer's Apprentice,"* Fantasia.

All the elements of a good scene are apparent as Mickey skips about to a musical beat.

154

foreign to Walt's approach to anything and especially in his constant shifting of his men, asking them to do things completely new day after day.

Walt never stopped kidding the staff about their efficiency and how much work they were turning out. Milt Kahl tells the story about Walt bringing a group of visitors into his room and saying, ''All right—show 'em why it takes so long.''

The end of the phenomenal growth of animation can be linked to the constant attempt to establish some kind of order for the production of the pictures. This brought about a perplexing chain of command for the animator, with Walt at the top. Though his ideas were supposed to seep down to us through the Production Supervisor, the Supervising Director, and finally the Sequence Director, they never quite did, and it was impossible for any of us to know what Walt really had in mind without seeing and hearing his ideas firsthand.

''I didn't want Walt doing anything about the rest of the studio,'' Dave Hand, then Production Supervisor, said, ''because he was so very valuable in the idea department.'' It was the thinking of the time that the sole job of the director was to deliver the idea of the scene to the animator and that Walt was to be shielded from all possible distractions.

When we questioned a piece of business in the sequence, the director said it was the way *they* had handed it to him, and we were not supposed to worry about it. *They* knew how it all worked, and this is the way *they* wanted it. To this day, we still are not sure who *they* were—all we know is that we were not among them. Isolating us in this manner was a crippling decision, most of all because very few people could interpret Walt for anyone else. So the handouts were carried out on a kind of assembly line basis: one animator would pick up three or four scenes that were ready, and then when the next man ran out of work he would pick up the next three scenes. We became interchange-

able—even though we were all very different.

For the animators who were more concerned with drawing or technique or visual effects, this worked out well enough since they had little interest in story or character delineation, figuring that was the job of someone else. But for many of us, this stopped the further development of character animation. With this piece-meal casting, there was no way to sustain a character or even to know the precise way he should perform.

We wondered how Walt would interpret our scene. How would he see it? Would he go for the pathos or the humor here? But there was no way to find out even why the scene was in the picture. The grand idea that was supposed to simplify procedures and make it easier for each person to do his own job with a minimum of distraction had developed into a restrictive separation of the talents. We were fast losing the stimulation that had come from the team effort.

In contrast, other phases of the business continued to flourish and grow in importance. The emphasis was now on the new elements: effects, mood, music, story, style; and, even though Walt demanded as much from his animators, animation was no longer considered a frontier. As Bill Tytla said, we could make a commonplace scene interesting; we had proved we were professionals.

Few were aware of the potential for better entertainment that was being lost or the way in which these decisions were ending the progress of the art of animation. Ken Peterson,[12] who did see the danger, said, ''The tragedy was that animation was not really recognized for what it was—the *heart* of the business.'' The shift had come just as we were beginning to realize how much could be done with this means of expression, this art form that was so fulfilling and rewarding.

Excellent animation was still being done and some discoveries were still being made, but they tended to be in the areas of refinement rather than in bold uses of

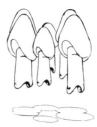

ANIMATOR: *Art Babbitt— Mushroom Dance. "Nut- cracker Suite,"* Fantasia.

One of our most charming moments on the screen lasted barely a minute and a half.

the medium. There was little inclination to experiment. We thought of safe ways to do the scenes rather than exciting ones.

This had not come about through any conscious effort to downgrade the animator or to limit his influence. To Peterson, the explanation was simple: "Two factors tended to bring about the isolation of the animator. One was the complexity of the animation production which led to a business of specialists [in creating new visual images on the screen], and the other was that the studio was expanding so fast."

By 1939 this expansion had forced some units to work miles away in buildings that could be leased in Hollywood. The whole *Bambi* unit was in a complex that once had housed another cartoon studio; one group worked in office space above the Ontra Cafeteria near Hollywood and Vine. At a time when we needed the stimulation of our friends, we were farther apart.

The moving of these units to other quarters did nothing to relieve the congestion in the main building where all of us were squashed together worse than ever. And having so many separate units working so far apart stretched the production procedures to the snapping point. The principle of squash and stretch that had built the studio was beginning to have a new meaning.

But soon we would leave the jumble of buildings on Hyperion Avenue, so full of memories, successes, failures, discoveries. We were sentimentally attached to those structures that contained so much magic, the rooms that had seen so many ideas develop, the buildings where so many of us took our first eager steps. Still, we were anxious to be rid of the annoyances and excited about all being back together again under one roof. In 1939 the move began to the glorious new studio out in Burbank. There, the explosion that had begun on Hyperion would be contained.

As the number of employees increased, Walt had less time for the personal contact that had been so important to the guidance and stimulation of his creative personnel. His time was concentrated on new ideas, the next picture, needed innovations, and planning for the future. The art classroom had been converted to a larger, fancier projection room known as Sweatbox 4, and Walt spent many hours there, leaving the routine work on the pictures to his supervisors and directors in both story and productions.

Instead of having the stimulating sessions with Walt in either story meetings or sweatboxes, the animators were now getting everything secondhand, if at all.

Frank Thomas and Milt Kahl started to improvise a lament which began, "Oh, Miltie-pie," (the friendly byname bestowed on Milt years earlier because of his explosive personality). "If I should die, please bury me in Sweatbox 4. Although I'm dead, I'll hear what's said, lying there beneath the floor."

Before the specific annoyances could be incorporated into verse and melody, everyone moved to the new studio in Burbank. Here, the elite meetings were not held in the sweatboxes, but in one of two identical projection rooms called 3C-11 and 3C-12,[13] with the second being the more important because it was right next to Walt's office. Now there was more than a closed door separating the animators from the knowledge of what Walt was expecting. There were two floors of magnificent building between them. Quickly the song recorded their problems.

> Oh, Miltie-pie, if I should die,
> Please bury me in 3C-12.
>
> Then I'll know why, but never cry,
> About the pictures that they shelve.
>
> I'll gaze upon, what's going on,
> And get it straight from Walt—
>
> And then I'll see who's blaming me,
> When it is not my fault!
>
> I'll get firsthand, the things they've planned
> That animators never know.
>
> See color shots, hear story plots,
> Gee, I can hardly wait to go.
>
> Yes, I like Forest Lawn, but when I'm gone,
> You know where I'd rather be. . . .
>
> I don't mean heaven, or 3C-11,
> It's 3C-12 for me.

The well-known phrase of resignation, "You can't win!" was just coming into popularity. One effects animator shook his head and added a second thought, "It's not only that you can't win—you can't even get out of the game."[14]

Sleeping Beauty

8. Burbank and The Nine Old Men

"You know, the only way I've found to make these pictures is with animators—you can't seem to do it with accountants and bookkeepers."　Walt Disney

The isolation of the animator did not end with the move to Burbank, but it was the turning point. Except for one final picture, *Sleeping Beauty*, where color stylist Eyvind Earle had a last magnificent fling, there were no special new breakthroughs by any of the supporting functions. The war and economic factors had forced a cutback, and the day of the specialist was over. With a smaller staff, team effort was stressed to an even greater degree, and Walt began to rely more and more on animation to carry the films. The first evidence of the animators' breaking out of their isolation was the creation of the Animation Board, which had been established as early as 1940 to help with the management of the animation department. Its members advised on hiring, firing, assignments, moves, promotions, and training; but, bit by bit, they were also determining what an animator should be and how he should be used most effectively. The personnel of this board changed according to the problems being considered, but by 1950 the board had settled down to a permanent group of nine supervising animators.

These key creators had an importance beyond their duties on the board and influenced the way pictures developed and the type of entertainment that was done. Although the supervising animators were still in their thirties, Walt joked about their responsibilities and

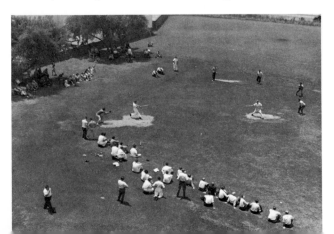

The new Disney Studio at Burbank, with spacious grounds attractively landscaped, resembles a college campus of the thirties—a concept of a pleasant place to work no other studio had.[1]

159

their wisdom and affectionately referred to them as his "Nine Old Men," after the nine justices of the Supreme Court. The board consisted of Les Clark, Woolie Reitherman, Eric Larson, Ward Kimball, Milt Kahl, John Lounsbery, Marc Davis,[2] and, the authors of this book, Frank Thomas and Ollie Johnston. We never thought of ourselves as some elite group, and the only time it even crossed our minds was when Walt made a kidding remark about his Nine Old Men being over the hill, or getting too decrepit to work, or losing all their old zip.

In later years, after Walt died, the press picked up this group's colorful title and used it as a glamorous way of linking these animators to him. The studio publicists kept it alive as symbolic of the old guard that had survived from the early days of animation, but their only requests of us were to pose for pictures—and that happened only twice in twenty years.[3]

Under this leadership, a new and very significant method of casting the animators evolved: an animator was to animate all the characters in his scene. In the first features, a different animator had handled each character. Under that system, even with everyone cooperating, the possibilities of getting maximum entertainment out of a scene were remote at best. The first man to animate on the scene usually had the lead character, and the second animator often had to animate to something he could not feel or quite understand. Of necessity, the director was the arbitrator, but certain of his decisions and compromises were sure to make the job more difficult for at least one of the animators.

The new casting overcame many problems and, more important, produced a major advancement in cartoon entertainment: the *character relationship*. With one man now animating every character in his scene, he could feel all the vibrations and subtle nuances between his characters. No longer restricted by what someone else did, he was free to try out his own ideas of how his characters felt about each other. Animators became more observant of human behavior and built on relationships they saw around them every day.

The Supervising Animator was given the flexibility of making changes and improvements after the scene was on his board. Changes that come after the animator has had a chance to live with his scene are often the ones that make characters really come to life. With

(Continued on page 164)

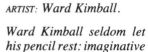

Ward Kimball seldom let his pencil rest: imaginative doodles done during an Animation Board meeting, circa 1957.

The second, and final, photo of the Nine Old Men. Front row, Woolie Reitherman, Les Clark, Ward Kimball, and John Lounsbery. Rear, Milt Kahl, Marc Davis, Frank Thomas, Eric Larson, and Ollie Johnston.

Key personnel occasionally had to become actors in studio films. Milt Kahl, Marc Davis, Frank Thomas, Walt, and Wilfred Jackson study Ollie Johnston's drawing during the making of a TV show promoting Sleeping Beauty.

ARTIST: *Marc Davis*— Bambi.

Story sketches by Marc Davis were an inspiration to the animator. Marc had great knowledge of animals and how they moved, as well as an unusual feel for entertaining business.

ANIMATOR: Frank Thomas—
Bambi.

Three years earlier this scene might well have been divided between two different animators. Under that old casting method, it is doubtful this type of action could have been brought off at all.

much of the sequence under his control, the Supervising Animator can plan a more effective way of using the animation to put over the story points, by changing footages, shifting scenes, calling for long shots, close ups, expressions, actions—anything that makes a stronger statement and richer characterization.

One of the first examples of this was the sequence of Bambi and Thumper on ice. The concept of an animator taking an idea like this and developing it into a sequence really sprang from the "milking" of a situation in the earlier shorts to get everything out of it. Norm Ferguson's Pluto and the flypaper and Pluto on ice were two of the earliest and most outstanding pieces of entertainment built by an animator. Fred Spencer was successful with this type of improvisation on Donald in *Moving Day*. But the Bambi and Thumper sequence had something that the Pluto and Donald sections did not have. That was a character relationship with strong beginnings in the story department, where it was worked out by a man who had a feeling for animation.[4] With this as a springboard, the animator continued developing this relationship, which only could have been done by one person handling both characters and completely controlling every single bit of action, timing, and cutting. Just how much we were really aware of the value of this type of casting then is hard to say.

Several years later, for whatever reasons, the mold was further broken on the three Uncle Remus sections of *Song of the South*, where all the supervising animators handled footage in large blocks. Bill Peet's great story work seemed to lend itself to this type of casting. He had developed entertaining situations with

strong character delineation, and the design of the characters inspired the animators to get a very loose handling in their work. But more important, Bill's business called for much personal contact between the bear, the fox, and the rabbit. Also, his relationships demanded split-second reactions between characters that would have been impossible to handle in co-animation.

This new way of working with character relationships encompassed the whole range of relations between two or more characters—from the broadest to the most delicate. It involved expression scenes that often registered the most secret thoughts and inner emotions of the characters, which as they became more subtle were also more revealing. With money in shorter supply, we cut out the frills and put our energies to work in a new direction, doing the most with what we had, making up for what had been lost in one area by concentrating on outstanding characters in entertaining situations. It was a new dimension in animation and the key breakthrough in reaching the audience.

Just as the concept of "life in a single drawing" had not been recognized as a dominant factor in animation that seemed to live, character relationship was not understood as a major contribution for many years. *The Grasshopper and the Ants* had brief moments of exciting relationships, and this could explain why it was so successful. The seven dwarfs had strong relationships, but these existed more because of story than animation. The animators at that point could not have developed this by themselves.

The Nine Old Men eventually were able to do it because they incorporated all of their own experiences (along with what they had learned from the top animators) into this new way of working—not just good animation, not just good drawings that moved in a

ANIMATOR: *Milt Kahl—*The Jungle Book

pleasing way, not just drawings that were funny, but drawings that *moved* the audience. As animation historian John Culhane said, ''Moving drawings became . . . *Moving* drawings!''[5]

Culhane says the Nine Old Men continued to attack the problems and meet the mounting challenges in animation—that Ichabod, with fear on his face, took the art a step up,[6] that ''Lounsbery's wolf in *The Sword in the Stone*, with its broad, comic, but terribly real frustration, and Milt's Shere Khan, a devastating caricature of the late George Sanders as a super stuffed-shirt tiger, were examples of acting by cartoon animals in the 60's that are considerably advanced from the cartoon animals in animation's so-called Golden Age in the 30's and 40's.''[7]

Obviously, animation was communicating with the audience better than it had before. More than acting, more than story, more than character by itself, something had happened that was allowing the animators to express themselves more fully, and the viewers noticed.

As Walt's interest turned to other things, the creative

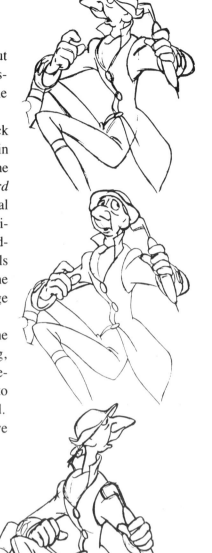

ANIMATOR: *John Lounsbery* —The Sword in the Stone.

ANIMATOR: *Frank Thomas*— Adventures of Ichabod and Mr. Toad

strength of the pictures shifted in favor of the animators. He had seen what they could do with material he might not have okayed in earlier years—they made it entertaining just through their skillful handling. Because of these skills, personality animation began to dominate the story material. However, we still needed strong stories, and these could not have been created without men such as Ken Anderson, Bill Peet, Erdman Penner and Don DaGradi who gave such a balance of talent and input of ideas with their different perspectives. Pictures were planned more with purely entertainment sequences—rich in personality and character—and these, in turn, helped the animator continually to develop his acting skills to higher levels.

John Culhane said that character relationships had gotten better and better. "In *Robin Hood*, there were so many vibrations passing back and forth between Prince John, the vain and mangy lion, and his gap-toothed snake sycophant, Sir Hiss, that it amounted to animated Sensaround."[8] And Culhane added this in a personal letter to the animator of these scenes:

I really did feel hypnotized in my theatre seat. In fact I felt the way that that long-ago radio producer must have felt who auditioned Edgar Bergen and Charlie McCarthy, and was disgusted with Bergen for stumbling over his lines until McCarthy snapped: 'Here, let me have a look at that' . . . and the producer thrust the script into the dummy's inanimate hands.

All of the Nine Old Men either had learned their art directly from the top animators of the thirties or been strongly influenced by their work. Les Clark had started

ARTIST: *Ward Kimball.*

Ward takes a friendly jibe at his aging fellow animators, Frank and Ollie.

with Ub Iwerks back in 1927, and he studied continuously from then on. Eric Larson, Ward Kimball, and Milt Kahl had all learned under Ham Luske; Frank Thomas and Ollie Johnston had been with Fred Moore, but they were strongly influenced by Ham and Bill Tytla. Johnny Lounsbery trained under Norm Ferguson, Marc Davis under Grim Natwick, but both of them studied the work of all of the top men. Woolie Reitherman was probably influenced more by Fergy than anyone else.

While no two of us were alike, we still had many traits in common. Foremost among these was the desire to put the finest possible entertainment on the screen. There were many arguments and disagreements among all of us on every conceivable issue. Still, no matter how exasperated we were with someone, it never entered our minds to question his motives. We knew that he wanted the picture to be just as good as we did.

For over twenty-five years this remarkable team worked together, dedicated to Walt and the medium and its constant improvement. Then Marc Davis was moved over to WED, our sister organization, to put his special abilities to work on the rides and shows for Disneyland, Woolie Reitherman began directing in 1961, Eric Larson eventually took over the all-important training program (to insure that new talent would reach its potential quickly), and in the mid-seventies both Ward Kimball and Les Clark retired.

In 1975, author John Canemaker paid tribute to the remaining four animators of the original nine. "Thomas, Kahl, Johnston and Lounsbery are a tiny but dazzling repertory company of 'actors with a pencil!'[9] With each new film, they change roles, but still retain their

ANIMATOR: *Ollie Johnston—* Robin Hood.

Subtle relationship between Prince John and Sir Hiss was achieved by one animator controlling the acting of both characters.

individual specialties, their star qualities, if you will.''

Johnny Lounsbery died suddenly in 1976; Milt retired in 1977; and, in January of 1978, we, Frank and Ollie, left the studio to write this book. A new era was beginning just as the one that had spanned nearly forty-five years of animation came to an end. Here is a closer look at these men in the order of their arrival at the Disney Studios.

Les Clark

When Walt hired Les Clark in 1927, he said, ''Well, you know this is only a temporary job, Les. I don't know what's going to happen.'' But as Les said, ''So it lasted forty-eight years!''

Les just kept going—and kept up! As Walt asked for the better drawing and greater refinements that left so many others behind, Les was able to adapt and continue in the front ranks of the animators, year after year. His drawings had appeal, were always gentle and warm and likeable, and his timing was always sensitive. He quietly went ahead perfecting what he did best, constantly at art class working hard to improve and to learn. There was much admiration for this quiet, thoughtful man, who came in with no art background yet through sheer determination and desire not only kept up but helped advance the art with his refinements of many fundamentals.

Walt was pleased with Les's Mickey in *Fantasia*'s ''Sorcerer's Apprentice'' and especially liked his delicate handling of the Sugar Plum Fairies in the ''Nutcracker Suite.'' However, the latter were not personalities but more like birds. Les said he had thought of hummingbirds, and this gave them a charm in timing as well as movement.

Les was a Sequence Director on *Sleeping Beauty*. From there Walt moved him into direction on TV specials and educational films. Just as he did in his animation, ''Les never settled for anything that wasn't top quality—his work always had that fine finish.''[10] One of his pictures, *The Restless Sea*, was a winner of many awards. He continued directing up until his retirement in 1976. He died on September 11, 1979.

Les Clark

Les Clark had a special feeling for the feminine quality in Minnie Mouse.

Woolie Reitherman

Woolie is the most physical of the group—with a compulsion to stay young and to squeeze in everything before it is too late.

Ken Peterson, who was Woolie's assistant on the dinosaurs in *Fantasia*, says, "You know how Woolie is. . . . He's gonna lick this if it's the last thing he ever does. The way Woolie is, he'll fight for entertainment—the drawing problems he had on his stuff—but he finally got it. Some of those papers, you know, when you'd go to clean them up, there was practically nothing left of them. They were all crumpled like old dollar bills—wrinkled and brown with different colored pencils. Nothing was ever finished; as long as he could flip it, there were going to be changes made." Woolie says, "My work had vitality and an 'I don't give a damn—try it!' quality." [11]

The Goofy that Woolie animated communicated with the audience in a way that only Woolie could have done it—this was a new type of animation. His timing, staging, texture, pacing, desire to do something different, good gag sense, knowledge of whether it was entertaining (and the ability to think of something else if it was not), all carried over into his directing.

Every story point, every scene, every line of dialogue had to be thrashed over a hundred times in the search for the essence of the material. Woolie would stubbornly argue his point; then, often to encourage a new way of looking at something or to probe deeper, he would switch to a new position hoping to bring out some fresh arguments. Always the search was for entertainment and audience communication.

Like Walt, he never seemed to run out of energy

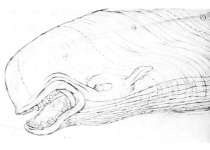

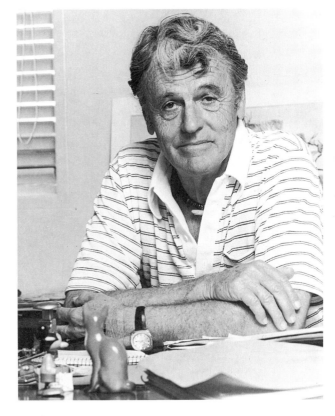

ARTIST: Woolie Reitherman —Pinocchio.

Woolie's animation captured the raw power of Monstro the whale.

Woolie Reitherman.

and would still be going strong at five o'clock while the rest of us sat in exhausted admiration. He was the only director ever to handle a feature alone and perhaps was the only one with the strength and stamina to keep track of all the people and what they were doing and be able to pull all the pieces together in the last hectic months.

His energy was boundless. As one animator said, "He doesn't even get jet lag."

Eric Larson

Eric's Figaro is one of the finest examples of pure pantomime ever done at the studio. The acting, texture in timing, and inner feeling for the character were remarkable things to achieve without benefit of dialogue. His flying horses in *Fantasia* were graceful in movement and convincing in action. He supervised the animation on the very difficult stag in *Bambi* and ani-

mated most of the likable old owl.

Because of his ability to handle every type of thing that could fly, Eric became known as a bird-man. He did everything from sincere birds who helped Cinderella make her bed to the craziest of them all, the Aracuan bird. In the Aracuan, Eric displayed a remarkable feeling for an imaginative character not based on an anthro-

169

pomorphic concept. And one might add that there was never anything in Eric's very dignified outward behavior to indicate that this strange incongruity could take place.

His quiet, mature judgment was respected even when he was young. Whenever a special committee was being selected, it was always Eric and somebody else. And when a serious conflict or disagreement arose in any large meeting, it was Eric who seemed to be able to soothe everyone with his "pour-oil-on-troubled-water speech," as Ward Kimball called it.

It was sometimes difficult to see how Eric ever got any work done. He had the largest crews of any of the top men, and there was always someone in his room with a problem, often nothing to do with production. Eric was always patiently listening, occasionally counseling, but somehow, in spite of all this, he was one of the best footage men in the studio. When and how he did it no one ever figured out. And to top it all, he was able to get footage out of most of his crew. At this writing, Eric is still in charge of the training program for the new talent coming into animation. Age has not diminished his empathy with young people.

Eric Larson

Ward Kimball

Not all nine of the supervising animators were interested in personality animation and character relationships. To Ward Kimball fell the mantle of true iconoclast of the group. He had tried and done successful personality animation on Jiminy Cricket, but soon found this style too limiting for his particular talents. He felt the proper use of animation for him lay further away from live action.

His conception and execution of the long song sequence in *The Three Caballeros* is a classic in the unrestricted use of the medium. The song was four minutes long with little or no business, and, after listening to it for a week, Ward says, "I decided to be optically literal. What you hear is what you see. When they say they have serapes—the serapes appear. And when the characters went out on the right—they'd come in on the left; they'd go out on the left, and they'd come in from the top. It was optically abstract."

Ward Kimball

170

TOOK   FOOK   SHOOK   NOOK   LOOK   SMOOK

Ward Kimball had the unique ability to make a funny drawing—not just the subject matter or the caricature but the actual drawing itself. While working on Peter Pan, he drew each of us as a Capt. Hook. From the left, Frank Thomas, Ward, Milt Kahl, Marc Davis, Clark Mallery, and Ollie Johnston.

Ward's approach to this was a new type of entertainment really too unique to pass on.

He was an excellent draftsman, with the rare ability to make funny drawings equally as well as serious ones. He had a better design sense than most and thought of imaginative ways of doing things. He never did what was expected, and to the consternation of at least one director never did the assignment the way it was handed out. His staging was tops, his timing unique, and he could show what was funny about a situation. He had a knack for picking out the special, little-noticed traits in almost everyone around him, and from then on that person would have a label on him. He was an excellent mime and could either act out these traits or incorporate them into one of his sharp caricatures.

Typical of Ward, he was also creative in his approach to teaching life drawing. He used the innovative idea of the "model in movement" to make his class more aware of the principles of animation, which encouraged the young students to think in terms of rhythm and action in their drawings.

Milt Kahl

Milt's great strength lay in his drawing ability and his conviction that animation drawings were really two-dimensional and should work in that plane—clear, simple, easy to read and understand. As one of four animators to work on the character of Pinocchio, he was given the assignment of animating Pinocchio as a real boy because of his careful drawing.

Milt's control enabled him to do the most subtle moves, leading to repeated casting on human characters. His Sir Ector and Kay in *The Sword in the Stone* were the best human figures ever done at the studio, and they were done without benefit of live action or the support of reference material. Though Milt actually preferred broad characters, he took great pride in doing assignments that were tough to draw. His unique sense of character design dominated the features for over thirty years, but it was so personal that it was often difficult for others to follow. He would deny this, saying, "Anyone who can draw, can follow it." What he really meant was, "Anyone who can draw like me can do this. . . ." He had remarkable powers to visualize, and as someone said, "Once he gets clear in his mind what he's going to do, it's as good as on the paper."

171

The Sword in the Stone

He was honest to the point of bluntness. Unlike many irascible temperaments who have filled the halls of history, Milt had a very sweet helpful side, when he chose. He gave unstintingly of his time and talent when it was to help the picture and almost as often to help a fellow artist who had a problem. However, he expected anyone coming for help to have worked hard and tried everything—to have done his best before coming.

Milt's farewell animation was his brilliantly done Medusa in *The Rescuers*. This time Milt had a character all to himself, and his rewards were great, as shown by this tribute: "The younger generation studies the scene in which Mme. Medusa takes off her makeup while plotting child abuse. The way that Milt Kahl accents Geraldine Page's fruity, cruel voice by making her tug extra hard at her false eyelash until her eyelid snaps back like a rubber band is like a drawing from Daumier's 'Sketches of Expression' series . . . but in movement!"[12]

JIMINY CRICKET

ANIMATOR: *Milt Kahl*— Pinocchio.

Jiminy Cricket is late for his first day on the job as Pinocchio's conscience and has to dress while running.
STARTS ON PAGE 253

Milt Kahl

Frank Thomas

Writing in *Millimeter* magazine, John Canemaker paid this tribute to Frank: "He has been 'sincerely' affecting audiences for forty years; he has made them laugh and cry, hate and fear, using basically a pencil he has charged with intelligence and humanity, tons of paper, and the 'persistence of vision'."[13]

No job was too painstaking, no research too time-consuming to lay the groundwork for a Thomas sequence. Each possibility had to be explored endlessly to find every last ounce of entertainment. His powers of observation and his acute memory for things he had seen and studied over the years gave him a vast reservoir of experience as he prepared his scenes for animation.

His analysis went past Ham Luske's rules. Through these powers he was able to portray complicated actions, attitudes, and acting. His great feel for character, acting, and entertainment can be seen in the many memorable sequences he "acted" in. The most famous but not necessarily the most difficult scene, the dwarfs crying around Snow White's bier, is said to have

Frank Thomas

173

extended the emotional range of our cartoons.

To have worked under Frank was to have been subjected to the most rigorous training imaginable. As one young animator said, "It is impossible to please that guy. He's never satisfied." The solution was not to try to master Frank's extremely complex acting patterns, but to study his approach to entertainment and his use of the fundamentals of animation. Frank's staging and his use of squash and stretch and the strong changes in body shape that gave so much life to his work were tangible things that have helped many young animators.

Walt cast him with Milt Kahl repeatedly because of Frank's knowledge of what the character should do and Milt's ability to draw it.

Like the rest of the fellows, Frank gave time to help others. His advice was sought on music, layout, background, and story as well as the animation. On the last few features, Frank would spend anywhere from six months to a year helping develop the story structure and situations, sharpening up and defining the characters and their dialogue—and then he would animate on those same sequences with a fresh eye.

Frank is a modest man, "frank" in his honesty, penetrating in his criticism, but always tempering it with humor.

Ollie Johnston

Like most of the group, Ollie was at his best when leading off on a character, particularly if the story and the characters were at a stage where they were still flexible. He was often the first to perceive that a character or a story point was not developing the right way

Ollie Johnston

and would work tirelessly to correct it. He had a vision of what it ought to be and was dedicated to seeing it come out that way. Through early experimental animation, he was able to show the potential for entertainment in the characters that would then be developed in future story situations. In doing this type of development he combined the appeal he had learned from Fred Moore with the sensitivity he had for the emotions of how the characters felt.

Colleagues agreed that Ollie carried acting and the feeling of the characters to the highest point. He had a sensitivity for good picture, imaginative layout, what the character should be doing, and how to arrange the scenes for the best effect. His knowledge of what was needed in a voice made him valuable in dealing with difficult decisions of whether the vocal talent was giving the animator the performance he must have to make the character think and act.

In an interview Ollie said, "I talk a lot about any scene I'm gonna animate and get the best ideas I can; and when I'm convinced I have the best way, then I put everything I have into executing it. But just because I have a good plan doesn't make it easy. Animation is inherently open to mistakes, and I could know exactly what I want to do and still have trouble. And I'd say to myself, 'Whatever made me think this scene would be easy?' or, 'I thought I promised myself last week I'd never make that same damn mistake again.'"

In spite of the usual problems, his footage output was always the highest on the picture, and the fact that he never looked upon animation as being easy helped him to emphathize with the young animators and assistants working with him. He knew that their problems required guidance and patience, and this he willingly provided.

His drawings of Mr. Smee from *Peter Pan* turned out to be a near self-portrait. Of course, this is not uncommon when the animator is really feeling the expressions. A young art student visiting during the production of *The Rescuers* glanced at the cat on Ollie's board—then at Ollie—and said, ''You look just like Rufus. Why you even wear glasses just like he does!''

The Jungle Book

Johnny Lounsbery

As is often the case, the pupil surpassed the master. Norm Ferguson had instructed well but Johnny had gone beyond what the legendary master had been able to do. His better drawing and bigger concept, not limited by old vaudeville acts, brought the bold, crude approach to new heights, using more refinement, more dramatic angles, more interest, and all without losing the main idea. His simple staging, appealing characters, good taste, strong squash and stretch, and controlled anticipations and follow through made a big bold statement, but they never lost believability. Hardly subtle, his characters were always fun to watch.

He was good at working with the young animators and did pose drawings that were an inspiring springboard to get anyone started. As a draftsman he was ideal for animation. His drawings were simple and loose and full of energy. They had volume and that elusive quality of life. He had some of Ham's ability always to find the way to go further in strengthening his poses.

Johnny's favorite of the characters he animated was Ben Ali, the alligator in "Dance of the Hours" from *Fantasia*, where he captured a cocky, spirited walk and attitude—one that was particularly unusual since it all had to fit the tempo and the accents of the prescored track. This work was a great influence on the other animators doing this section, many of them animating for the first time. He had an especially good way of working to live action, being able to adopt

John Lounsbery

some of its subtleties without losing the strength of broad cartoon action.

Johnny tended to be an introvert, but asserted himself on key decisions. He had his own special way of looking at things, and no matter how bad they were he always had some funny observation to lighten the situation. At the time of his death, Johnny was directing sequences on *The Rescuers*.

Marc Davis

Marc Davis is an example of a talent being shifted to where it is most needed. This happened to many of the men since no one had been trained for the jobs that were being developed at Disney's. Several men actually created their jobs by doing something particularly well—and that is how we got the great results.

From careful cleanup on the delicate drawings of *Snow White*, Marc moved to story sketch and character design on *Bambi* because of his ability to draw animals. After doing outstanding work in these areas

he was given his first chance at animation on the characters of Flower and his girl friend. After *Bambi*, the very versatile Marc returned to the story department, where he designed the Eagle and Octopus section of *Victory Through Air Power* for Bill Tytla to animate. Due to some careless oversight, he never received story credit on either *Bambi* or *Victory Through Air Power*.

In an interview, Marc expressed this philosophy: "To be an animator, you have to have a sense of the

dramatic, a feeling for acting; you have to be a story-teller."[14] In his own work Marc also added these qualities: more appealing attitudes, better drawing, and the convincing movement that came with this drawing ability. He saw a unified relationship of all parts of a character and on the flamboyant Cruella deVil made use of everything from her bony elbows to her posturing through her erratic movements.

On Marc's Maleficent, he showed a flair for the dramatic based more on powerful shapes in his design and strong use of color than on broad action. He had a feeling for the importance of a good layout and never overlooked the value of props such as the raven and the staff and made sure they were part of the overall picture.

Marc is a very gentle person, but with strong convictions that he holds to tenaciously.[15] He has a special sense of humor that usually has some unexpected twist to it. He is a very successful teacher, specializing in drawing for animation. His main courses were given in night school at Chouinard's, and many of his students later followed him to Disney's.

Marc Davis

Sleeping Beauty

Refining Techniques

Under the leadership of the Nine Old Men, the original animation principles were refined, perfected, and extended. By 1960, the characters' actions had become so sophisticated it was almost impossible to isolate the elements making them work. Squash and stretch, follow through, secondary actions, all were so subtle and interrelated that only the entertainment in the scene was obvious.

ANIMATOR: *Frank Thomas*—Bambi.

Overlapping action became more than just a way to avoid stiff action when Thumper tried to teach the young Bambi to say "Bir-d!"

ANIMATOR: *Milt Kahl*—Pinocchio.

Pinocchio is near panic as he begins to turn into a donkey. A lesser animator might have made the reactions so violent and active that the drama of the scene actually would have been lost. Do not confuse action with acting.

1   5   9   10   13   16   18   2

ANIMATOR: *Eric Larson*—Bambi.

In this quiet scene, the old owl advises some young birds visiting the new baby deer that it is time to go. The situation required a restrained move, but one with clear definition. Do not confuse subtlety with vagueness.

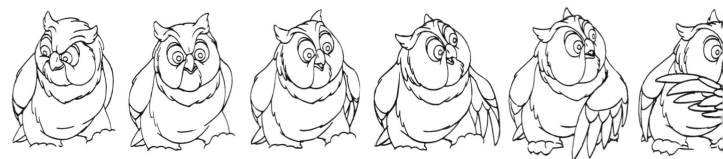

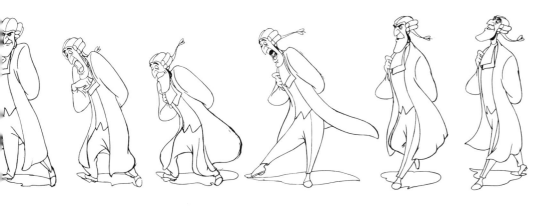

ANIMATOR: *Ollie Johnston*—
Adventures of Mr. Toad.

Some animators have claimed, "Each drawing isn't important, it's the movement." However, for clear staging and clarity of action, every drawing in the scene must show the attitude and the acting. This scene had good texture in the timing, contrasting the measured, precise steps at the start with the unexpected whirl and accusing point at the end.

27   28   40A   40F   40H   40K   42   43   44

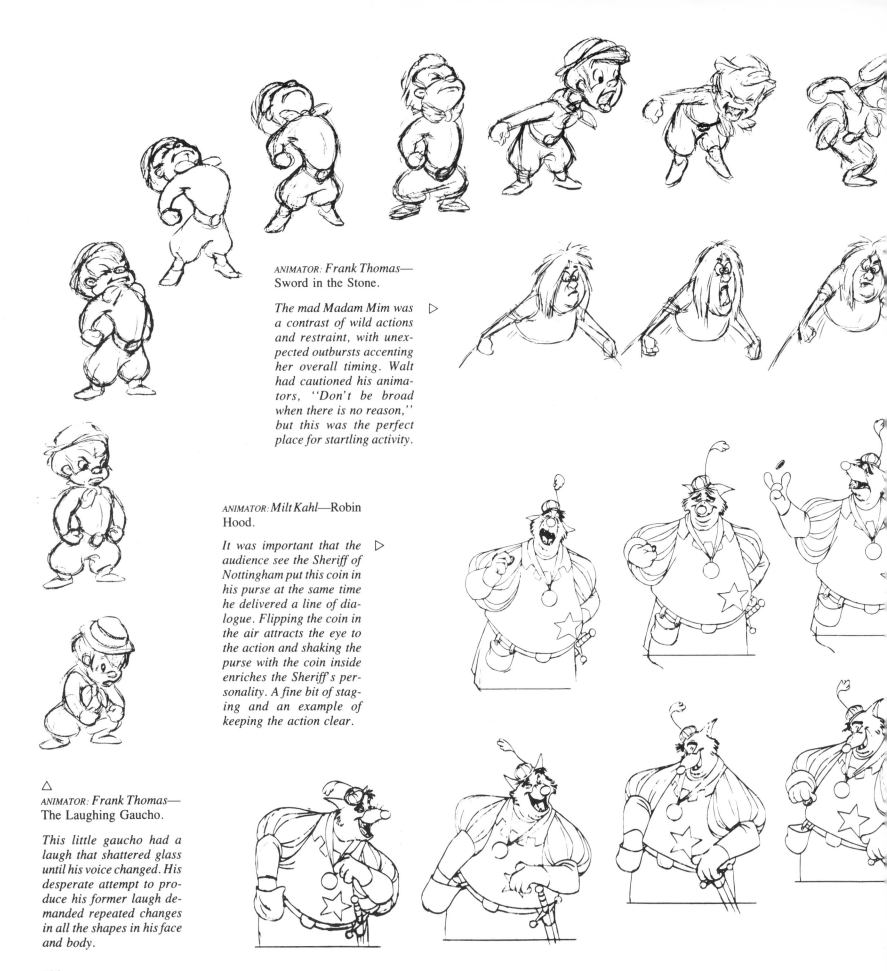

ANIMATOR: *Frank Thomas*—Sword in the Stone.

The mad Madam Mim was a contrast of wild actions and restraint, with unexpected outbursts accenting her overall timing. Walt had cautioned his animators, "Don't be broad when there is no reason," but this was the perfect place for startling activity. ▷

ANIMATOR: *Milt Kahl*—Robin Hood.

It was important that the audience see the Sheriff of Nottingham put this coin in his purse at the same time he delivered a line of dialogue. Flipping the coin in the air attracts the eye to the action and shaking the purse with the coin inside enriches the Sheriff's personality. A fine bit of staging and an example of keeping the action clear. ▷

△
ANIMATOR: *Frank Thomas*—The Laughing Gaucho.

This little gaucho had a laugh that shattered glass until his voice changed. His desperate attempt to produce his former laugh demanded repeated changes in all the shapes in his face and body.

181

ARTIST: Glen Keane.

Forty years later the principles of communicating through drawings is carried on by new animators. These story sketches for The Fox and the Hound *have strength and dramatic impact in the design. Placing the bear high on the screen makes him look big and powerful.*

ANIMATOR: Glen Keane— The Fox and the Hound.

Glen carried this feeling over into his animation, retaining the great scale while adding the excitement that comes from movement.

We had been taught always to look for things live-action people wish they could do, but too often the story material demanded careful drawing and subdued action. Then story-man Bill Peet gave us the wizard's duel in Sword in the Stone, a perfect use of animation, maintaining personalities through a surprising change in forms and exciting action.

9. Our Procedures

"The ideal set-up would be the storyman, the director, and the layout man, as well as the musician, operating as a sort of story unit. They all should be keenly interested in the picture. No one person should dominate to an extent where he would keep the others from entering into the production and freely expressing themselves."

Walt Disney

In spite of constant efforts and persistent claims, Walt never did build an organization in the strictest sense of that word. What he built was a loosely unified group of talented people with particular abilities who could work together in continually changing patterns. They did this with a minimum of command and a maximum of dedication. What Walt wanted was the greatest creative effort—not the most efficient operation. There were titles and departments and job classifications without end, but they had more to do with responsibility than authority.

It was the person with the better idea who was on top, regardless of his job. Still, this recognition often survived only a day, as some other idea was embraced in the process of endless growth. The slang of the day had characterized the ideal hero with glowing, flaxen locks as "The Fair-Haired Boy," and at Disney's that role was apt to be so transient that the "fair hair" was assumed to be an easily transferred wig. The employee wanting an update on developments in his projects would ask, as he arrived for work in the morning, "Who's got the wig today?"

This method worked because Walt was the boss—not just because it was his studio or that he had the authority to get what he wanted, but because his ideas were the best. Many times we could not understand what it was he wanted, but never did we lose confidence in him or his ability. We could question his judgment, or his emphasis, or the way he went about achieving a result, but it was with the knowledge that Walt's way

FACING PAGE: Pinocchio

The Rescuers

always was a very good way. Usually each of us felt, "Why didn't I think of that?" but every so often we secretly would feel, "My way is better!" and occasionally it would suddenly seem so to Walt, too. He relied heavily on his staff to feed in creative ideas.

In understanding Walt's methods, it is important to realize that he was not in the animation business to make money. As he said, "Money—or rather the lack of it to carry out my ideas—may worry me, but it does not excite me. Ideas excite me." He was more like a man with a hobby than one with a commercial enterprise. He was doing what he wanted to do and hoped that others would share his curiosity and excitement about the potential in what they were doing. He put all the money gained back into the next picture because that was where the fun was, and he certainly never reached a point where he did not know what to try next.

He did not dream a big, overall dream; he made it up as he went along. Each thing he did suggested something else, something new, something that had never been tried, something an audience might want to see. He realized that he could not explore these areas without better talent around him, so he was always adding to the staff. "Never mind the classification, just get that guy in here." Talent, ability, new ideas were the important matters.

His amazing faculty for casting his men on assignments that would bring out unexpected talents extended down to the least employee. When Dave Hand was production supervisor he saw this happen over and over:

I think Walt had an uncanny way of finding just the right place for a "lost soul." Admittedly, because money had no relationship to his finding the right job for the right man, he would direct the movement of the creative talent . . . from one place to another. In my position, I was ready to give up on some little guy and would so express myself to Walt. Many times he would say to me, "No, Dave, let's move him over to this spot in this department. Maybe he'll work out there." And even at times, if the "lost soul" didn't make it in that department, Walt wouldn't give up on him; we would have to try yet another spot. To my amazement, some of these "lost

souls" became valuable contributors towards our production progress. And most others would find a niche that satisfied the studio and them.

Possibly the most elusive part of this casting, and the part that Dave considers to be of the "utmost importance," was the building of the material from the first days in story toward the men who were going to handle it. The story crew was selected for the interest they might have in a type of story situation, and, very soon afterward, as the entertainment values were emerging, the director would be selected. The storymen knew this director's talents and automatically started shaping their business along his lines. At the same time, the men who eventually would animate this film were chosen, and everyone worked to provide the type of material they did best. "Even in the story development period, the business being considered (perhaps unconsciously) is thought of relative to a certain animator being able to handle it," Dave said. "I believe it to be a most important part of having the picture come out with quality at the other end."

This is obviously the opposite of approving a script, preparing the scenes, and then calling in any available animators to complete the work. It also pinpoints the subtle working relationships that made an established organization impossible. Any attempt at describing how the pictures were made has to be done in terms of the men who made them and how they felt about their assignments. There were constant experiments in innovative procedures (some successful, some quickly discarded), but through it all there was a perpetual shifting of job responsibilities and opportunities. Making a film became a sequence of associations, with the whole process kept extremely flexible until a good product actually had been assured.

Of all the methods tried, we list here the most successful, and, in most cases, the ones that produced our greatest films. No two pictures were done exactly alike since Walt always searched for a still better way, but the procedures presented here show the way the best work was done at each stage. Perhaps it was an unusual way to make films, but it brought inspiration in the conception, control in the production, and success at the box office. It took years to find these concepts, and few of them are quite what anyone would expect.

Aristocats

From left to right:

1. Roy Williams, Homer Brightman, and Ted Sears.
2. Ollie Johnston, Milt Kahl, Woolie Reitherman, John Lounsbery, and Frank Thomas.
3. Jack Boyd, George Bruns, Ken Anderson, and Les Clark.
4. Ben Sharpsteen, Jim Algar, and Bill Roberts.
5. Winston Hibler, Joe Rinaldi, Clyde Geronimi, and Ed Penner (seated).
6. Bill Peet, George Stallings, and Wilfred Jackson.
7. Charlie Philippi, Walt Disney, Ken O'Connor, and Ham Luske.
8. Basil Davidovich, Don Griffith, Woolie Reitherman, John Sibley, and Dick Lucas.
9. Herb Ryman.
10. Al Dempster, Bill Layne, and Art Riley.
11. Carl Barks (with pointer) and group.
12. Mary Weiser, Dot Smith, and Grace Christianson.
13. Al Dempster, Dick Anthony, Ralph Hulett, and Eyvind Earle.
14. Claude Coats, Wilfred Jackson, and John Hench.
15. Art Riley and Ray Huffine.

The Team

The basis of the Disney method of making a film always has been team effort, where constant discussion and daily arguments replace rigid procedures. Walt realized that each person connected with the film had to feel that what he did was the element that made it all work. This meant keeping everyone involved in the searching and the trying and the evaluating that went on through the whole production. Walt summed it up very simply, "Everyone has to contribute, or they become laborers."

Frank Lloyd Wright once was trying to pinpoint the blame for something he did not care for in one of our films. When we explained that we all shared in the responsibility since we worked so democratically, he snorted, "Democracy! That's not democracy—that's MOB-ocracy!" It is true that many artists cannot adapt their talents to the group effort. Highly specialized ideas are nearly always beaten to the ground, with preference given to more solid entertainment, since the base must be as broad as our audience. Personal preferences succumb to the majority rule, or the director, or the producer, but in the exchange of ideas there is a stimulation that no individual could generate in himself. Our procedures tried to make the best use of this collaboration by adding constant opportunities for it to flourish.

13

ARTIST: *Gustaf Tenggren*—Pinocchio.

ARTIST: *Kay Nielsen*—
"*Night on Bald
Mountain*," Fantasia.

ARTIST: *John Hench*—Cinderella.

ARTIST: *Mary Blair*—
"*Johnny Appleseed*,"
Melody Time.

ARTIST: *Eyvind Earle*—Sleeping Beauty.

190

*Mary Blair and Ken An-
derson discuss drawings
they have done in relation
to the needs of the film.*

ARTIST: *Mel Shaw*—
The Black Cauldron.

ARTIST: *Ken Anderson*—
The Rescuers.

Stylist

Each story seemed to call for something new in the way of style and design to match the mood of the material; so, before any actual story work was begun, Walt would look for an artist of unique ability to make some drawings or paintings that would excite everybody. From outside the studio he brought in top illustrators of children's books, such as Kay Nielsen and Gustaf Tenggren, to explore the visual possibilities of a subject. Within our own staff were highly talented stylists like Albert Hurter, Mary Blair, Don DaGradi, and Ken Anderson, who knew the production problems and could suggest specific layouts or character sketches as well—to help get their ideas into the working elements of the picture. But more often, these stylists were not supposed to concern themselves with the details of making the picture. They were trying to create a way of visualizing the whole concept so that it would be attractive and fresh and establish an integrity of design for both characters and locales.

These "inspirational sketches" started the whole staff thinking. As one animator said, "There is something exciting about animating on a sequence that has an imaginative locale—a make-believe place that would be exciting to be in. Like the Snow White setting—a fanciful world. The settings in *Pinocchio*—Geppetto's shop full of all those dolls—the inside of the whale, or

ARTIST: *Vance Gerry*—
The Sword in the Stone.

The stylists influenced the whole appearance of each picture, yet their work was never seen by the public. They were part of a large group of artists who inspired, created, planned, and suggested but did not make the actual drawings and paintings for the films. The design, color, mood, locales, characters, and fantasy worlds all started in the inspirational sketches of this select group.

191

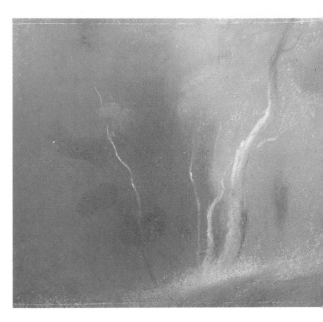

Occasionally several different stylists were assigned to the same picture in an attempt to find the most suitable style for a special film. For Bambi, *many artists tried to capture the realism of the deer in the forest and the poetry of Felix Salten's book. Tyrus Wong brought a magnificent oriental tradition to the material.*

Pleasure Island—the locales inspire ideas for layouts and exciting scenes that you can't feel in the ordinary situations. It stimulates your imagination so that you think of more unusual ideas."[1] No one had a chance to get bored or stale or feel he was just doing the same thing over and over. Everyone got a lift from having fresh talent continually suggest new concepts.

There were times when the dramatic or charming styles suggested could not be maintained in the actual animation—to everyone's disappointment. Possibly we were just not good enough to convert the strong designs to our type of animation, but we felt that as long as we were achieving our audience identification through sincere, believable characters in real settings (no matter how fanciful), we had to keep certain fundamentals of animation. We experimented with other types of movement that might fit the suggestions of the stylist, but they always seemed to lack life. No matter what we tried, we were never able to adapt our techniques to the restrictions of an incompatible design.

We all loved the crisp, fresh drawings of Mary Blair; and, since she always worked in flat colors with interesting shapes, it seemed that her work could be animated with wonderful results. Although we kept the colors, the relative shapes, and the proportions, once Mary's drawings began to move by the principles of

animation that Walt had decreed they often lost the spirit of her design. It was no problem to move the drawings artistically, keeping exactly her suggestions —and some very interesting innovations came from those efforts—but as soon as it was necessary to tell a story with warmth and personality it all broke down. We had proved in *Fantasia* that any shape could move in almost any manner to match the verve and excitement of a strong musical track—as in the stirring dances in "Nutcracker Suite" or the abstract designs of "Toccata and Fugue"—but this movement could only illustrate a story concept; it could not sustain it. There is possibly a way to do both. We just never found it.

Ken Anderson felt the problem went deeper. "Mary's style . . . doesn't adapt that well. . . . When you made any adjustment at all, they were not Mary Blair's. . . . But if you had movement and color against that background, it's a good question as to whether it would have been as wonderful a thing to look at." It may be that certain designs simply should be left in their static form, suggesting their own dynamics through their relationships. Animation has its own language, and it is preferable to develop its own elements rather than try to force it to duplicate or augment another art form. After all, animation is as much a separate medium as ceramics, carvings, tapestries, frescoes, or prints.

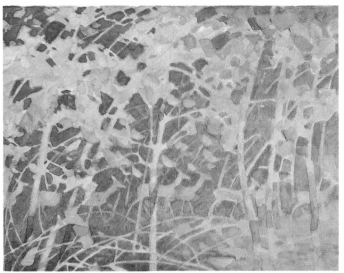

ARTIST: Art Riley—Bambi.

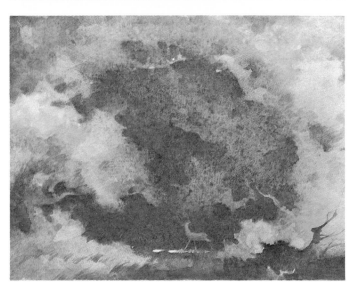

ARTIST: Maurice Noble—Bambi.

Scene from the picture shows influence of the stylists.

193

How The Storyman Works

In The Fox and the Hound, *the fox was raised on the farm but now has been turned loose in the woods. Seeing a beautiful vixen, he wants to get acquainted. At this point, he is more like a teenager than a real fox. The vixen is fishing by a stream, and he rushes over to help, without knowing anything about catching a fish.*

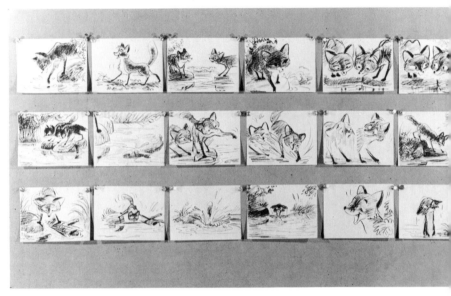

Vance Gerry explores the possibilities of the situation, trying many set-ups, different ways of staging possible business, and alternate views. He wants to keep the girl attractive and the hero likeable, with both very interested in each other.

Vance tries to find a continuity without dialogue that is entertaining and right for both characters. He keeps his drawings simple, looking for body attitudes and ways to enhance the charm of the situation and the characters' appeal.

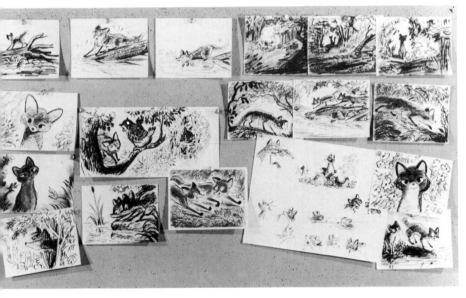

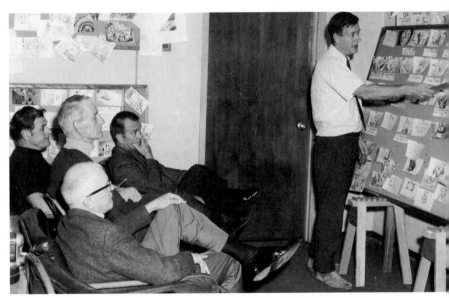

Good drawings that do not quite fit the storyman's current continuity are pinned on a second board called the "goody board." They will stimulate ideas at the next meeting and may be used to pin up an alternate continuity.

Very little of what Vance draws will be in the final film, but his early explorations will have influenced everyone who works on the sequence.

Vance presents his board to the Production Unit. Behind Vance is Woolie Reitherman, then Ken Anderson, Larry Clemmons, and, in front, Milt Kahl.

It was always difficult to pin the sketches up in a straight line. If the line went up at the end, it was said that the storyman was an optimist; if it went down, he was a pessimist.

194

Storyman

Writers of proven skill had been brought into the studio, but they were seldom given a chance to write. A script could be used in the beginning to show suggestions of what might be done with the material, but more often the ideas were talked over, tossed around, beaten to death, changed, discarded, revamped, built upon, and "milked" without a single word being put down on paper. Since animation is a visual medium, it is important that the story ideas, the characters, the business, the continuity, and the relationships be presented in visual form rather than in words. So the storyboard was invented.

The first sketches to be pinned up were not the continuity of proposed action but general illustrations of the idea: groupings of characters, situations, locations, the first attempts to visualize this story. Gradually, as choices were made, more of a continuity was seen, and, eventually, sketches emerged that defined actual scenes that might be on the screen. Through all these changes, as ideas grew into something better or failed to hold up, or were found to be too elusive to capture in still drawings, sketches were pinned up and taken down, day after day. It is a very flexible way to work.

The assignment sounds deceptively simple. Find the entertainment values in the story situations, then present them visually through the feelings of the personalities involved. Until the spectator can see an incident through a character's eyes, there is no life and very little warmth. So the discussions were not so much about "What happens next?" as about character relationships and the funny things that people do.

A truly entertaining idea does not come easily, and humor had to be considered a very serious business. A gag was never accepted just because it was funny; it had to work just right for that spot in the story and for that particular character. One new man was stunned at his first story meeting. "Everyone was so grim," he said. "No one was laughing. I thought, 'Funeral directors have more fun than this!'"[2]

Walt seldom had a single storyman working alone, because he felt that two or three men working together would generate more ideas and give greater scope to their subject. Often it was a combination of a storyman and a story sketch man who sparked each other, either through stimulation or sheer irritation. When anyone was trying to prove that his idea was the very best possible, he would work harder to make it as interesting and definite and clear as he could. The storyman did the talking in the meetings, which gave him a definite advantage in presenting his own ideas; but the sketch man could control the appearance of the boards by staging rival suggestions less dazzlingly than his own. Usually some agreement could be reached before Walt came to see the boards, but often a certain testiness could be discerned as the storyman started his presentation with the offhand remark, "The sketches aren't very good, but. . . ."

When the men in the story unit felt that they had something to show, they would call for a meeting. More often, Walt would barge in unannounced to see how things were going. Since he had a habit of prowling through the rooms at night to see what ideas were being generated, this type of visit usually meant that he had seen the storyboards and wanted something different—though this was never mentioned. He would feign innocence with, "Whatcha got here, guys?" and the "guys" would be caught so unprepared that they could respond with neither a hard sell nor an alibi. So they listened, and learned. As Dick Huemer said, "Walt was his own best storyman."

If Walt felt that some solid ideas were beginning to show up, or that some fresh ideas were needed, he would call in other storymen to get reactions. For quite a period he had what he called his "shaping crew," who followed him from room to room giving their thoughts and suggestions. One disgruntled storyman who preferred to work completely alone complained about this "convention" method of building a story, and top storyman Ted Sears summed up the situation best with this pungent remark, "There's nothing worse than someone who comes in with a fresh eye!" But out of this system came wonderful stories, filled with rich ideas that gave the animators the greatest help in the world. One of them commented in later years when he viewed an old film, "You get the feeling that every last frame of that thing has been worked over until it's perfect!"

If a story meeting was not successful, other storymen would bestow the "Bomb of the Week" award on the hapless drawings. If the storyboard was approved, it would receive the coveted "1st Prize."

Walt wanted the whole staff to participate in the building of each picture, and he encouraged everyone to submit gags on the current story. Here are some of the suggestions turned in for the dwarfs in Snow White.

196

Story Sketch

"A story sketch is not geography—it is not continuity —and it is not a diagram. Nor does it merely illustrate the dialogue for the sequence. Those are all the common mistakes of the beginning story sketch man. The story sketch should show character, attitude, feelings, entertainment, expressions, type of action, as well as telling the story of what's happening. When you look at a board, it should reflect the feeling of the sequence so the viewer starts to pick up some excitement and stimulation."[3]

The story sketch is somewhat comparable to the *New Yorker* cartoon drawings of the thirties, when Harold Ross personally reviewed all the drawings submitted. He was critical of the staging, the characters, the whole idea; in fact, very little of the original work ever pleased him, and he was especially upset if he could not figure out where he as the viewer was supposed to be while observing this situation.[4] Marc Davis used to give his art classes the assignment of trying to improve on the staging of a *New Yorker*

cartoon. He knew it would be almost impossible to do, and very soon his students realized this, too.

A story sketch man at the studio was usually an artist who had a special interest in illustration, design, appearance, and character. His staging influenced the layouts that followed, his approach established a style for the picture, and his arrangement of the scenes and their storytelling value became a guide to the cutting and presentation of the ideas in their final form.

Whereas the stylist had been asked to make beautiful drawings in full color with no restrictions other than the creation of an exciting illustration, the story sketch man was faced with the problem of making everything work and fit together and match the situation on his storyboard. He tried to be flexible and keep an open mind, because he knew that in the story meeting his ideas would be only springboards to new and greater suggestions.

It was difficult for the story sketch man to maintain a feeling of detachment at these sessions, since he

This sequence comes early in the film The Sword in the Stone, *and it introduces both Wart, the young hero, and the sullen and oafish Kay. These drawings by Bill Peet reflect the experienced story sketch artist's knowledge suggesting action, locale, relationships, and the appearance of the characters.*

197

SLEEPING BEAUTY
2082
RUFF
SUGGESTIONS

Suggestions for costumes by Tom Oreb, for Sleeping Beauty.

In Peter Pan, *Captain Hook has captured Tinker Bell and is trying to make her divulge the location of Peter's secret hiding place. Pretending friendship, he plays on her jealousy of Wendy, and finally wins her over. She marks the spot on the map.*

Don DaGradi explored camera angles, staging, acting, character development, locale, and props in these early sketches.

was the first one to put up a drawing with his heart in it. The artists who followed would be just as vulnerable, but he was the lead-off man. Even though there were attempts to soften the blows ("We're not criticizing you, it's just the idea we don't like!"), the fact remained that the sketch man had believed in the drawing when he made it. Because their contribution to the whole picture was so great, only artists who drew with a special appeal or a sensitive style were put in story sketch, and the very sensitivity that made them valuable was what made them so depressed when the storyboard was changed. And it was always changed. That is the point of a storyboard.

Occasionally a story sketch man would become too personally involved in his work and let his ego blind him to the needs of the overall story. There was a time when one such harried artist could not stand the treatment his lovely drawings were receiving. As a particular favorite was being tentatively folded over, he cried out, "Walt, you can't do that! Not that one!!" Walt did not respond directly but carefully and deliberately

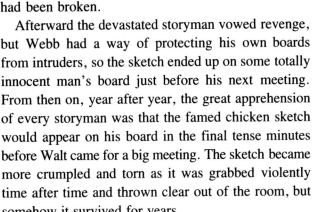

pulled that sketch and the next three clear off the board, tearing the corners where the pushpins had held them captive; then he released the tattered paper to let it flutter helplessly to the floor. He seemed to be engrossed in the picture itself and totally unaware of what he was doing to these "masterpieces," but the message to the sketch man was unmistakable. No dialogue is needed if pantomime can tell it all.

Webb Smith was a great storyman who drew in the old cartoon style and became not only one of the best gagmen but one of the most innovative pranksters. Once, he had been ridiculed by other storymen for a particular drawing of a chicken on one of his storyboards, and he felt that some form of retaliation was in order. Just minutes before his co-workers were to have an important meeting with Walt, Webb slipped into the room and pinned the chicken sketch right in the middle of a storyboard. The storyman usually tried to work up a fine pitch of enthusiasm as he told his story, hitting the boards with a pointer, talking fast, and laughing as spontaneously as he could in hopes of selling Walt the ideas being presented. Totally unprepared for a chicken in the middle of his story, he was deep into the action as he approached the interloper: "Donald comes roaring around the corner, see, and he slips on this crazy old rug here, and then he crashes into this lamp, and he's getting madder, and then this chicken comes and he — uh — he goes an' — he comes — he comes in here an' — well, anyway, Donald comes along here somewhere. . . ." The mood had been broken.

Afterward the devastated storyman vowed revenge, but Webb had a way of protecting his own boards from intruders, so the sketch ended up on some totally innocent man's board just before his next meeting. From then on, year after year, the great apprehension of every storyman was that the famed chicken sketch would appear on his board in the final tense minutes before Walt came for a big meeting. The sketch became more crumpled and torn as it was grabbed violently time after time and thrown clear out of the room, but somehow it survived for years.

Joe Rinaldi stages a gag in the fewest number of drawings.

Joe Rinaldi wanted Tinker Bell to look more like the popular bathing beauties of the time, as in his sketch at upper left. Don DaGradi searched for the best angles to make her look small and feminine.

Director

There was a greater variety in "Music Room" procedure than in any other area, with Walt's leadership being the only constant factor. Walt worked best when he was uncluttered with details and able to let his imagination run free, so the director's job began with the process of picking up the pieces and trying to make them all fit together. Many different men were tried in this position, some coming from the ranks of the storymen who had a special sense of the whole picture, and others from the animators who had a knack of working with younger artists. Layout men were tried, assistant directors, and even people who seemed to float between departments without any real cate-

A production unit for Sleeping Beauty: from the left, director Eric Larson, story sketch man Joe Rinaldi, sketch man and stylist Don DaGradi, supervising animator Marc Davis.

200

gory to call their home. Many of these choices survived for only one picture.

Walt never wanted to be told that he could not do something, especially if the reason was a technicality or restriction of production. Still, he was realistic enough to know these annoyances had to be considered, so he put key men in the unenviable position of having to say, "No," when the ideas were becoming too impractical. He could not tolerate a "yes man" at any time, but he bristled when he received any negative response—it brought his creative drive to an immediate halt.

At times the directors felt like little more than clerks, trying to put Walt's ideas on the screen, while at other times they were expected to make sweeping decisions that affected the whole studio. It depended upon where Walt's interest lay. If something excited him, he would be deeply involved, telling everyone what to do; while if he were more interested in some other area, he left surprisingly big decisions to his directors, often by default.

The most successful arrangement was the Production Unit, where responsibility was shared. The director made the decisions but was aided by his layout man, a couple of supervising animators, and possibly a story sketch man on loan to draw up the new changes. Just because the storyboards had been moved down to the Music Room did not mean that they had been approved entirely. Hopefully, the storyman still could be persuaded to join this crew in the process of refining and developing without feeling that all his careful work was being thrown out.

Sleeping Beauty

The Jungle Book

Recording

Walt wanted to "find" his characters before going ahead with other story sequences or even the experimental animation, so the production unit began searching for voices as one of its first assignments. By this time, we all knew the type of character we wanted in our story, but to find the precise voice that made him just right was always a very demanding process. For Geppetto we had wanted a gruff, crotchety old man, who had a heart of gold but was accustomed to having his own way since he lived alone with only his pets and his dreams. On the storyboards this had seemed ideal. There was warmth revealed in his inner feelings and humor in his put-on crankiness. The perfect voice belonged to the character actor Spencer Charters, and

TEMPORARY MODEL SHEET OF GEPPETTO # 2

PINOCCHIO ∽ Ƒ 3

COMPARATIVE SIZES OF PINOCCHIO TO GEPPETTO AND TO ROTO — PINOCCHIO IS ONE HALF SIZE TO GEPPETTO.

Our first Geppetto in Pinocchio *had many characteristics of Doc, the lead dwarf in* Snow White, *which were combined with the physical appearance of the actor who did the voice. When we switched to a new voice, a completely new character emerged.*

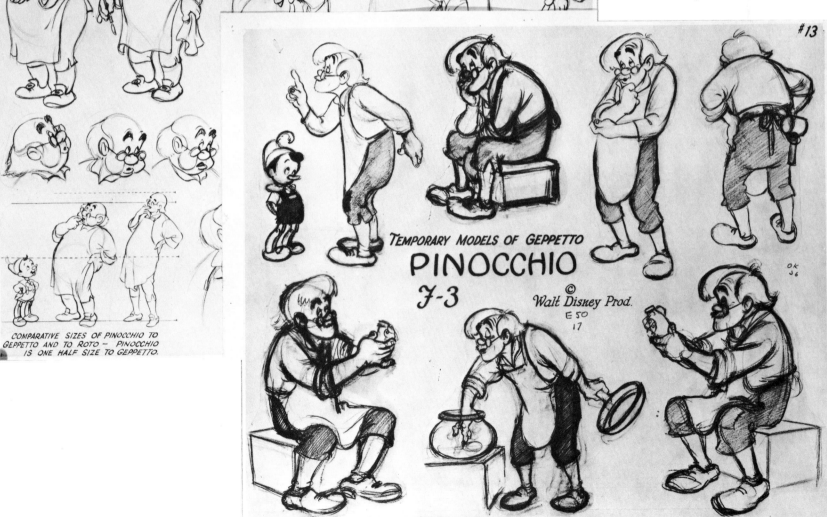

TEMPORARY MODELS OF GEPPETTO

PINOCCHIO

Ƒ-3

© Walt Disney Prod.
E 50
17

13

203

Pat Buttram always added an extra dimension to the characters he portrayed. As a writer, gagman, and comic, he helped build such personalities as Napoleon, the farm dog in Aristocats; *the Sheriff of Nottingham in* Robin Hood; *Luke, the shiftless muskrat in* The Rescuers.

Eva Gabor gave elegance and charm to Duchess in Aristocats *and determination and compassion to Bianca in* The Rescuers. *She wanted more comedy in her roles but we needed the warmth and sincerity she projected with her distinctive voice.*

our first model drawings were influenced by his appearance. But, after nearly 100 feet of experimental animation had been done, it became apparent that the hidden nuances that should have given the warmth were not as evident here as they might have been in live action. The character seemed abrasive and too strong in his manner. We had made a serious mistake.

With just one sequence in work and only the experimental animation involved, it was still possible to back up and start over. The search now was for a mellower man, more gullible, and with an old-world charm. These qualities were found in Christian Rub. The character was redesigned, the dialogue changed to fit this new attitude, the sequence rebuilt around a different personality; eventually there emerged a lovable old woodcarver who was both memorable and believable.

For a long time Walt considered recording the voices as part of the storyman's responsibilities, since he had been deeply involved in writing the dialogue and knew so well what the lines were supposed to do for the sequence. In the fifties, this idea was gradually abandoned as more value was found in having the director and the animators on the recording stage. It is very important that the animators be able to "see" the attitudes and expressions when they close their eyes and listen to the voice. Too often great voices or great actors prove disappointing in this regard; it is not a matter of talent or experience. The quality of the voice

itself either brings pictures to the animator's mind or does not. The animators were also found to be more alert to the little sounds, the grunts, the sighs, the vocal mannerisms that gave the specific touches they needed to make the cartoon drawings live. Personality is revealed not so much in speeches as in mannerisms, and more entertaining characters are created with the little sounds rather than the actual dialogue.

It was also discovered that many times the person who had brought the sequence up to this point was now drained of ideas; a fresh talent taking over and working with the actors could adjust more readily to the problems of the recording. If the voice everyone liked reflected a slightly different personality from the one planned, there had to be a shift in our thinking. It was important that this new interpretation be evaluated for what it offered. There often would be unexpected entertainment potential in a voice or characterization that a person with a preconception might miss. When Peter Behn tested for the bunny that was later to become Thumper, the reaction of the casting director was, "Get that kid out of there—he can't act!" This is the danger of one man trying to do it all himself. It is easy to become so determined to get what you think you want that you lose sight of what you actually are being offered.

The difficulty of making this kind of judgment is compounded by the "tin ear" that everyone gets as he listens to lines being said over and over. Soon the

a climax of feeling. Other actors became overstimulated and neglected subtleties of the character they were trying to portray. Usually nothing was lost in having actors record their lines separately, because a good coach could bring out refinements in a performance possibly missed in a group recording. Another advantage to separate recordings surfaced when either the animator or the director later decided to alter the amount of time between two lines—perhaps to change a character's facial expression. If both voices had been recorded on one track, with natural overlapping, it would have been impossible to open up the sound track.

We always tried to record only a portion of our dialogue in the first session. On the shorts it did not matter too greatly, since there was never much dialogue in them anyway. However, on the features, our contracts usually called for five sessions over a period of at least two years, and occasionally we had problems in finding the actors when needed again. (Phone calls to Europe, Japan, and New York were required

Phil Harris, left, and Sebastian Cabot provided rich characters as the voices of Baloo and Bagheera in The Jungle Book.

Phil Harris and Scatman Crothers study Aristocats *storyboards of the sequence they will record while the production unit offers suggestions and clarification. (Woolie Reitherman points to the board, Frank Thomas is behind Scatman, Danny Alguire stands in front of Ollie Johnston.)*

performances all sound alike and no one can judge if they are what is wanted. Once again, the team effort of sharing the responsibilities offered the best solution. So the director of the sequence was asked to direct the recording session, with most of his unit around him making suggestions, listening, discussing, considering. The recording that was approved on that day would be around to haunt them all for years to come—it was important that it be the best everyone could do.

Very seldom did the actors record all the lines without stopping; they took a page or two of the script at a time. This gave them a chance to listen to what they had done and the director a chance to make suggestions. Separate bits of recording of the same lines were "takes," and they were numbered and referred to as "Take One" or "Take Two" (or occasionally even "Take Fourteen") when selections were made later of the best lines done. This sometimes led to rather confusing instructions to the assistant director: "There's a better take in Take 3, so take Take 2 and cut off the end, then take that third take and take it clear to the end."

Some actors worked well together, giving a natural, conversational quality and building the whole piece to

Sandy Duncan, voice of Vixie in The Fox and the Hound, *with directors Art Stevens (left) and Ted Berman.*

one day to locate Peter Ustinov, who was working only a half-mile away at the NBC Studios in Burbank.) We needed time to develop our characters and build stories through their personalities. Jim Jordan, once famed as Fibber McGee, was hired to do the voice of our albatross in *The Rescuers*. He became alarmed when we outlined our extended timetable and snorted, ''Huh! You better get me all at once! I'm seventy-six, y'know.'' Years later he was still recording voices for us on other pictures.

We learned to be very careful about choosing the voice of a fine performer if it did not sound entirely natural and casual. An outstanding stage voice, or even a straight voice, gave the animator very little visual help. Similarly, the phony voice or fabricated voice of the imitator proved to be a problem because it never had sincerity. In a parody or a satire the ''put-on'' voice works well, but it fails to convince an audience where believability is required. The straight voice will keep the character dull, and the phony voice will lose the audience.

A difficult moment comes when a top talent does not give a performance with either life or entertainment in the first session. Is this an off day? Is the material at fault? Should we look for someone else? We asked the very talented Sandy Duncan to do the voice for our lady fox in *The Fox and the Hound* because of her fresh, disarming manner and her ability

to give any line an unexpected charm. But though her performance was exceptional, the reading was disappointing, lacking the crispness and definition we had anticipated. Experience told us the trouble had to be in our script, and more work would be needed to give Miss Duncan a clear character and a stronger situation. We realized that we really did not know our little fox as well as we thought we did.

Back at our desks, we looked for business that gave changes of attitude, something to bring out real concern, a situation that would show Sandy's cute, zany side, and make use of the wonderful warmth she could give to almost any material. We wrote and talked and rewrote, and when she came in again the script gave her the opportunities she needed. Her performance surpassed our original hopes, giving the integrity, the surprises, the textures, the appeal that we needed.

This kind of building and adapting naturally made extensive changes in the storyboards, and the storyman was either enthusiastic about the great new possibilities that were now opening up, or he was slightly jaded about all his careful work being aborted. Since the new suggestions had come under the director's control, it was only natural that he keep the boards and incorporate the new ideas. However, the changes were not always successful or easily made, leading one storyman to pin a large sign over his door that read, ''It was funny when it left here!''

Assistant Director

This individual is neither an assistant nor a director. He is a troubleshooter and record-keeper who has the job of making order out of the sweeping criticisms and creative thoughts of the director and the production unit. He works in areas where things constantly can go wrong. Frames can become lost more easily than cattle on the range, and, as with the stray dogie, a missing frame *must* be found—which is incomprehensible to live-action editors, who measure their film in arm lengths. Every last frame of a cartoon must be controlled if there is to be any sync with the voices, the music, the sound effects, or even to match one track to another.

After a recording session, the assistant director takes the selected lines and, with the cutter, splices them together so they will play like a radio script. Everyone listens, criticizing the assistant for not leaving enough time in some places, putting in too much in others, and occasionally for having cut in the wrong "take" somewhere else. When the track is approved, it is written up on grey sheets of paper marked with many lines, each one indicating a single frame of film on the track. The start and end of each take is noted as well as the location of the words within the take. Any change in the tracks from then on will be made on these grey sheets, crossing out some frame lines, patching in others. In this way, these "greys" become the living record of the picture, recording each shift, each change, cut, replacement, switch, addition—every whim of the director and animator.

Before long, these greys will be so patched and tattered that they are almost unintelligible, but records of another type kept at the same time will take over. Called "bar sheets," they continue to be "the bible" of the Music Room right on to the end of the project. This method of record-keeping for every piece of film,

whether sound or picture, was developed in the first days of working with music and is more fully explained in the chapter on "The Disney Sounds," but it must be mentioned here in relation to the responsibilities of the assistant director.

The bar sheets are a chart on paper of everything on the reels and on the greys. In a simple example, a take has been selected of Grumpy saying, "I don't know, but I'm agin 'em." It runs 3 feet, 6 frames, and the voices of the other dwarfs have been cut into the reel in relation to that footage. Now, the animator finds that the line lacks the emphasis he feels for that spot and prefers an alternate take, which had more vitality. The director agrees, so the line is replaced. But the new line is shorter, running only 2 feet, 14 frames. Eight frames must come out of all tracks for them to work with this new replacement, but it all can be done on the bar sheets first.

As one well-trained assistant explained, "You do the cutting on paper, in effect, and if your bar sheets are accurate, the assistant director doesn't have to spend time in the Cutting Room. The cutter just does what's on the bar sheets!"[5] That is certainly the ideal situation, but in actual experience it is seldom that easy. What works on paper may not sound right to the ear, and after trying a little change here and shifting one track to a new location and moving the music up earlier—somehow nothing may seem to fit together anymore.

There is no more desolate feeling than being cooped up in the cutting room late at night with the film all over the floor, with nothing in sync anymore, no apparent way to get back into sync, and the "greys" not reflecting what is on the tracks. Somehow this usually occurs when there is a crucial meeting scheduled for first thing in the morning to look at the reels.

Cutter

The cartoon cutter has none of the latitude of his live-action counterpart to determine lengths of scenes or choose which shots shall be used. His job is concerned, first, with keeping, marking, and storing all of the

film, and, second, with keeping the all-important sync. In order to have everything as flexible as possible while the animation is bringing out new ideas, the sound should be kept on separate tracks. Even the simplest film will have four tracks: two of dialogue, one of sound effects, and one of music.

The cutter must list and save every take that has been made of each voice talent: the selected takes that were tried in the reels, the replacements and alternates that were considered, and, finally, all the thousands of tiny scraps that were extra sounds some animator liked but could not find any place to use. At the end of the picture, he will be searching desperately for many of these. The job seems more like that of a librarian than a film editor, especially if the assistant director has done his job well, but, actually, there is much creativity and clear thinking demanded of the cutter.

The whole unit may be eager to listen to a newly recorded track, but the laconic cutter makes everyone wait until he has scribed his takes and put everything in order. In addition, he never uses his master track for anything. He works entirely with prints so that the director can try any ideas he wants without jeopardizing the original. Cutters usually seem uncooperative since they are reluctant to take a chance just to hear how an idea will sound. A baleful eye greets the exuberant animator who claims, ''We can tell in a minute if it's going to work and then we can put it right back the way it was!'' Somehow, it never quite goes right back, and hours are spent trying to find out why.

Character Model Department

In the mid-thirties, no model sheet of the characters was official until it bore the seal, ''OK, J.G.'' Joe Grant, artist, writer, designer, and, at one time, producer, was the studio authority on the design and appearance of nearly everything that moved on the screen, and his taste and judgment were largely responsible for the pleasing style that identified the Disney product during that period. He collected under his wing, in the Character Model Department, a strong group of very talented artists who made inspiring and stimulating sketches of all the new characters being considered.

Joe's drawings were done predominantly in soft pastels, but his crew could handle every dramatic and flashy medium known to artists. This was always a source of annoyance, and envy, to the animators, who were restricted to line drawings and flat color. Joe seemed to have an endless supply of lovely sketches in his pockets, suggesting a nicer effect, a softer look, a more interesting shape, and Walt asked repeatedly,

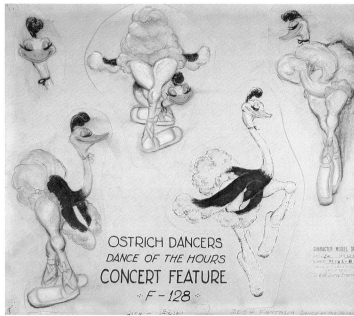

ARTIST: *Campbell Grant*

ELEPHANT POSES
"DANCE OF THE HOURS"
1-039

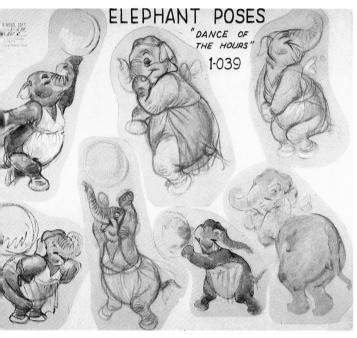

ARTIST: *Martin Provensen*

Sculptors Charles Crista-
dora and Duke Russell were
part of a small department
of artists who turned the
drawings into three-dimen-
sional masterpieces.

ARTIST: *Jim Bodrero*

ARTIST: *Jim Bodrero*

WIND IN THE WILLOWS
"TOAD SUGGESTIONS"
- 2011 -

The Character Model Department eventually expanded to include three sculptors who translated the drawings into beautiful, little clay figures of each character. These were cast, and a limited number of plaster models, painted in the colors suggested by the "Color Model girls," were distributed to the animators. There were no elusive smudges here but hard reality in forms and shapes magnificently done, and they were a great aid to the whole animation department. Unfortunately, they were so good that Walt started giving some away to VIP's as souvenirs, while others became permanent decorations in the offices of top personnel. The rest had a way of disappearing, especially as we neared the end of a picture.

"What ya got there, Joe?" Joe would casually reveal his little masterpiece, causing Walt to exclaim, "Yeah . . . yeah! Look at this, guys, isn't that better? Why don't we draw it like that?" However, there was no way an animator could duplicate in line what had been captured with a slight smudge of chalk. Although stimulated by an improved appearance for the character, we were completely frustrated by the technique.

PRODUCTION FI
"SNOW WHITE"
WITCH MODE

FEB 25 1937

The whole department was disbanded in the economy moves brought on by the second World War, and it was never reorganized. Only one or two of the men ever returned to the studio.

The Story Reel

The storyboards must now be altered to match these wonderful sound tracks, so a recording is made that can be played while the crew watches the storyman point to the familiar sketches. It is one thing to ''tell'' a board, making the parts spirited or peaceful by the pitch of the voice combined with the tempo of the presentation, but it is quite another to create any of this drama while trying to keep up with a sound recording that races through the slow parts and drags forever where it should be exciting. Obviously, something must be changed in both sound and picture. This is the beginning of the continuing changes on the greys, and they are erased, patched, and revised as the tracks are repaired to match the new drawings that will condense some actions and expand others.

This process is repeated until a rough approximation is achieved of the way the sequence eventually will appear. Someday this film is going to be projected on a screen at 90 feet a minute, and the sooner we start seeing it at that speed the better off we are. We can love the individual drawings on the storyboard, let our eyes linger over them, revel in the color and the details, but that is not the way the audience is going to see our picture. The drawings will flash by much too quickly to be appreciated by themselves. Each image will add a tiny bit to the whole concept, and this larger picture gradually growing in the audience's imagination is the important one that demands all our attention.

Once the tracks and the drawings seem to relate in a comfortable manner, the director ''times out'' his sequence so it can be put on film. With the greys on one side of him, the record player on the other, and the boards in front, he wrestles with the refinements, the actual frames involved and the precise staging required. Still more corrections are needed in the drawings, and the whole process may take several days, but it is worth every minute of the struggle.

When the director is through, the story sketches are numbered, sent to camera to be exposed at the footages marked on the greys, and, the next day, Presto!:

the director will see his whole sequence on film in running form. This is the Story Reel. It is a revelation; it is impressive—but it is also full of surprises; so more corrections are made. Since it is almost as easy to change a sketch and reshoot it at a different footage as to change it on the storyboard, revisions can be quickly made and tested. A few pertinent sound effects are added to give a little zest, and some pieces of old music might be played alongside to suggest a mood. It is easy to experiment with the reels at this stage, making them twice as long, or shorter, bolder, gentler, more exciting—the picture must be allowed to grow into something better.

Adding the element of *time* to the story business always makes a startling difference. It is one of the most difficult shifts for a storyman to make, and often he cannot see why his approach was not better. It is true that certain types of gags are more suited to presentation in a still drawing, but some situations that sounded very funny when told from the storyboard suddenly become very long and over-built, while others go racing past the spectators before they have a chance to grasp what is happening. The ideas must be converted so they will work on film and move the sequence closer to its final form.

Everyone studies the completed reels. Does the sequence play the way it was originally planned? Does it develop naturally? Is it repetitious, does it just lie there, is it confusing? The layout man can see what areas are staging well the way they are and what parts need more development. He has found out where he must strengthen and where he can save himself needless work. The animator can visualize his intended scenes not only in relation to the time allowed but to the other scenes in that section, and the storyman can see if his ideas are actually working in this visual form. It is only one step in the whole production procedure, but it is a vital one that will speed up all of the following functions as well as guide everyone toward a better picture.

Layout

The layout man has the responsibility for the appearance of the picture, scene by scene, and as a total film. If a special style has been set for the production, he adapts this work to the bread-and-butter needs of the scenes. He works with the director on the staging and dramatization, building on the ideas of the story sketch man. He designs the backgrounds, suggests the pattern of action for the animator, indicates camera positions for the most effective shot and the cutting that will tell the story in the most entertaining way.

In live action films, this important cutting, or editing, as they prefer to call it, is done after the film has been shot. The arrangement of the pieces can give the picture special meaning, excitement, suspense, purpose, or just as easily make it a dull conglomeration of tedious, endless scenes. The same potential exists in the animated film, but we must operate in reverse! We

have to make our decisions when the film exists only in our dreams. It is far easier when there are tangible strips of film that can be spliced together and tested and judged.

In theory, the layout man plans his sequence carefully in rough sketches, working back and forth to find the best way to solve all of the problems inherent in any film. Surprisingly, one of his biggest headaches is in keeping the directions clear and consistent as the characters move across the screen or exchange looks during dialogue. As long as the scenes were presented as seen by an audience watching a stage performance, there had been little problem. But once the camera moved among the actors and through the sets, it became more difficult to keep the audience oriented. Since the scenes were planned to stage the business rather than clarify the precise location of the characters, there

Page from the Layout Book (which was standard at that time) for Snow White. *The action sketch is at the top, the locale and mechanics at the bottom. Scene 1: Snow White comes down stairs, runs across room to kettle in fireplace at left.*

Scene 3 from Layout Book: dwarfs come down stairs, exit to right. Snow White had gone to the left! The position of the camera has been shifted for this scene, but the audience still sees Snow White go one way and the dwarfs go the other —which is why the layout men say that keeping directions clear is their most important job.

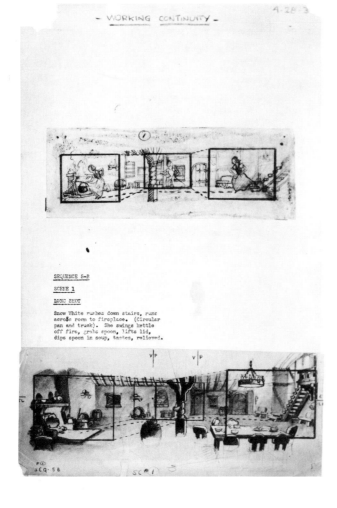

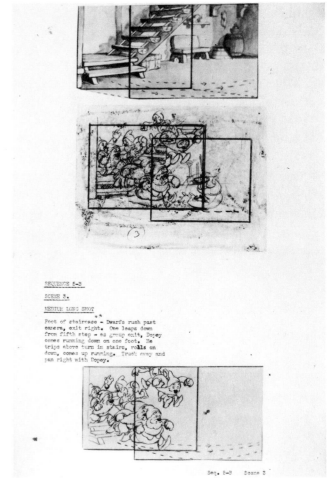

212

Rough layout drawing of Prince John's castle in Robin Hood, *showing the geography, the character relationships, the design and the style of the picture. All of the other scenes in this sequence will be based on this master drawing by Don Griffith.*

The type of pictorial shot below is more fun to do. There are no characters to worry about, just a good drawing with a strong mood to fit the situation.

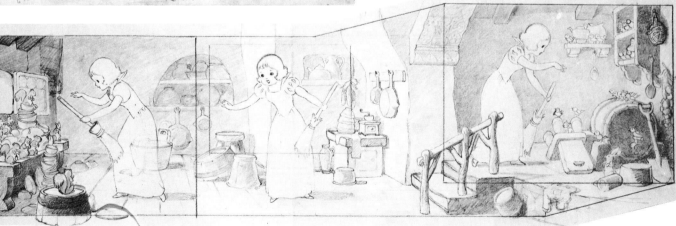

Layout sketch with suggested camera move. As Snow White gets to her feet, the camera follows her up, losing the animals. Less to draw, less for the audience to watch.

Full-sized layout sketch with the figure in it—will it work as planned in the Layout Book? The girl must run about to instruct the animals on what to clean. The length of the soundtrack did not allow for this much movement; so, eventually, this action was done in a close-up.

Imaginative Staging Helps the Sequence

Basic staging problem: the old dog in Lady and the Tramp *is supposed to turn away from the irritating singing coming from the left. This preliminary staging had no strength in the acting.*

With these drawings, he can now turn his back to the sound, giving him a definite change of attitude.

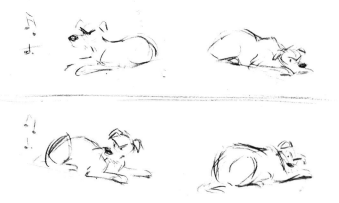

In the final drawing, he not only turns away from the sound but covers his ears as well.

Bernard, the secret agent in The Rescuers, *is slipping down the moist walls into the blow-hole below. This first layout lacked strength in portraying his predicament.*

This more imaginative approach immediately added interest and involvement.

EXTREME ACTION IS BEST ILLUSTRATED BY MINIMIZING BACKGROUND ELEMENTS, AND OTHER THINGS THAT WOULD DRAW ATTENTION AWAY FROM THE ACTION.

STAGING (PERSPECTIVE)

 USING A "DOWN SHOT" (HIGH HORIZON) CAN CAUSE PROBLEMS....

...UNINTERESTING OR EMPTY SPACES

...GREATER DIFFICULTY IN DRAWING RECTANGLES AND CIRCLES IN PERSPECTIV

CHARACTER SIZE RELATIONSHIP IS MORE DIFFICULT.

(HERE ARE THE SAME CHARACTERS SET AGAINST A LOW HORIZON.)

A DOWN SHOT SHOULD BE USED THERE ARE INTERESTING OR IMP THINGS TO LOOK DOWN AT.

It was difficult to give the feeling that Penny was really down in a cavern in The Rescuers *until this shot was conceived. With layouts like these, the animator will try to make his characters move properly, no matter how difficult the angle or perspective for his drawings.*

Carson Van Osten of the Comic Strip Department prepared these sheets to explain the importance of staging to young artists.

were constant examples of someone apparently looking away as he spoke to a companion who was not showing in the scene. Arguments raged and diagrams were produced to prove that a concept was correct: "The camera is here. Mickey is here. And Donald is there! He has to look to his left to talk to Mickey!" But regardless of analysis, it never looked correct to the viewers unless a clear direction from one side of the screen to the other had been established.

There is more fun in drawing up the big pictorial scenes that show the whole set-up and establish both the mood and the details of the locale. Often the pictures on the screen will tell as much about how someone feels as the acting; it is a combination of the mood and the relationship of the character to his surroundings.

With the exception of the first four or five features, most of this procedure has remained only theory for the layout man. The animators need work before there has been time to plan anything, the background painter is waiting to experiment with techniques and colors, the director wants him to make some sketches to repair the story reels, and, somehow, the part he has been thinking about has been revised before he even had a chance to put any thoughts down on paper. Some men can adapt quickly to such changes, trying one idea after another on the spot, but most need time to adjust. As one remarked, "I can't do sketches on my lap like

Ken Anderson. . . . I have to go back to my desk and think about it a little."

Here is a list of some of the things the layout specialists think about, taken from the scraps of paper pinned to their desks. They come primarily from Ken O'Connor and Don Griffith, with a few from Ken Anderson, but much of the wisdom goes back to their teachers.

1. One quick look is all the audience gets—keep it simple, direct, like a poster; it must sell an idea.[6]
2. Fancy rendering at a later date cannot save a poor original conception.
3. Always keep screen directions *clear*. This will be your biggest headache—don't overlook it.
4. Keep informed on: art in history—architecture, costumes, landscapes.
5. Keep informed on: styles, mediums, textures, surfaces, composition, drawing.
6. Keep informed on: technical information—effects given by different lenses, ground glass, filters, gels. What the optical printer can do for you.
7. Mood can be established by timing and movement:

> Sad or Quiet—long scenes with slow moves on pans, trucks, and characters.
> Happy or Excited—short scenes, fast cuts, quicker moves on camera and characters.

Charlie Philippi stands before the giant rough layout of Pinocchio's village. This scene was supposed to create a whole new artistic dimension for the cartoon. Made up of many moving parts, it went beyond even the capabilities of the multiplane camera and cost a staggering $48,000, almost twice the price of a complete short film at that time.

In contrast, the water scene had no animation other than some seagulls, and movement was simulated by using a distortion glass; yet it got an ovation at the premiere. The expensive, complicated shot went by virtually unnoticed, causing Walt to remark, "Never again."

Cinderella

Layout man Ken O'Connor built an actual model of the coach and photographed it as an aid to drawing in changing perspectives.

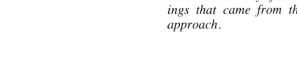

Final cels of the coach show the accuracy of drawings that came from this approach.

A circular pan is suggested in the preproduction planning of Cinderella's coach on its way to the castle.

Four Ways to Plan and Make the Layouts

1. The Thoughtful Thumbnail

Developed by Ken Anderson and Wilfred Jackson for *The Song of the South*. With their knowledge of staging, layout, and visual communication, they worked from the storyboards in small thumbnail sketches, trying one way after another. When a continuity finally was found, the animators were called in to criticize and suggest still more ideas. With Ken's amazing ability, sketches were made as fast as the men talked. These became the basis for the final layouts, cutting, and staging, and showed the animator where his scene fit into the full continuity.

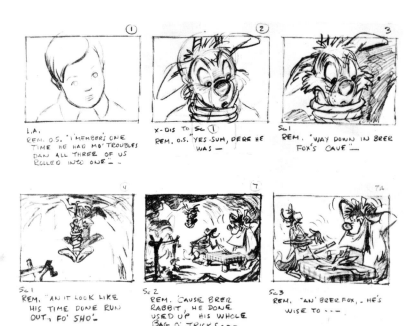

2. Traditional

More thought is put into visualizing the actual layout so that everyone will know exactly what is being planned and can judge if it will work properly. Changes still can be made, but they generally are confined to small things, such as extending the drawing so a slight pan move can be used, or moving a piece of furniture to make more room for the character in the scene. This method works best if the layout man has had enough time to plan the staging for the whole sequence.

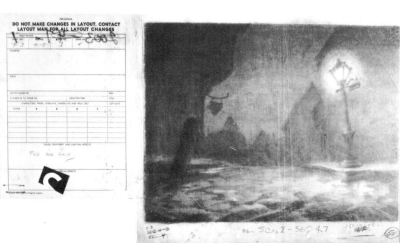

3. The Multiple Choice

Also contributed by Ken Anderson, the idea here is to stimulate everyone to the possibilities in a situation and a locale, giving the director, layout man, and animators a chance to choose the staging and layout each liked best. Ken inspired us with the possibilities in the visual presentation, going far beyond business and staging.

4. Long Shot or Establishing Shot

For *The Fox and the Hound*, Don Griffith established with this master shot the houses of the hunter and the widow, the distance between them, and the details in the terrain. For the whole picture, this layout then became the guide for all business in this area.

A scene of a closer shot along the fence is planned, keeping all the spatial relationships established in the long shot. No matter what camera angle is chosen, everyone in the unit knows what should be shown in such a shot.

Experimental Animation

With the voices recorded and the lead story sequence approved in the story reel, it becomes time to start the experimental animation. The term is misleading in some ways. It means that a supervising animator will now take these ingredients along with the suggestions for the appearance of the main characters and, putting it all together, see if he can come up with a personality that comes to life on the screen and is interesting enough to hold the picture together.

The sequence that is chosen for the first story work involves the main characters coming together in an interesting situation. For instance, the first sequence of *Pinocchio* was the one in which all the characters are introduced in Geppetto's house. The action here is subdued enough so that everyone can observe the appearance of these new figures, and there are enough personality traits apparent in what they do to show who they are and how they act.

Some animators prefer to start with the acting, revealing the personality of the new character through what he does and leaving the refinement of his appearance until they know him better. Others feel just as strongly that the appearance is primarily a drawing problem that must be conquered before any acting or movement is attempted. Animators, like artists and actors everywhere, are all different, and they each have to find their own approach to their work. Much of the strength of the studio actually has come from just these differences in the individual animators, which

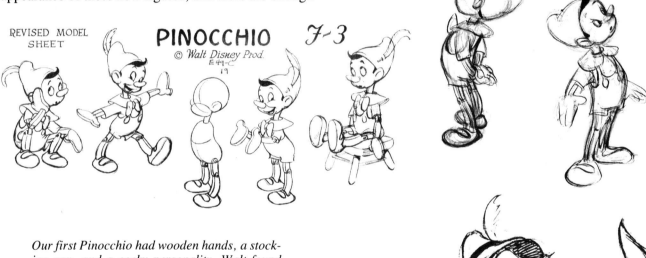

REVISED MODEL SHEET   PINOCCHIO ℐ-3
© Walt Disney Prod.
E44-C
19

Our first Pinocchio had wooden hands, a stocking cap, and a cocky personality. Walt found this to be too brash and lacking in appeal, so we stopped animating until a new design could be found, matching a new story concept of the character.

Fred Moore's drawings at upper right suggested more innocence and the proportions of a boy rather than a puppet.

Milt Kahl's drawings of the chubby, naive little boy in the Tyrolean hat became the final model when we resumed animating six months later.

221

◁ Pinocchio

account for the variety of feelings and characters they can portray on the screen.

The general appearance of the character can be almost any design that fits the story and the overall style of its presentation, but the specifics of how he is drawn depend entirely on what business he has to do, what attitudes he must show, and what expressions he will have. The voice will suggest many facets of his personality, but the needs of the story and his place in it are the major considerations. Once you know what you want him to do, you will know how to construct him so that he can do those things best. His job as an animated character is to communicate story ideas in the most entertaining way, and just being alive is not enough.

We must study the design carefully, questioning the shape of his whole figure, his costume, his head, cheeks, mouth, eyes, hands, legs, arms—even the setting he is in and how he relates to it. Is the scale correct? Is it drawn to give the best advantage to the character? Does it support and fortify his personality so that he feels dominating or timid or clumsy or defiant, or whatever he is supposed to be? This is as much a part of the problem as the type of movements he has, the timing of them, and the acting in both body attitudes and facial expressions.

However it is done, eventually there will be about 75 feet of film animated and projected for all to see and criticize. It is interesting that the reaction always follows the same pattern. If the characterization is weak for any reason, the drawing is criticized. If the business is weak, the characterization is criticized. For some reason, the original business, also being tested at this point, is assumed to be infallible, and only the new figure's appearance is torn apart.

One young animator was quite shaken by the criticism of his scenes. "The best drawing in the world wouldn't have helped because it would still be empty; it was because of the emptiness in the business that they criticized the scenes." He went on to explain, "I can't make a drawing until I know *what* I'm trying to draw."[7]

If the business *is* right and the animator made the right choices on his drawing and acting, everyone is elated. There may be tiny suggestions about details, appearance, or ways of doing something, or, more

Very few characters require the tight, careful drawing found on the queen in Snow White.

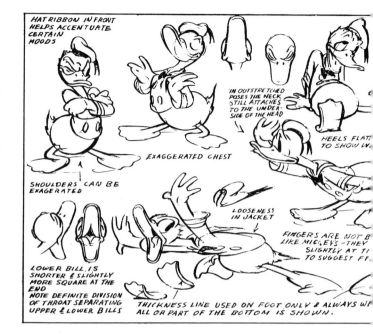

likely, a way to build to an even more entertaining action, but the main reaction is one of enjoyment and excitement.

Walt seldom complimented anyone, letting us feel that sheer perfection was the standard he expected of everybody. Nevertheless, we will always remember his reactions to our experimental animation of Bambi and Thumper. He had been concerned over our ability to make four-legged characters have enough personality to sustain a whole feature, but when he saw our first efforts he turned to us with tears in his eyes, "Thanks, fellows," he said, "That stuff is pure gold!" It was one of the few times we can remember his coming right out with a sincere compliment. Les Clark, one of the earliest animators at the studio, remembered its happening twice in 39 years, when Walt said he particularly liked the Mickeys Les drew; usually his approval was indirect or buried in some other thought. He did not like to expose his feelings, and it was impossible to thank him for anything. He would cough and scowl and mutter, "Yeah, uh—well, say, we've got to get going on this thing, y'know; it's gonna get way out of hand if we don't pay attention here. . . ."

With the experimental animation approved, everybody could go back to work with a new idea of what this story is going to be and how it is going to be told. Once the characters have been seen as living and acting and showing very definite, specific, and, especial-

ly, entertaining personalities, everyone knows how to handle them. The storyman can now start on the next sequences with more confidence; the layout man can work with more precision; and, also, very important, the "inspirational sketch" man can start exploring new situations that will give these characters their best chance for great performances. The rest of the animators are brought on as suitable work is found for them, although it may be six months before everybody can be working full time on the work each does best.

The Handout

The animator gets more than just a scene and a pat on the back when he picks up his work from the director. There is a tape or record of the sound track, along with an exposure sheet, which is not only an exact copy of the scene as it appears on the greys, but it also contains suggestions for accents to be caught or certain staging to be maintained. The animator will get a copy of the final storyboards so that he can see how his scene fits into the whole sequence, and he will have the layout showing the size of the characters, their suggested positions, the extent of their movements, and the area in which they are working. In addition, there is a full scene description which reminds him of why the scene is in the picture, what it is supposed to achieve, and what has been considered entertaining about it.

When we were younger, the director and the animator acted out everything for each other, down to how Pluto would eat out of his dish. The handout of only a few scenes could take the whole day because the idea was to pack as much entertainment as possible into that continuity, and we knew it could be still better, no matter how good our last version sounded. Elsa Lanchester said of the business she had worked out for one of her scenes, "There's always a better way, you know. No matter how good it is, there's always a better way, and you have to keep trying, don't you?" Back in the thirties, we talked of how Chaplin would do the scene, or perhaps Buster Keaton, or one of the fellows in the studio whom we both knew, and we climbed on the table and over the chairs and all over the room chasing imaginary cats or villains or whatever.

One day Wilfred Jackson was disturbed by violent sounds coming from Bert Gillett's room directly above him. "I heard this terrific music going on with thumping and bumping—I thought they were moving furniture or something." Gillett was the other director, and

Jackson was used to the sounds of a musician working out a pattern as Bert jumped from his table to the floor repeatedly, trying to capture the timing of fleas jumping off Pluto's back, or even the "thump-clop, thump-clop-thump-clop" as Peg Leg Pete ran after Mickey. But this sounded more sinister, and Jackson just had to go up to see what was going on.

His eyes popped as he opened the door. "Here was Frank Churchill over at the piano with his cigarette hanging down, with his eyes closed and his foot stomping away," while on the other side of the room, Bert had Fred Moore up against the wall and was swinging wildly with his fists. Fred was trying desperately to duck and break away, but was doing little to defend himself. Jackson stared in horror, wondering if he should call for help or try to stop the fracas by himself. Suddenly it all stopped, and the three men walked back to the big table and looked at the exposure sheet, marking down actions and timing. They were working on a scene from *Ye Olden Days* where a big horse has a fight with a donkey.

There was always great value in this process of acting out a scene. The animator even had his assistant do it when back in his room, so he could see how the scene looked and determine the best angle for drawing it. This helped in deciding how best to use the time for putting over the business, as well as noting all the tiny details of the action.

The handout is not finished when the animator takes his scenes and layouts and tracks and readings down to his room. He is still turning things over in his mind. The director has told him that these particular scenes are the most important ones in the picture, with the best entertainment potential, that probably no other animator could do them as well, and that he really will make a name for himself on this picture. The animator listens to a record or tape of his sound track and wonders if they really picked the best take of the dialogue. He looks at the layout and wonders if this is the right way to stage the business. Is the character too small for the expression to read? Maybe it should be two scenes. He makes some thumbnail sketches, studies the photocopy of the original storyboard, then storms back up to the director's room with a whole new idea. "Hey, wouldn't it be better if we did this in a close-up, facing the other direction and saying this second line of dialogue first? Then we could add a gulp, and maybe a sigh, and then go into that other line. . . ." The layout man turns back to his desk muttering something that no one hears as he starts a new layout.

The director must listen because he may get back a scene without any life if the animator does only what he is told to do. Perhaps he is not thinking about the scene in the same terms as the director, and that possibility, coupled with the likelihood of a mechanical performance otherwise, makes the director do some thinking. He has an opportunity, now, to get a scene that sounds different from what was planned, but one that has enthusiasm behind it and a good chance to be just as entertaining; it is worth considering.

A compromise is reached, the track is shifted, the scene description changed, new layouts made, exposure sheets and greys are corrected, and the enthusiastic animator returns to his drawing board. The handout is over.

Supervising Animator

The supervising animator is responsible for training the young animator assigned to him. Ollie Johnston, left, and Glen Keane discuss a scene Glen will animate in The Fox and the Hound.

This title meant that the individual was responsible for the work done by the men under him. Ordinarily, he would be assigned anywhere from one to seven or eight animators of varying talents. If they were strong, experienced men, he had little to do. They would pick up their work from the director and do the scenes by themselves. The supervising animator would talk to them about the character they were doing, exchange ideas on how to keep him consistent in appearance, suggest business that might fit into their section of the picture, or discuss further ways they all might develop the character. He might also commiserate when things went wrong or try to defend his animators if they were unjustly criticized.

When the animators were less experienced, the supervisor did whatever was necessary to help them get a satisfactory result. He was present at the handout, making suggestions and being sure that these men understood just what was wanted. In some cases, he made the key poses for each scene and even shot them on film as a guide for how the scene should work. Afterward, both drawings and film were turned over to the new animator, allowing him to concentrate on just the movement within the drawing rather than worry about all the other aspects of doing a scene. This young artist still had the problem of making that movement convincing and entertaining with the quality of life we wanted; his energies could easily be dissipated if he were expected to do too much all at once.

We estimated that it took a year and a half to learn the basic fundamentals of animation and another five or six years to be at all skillful. Even so, we never outgrew the concept of helping each other, exchanging drawings and sharing ideas. It was the basis of the team effort and enabled us all to do far better than we would have by ourselves.

Photo by Dave Spencer

The Animator

Story, layout, painting, styling—these are creative jobs, difficult and rewarding and interesting, but essentially concerned with solving problems in the most artistic manner. Only animation is magical. This is its appeal. The creative artist can make something here that exists and breathes and thinks for itself, which gets back to our test of all great art: does it live? Techniques can be copied, mechanics can be duplicated, and even the drawings themselves traced, but the spark of life comes only from the animator. His taste, judgment, and ideas are unique with him and his animation. It is a highly individual effort.

As a person, the animator may be shy or introverted, arrogant or domineering, quiet or pensive; it no longer matters. Personality traits fade away as an artist enters the private world of the drawings on his board. Through the characters he creates, he can be adventurous, crafty, funny, evil, lovable, athletic; he can be a bird, a flower, a snowflake, a shaft of light. This is a very attractive prospect to most of us.

At times his scenes appear to be controlled too much by others; the design of the character, its personality, the layout, the amount of footage are all determined by someone else. However, as a contributing member of the group, the animator undoubtedly will receive more stimulation than restriction from this process.

While the layout man was thinking primarily of storytelling and design and mood when he suggested the locale and the props, he undoubtedly had strong ideas of how the character should act as well. Equally strong ideas were held by the storyman, the director, and everyone else who had contributed to the scene up to this point. Now the animator must build on the work and the ideas of all these people, selecting and discarding carefully, sifting and judging, suggesting and changing, until he has found a pattern of action that is just right for him. He must understand it and feel it; it must be his own, regardless of where the ideas came from. It is this personal thinking of the animator that makes the scene good, not the reliance on others to tell him what to do.

This does not mean that he is obliged to change the business or feel compelled to think of something completely new. First, he must listen and try to appreciate the values of the scene as it stands. More than one top animator has ruined excellent story material by insisting on animating a scene when he does not understand the humor in the story situation or feel the action.

The animator works back and forth through his scene until he has made the drawings that control the movement. He might have to make a drawing for every frame of film, or his key drawing might occur only every foot, depending on the particular action. The number of drawings is immaterial, because as an artist he would be drawing day after day in any job he has taken. Here, his drawings happen to be in continuity and related in a very special way. He discards far more than he keeps in his attempt to capture on paper his feelings about the scene, so his concern is not how many drawings he has made, but how well they depict the vision in his mind.

ANIMATOR: Ollie Johnston—
The Rescuers.

Animator's sketches of the attitudes and poses of a little girl helped determine how the scenes could be played and which positions had the most appeal.

The idea for this scene in The Fox and the Hound *comes from an inspirational sketch by Mel Shaw of the foxes meeting in a romantic setting.*

Vance Gerry develops the situation in his story sketch.

Rough layout of the specific scene by Don Griffith shows the approximate positions of the characters in a close-up of the setting.

Animator Glen Keane fits his action into this set-up.

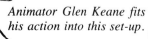

The background is painted from the clean-up layout by Jim Coleman. When it is combined with the cels painted from the animation drawings, all the parts should fit together into one picture.

◁ Don now can produce a cleaned-up layout that matches the actual animation that has been done in the scene.

These rough animation drawings from The Jungle Book *establish the action and capture the adoration that the boy Mowgli has for his new friend Baloo, the bear.*

High-quality clean-ups are required where the drawing of the eyes and the subtlety of the expression are the key ingredients in the scene. These were done by specialist Dale Oliver and projected amazing life on the screen.

Before Walt Stanchfield moved into animation, he made a whole booklet of the common problems and mistakes of the beginner in clean-ups. these are two sample pages.

STRAIGHTS AND CURVES

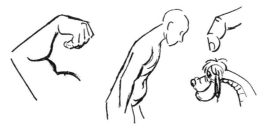

USUALLY THE PART OF THE BODY WHICH IS CURVED IS THE MUSCULAR OR FLESHY PART WHICH BENDS OR FOLDS INWARD. THE STRAIGHT IS USUALLY THE BONEY PART WHICH STRETCHES OR PULLS TIGHT WHEN BENT. THINKING OF THIS WILL HELP DETERMINE THE STRAIGHTS AND CURVES IN AN OBJECT EVEN IN A RELAXED POSITION.

THE REVERSE WOULD BE TRUE WHEN THE FLESHY PART IS AGAINST SOMETHING RIGID.

OR AS IN THE CASE OF THE GROUPING OF HAIR OR FEATHERS.

AVOID MONOTONOUS SHAPES

RATHER USE STRAIGHTS AGAINST CURVES

AVOID STATIC REPETITIONS

VARY THE SHAPES EITHER IN SIZE, SHAPE, OR DIRECTION.

AVOID PARALLELS

VARY SHAPE

AVOID EVENESS IN HAIRS, FEATHERS, FINGERS, ETC.

VARY THEM IN SIZE, SHAPE, DIRECTION OR DISTANCE APART.

Assistant Animator

Gradually we developed a professional class of "clean up men" who took pride in their work. It was their skill that made the pictures look so fine, yet for a number of years they never got screen credit, nor even the salary they deserved. They sometimes were compared to a blocking back on a football team who clears the way for the star runner to make the yardage and the headlines, and it was true that they had to take their satisfaction from the success of the sequence on which they had worked.

They studied line drawing, training on Holbein, Degas, Daumier, Da Vinci; they watched drapery in movement, noting the difference between filmy scarves, woolen skirts, flowing capes, and even baggy pants; they learned the value of a sharp, crisp line against a large, soft shape; they knew how to keep a design in the free-flowing changing shapes of animation rather than make a rigid copy. They always extended the arcs of the movement, squashed the character more, stretched him more—refining while emphasizing both the action and the drawings. They understood the business of the scene, what it was supposed to achieve, worked closely with the animator in deciding which parts were developing well and which parts needed a little help, and they could see the characters start to live as they "rolled" the drawings on the pegs. This required a special kind of talent as well as study—not every artist could master it.

The best working plan seemed to be the small unit of only a few men who, with the animator, carried the full responsibility of doing everything on their own scenes. An ideal group would include an assistant animator who was experienced enough to make simple animation changes and corrections, a second assistant who drew well but was just learning his job, a reliable breakdown man, and an eager inbetweener who could double as bookkeeper and handyman. This last category included everything: threading the film on the Moviola, taking a test over to the cutter, running up to the Music Room for a corrected layout, or even prying the reels away from a distraught assistant director "for just a couple of minutes; we want to see how it looks cut in the reel!" Together they budgeted their work and met their deadline. No other system retained as much quality or moved as much work without losing control of the way it was done.

Assistant animators who had this much ability were seldom content to stay in this position for more than a few pictures. Some went on into animation, but most went into other types of jobs where their interest in detail, refinement, and design was stressed. Undeniably, it had cost more to have a clean up man redraw the complete scene, but it was the only way we could have produced the rich characters of the first features. In later years, as costs continued to soar in all departments, a new procedure called "Touch-up" was instigated. It asked that the animator draw slowly and carefully enough so that the assistant need only touch-up the drawings here and there to make them ready for the Ink and Paint Department. By this time all of our animators had become more skillful and were able to adjust to the new idea without noticeable damage to the product. Top quality clean up work is needed on only a handful of scenes in any sequence, and a great variety of shortcuts can be used on the balance to make them acceptable.

Unfortunately, the assistant's work over the years has been considered an area where money can be saved. The production manager watching the money will have been frustrated through the early days of production since there is no way for him to measure ideas or work in progress. But once drawings have been made, a smile envelops his face. Here is something that can be counted, checked, timed, and followed through the plant. The term "pencil mileage" is heard often as the number of artists plus the speed of output is balanced against "footage to be done." Between trying to please the animator who wants the best and the manager who wants the quickest, the assistant must reach a compromise that still satisfies his own standards.

Pose Test

The quickest way to see how a scene is going to play is to shoot what we call a "pose test." While the animator is setting up his scene, figuring the size, the movement, the acting, he is making rough drawings that will become the basis of the actual animation. Now, instead of refining those drawings and relating them to each other, he sends them to camera just the way they are. They are the key poses for the scene and show how the scene is being planned. By shooting them at no less than 4 frames apiece and no more than 24, both the director and the animator can see if the action will be strong enough, or too strong, and if the amount of time allowed for the scene is going to be right. When a series of pose tests are cut together in a reel, there is

quite a good feeling of how that part of the sequence will play.

There is also a possibility that the scene may look funnier and more interesting in poses than it ever can in full animation. Fred Moore had a famous scene in *Snow White* that always worked far better in the pose test. The scene showed Dopey and Happy very concerned about the magical powers of the evil queen. Grumpy had just informed them that she might be in their room "right now!" Fred used about eleven poses to show Dopey looking from side to side, then glancing at Happy's beard, lifting it, searching under it, then receiving a "bonk" on the head. When this pose test came back from camera, it had a surprising crispness that gave excitement and a feeling of nervous apprehension. There was a big laugh the first time it was shown in sweatbox, but that was the best the scene ever looked. From then on it went down hill. Fred made new and better poses as he animated the scene, but the crispness was gone.

After several unsuccessful tests, in desperation he went back to his original poses and tried to work between them, hoping to recapture the sparkle that was in his first pose test. That was even worse. He never did find the right combination of timing and spacing and regretted ever having posed the scene in the first place. The sweatbox note shows Walt's effort to get more life in the scene:

Scene 31   Shoot corr.   ruff.

Drawings for a pose test of José Carioca by Fred Moore. Each space between the lines of the "exposure sheet" represents a frame of the film and tells the cameraman how to expose the drawings in the scene. Only the poses (numbers circled on sheet) will be shot on this test. The exposure sheet also shows the placement of the dialogue, the length of the scene, and any special instructions.

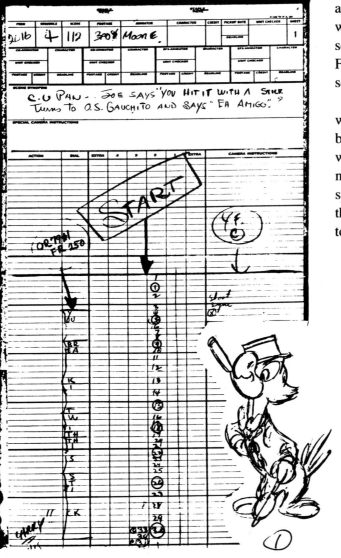

230

Be closer at the start of this scene, and as you pan up, come back at the same time.

The minute Dopey looks under the beard, have Happy turn right around and hit Dopey, taking out the stall you now have. Happy would take it just as the extreme was reached and turn right to hitting Dopey.

Fred, you suggested that Dopey's head, from the bonk, would go down and pop up again. . . . Walt okayed it.

Despite some negative aspects, pose tests have a distinct value, as we discovered when working on *Bambi*. The sequence of the young deer on the ice with his friend Thumper was about to be cut from the story as being extraneous business. The animator who had hoped to work on this section was appalled.[8] The

dialogue that had been recorded was excellent; the story sketches showed clearly what great entertainment there would be in the situation; it would be a wonderful sequence to animate.

A meeting was scheduled to make the final decision, and the animator was determined that this material should get the best possible chance for approval. For three days and nights he worked, posing scenes, roughing out new sketches, making out exposure sheets, shooting held drawings and story sketches, until he had a running reel on the main part of the sequence. It was crude, but it sold the idea. Without the pose tests showing the possibilities in timing and reaction, the sequence would have been cut from the picture. As it was, the relationships were built into even more entertaining actions until that section became a high point in the whole picture.

The Work Reel

When the animator has film on two or three of his scenes, he wants to see how they play in continuity. By themselves, they may look just great, having life and sparkle and clarity, or they may be a complete disappointment. All of this can change completely when the scene is viewed as part of an overall continuity. After all, they have been planned to work in sequence and that is the way they should be seen. The dull scene may have just the subdued feeling needed for that spot, and the active one may be entirely too violent. The only way to be sure is to cut them into the story reel, replacing the story sketches that are occupying

this spot in the picture. Here, they will benefit from the suggestion of activity and personality in the scenes just preceding, as well as the ones that follow.

As each animator continues this practice, the story reel gradually becomes the work reel, or the ruff reel, since it contains all the scenes of rough animation. Coupled with the matching sound reels, they are constantly changing with the latest revisions of footage and scene cutting. As each new test comes in, there is usually a request for the addition of a sound or a slight shift in position for better sync. In this manner, the work reels, at all times, reflect the progress of the

sequence and show whether the anticipated entertainment is actually there.

Everyone can learn something from them, even in this rough form. The layout man might discover the mood and design is not as evident as he had hoped, or the background man can find out how long a certain background will be on the screen and how much of it will be covered by the figures. The director wants the work reels for his sweatboxing, the animator needs them to study his changes, and the assistant animator must check the scenes he is to clean up. Throughout the day, the assistant director will be trying to grab the reels so he can make all the changes that were requested yesterday. They are a popular and necessary item.

How Does it Look?

We never made a picture starting at the beginning and working straight through to the end. We began with the section that gave the best opportunity to get hold of the characters, then moved on to a sequence that either had the greatest entertainment potential, or was needed most for the development of other phases of the picture. There was no possibility of establishing a flow this way and very little chance of finding a balance of fast to slow, excitement to serenity, pathos to comedy. The individual sequences were not handled like a short, but they were complete in themselves and high in interest. We were curious about how it would look all cut together.

We knew it was fairly easy to make an interesting picture that would run only ten minutes. Most people will watch almost anything that is fresh or funny or surprising for that long. Twenty minutes is an ideal length for an animated film, and even a half-hour show offers few real difficulties. The audience can be kept dazzled or persuaded or laughing, maybe even crying a little, in that amount of time. But beyond a half hour, troubles start mounting. A feature-length film requires very special considerations. It is important that it be seen in some kind of running form as soon as possible.

Eventually, the day comes when this can happen. However, there may be blank film on the picture track with newly recorded dialogue carrying the intent, and there will be many areas with only still, inspirational sketches giving just the barest suggestion of what is to come. But between the story reels and the work reels, and the bits of completed animation, perhaps even some in color, the staff can follow the story, and for the first time see what their picture is going to be.

There was enormous excitement when that point was reached in the production of *Snow White* and a special evening showing was arranged out on the sound stage, the building then doubling as a theater. Everyone wanted to see the film, but there was only room for the key personnel in the four rows of seats at the end of the stage. Getting ready at home, Walt was nervous, anxious, critical, tense, eager. He suddenly called to his wife, "Hurry up, Lilly, or we won't get a seat!" Lilly, who had a much more pragmatic view of life than her intense husband, turned in disbelief. "Do you mean to tell me that in your own studio they won't even save you a seat?" Walt was flustered and tried to cover up, muttering about how late it was and wanting to get there early and you never could tell what might happen, and it *was* a very important occasion! We *had* saved them two seats right in the middle; as a matter of fact, there were four seats there, since no one was sure he wanted to be sitting right next to Walt at such a crucial screening.

Seeing the picture all together for the first time is always a startling experience. Somehow it has picked up a life of its own. In some ways it is like one of your children. It may not be what you expected or what you told your friends you would have, but there it is, and it is yours. Up until now you have been living on dreams, believing that the picture would be a certain way and would tell a certain story and have these wonderful characters that everyone would really love. Now your hopes and dreams are over; *this* is what you have, and this is what you have to continue molding and shaping on a very practical basis. The picture probably has some fairly good moments here and there, but it will never look just right all the way through. If it is sup-

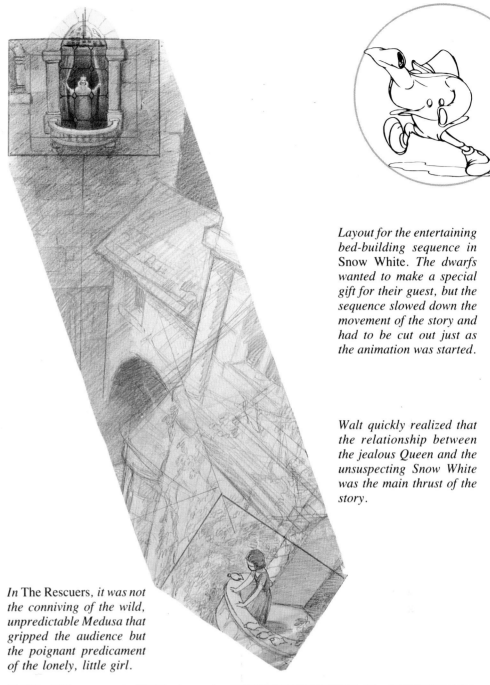

posed to be exciting and is not, now you must do what you can to make it exciting. If it needs suspense, put it in. If it is too long, trim it, and if it is too short, add—but add very judiciously. If it is redundant, or fails to make its points—whatever the problem—you must work with these pieces of film until they become the best picture you can make of them.

Too often the money is all spent by this time and someone is screaming that the picture must be completed in any form, "Just get it done!" But that is a sad decision. This is the very time when the most creative work must be done. Famed film director Blake Edwards said in an interview,[9] "It's nothing to bring a picture in on schedule or under budget. The hard part is making a good picture—I don't care what your schedule or budget is!"

When making *Snow White*, we thought that our main entertainment would be with the dwarfs and the funny things they would do in trying to solve the problems

Layout for the entertaining bed-building sequence in Snow White. *The dwarfs wanted to make a special gift for their guest, but the sequence slowed down the movement of the story and had to be cut out just as the animation was started.*

Walt quickly realized that the relationship between the jealous Queen and the unsuspecting Snow White was the main thrust of the story.

In The Rescuers, *it was not the conniving of the wild, unpredictable Medusa that gripped the audience but the poignant predicament of the lonely, little girl.*

The exhausted dragonfly Evinrude in The Rescuers *grew from an incidental part to a major role in the film.*

brought about in their lives by an unexpected visitor. The queen and the girl were necessary parts of the story, but we would not dwell on them. When we saw the whole picture in a very rough form that exciting night, it was immediately evident that the tension between the vain queen and the girl she was determined to kill was the main drive of the picture, and anything that interfered with this story progression seemed extraneous. As a result, two whole sequences featuring the dwarfs were cut out as well as a comic fight between Doc and Grumpy; the sequences that carried our main story points were strengthened and made even more dramatic. Partly through luck, but

The two farm dogs in Aristocats, *Napoleon and Lafayette, were so successful in their first sequence that the story had to be changed so they could come in again.*

ARTIST: *Ken Anderson.*

The Swamp Volunteers in The Rescuers *were cut down from a dedicated home guard that drilled and marched incessantly to a handful of helpful little creatures of the bayou.*

largely through keeping our procedure flexible, we ended up with the best balance of story–character– sequence relationship we ever achieved.

While working on *The Rescuers*, we thought that the greatest interest would be with the two mice and their overwhelming problem. We worked to make them small and inept, but determined. Medusa, we felt, would be a spectacular villain, slightly mad, powerful, and a constant threat. The crocodiles would be invincible, stupid, and chilling. They would be the scary part of the film. The little girl would have to be done very carefully because she was presented as a real girl, not a caricature, and since she would be difficult to do we tried to keep to a minimum the scenes she was in. We believed our big entertainment would be in Medusa and Snoops trying to outsmart each other in their attempts to get the diamond for themselves, and in the mice trying to outsmart the crocodiles.

Instead, when we saw all the pieces put together, the only thing anyone cared about was the predicament of the little girl. Medusa was a wonderful, flamboyant clown, Snoops a bumbling, ineffective partner, the crocs only dim-witted louts, and the mice just cute little characters trying to do their best. But the girl! Your heart went out to the girl and the terrible situation she was in. It was not the villains surrounding her who built the anxiety, but the predicament itself. So we strengthened the sequences that featured her, paying special attention to anything that would create more pathos. We staged her scenes for the most impact we could get, and used the sad and quiet moments featuring her for a balance to the madcap activities of the rest of the cast. We used less of Medusa than we had planned, cutting out one whole sequence and trimming others, so that she would have a brisk, crazy tempo whenever she was on the screen. The crocs were cut down to relatively minor parts. The climax was now centered on the situation down in the cave, with the heroes facing the mindless force of nature rather than any direct confrontation with the bad guys. At the time, it seemed we would never be able to make the film come off with the proper balance, spirit, texture, fun, heart, and tempo we needed, yet the public acceptance, once the film was released, proves that it was worth every headache and extra dollar spent.

Some directors stubbornly hold onto their beliefs of

what the picture is saying and cannot detach themselves enough to see what they actually have up there on the screen. Woolie Reitherman has an amazing ability, as a director, to pull himself back and view the product impartially. He readily admits the weaknesses and the strengths of what he sees just as if he had nothing to do with the film up to that point. As he commented with a sigh, "You've got to find what's working—not what you thought would work, and not what's in your heart, but what's up on the screen!"

Among the things up on that screen that are working might be an incidental character who, because of an unusual voice or special animation or even sound effects, is starting to click with the audience. The farm dogs, Napoleon and Lafayette, in *Aristocats* and little Evinrude in *The Rescuers* are examples. We always tried to build on the scenes with such characters and even considered bringing them back into the picture in another sequence. Often we found that some clumsy story point could be told in a fresh and interesting way simply by telling it through this new personality.

Our best advice, at this point, is to develop and strengthen what is good; edit out and shift emphasis on what is not coming off; stay away from the commonplace and the hackneyed; constantly search for new things the audience has never seen before—but tell it all with the same old values and fundamentals of communication.

No one can say that any one of these steps in our way of making a film is more important than any other. They are all needed. The two most important procedures are certainly (1) to involve the whole staff in the production, and (2) to keep the picture growing and improving, constantly, right up to the moment of release. Many ideas that sounded great in those story meetings become sodden and lifeless when seen on the screen in relation to the rest of the business, and the sooner these elements can be discovered the sooner they can be corrected. Many other story ideas that were only "touches" will come to life in animation with so much entertainment that it is foolish not to get the full value from them, even if it means adding considerable footage.

Someone outside the studio once stated that it probably was easy for us to make a film now that we had done so many; we must have found the formula. Woolie

retorted, "On every picture, you're in a learning process! It's not so much an application of professional knowledge as constantly learning!" He went on to say, "It is always new, or it had better be. On each film, you start from scratch, make the mistakes, pick yourself up time and time again, yet never give up. You must keep your belief in the picture and your faith in yourself. For a picture to end up good, it must be treated like it was the very first one you ever made."

Animating at Disney's was exciting, but it was also extremely difficult. We were under great pressure and had tight restrictions on time and money, although seldom were they both imposed at the same time. If an animator was doing excellent work, he was told not to worry about the budget, but "could he work overtime to get more of that kind of footage in the picture?" The demand for sheer perfection in execution, along with the constant search for top entertainment values, creates far greater pressure than the requirement to complete a job by a certain deadline.

When an outstanding scene of animation was done, everyone somehow expected the animator to do that well from then on, and even thought, hopefully, that he would continue to improve, as well. A few weak scenes in a row and the animator could be considered to be "in a slump" or, worse, "slipping"! There was a clichéd remark in Hollywood during the thirties about actors and directors: "You're only as good as your last picture." One of the top animators at that time adapted it to animation, claiming, "You're only as good as your last scene!" It was a joke with an uncomfortable twinge of truth in it, and we all felt a compulsion to do our best constantly and try to keep moving that standard ever higher.

Munro Leaf, who has written considerable fantasy and magic himself, wrote these words after he had seen *Snow White*. "If you come right down to it, there isn't a live thing in the picture. Technicians can tell you how it is all done with ink, paint, photographs hooked one on to another and garnished up with sound effects. I'd hate to call a technician a liar, but somebody is going to have a tough time telling me that good, beautiful Snow White, her prince, the wicked queen (who is really wicked when she settled down to it), and all seven dwarfs, and the hundreds of birds and animals came out of any ink or paint pots."[10]

Seven Steps in Animating a Scene

When you picked up the scene from the director you were given the story sketch, the layout, the exposure sheet, the sound, and a full description of the action. Now, what do you do?

1. Think

What is the scene in the picture? What is the entertainment potential in the business? What should I have the character do? How can I best show it? "Don't start animating before the idea is worked out. Know exactly what you are going to do before you start."

2. Thumbnails

Work out your ideas in small size before making a big, complicated drawing. First, you will test:

A. THE STAGING

Example 1

ARTIST: *Marc Davis*—Cinderella.

Cinderella is awakened in the morning by a friendly bird. This is the introduction of the heroine, and it is important to show what kind of girl she is. She must be appealing, not merely pretty.

Example 2

ARTIST: Frank Thomas—Robin Hood.

Thumbnails research attitudes for Robin Hood when disguised as a stork competing in the tournament of the Golden Arrow.

B. THE CUTTING AND CONTINUITY

Be familiar with the whole sequence so you will know just how your scene fits in. With the director and the layout men:

1. Plan carefully which character you will have your camera on to get the most entertainment.
2. Plan when to use a two-shot, a long shot, or a close-up.
3. Look for opportunities to get depth and perspective and avoid too many scenes in a row that are flat-on.
4. Try to change angle when it is possible or logical, but do not do anything to confuse the viewers.
5. Do not pick an angle that is tough to draw just to be doing something different; it will take longer to animate and will not be as effective. Choose the angle that is most helpful for your business. Example:

ARTIST: Ollie Johnston—Robin Hood.

Robin Hood, disguised as a gypsy fortune-teller, is trying to capture Prince John's interest. Little John, behind the curtains, puts fireflies into a glass container to make a glowing, mystical crystal ball from the spirit world.

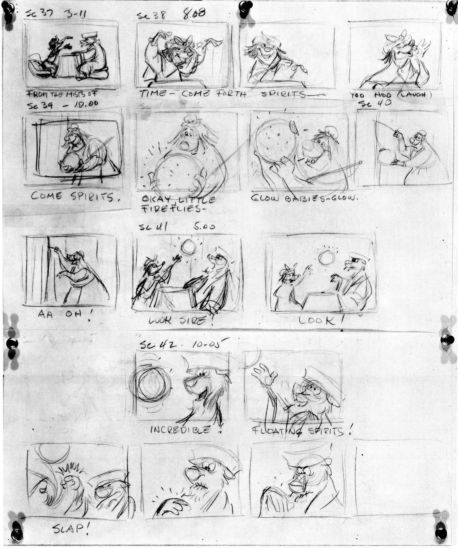

3. Mechanics of Presentation

With a rough continuity and scene cutting established, the individual pictures should be checked and developed.

A. PERSPECTIVE

Be sure to match the perspectives of the layout. If the feet do not fit on the background, how can you show how much they lift up?

Examples:

ARTIST: *Degas*—
Rest Period.

The feet are well planted to show the perspective and give dimension to the drawing.

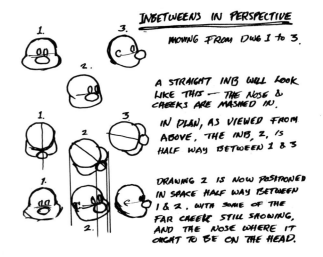

INBETWEENS IN PERSPECTIVE

MOVING FROM DWG 1 TO 3.

A STRAIGHT INB WILL LOOK LIKE THIS — THE NOSE & CHEEKS ARE MASHED IN.

IN PLAN, AS VIEWED FROM ABOVE, THE INB, 2, IS HALF WAY BETWEEN 1 & 3

DRAWING 2 IS NOW POSITIONED IN SPACE HALF WAY BETWEEN 1 & 2. WITH SOME OF THE FAR CHEEK STILL SHOWING, AND THE NOSE WHERE IT OUGHT TO BE ON THE HEAD.

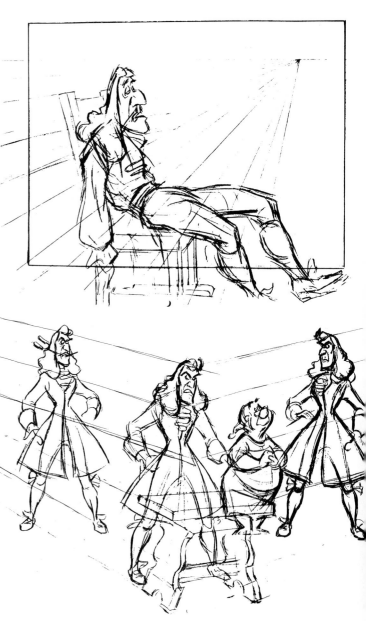

If you draw two or more characters in a scene, do careful key drawings for size relationship and staging. Have good eye contact if characters are looking at each other!

238

B. SCALE

Check all layouts for the scale you need in a picture. Examine your sequence for "pictorial" shots that will remind you of the size of the characters you are animating. The scale of the characters to the things around them, and to each other, is an important part of making them believable, as well as giving them charm and appeal.

Examples:

ARTIST: Bill Tytla—
Brave Little Tailor.

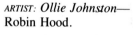

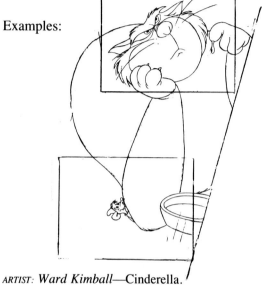

ARTIST: Ward Kimball—Cinderella.
Long diagonal pan accentuates the scale.

4. Solve Special Drawing Problems

Be sure you can communicate your idea and not be stopped by insurmountable drawing problems. Work them out in thumbnails or full size, but do not proceed until they are solved.

Examples:

ARTIST: Ollie Johnston—
Robin Hood.

Page of drawings to find the best way to show Robin Hood as a gypsy peering over the edge of a crystal ball.

ARTIST: Gustaf Tenggren— Pinocchio.

ARTIST: Milt Kahl—
The Sword in the Stone.

239

5. Double Check Your Ideas

Once you have your ideas clearly defined, check your layout to be sure it will work as planned. Does it allow enough space for the actions you are considering?

"Don't accept your drawings too quickly; try them out on someone else."

Example:

Layout from Snow White *with construction of Dopey drawn in to show height, scale, cast shadow, and perspective.*

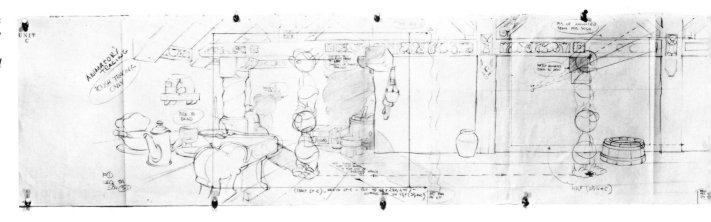

6. Blow Up Drawings Full Size

Individual sketches do not always relate to each other on the pegs the way you thought they would. Rough out all the key positions of the scene, based on your thumbnails and research drawings.

Examples:

ARTIST: Frank Thomas—
Peter Pan.

ARTIST: Ollie Johnston—
Reason and Emotion.

Drawings with this much movement present a special problem: can the activity suggested in the thumbnails be maintained within the limits of the field border?

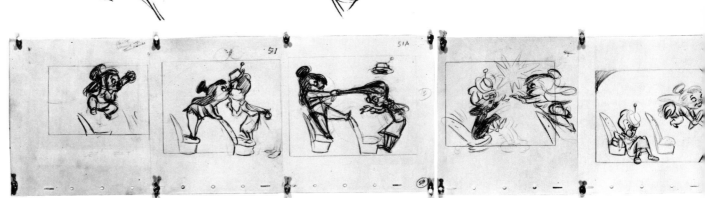

7. Put the "Juice" in it.

With all the staging problems solved, the animator can now concentrate on individual actions, timing, expressions, and making the drawings that will give life to the action.

The scene is a close-up of Captain Hook telling his valet in the next room of his plan to trick Tinker Bell into revealing the location of Peter Pan's hiding place. During his dialogue, he is putting on his finest clothes, down to a gold-plated hook.

These are the drawings blown up from thumbnails that determine position, perspective, size, and movement in the scene. There are twenty-eight frames between drawings 2 and 3.

Within that area, key drawings are made of just how the hook will be put in place. These drawings are called "extremes" or "keys." The animator controls the timing with charts on the drawing noting the position of the inbetweens in relation to the extremes.

The breakdown man does the main inbetweens that may contain special drawing problems.

The inbetweener makes the remaining drawings that will complete the scene. In this type of complex and sophisticated action, there are no mechanical inbetweens. Each drawing has to be considered a new phase in the overall action. The cartoon character must be alive on every drawing.

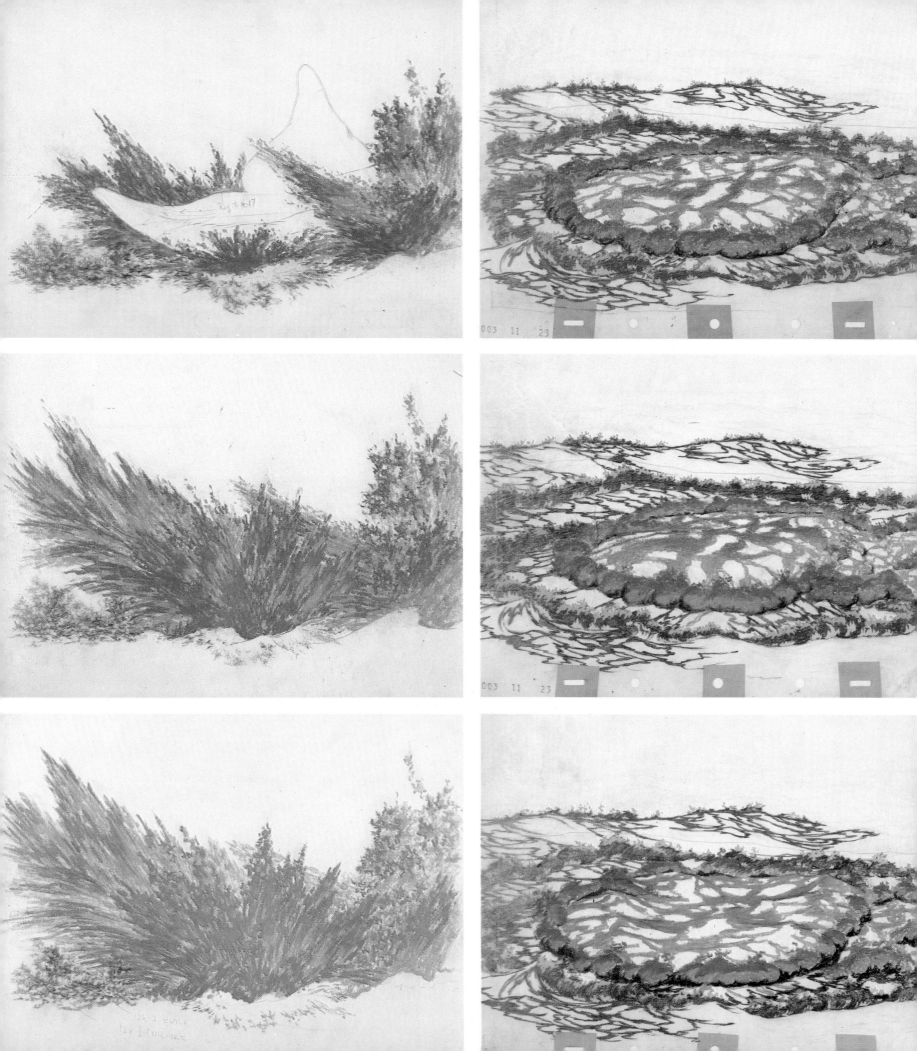

10. How to Get It on the Screen

"It's possible to do darn near anything if we figure out certain definite things. . . .
We can do anything we think of with this."
                                                                          Walt Disney

Shortly after *The Rescuers* was released in 1977, a friend remarked, "I love those characters! I think they are probably the greatest Disney has ever done." Undeniably the animation of the characters is what attracts an audience, but many other elements play a vital role in a successful picture: the colors, the beauty, the visual effects, the locales, and the music. The creation of our fantasy worlds took as much dedication and knowledge in the other departments as it did in the animation, and it occupied much of Walt's interest as well.

When he sat in those first meetings looking at the glorious color sketches from the stylist or the inspirational artist, an image was forming in his mind, a total concept of what this picture could become—how all the parts would fit together, how it would look, how it would sound, and how it would make people feel. It was a slowly developing concept, but all the parts were closely related right from the start.

He began to see a place that was real, inhabited by characters that were real, whether they were dwarfs living in a land of magic, or a wooden puppet being chased by a monstrous whale, or tiny fairies spreading drops of dew at night. In his imagination it was all coming to life—mythical, but believable. This was not a dull, humdrum type of reality but one that sprang from dreams: a land where one could feel at home, yet where everything was fresh and new and different. To achieve this on the screen, great attention has to be given to the locales—the size of the furniture, the props, the trees, the animals, the shadows they cast, the air they breathed, the clouds that floated over them, the rain—it all had to be right, just what you would find in such a place.

The inspirational sketches often had shown much of this, but they were only a handful of still drawings, usually done in a medium unsuited to production work. One question always had to be faced, "How do you get it on the screen?" This major question broke down into a myriad of little ones: how can we get that soft

Fantasia

◁ Pinocchio—*water action studied in the Effects Department.*

Soft edges and delicate shading were a challenge to animators only recently expert in line drawing. Getting the same effect on the screen was the problem of Special Effects technicians who constantly were asked to achieve the impossible.

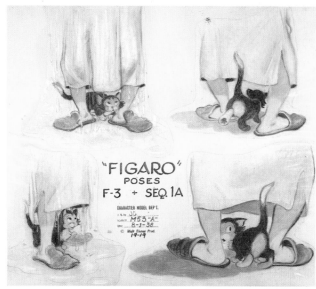

"FIGARO" POSES F-3 + SEQ. 1A

Albert Hurter made drawings of the dwarfs in a group, using shadows to define the forms and add clarity to the arrangement.

shadows were shown on the walls, adding to the spooky effect, but Walt saw more than that. When the dwarfs were grouped together there was not a flat row of seven cartoon characters, it was more of a painting, with the figures in the foreground in darker colors, giving interest and definition to the group. He wondered if his staff could do something like that. He wondered if the men would get fresh ideas on lighting in general if they actually could see a replica of the dwarfs' home.

Albert Hurter, the sketch artist whose imaginative drawings inspired the style and appearance of many Silly Symphonies, had earlier been assigned the job of drawing all the nooks and crannies of this special house. His Swiss heritage and keen powers of observation made him ideally suited for capturing the storybook charm of a cottage that dwarfs might have built, and now he had so many drawings of the stairs, the beds, the windows, the fireplace, and even the kitchen sink, that the whole structure almost could be visualized.

Walt said, "Someone could probably build a model of that house just from these drawings. Y'know, that model we had of the old mill was a big help to everybody in visualizing that picture, and in planning the scenes and camera angles. Let's get Ken Anderson in here." Ken already had been transferred from animation to layout because of his architectural knowledge, and now his formal training would be put to further use. Walt asked him to build the model on a scale of one inch to the foot, interpreting Albert's inspiring sketches into real shapes and distances. With Walt's enthusiasm and curiosity clearing the way, the dwarfs' cottage soon emerged as a reality, complete with furniture and props.

Everyone crowded around to see how it looked all

edge?; how can that brilliance of color be attained?; how can we get that elusive feeling of glowing light everywhere?; how can that overall effect be captured in our crude medium?

While the background man thought mainly of color and the layout man of drawing, Walt was always thinking of a different approach that might open up something entirely new. At the start of *Snow White*, he studied the first drawings of the dwarfs searching through their house for the unknown intruder. Great

together, fascinated by the relationships that were now so evident. A few excited moments later, Walt had another idea. Why not take Margie Bell (who had been hired to do the live action of Snow White herself) and shoot film of her on the stage, pretending to come through a door, entering the room, looking about in wonder, seeing a small chair and running over to sit on it? This could all be done with the measurements of the model of the cottage blown up to full size. Then on another reel of film, we could shoot the model house, matching the same camera moves—only this time in miniature measurements. This film would be printed on washoff relief cels (a newly discovered photographic process for printing directly onto the cels) and later combined with the film of the girl. If the distances were measured accurately, it would appear that Margie was inside the dwarfs' house!

It nearly worked. Forty years later, TV cameras using video tape were regularly combining the action of full-size actors on one camera with a miniature set on another, but in 1935 there were too many problems for the idea to be practical. For one thing, the cels were nitrate and the developing chemicals caused an unpredictable amount of shrinkage on each picture. With no consistency from one to the next, the quality of the whole process was in constant jeopardy. Walt continued to search for a way to make backgrounds three-dimensional, even having them animated in changing perspective on several pictures. While this gave startling effects for individual scenes, it further separated the flat characters on the cels from the rounded forms in the background by contrasting the two different techniques.

The model of the cottage was far from wasted since it was used extensively by both the story sketch men and the layout men to determine what they should show when presenting any piece of business. The story people had the job of making the house seem real through the activities going on, and the layout and background personnel had the responsibility of making those suggestions work in a practical way. They cut out little figures that would throw shadows on the walls, then shifted the lights for a variety of effects; they created pictures that had a new authority, for this was no longer a make-believe house—it was there before them in a very real state.

The work of the layout men reflected this stimulation in everything from the design of the specific scenes to the presentation of the whole sequence. More effective camera angles, interesting groupings of the characters, use of perspective to give dimension, types of scenes to build the mood—all were handled so skillfully that the spectators neither noticed nor wondered. They were completely absorbed in what was happening on the screen.

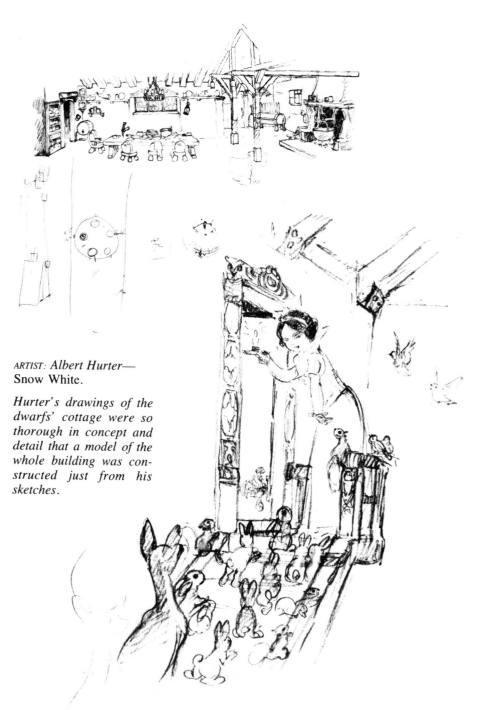

ARTIST: *Albert Hurter*— Snow White.

Hurter's drawings of the dwarfs' cottage were so thorough in concept and detail that a model of the whole building was constructed just from his sketches.

245

Four Styles of Background Painting

PAINTER: *Walt Peregoy—* 101 Dalmatians.

1. The painting technique for 101 Dalmatians: *flat areas of color to match the handling of the flat values on the characters, with all the details and drawing left in line on a covering cel. (On the left, the painting without the lines; on the right, the completed background.) This idea, pioneered by Ken Anderson, made a perfect wedding of characters and background.*

PAINTER: *Claude Coats—* Lady and the Tramp.

2. For Lady and the Tramp: *romanticized handling of nostalgic sets, with soft edges and full painting. In this type of background, plain areas must be left for the character's actions to avoid conflict with the background detail.*

246

PAINTER: *Sam Armstrong—* Snow White.

3. For Snow White: *the delicate watercolor techniques popular in book illustrations of fairy tales. Shadows, tints, and special colors were needed, scene by scene, to help the characters fit into this world.*

PAINTER: *Eyvind Earle—* Sleeping Beauty.

4. For Sleeping Beauty: *intricate design and a mosaic of close values in carefully controlled gradations. Ordinarily, a character would be completely lost in so much activity in forms and colors, but the cel of Briar Rose placed at the right shows that these characters stood out because of the bold simplicity of their design.*

Backgrounds

The background painters were experimenting, too, trying to capture in water color or tempera[1] (mediums easy to change if necessary) the same effect the stylist had achieved with chalk or inks or some special build up of paints. Taking the layout suggestions as scenes that actually would be in the picture, and surrounding himself with the original sketches that Walt had liked, the background painter searched for ways to duplicate an elusive effect.

These painters are not the same as easel painters, even though they share many of the same talents. The background painter must know color very well, possess a good sense of design, know how to pull a picture together, and be able to handle his medium extremely well. He may even have some reputation as a painter of landscapes or abstractions, but here at the studio he has a very special assignment. He must stage the character and support the action. That comes before anything else. His work may be dramatic, startling, powerful, or thrilling, but it must still be only a background for the action.

There should be nothing behind the animated figures that distracts in any way. Too much detail, busy shapes, eye-catching forms are all confusing; too much color, too much dark and light pattern, colors that conflict with the figures are all disturbing. The background artist is asked to paint a woodland glade, but not to have any trees or bushes in the middle where the

characters will be working. He is told also to keep the handling very simple on the left side because a horse will be standing there, not moving much but still occupying the space. And the grass at the bottom cannot be harsh or realistic with individual blades, because that will draw attention away from the actors; nor can the grass be too soft and fuzzy either, or it will appear that the characters are standing in a cloud. There must be a solid plane for their feet to match, and it must be green because it is grass, but it cannot look like grass or be a major part of the design. The areas where the painter *can* show the leaves and branches and the beauty of this romantic spot are along the top, down the right side, and in a tiny patch over on the left beneath the horse's belly. It is not easy.

If the background has been designed around the characters and the action in the first place, this may be all that is needed to give a great effect. Subtle tones (close in value) behind the figures and along the "path of action" can suggest much while actually showing very little. This is possible to do, but a definite challenge.

Another way to keep the character completely clear at all times is to hold down all the elements in the background so that they frame the actor as if he were spotlighted, or working in a "pool of light." This will not give the excitement found in a strong design, but it will insure that the animation reads well throughout the scene.

The background man is particularly frustrated by

ARTIST: *Al Dempster*—
The Jungle Book

Pictorial scenes or establishing shots require the background to dominate the characters since the scenic picture is more important than the action. The animator must make his drawing fit the background. The preliminary sketch on the left established the color and treatment for the final painting, right.

close-ups. There may be a long shot with a busy brick wall behind the figures or a shelf full of toys, and on the next scene a close-up of the character. The painter thinks, "Ah! Now I can show all the texture and the bumps and scratches on these objects." There is really no need to keep the same background on such a cut, and the painter will ruin the scene if he tries. A plain colored card would be far better, or just the faintest suggestion of the things seen in the long shot. Actually, a live-action camera moving in this way probably would have the background out of focus, and that would be the easiest solution.

ARTIST:
W. Richard Anthony—
Bambi.

In Bambi, *the background painter kept the busy forest details from conflicting visually with the animals by, first, making his painting reflect the overall mood rather than show blades of grass: second, keeping a "path of action" clear of any extra drawing; and, third, adding a feeling of light where the characters were working.*

A very effective scene in *The Jungle Book* showed the panther sitting on a tree limb with only the luminous mist of the tropical night behind him. In the foreground was a small cluster of leaves and a flower drawn very crisply, but with just enough individuality to give the scene realism, beauty, and character. It took years of experience to know that this would be best, but, literally, only minutes to paint.

Painting backgrounds is a challenging and complicated assignment, but one that offers vast opportunities to the artist. Successfully done, the backgrounds contribute much to the audience's enjoyment and, like music, can create a depth of feeling in the mood and enhance the dramatic quality of the whole film. Walt felt this was so important that he asked the background men to try several different paintings of the key scenes with a variety of colors and techniques to stimulate their imaginations and help them find the best approach. These were shot in color and judged from the film so the artist could find the most successful handling before facing the restrictions of supporting the animation.

The background painter works closely with the layout

This extremely simple background in The Jungle Book *gave just enough detail to support the idea of the scene without conflicting with either the character or the mood.*

ARTIST: Al Dempster— The Jungle Book.

A background is painted three different ways as the artist searches for the most effective appearance for the desolate, black pool where the young Mowgli, friendless and miserable, will meet the vultures.

man, from the early experiments that develop the color key and style to the design of the effects animation that will surround the characters with all manner of natural forces. But adapting the style and the color on a flat piece of paper is only part of the problem. There is still the matter of getting it to look right in the finished film on the screen.

Effects Department

The effects animator is a special kind of artist: he has a curiosity about the way things work, a feel for the mechanical, and usually sees great beauty in the patterns of nature. Some effects animators have been fascinated with pure realism and have tried doggedly to duplicate it, while others have created spirit in the movement of water and lava, drama in fires and storms, and astonishing loveliness in the handling of falling leaves and snow. During the making of *Snow White*, the Effects Animation Department grew to a total of fifty-six men and women, many proficient in special techniques, all amazingly patient as they drew endless tiny shapes.

Originally, character animators had done all of the effects in their own scenes: rain, smoke, shadows, tears, clouds, dust, speed lines—even throbbing lines to represent pain and question marks to show confusion. But Walt felt that these all lacked style and asked his men to be more observant and to draw more accurately. They observed, and as soon as someone noted that the image of a real object moving fast is blurred on film, every animator tried to find his own way of drawing a blurred image in cartoon terms. In attempting to outdo each other, these animators created shapes that became designs in themselves, dominating the scenes, and the inkers were puzzled as to whether these concoctions should be traced in ink, painted on top of the cel, drybrushed, or done in different colors.

A favorite device for portraying an arm or a leg moving very fast was to draw a series of after images following along. Unfortunately, this always looked more like spaghetti trailing the limb than a true blurred image. Carleton (Jack) Boyd, who later became head of the Effects Department, still laughs about those days. "Four feet of wet spaghetti! It looked awful—but

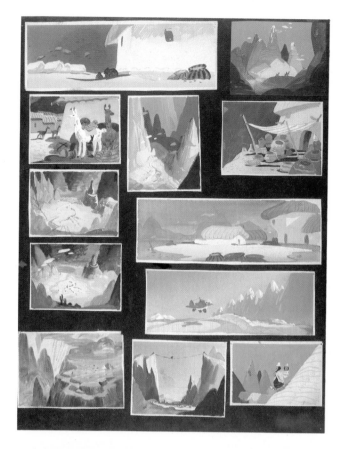

ARTIST: *Art Riley*— *"Little Pedro"* and *"Lake Titicaca."*

The little airplane on his first mail route over the Andes and Donald Duck as a tourist in Bolivia called for some new ideas in color and design. The background painter suggested a fresh and appealing style in these experimental sketches for Saludos Amigos.

ARTIST: *Ralph Hulett*— Chantecler.

The talented painter can make ordinary scenes interesting through striking color relationships. Thousands of beautiful paintings and drawings were made for this proposed feature before Walt decided it was not right for us.

251

we were trying to find out how to do it. It took a lot of mistakes before you found out what you could do.'' This type of personal expression came to an abrupt end when Walt eventually set up the Effects Department to standardize the procedures, unify the appearance, and control the quality.

With new importance given to what always had been secondary animation, the men selected for the new department seldom could hold themselves down to a supportive role. Even though they were aware that their work should be subordinate to the main action of the scene, the enthusiasm that led to the experimenting also swept away care and much of their judgment. Again, it was Jack Boyd who shook his head and laughed as he thought back on a scene he had once done. ''I had just discovered water! I was a star! You guys did a wonderful job on the character animation, and I came along with a splash and destroyed you!''

Then with a sigh, ''Now I shudder to think of that stuff.''

Shadows were another problem. These had been done in a very simple way from the earliest days because they anchored the figure to the ground. Without some kind of contact with the background, the characters seemed to float around, walking on air, no matter how much weight had been animated into their movements. Just a circular shape painted around their feet in an unobtrusive grey defined where they were standing, and as they walked about or jumped it continued to show just where they were. Being opaque it covered anything on the background that it passed over, unless it had been carefully animated to fit the shape it encountered. Too often an easier solution was to ask the background man simply to paint out the offending object and leave a barren path in its place.

As the quality of the pictures approached that of the better book illustrations, this crude shadow was replaced by one done with a transparent paint that gave a much more realistic appearance. Since this darkened the background without obliterating any of the detail, the spectator could now see every rock and pebble right through the shadow, and the background painters became much happier. Unfortunately this wonder paint dried very quickly, leaving streaks and puddles that varied in density from cel to cel, causing the shadow to look quite agitated on the screen as it wiggled and jittered.

When the paint was very cold it was somewhat easier to use, and if it were confined to small areas that the ''girls'' could paint quickly and deftly, a satisfactory result could be obtained. So the painters worked close to the refrigerator and moved fast, but the shadow was still only one shade and there was no control possible if a slight variation was desired. More than that, it was impossible to paint large areas on the cels and keep any consistency in the quality.

A far better result came from painting the shadow completely black, but photographing it at only partial exposure. This way, there was complete control. The shadow would be light when it was shot at thirty percent exposure or very dark when shot at seventy percent, and between the two almost any shade could be obtained, enriching the appearance of the scene in both design and color, since the shadow darkened the existing color without disturbing the harmony of the relationships.

This was just what was needed to make the group of dwarfs match the quality of those first sketches. A mask over part of the scene changed the values on the figures whenever they entered that area, without requiring any new painting, or, especially, a whole new set of colors. Now, the dark and light patterns of the scenes could be created in a very simple way, but in a way that added depth and luminosity to an amazing degree. The shadows that the dwarfs cast on the walls contained rich, subtle colors that were not on anyone's palette, adding to the enchanted feeling of the whole cottage. At the same time, controlling the shades on the figures in the group prevented them from looking like a police lineup.

These double-exposed shadows required that the scene be photographed twice, once with them and once without, which was not only a headache for the cameraman but doubled the expense of his efforts. Not too much later he would be shooting scenes ten and twelve times for special effects, so the problems of a second pass became minimal. However, in the lean years, the double-exposed shadows were among the first things to be eliminated in the drive to cut expenses.

More dramatic background painting with very careful matching to the character achieved many of the same results, or created a surface so dark or textured that it would not show a shadow. In *The Rescuers*, the sequence of the mice and the girl down in the cave with only a tiny lantern would have been an ideal place for shadows to augment the suspense and the drama of the situation, but since the sequence was frightening enough the way it was the decision was

ANIMATOR: *Cy Young—*
"Nutcracker Suite,"
Fantasia.

Only an extremely sensitive artist could have animated this sensuous, white blossom that became a twirling ballerina.

made to leave off the shadows and paint the walls dark and wet instead. The shoes and feet of the characters were painted dark also, so they would be almost a part of the background, giving the feeling that they were already in shadow.

Through the early thirties, the entire Effects Department consisted of only two men: Ugo D'Orsi, a straightforward, stubborn, and dedicated Italian, and Cy Young, a quiet and sensitive but equally stubborn Chinese, who loved to play the bass fiddle as a hobby. Both spoke with such accents that most of the staff had difficulty understanding what they were saying, and communication between the two was almost impossible, especially when tempers flared. Since they did most of the careful work themselves, they needed only a single assistant between them, and a major part of his job was to act as interpreter, diplomatic emissary, and peacemaker. Still, few animators have surpassed the delightful results that these two men slowly and delicately achieved with their innate sense of design in motion.

Who can ever forget the lovely white blossom-ballerina in *Fantasia* floating gracefully to a caressing landing on the surface of the water, only to be reborn and rise up inverted, swirling and spinning as she danced off with her colorful companions? That was Cy Young at his best. Rarely could others create such poetry and sensuality in a mere blossom's falling into a pond.

Ugo showed more intensity and force in his work, but was equally sensitive to the total design. Typical of his drawings were the crashing waves that heeded Mickey's commands in the dream sequence of "The Sorcerer's Apprentice." The director of the picture commented on "the amazing patience and tenacity [Ugo] displayed in doing the filigree waves and foam . . . he 'pioneered' those . . . patterns practically out of his imagination, long before the help of research photography."[2]

Both Cy and Ugo were determined to get realism into their work and studied constantly to increase their understanding. One day they were discussing a scene involving a witch's kettle bubbling over a fire. As

ANIMATOR: *Ugo D'Orsi—* *"Sorcerer's Apprentice,"* Fantasia.

A special talent turns a tedious "effects" scene of the crashing wave into a memorable work of art.

drawn on the layout it was an old pot, rusty and partially covered with soot from years of cooking. Cy felt that light from the flames would be reflected evenly over the whole pot; Ugo claimed that the light would be only on the portions not covered by the soot, since soot has no reflective power. Each man was adamant, and, since there was only one way of proving who was right, a fire was built in an empty film can in the middle of the floor, with the shade from a goose-neck lamp inverted over it as the pot. Soon the flames were dancing merrily.

While everyone else was screaming, "Put that fire out!" the discussion grew into an argument. The whole surface of the lampshade was indeed bathed in glowing light as the flames enveloped it, but there was no soot on it—as yet. People were running about, and excited protests were now coming from far down the hall, but still the two animators fanned the flames earnestly— their faces right down at the floor—and studied the curved bottom of the shade.

The linoleum had begun to curl on the floor before a brigade of Dixie cups could be organized to douse the flames and send the frustrated effects animators back to their desks—with the point still unproved. Maybe it was inconsequential anyway and hardly worth considering, but that intensity of feeling and the driving desire for knowledge were typical of their approach to assignments.

By 1935, new men were coming into the Effects

Department in a steady stream, and most of them were full of ideas. One of these was Josh Meador, a newcomer with an unusual combination of talents. Young and individualistic, Josh was an excellent draftsman, painter, designer, and he possessed great technical ability as well. By the end of *Pinocchio* in 1939, he had taken over the department, and for *Fantasia*, only a year later, he had well over a hundred men and women turning out the most impressive effects animation ever seen. One of them said, "Josh was continually shooting live action and experimenting with the stuff—water and smoke and all those things. He was really very thorough with his research work. He didn't just sit down and animate water, he went out and shot some water, then took it home and studied it. In those days you did that—you went home and practiced drawing."[3]

Some things just could not be drawn in pencil lines: wind, fog, drizzling mist, a thick cloud of dust, and almost all kinds of snow. Blaine Gibson, animator and sculptor, who was in the Effects Department for nearly ten years said, "It is quite a challenge to do something like that; when you put a line around something, even though you only give it a partial exposure, right away it's something that's different than what it is!" That fact did not stop Josh.

The next storm, he was out with his cameras shooting the marvels of nature against a black background, and before that winter was over he had a whole library of

Three leaders of the Effects Department study bubbling mud in a Studio vat. From left, Jack Boyd, Josh Meador, and Dan Mac-Manus.

Inspirational sketch—*"Sorcerer's Apprentice,"* Fantasia.

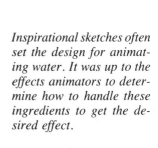

Inspirational sketches often set the design for animating water. It was up to the effects animators to determine how to handle these ingredients to get the desired effect.

ANIMATOR: *Josh Meador*—Alice in Wonderland.

The story sketch of Alice floating in the bottle shows a very simple design for the water effect, but in the actual scene this was not enough. The sea was so vast, it was impossible to tell how large Alice was or how far away she might be. The addition of large bubbles gave the needed scale to keep her very small.

ANIMATOR: *Dan MacManus* —Bambi.

Drawings for the splash of a single raindrop in the passing storm in Bambi *reflect study and observation by the effects animator.*

ANIMATOR: *Paul Kossoff—* "*Rite of Spring,*" Fantasia.

Imagination in both design and movement was needed for this scene of lava flowing down the primordial landscape.

ARTIST: *Jules Engel—* "*Rite of Spring,*" Fantasia

The "Rite of Spring" in Fantasia *called for mist, rain, smoke, wind, water, falling rocks, fire, and flowing lava. Just four years earlier, none of these effects could have been animated convincingly.*

ANIMATOR: *Ed Aardal—* "*Rite of Spring,*" Fantasia.

There was no way to study volcanic eruptions in prehistoric times, but this outstanding scene was created from inspirational sketches and suggestions of raw power in Stravinsky's music.

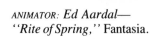

256

rain: soft rain, hard rain, heavy rain, blowing rain, swirling rain, drizzling rain. These were printed onto special papers, so they could be combined with the animated rain as needed to get any effect wanted. Josh had been told, "When I look at rain, I don't see a lot of black lines around every drop. Sometimes I don't even see the drops, just streaks of light, and little splashes on the ground." The animator's drawings by themselves could not give this illusion, but by combining them with photography of real rain, it was possible even to capture the mood of the rain. There was dreary, weeping rain for the sad sequence in *Snow White* when her friends wept at her death; there was the fury of driving, stormy, excited rain shortly before, as the dwarfs

chased the witch up the rocks; and after she had fallen, the steady, drenching, heavy rain that seemed to wash the evil memories away. A few years later, a whole sequence of effects animation depicting a summer storm was a high-point of entertainment in *Bambi*. The effects had become an integral part of the film, contributing drama and excitement and mood, as well as the vital element of making everything so believable.

Of all the natural elements that had to be drawn in pencil lines without shading, water was the most difficult. The combination of transparency, elasticity, weight, mobility, and consistency, together with the many moods associated with bodies of water, made it impossible to handle realistically. It had to be repre-

Excellent effects animation of water and foam makes this scene from Pinocchio *exciting and convincing. The relative size of everything from monstrous whale to tiny figures on the raft gives a startling scale to this imaginative set-up.*

257

sented in a design the audience could accept without question. As one animator said, "You had to draw some kind of effect that would give the impression of water without costing a fortune," yet what could anyone draw in line that would look like water? "You weren't just drawing the crest of a wave, you were moving the highlights and shadows and all the color indications that were so important to the animation."[4]

If it was a large body of water, the animator had to think in terms of the mass, the perspective, the depth, the movement of it, all going back into space. And he had to be careful that he did not have everything moving the same amount and at the same speed, which would give a type of rhythm to the action that would kill any feeling of realism. Ed Aardal was one of those who had a special affinity for large water action, which he attributed to his year spent on a fishing boat off Alaska. "When you lived all that stuff," he commented, "you kind of memorize it—you got the feel of it."

One animator admitted that he had tried to fake his handling of the water in a scene instead of taking the time and effort to study real water and make it right. The work was criticized immediately, and a more experienced man was called in to take it over. Nothing but the highest quality was accepted, and although water was the most difficult effect to do, and the most expensive, most of the men in the department felt that the audience remembered impressive scenes of good water animation longer than any other effect.

It was not only a matter of representing nature—each film had its own design concept, and the drawing of the effects had to comply. Someone would try many different ways of depicting whatever it might be—water, smoke, frost, or sheen—searching for a way of drawing that was compatible with the style but still allowed the necessary freedom of movement. He would try complicated groupings of colors and patches, highlights and sparkles, drybrush, airbrush, any effect that pictorially would be convincing and exciting. During the period that Josh Meador was in charge of the department, he was a source of many suggestions, since he had such a feel for design and form and color.

The experimental sketches were shown to the director and his crew, and decisions were made as to which design was best for this particular job. Often a few color tests were shot to be sure of the results before embarking on the expense of animating an elaborate concoction. Josh would break down the elements of his sketch, figuring what the animators would do, what should be added by the inkers and painters, and what would be done by the cameraman with exposures and special lenses. It was often difficult for the animator to visualize how his limited portion could possibly produce the exciting drama that had been described.

Walt had set the standard, and that way of doing things persists to this day: it must be the very best you can do; and, if properly prodded, you can always do far better than you think you can. During the making of *Pinocchio*, the animators were experimenting with various ways of handling bubbles, trying to get something on the screen that looked wet and shiny. They carefully animated the circular forms, keeping them rubbery and fragile, with changing shapes; but most of their effort went into the choice of inks, of colors, highlights, and the techniques that would make these circles look like real bubbles. The animators finally shot an assortment of experiments in color and ran them for Walt so he could choose what he wanted. He surprised them all by commenting not on the lines and colors, but the quality of the animation. "I like these —the others look too heavy. The bubbles should be full of air." Who else would even notice if an animated bubble looked heavy?

Bubbles created an unusual chorus as each reflection added another voice to Cinderella's song. Enormous technical problems were combined with the normal difficulties of animating a screenful of bubbles to achieve this effect.

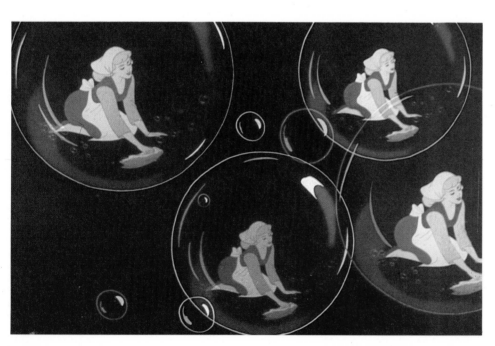

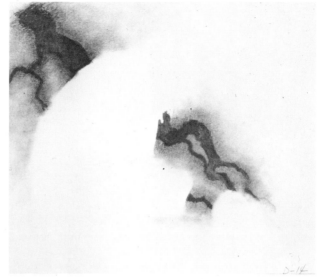

ANIMATOR: *Norm Ferguson*
—Alpine Climbers.

Pluto has been rescued from a snowdrift by a St. Bernard with a brandy cask. Warmed through, Pluto's run is now interrupted by a violent hiccup.
STARTS ON PAGE 299

The story sketch below of the threatening Tyrannosaurus Rex in ''Rite of Spring'' suggests forked lightning as a backdrop.

ANIMATOR:

Carleton (Jack) Boyd—''Rite of Spring,'' Fantasia

Drawings from the scene as animated show how the spectacular flashing effect was achieved. Alternate frames of black and white double-exposed over the drawings gave the shimmering, dazzling look of real lightning.

The lightning flash during the April shower sequence of Bambi *created a special X-ray effect.*

For "Night on Bald Mountain," Fantasia, a strong design was needed to make the smoke and flames conform to the style of the whole film. The action itself was still realistic and very convincing. A frame from the final film shows how effective the scene became with all parts fitting the total concept.

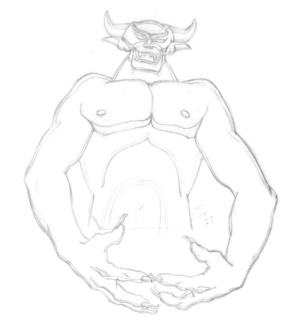

Special Effects

Pinocchio is swimming madly to escape the powerful charge of Monstro the whale. He is surrounded by fish, all dashing for their lives. He finally breaks to the surface and apparent freedom, but the monstrous form rises from the depths, and his huge jaws close with a heavy sound on all who had tried to elude him. It is an exciting moment—the audience should feel the tension, the suspense, the desperation of the characters trying to escape.

The animation of Pinocchio is good and does exactly what is needed for those scenes. The fish are well animated and the effects of bubbles and streaks and speedlines all give the impression of great effort and speed. But something more is needed. It does not have that rich look of a first-class illustration. Is there any way to get a watery effect here? After all, Pinocchio is

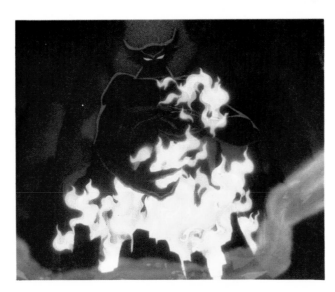

way down there and ought to look different. And what about Monstro? How can we make him look huge? Of course we need the other characters to be much smaller to give the proper scale, but how about some shading on the whale? One continuous tone over his entire bulk will never give the illusion of volume. What will take it out of the thin, flat world of the line drawing, and get it into the depth and dimensions of the shaded drawing and the painting?

To get the watery effect, a panel of glass was ground with the same type of ripple found in low-grade window glass. When this panel was placed over the cels under the camera and pulled slowly through the scene, the images beneath it writhed and wiggled just as objects do when reflected in a lake or especially when seen under water.

For the tiny figures in long shots (figures too small to be drawn accurately or painted), washoff relief cels could be used since this permitted normal-size characters to be reduced to very small size, or blown up large, as well as repositioned or even made into multiple prints.

To get the shading on Monstro, someone devised a "frosted" cel treated to create a tooth on the surface that would take pencil, pastel, chalk or crayon, with smear or smudge or careful shading. Once the drawing was completed in full color—it was really more of a textured painting—a special procedure cleared the cel to its normal transparency with the artist's original work ready to go under the camera. Now artists could work in the colors they wanted and the shading they needed to explore new dimensions in visual effects.

The men who solved these problems were the skilled craftsmen of diverse backgrounds who had been thrown together in the catchall department, Special Effects. Walt always had been skeptical of theory and philosophy, preferring to have practical artisans around him who could get right down to work with their hands. For some reason, he had a distrust of engineers as men who designed primarily for themselves without regard for the intended use of the product and he refused to have anyone on the staff with the title, "Engineer."

There were only three categories for a technician: camera, sound, or special effects. Bill McFadden had a degree in aeronautical engineering, which had nothing to do with either camera or sound, so obviously he

EFFECTS ANIMATOR:
George Rowley—
Pinocchio.

Small flames generally have a mild, undulating pattern, back and forth, combined with a slight up and down action.

Large flames have an elaborate pattern of dancing shapes, curls, parts breaking off and carried up, combined with violent activity within the shapes.

The magnitude of the forest fire in Bambi *was conveyed best by moving a distortion glass over a dramatic painting. A separate glass was used for reflections in the water.*

261

Different distortion glasses were used to give a watery feeling at the end of the spring storm in Bambi. *At first, there was only a light distortion as the sunset reflects in the pool.*

When water droplets disrupt the image, a heavier distortion is used. (The ripple rings were painted in lacquer on the cels, with no inked outline.)

The distant details that make this scene so believable were achieved by using wash-off cels to "blow down" the drawings and frosted cels to add texture to large surfaces.

Frosted cels have a rough surface on one side that will take pencil or crayon with shading and texture. Later, the cel is "cleared" so it can go directly under the camera. Effects animator Jane Fowler Boyd checks her drawing of flames.

had to be in special effects, along with the model makers, theatrical craftsmen, painters, machinists, carpenters, and the other individuals trained in the profession that was never mentioned: engineering. The men in this conglomerate never knew what they would be doing next or how it might relate either to their training or the last job they had just completed. They might be asked to find a way to photograph an amoeba, or build a whole new camera, or a piece of furniture, design a building, or string beads on black threads to represent stars in the firmament. Few people at the studio knew who these men were or what they did, but everyone saw that amazing scenes were appearing on the screen. As one employee said, "You can't believe how many people it takes to do something like this."

Bill Garity, an expert on camera lenses, was nominal head of the department, but Walt worked with each man on an individual basis, asking questions more than assigning jobs. As one of them said, "The two questions Walt asked most were, 'Can you do it?' and 'What can you do here?'" They were called into sweatboxes and story meetings and often just sat around listening, getting the feel of what Walt was after. Then

262

The Ingredients of a Scene

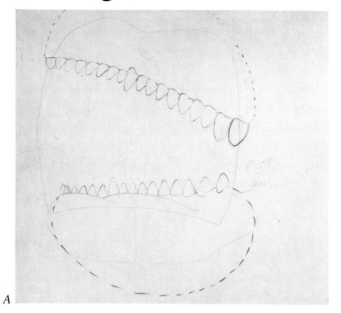

A

B

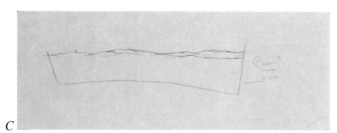

C

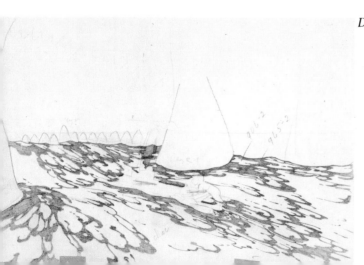

D

E

F

G

H

Geppetto and Pinocchio try to push their raft into the ocean when Monstro the whale opens his mouth to sneeze. The scene lasts barely four seconds on the screen and shows the amazing concept of what made a good-looking picture for this place in the film. The separate parts are:

A. Monstro's teeth and upper jaw.
B. Seagulls in distance.
C. Wave action on distant ocean.
D. Water running into mouth.
E. The raft.
F. Water splashes over the teeth, raft, and characters.
G. Pinocchio and Geppetto pushing the raft.
H. The kitten Figaro.

Not shown: double-exposed smoke filled the top half of the scene, from the fire that Pinocchio started.

The "draft" of the picture records each scene by number, description, and footage, as well as who animated it. Sequence No. 10.7 of Pinocchio shows Scene 1 as 6 feet 4 frames and drawn by six animators.

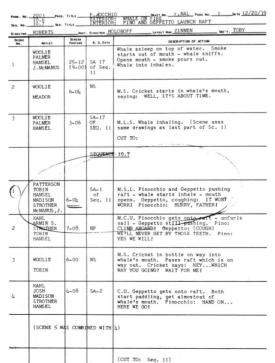

Prod. No. 2001 Prod. Title PINOCCHIO Draft No. FINAL Page No. 1 Date 12/20/39
Seq. No. 10.9 Seq. Title EXTERIOR: WHALE ON FIRE / INTERIOR: PINO AND GEPPETTO LAUNCH RAFT
Director ROBERTS Asst. Director HOLOBOFF Layout Man ZINNEN Sec'y TOBY

SCENE NO.	ARTIST	SCREEN FOOTAGE	B.G. DATA	DESCRIPTION OF ACTION
1	WOOLIE PALMER HAMSEL J. McMANUS	25-12 (9-00)	SA 17 of Seq. 11	Whale asleep on top of water. Smoke starts out of mouth - whale sniffs. Opens mouth - smoke pours out. Whale into inhales.
2	WOOLIE MEADOR	6-04	NS	M.S. Cricket starts in whale's mouth, saying: WELL, IT'S ABOUT TIME.
3	WOOLIE PALMER HAMSEL	3-06	SA-17 OF SEQ. 11	M.L.S. Whale inhaling. (Scene uses same drawings as last part of Sc. 1) CUT TO:
				SEQUENCE 10.7
(1)	PATTERSON TOBIN HAMSEL MADISON STROTHER McMANUS, J.	6-04	SA-1 of Seq. 11	M.S.L. Pinocchio and Geppetto pushing raft - whale starts inhale - mouth opens. Geppetto, coughing: IT WONT WORK! Pinocchio: HURRY, FATHER!
2	KAHL ARMIN S. STROTHER TOBIN HAMSEL	7-08	NP	M.C.U. Pinocchio gets onto raft - unfurls sail - Geppetto still pushing. Pino: CLIMB ABOARD! Geppetto: (COUGH) WE'LL NEVER GET BY THOSE TEETH. Pino: YES WE WILL!
3	WOOLIE TOBIN	6-00	NS	M.S. Cricket in bottle on way into whale's mouth. Passes raft which is on way out. Cricket says: HEY...WHICH WAY YOU GOING? WAIT FOR ME!
4	KAHL JOSH MADISON STROTHER HAMSEL	4-08	SA-2	C.U. Geppetto gets onto raft. Both start paddling, get almost out of whale's mouth. Pinocchio: HAND ON... HERE WE GO!
				(SCENE 5 WAS COMBINED WITH 4)
				(CUT TO: Seq. 11)

as the pieces of an idea started to come together, Walt would start calling in the men who might do the work, carrying it to a more advanced stage. "Hey, let's get Joe in here—and who's that little fellow who built that thing for us? You know, that guy from camera; get him in here, too. And see if you can get a musician, too; these guys will have to work together." Cameraman, carpenter, stylist, colorist, technician, artist— they formed teams as needed, with no money for expenses, no time to research, only their own inventive minds and Walt's enthusiasm to guide them.

Once they were asked to build an arrangement that could hold separate layers of artwork at varying distances from a still camera, so that the ensuing photograph would have the appearance of depth. It was built of wood and glue and tape—as Bill McFadden said, "You couldn't build anything without tape, y'know." But it worked and Walt liked the result and suddenly was talking about building another one, larger and more complicated, that might be used for shooting animation. This was more of a problem and called for engineering knowledge, but on the records it was built by Special Effects! And so the first multiplane camera was born.

Four years later the men were still working with tape and glue, but now they were creating exquisite, delicate scenes for the films. *Fantasia* was a particular challenge to their creative minds, with all of its unprecedented effects. To get wraiths rising from the graves in the first scene of "Night On Bald Mountain," they devised a method of reflecting the artwork onto a piece of bent tin, much like the mirrors in a fun house. It gave an eerie effect, but to avoid other reflections each

frame had to be a three-minute time-exposure with the room completely dark. With the time needed to make all the moves and changes before the next frame could be shot, the men barely could do 16 frames an hour. That was only one foot of film, and some of the scenes were over 20 feet long!

Sitting there in the dark, hour after hour, they could not keep from nodding, but someone in the three-man crew always managed to keep things going by singing out the hour or the footage or the next move to be made. One of them remembered after an all-night session that he had heard, "Three o'clock," and a little later, "Four o'clock," but that the next number was "Six o'clock!" What had happened to five o'clock? No one knew at first, but groggy confessions revealed that all three men had fallen asleep at the same time and slept for nearly two hours before some inner alarm awakened them.

Early in this exhausting schedule the final plans were made for shooting the last scene in the picture. It was the ending shot of the "Ave Maria" segment, which had run into several delays, putting it far down on the schedule. There had been many suggestions for the content of this crucial scene, ranging from stained glass windows to towering cloud formations that symbolized inner feelings of great magnitude. But Walt decided on a long, continuous scene, nearly 220 feet in length, that would start with an impression of the interior of a large Gothic cathedral. From there, the camera would move slowly and steadily through the dimly lit interior while a shaft of light dissolved in, cutting across the image. Then a vertical shaft of light would spread as giant doors opened on a fantasy world just

THE HORIZONTAL MULTIPLANE CRANE
LIVE ACTION CREW NECESSARY

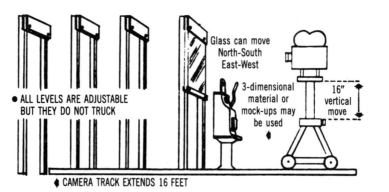

Drawing in the Layout Manual explains the procedure for reflecting images onto a bent and rippled sheet of tin for another type of distorted image.

Diagram in the Layout Manual of the horizontal camera crane devised for the final shot in Fantasia. *Amazing effects were obtained by painting large images on panels of glass and moving the camera slowly through them. Pictures taken from the "Ave Maria" section in* Fantasia *show how this looked on the screen.* ▷

at dawn, giving a spiritual feeling for the end of the picture.

The special effects men looked at each other. No camera they had could move that slowly and continuously—why, it would have to be 40 or 50 feet above the drawings. Maybe the camera could move horizontally, but even if it were put on some kind of little carriage and moved along a track, a crew could never get it in precisely the same place a second time to make the dissolves Walt mentioned. And even if they were able to calibrate the camera moves some way, the artwork would have to be on panes of glass at least three or four feet wide, and mounted on some kind of stand, and those stands would have to be moveable, too. It was out of the question, it could not be done. How would they ever control the light, what kind of room would they get, and would it not be impossible to do away with the reflections off the glass? There was just no way that this could be done, especially in the few remaining weeks before the deadline for the picture.

So Walt had the carpenters knock the seats out of the end of the sound stage (which was at least 45 feet across), shut down the recording sessions, and he told them to go ahead! A couple of cameramen, two or three carpenters, two inventors, and an artist, and the project was begun. A partition was built across the end of the sound stage, and behind it strange things began to appear. A special stand mounted on rubber wheels was built for the camera, and on the side, pointing rigidly to the floor, was a metal pointer. On a wooden rail nailed to the floor tiny numbers were marked in black and red and blue pencil, all carefully measured

from one end of the stage to the other. Set astride the camera track and the marked rail were large stands holding panes of glass with surprisingly little color painted on them. Most of the effect would be in the lighting and the camera exposures. Today it would be called a "Mickey Mouse" contrivance, but everything seemed to work, to be sturdy, and to offer the necessary control. The tape would certainly hold for one time through; as with most of the studio set-ups, this was never expected to be used again.

With barely three weeks left before the deadline and only days after those men had fallen asleep filming the spirits rising from the ground, the crew started to shoot this last scene. With everyone carefully checking and rechecking, each man made his moves as the lead cameraman read from the elaborate exposure sheet and the camera inched its way across the stage. The crew who had built the set-up stayed on to do the shooting, even the carpenters. Since they knew how it was supposed to work, it was assumed that if anything went wrong they could fix it more quickly than anyone.

On that crew was a young and eager Bob Broughton, who would contribute his talents to the Special Effects Department for another 40 years. They shot nights and they shot days, and the only time they had a break was the one night of the week Walt played badminton on the stage from 7:00 to 10:00 in the evening.

It took just over six days to shoot it all, and the men fell into bed while the film was being processed at the lab. The next day a very anxious group assembled to see how this wonder of wonders looked on film. It was beautiful! There was not a jerk or wobble in the whole thing, but there was a major difficulty. In one of those

Fantasia

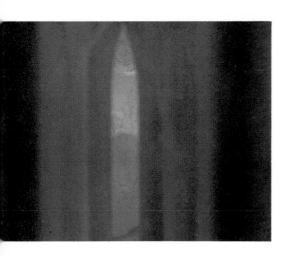

unfathomable vagaries of the human mind, someone had put the wrong lens on the camera; so in addition to the magnificent artwork, the camera had recorded the stands, the track, and even the busy workers running around during the week of shooting!

It had to be done over. The deadline was now only days away, but this was not the deadline for camera work, or for the lab, or for the answer print. This was the premiere showing of the picture in New York! No picture ever had been premiered with the last 200 feet missing. The filming had to be perfect this time. The crew shot for three days and nights, stopping for a brief rest during the badminton games—then back to the figures on the floor and the careful moves. All was going well, coffee was keeping the crew awake, and a quiet determination had settled over the whole process when suddenly, late in the evening of that third day, there was an earthquake! Not a big, shattering one, but a rolling, shaking movement that froze the men in their tracks. Rocking and vibrating before them was the line of wooden stands holding the glass panes! The men held their breath, but it was over as suddenly as it had begun. No glass was broken, nothing was off its mark, the track seemed intact and straight, but how could they be sure? If they went ahead and completed the scene and it turned out to have a jump or a jerk or a false move, it would be ruined and there would not be enough time to reshoot it before opening night. If they started all over again, they barely would have time to finish it before that important date. What if there were a delay for any reason? Was that cutting it too thin? This was a big decision—for someone else to make. The crew went home to bed.

The next morning the department heads decided it would be better to chance another earthquake, fire, or flood and go for a take they could be sure of; so once again the crew rolled the camera back to the starting mark, checked the lens, put in new film, and started one last time. Walt cancelled his badminton and barred everyone from going on that stage.

With only one day to spare, the crew finished shooting and rushed the film to the lab. There were no disasters on the stage or at the lab, and the men had done a perfect job. While they took a week's vacation, someone else jumped on a plane for New York with the precious film under his arm, arriving in the after-noon with a good four hours to spare! It was spliced onto the end of the picture and that is the way it was run night after night until a new print could be made of the whole last reel.[5]

Why did these men work so hard, so persistently, so eagerly? Why did any of us become so dedicated, so unquestioning, so determined? Was it just that we were young and that the work was exciting? Each assignment seemed impossible at the start; yet a way was found to do it, and to do it so well that the whole staff was awed by the results. The exhilaration of breaking through barriers to new frontiers was more than any of us could resist.

Orville and Wilbur Wright wrote letters home from Kitty Hawk that they were being eaten alive by the sand fleas, constantly irritated by the blowing sand that got into everything, half-frozen every night by the cold winds, straining to read their diagrams and figures with inadequate light in the evenings; yet they were so excited about what they were doing, so stimulated by the tiny successes of each day that they felt like kids again and could hardly wait for the light of dawn that would bring them new opportunities.[6] Possibly not every inventor has the chance to experience this sensation, for often inspiration ends up in perspiration and compromise and drudgery. Fortunate are those who have known the exhilaration of the creative process.

With the beginning of the second World War, all of this came to an end. Our highly trained and talented men were drawn into the war effort where their special skills were more urgently needed. Only a couple of the younger men returned to the fabled Special Effects Department, but the work was different. Economics was calling for experimentation, but in efficient methods rather than in new fields.

By that time, Ub Iwerks had returned with his own type of creative invention. It had been barely a dozen years since he was known as the greatest animator in the world, yet now he had given up drawing to concentrate on his inventions, finding more productive processes, building new devices, creating artistic effects. Part of his genius was his ability to go directly to the heart of the problem when something was not working. Where others tried to fix the failing part, Ub instinctively went right to the thing causing the problem. Where others looked for a way to get the job

done, Ub found a way to make it into something better. He understood cameras, projectors, lenses, cels, paint, and film, yet he also understood the artist's difficulties, the ingredients of a quality product, and, most of all, Walt's dreams.

The Special Effects Department became more sophisticated, replacing haphazard tactics with orderly procedures. Instead of the contraptions built with tape in such a casual manner, the new devices were built to work and to last. A machine shop was assembled to make precision instruments and intricate mechanisms that would assure repeated quality in the visual effects. The men in the department became some of the most highly skilled in Hollywood and occasionally were lent out to other studios when very special effects were needed.

The unforeseen and enormous problems of Disneyland and Walt Disney World drew Ub away from the film work, and Eustace Lycett took over the department. Eustace was one of the "kids" from the earliest days, and together with Art Cruickshank and the rest of the crew could handle any problem tossed to them. Seasoned, experienced, creative, their skills were needed more often on the live action pictures than on the carefully budgeted animation features. For *The Black Hole*, they had to think up the answers before anyone was quite aware there would be a problem. They knew there would have to be a device that could hold a model spaceship and move it in every possible manner. In addition, they would have to have a camera on a mount that could make any move to match, and the whole would have to be coordinated by some mechanical mastermind. They sat around in a circle, discussing, first, what they would have to have; second, what type of thing would do it; and, third, how such a thing could be built. This approach was reminiscent of creating the homemade contraption for the last shot in *Fantasia*, but the results were dramatically different. The men developed something so intricate and complicated, yet so simple in appearance and operation, that it seems to be a highly sophisticated robot—which is just what it is, although they prefer to call it a "computerized camera." As long as these men can come up with answers before we realize there is a question, the films will continue to combine fantasy and believability in a very real way.

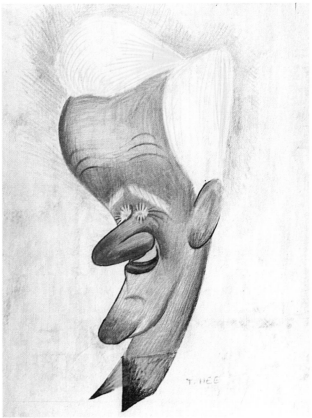

Caricatures by T. Hee of Hugh Hennesy, top, and Lou Debney, bottom. T. claimed that everyone had a color that was determined by individual personality and character.

Color

Before 1932, the only full color cartoons anyone had ever seen were in the Sunday newspaper comics, so it was only natural that when the first animated cartoons appeared at the labs, the technicians tried to match their harsh and gaudy and brilliant colors. When the original art material was sent over to show the delicate gradations that had been so carefully painted, the reaction was still, "Why do you want that? This has more punch and sock to it!" Gradually their attitude changed, but somehow the film did not. For years Walt battled with Technicolor to get them to give him the exact colors his artists had painted, until everyone began to realize that it was the color system in the film itself that was too crude to control to such a fine degree.

It worked quite well for all the hues in a middle value, but once the colors started getting to the lighter shades they bleached out quickly. Teeth that were supposed to be merely clean became so chalky they fairly leaped out of the mouths, whites of eyes glared like headlights, soft foam on water looked like piles of popcorn. And on the other side of the scale, anything slightly dark went almost black.

To get a cream-colored dress or a soft bluebird was not easy, and a black dog, like the Scotty in *Lady and the Tramp*, was almost impossible. If he were painted darker than a medium value, he went too dark to see any detail or facial expression. Careful shades of grey had to be selected, and the feeling of a black dog came from painting the backgrounds very light behind him.

Every color system on film has its own strengths and weaknesses that somehow must be mastered by the craftsman who wants to put his color theories on the screen. It is often an annoying and frustrating gamble but it is worth the effort if one is at all concerned with the appearance of the product. T. Hee, brilliant caricaturist, stylist, and director, claims that, "Color is equally important to the drawing itself." It supports the whole idea being presented, certainly, and it controls the mood completely, leading the audience as surely as the music track from one feeling to the next. More than that, colors have their own vitality, making characters as well as situations exciting, restful, happy, or even funny.

Colors used on Lady for all normal lighting. Lady and the Tramp.

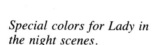

Special colors for Lady in the night scenes.

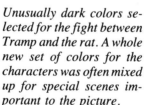

Unusually dark colors selected for the fight between Tramp and the rat. A whole new set of colors for the characters was often mixed up for special scenes important to the picture.

The delineation of any personality almost starts with color. Costuming has been an essential part of the theater from the beginning, but slightly less understood by many is the impact and potential of the colors themselves. T. Hee is more sensitive than most when he claims, "On some of the caricatures . . . I would make the guy's face green, because of his character . . . he didn't look good in any other color. . . . And other people, I would make their faces completely red, and their faces were not red. . . . Red is vibrations and green is vibrations and all of it is electric and it's alive and if you're around a person for a little while . . . he takes on a color!"

A color sense is like any other talent; an artist either has it or he does not. Relative values can be learned, but the primary approach always will remain, making that artist orthodox or sensational, dark and mystic or sparkling, realistic or abstract, no matter how well he ever learns to put colors together. This is a constant concern to the producer who wants a special feel to his film. Even if he has a dozen color stylists and background painters, seldom will any be exactly right for the proposed subject. There must be conferences, criticisms, suggestions, and expert guidance to obtain a result that has the full compatibility of idea and graphic representation.

The man selected will have the responsibility for creating not only a color key for the whole picture, but the basic appearance of the characters in the various sequences. The director always may have visualized his heroine in a pink gown, but if pink does not fit the color scheme being suggested, he had better be prepared to change his concept, perhaps radically. The ephemeral world of a "Nutcracker Suite" or the quaint realism of Geppetto's house only can evolve as the colors work together perfectly. The background man seldom will have complete authority in this area, since no film is fully successful when one function has dominated. To see that a balance is maintained, the director and his layout man work closely with the painter while the producer watches the results carefully.

Further help comes from the Color Model supervisor, who must have considerable ability to qualify for her job. She knows the Ink and Paint Department well, knows what is easy to do and what is difficult and time consuming, approximately how much any process will cost, what colors are available, and even which ones are stable or cause problems. In addition, she is a fine artist and has a good color sense. She knows how much the thickness of a cel will darken a color and what to mix to compensate for the loss. To the uninitiated, the list seems endless.

As one of the women put it, "You had to know every other aspect of the business to do your own work, and be creative about it. . . . We're like a liaison between all the departments."[7]

Finding a set of colors that will work with the general scheme, the specific background, and the needs of the character is only the beginning of the problems the Color Model expert faces. All of the earlier work has been done on paper with a variety of techniques, and now a way must be found to achieve an equivalent effect in flat shades of tempera paint within outlines on a cel. Handsome, appealing characters like Jiminy Cricket or Thumper look so right that the average person has great difficulty in imagining their being any other way, but they all took imagination, dedication, and persistence.

One small example is the expense that will be incurred in putting any character on the screen. To begin with, each color represents an expense in itself by the time it is mixed, put in small jars, dispensed to the painter, put in the exact area on the cel, and then allowed to dry. Each use of color adds an additional expense, so the Color Model advisor speaks up early when she sees a bit of questionable detail on the animator's drawings. That item will have to be drawn many times, have a color selected, be painted on hundreds of cels, and, finally, checked carefully. We were told, "Each button costs ten thousand dollars!" and we became very selective in our decorative additions to the characters. The question is constantly asked, "Is it worth it?" "Do we really need that extra button?" "How about the buckle on the belt—does it really need three colors?"

Jiminy Cricket had 27 colors in *Pinocchio*, but when he appeared later in the *Mickey Mouse Club* films that number was cut to nine. Almost any character will have that many colors, no matter how simple he is. There are always lots of little places to paint, such as inside the mouth, the eyelids, the bottom of the feet; a person does not ordinarily think of these as having a

Pinocchio

different color, yet it is needed for definition.

Everyone knows if the character is a drab little guy, a flamboyant extrovert, a deceitful villain, a sweet motherly type, but the selection of the exact colors that go together to create this appearance is a matter of personal preference. The better the taste and judgment of the color model experts, the more handsome the character will be. These challenges are compounded by the fact that colors that appear right in a daylight setting become garish against a nighttime background. Often a different set of colors will have to be chosen for the night scenes or for some other unusual sequence with a special lighting or mood. And the problem does not stop there.

It is not enough to choose colors for one character that will work throughout the whole film. His colors also must be related to those of all the other characters appearing with him in all the sequences; and, inevitably, the shades and hues that seem perfect for one figure clash and fight with the perfect selections for the character beside him. Then when that annoyance is solved, the next sequence introduces new figures who upset everything that has been decided up to this point.

There is still more. Often there will be more than one character representing a general type of person in the story. There might be two bad guys working as a team, or three fairies who are always together. The ultimate, of course, was seven dwarfs. Setting the color models is a difficult and time-consuming procedure. It takes more than one nice sketch to find the answers.

If the picture is designed to be realistic, bright colors on the characters will be a problem, causing the background painter constant headaches as he endeavors to fit the figures back into his painting or maintain a successful color scheme for mood. Snow White running through the woods in terror is a good example of colors that adapted as well to the threatening forest as they had previously to the sunny glade where she had been picking flowers. Muted colors and a moderate range of hues give the painter far more latitude in creating exciting pictures on the screen. A character that is all one color will limit the backgrounds to about two sets of colors for the whole picture; any other combinations will be muddy, too light, too colorful, too dark, or just bilious.

Black is a complete absence of light on the screen and thus becomes a hole rather than a color. While it may add accent and sparkle to a still drawing, it has a tendency to suck the life out of the object when it is projected. In *Sleeping Beauty*, the bodice of Merryweather's peasant costume was black; and while it made a brisk pattern in the overall design, there was an amazing loss of vitality in the scenes in the color print compared to the rough pencil animation.

Black details also tend to blend into the darker areas of the backgrounds, causing them to lose their identity. The marcelled waves of Captain Hook's hair in *Peter Pan* caused much consternation in the Inbetween Department because the contour could not be a straight inbetween of the lines, but had to be a complete drawing of the hair in a new position. However, his hair caused even more consternation in the final film as it faded into the dark shapes in the background in scene after scene. We could have saved ourselves a lot of work and money if we had known that the colors behind him were going to be that dark.

As a film, *Pinocchio* is undoubtedly the most gorgeously intricate that ever will be done. *Fantasia* had more impressive scenes and visual surprises, but for richness of handcrafted detail, *Pinocchio* will never be surpassed. Walt knew that he wanted a picture with a great feeling of atmosphere, with dimension and space in the backgrounds. He wanted dimension in his characters too, with an emphasis on depth and roundness in the actions. To aid in this, the Color Model advisors, working with the background painters, the color experts, and a special group of effects animators had developed several techniques that changed a flat area of paint into a rounded form. They used a blend that was rubbed on, drybrush that was stroked, and airbrush that was sprayed on.

Gradually one department after another was created to control these special processes. The airbrush department alone had over twenty women in it, all adroit at controlling the delicate spray that softened harsh areas of color. The kitten Figaro had both airbrush and drybrush on his face to give him the soft, furry look so typical of a kitten. Since there was no way of making these particular effects exactly the same way twice in a row, there was bound to be a flicker and a crawling when it was finished, but it helped the appearance so much that the decision was made to use both techniques.

It was imperative that this work be started early so there would be time to experiment. This had the added advantage of keeping the whole crew excited as they saw new effects being created for the picture even though their own part of the production at that time might have been minimal or routine. It also gave the animators a chance to make their own suggestions and even to incorporate emerging ideas into their handling of the characters. When Walt started *Fantasia*, many of the pictorial suggestions were so different from the standard appearance of cartoon material that a special crew of color experts was combined with the technicians and cameramen to see what could be done in this new direction before committing the whole studio to the project.

Typical of the new men were established painters such as Lee Blair, Elmer Plummer, John Hench, and painter-teacher Phil Dike, who was put in charge of all color. Everyone was encouraged to experiment in techniques, design, and effects. As John Hench said, "That was one thing; if you wanted to do something Walt would let you do it." John got into backgrounds, which soon led to a curiosity about what happened in camera. He had done some photography, so he tried different tests to see what effects he could get. This led to three years in the fabled Special Effects Department doing everything. At one time he even did some effects animation. His sense of design led to work at WED, the "Imagineering" subsidiary company that created Disneyland and Walt Disney World. He later became one of WED's chief executives.

Walt tried these men here and he tried them there, as he found out what they could do best; and with his incessant drive to place an individual for maximum creative output, he started them developing his radical ideas for a concert feature film. Like the stylists, they were unhampered by past experiences on cartoons, and were free to express an idea in the medium that best suited them, without regard for how it eventually could be duplicated on cels.

At one meeting, Walt's eye was captivated by a series of soft pastel sketches on black paper showing a tiny fairy spreading dewdrops on the plants at night. Walt particularly liked the delicate handling and the glow that seemed to surround the figures, and he wanted both of those features kept in the final form, no matter how it was done. To the assembled artists, some old and some new, he said, "I say there are possibilities in those backgrounds down there . . . and with our dewdrop fairy there's a chance for a different treatment. Get away from the vivid colors and get a night color for her. . . . Our backgrounds should be done in a fantastic way when rendering them; so I say, let's open up and give us something that hits us, BOOM!"

When the meeting was over the puzzled technicians asked each other, "How the dickens are we going to get this thing on the screen?" The new artists wondered, too. Obviously, more painting was not the answer. They would have to explore all the technical devices and processes that might help them, as well as think up some new things to try in every area. Studying the sketches, they gradually found certain elements that could be drawn, and others that would have to rely on what the camera could do: the lenses, the filters, the double and triple exposures. Still others might be handled with special work on top of the cels: airbrush, oils, smudges, blends.

They tried a first test and looked at it long and hard. "Gee—it doesn't look anything like the sketch Walt liked; what do we do now?" All the experts sat in on these showings, offering suggestions from their own limited knowledge, and the materials were prepared for a second try. Finally a way was found—it might have taken as many as twenty separate exposures under the camera, or a mask to block out light from underneath, or a soft multiplane effect with slightly out of focus edges; each scene was different, each took imaginative exploration, but each eventually surpassed the original sketch in every way. Those dewdrop fairies glowed and shimmered, were feminine and delicate, and worked in backgrounds of pure magic.

The white ballerina blossom that floated so gracefully down onto the placid, black water was inked in a white outline that matched the color of the petals. But she still looked too harsh, too chalky. The scene was shot again with a slight diffusion that helped, but it was not until separate exposures intensified the light that she seemed to glow with a pristine beauty, filmy and radiant. Elmer Plummer had designed the scene, knew what he wanted in values, and worked with the men in Special Effects until they got it; but he still painted the background himself to be sure that it would look just the way he wanted it.

Elmer explained his position this way: "I was a bona fide artist and had pictures hanging all over this country, watercolors and oils, and all of a sudden I found myself doing story sketch in pastel, but done in such a way that it was hard for a guy who was not a pro—who did not know the technique—to put it down the same way." Walt relied on this uncompromising insistence on exact values and relationships to get the new effects he was seeking on the screen. The commercial artist who might say, "That's good enough," would never have the persistence or the judgment to know the difference. It often took great persistence.

One of the most impressive scenes in that sequence is the pride of the harem in the Arabian Dance, the delicate, white fish with the long flowing tail, surrounded by her bevy of maids. As their black, semitransparent tails enshroud her at the start, there is a

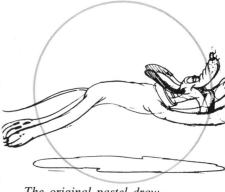

The original pastel drawings that started a new way of thinking about the uses of animation. "Nutcracker Suite," Fantasia.

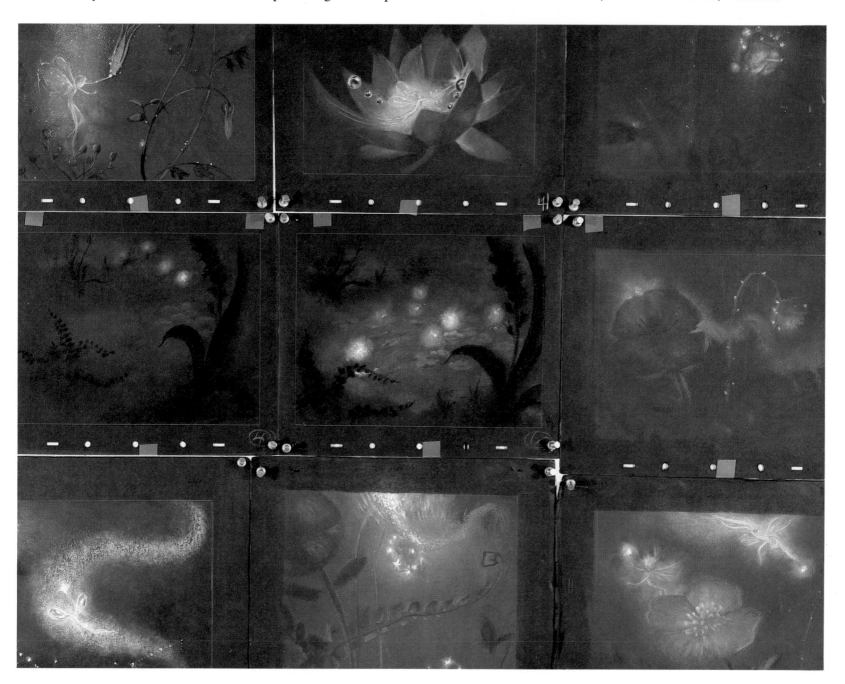

273

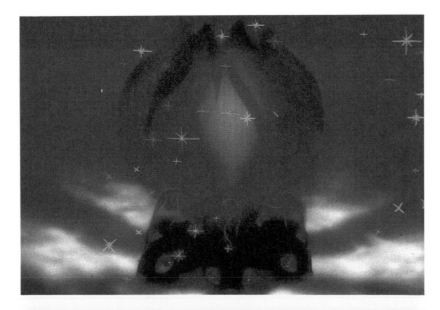

scene or buried under layers of paper. The action eventually was broken into three scenes, which made it easier to carry, but it still took just as long to shoot.

The success of these glorious scenes was due in large measure to Phil Dike, the studio's color coordinator. He had an ingenious solution to the problem of getting a satisfactory result from the elusive capabilities of the film being used. He asked Technicolor to print a scene as far to the red side as they could (what they called ''out of line''); then, gradually, on successive prints, he had them come back, one stop at a time, to normal. Then he ordered the same thing with the blue. This way he knew what he could expect, what hues were on his palette, and could work to their limitations.

These experimenting artists had further difficulties with the slightly more organized departments that surrounded them. Walt had a way of telling one person to go ahead and get what was needed, to do whatever was necessary to complete the job—without telling any of the other people who would be involved in such a project. When these new men went to another department and announced that they had to have a certain thing, or something had to be done a certain way, or they needed six inkers right away to do some work directly for them, there were all sorts of departmental jealousies and wounded egos. Supervisors were trying to solve new, unheard of problems, run their departments efficiently, and still give Walt what he wanted; so, when some outsider came in with an idea of taking over for a while, there naturally was some conflict. No one could ever run to Walt and ask him to straighten it out or define lines of authority, so each man had to be his own diplomat and do what he could to get others to cooperate.

That was the worst part of Phil Dike's assignment. He was respected and he was liked, but he had to work entirely through other people and their departments, with words as his only tools. He could not paint it for them, or shoot it for them, or change a lens for them, and since he worked primarily with other artists there was no end of opinions on what the color should be and how it could be obtained. But Phil was very diplomatic, always took the blame, and somehow saw that the most beautiful scenes ever done in animation were captured forever on film.

filmy light provocatively gleaming behind this host of veils. Never has an object on celluloid looked so diaphanous and delicate. When this effect finally had been perfected, it presented an enormously complicated job for the cameraman, but that was nothing to the shock he received when the completed scene was brought to him.

The stack of drawings was far more than one man could carry—the scene was over 100 feet long—and it looked like a small mountain, for it included not only separate drawings for the fish but for all of the sparkles, the effects, the shading on the tails and the fins. Each level added another group of drawings. In fact, the scene had been so unusually large that the animator, Don Lusk, and his assistants had been the subject of several gag drawings showing them dwarfed by the

Ink and Paint

There comes a day when the animation drawings have been completed. The scene works in continuity, the character acts as he should, his expressions communicate strongly, the layout supports his actions, and the details of costumes and props are all accounted for. On that day, a big check goes up on the production chart. But the drawings are far from finished. They only have been approved as working correctly. Now they must be put into their final form, the way the audience will see them.

In the twenties, the drawings were inked directly on the papers they were drawn on, with no shades of grey except for textures, dots, and decorations that could be done with a pen. Celluloids were used only for the background and "held" objects that did not move. This saved the tedious work of redrawing everything in the picture for every single frame. Winsor McCay had felt that this constant tracing brought a breathing effect and a life to the total drawing that was an integral part of the art form, but few who followed shared his diligence and dedication. He rightfully accused them of making a commercial trade out of the art he had developed.

Unmoved by this criticism, the men in the studios continued to search for easier and quicker ways to get their films completed. As long as the background was on a cel on top of the drawings, the action of the figures was restricted to the open areas, and this limited the types of gags that could be used. Then one artist wondered why the figures could not be on the cels while the backgrounds were drawn on the paper underneath. Instead of being done as simple ink drawings, both the characters and their locales could be painted in all the shades of grey as well as black and white. As long as the paint used was opaque, the painted figure on the cel would block out the parts of the background he was covering, while the clear cel had little effect on anything else in the scene. Earl Hurd is credited with this discovery, or invention, and there has been no essential change in the procedure in fifty years.

It is one thing to say that the drawings were traced onto the celluloid, but quite another to do it. Anyone who has tried to draw on glass with a pen will recall that nothing might come out of the pen at all, except a long, fine scratch. You draw slowly, you draw fast, you make little strokes, you use sweeping lines, then suddenly, for no reason, Ggrbloob! a huge splatter of ink comes out all at once. The same is true of tracing onto a cel. It seems the ink must be "floated" on rather than etched in to be successful.

In New York, it was felt that only men could master this difficult art; in Hollywood Walt assigned two women to the job, and when he could not pay them he married one and made the other head of the Ink and Paint Department. The two ladies in question never denied the story, although they exhibited knowing smiles as they listened to Walt's retelling of it over the years.[8]

Mary Tebb remembers the days that followed because she inked all of *The Skeleton Dance* by herself, ribs, skulls, and vertebrae. She asks herself now, "How did I do it? I don't know. I was young. I see it now and I'm amazed!" But it was simpler then with a heavy, untapered line around everything and none of the refinements that would make each cel such a work of art in only a few more years. It was Walt, as in all the other functions, who gradually raised the quality; he asked in a way that showed he expected the girls to be able to do it. In Mary's words, "That's what made him great, I think, because he brought out from us more than we thought we had."

Painting is not as difficult as the inking, but it still takes patience, organization, and considerable skill. Mary explained the job this way, "You have to learn how to do it right first: learn how to mix your colors, read your model, put the right paint on the right thing—how to dry it—and be sure you don't do it on the front side of the cel instead of the back. It sounds easy, but it's amazing how many people can't do it!"

On drawing after drawing there are little areas that could be anything: part of the flowing hair, the skirt, a tail, a ribbon, or even a hand behind the back in the middle of an action. Looking at the drawing by itself, there is no way of telling what it might be, or what color should be put on it. Sometimes a check of the drawings in sequence will reveal the identity, but often a full conference must be called. "What is this thing showing through here supposed to be?" To avoid this kind of confrontation, the animator's assistant usually

When we made Who Killed Cock Robin? in 1934, Jenny Wren's cheeks were painted with circles of pink paint. The outline was inked in the same color but the effect was still like clown make-up.

For a more natural look on Snow White, the artists in Ink and Paint suggested a delicate tint of rouge, carefully rubbed on top of the cel, and a little drybrush on the black hair to soften its contrast with creamy skin.

Example of drybrush is shown on Geppetto's hair in this sample cel from Pinocchio.

The completed cel of Cleo in Pinocchio shows the combination of self-ink lines, transparent paint (on the fins), and the subtle use of "blend."

writes little notes on his drawings explaining any mysterious forms created by the movement.

The women who had worked up to the more important jobs continually were looking for ways to make the individual cels look more appealing. They did not like to see crude, barren work going through the plant, even though they knew that probably, in action, these drawings would do the job. Still, if the drawings could be made to look better, to have a bit of shading, or a smudge, or one more color, or a bit of detail that would really make the work sparkle, they would suggest it.

Looking at a cel of Snow White, some of the women felt that the black hair looked unnatural and harsh, so they tried adding a wisp of drybrush in a lighter grey to soften the edge of her hair. It helped immensely, so they proceeded to add it to every cel all through the picture, with no indications from the animators, and nothing to guide them but their own sense of what looked right. This had to be done on top of the cels, and the only way to be sure the effect was working from one to the next was by flipping the whole sheet of celluloid, heavy with paint. It was tiring and risked cracking the paint, but there was no other way.

No one quite remembers who first suggested the idea of inking the outline of an area with the same paint that would be used to fill in the area, but it revolutionized the appearance of the characters. Each space that is a separate color must have an outline around it defining it from the area next to it. The hat is one color, the hair another, the face still another, and so on. When these outlines are done in black ink, there is a heavy, crude look that is fine for Peg Leg Pete but unacceptable for more delicate characters. Colored inks were tried on the first color films and were an improvement, but when a look of quality and careful shading was needed, they were still too strong. So someone came up with the idea of inking with the same paint that would be put on the back of the cel. This paint was thinned down to the consistency of ink and made slightly darker to match the greying effect of the thickness of the cel on the color beneath it. Now there was an outline that was scarcely noticed on the screen. The way was open for soft color changes on any form, the delicate shades and subdued values that gave the beauty Walt had been seeking.

This type of refinement was particularly needed on feminine faces whether they were human or animals. A strong outline around any parts of the head changed the feeling, as indicated by this note from a *Pinocchio* directive: "When Pinocchio is a puppet, before he comes to life, we are going to have the black line where his neck joins because it looks mechanical, but when he comes to life, it spoils the cuteness to have those lines in black so we just ink this in the same color as his neck so you don't get any hard edge here."

Before long, the characters had more colored lines on them than the black, and they became so involved that the Color Model experts had a whole page of notes on just the inking, aside from the notations of the colors themselves. The name accepted for the colored line became a "self-ink line," and even after the inkers were replaced with duplicating processes, there was still the need in critical areas for this kind of finesse.

Still more refinements were suggested—many more. One that was quite important for a few years was called the "blend," a waxy little crayon that came in various colors and could be rubbed on top of the cel to slightly darken the color underneath. With the realistic painting and strong dimension in the backgrounds, the cels with their flat colors were beginning to look like display cardboards. The self-ink line leading to another shade had helped, but now with a transparent smudge effect available in the blends, a turning edge could be suggested. As with the drybrush, it required flipping the painted cels to be sure the work followed through in both placement and density from cel to cel; it took time and judgment to put on just the right amount in the right places, but it added much to the appearance.

The blend was such a successful addition that even Mickey and Pluto were given a face-lift in *The Pointer*. Mickey's cheeks were not only round and shaded, but they had a light bit of healthy color; Pluto's wonderfully flat lack of anatomy suddenly sported shading that made him look like a collection of old telephone poles. In the next picture, he had all of his former cartoon floppiness restored.

However, when the blend was tastefully used it created marvelous effects. In some cases, the self-ink line would be rubbed off after the area had been painted, and the place where the two colors came together was

tion, a whole little department evolved, consisting of people who were adept at their own special effects.

When that mammoth scene of the fish from the ''Arabian Dance'' arrived at Ink and Paint, it was this group who put the transparent paint on the fins, the drybrush on the tips of the tails, the sparkles in the water, the highlights on the bubbles—all the extra work that had to be matched and checked and followed through until finally the cameraman placed them on his pegs, one by one, in successive exposures, to create the mystic and shimmering spectacle of this piscatorial harem. The trails of fairy dust marking the paths of the dewdrop fairies, Tinker Bell in *Peter Pan*, and every other object glowing with iridescent matter were the work of this specialized crew. Difficult and demanding as it was, it was the essence of fantasy. Story and animation, layout and background, special effects and camera could all create incredible illusions, but the visual stimulation that came from this patience and care and skill added a touch that could not be duplicated by anyone else.

Actually, there was more involved here than just artistic endeavor. The transparent paint that produced the appealing filmy effect on the screen was made from the bile of an Asian ox, and was smelly and unpleasant to use. When this paint was employed for

A cel from the last picture to be inked, Sleeping Beauty, *shows the number of colored lines used. Every cel was a highly complicated job for the inkers.*

Airbrush was used in special cases for a heavy turning edge; in this case, on the body. This Snow White *cel also shows ''blend'' used between the face and cheek coloring.*

covered by the blend so that it became invisible. Walt was as amazed as anyone. ''This is very effective! I think we are certainly on the right track.'' Then, remembering his continuous financial problem, he cautioned, ''But let's be very sparing with this blend and those things. That is what will hold up the works; all that blend will slow it up.'' Later he commented again, ''I say watch this blend business, and not do a lot of unnecessary work. It is too expensive, too. We must keep from going broke on this picture.''

Most of these innovations had been worked out by the Ink and Paint supervisors and the Color Model advisors since the rest of the department was too busy producing the cels to do any experimenting. Walt asked, ''Can't we do something here. . . ?'' and the women thought back to their art school days, or their childhoods, for any materials that might give a new effect. As the demand grew for this elaborate decora-

Fantasia *called for the most elaborate cel work ever attempted. This original cel dating from 1939 shows the variety of work done for each frame of film in the "Nutcracker Suite": colored lines, drybrush, airbrush, transparent paint, stipple—all in addition to the difficult job of tracing the pencil drawings in the first place.*

shadows, it was imperative that no outline be seen, so the inkers had to trace the drawings onto the cels in what amounted to invisible ink. The painters complained that they not only had to work fast but could not even see the line they were working to!

The washoff relief cels had the emulsion on the back of the cel where the paint was to go, and extreme care had to be used or both would come off the cel together. Becky Fallberg, who was later head of the department, says, "Oh, it was horrible! Everybody moaned when they got those kinds of scenes." There even was trouble with the cels themselves, especially when the only ones available were made of the highly flammable nitrate. One shipment would be yellow, one grey, one set would buckle, the next would warp, and all would shrink once they were cut to size.

When the animation on *Bambi* started filtering through the Ink and Paint Department, a new problem arose. The legs of the deer had to be strong and rigid for the animal to be convincing. The assistants and inbetweeners in the animation building had taken great care in practically tracing the legs during a scene of little movement, but now the inkers found they could

A combination of stipple and inking in a variety of colors was used to represent fairy dust and sparkle effects. Here, Merryweather shoots a bit of magic from her wand in Sleeping Beauty.

Hours of tedious work were required to trace all the elements in a comprehensive drawing such as this from Lady and the Tramp.

ists no longer could be held together. When peace returned four years later, the concentration was on better ways to achieve the same result that once had cost so much in time and effort. Since no records were kept in that era when procedures changed with each scene, gradually people forgot how things had been done. Before long, the equipment that once produced the great effects—the drum that had cleared the frosted cells, the mechanism that had processed washoff relief cells, the inventions that had held detailed work together under the camera—was all rusting on the back lot, and newcomers walking around the lot at noon wondered why anyone would keep junk like that around. Just a few years later, it was thrown out because the interest was in new procedures.

The primary concern was to free the inkers from the

not copy these drawings accurately enough to avoid the jitters and wobbles that always managed to creep in. Since the moves were so small and no knowledge of animation principles was involved, the Ink and Paint artists suggested that they do the inbetweening on the cels, eliminating the extra drawings that were causing the trouble. There were many days during the making of the picture that they regretted having made the offer, but the results were magnificent.

This type of dedication, in addition to the ten long weeks of training before anyone even was hired, led to the most beautiful inking ever done. The tapered lines and the sure, deft touch made each cel a work of art. Before the war there were many talented candidates to choose from for this work, and the ones selected were fine artists in their own right. Betty Kimball admits, ''The inkers were very good at drawing. . . . They had to be, because they had to get that feeling of the animator's drawings in their ink lines, and it's very hard to control a pen on that slippery celluloid.''

Mary Tebb felt that the morale of the staff was reflected in the work they produced. ''I think that's one reason why the product itself is . . . still beautiful . . . because it was done by dedicated people.'' There is certainly some elusive reason why the pictures never look dated, beyond the styles and fashions in both art work and humor.

With the second World War came economic problems, and the immense staff of highly skilled special-

tedious process of endless tracing, so they could devote their time to things that really counted. There was a drive on the part of the animators at the same time to find some way to duplicate accurately their own crisp, strong drawings on the cels. The women were good, very good, but their work was still a tracing, and tracings never have the vitality of the original. In the late fifties, Ub Iwerks adapted the Xerox process to our needs, creating a great machine that copied the drawings on an electrically charged plate. There was very little delicacy in the result, and a light line was apt to drop out entirely, but the animator's drawing was there, strong and irrevocable in the blackest of lines. In fact, this heavy, black line put us right back into the 1920s, before the refinements of inking had begun.

Other colors that the Xerox Corporation could offer were no better, so we attempted to make the dark outline look more acceptable by using it as the style of the whole picture, backgrounds and all. *101 Dalmatians* was the result, spearheaded by the multitalented Ken Anderson; the linear quality of the artwork gave a crisp, handsome look, especially for a film about black and white dogs. The animators were very pleased, but Walt felt it lacked the delicacy and the care that the old pictures had achieved. Many in the audience felt the same way, saying that they missed the elegance of the prewar films. It was not until we had perfected a grey line for *The Rescuers* that we were able to lose the harsh outline and regain a soft look. That simple change brought raves from critics who claimed we had developed a whole new style for this picture.

Lady and the Tramp

The rabbit children and their turtle friend from Robin Hood. *The animators appreciated the faithfulness of reproduction using the new Xerox process instead of hand-inking the cels, but they missed the delicacy in the faces that colored ink lines had given.*

Many stories seem to call for a final shot of the main character walking away into the distance while the camera pulls back slowly—usually up into the sky for a picture of the sunset or the moon or a title that says, ''The End.'' This was always almost impossible to animate, because of the dual problem of making the figure just the right amount smaller with each step while keeping the same spirit throughout. The camera usually pulls up into the sky because the character looks so terrible that he is ruining the whole concept; and, even though the scene needs to continue for at least nine feet, it would be impossible to keep him on the screen any longer.

But with the Xerox machine, all that has changed.

We need to animate only one complete step of the character walking away from us, and it can be any size convenient for us to draw. Once the action is checked and approved, the drawings are sent to the Xerox Department where they are blown down to the correct size for the scene. More than that, the drawings are repeated over and over, smaller each time, so that theoretically our character can keep walking forever. From a practical standpoint, the painters cannot paint him after he reaches a tiny size, but usually that point is not reached until the needs of the scene have been well met.

The one problem that remains to be solved is brought about by the very procedure that saves so much effort.

Bianca from The Rescuers. *Thin pencil lines and a medium grey toner in the Xerox machine finally gave us the soft appearance once more. Colored lines added to a cel of this kind recaptured the delicacy we had enjoyed with the inking, at a fraction of the cost.*

Any small, insignificant, hardly noticeable error in the movement is magnified by repetition. A slight limp, a gimpy walk, an unnatural roll to the body, a foot that picks up too high, a leg that pushes into the ground, any little thing that would never be noticed in one step of an ordinary scene, becomes amplified with each repeat until the character looks as if something is terribly wrong with him; and as the camera soars up into the sky, most of the audience is wondering if someone should not go help the poor fellow before it is too late.

There continues to be a need for good inking, but it is in small areas where a self-ink line is used or where some interesting effect is desired. The long hours of endless copying have given way to special work that requires the same skills, but now the inkers can concentrate on just the things that will make the picture look its best while costing the least. With a giant machine to take over the dull parts of their jobs, they now can devote their time to the projects that a machine cannot do.

From time to time, the key creative personnel felt that some of the Ink and Paint artists who had done superb work should get screen credit for their efforts. It would be impossible to mention everyone, of course, but a few, with unusual talents, or that extra bit of dedication, should be recognized. This never occurred for several reasons. First of all, in the early years, no one got screen credit. Walt had known that the audience would respond better to one name—one product that easily could be remembered—than to a long list of unrecognized names. Still, he was appreciative of creative effort and felt the person who did an outstanding job should be given credit for it.

On the comic strip he had tried to replace his own name with those of the men who actually were doing the continuity and the drawings, but he was told by the syndicate that such a change would kill the strip. The public knew Walt Disney and that was the name they wanted to see on the drawings, regardless of who made them. When he embarked on the feature films, however, there was a precedent already set from the live action films that justified the naming of his key people. But by that time, there were over 600 members of his staff putting in long hours, working with complete dedication to the studio and devotion to the films. Most of them were unconcerned about screen credit, preferring to be known as just part of the team.

Still, it was impossible to list even half the number of people who really had struggled to make each film an outstanding experience for the theatergoer.[9] Assistants, inbetweeners, cutters, sound men, cameramen, and, especially, the ''girls'' in Ink and Paint had to be left out, even though the films could never have been made without their sustained efforts. Some people claimed that this work was only a craft and not at all comparable to the creative thinking done by the ''men in the main building,'' but we relied heavily on their skills and their ideas, and they never let us down. We loved those girls. Still do!

EVINRUDE

Jim Macdonald makes the sound for Evinrude in The Rescuers.

11. The Disney Sounds

"I think a good study of music would be indispensable to the animators—a realization on their part of how primitive music is, how natural it is for people to want to go to music—a study of rhythm, the dance—the various rhythms that enter into our lives every day."

Walt Disney

Music

Work was still being done on the last segments of *Fantasia* when the *Bambi* crew moved into full production, and Walt was kept hopping from one projection room to the next to keep up with the reels as they progressed. One day he was called into a meeting on the forest fire sequence in *Bambi* just as he finished viewing the work reels on Beethoven's *Pastoral Symphony*. The *Bambi* picture reel was only half completed, but the intent was clear and the musician, Ed Plumb, was eager to present his ideas on the score he was writing. Halfway through his presentation, Walt stopped him and asked the projectionist if the *Fantasia* reels were still up in the booth. They were, so he asked to hear the storm music from the *Pastoral Symphony* run in sync with the *Bambi* reel. We were stunned by the power of the music and the excitement it gave to the drawings.

When it was over, Walt turned and said, "There, Ed, that's what I want. Something big! See the difference?"

Ed's look was part shock, part disbelief, and part pleading, "But, Walt—that's Beethoven!"

Walt responded, "Yeah. . . ?" and waited to hear some reason why Ed could not write the same sort of thing. It was no more than what he asked of his whole staff day after day.

Music is undoubtedly the most important addition that will be made to the picture. It can do more to bring a production to life, to give it integrity, style, emphasis, meaning, and unity than any other single ingredient. With the surge of a full orchestra, there

Musician Ed Plumb, center, with the composers of the songs for Snow White. *Left, Frank Churchill and, right, Larry Morey.*

will be bigness and majesty and soaring spirits; with a nervous, fluttering melody line on a single instrument, or pulsating drumbeats, there will be agitation, apprehension, suspicion. Music can build tension in commonplace scenes or ease it in ones that have become visually too frightening.

At times there is value in playing counter to what is being seen. Chaplin writes of his troubles in getting arrangers to realize that the music behind his tramp character should not attempt to be funny, but should strive for an emotional dimension. "I wanted the music to be a counterpoint of grace and charm, to express sentiment, without which, as Hazlitt says, a work of art is incomplete."[1]

Still other times require the music to express an attitude that cannot be shown strongly in moving draw-

The trio from Kansas City pose with the animation staff in 1927. Front row, from left, Ub Iwerks, Walt Disney, Carl Stalling (the first musician). Back row, the artists: from left, Johnny Cannon, Wilfred Jackson, Les Clark, Jack Cutting.

ings. Feelings of isolation, rejection, an awareness of beauty, a sense of growing strength, of hope, of devotion—these are all inner emotions that are difficult to show. Fortunately, this is the area of greatest strength for music, and the musician who feels the mood in your film can make it all intensely moving.

Since music is so closely associated with most of the major events in our lives—nursery songs, campfire songs, school songs, religious songs, dances, weddings, and, finally, funerals—it becomes the soul of our memory, forever coloring our impressions. Just the playing of a familiar theme brings back the emotions of past experience, and through associations we can be made to feel empathy even for peoples of distant cultures. This becomes a vital element in making fantasy worlds believable—not just as a place observed from the comfort of our theater seats, but a region we actually inhabit for the duration of the film.

Before the days of sound, it was the organists and piano players in theaters across the country who used the magic of music to transport audiences to other lands and other times. In a primitive and very direct way, these musicians communicated with the viewers, leading them from one emotion to another as the story in the film unfolded. From opera they took themes of passion and torment, descriptive passages and mood-setting phrases. In folk songs, popular songs, sentimental ballads, they found melodies with strong

connotations that created an immense emotional response. Movie theater musicians had a special feeling for just the right music to fit any situation, the background to recall tunes from everywhere, and the ability to improvise constantly, adapting new ideas to old songs. Their music communicated: Danger . . . Romance . . . Loneliness . . . Cold . . . Joy . . . Longing . . . Bravery. . . .

Walt brought men in from all over the country to help develop a new use of music in a whole new kind of entertainment. They included Carl Stalling, who had once played for the Laugh-O-Grams back in Kansas City; Bert Lewis, also from Kansas City; Frank Churchill, who wrote the music for the famous flypaper sequence with Pluto, and "Who's Afraid of the Big, Bad Wolf," and all the songs for *Snow White*; Leigh Harline, who was most famous for "When You Wish Upon a Star" but had done the music for such diverse subjects as *The Grasshopper and the Ants* and *The Old Mill*; and Ollie Wallace, who composed the score for *Dumbo* with Churchill and was best known for "Der Fuehrer's Face." These men were joined by Albert Malotte, who achieved more fame as the composer of "The Lord's Prayer," and the highly talented Paul Smith, fresh out of university and full of musical ideas. His adaptation of cartoon techniques in the scores for the *True Life Adventures* several years later added immeasurably to that series of live action films. Buddy Baker also contributed to both live action and cartoon, showing equal facility in symphonic suites or comic chases.

Each of these men had a great sense of melody and a unique ability to orchestrate very special feelings. Of them all, Frank Churchill probably had the greatest feel for the animated film, as his score for *Snow White* showed so well. The bubbling quality and friendly spirit of the section in which the animals take the girl to the dwarfs' cottage was especially appealing, and we asked Ed Plumb what gave the music that extra something. Ed squinted his eyes, "Y'know, I've memorized every note in that orchestration and I still can't figure out what does it."

After Frank Churchill's death, his room was given to Ollie Wallace. Ollie was peppery, spirited, and always had a twinkle in his eye, so when he claimed that Frank's spirit was responsible for the great melodies that continued to come from that room we nodded our heads and smiled. But one day he was scowling and professed great annoyance. ''That Churchill hasn't written a decent note in the last three days!''

In 1928, no one knew how the drawings of the cartoon and the notes of the music could be planned together. It was easy enough to improvise a score to a completed film, but to figure out ahead of time where the beats would occur on the drawings was beyond everyone. Walt insisted there must be a way the two could be worked together and be controlled and built upon and changed. What kind of graph or chart or score could be devised that would bring the music and picture together?[2]

The newly arrived Wilfred Jackson had the answer with his metronome. He reasoned that if the film ran at a constant speed of 24 frames a second, all one had to do was determine how much music went by in a second. Although his knowledge of musical structure was rudimentary, he did know bars and beats and staffs and signs, and since the tunes being used for these first films were rather rudimentary themselves it all worked out quite nicely. A new language had been discovered.

It seems simple enough now, but Dave Hand reported that animators in New York were baffled and tried over and over for a year and a half before figuring out a way to establish where the accents would occur while making the drawings. Jackson's system was easily expanded to include variations in tempo and other time signatures, and as long as the song adhered to a strict beat it could be written out from beginning to end.

The director knew what part of the song would be heard during any action he planned, and the musician knew what movements were being planned to go with the music. The animator knew that if he had his character slide from early in Measure 54 to the middle of Measure 55, there would be either a slide whistle or an instrumental glissando to back him up on the final sound track.

The musician and the director worked closely together in the same room, planning the entire picture before any animator began a scene. Wilfred Jackson told of these sessions in an interview: ''First the musician would suggest tunes for the various sections of the picture to get the mood or general type of action for each part. He would patiently play the same phrase

over and over again while the animation director visualized and timed the action in his mind. Working back and forth, the musician would sometimes change elements in the score to enhance certain actions, or the director would modify some piece of business so that it worked better musically. When both were satisfied, the director would mark the action down on the 'dope sheet' [Bar Sheet] while his partner sketched out that part of the music score. Then they would move on to the next little piece of action.''

This close cooperation became the standard procedure as other musicians were added to the staff. It was a long and tedious process for musicians more adept at improvising through inspiration, and they often wished they could withdraw from these daily meetings after laying out some basic footages and the number of bars in a verse or a chorus. Even after the director had worked over every last movement in the picture, stretching it or condensing it to fit the pattern of the beats, there was still the animator who had to be satisfied, and he inevitably had more refinements and ideas that built on what already had been done. There were other times when the animator simply could not put over all the business demanded within the footage limitations imposed by the music, and then the musician would be asked to add just one more little beat to his music—just one? Astounded at this lack of comprehension of the basic mathematical structure of music, the musician would insist on a full measure, or better yet, a phrase, but that only seemed to add more problems. The action could not be padded by that much. So the ''3-12 measure'' was invented.

To a measure containing two beats, an extra beat was added, creating a measure of three beats. When the first musician gave in to this compromise the tempo was in 12s, twelve frames to each beat, so it was called a 3-12 measure; but the term persisted regardless of tempo for years. It was like adding an extra step on one foot in a march; instead of ''Left, right, left, right,'' it became, ''Left, right, right, left, right.'' When an animator with a musical background asked how this was possible, he simply was told, ''Oh, Churchill knows how to do it!''

Walt used to claim that Frank Churchill always slept through the story meetings and never listened to his first instructions, but Frank hardly can be blamed. He knew that no matter what ideas were tossed out, and no matter how enthusiastically they might be received, that would have little bearing on the music he eventually would write. By the time footage was added, phrases repeated, sections cut out, and everything plastered together with an assortment of 3-12 measures, any original plan would be so butchered there would be little of it left. He figured, correctly, that he would do better to wait until the decisions had been made and the footages set, and then he could write a score with integrity and flow, regardless of what had happened to the so-called structure. He would sit at his piano penciling in his melodies and muttering, ''This note is for the director, and this is for the producer, while this little note down here is for the animator, and this is for the director's Aunt Tilda, and this is just for me!''

It was not an easy procedure for anyone, but that close collaboration was the very thing that produced the new art form. From the advent of sound to the late thirties, music and animation had been one. Wilfred Jackson expressed the general feeling: ''I do not believe there was much thought given to the music as one thing and the animation as another. I believe we conceived of them as elements which we were trying to fuse into a whole new thing that would be more than simply movement plus sound.'' Jerome Kern recognized the artistry in this process and claimed that a distinct new musical form had been created. He termed it ''the use of music as language'' and credited Walt with making an outstanding contribution to the music of his time—possibly the only real contribution of the twentieth century![3] The effect of absolutely everything being related to the musical beat became so well developed that, in the musical world, ''Mickeymousing'' became the name for music that accented or echoed every action on the screen. As a way of scoring, it was not limited to cartoons, but also was used with good effect in such pictures as *King Kong*, matching the huge ape's ascent of the Empire State Building with dramatic progression in the orchestration.

If this close integration of music and action had been a headache to the musicians, it was equally demanding for the animators, forcing them to become more crisp in their thinking and better organized in their statements. They always had been required to get across the story points in the least amount of time, but they had never faced the discipline of working to the rigid pattern of a beat. Where ordinarily they would have taken an extra eight or ten frames to complete an action, stage a pose, or register a look, the music made them search for the absolute essence of the idea—that and nothing more. No frills, no extras; get right to the point. It is doubtful if they ever would have achieved this concise distillation without the constant pressure that demanded they find a way. Looking back on it now, we can see that it was valuable and necessary training. Unlimited footage nearly always lulls the animator into a slipshod performance.

While the shorts featuring Mickey and action gags were giving the musicians such problems, the Silly Symphonies were pushing into a new relationship of music and animation. Here, the integrity of the music was more important, and the action had to do the adapting. When a theme from Rossini or Schubert was used, it had to be used intact or the whole effect was

Bar Sheets

The exposure sheets were short and only represented enough footage for three or four beats to a page, and Wilfred Jackson wanted to see the whole song spread out before him like sheet music, so he originated the ''bar sheet.'' This often was called the ''dope sheet'' since it eventually contained all the dope on both the music and the actions, but its essential purpose was to lay out the bars of music in long boxes that could be viewed together. On these were the tempos of the songs, written in terms of the number of frames between each beat, and a notation of the start of the music, which part was verse and which chorus, any repeats that might be used, and where the music might start into a second song. Everything was penciled into these boxes, even the location of sound effects and words of dialogue.

Along with this was written information about the scenes, the starts and cuts and the pattern of actions. With all the information in one location, it was easy to see how any change on one part would affect any of the other parts, and corrections could be made quite simply—on paper. Disaster followed when someone forgot to correct the animator's exposure sheets or notify the cutter, or made any revision without telling everyone concerned, but that sort of confusion was spoiled. There were no 3-12 measures here, and considerably more work was required to find actions that fit the music, told the story, and still built a personality. A move that was right, visually, would seldom match the sound on the track at that point, and the animators had to become more like choreographers, trying to build a unified statement in movement rich in emotional content and with a cohesive flow—all within the confines of an established score. The visual material could not be choppy or fragmented; it had to have the same unity as the music.

In those first symphonies, the actions had been simple, staying with dance steps and runs that easily could be made to follow the beat of the music. But with Walt's insistence on humor and personality, the films built quickly into stories that demanded the acting match the tempo, too. This reached a peak in 1935 with *The Band Concert*, which combined well-known music with strong personalities and a situation played entirely in pantomime. It was a rare combination, reflecting still another use of music as language. As one producer said, "Who else would take a band concert out of Walt's boyhood, mix in 'William Tell' and 'Turkey in the Straw' and a Kansas cyclone, and come out with a performance that would enchant Toscanini?"[4] (Typical of Walt, he did not stop there but began thinking of an even bigger use of the same principle. He called that one *Fantasia*.)

In addition to the stories that called for spirited music, there were sequences that called for a mood to be established by a special theme. In many instances, the feeling of this score would influence any further development to such an extent that it was decided to record the sound first and work to its limitations. There is a special feeling in work that is done this way that is not found in other methods, but it is more expensive because of the demands it makes in all the creative departments.

---

fairly normal in those days.

We took a line of music . . .

erased the notes and the staff lines, leaving this, which denotes the bars, or measures, of the song.

It was called a bar sheet.

Listening to the metronome we determined the tempo wanted, and that decision gave us the number of frames to each beat: 8s, 9s, 10s, 16s, whatever. The structure of the song determined the number of beats to the bar, 2, 3, 4, or 6. The more sophisticated rhythms were not then considered.

We wrote up a song's musical beats like this. In this example, there are two beats of 12 frames to each bar.

A bar is thus 24X long.

Now we added the scene starts and cuts, noting how many frames before a bar, or after a bar it might be. If a scene were shifted, it was erased and put in its new location.

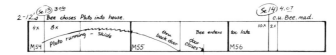

Next came the action, timed to the beat of a metronome, then written on the bar sheet, relating the action to the beats. Now we knew just how many bars were needed for each bit of business.

Later, dialogue was added, showing where the take started and ended. Location of sound effects were noted, too. (There is still no music suggested, just the beats.)

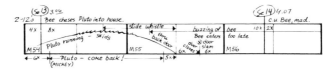

289

Timing, Spacing, and the Metronome

The action in a scene was planned by the animator and the director at the time of the handout. If there was music, there would be either a prescored track or a tempo set by the musician that could be marked on the exposure sheet. When a metronome was set to that tempo, those written beats became audible, giving a good indication of the amount of time for the action of the scene. If there was no sound to use as a guide, the metronome was the only way to determine the length of any of the action.

A setting of 12s (twice a second) was usually used, which meant that a beat came every 12 frames. This just happens to be the tempo of all marches, and offers a good alternative when no metronome is handy. Whistle any well-known march until the rhythm is well established in your mind, tap your foot and have a friend count the taps as you act out the scene. You will not be more than a frame off. Milt Kahl once proclaimed in a lecture, "Everyone walks on 12s—unless there's something wrong with them!" Walt Stanchfield immediately drew a sketch of a man at the doctor's office saying, "Something's wrong with me, Doc. I've been walking on 13s."

With the metronome running, the moves were tested; how long does the character walk, how many steps does he take, when does he stop, how long is he held? It was all noted on the exposure sheet, corrected, altered, and tried still another way, until the very best pattern of action had been found. It was called, "Finding the quickest way to do the most."

To conceive of a series of actions that would put over the story point, keep the personality of the character, and be imaginative enough to be entertaining was a big assignment. To do it all within the limits of the allotted footage, with a feeling of accents to match the beat and gestures that gave sync and rhythm, took more than mere drawing ability.

A visitor walking through the halls would hear the scattered ticks and tocks coming from several rooms at the same time, as the animators listened and acted, considered and timed. That metronome was a stern, unrelenting taskmaster, but it was responsible for packing more entertainment into small amounts of footage than any other procedure.

The inspirational sketch by Mel Shaw that suggested the scene.

EXAMPLE #1.

The scene with no sound track for a guide.

Scene description: Animals playing; fox in water; hound dives in, splashing water all over his friend.

Tempo: Set metronome on 12 beat.

Footage: Undetermined, but keep brisk and busy.

In this scene from *The Fox and the Hound*, there had to be the spirited feeling of two kids in the old swimming hole. The animator decided to start the scene with the fox alone in the water, then bring the hound in on the ninth frame. Listening to the metronome, he determined that the dog should run for 16 frames before he jumped. For the dive, the pup should have a big leap with a float-

ing feeling—in contrast to the busy action of the run. Again going to the metronome, the animator tested different types of leaps, with the one that took two

Charting the action in this manner on the exposure sheets gave the animator a chance to see the relationship of all the moves in his scene as well as the precise number of frames to be used in any action.

The bouncing ball has only one frame of contact with the ground.

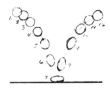

These twelve frames can be written on the exposure sheet in the form of a chart, like this:

A man landing and jumping contacts the ground for six to eight frames.

Charted on the exposure sheet, it looks like this:

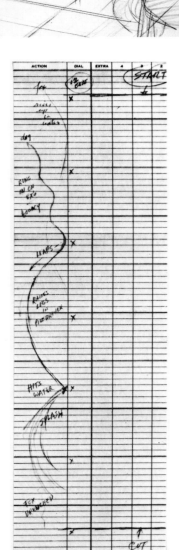

The animator makes a chart showing where the pup's head will be on each of the drawings in the run and jump.

beats, 24 frames, being the best. This was charted on the exposure sheet, with the 8 frames blank at the start, going 16 frames for the splash, and another 8 frames at the end to see the picture of the fox drenched, but laughing. The whole scene came to 4 feet 8 frames, or 3 seconds.

The layout was checked to see if there was enough room for the pup to run for 16 frames from the field border to the edge of the water; then drawings were made of the size of the dog and his attitude throughout the action. All that remained was to determine the spacing, how far he would move on each drawing, and this was a simple matter of taking the distance from the first drawing to the spot where he jumped, and dividing it into 16 equal spaces. Each of these became the position of the pup's head as he progressed on his run. To keep this run lively, an 8 frame gallop was chosen, which gave the pup a happy, bouncing movement as he entered. With confidence in the timing and the path of action, all of the animator's energies could now be concentrated on making drawings of a playful pup in a mischievous mood.

When the procedure is written down step by step this way, it seems like an involved and tedious process, but actually it takes only a matter of minutes. The big advantage is that it gives the animator a chance to think about his scene, play with the ideas, and turn it all over in his mind before he is committed to a specific action. The steps that sound so mechanical in writing will all stimulate his imagination, and increase both the fun of doing the scene and the probability that it will come out on the screen just the way he has visualized it.

A closer shot of the action of the fox and hound playing in the water. With no solid surface beneath their feet, perspective becomes important as the only means of establishing the level of the water. A grid is drawn to remind the animator of the drawing restrictions as he bobs the characters up and down to give the feeling of being in water. The timing of the actions, which are matched to this perspective, is the only way of achieving this illusion.

The exposure sheet with the action notes for the run, the jump, and the splash.

When Pluto was sniffing, his nose hit the extreme up and down positions on every other frame.

On the exposure sheet, the chart looked like this:

291

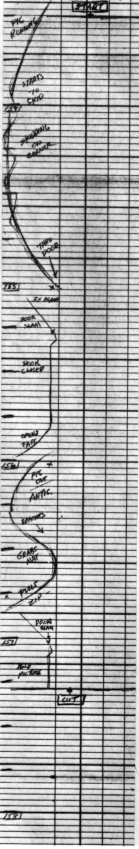

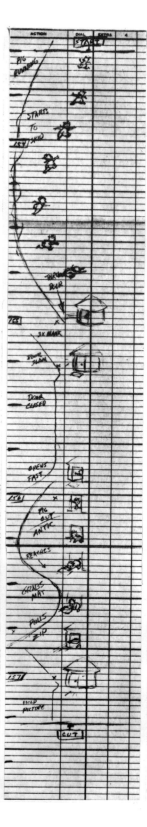

EXAMPLE #2.

Working to music in an established tempo.

Scene description: First little pig runs into his straw house, slams door. Welcome mat is in front of door. He opens door, pulls in mat, slams door again.

Tempo: two 14s, or 7 frames per beat.

Footage: 6 feet 10 frames.

First, we determine the main accents we want to catch in the action. They are:
1. Going through the door.
2. Slamming the door.
3. Opening the door.
4. Pulling the mat in.
5. Slamming the door again.

Second, we study the exposure sheet and the lay-out and consider the big elements of the scene. Setting the metronome on a 14 beat, we try to visualize the type of action that will be best for this situation. We want to see the pig struggle excitedly and skid on the corner as he attempts to reach the door. (This gives the audience a chance to share his emotions, and the musician an opportunity to support the action.) The best accent musically for him to dash into the house would be on Measure 155, with the door slam coming 7 frames later on the up-beat.

The next big accent, for the opening of the door, comes on Measure 156, just 21 frames after the door slam. The door must be closed long enough to get the picture of the house with the welcome mat at the doorstep, but not so long that the tempo is spoiled. As the door is opened, the pig anticipates for a meager 7 frames, dives for the mat, and grabs it on the next beat, then pulls it in very fast. The ensuing door slam could come on the downbeat of Measure 157. Acting all of this out to the ticks of the metronome shows that this pattern is possible. It is fast, but allows time to see everything—the excited face, the reach, and the grabbing of the mat—and still leaves a picture for 8 frames before the cut. Adding sketches of the positions of the little pig throughout the action helps to prove out the planning. The action will be brisk, but when it is charted on the exposure sheet it is all clear and looks interesting. It is time to start animating.

292

The whole section of *Snow White* that showed the heroine lying on her bier while her friends mourned was planned to a prescored organ track that set the length and the mood of anything that would be done visually. No one came out of the theater whistling that song, but it was a great piece of music and did more to choke up the spectators than is generally realized. The number of scenes was carefully planned as well as their content, so that there would be no busy scenes, no fast moves, nothing that would contradict the feeling in the music.

The animator had to play this track over and over to maintain the right feeling in his drawings and his actions.[5] It was necessary that he saturate himself with this spirit to capture a similar mood in the animation. Unfortunately, next door, Fred Spencer was trying to animate as much life and vitality as he could into the dwarfs as they sang and danced for Snow White in the Entertainment Sequence. As the dreary organ tones of the mourning section seeped through the walls, Fred turned up the volume on his record of the yodeling and singing. This quickly enlivened the funeral next door, destroying hours of getting into just the right mood. There was pounding on the wall from both sides and fierce shouts of, "Cut out that sad stuff!" answered by "Stop that dancing in there!!"

Prescoring

In *Fantasia*, most of the music was "free tempo" and did not adhere to a strict beat, which created awkward conditions for the use of the bar sheets. With one bar being 42 frames and the next 47 and the next 45, there was no way of getting a consistent measurement for a chart. Instead, the tracks were "read" by the cutters, the same as they read the dialogue tracks, writing the notations on the "greys."

Measure numbers were written on the sheets, along with special accents and any other placements the director or animator might need. Action notes were written on the greys beside the music reading. In this case, bar sheets were kept more as a record than a working procedure.

The ultimate in working to a prescored track was *Fantasia*, and many extra story meetings were held to find the best activities to show during all parts of the music. The Silly Symphonies had taught the staff the value of letting music speak its message uninterrupted, so the animators were well-prepared for an extremely difficult job: never enough time in the music to do what needed to be done in some sequences, and far too much time in areas lacking ideas in the first place. The years of training produced unsurpassed scenes of deceptive simplicity.

Walt had discovered very early how much the music could do to establish a mood and how much it aided in communication with the audience. It did not have to be a symphonic score or even a great piece of music, as long as it contained the essential element of communicated feeling and was right for that spot in the picture.

Charlie Chaplin wrote of his own discoveries and feelings: "Even in those early comedies I strove for a mood; usually music created it. An old song called *Mrs. Grundy* created the mood for *The Immigrant*. The tune had a wistful tenderness that suggested two lonely derelicts getting married on a doleful, rainy day."[6]

Walt had a similar kind of reaction to the emotion suggested by music, and while he did not pretend to know how it was constructed or how it worked he always knew just the feeling he wanted it to give. During the making of *Snow White*, a sequence had been planned showing the dwarfs assembled in the woods outside their cottage. They were trying to think of a present they could make for the girl who had come to stay with them, and as they thought a musical vamp gave the feeling that something was about to happen. One by one they would have an idea, leap up, make their announcement, have it rejected, then wilt back into despondency, and more thought. Walt wanted the music to echo their attitudes, and his reactions to the proposed score is typical of his feelings about the music in every picture: "Right now you have too much sharpness and 'boom-boom' of the piano. When one of the guys gets an idea, the key should change. When he lifts up the music goes with him, and when he sits down the music should go down. . . . I don't like the idea of the music jumping at you. I see it lifting up with them. . . . As each guy who thinks he has a rare idea is voted down, the music goes right into the wilt down. . . ."

Music Not Prescored

Most animation on the features was not done to a prescored track, and with the emphasis on acting and mood the scenes were better supported by a free tempo type of music than by the rigid beat. In those cases, the musician would ask for a dummy score to be made up showing him what he had to match and where things happened. A music check was made of the whole section with all the accents, the footsteps, jumps, staggers, displays of emotion, or strong looks. Footages were marked for each of these, the same as on the bar sheets, but the choice of how to tie all of them together was left up to the composer. If they happened to fall in rhythmic patterns, he could use a fixed tempo if he chose, or he could do it all to a free beat.

Jim Macdonald devised an interesting way of making a precise guide for the musician with this problem. On a reel of blank film, he punched out holes that would make clicks and pops when the film was run on the sound head. These sounds were timed exactly to the action on the film, so the musician could hear where these accents came while writing a score to match.

The public continued to enjoy seeing cartoon characters move in close relation to music; there was something fascinating about it and something that felt right to them. However, it had to be done tastefully, with more nuances and surprises, carefully avoiding the choppiness and "ricky-tick" sound of the early cartoons.

Surprise Accents

The audience feels comfortable when led to believe that certain things will happen and in fact they do. The character walks in rhythm with the music; he accents his movements on the beat; it feels right. The opposite must be true of the surprise gag, the unusual, the startling. These accents should come on the off beat, the up beat, somewhere in the middle of the measure, where they are least expected. The audience is led to anticipate one thing, and the continued accents on the downbeat fortify this sense of security. To be a surprise, the sound must come at a totally unexpected place in the music.

Walt also suggested there might be feelings of dissonance in the harmony, for the sake of comedy, and to show that there was no agreement in this group. Without just the right feeling in the music, he thought the whole idea of the sequence was ordinary and not worth doing. He commented at the end of the meeting, "It is important that we work out a good musical pattern on this or else we had better give up the idea and try to work it out in some other way." The sequence eventually was cut out of the picture.

Walt was just as critical of the songs that were suggested for the characters to sing. One musician reported that Walt could get his ideas across almost without using words, because his criticism was always in terms of the feeling he wanted. He knew that a merely pretty song with a nice melody would soon

Snow White

become ordinary and drag his picture down. The song had to have a freshness and a vitality and something extra before he would accept it. If it did not make him feel the way he wanted the audience to feel, he would ask the composer to try again.

As he started work on *Fantasia*, he was very honest about his lack of musical knowledge, and it did not worry him in the least that his reactions were those of the man in the street. Leopold Stokowski was immensely helpful and spent some time explaining the construction of a musical number and the relation of the form to the reaction of the listener. He concluded, "If our picturization is contrary to the music, it will confuse the public; if it is in form, it will be clear and pleasing and they will enjoy it."

Walt's response was less erudite. "There are things in that music that the general public will not understand until they see things on the screen representing that music. Then they will feel the depth in the music. Our object is to reach the very people who have walked out on this 'Toccata and Fugue' because they didn't understand it. I am one of those people; but when I understand it, I like it!"

Inevitably as the work progresses on any sequence new ideas pop up, and surprisingly often these ideas actually will strengthen the music, since they sharpen the definition and emphasize exactly what the composer is saying. If truly creative people are involved, the musician is quick to realize the improvements and eager to adapt his score if that is still possible. The happiest solution to all of this was the "temp (temporary) tracks" that were used so extensively throughout the thirties, forties, and fifties.

In concept, the musician would record his ideas in a purely temporary form as a guide for all the production that would follow. In some cases, a small orchestra was brought in and the work so carefully planned that the result could be used for production—if desired. In others, the studio composer would play his score on the piano or organ.

The advantage of this early test recording is obvious. It presents a strong musical concept that is stimulating and inspiring. As the director and animators develop the graphics, they are guided but not restricted by this track. Being temporary, the music can be changed and new ideas tried; the man who wrote it is standing by to help decide just what those changes should be and where in the score they should come. He is not beaten down by what seems like daily trivia, but is available when help is needed; and having made his initial statement of how he believes the music should be, he exerts more influence than when he tried to do instant composing in the room with the director.

The best music was achieved when it could springboard from the hours of thought and refinement that had gone into the story development and acting. If a sequence is well balanced, builds properly, has life, good textures, and a flow, the musician has a much better chance of writing a superior score than if the picture is dull, lifeless, and spotty. Even the grandest score will seem unimpressive under those conditions.

With a smaller crew and extended schedules for the pictures in the sixties and seventies, it was no longer possible to keep a musician on full time, so we shared one with the live action units. George Bruns worked equally well in either medium, writing "Davy Crockett" for the live TV show at the same time he was adapting Tchaikovsky's ballet score for *Sleeping Beauty* to our animated version of that classic fairy tale. George was big and easy-going, but he worked very hard and produced a seemingly endless string of fresh melodies and haunting scores.

He did temp tracks, prescored some selections, orchestrated songs, jumped over to the live action shows, then back to consult on the best musical treatment for the next sequence in the cartoon. When there was more to do than he could handle, he suggested that we find a piece of music from an earlier picture and "track" our picture with that. It enabled us to find just the mood we wanted, the tempos and phrasing to support our action, and kept us from wearing him out with too many changes.

When the time came to write the final score, George was fresh and enthusiastic, suggesting more effective ways to present our concepts, and writing lovely new ballads in the same tempo and feeling as the ones we had used for our "tracking."

All of our feature cartoons took anywhere from two to five years to complete; so no matter what the involvement of the musician during the formative period, there was still much to be done in the final days.

Sound effects were a very important part of the musical score, requiring musicians with unique talents—most were percussionists with stage bands. Here, Frank Churchill conducts as Walt listens (lower left), Bill Garity balances the sound (right foreground), and Wilfred Jackson follows the score in his dope book.

The composers of "When You Wish Upon a Star," as caricatured by T. Hee. Musician Leigh Harline, at the piano, and lyricist Ned Washington, on bended knee, selling the song.

Invariably there were many surprises and changes from those first excited plans. The director has gone through the reels with the musician hour after hour, discussing, planning, changing, humming; but he is never sure that the musician understands what is wanted, and the musician has an even more difficult time getting his own ideas across since the language of music is not something the director understands. Sometimes the music will lack the magic anticipated, and whole sections of the film will seem to fall short of what they might have been; but just as often, everyone will be startled by how much more powerful and intense the actions have become when fortified with the music.

We had worked hard on *The Rescuers*, trying to make the mice seem very small and inadequate to the task facing them, but the confidence and spirit in the voices seemed to dispel any concern we could develop for them. When Artie Butler wrote the music, he felt the predicament of the mice acutely and wrote music that immediately made their task enormous, while somehow keeping them virtually helpless. When they tried to move the huge diamond from its hiding place, the score added a good one hundred pounds to the weight of the gem. The animator exclaimed, "I tried

to make the mice strain and heave and use every bit of their strength when they pushed against that diamond, but this—this exhausts me!"[7]

Such effects are not evident in a piano track or even when played with a couple of instruments on a temp track. It takes the full voicing of the orchestra to bring the music to life, and until that time the director must go on faith that the score will fulfill his hopes and dreams. There is no way a single musician with only a small piano and an enthusiastic voice can convey the feeling or spirit that will come from the same notes played on all the instruments. This is unfortunate, since twenty-five musicians sitting on the stage awaiting instructions have an uncomfortable effect on a director's judgment of revisions when the first rehearsal reveals a different feeling in the music than had been anticipated.

All the other functions in the making of a film are built through constant testing and correcting and keeping the best relationship to the whole, and in the beginning music was done the same way. For over forty years, great scores have continued to bring new life to the studio's most popular films, even though the techniques of matching sound to picture have changed so

completely. It encourages one to believe that there still are many more ways, exciting ways, inspiring ways, to meld music and picture together.

Songs

When there were songs in a picture in addition to the musical score, they were written and recorded very early, so they could be integrated carefully into the story development. Walt was adamant about songs that stopped the flow of the story while some singer demonstrated his prowess, and he insisted that the only use for a song would be to pick up the tempo of the story and to tell it in another way, while adding to the emotional content of the sequence. A good song should make the audience feel more deeply about the situation.

Once a song had been accepted from the composer, a ''demo'' record was made approximating the length and structure being considered. The vocal might be on a production track (one that could be used in the final), but it would be far better on a temp track, with the accompaniment only a piano or small group that could be replaced later when all final decisions have been made. In the recording business, when a vocalist is recorded, the song itself and the singer's style will dictate the number of choruses and the right arrangement for that number. In a film, the structure must be dictated by the needs of the story. Bill Peet once cautioned a composer who wanted to control the presentation of his melody: ''You're better off writing to the material in the picture, because your song will end up being more unique. Instead of writing what you think is good and asking for the picture to adapt to it, remember that the cartoon material has been worked over and over; it has more thought, depth, and entertainment in it than you realize. You'd better use it!'' Of·course, it is possible to write such special material for a song that it becomes little more than a novelty, but if it works well for the picture and progresses the story situation, it still will have great value.

A song that catches the exact mood of the sequence and expresses it in a fresh and memorable way will do wonders for the film, and for the composer, too. Leigh Harline and Ned Washington's lovely ''When You Wish Upon a Star'' served double duty, introducing us

to a cricket with a gentle personality as well as setting a mood for the whole picture to follow. The next song, ''Little Wooden Head,'' captured the spirit of Geppetto and gave us a chance to introduce the wooden puppet in his lifeless state. Without that song with the melody that seemed to fit an old-world music box, the sequence of introducing the puppet to the other residents of the toy shop would have been full of dialogue, contrived gags, and lengthy business. With a song that fit the situation, it was full of melody and fun, and did much to show the audience how this woodcarver lived.

Once the song was recorded, the storyman could start precise work on his storyboard, adapting the general ideas to the mood and measures of the music, or suggesting changes that might help both picture and song. With only a demo track, changes could be tried and the structure of the music altered to fit the growing needs of the storyboard. In some cases, the vocal would remain, but if it has been recorded on a separate track, changes in the rest of the music would have no effect on it anyway. Now, when the board looks promising, and the length of the song feels right, the sketches can be shot and added to the story sketch reel. Once more they are changed and shifted, redrawn and reshot, until everything has the proper flow. There still will be improvements later on, as new ideas keep coming, but for the most part, they will be only touches that add spirit and character to the performance. Animating to music is difficult and expensive and it is wise to know exactly what is wanted before anyone starts.

Sound Effects

Funny sounds always have been an integral part of cartoons. It is almost impossible to think of the early films without the slide whistle, ratchet, pop-gun, xylophone, and bells. These had all been written in as part of the score and were not recorded until everything on the picture was completed. The animation had been done to a specific beat, the actions were all marked on the score itself, and four or five percussion men were now brought in with the orchestra to record the whole picture in one long, complete take of everything that would be on the sound track.

As technical knowledge advanced, it became possible to do the different parts of the sound separately and

The layout drawing for The Old Mill *shows the decaying timbers and interior structure that would creak ominously in any storm.*

combine them onto one track at a later date. Now if someone hit a wrong gong or scraped his sandpaper block once too often, the whole seven-minute take did not have to be done over. But a larger advantage was that now the way was open to experiment. The music could be recorded in separate takes called "cues," the voices could be done over and over until just the right inflection was captured, and the sound effects could be recorded individually, speeded up, run backward, or built out of two or three separate parts.

For *The Practical Pig*, in 1935, the sound effects men had to get the juicy impact of a ripe tomato hitting the big, bad wolf in the face. A wet washcloth had too much impact, a spoonful of grease was too wet, and a cup of water had too much splatter. The sound finally was achieved by combining the three best sounds over the blatant sound of the "razzberry," the impertinent noisemaker made of two loose pieces of rubber. None by itself sounded anything like a tomato, but together they had the feeling needed to match the action.

As Jim Macdonald says, "The sound man must think about what the sound is going to do for the picture—not just how it ought to sound." Jim was the most creative and dedicated of all the sound men, staying at the studio for some forty-two years, then continuing to come in for sound effects sessions after that well into his seventies. Originally brought in as a drummer to handle some of the sounds for those early cartoons, he was offered a steady job because of his imagination and sense of entertainment. He says that the sound effects man must "feel" the effect, even as he makes the sound, and in support of this philosophy threw himself violently into everything he did, from pounding on a door to choking himself with the hiccups. Being a musician he saw to it that the sounds always fit properly into the score, and being an entertainer he made sure the sound was the best that could be gotten for that spot. Good sound effects will add life and excitement to a film, whereas drab, ordinary sounds will quickly drain what life there might be in the action.

There were always changes in the ideas and the material as a picture developed; but when the studio embarked on the feature cartoon, the period for this experimentation stretched to three years or more. This meant that there would be endless changes in the sound

tracks as a good track inspired better business, which, in turn, built an even better track. No department was free of Walt's constant building and improving. Any new idea had to be tried out before a decision could be made about its actual value, and this led to test tracks and test recording and test music.

No studio could afford to bring in specialists every time there was a new idea to try, so members of the staff who were particularly inventive and creative—along with their other talents—were asked to do the experimenting. If it had to do with music or sound, it was usually someone from the sound effects department, and most often Jim Macdonald.

With considerable ingenuity and a great deal of blowing and accompanying dizziness, a track had been recorded for the organ that Grumpy played in the dwarfs' house. It was only a first test, but it involved everyone in the studio who could read music, plus a handful of competent musicians and all the sound effects men, some thirty of us in all, blowing on bottles and jugs and strange homemade instruments. The most demanding part was for the man who blew over the giant jug for the lowest bass notes. That part had gone to Jim. When Walt heard the track he exclaimed, "Yeah! That's a happy song . . . a happy group! Somebody should be yodeling," and he turned to look at Jim. "Why don't you get down on the stage and try to yodel?" As Jim said, "I had never yodeled in my whole life, but when Walt said, 'Yodel!' you yodeled."

And yodel he did, over and over, for a couple of years while they built the track into a happy sequence with just the right amount of singing and playing and fun. When everything was finally approved, a professional group of yodelers was called in to give the ringing, authentic sound, but the structure and the length had been worked out by amateur yodeler Jim Macdonald. He commented, "I was always doing voices for actions where they didn't want the actor to hurt his voice—grunts, strains, screams, gasping. . . ."

In *Aristocats* there was a scene of the alley cat O'Malley nearly drowning in the river. Phil Harris played the part and was not only willing to do anything we needed, but invariably found a way to make it all the more entertaining. Still, drowning did not seem to be a suitable application of his talents. We had used some miscellaneous gasps and coughs he had done for

us as we built our continuity and business to its climax, but then we called upon Jim. After looking at the film he recommended that he do it all in one take as he watched the film on the screen, rather than in separate pieces as he usually did. He brought out a big tub, filled it with water, and then with the mike in place and his chin half submerged, fixed his eyes on the screen and gave the order to roll the film. He not only matched the action precisely, but inhaled at least as much water as the cat in the picture, and ended up just about as nearly drowned.

Jim had a woodworking shop in his garage and would spend hours building gadgets that might make sounds for special sections of the pictures. When work was beginning on *The Old Mill* he saw that there would be a need for many different kinds of creaks as old, rotting parts of the structure would turn. He conceived of an elaborate contraption of drum heads, string and buttons and supports, and a wheel for tightening it all, figuring that with a bit of rosin and a bow he should be able to get some exceptional groans. What he got was a perfect foghorn! So he recorded that, which is still the one used today, and returned to his shop to start a new idea. It is very important that the effects man have enough time to think and play around with ideas if the sound is to be at all unusual, or just right for the picture. Many times it is necessary to run the recorded track through some of the sound equipment, to rever-

berate it, or take out the lows, or speed it up, or combine it with other sounds. When the day comes that the director is down on the stage to record, the sound effects man must be ready. It is then too late to experiment.

Every sound that is recorded eventually goes to the Sound Effects Library for use in other pictures. Over the years this enormous collection has been built into a treasure house of nearly every sound in the world—except the one, special, elusive sound that you want. There are fifty different coughs, whistles, footsteps, creaks, and foghorns, and these are widely used to build the test tracks, but when the picture is finally all put together, there is always a long list of needed sounds that should be done a little differently for this particular picture.

If the sound is part of a story idea or related to a character, it is always recorded early, so the animator can work to it, rather than trying to fit it in later. As the idea for the exhausted dragonfly in *The Rescuers* was developing, Jim was told of the problem and immediately started searching for things he could use. A power saw with its varied whines and straining noises seemed like an obvious choice because it sounds so determined and desperate, but it did not prove as flexible as a little creation of brass tubing and an air hose combined with a rubber membrane over a kind of drum that Jim could play like a musical instrument. It was when Jim added the panting and wheezing on the end of the buzzing sounds that the character of Evinrude finally leapt to life. That sense of entertainment in commonplace sounds is a very special talent.

It is the assistant director's job to build his tracks and keep them in sync and growing to match the needs of the picture. So it falls to him to rummage through the sound effects library for the most appropriate sounds he can find, and, also, to decide just how many he should put in. Too few can make the film sound spotty, too many can make it sound ridiculous.

At the start of the war in 1941, Ward Kimball and Fred Moore were animating a long, involved scene of a small soldier going through all the things a soldier is trained to do—drilling, manual of arms, saluting—everything except making his bed and KP. There was an eager assistant director at the time who was just waiting for his big chance to show what he could do.

The inventive crew of the Sound Effects Department creates a variety of creaking sounds to match the drawings. From the left, Earl Hatch, Jim Macdonald, ''Rusty'' Jones, and Eddie Forrest.

299

The suggestion was made that the scene would get over better even in its rough state if it had a few sound effects. Ward and Fred cautioned the assistant that if the effects were too real the scene would be dull, while if they were too exotic it would become silly and lose its strength. But the right sounds, carefully chosen, would give a sprightly character to the whole thing.

Three hours later the beaming assistant returned with the film and put it on the Moviola with the sound track he had concocted beside it. On the opening frame of the scene, there was a ratchet sound as the soldier's arm came up in a salute, followed by a ''ping!'' from a tiny bell as the fingers touched the forehead. This was followed by ''sproings,'' wheezes, thuds, claps, squeaks, one after the other, accenting every last little move the animated character made. Fred and Ward looked at each other in amazement, back to the film, back to each other, then broke into convulsive laughter. They fell to the floor and could no longer see the film, but the parade of unlikely sounds continued on and on, popping and bleeping, like something gone mad. The longer it went, the funnier it got, and once Fred and Ward had started to laugh, there was no stopping.

The assistant's beaming look of anticipation had long since dropped to a more defiant attitude, then to a grim set of determination. He stared doggedly at the film clacking through the Moviola, intent on seeing his masterpiece through to the end no matter what. Then he quietly turned off the machine, took off the film, walked out of the room with his track under his arm without uttering a word. The gales of laughter had naturally attracted everyone else in that wing of the building, and now curious heads were thrusting into the room. Not realizing the source of the humor, they let the assistant walk right past them, and that very special track disappeared forever.

Occasionally the sound effects man is asked to come up with a sound for something that cannot possibly make a sound of its own: for instance, the sound of a spider web shimmering with dew. Walt insisted that there should be a special sound, and though he could not describe it exactly he gave the impression that everybody knew what it should be. Jim Macdonald was given the assignment at that point and turned it

over in his mind for several days. It should be like a wind chime, he thought, soft and delicate, without the impact of glass hitting glass; it had to be something else.

Jim found his answer in some pieces of duraluminum left over from a new panel installed in the sound department. He cut the material into small pieces and suspended them from a plywood frame, and when he shook the whole thing an amazingly light and shimmering sound came forth. Walt liked it so well that he asked Jim to tune it chromatically so that a glissando could be played, or maybe even a tune. It was never enough to give Walt what he asked for. That always stimulated him to even more elusive, but undeniably better, ideas, and especially ideas that never would have been thought of in the beginning.

One of Jim's greatest accomplishments was the sound for a giant magnet. This actually was intended for a ride at Walt Disney World, but Marc Davis, who had helped develop the ride, knew from his years of animation training that the key factor in making the whole idea work was to have just the right sound. He called Jim out of retirement to find it. The fascinating thing is that Jim went right to objects that make no sound! That is, no sound the human ear can detect. A heavy-duty soldering iron operating on 60 cycles held close to the microphone gave off a very low, rhythmic hum. A de-magnetizer used for taking static electricity out of scissors before cutting tape gave off another sound that barely could be recorded, and, finally, Jim got a large cymbal and gently brushed a tiny piece of cotton against the edge. No sound could be detected on the stage, but the tape machine was picking up strange vibrations. These three sounds were taken to the dubbing panel in the theater, where the tracks were mixed and switched and altered, and raised in volume until the sound could be heard by human ears. It was a slow, pulsing, indefinable sound, and it started to make everyone there sick. As they bolted for the door, the annoyed technicians yelled back at Jim, ''You can't put that in Disney World!''

But Jim continued to play with his sounds, feeling like a mad inventor, until he had them at the provocative stage just short of producing illness and just past recognition of it as sound at all. It was more of a feeling, and it felt like a magnet should sound!

FACING PAGE:

Cobwebs never have been known to make a sound, but Walt felt this one in Alice in Wonderland *needed a special effect. Jim Macdonald eventually found a good effect that sounded just the way a cobweb looks.*

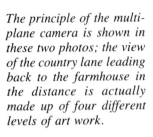

The principle of the multiplane camera is shown in these two photos; the view of the country lane leading back to the farmhouse in the distance is actually made up of four different levels of art work.

Photo by Dave Spencer

12. The Follow-up Functions

"No one person can take credit for the success of a motion picture. It's strictly a team effort. From the time the story is written to the time the final release print comes off the printer, hundreds of people are involved—each one doing a job—each job contributing to the final product."

Walt Disney

ANIMATOR: Ollie Johnston— Lady and the Tramp.

The old bloodhound Trusty tries to pick up a scent on the wet streets. More than just another walk, there is purpose and determination in his continuous searching.

STARTS ON PAGE 363

With the writing of the music, the last truly creative function has been completed. Some members of the staff already have new assignments and are excitedly exploring the next project, but there still are several crucial jobs to be done and decisions to be made that greatly affect the final appearance of the picture. Usually all the money budgeted for the film has been spent, and the big push is to "get it out" in the quickest way possible; yet too many compromises at this stage could destroy much of the value of the work already done. Fortunately, there are still dedicated people left who will see that this does not happen.

The scenes must be checked over and over to be sure that all parts work correctly. The artwork must be photographed by the Camera Department, all the different sound tracks must be combined onto one track, and then the lab must face the impossible task of getting the colors on the film to look the same as they were painted. While these jobs are not glamorous, they are vital in averting the seemingly endless string of one process or another always going wrong. Frantically trying to control these processes and keep the picture moving is the Production Manager.

Someone has to assume the responsibility for seeing that there are no bottlenecks, that scenes move through the organization smoothly, that directives are being carried out, that costs are held to a minimum, and that the producer understands why the project is not being completed on schedule. It does not have to fall to one individual. It can be shared by a small group of overworked artists with a special loyalty to the whole production. However, it is the one person with the official title Production Manager who can be blamed, criticized, questioned, and sent to take care of things.

His job was easy when the picture slowly was taking shape in the Story Department, the director was testing voices, and the experimental animation was being done. Not much money was being spent, but the creative process is impossible to control anyway. However, once the work has been passed by the animators to their assistants, drawings can be counted, deadlines imposed, schedules arranged, and work organized.

The picture is in full production at this point, and suddenly everything is going at once and in all directions. There is not enough time in any day to check even half of it, especially if the crew is behind schedule and working overtime to meet a deadline—which, somehow, nearly always happens. Nothing seems to be coming out quite the way it was planned, and no one really knows why. Everything conceivable for keeping production moving has been tried at one time or another, but a sense of devotion to the product brings the best results. Nevertheless, the Production Manager will tell you that too much devotion can cost too much money, too!

Checking

One of the best ways to keep work flowing smoothly is to have each scene checked carefully before it moves on to the next department. Once the animation is completed, it should be checked for technical problems. The drawings may have worked well in test camera, but someone has to adapt them to their final form on the cels. Are the characters on the right levels to match the other scenes in the sequence? Should some of the

303

levels be combined? Will the pan moves and trucks work smoothly? Is the action completed out to the field borders? Will it work under the camera?

Before we had checkers it was up to the cameraman to keep a close watch on the drawings on his stand as he was shooting, but that usually was too late. Typical of this situation was an incident on *Mickey's Kangaroo*. After shooting nearly half the scene, the cameraman noticed that Pluto was snarling as if he were guarding his dish, but in a peculiar way he was standing in it—though not quite in it. His foot covered part of the dish, but it did not match the curve or the shape of it. The clean-up man was called over to explain what was intended, and he immediately cried, "Someone has moved the dish! It's supposed to be over here right under Pluto's teeth, not back where his foot is!" A call to the background man produced his copy of the layout sketch and his notes on the scene. He was blameless.

Another call; this time to the layout man, who came with all his drawings to prove that the dish always had been in the same place. Now the animator joined the assembled group, and after more discussion he recalled moving the dish so there would be room for Pluto to run in and leap into this defensive position. He had made a tracing of the location of the dish and marked it on his copy of the layout. It was surprising to him that the layout man did not know about it, and he wondered why the final animation had not been checked before going ahead.

They all stared bleakly at the completed set-up on the camera stand. The cels then went back to the production rooms where adjustments were made until the scene worked properly, but much time was lost in all departments through mistakes that somehow slipped past everybody. Rather than establish blame it seemed more important to prevent it from happening, so the position of Checker was created.

Very soon it was discovered that one checker was not enough. In addition to the check for mechanics and technical problems, there had to be a check for missing detail, for clear instructions to the inkers, for missing lines around color areas, for registry of one character to another or to an object on the background. In Ink and Paint they needed additional checking before a scene was painted, and still another afterward to make sure everything was on the cels and following through perfectly. Some of the amazingly complicated scenes from *Fantasia* even required a specialist in checking, since the components were so involved and interrelated that hardly anyone even knew what was supposed to happen.

Only certain individuals should be checkers. The job calls for a special personality makeup more than an artistic talent, and not everyone can adapt to the demands. Complete concentration and an "eagle eye" are needed hour after hour to ferret out the smallest errors—but in the process a huge one should not go by unnoticed! The checker must be a detective, completely dedicated and above personal involvement. Such individuals scarcely can be blamed for screaming, "ah-HAA-aa-a-a!!!" when they discover a mistake, but that outburst does little to endear them to the person who made the error. No one does sloppy work on purpose, and somehow a distressing air of recrimination seems to hover around a visit to the checker's room. For some reason, the feeling is reminiscent of being called to the principal's office.

Blue Sketch

New procedures were suggested constantly that would make the checker's job simpler and eliminate some of the expense created by needless errors. The "Blue Sketch" was one of the most practical.

One time a background painter was given a layout showing an ominous evening sky with the vague shapes of tree branches silhouetted against the clouds. The color key that styled this sequence showed a greenish sky with an evil look. The background man was intrigued. Here was a good-looking design, simple yet dramatic, and an impressive painting could be made of this. He carefully worked out the lacy fingers of the branches, the contrasting shapes and colors, with subtle shading in the clouds. The whole thing was alive and would make anyone look twice. The only trouble was that the background painter had not checked to see what action took place in the scene. It was actually a close-up of a large and formidable character who blotted out all the trees and most of the sky—only bits of painting around the edges showed. This was a great disappointment for the painter as well as a waste of

talent and time. Something had to be done to keep this from happening again. That was when someone thought of making a "blue sketch" of the scene.

When the action of the rough animation has been approved (what we called "OKed for Clean Up"), the scene is picked up by the Layout Department and checked for all the extremes of movement. A composite tracing is made in colored pencils (predominantly blue) that shows the size of the character, how much of him is showing, how high he goes on the paper, his lowest point, his maximum move to the left or right, any contact he makes with parts of the background, as well as the first and last drawings in the scene. These essential movements of the character are recorded so that everyone will know just where he goes and what he does in that one scene. It reveals changes the animator may have made in the whole set-up that the layout man possibly does not know about yet, and it indicates to the background man the main areas of activity and those places that should be painted simply.

Even so, the element of human error will not be shut out. There was a scene in *The Jungle Book* that is still a mystery to all involved. The boy, Mowgli, was to be shown running through the jungle after he thought he had been double-crossed by Baloo. The feeling needed to be one of desperation, with more abandon and floundering than speed. The animator who was to do the scene remembered a piece of live action film showing a boy push aside some branches as he ran into a thicket. It seemed like a good action that would fit both Mowgli's attitude and the situation, so the film was brought up and the animator studied, made notes, and sketched until he could adapt the action to the restrictions of his scene. The boy threw up a protective arm, ducked his head, twisted his body, then leaned back, all giving him more thrust when the branches were pushed aside and he burst through, continuing his forward progress. It was a good action and difficult to capture, but worth it for the extra quality it would give the picture.

All of the key positions of the characters in a scene are traced onto a single sheet and checked against the final layout. In this example from The Fox and the Hound, *there is, first, the pup coming out of the hollow log; next, his contact with the fox; finally, the last drawing of the two playing. This shows the background painter where the action occurs in the scene.*

305

This type of action would not show up on the blue sketch, and none of the people who worked on the scene took note of anything special about it. The effects animator who did the final drawing on the branches stayed as close as he could to the action the animator had defined, but he felt the leaves needed to be bigger to match the new model and even added a few more to increase the overall mass. The layout man, thinking more about dense jungle than the boy's problem, also increased the size and number of the leaves. Finally, the background man, looking at the layout and the effects animation, added a bit of lush growth of his own that was appropriate to the jungle, but by then the action was completed covered! The boy simply ran behind some dense bushes and came out on the other side, still running.

Money and time and effort had gone into shooting the live action, animating the scene, cleaning it up and inbetweening it, making the layout, and painting the background. At this point in the production, which artist should change what he had done? A conference was held and the decision was based on expediency: leave it the way it is; the audience will never know what they are missing. The best procedures always have a way of breaking down, and only close contact between the individual artists can keep everyone working toward a common goal.

Bill Cottrell began his career working on one of the first cameras used by the Disney cameramen. Later he transferred to story, eventually becoming a story director. He was the first employee to be at the Studio fifty years.

Camera

The first animation camera was suspended from a wooden frame so it would point straight down at the drawings on a table. There was nothing fancy about it and most filmmakers built their own. Since the drawings had to be held in register so each always would be in the same place, various methods were tried, with holes punched in the paper that matched little metal pegs becoming the most successful. To hold the drawings absolutely flat while photographing, a large piece of heavy glass, called a platen, was placed over them. This was even more important when cels were involved, since they had a tendency to curl and reflect light back up into the camera lens.

Before the button is pushed to shoot a single frame of film, the whole set-up of drawings and background must be checked visually to see if it looks right and is completely free of foreign matter. A speck of dust or a curious fly can ruin an expensive scene, so an air hose is kept handy to blow off anything that should not be there.

In the twenties, two cameramen were needed to shoot a scene since the camera had to be turned by hand. One man stayed up on top and carefully turned the crank one turn, trying to keep a consistent speed and rhythm throughout; the other arranged the drawings on the pegs. At Disney's, it was the ubiquitous Ub Iwerks who rigged up an automatic switch so everything could be done by one man seated at the camera table.

As filmmakers' ideas expanded, they found a need to move the camera up and down so they could come in closer on a scene or pull farther back during the action. A calibrated post replaced the wooden frame. A short time later, they wanted to move the camera either to one side or the other, and then they also needed to twist the camera as much as ninety degrees for special shots, and to move the drawings through at right angles to their normal position. This was called a vertical pan even though the art work remained perfectly flat. The pegs at both top and bottom were placed on bars that could slide, and then auxiliary pegs were introduced, and then a contraption that would move the pegs in any direction.

According to Bill Cottrell, who was the whole cam-

era department in 1930, Walt had constant ideas for improvements on the camera and kept asking for additions that would allow more flexibility. His ideas continued on into the film itself and what effects were possible there. Bill said, "He asked me to experiment with color on film—to put silver nitrate on the film and see what happened. The picture *Night* was printed on blue stock, and we had a fire sequence that was printed on red."

By the sixties, the cameras and animation stands could do almost more than most animators knew how to make use of. These giants were expensive, and few of their fancy gadgets were used very often, but when needed they were wonderful to have. It was always a question of whether it was cheaper to have the cameraman shoot the scene six times (each time with a different exposure, and different material, until a very special effect was achieved) or have an enterprising young artist draw it all by hand. Sometimes there was no question since the effect could be obtained only by the camera work, but now and then an enthusiastic and competent cameraman could talk the producer into more expense than really was necessary.

There was a period in the mid-thirties when every new employee in the creative fields had to work in the Camera Department six weeks to learn how the pictures were put together physically. It sounded like a great idea because it educated everyone in the major tools they would be using in putting their ideas on the screen, but in truth it was a fiasco. The need for an unusually sharp eye and complete concentration, combined with the almost unlimited potential for error after error, was more than most artistic temperaments could tolerate. Expenses soared and the productivity of the department itself dropped to an all-time low. The idea was abandoned, but for years cameramen seemed to cast a baleful eye at any animator who came visiting. It was unfortunate, because animators must have some technical knowledge just to animate well and should know what assistance the camera can give them in achieving their results.

This all led inevitably to the huge, shiny, mysterious monster that was kept hidden behind signs saying, "No Admittance" and "KEEP OUT": the multiplane camera. Solidly engineered, it was built to withstand every kind of ill treatment, but it was awkward to get

around and unbelievably heavy. The light-weight metals were hardly known at that time, and four strong men were needed just to lift the frame that held a single animation level. As many as eight 500 watt bulbs were in a bank of lights for one level, and when all levels were lit the heat was oppressive.

Somehow this camera captured the imaginations of both artists and the public, either because of its overwhelming size or its impenetrable workings or the possibilities of what it could do. The principle of its operation is simple and easy to explain, but making it work is quite another matter. The complications are suggested by the fact that less than two years after its initial use, a manual had to be prepared that began: "The Multiplane Planning Board is a body headed by the Direction Unit and Camera Coordinator and a representative of the Engineering Department. The function of this board is to work out the ways and means of accomplishing Multiplane shots. . . ."

Basically, the multiplane apparatus makes use of several layers of glass, each with some scenic material on it and placed at a varying distance from the camera. For an average shot, the background itself would be eight feet away, the first level six feet, the second five feet, then another at four feet, and maybe a fourth level at only two-and-a-half feet. As many as six levels have been used and shot from a distance of 14 feet, but that is not an average set-up. Assume the scene called for the camera to move in through the artwork and progress to the right slowly. The amount of the move on each part would have been very carefully calculated by an engineer, and all that is left would be to run through the scene to see if everything works as planned. On the regular camera, there is no run through. If a scene has been checked and approved, it will work on the camera, and it does. The cameraman shoots it just as the exposure sheet is marked. On the multiplane camera, it is necessary to test the markings.

The lights are turned on, the first cels are placed in position, and the technicians take their places beside each of the levels. Up on top the cameraman is peering through the lens, but there is no film in the camera. First, the level with the featured artwork is lit with the proper intensity, then the other levels are lit separately, so that each gives the best artistic appearance to the whole scene. Two big problems plague the crew endlessly: first, reflections that bounce off the shiny cels into the camera lens, and, second, light from a lower level that occasionally shows through the paint on the back of the cels.

The reflections took all kinds of ingenuity to conquer, from adding neutral density glasses under the camera lens at a forty-five degree angle (to "reflect the reflection away") to leaving the offending level dark for one shooting, then lighting it by itself for a second run-through. Expensive and tedious, but as the crew said, "We were shooting most of the stuff with multiple exposure anyway."

Conquering the light leaks was easier—for the cameramen. This involved sending all the cels in that level back to the painters for another coat of paint, this time in heavy black. (Later white paint was used for this

backing.) The painters were annoyed at having to do this extra work, because only one frame had a light leak, and a piece of black paper slid underneath the cel would have stopped that in a hurry. After years of protest from the painters it finally was agreed that this was a good idea.

Work in camera completely stopped while the painters fumed and painted the back of every last cel on that level. When work resumed later that day, or maybe even the next, the camera crew started over again to make sure everything would work smoothly with this new correction. They could not check every frame of a scene but did have to run down to all the critical points, checking the camera moves, the appearance of the scene at that point in the camera finder, the light leaks on other levels, and the constant reflections. In spite

The camera room at the Hyperion studio, 1937. The standard camera crane, at right, is dwarfed by the first multiplane camera taking shape at left.

of the most careful planning, sometimes they would find that they were overshooting a painted area or removing a level before all of its parts were out of the camera field.

As the camera was lowered closer to the artwork, new problems appeared because of the change of angle from camera to lights. Alterations that corrected a condition at one point always seemed to create a second problem at another. So hour after hour the camera crew backed up, changed the equipment, started forward, backed up, started over, changed something else, until all parts of the scene were working flawlessly. This literally took days, even with a full crew of five or six men, but eventually they were ready to shoot the scene.

It is easy to see why operating the multiplane camera was so expensive and why it was used less in later years. Just to set up for a held position with the background out of focus took longer than on the regular camera, but the results were unsurpassed. There was also a time factor in just shooting the film: to get the depth of field in the focus for such a distance, a time exposure of some eight or nine seconds was required for every frame of film. In addition, there were 22 possible adjustments that could be made before each frame was shot; not all were used on every frame, but all had to be calculated and written up and checked for *each frame*. The exposure sheets were so complicated that only highly trained technical men could write them—or read them.

In spite of the complications, there were three separate multiplane cameras working around the clock for

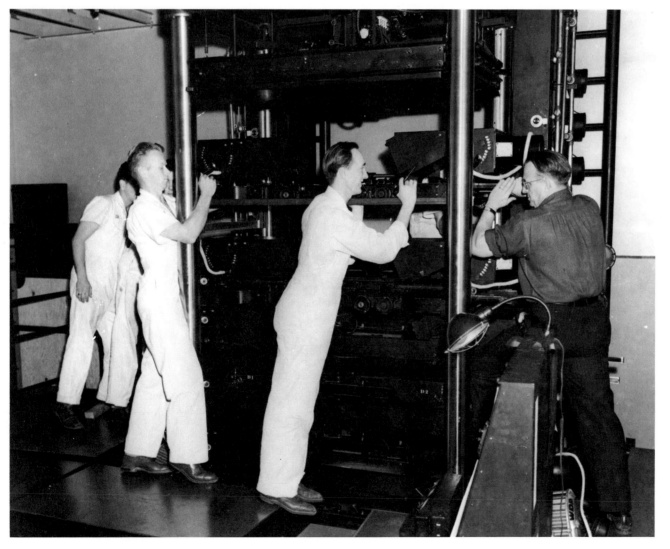

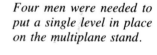

Four men were needed to put a single level in place on the multiplane stand.

many months. One cameraman said, "I worked almost a year on *Fantasia*, 12 hours a day. I had the night shift. I'd come in about 6 o'clock and I'd never get home till 8 or 9 in the morning." He remembered the special problems of shooting a little scene that would be on the screen for a mere three seconds, yet it had to be shot 12 separate times to get the subtle effects that came only from multiple exposure. "You'd do one

The cameraman uses an air hose to clean dust off the cels before closing the platen. This procedure is followed on each level containing cel work on the multiplane camera.

Usually only the cameramen were allowed in the multiplane room, but, occasionally, a few painters were called in to alter the cels so the shooting could continue with a minimum of delay.

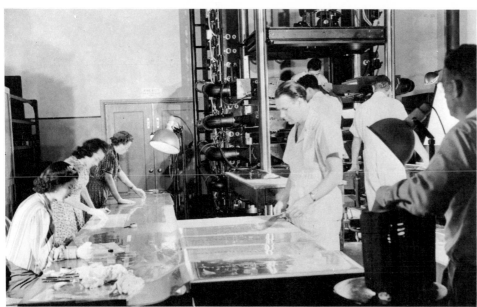

and then you'd do another, then a distortion; you'd do a diffusion, you'd do mist; if you'd make one mistake after you start. . . ." He shook his head at the painful memory. "You had to absolutely duplicate every move. With four or five guys—you've got a guy there, and a guy there—and a—you'd never make that film today, I guess."[1]

Few inventions have made such a difference in the appearance of the product as the old multiplane camera. When it was first used it was very special, and the public heard enough about it to know that it meant quality in production and visual excitement. It was good publicity, a great advertising item, and the name appeared prominently in our ads. We were amazed one day to see an ad for a Warner Bros. live-action feature, laid in the wooded hills of magnificent mountains, that claimed the whole picture had been shot with the "Glorious Multiplane Camera!" A good publicist cannot seem to pass up anything that is hot at the time!

In later years, when the most often heard question is, "How can we get the same effect for less money?" layout men increasingly have gone to the optical printer for their answers. Assorted wonders daily come out of this device: among them a combining of different strips of film that in many ways duplicates the work of the antiquated multiplane camera, long since priced out of existence. In this process, called bi-pack, the character is shot on one piece of film and the background is shot on another. In the printer, the two pieces of film are combined—sometimes revealing a bit of telltale rim-lighting, but usually producing a surprising feeling of depth to the scene. For a character racing straight toward the camera, or going away, or for the camera to pan with the character through certain landscapes, bi-pack gives the best illusion.

The men in Special Effects operate the process lab, and it is not in their makeup to do anything over and over without asking questions. When head layout man Don Griffith went over to ask about the best way to plan a scene he had for bi-pack, he was told, "Why do you want bi-pack? Why don't you use two-strip?"

Don asked, "What's two-strip?"

He is not sure that he understood the answer, but, as he says, "The main thing is that they can do it!" The master peg that used to slip and cause the annoying

The Multiplane Camera

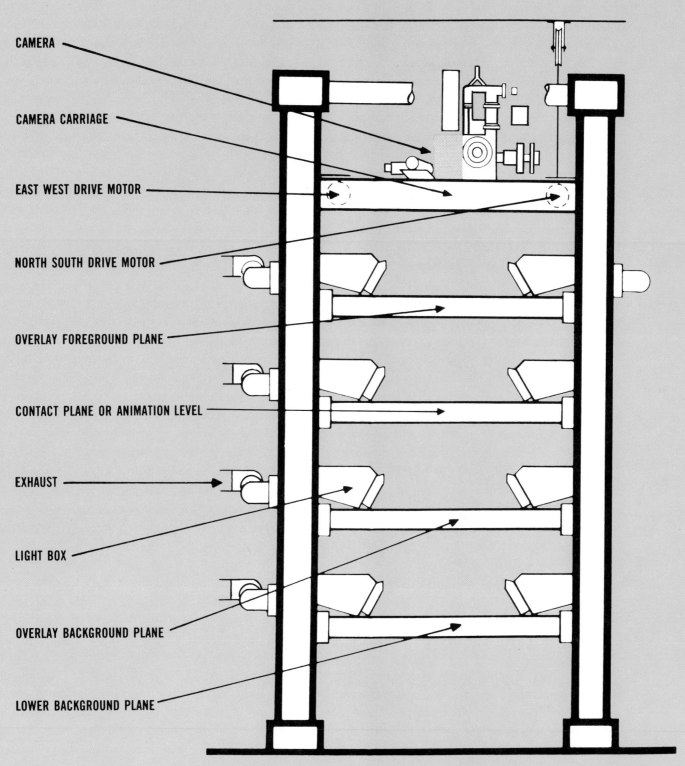

CAMERA

CAMERA CARRIAGE

EAST WEST DRIVE MOTOR

NORTH SOUTH DRIVE MOTOR

OVERLAY FOREGROUND PLANE

CONTACT PLANE OR ANIMATION LEVEL

EXHAUST

LIGHT BOX

OVERLAY BACKGROUND PLANE

LOWER BACKGROUND PLANE

rim-lighting has been eliminated, and three and four strips can be combined simultaneously, and a soft focus can be achieved on one level (as in the old multiplane), and even a see-through effect for an overlay is possible. While Don Griffith is excited about these accomplishments, Art Cruickshank, veteran of the Special Effects Department since the thirties, still likes the multiplane camera best. He wishes it could be used again, because nothing can take its place in achieving great effects. "The bi-pack is okay for a couple of levels, moving in and around, but for a full, six-level scene, it can't do the same thing at all."

Several exceedingly alert minds around the world have come up with a computerized multiplane camera that makes all the moves of the separate levels automatically, and this eliminates those four or five technicians who stood around waiting to make a small move on their level hardly often enough to remember if they had done it in the first place. Now, when they automate the position of the lights, their relation to the camera and to the cels, and figure how instantly to effect changes in the cels themselves as necessary, it may be economically possible to start planning those involved scenes again. There are many ways today to make the old device less cumbersome: for instance, the use of smaller lights that throw out as much actual candlepower as the old bank of 500 watt bulbs but with virtually no heat.

More likely, however, new uses will be found for the astonishing electronic inventions that become available to the imaginative producer and director almost daily. Then, the venerable old giant that stimulated so many wonderful concepts and made so many visual dreams come true, can be retired to the museum. It proved that creative men with determination eventually can find a way and that the artist who is alert to mechanical aids can find the assistance he needs to put his ideas on the screen.

Dubbing

This is the original name for the process of combining all the sound tracks onto a single track that will be printed on the film along with the picture. Somehow, the dialogue, sound effects, and music all have to be dubbed together without losing any of the special values that each has brought to the picture. Proper balance between these sounds can give the film more life and sparkle, while a lesser job will leave it muddy and undistinguished.

Since the process actually calls for recording everything a second time, it also has been called re-recording, or "re-re." This presents another occasion for diplomacy and compromise. The sound man has high standards for what constitutes good sound, and he is very aware of what other sound men will say about his work. Most potential conflict here comes from the sound man's very best effort to get clear, pure sound on the tracks when that might not be the goal of the director. He may be after the reality of voices half-lost in a crowd, the confusion of noises in strong activity, the impact on the listener if he were there! The sound man wants to hear every sound clearly and distinctly; the director wants emotion and involvement.

There are no absolutes in sound; it is all relationships. You can have more highs, or more lows, less of this, or a touch of that, or a bit of reverb. It is complex, and it is all controlled by a system of dials and regulators and buttons that only the "mixer" may touch. Through this system go all the sound tracks at the same time, and there probably will be as many tracks as there are sound heads on which to run them, even when the music has been re-recorded previously and is now on one track. If the music track is run at a level that gives it an opportunity to have real meaning, the dialogue cannot be heard. If the dialogue is brought up, the music cannot be heard. And if the sound effects are given a chance, they are apt to blast you out of your seat. It is a ticklish business with constant discussion of what should be done. Very rarely will there be any agreement.

The assistant directors and the cutters spend long hours preparing for dubbing sessions, because all the tracks must be in order, with no dirt or scratches, and old duplicates from the work tracks must be excluded. This is the time they discover that the irreplaceable piece of film they thought had been misplaced is actually lost! This is also a time of hope that the dope book containing the bar sheets has been accurately kept up to date, because this is the supreme authority on the status of both the picture and the sound tracks. From now on these two will be worked on separately, and it

is highly advisable that they fit together perfectly when eventually they are printed side by side on a roll of film.

Often, additional reels containing the sound will be made up just for the dubbing session so that one take of dialogue can be moved off the reel that contains phrases too close together or too different in volume. There must be enough time for a dubber or mixer to turn his dials when he balances everything. A low whisper cannot be right next to a yell on the same track; it must be moved to another reel where it can be controlled better. After the sound has been checked and shifted and measured and replaced, cue sheets are made up that show the sound men just what is on each track, how long it runs, and what comes up next. These become the guide as rehearsals bring out suggestions and notations of what to try on the next run. "Hold the music down just a bit and bring up that hoarse cackle—it's getting lost in there."

These practice runs can take all day on a complicated sequence, and in the early days there was no stopping to correct a mistake. Whatever happened, the reels had to run to the end, then be taken off, wound back, and threaded up again on the sound heads, one after the other. With ten reels, and a confused sound man, even a speedy projectionist could not make up for the delays. One assistant director says his blackest days were spent on those rehearsals, for after the proper setting for each dial had been determined for all the places in the whole reel the director would be called over to listen for the first time. While he frowned with critical appraisal, the film might roll by for 700 feet with perfect balance; then, for no apparent reason, a crucial line of dialogue would not be heard, or a sound effect would be muffled. The director's comment would be, "Call me when you've got the bugs worked out," and he would return to his room while the reels were run back, re-threaded, and made ready to start over again from the beginning.

New equipment and inventions have greatly simplified this whole procedure now, but there are still decisions to be made, torn film, parts that sound thin no matter how the dials are turned, heavy, tubby sounds that cannot be made to match, frantic trips back to the cutter's room to shift or replace a tiny piece of sound. Re-thread and start over again. . . .

Answer Print

Anyone who has shot color pictures of a vacation trip knows that the slides or prints never come back looking exactly the way the scene appeared to the eye. The pictures are a little bluer, or maybe redder, or in some strange way not in the same balance at all. The same thing happens when film is shot of the completed artwork and sent to the lab to be developed.

These scenes come back as "dailies" and are eagerly studied by a concerned staff. The representative of the lab explains that "dailies" are never true in color since they are printed in whatever bath is available at the time. He assures everyone that the negative is good and that all this will be corrected when the lab makes the Answer Print. The big trouble is that the lab cannot always do it. As John Hench grumbled after hours and hours of experimentation, "Film just won't do what you think it should!"

The results improve each year with new chemicals and processes, but for four decades it was a thorny problem that took much energy and many meetings. Walt even hired two key men from Technicolor to advise on what could be done to insure a certain result in the final printing, and magnificent results were often obtained one way or another.

If a certain visual effect really is needed in the film, it is wise to experiment early to see if a cooperative lab can help in any way, for after the print has been made there is very little that can be done. It can be darker, or redder or lighter or bluer, which might make the overall scene read more clearly, but it cannot achieve a whole new color balance. That only can be done by changing the original artwork to make use of such capabilities as are available at the lab. It is often a disappointing compromise.

Foreign Versions

Ordinarily one does not think of the special problems of making a foreign version of a film until after the initial release, when the box office receipts indicate whether the venture is justified or not. At Disney's the foreign market always has made up a large percentage of our revenue, starting with that first recording of *Snow White* in another language.

The Rescuers

Since the shorts were based on sight gags, the sound tracks had been mainly sound effects and music. The occasional, "Hi, Minnie!" and "Yoo-hoo!" were hardly important enough to be translated into French, German, Italian, Spanish, and Portuguese. But with the coming of the features, new considerations had to be faced. The man Walt chose for this diplomatic and creative job was Jack Cutting, who had started as an inker, worked his way up to animator, then switched over to be the first assistant director. In that job he learned everything about putting a picture together, both physically and artistically, but his talents lay beyond that. It was his feel for the characters themselves and what made them work in the picture that made his versions in other languages so unique. He did not try to match a deep voice, or a whiny voice, or a raspy voice, but went instead for an actor who could project the same personality as the original, regardless of the voice quality. Jack knew and understood the character relationships and how they should play against each other, and he searched until he found actors in other countries who could capture the same feeling that was in the version we had made.

He traveled often, lived in Europe for much of each year as he learned the languages, and became acquainted with technicians in the studios and performers in the night clubs and in the films. He worked with the dialogue writers and interpreters in finding the best way to keep the spirit of a line rather than just the words, and used his training and his judgment in coaching the voice talent during the recording sessions. This recording was always done in the native country whenever possible, partly because of the availability of busy actors and partly for the natural feeling that came to the phrasing and expressions.

As the popularity of the pictures grew in Europe and Asia, more and more languages were dubbed in with the original music and sound effects: all of the Scandinavian countries were represented, as were the Middle East, Japan, Korea, Thailand, and even India in a Hindi version of *Bambi*. If a picture was popular in one country, it was equally popular around the world, but occasionally one country would pick a favorite and treasure it above all others. Japan always has loved *101 Dalmatians*, and Germany made *The Rescuers* the highest grossing picture of all time in that country.

As animators we wonder about this popularity of our work in other lands. When we have labored so hard to get good sync—the very best acting to match the voice track and to convince audiences that the voice is really coming out of this cartoon character—we are puzzled that the figure still can come alive when his voice is changed. Do we worry too much about making the lips and the mouth and the whole face speak the lines, or is it this very concern that makes the character convincing even with another voice? Is it the care that Jack Cutting used in choosing a personality that would match what we already have animated, or is there more magic in this medium than we have suspected? However it happens, it is extremely gratifying to know that our work and our views on entertainment are bringing happiness to peoples of all races all around the world.

That's My Character!

Everyone who has worked on a picture will feel that he made the personal contribution that caused the cartoon character to come alive on the screen. The storyman naturally will feel that the character is *his*, because, after all, it was the story work that determined what kind of an individual this figure would be; and the story sketch man smiles because he drew the new character, made the expressions, showed how he would look; and the director knows that it was he who pulled all these talents together and kept insisting that the figure act a certain way; and all the time the actor who did the voice is saying, "Well, I know he's my character because he's me; I did him!" And the animator nods knowingly, because no one can deny that he set the final model and brought him to life, and the assistant knows that without his work the character would never have reached the screen. The person who selected the colors, those who painted the cels, even those who carefully checked to see if this character had all his buttons; the cameraman who shot the scenes; the sound mixer who gave the special sound to the voice—to all of them, he is *their* character! This is as it should be. Unless everyone feels this closeness to the end product, the dedication will not be there and the necessary care will not be taken to insure that the end result will be the finest anyone can do.

Alice in Wonderland

HOW MANY DRAWINGS DOES IT TAKE?

Twenty-four frames of film are projected every second, with several drawings on each frame.

There is the background drawing throughout, plus as many as four levels of drawings laid over it. For instance:

A. Mickey's legs and feet (which do not move).

B. Mickey's head and body (which do move).

C. Pluto.

D. Pluto's tail (which wags intermittently).

Probable average of 4 drawings per frame times 24 frames per second = 96 drawings.

96 drawings a second times 60 = 5760 drawings a minute.

The picture is 80 minutes long.

There are 460,800 total drawings for film.

But those are just the finished drawings (which will be put onto cels and painted, for another 460,800!).

It began with the inspirational sketch man. He undoubtedly did 1000 drawings, counting sketches, doodles, research, and final.

Next, the story sketch men. Each man does at least 20 drawings a day, 100 a week, 5000 a year, 15,000 during the three years it takes to make the picture. Five men would easily do 75,000 drawings on each feature film.

The layout man does about half that many; three layout men: 22,500 drawings.

The animator makes at least five drawings for every one he keeps, but he does only about a fourth of the actual drawings in the scene. That would be 115,200 times 5 = 576,000 drawings from all the animators combined.

The inbetweeners do the 345,600 left in the scenes, once in ruff, once in corrections, and again in final: perhaps 1,036,800.

The clean-up men redraw all the animators' drawings, keeping only about one of every three that they draw. 115,200 times 3 = 345,600.

Drawings by all personnel of gags, caricatures, maps of how to get to someone's house, explanations and suggestions for new staging would easily total 2000 drawings.

This makes the following grand total:

Inspirational sketch	1,000
Story sketch	75,000
Layout	22,000
Animators	576,000
Inbetweeners	1,036,800
Assistants	345,600
Finished cels	460,800
	2,517,200
Miscellaneous sketches	2,000
Total drawings	2,519,200

WHY DOES IT TAKE SO LONG?

A feature film must be one hour ten minutes long, minimum. At ninety feet of film projected every minute, there are 6300 feet to be animated. However, most Disney films were about ten minutes longer, totaling 7200 feet.

Ten feet a week was the average output of an animator on this type of action; some did more, some less. The crew usually had ten men who could do this.

Ten men doing ten feet a week would take 72 weeks to do 7200 feet. Add to that holidays, vacations, winter colds, a touch of flu, slumps, mistakes, and a scene or two that has to be done over: 78 weeks

total.

There are six months of research before the film goes into production. There is one year of work on story, planning, styling, experimenting, and recording before animation is begun.

Animation takes a year and a half.

Six months follow-up time needed for clean up, color, music, camera, etc.

Grand total: three years six months, if there are no catastrophes. (Twenty animators doing fifteen feet a week could do it in six months—but there are not twenty animators who can do even ten feet a week!)

13. The Uses of Live Action in Drawing Humans and Animals

"This is a very important thing. There are so many people starting in on this, and they might go hay-wire if they don't know how to use this live action in animating."
Walt Disney

Our term "live action" refers here to the filming of actors (or animals) performing scenes planned for cartoon characters before animation begins, as compared to "regular animation," which develops entirely from an artist's imagination. The direct use of live action film has been part of the animation industry for years—as an aid to animation, a companion to animation, and even as a replacement for animation. From time to time, almost every studio has fallen back on a strip of live film to perfect a specific action animators were not able to capture. At the Disney studio, filmed action of humans and animals was used in many ways to do

many jobs, and it led to some important discoveries. Live action could dominate the animator, or it could teach him. It could stifle imagination, or inspire great new ideas. It all depended on how the live action was conceived and shot and used.

In the early 1930s, animators drew from the model regularly, but as the necessity grew for more intricate movement and convincing action in our films, this type of static study quickly became inadequate. We had to know more, and we had to draw better to accomplish what Walt Disney wanted. Some new way had to be found for an artist to study forms in movement, and

Helene Stanley, left, portrays the gentle Anita in 101 Dalmatians, *while Mary Wickes is her overbearing, flamboyant friend Cruella DeVil. Each actress contributed her own ideas on personality and mannerisms within the framework of the action devised for this particular scene.*

ANIMATORS: *Milt Kahl, Anita; Marc Davis, Cruella—* 101 Dalmatians.

The animators' drawings show the freedom used in interpreting the action on the photostats. Milt, animating Anita, chose not to use the cringing body position suggested by Helene, while Marc went even further with Cruella, adding the thrust to the neck and a thin, bony body. By working closely together, the two animators were able to make the drawings match in size and scale, while the performances of the actresses maintained the personality relationship.

for this to be useful it had to relate to the work on our drawing boards. Running film at half-speed in our action analysis classes was helpful for a general understanding of weight and thrusts and counter thrusts, but the principles were not directly applicable to animation. Our instructor Don Graham had chosen certain film segments as clear, isolated examples of movements he could use in his lectures, but, while they gave us insight into articulation, they were still essentially classroom exercises.

One day, during a discussion of how the *Snow White* dwarf Dopey should act in a particular situation, someone suggested that his actions might be similar to those of burlesque comedian Eddie Collins. This led to everyone's going down to the theater to see the exceptional Mr. Collins perform. We invited him to the studio, and a film was shot of his innovative interpretations of Dopey's reactions—a completely new concept that began to breathe life into the little cartoon character. Dopey had been the "leftover" dwarf, with no particular personality and not even a voice; so, now, to see the possibility of his becoming someone special, and, particularly, someone entertaining, was an exciting moment! And best of all, everything Collins had suggested was on film.

There was nothing in the film that could be copied or used just the way it was, but as source material it

was a gold mine. Freddie Moore had the assignment of doing the experimental animation on Dopey, and he ran the Collins film over and over on his Moviola, searching not so much for specifics as for the overall concept of a character. Then he sat down at his desk and animated a couple of scenes that fairly sparkled with fresh ideas. Walt turned to the men gathered in the sweatbox and said, "Why don't we do more of this?"

Immediately other comics were brought in—entertainers from vaudeville, men who had done voices for the other dwarfs; all were put before the camera. No routines were filmed, just miscellaneous activities and expressions that might help delineate a character. Our own storymen who had a special talent for acting were dragged to the sound stage, and animators even photographed each other. As Bill Cottrell said years later, "It all seems so amateurish now—but it was fun! It *was* fun!" And that spirit of fun and discovery was probably the most important element of that period.

Now we had film that had been shot just for us, directly related to the characters we were drawing, and even though the acting was crude, we all picked up ideas to enrich our scenes. We quickly found that there were two distinctly different ways this film could be used. As resource material, it gave an overall idea of a character, with gestures and attitudes, an idea that

320

could be caricatured. As a model for the figure in movement, it could be studied frame by frame to reveal the intricacies of a living form's actions.

At that time, the only way of studying live action frame by frame was to trace the film on our rotoscope machine. This was simply a projector converted to focus one image at a time, from below, onto a square of clear glass mounted in a drawing board. When drawing paper was placed over the glass, tracing after tracing could be made, each sheet kept in register by pegs at the bottom of the glass. It was tedious work and time-consuming, but this was the way it had been done for twenty years.

Naturally, Walt changed that situation in a hurry. He had the film processing lab work out a system of printing each frame of a film onto photographic paper the same size as our drawing paper. These sheets, which we called photostats, were then punched to fit the pegs of an animation desk, and the animator could now study the action by flipping "frames of film" backward and forward, just as he did his drawings. Here could be seen every tiny detail of changing shapes and relationships in the movements. At last, the animators could study all of the mysteries that had intrigued them so long.

We were amazed at what we saw. The human form in movement displayed far more overall activity than anyone had supposed. It was not just the chest working against hips, or the backbone bending around, it was the very bulk of the body pulling in, pushing out, stretching, protruding. Here were living examples of the "squash and stretch" principles that only had been theories before. And here was the "follow through" and the "overlapping action," the changing shapes, the tensions and the counter tensions, the weight shown in the "timing," and the "exaggeration"—unbelievable exaggeration. We thought we had been drawing broad action, but here were examples surpassing anything we had done. Our eyes simply are not quick enough to detect the whole gamut of movement in the human figure.

Some actions were so complicated they were impossible to draw in caricature, and many of the moves that gave touches of personality were too subtle to capture at all. The tilt of the head as it turned, the changing shape of an eye, the slight swelling of a cheek in a

The animation of the wicked, scheming stepmother in Cinderella *was based on the strong actions and expressions of Eleanor Audley. These photostats show the relationship of the features and the timing of the move, but the face had to be redesigned to match the other characters in the picture. Nothing on the photostats could be traced or copied, but they still gave an excellent guide for the action needed in the scene.*

321

fleeting smile, the raising of a shoulder as the body leaned forward—these were the precious elements of life revealed by the camera.

But whenever we stayed too close to the photostats, or directly copied even a tiny piece of human action, the results looked very strange. The moves appeared real enough, but the figure lost the illusion of life. There was a certain authority in the movement and a presence that came out of the whole action, but it was impossible to become emotionally involved with this eerie, shadowy creature who was never a real inhabitant of our fantasy world.

Not until we realized that photographs must be redrawn in animatable shapes (our proven tools of communicating) were we able to transfer this knowledge to cartoon animation. It was not the photographed action of an actor's swelling cheek that mattered, it was the animated cheek in our drawings that had to communicate. Our job was to make the cartoon figure go through the same movements as the live actor, with the same timing and the same staging, but, because animatable shapes called for a difference in proportions, the figure and its model could not do things in exactly the same way. The actor's movements had to be reinterpreted in the world of our designs and shapes and forms.

As long as we remembered to use the photostats only as a reference in making our own statement of what should be in the scene, our animation was never tight or restricted. Our drawing ability had to improve, our knowledge of anatomy and acting had to increase, and our judgment had to develop, but, with an apprehensive Walt Disney watching every line we made, progress was automatic—difficult, but expected. Our animation picked up a crispness, a force, and a richness it never had before. This took study and analysis and careful work, but once a movement was understood it easily could be incorporated into cartoon terms. We had made the big break with rotoscope.

No one knows for sure why a pencil tracing of a live action figure should look so stiff and unnatural on the screen, unless there simply is no reality in a copy. The animators had learned this in art classes, but, somehow, studying film of a moving model made them think that live action was different. The camera certainly records what is there, but it records *everything* that is there, with an impartial lack of emphasis. On the other hand, an artist shows what he sees is there, especially that which might not be perceived by others. His drawings can be closer to the true realism of an object because he can be selective and personal in what he chooses to show. From the photostats, the animator chooses only those actions that relate to the point of his particular scene; then he strengthens those until they become the dominant action, with everything else either eliminated or subordinated. What appears on the screen is a simple, strong, direct statement that has clarity and vitality. The spirit and life have been gained by adapting the human form to an artist's own designs, the shapes and forms that he uses in reaching an audience. This is no more than what artists always have done. Michelangelo's magnificent statue of David, for all of its power and beauty, has such distorted normal proportions that David would be a strange looking apparition were he to be met walking down the street. The celebrated Venus de Milo could not even fit into modern clothes, and most of the other classic beauties of art, who have enthralled men for centuries, would attract only stares of amazement at a social function. The point is: a work of art is never a copy; for it to have meaning to people of many generations and numerous cultures, it must be the personal statement of an artist.

The first live-action films we had shot were for reference only, and it was pure chance that something fit either our story continuity or our sound tracks. But it was not long before one of us had picked out an action he liked on a piece of film, synced it up with his sound track, made a couple of adjustments in timing, and then incorporated that action into his animation. Soon we were shooting film for specific scenes or special actions, so that an animator would not have to spend too much time searching for relevant material.

As a director shot more and more of his cartoon continuity in sequence with live actors, he began to realize that this was a wonderful opportunity to check planned business and staging before it was animated. This was also an excellent way of establishing early communication with the animator himself, for here was something tangible to discuss. The action was on film, and the director and animator could build from there, adding or cutting, doing more or doing less,

Actress Helene Stanley devised a light dance step for Merryweather cleaning the house with magic in Sleeping Beauty. *Later work on the sequence determined that the action would be better seen in front view, which was no problem once the action was understood by the animator.*

1. First a drawing was made over the photostats, tracing action the animator wanted to retain, emphasizing points that made the movement unique, and noting the relationships and timing of all the parts.

2. Setting the photostats aside, the animator worked from his own drawings to capture the same action in the proportions of his cartoon character, who, at this point, was turned around to face the camera.

3. Using this second set of roughs as he would on any scene, he proceeded to animate normally. Occasionally he referred back to the photostats one more time for some fine point that did not seem to be working or to solve a difficult drawing problem within an action. After all, that is what a model is for.
(ANIMATOR: Frank Thomas —Sleeping Beauty.)

strengthening or modifying; but, at least, they were starting from the same point.

All of this demanded more care in the planning and shooting of live action film. If the image on the film was right, a weak animator could get by with it and a good animator could make it even better. However, if the live action was poorly planned, or staged in a confusing manner, it would cause trouble for everyone, and the director would do better to throw the film away and start afresh with the animator and his storyboard. Essentially, the film should be considered a further step in the visual development of the story material, like an advanced story sketch, and it should be shot with that purpose in mind. Before going over to the sound stage, the director should take a hard look at the scenes he is planning to shoot and ask himself:

Is this material really ready to go into animation?

Does the business fit the story? The character? Is it right for the mood, the tempo, the overall idea?

Is it entertaining? Is it just somebody saying some necessary dialogue, or is it a situation that gives the actor a chance to build and contribute?

If we happen to get some funny action or new business, will it fit? Can this be used easily and effectively? Does it animate as it is? Will it make a good scene? Would I be excited if I had to animate it?

Am I helping the animator by shooting this, or will it be tough to handle once it is on his board?

And when the director is on the stage with the scene rehearsed and the actor ready, he should remember renowned film director Stanley Kubrick's final check: "Is anything happening worth putting on film?"

Unless a director is exceptionally wise, or an animator himself, he should ask the man who ultimately will animate the scenes to help plan the business on the stage. Almost always when someone else shoots film for an animator the camera is too far back, or too close, or the action is staged at the wrong angle to

reveal what is happening, or it is lighted so that what you want to see is in shadow. Occasionally the footage will show only continuity of an actor moving from one place to another, or just waiting, or getting into position to do something interesting later on. The action must be staged with enough definition and emphasis to

The whole production unit often participated in the shooting of crucial actions. In this scene for Sleeping Beauty, *from the left, layout men Ernest Nordli, Don Griffith, and Tom Codrick check their layout continuity; performers Ed Kemmer and Helene Stanley discuss their roles with the director, Clyde "Gerry" Geronomi; supervising animator and sequence director Eric Larson reviews the script while production designer Mac Stewart makes sure the camera position matches the scene that has been planned.*

Actor Hans Conried portrays Capt. Hook and artist-comedian Don Barclay gives a very imaginative performance as Mr. Smee in this scene from Peter Pan. *The prop man rocks the boat, creating an action that would be difficult to animate convincingly, while an unidentified child actor plays the stoical Indian princess Tiger Lily.*

Cinderella.

When a pretty girl or a handsome prince are presented romantically, they must be conceived as "straight" and drawn realistically and carefully.

101 Dalmatians.

If the shapes in the face and body can be caricatured just a little, the characters will be easier to animate and more convincing to the audience, as in this scene of Roger teasing his wife Anita in 101 Dalmatians.

101 Dalmatians.

The Baduns were the henchmen of Cruella deVil in 101 Dalmations, *but their stupidity made them a constant liability. The grotesque design enhanced the slapstick routines and semiserious business of these second-rate villains.*

be extremely clear, but neither overacted nor so subtle that it fails to communicate.

Great care in the shooting produced scenes on film that were so succinct, so rich, and so well staged that they could be cut into the continuity reel almost like a first rough test of animation. However, they were not the straight pieces of acting one might expect in a live action film, because these imaginative scenes had been carefully planned for the medium of caricature. Usually we used actors whose talents included comedy, inventiveness, and creativity—as well as considerable theatrical experience. As the result of building scenes with such people, incorporating new ideas, searching for a way that communicates better or offers more entertainment, the live action film gave the animator a springboard to go beyond what he could have imagined himself.

We photographed anything that might prove helpful, and soon we discovered that the timing of a clever actor could make a mild gag hilarious, that an experienced stage comedian would offer sure ways of staging a scene's business, that another talent might suggest ways to put life into actions that had been conceived simply as continuity. Some actors gave back only what was asked of them; others were eager to take over and tell us how to do our whole production. In between, there was a group who enjoyed working on a role, building character, and finding ways to make it memorable.

Many times a performer would devise a piece of business so funny, so unusual and appealing, that everyone would be sold on it immediately—blinded to the fact that its length would slow down the pace of the story. Just because some business is funny does not

necessarily make it right for that place in the picture. It is very difficult to judge whether a suggested way of doing something is worth the extra footage or whether it can be shortened in animation without losing its value. Comedy routines and personality-building both take time; they cannot be rushed. The director and animator must decide whether they are gaining important development with this piece of entertaining action, or just stretching out the picture.

Usually we did not use the same person for both the acting and the character's voice on the sound track, since we found that actors had a tendency to give the same interpretation to both performances. What we wanted was someone who could add to the physical performance, come up with a new dimension, a way of doing it that no one else had suggested. To get that, we needed an inventive actor fresh to the whole idea, with no preconceptions to limit his imagination.

The sound track was on a record, which could be played over and over while the actor was rehearsing and trying out ideas for timing and character. Then, when the scene actually was shot, a recording was made of the sound as heard on the stage by the actor. After a "take" was chosen several days later, this recording was replaced by the original track, matching in sync what had been recorded on the stage. If new actions had been devised that required more time between lines of dialogue, there was no way of changing the track at that point; so, the needle was lifted from the record and the scene was shot "wild." After the film came back from the lab, the director and the animator juggled the picture and the sound track back and forth until they had the best sync they could achieve. Sometimes a new interpretation would develop

that necessitated doing the dialogue over with a different phrasing or expression; that sequence would be marked for a retake the next time the ''voice talent'' was at the studio—another reason for not recording all of the sound at one session.

It became increasingly important to choose just the right actor for this type of live action, since it would have such an influence on the development of a character's personality, and even on the entertainment value in the picture. Some comedians were versatile enough to suggest antics for characters in one picture after another, but for the most part we wanted a different actor for each role. Obviously, the Huntsman in *Snow White* could never be portrayed by the same man who would do Mr. Smee in *Peter Pan*.

Occasionally, there will be a cartoon character requiring such a subdued role, or such careful planning, that there is virtually no room for new concepts from the actor. Once the role comes to life with the proper voice, the visual image should match, and nothing more. The Huntsman needed no more personality, no more acting; his scenes had been so well conceived that he had only to look convincing to make his sinister role believable.

Of course, there is always a big problem in making the ''real'' or ''straight'' characters in our pictures have enough personality to carry their part of the story. Animator and director Woolie Reitherman has said, ''The art of animation lends itself least to real people, and most to caricatures and illusions of a person.'' The point of this is misinterpreted by many to mean that characters who have to be represented as real should be left out of feature films, that the stories should be told with broad characters who can be handled more easily. This would be a mistake, for spectators need to have someone or something they can believe in, or the picture falls apart. In *The Rescuers*, the young girl Penny was surrounded by a whole cast of broad characters; but, while they enriched the story, they did not carry it. As Woolie said afterward, ''Naw, the little girl was so believable! All those things around her were great, but you needed that sincerity.''

The sincerity in that case came from careful planning of the scenes to make use of the most appealing aspects of this little character. Some miscellaneous scenes had been filmed of two different five-year-old girls, so that the animator could study how a child of that age moved, but there was no attempt to record special moves or actual scenes after that. Instead, the effort had gone into finding the right things for her to do and the best way for her to do them. It is axiomatic that boy or girl characters can be done more easily in live action than in cartoon, and that one should not do things in a cartoon better done in live action. However, if that philosophy had been followed over the years, there would have been no *Snow White*, no *Cinderella*, no *Peter Pan*, nor most of the features that the Disney studio produced. To make a ''straight'' character convincing and interesting requires great creative effort. It may take imagination and a knowledge of both story and animation, but there is always a way—if the staff is smart enough to find it and willing to work hard enough to accomplish it.

Generally speaking, if there is a human character in a story, it is wise to draw the person with as much caricature as the role will permit. Early in the story development, these questions should be asked: ''Does this character have to be straight?'' ''What is the role

ANIMATOR: Ollie Johnston— Reason and Emotion.

The broader the design, the greater the communication, and the more fun for the animator. The essence of pure, undisciplined emotion was embodied in this chubby lady for the film Reason and Emotion. *Without the restrictions of realism, the animator was able to make her appealing, and even a little sexy.*

Snow White

we need here?'' If it is a prince or a hero or a sympathetic person who needs acceptance from the audience to make the story work, then the character must be drawn realistically, but not necessarily in a restricted manner. In *101 Dalmations*, Roger and Anita had to be treated as real people because of the genuine concern they had for their pets; yet they were drawn with less realism than the prince in either *Snow White* or *Cinderella*. The design of the whole picture, as well as the treatment of the story, permitted the animator more freedom in representation. The Baduns and Cruella deVil had broader roles and could be drawn with more caricature, which immediately made them more interesting and stronger. In *The Rescuers*, the little girl had to be drawn sincerely because she was the heart of the story; Medusa and Snoops could be wild, comic figures because they were not sinister.

Whenever two or more animated characters are in the same scene, interrelating in ways that are true to their own personalities, live action staging can be particularly helpful. Technically, it is difficult to animate two characters sharing a space, moving them about without their stepping on each other, while keeping a general feeling of dimension and volume in the scene. The problem is compounded if some critical acting is required at the same time. When the scene is shot with this in mind, and the actors move around in a way that is helpful to the animators, everyone will benefit.

Les Clark was given the scene to animate of the three dwarfs dancing with Snow White—the only long shot that showed the dimensions of the dwarfs' room and the scale of the characters through their movement. Animating the decrease in the girl's size as she moved away from the camera was controlled by working from the live action film, but the matching perspectives of the dwarfs that Les animated from imagination made the scene amazingly convincing and added credence to the whole sequence.

Any dancing scenes in a story should be shot early and planned throughout the musical number, rather than handed out piecemeal when an animator needs them. Obviously the choreography will be richer if a dancer plans it all, instead of leaving it up to the unresolved fantasies of some storyman. In the scene Les had, there was a special problem with Snow White's hand positions. Just how high can a dwarf reach up comfortably to dance with a young girl? The height of each dwarf had to be planned, not in relation to the girl doing the live action but to her cartoon proportions, derived from the photostats of her dancing. For the scene to be effective, it was important that the dwarfs should not strain or be awkward as they reached to take her hand. Fortunately, with Ham Luske shooting the live action, all such details were carefully covered.

It is not worth the trouble of filming simply to record a change in size as a character comes closer to the camera, but if a major part of the design of a scene is based on startling perspective or the relationship of several characters working in perspective, then a great deal of the animator's time may be saved by first proving out the effectiveness of the scene on film.

The same strategy applies to the action of the inanimate objects that might be in a scene. Rolling barrels, falling trees, avalanches, moving cars, wagons, and trains are all time-consuming and tedious for an animator to master, and they are questionable expenses in the animation budget when tracing such things from photostats will give just as good results, if not better. In *Pinocchio*, Stromboli locked the little fellow in a large bird cage made of bent sticks, which bounced and swung as his wagon bumped along the cobblestone streets. The cage even had a small perch inside that was swinging in a separate action. This intricate object would have been almost impossible to draw in the first place, let alone to capture the weight and convincing movement of its action. However, the point of the scene was not the cage but Pinocchio's reaction while inside, calling for help. That action in itself was difficult enough for any animator, and fortunately there was no need to add more expense to the scene by having someone work over and over on the drawings of the swinging cage. A model cage was built at half size, and it was filmed so it appeared to be the right scale and weight for both the little puppet and the wagon. The animator then worked with tracings from photostats of the swinging cage, attempting to match the acting he wanted with the changing perspectives of the bouncing cage. It was a nightmare to animate, but a spectacular theatrical device.

In 1948, Walt Disney had money problems (again). *Pinocchio* (which had been finished in 1940) had not

The model of Cruella's car was painted with black lines that made it look like a drawing when reproduced on the photostats. The image was cut out and pasted on a cel, then copied by the Xerox process like any drawing. Once it was painted in flat colors, as shown here, it looked just like the other cels in the picture.

The climax of 101 Dalmatians *featured a collision between two cars driven by the villains. Shooting the scene with models of the cars are from the left, layout man Basil "Dave" Davidovitch, animator and model maker Dick Lucas, effects animator Jack Buckley and, at the camera, Ed Cook. Such actions would take hours to animate without this kind of help.*

Tracings from photostats of the bird cage that imprisoned Pinocchio gave the realistic action that was needed while saving the time that would have been required to animate such a difficult assignment. Even more time was saved by drawing the back of the cage on one level and the front on another so that Pinocchio could be sandwiched between the two without tedious registration to the bars on every drawing.

yet paid for itself, *Fantasia* looked as if it was always to be in the red, *Bambi*, Walt's favorite picture of all, was still not in the clear. The solution to the studio's financial bind seemed to be another cartoon feature along the lines of the successful *Snow White*—rather than anything experimental. Although "package pictures," like *Make Mine Music*, did not have the production difficulties of a storytelling cartoon feature, they had not been very profitable either. A new, less expensive way to make the projected *Cinderella* as a full-fledged animated feature had to be found. Reasoning that animation was the most costly part of the business, Walt felt that everything possible should be done to save the animator's time, to help him make that first test "OK for cleanup" without correction. He turned to live action to solve his problem.

All of *Cinderella* was shot very carefully with live actors, testing the cutting, the continuity, the staging, the characterizations, and the play between the characters. Only the animals were left as drawings, and story reels were made of those sketches to find the balance with the rest of the picture. Economically, we could not experiment; we had to know, and it had to be good. When all of the live film was spliced together, this was undeniably a strong base for proving the workability of the scenes before they were animated, but the inventiveness and special touches in the acting that had made our animation so popular were lacking. The film had a distinctly live action feel, but it was so beautifully structured and played so well that no one could argue with what had to be done. As animators we felt restricted, even though we had done most of the filming ourselves, but the picture had to be made for a price, and this was, undeniably, a way of doing it.

By the time we were starting *Peter Pan*, we had learned to get further away from any actual use of the live action scenes, restaging them after seeing weaknesses, using the film as a starting point from which to build and invent and enrich. We had been shown the way to go, but we had to do the "going" ourselves, and the picture was better for it. We recaptured much of the fantasy and magic in the features made before the second World War.

Animators always had the feeling they were nailed to the floor when their whole sequences were shot ahead of time in live action. Everyone's imagination as to how a scene might be staged was limited by the placement of the camera, for once a scene had been shot it was very hard to switch to a whole new point of view—even though in animation it is quite easy to hang the camera from a star, or a nearby cloud, or let it drift with the breeze wherever it is needed.

Animals

If an animal in a film is wearing any kind of costume, he can be handled with human attributes and the audience will accept him. In contrast, if an animal in his natural fur should suddenly stand up and start gesticulating, the viewers will feel uneasy. Put a cap on him, or a tie, and he can swagger around, gesturing and pointing like any ham actor.

Stranger than that, if the story parodies human activities, as in *Song of the South* and *Robin Hood*, there is no need to restrict a character's movements by the limitations of its animal body. The character can have human hands, fingers, a human pelvis, and feet with shoes. Of course natural animal drawing or realistic action will always add sincerity and interest to this type of film, but it is not truly needed to tell the story. On the other hand, if the story is man's view of what the animal world is like, as in *Lady and the Tramp*, *101 Dalmatians*, and *The Jungle Book*, the animals must be completely believable or the whole premise will collapse.

There was a unique situation in *The Sword in the*

Studies of hunting dogs for The Fox and the Hound *by Mel Shaw. This type of character has to be treated as a real dog throughout the picture.*

The animators agreed that the characters easiest to animate as well as most fun to draw had been the animals in the Uncle Remus stories of Song of the South. *Ken Anderson remembered those days when he suggested his version of Richard the Lion-hearted for* Robin Hood.

In The Sword in the Stone, *the wizard Merlin turned both himself and young Arthur into squirrels. They had to be drawn in such a way that they would look like the other squirrels yet still be recognizable to the audience. Here they are approached by an eager young female who wants Arthur for her mate.*

The animation of animals in Snow White *was a major step forward at the time. Just four years later our knowledge had increased to the point where we could handle more realistic drawing convincingly.*

ANIMATOR: *Jim Algar*— Snow White.

ANIMATOR: *Ken O'Brien*—Bambi.

Stone that called for special decisions. The young Arthur had been turned into a squirrel by Merlin, the magician, so that the boy could gain a better understanding of the world of nature. While in this guise, Arthur met some real squirrels who accepted him as one of their kind, even though he could not speak their language. The problem was to animate the boy so that he would be believable both to the audience and to the squirrels. If he were just a boy running around in a squirrel suit the audience would have no trouble recognizing him, but would people believe that real squirrels could be fooled so easily? If the boy were animated as a genuine squirrel, it would be impossible to preserve his character—or the humor in a situation based on Arthur's being a misfit in a foreign land. The compromise was to have the boy limited in his actions by a squirrel's body and appearance, yet retaining his own thoughts and mannerisms. He had to move like a squirrel, but a rather inexperienced one.

When we say "real," we mean only what the audience accepts as being real, for obviously a real animal cannot act or emote as broadly as animators require. The more an animator goes toward caricaturing the animal, the more he seems to be capturing the essence of that animal, and the more he is creating possibilities for acting. For example, if we had drawn real deer in *Bambi* there would have been so little acting potential that no one would have believed the deer really existed as characters. But because we drew what people imagine a deer looks like, with a personality to match, the audience accepted our drawings as being completely real.

Of course, style and design are part of this, too. A caricature cannot be made without them. But the big point is that characters on the screen appear to be most real when they can be animated to have personalities, and this only can be done when there is potential for movement in all parts of the body. In other words, the more realistically animals are drawn, the less real they will appear on the screen.

The animals in *Snow White* were crudely drawn compared to those in *Bambi*, yet they all behaved the way they should to work with the girl in that story. And some people even thought the animals were real. Since it certainly was not the drawing that made these creatures so convincing, it must have been the acting in the animation.

When learning to draw anything, it is important that the artist go to the source. Afterward he can make any use of his knowledge that he chooses, but in the beginning he must study the real object, whether it be a zebrula or an aardvark. If Disney artists were going to animate a fox, they would try to get a real fox to study and photograph, and, if possible, feel. Nothing matches the learning that comes from feeling an animal's bones and muscles and joints, to discover how they are put together and how far they can move in any direction; it is always surprising. The artists would get illustrations of fox skeletons to help in understanding why a fox looks like a fox. How is he different from other animals? Then they would get film of foxes in action to

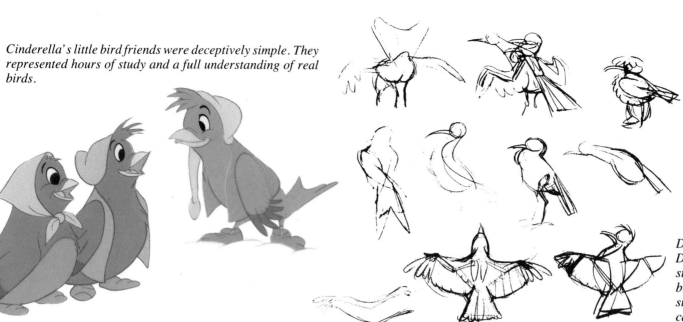

Cinderella's little bird friends were deceptively simple. They represented hours of study and a full understanding of real birds.

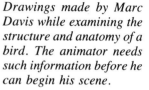

Drawings made by Marc Davis while examining the structure and anatomy of a bird. The animator needs such information before he can begin his scene.

Director Woolie Reitherman had a pet fox that we could handle, photograph, and study as work was starting on The Fox and the Hound.

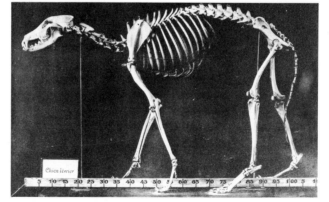

Major differences between a fox and a greyhound are immediately apparent when their skeletons are studied. The fox seems crouched, ready to dart, with his legs well under his body and his pelvis tilted down. Most dogs stand more erect than the fox and move with quite a different rhythm.

Les Editions Guerinet.

study their movements and their timing. What makes this animal a fox? What attitudes or actions are unique to him?

Nearly always, film was available on virtually any animal, because of the studio's great live-action series, *True Life Adventures*. The animators drew from this film, traced off bits of action and timing to study, tried to draw actions in successive drawings, and then went back to study some more. They found that the amaz-

ing photographs made by Eadweard Muybridge[1] nearly a hundred years ago were good for reminding them of what the animal does, but his cameras did not always catch the extremes or details of relative timing, and the pictures could be misleading if the animators were unfamilar with the animal or the action. Since it is always hard to figure out the bumps and shapes in still photographs, live action film is more useful; you can see a roll developing, or pulling out straight, or a

The Human Figure in Motion, Dover Publications Inc., Plate 142.

Muybridge's Complete Human & Animal Motion, Dover Publications, Inc. Vol. 3 (of 5 volumes)

The sequential photographs taken simultaneously from three different angles by Eadweard Muybridge in the late 1800s provide the best general reference available for any student of action and motion. The thrust of the body, the straight leg on both the jump and the landing, and the bulging tissues in the low positions are all clearly evident in these photos— what we call "squash and stretch." Note also the secondary action of the arms to maintain balance.

Sketches by Ollie Johnston. What makes a kitten cute and appealing? The animator tries to discover this by sketching from film taken for Aristocats.

The Rescuers

bulge coming up, or a joint moving under the skin much more clearly.

Many people get the idea that production stopped for six or seven weeks while everyone learned to draw a new character. That would have been a lovely way to gain knowledge, but it was not economically feasible. Other than a special class that might start at 4:30 PM and go until 6:00 (one hour of our time against a half hour of Walt's), all of this research was done while keeping up our footage on the current production: after hours, weekends, noon hours, whenever we could squeeze in some extra time. Each man wanted to do

Walt never outgrew his interest in farm animals and the human characteristics they seemed to possess. Here he visits a farm in England.

Frank Thomas studies the "Cinderella Dog" that modeled for Tramp in Lady and the Tramp. *There had been disagreement on the type of dog we should draw for our male lead until one night storyman Ed Penner saw the perfect model disappearing into the bushes. Like the hero in our film, he was a stray and could not be found again for several days. Eventually he was located in the city pound, just hours away from the gas chamber. Ed bailed him out and returned triumphantly to the studio, where the dog was discovered to be a female and less than a year old. Still, we filmed her, sketched and studied, and eventually boarded her in a kennel with other canine movie stars.*

Eric Larson studying dalmatian pups at close range.

From the left, Bernard Garbutt, Marc Davis, Retta Scott, and Mel Shaw sketching at the zoo during the making of Bambi.

his best, and when he saw others drawing better he quickly tried to learn what they knew.

This sharing of knowledge speeded up the whole learning process and kept a stimulating atmosphere alive. If one of us started to fall behind, Walt might say, "We can do better than that!" as if the individual were not as important as the whole team effort. However, he was more apt to say, "Why don't you go see Marc Davis? He's got some nice drawings of those deer. Y'know, he doesn't get all tied up in the anatomy; yet they look real, and they've got an appeal and a personality. You oughta go look at them; Marc might be able to help you." And Marc would, and so would Milt, and Eric, and any of the sketch men working ahead of the animators, developing ideas.

Of these men, Bernard Garbutt had the most perplexing talent. He knew animals and how they moved and how they did things, but he never drew from an action standpoint. There were no thrusts, no muscles, no coiled springs, just a clear, simple outline of the animal in movement. We would go to him with a specific problem: "I've got this deer getting up, and I know

the hind end comes up first. Then I put out his front legs. . . . I think that's right, but what happens to the head at that point?"

Garbutt would perch on the edge of the table, more like a bird than a draftsman (he never seemed to sit in a chair), and start explaining, and while he talked his pencil would start making a thin line that seemed to meander aimlessly across the paper. We would turn our heads first one way, then the other, trying to see what he was drawing, but the lines resembled a tangled cobweb as much as anything else. Then, suddenly, we saw a deer in the precise phase of the movement we had described; only Garbutt was drawing it upside down so it faced us.

While we were blinking and trying to absorb that combination of rendition and explanation, he would continue: "Now with a camel, he'll put this leg out first and keep his head down. . . ." When he had finished drawing a camel getting up, he would go on to the buffalo, just so we would have a thorough understanding of what was unique about the deer in this particular action. In ten minutes we had a whole

Typical drawings by Bernard Garbutt; gentle and accurate.

337

course in comparative anatomy, illustrated with gentle little contour drawings that had no boldness or vigor, just surprising accuracy.

We had another unique talent in Retta Scott, the first woman at our studio to have an interest in animation. She had an astounding ability to draw powerful, virile animals from almost any perspective and in any action. At one point in *Bambi*, we needed some convincing and frightening hounds to chase our heroine Faline, but none of the animators was advanced enough in his understanding of hounds to tackle the assignment. Retta could draw the dogs in any position, and she knew the attitudes and the mood, but she was inexperienced in the art of relating one drawing to the next. So the supervising animator, Eric Larson, set the scenes up for her and showed her what needed to be done. With typical modesty, Eric says, ''I worked with her on the timing, but she did it all; she worked and worked on it.'' However it was done, between the two of them there appeared on the screen one of the most chilling and exciting pieces of action ever to be animated.

Another imaginative bit of problem-solving called for in *Bambi* was the drawing of the stag's majestic antlers. To follow through the perspective of each bony prong as the head moved about was just too complicated for even the most mechanically oriented artists, and the first filmed tests of the animation drawings revealed rubbery, wandering antlers—a distressing loss of majesty in what should have been the stag's crowning glory. So, a miniature plaster model was made of the stag's head with the full complement of antlers atop, and this was placed beneath the glass of the old rotoscope machine. Up on the drawing board, the artist

ANIMATOR: *Retta Scott with Eric Larson—* Bambi.

Vicious hunting dogs have been unleashed to track down the deer in this scene from Bambi. *Knowledge and drawing ability are combined to make an exciting action, so real it makes the audience gasp.*

had the first drawing of a scene with just the head of the stag carefully drawn in. He slowly turned and tilted the model underneath until the head lined up exactly with his drawing. This done, he simply traced the horns. That drawing completed, he moved on to the next; with a slight change in the model, more horns were ready to trace. The result was perfect—a bit tedious, but not nearly so demanding as the attempt to draw it all in perspective from imagination.

Rico Lebrun had been hired as we began to work on *Bambi* because of his knowledge of animals and his ability to teach. He felt strongly that the only way to learn all about an animal was to get your hands on it and move it about and feel how the parts worked. He started a search for a young fawn, but since none was then available we contented ourselves with studying what film we had and observing older deer at the zoo. One day, Rico got a call from a ranger in the Forestry Service who had come upon the carcass of a very young fawn, no more than two days old. It was still in good condition, and he could have it! Rico was ecstatic.

That night in class, we crowded in close to watch the movements of the legs and the back and the head as Rico turned the body round and round, testing the articulation of each joint. He was enraptured with his model; we were a bit more reserved—after all, it had been dead for three or four days. Excitedly, he announced his plan to remove the outer layers, a little each night, so we could learn all the intricate workings right down to the skeleton. The whole procedure might take ten evenings in all.

The next night, we stood farther back as Rico re-

The fawn that had been the model for so many inspirational sketches had grown up by the time the animators started on the picture. Here, Rico Lebrun shows Frank Thomas how the head fits onto the neck. Also watching are Retta Scott and Bob Youngquist. (Man in foreground is keeper for the deer.)

The deer showed more interest in Ollie Johnston's drawing than in her job of posing for the class. In background, Milt Kahl, left, and Bill Shull.

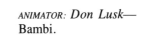

ANIMATOR: *Don Lusk—* Bambi.

Drawing problems were more of a threat to the majestic stag in Bambi *than the bullets of the hunters. No one could draw the imposing antlers so that the volume and perspective were constant from drawing to drawing. The accuracy seen here came from tracing a plaster model that could be turned in any direction to match the animator's drawing.*

*Expert model-makers con-
structed a jointed armature
of a young deer for the animators to study while working on* Bambi. *Based on
Rico Lebrun's drawings,
everything moved correctly,
right down to the toes.*

(5) *Remember, it must
squash and stretch in movement.*

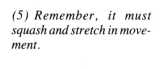

Tails and Ears Are Important Too

(1) *Ears are an important
part of the attitude on any
animal.*

(2) *Hair can be a key to
personality, and many times
will show how a character
feels. Scraggly hair gives
an unkempt, irritable look.
Smooth and sleek fur is soft
and feminine.*

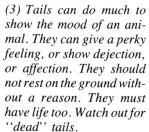

(3) *Tails can do much to
show the mood of an ani-
mal. They can give a perky
feeling, or show dejection,
or affection. They should
not rest on the ground without a reason. They must
have life too. Watch out for
"dead" tails.*

(4) *The neck is often passed over when considering
parts of the anatomy that
can help show an attitude.
It can be arched for bellig-
erence, show alertness, be
cocky with chest out, or indicate anger.*

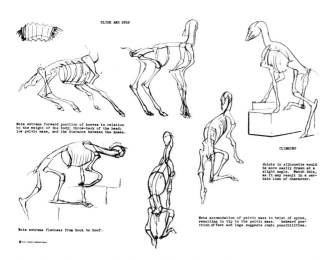

Drawings by Rico Lebrun of the skeletal construction of a fawn in various positions, done after his exhaustive research on the cadaver he brought to class.

Attitudes for acting—Frank Thomas.

Structural analysis—Marc Davis.

Action sequences—Ollie Johnston.

removed the skin—so we could examine the muscles and the tendons and the remarkable engineering principles revealed in this wonder of nature. Unfortunately, each time he contracted or extended any part of the cadaver a rich aroma was pumped into the air. He called to us, ''Hey, fellas, get in here close where you can see what this thing is doing.''

We answered warmly, ''Oh, we can see just fine from back here!''

In spite of this unique opportunity to gain vast knowledge, attendance at those evening classes began to fall off. However, Rico's enthusiasm seemed to increase in direct proportion to the odor, which no longer could be described as merely pungent. Our noses finally turned us all away, but not his. He stayed with his prize until it was only bones. In the end, Rico furnished us with a wonderful set of drawings that we studied with considerably more relish.

While it is extremely helpful to understand the anatomy of an animal, its movement and timing and balance and rhythm are just as important from an animation standpoint, and probably they all should be learned together. This is a comforting thought if the subject is a lion, or tiger, or rhinoceros, or any large, wild crea-

Exhaustive research was always done as the animators began a new character. Sketching directly from the film often catches the spirit of an animal and the essence of his movement. For 101 Dalmatians *we used our filmed action this way more often than on photostats.*

341

ture. We had little desire to probe with our fingers the inner workings of the orangutan while animating King Louie for *The Jungle Book*. A few charts of comparative anatomy and some reels of film told us as much as we wanted to know.

Long before our artists encountered Rico's fawn cadaver, they had been studying the general behavior of real deer at close range. The studio had been sent a pair of fawns from Maine that were kept in an area alongside the animation building, and the artists had only to glance out the window for stimulation and reference to the real thing. Despite the great value to the artist in directly observing an animal in its daily activities, when a story called for a rare or unfamiliar action from a deer it was still a major problem for the animator. In the first sequence of *Bambi* we needed to portray those initial few minutes in a fawn's existence, when it is wobbly and vulnerable and puzzled by the world, and dependent on its mother. However, nature endows fawns with a strength and coordination that develops so quickly that within only a couple of hours they are very different creatures. When the San Diego Zoo phoned to say they had a doe ready to foal any day, the studio shipped a film crew down there immediately. They set up their equipment just outside the deer's enclosure, at a spot that gave them full coverage of every part of the pen. There was no place the doe could have privacy if she desired it. Although she

had given all signs of being ready to deliver, a long night's vigil produced nothing. Nor the next day's either. The weary crew prepared for the second night under the watchful gaze of large, doe eyes. Morning came and the prospective mother was calm and reserved. The crew was exhausted.

When nothing happened during the whole day, no signs, no indications of any kind, the crew decided to get some sleep and come back about midnight, having been assured by the zookeeper that most births occur during the small hours of the morning. They were gone for barely five hours and returned still groggy and bewildered from too little sleep, but they were even more bewildered to gaze upon a frisky, playful five-hour-old fawn prancing about the enclosure. The crew went back to bed.

In contrast to live action films of humans, scenes of animal action seldom can be spliced into any kind of helpful continuity. There might be a short sequence of action scenes in a run or a fight that could be pieced together from scraps, but more often the animator has to be inventive, to find a specific place where he can use a particular action. Hopefully, he can find some film of an animal flopping down in an exhausted state, or one getting to its feet with a feeling of tired, aching muscles, or a spirited, excited turn, breaking into a run—all movements that suggest an attitude. Against this, the animator can place a line of dialogue delivered

ANIMATOR: *Hugh Fraser—*The Adventures of Mr. Toad.

The weasel has a long body, a stealthy appearance, and is assumed to be sneaky and up to no good. As a cartoon character, he became a fast-moving hoodlum.

with the same type of feeling, and with a little adjustment here and there (to improve the sync and match the phrasing) produce a scene with convincing action and believability.

For *101 Dalmatians*, scenes were shot of a dog running up stairs, stopping and turning, coming down the stairs, straining on a leash—all of which were definite aids in timing scenes for the picture and assisting animators to achieve natural-appearing action. But the scenes that brought the characters to life were the ones imagined by the animator, showing what the dog could have done, in ways the dog would have done it.

In addition to movements needed for scenes and continuity, many miscellaneous actions were filmed in trying to capture something of the individual animal's own personality. These natural movements proved to be the most helpful, since special meaning could be given them by adding dialogue, or music, or sound effects, thereby interjecting an extra quality into the behavior.

Probably the most important rule for any kind of animal photography is, "Don't be afraid to waste film!" To get the natural, the unexpected, the rare moments, there must be unlimited patience and a running camera. The director who is determined to get only what is called for in his script, and get it right, will miss the wonderful things that make an animal what he really is. The animator who leaves the whole tedious business to others will miss the firsthand knowledge that only can come from being with the animal while attempts are made to capture its unique attributes. The best actions are invariably unplanned.

When the casting was set for us to animate the geese in *Aristocats*, we borrowed a camera from the studio and visited a friend's ranch. He had two geese, some assorted chickens, and a decrepit, tattered white turkey who had an amazing desire to star in a screen test. The whir of film running through the camera caused him to strut about with his three or four remaining tail feathers askew, but it made the geese run away.

As the geese ran, we were amazed to see how closely they stayed together, with their necks almost intertwined. We had expected the roll of the body as they paddled about clumsily, but the way the two geese worked together was startling. At once a kind of character emerged for the two, which went beyond the dialogue we were contemplating for a pair of silly spinsters on a walking tour of France. The film we took seemed to have an almost constant overlay of the preposterous turkey, but behind him were always these two heads peering around, keeping their eyes on the camera and the highly suspect man behind it. We sketched from the film and from our memory, for once we had seen these girls in action, nothing could erase the reality of their intense skepticism. The nicely

designed drawings of geese that we had seen on the storyboards were suddenly two very real personalities bustling about with their own private dignity—haughty, appraising, critical, and funny. They were real geese, with all the movements of real geese, but they had revealed the personalities that could be understood and shared by all humans.

Finding entertainment in a personality does not mean making a clown out of that character. It means only that one is relating to qualities common to all individuals, and there is no loss of dignity inherent in that process. The personality traits can be heroic, altruistic, or noble; it is the use made of them in the story situation that determines whether they are comic, or cute, or stupid, or mean. There are many ways of being entertaining, and the challenge is to the storyman to create situations where these individual traits can be brought out in an entertaining way.

Many animals have their attributes already defined by the legends and stories of various cultures. A coyote is a cunning and wise hero to the American Indian, and a villainous predator to the sheepman. To most people, a rabbit is nervous and almost completely helpless; a wolf is all villain, whether he is slavering or deceitful; and the beaver is hard-working with no sense of humor. When casting a picture with "good guys" and "bad guys," these are important considerations. The "good guys" have to be small, ineffectual, cute, and associated with nonviolence. It doesn't matter if the real animal is that way or not. You are playing off images in the viewers' subconscious, and if people

grew up thinking a certain way that is where you must start. To have a mean and cruel kitten terrorizing a family of nervous, flighty bears is an uphill fight for everybody.

Still, there is considerable room for variations. In *Robin Hood*, some of us thought the Sheriff of Nottingham would be more interesting if he were a goat. As the story was structured, there was no need for him to be a crafty villain; he was only stupid, bossy, and unconcerned with the people he might be hurting. A goat with a thick skull could do this much and give the animators a new animal to draw that could open up fresh ideas.

The director of that film felt just as strongly that the Sheriff should be a wolf, because the audience believes the wolf to be a villain. The fact that recent research has shown him to be a good family man and a fine fellow will do little to change ideas that are centuries old. In addition, the goat has no established role in legend, and we would have the burden of proving that he was good or bad or indifferent. Developing that image could waste precious footage that might be better used to show entertainment in the specific kind of villain he was.

The most provocative discussions come when the story calls for a mythical creature, or one that has not appeared in tale or legend. A dragon is known to be ill-tempered and sullen, so that is not too much of a problem. But other pictures may include creatures with no connotations. When Woolie Reitherman was animating the dinosaurs in *Fantasia*, Walt told him to

beware of any human personality traits, "Don't make them cute animal personalities. They've got small brains, y'know; make them real!" It was a disarming request since there was little research possible on what a real dinosaur might have been like, but Woolie was not bothered. He dipped into his imagination, combined that with a few raw animal things he had seen, and, working closely with Bill Roberts, who was directing that sequence, came up with scenes of dinosaurs that seemed to be just the way people always imagined these giants should be, if ever they had thought about it before! Fortified by Stravinsky's magnificent score, they created, together, a stirring film that never can be forgotten.

The Triceratops and Stegosaurus live again through the magic of animated drawings.

ANIMATOR: *Woolie Reitherman—*
"Rite of Spring," Fantasia.

Who knows how a dinosaur walked millions of years ago? The animator drew, erased, corrected, and drew again before getting this convincing walk on the Tyrannosaurus Rex.

A 16 pound bowling ball is rolling down the alley. It has a smooth, continuous, evenly spaced progress.

It is not erratic; it does not speed up and slow down, then speed up again.

It does not change direction abruptly (unless it meets something stronger). How much an object weighs is shown by how much effort is required to move it, to stop it, to change its direction. These are shown through Timing, Arcs, and Squash and Stretch.

If the object is a character, a leg is put out to take the weight, squashing and absorbing the force of the move.

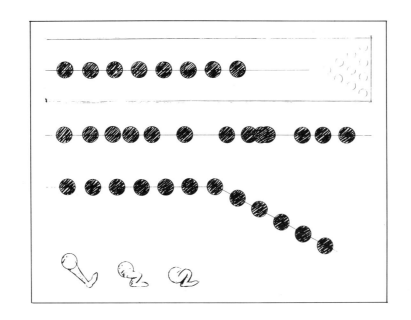

In 1928, Mickey had charm but no weight as he turned a corner without regard for support or gravity.

The Rhythm Walk

This spirited walk with the bounce in the middle was used by everyone in the early thirties. It was always done to a musical beat, giving a happy, energetic feeling to the action and a jaunty attitude for the character. Combined with some carefree whistling, it did much to establish Mickey's personality.

(146) Mickey starts a normal step, lifting his body high.

(148) In the middle of the step, he dips down.

(151) Then up again to a high position on head and body.

(154) Finally, the low, "squash" position as he places his foot to complete the step.

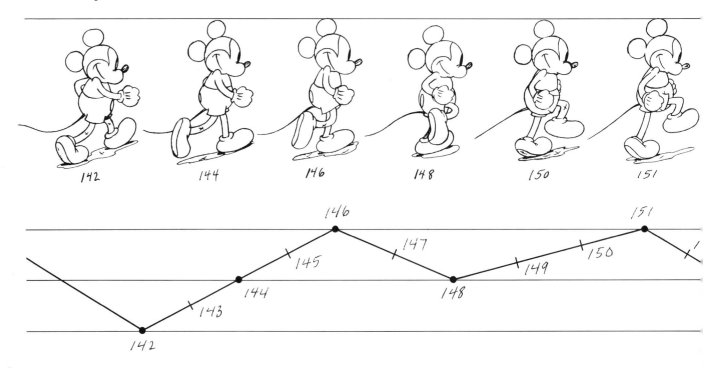

346

Walks THE IMPORTANCE OF WEIGHT

Walks always have become troublesome and complicated to animate. The action can become so involved with weight distribution and balance and secondary movements that every single drawing becomes a headache, yet they can do so much to reveal personality and attitude that they are one of the animator's key tools in communication. Many actors feel that the first step in getting hold of a character is to analyze how he will walk. Even the most casual study of people on a busy street will reveal dramatic differences in how they achieve simple locomotion: long strides, short steps, determined waddling, bouncing, mincing, swaggering, rippling; there is no end to the variety.

In the early cartoons before sound came along, there were few attempts to make walking anything more than a means of moving the character to a new position on the screen. There was pacing back and forth, occasional dragging of feet in sorrow or despair, or purposeful striding as the hero fought back, but no animator tried to establish character by the way the figure walked. With the introduction of sound there came the "rhythm walk," with its extra bounce in the middle that gave life and spirit to a mundane character

in everyday activities. Once the character went into action, it was the same old business of moving the body where the animator wanted it to be, then adding legs and feet underneath moving up and down.

A marching soldier will make a sharp 90° turn at the corner. But if he is running fast, he will swing wide, slipping and skidding and leaning into the curve to keep his balance.

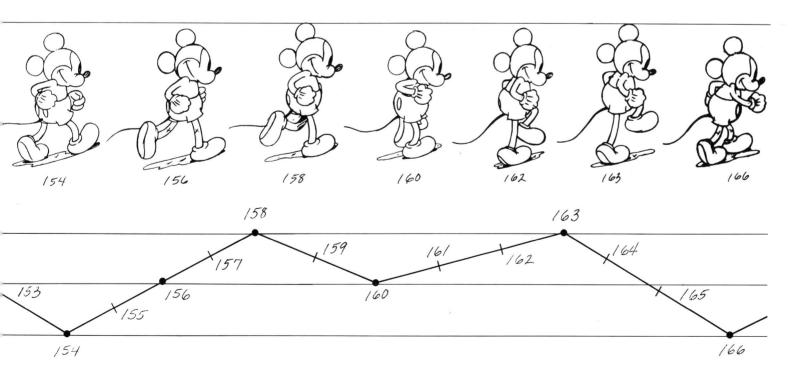

Walks   THE IMPORTANCE OF WEIGHT

ANIMATOR: *Frank Thomas*—
Robin Hood.

Robin Hood runs in to pick up the last sack of gold. He places his foot well in front of his body and slides into position, lifting the other leg and planting it to help support the weight of the gold as well as to start his change of direction.

It was the realization that the cartoon figure could not be believable without convincing weight that really changed the animators' thinking. The principles of squash and stretch were beginning to be understood and provided the procedures and the tools for displaying the new discoveries. Basically the principle was that a moving body could not be shifted in direction without encountering resistance from something in its present path of movement, causing it to turn.

The scent of perfume floating through the air, from Moose Hunt.

ANIMATOR: *Frank Thomas*—
The Rescuers.

Luke, the muskrat, is running with his jug when he meets a crocodile, makes a wild, scrambling take, reverses direction and zips out. Through this impossible action, the jug is timed realistically, with a full arc and convincing weight, which makes everything else seem believable too. If the jug had flipped about like a piece of cloth the whole scene would have been just another frantic cartoon take.

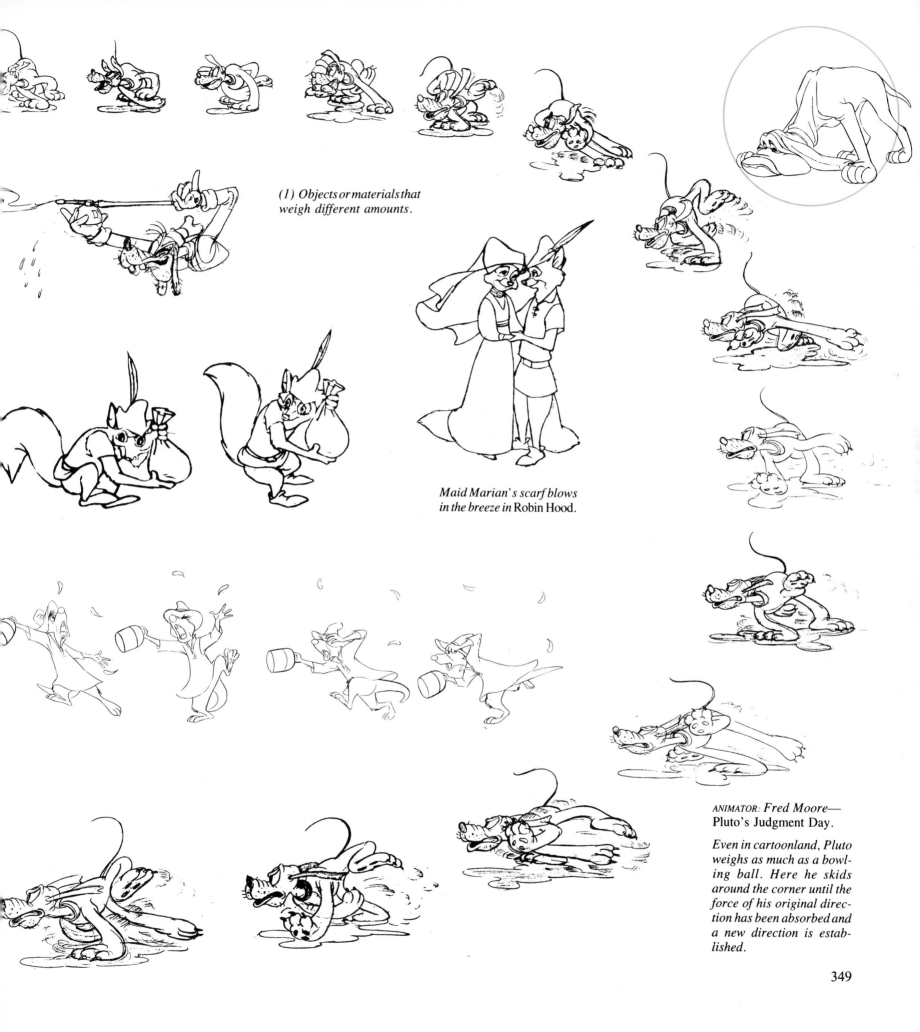

(1) Objects or materials that weigh different amounts.

Maid Marian's scarf blows in the breeze in Robin Hood.

ANIMATOR: *Fred Moore—* Pluto's Judgment Day.

Even in cartoonland, Pluto weighs as much as a bowling ball. Here he skids around the corner until the force of his original direction has been absorbed and a new direction is established.

ANIMATOR: *Ollie Johnston—*
101 Dalmatians.

Pongo has seen a beautiful girl with a young female dalmatian go into the park. Straining on his leash, he drags his master in pursuit of them.

(2) The elements can influence the feeling of weight.

ANIMATOR: *Fred Spencer—*Moving Day.

Donald is trying to get a fish bowl off his rear by tying suspenders around it and attaching the other end to a piece of furniture. Here he is running and slipping as he reaches the full tension of the suspenders.

Roger and Anita, from 101 Dalmatians, *have fallen into the pond. The water has made all of their clothes heavy and limp and sagging.*

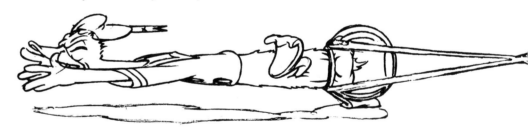

The weight of the engine is shown as it skids to a stop, and the added touch of the coal flying momentarily into the air helps the effect.

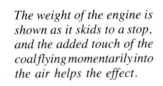

350

(3) Weight is revealed by
how hard a character has
to push or pull against an
object.

ANIMATOR: *Milt Kahl—*
Pinocchio.

*The first roughs of Pinoc-
chio happily skipping off to
school show the amount of
looseness that is possible
in the movement of even a
wooden boy.*

ANIMATOR: *Frank Thomas—*
Pinocchio

Walks   FOUR-FOOTED FRIENDS

By the time we had finished our work on *Pinocchio* in 1939, the animators had done skips and runs, casual strolls, walks with enthusiasm, with tired feet, with apprehension, and with heavy-footed rage. In one scene, Jiminy Cricket even dressed himself while running full speed; and in another, Pinocchio, as a puppet, was made to simulate a walk with strings.

Then Walt Disney decided to make *Bambi*. This was to be a picture of beauty and mood, of philosophy and poetry, contrasting the intimacy of a dewdrop on a blade of grass with the excitement of young bucks leaping about on a meadow. *Bambi* had less story, by far, than the other features, being more like the pictorial Silly Symphonies, but it had strong character relationships, neither cartoon relationships nor caricatured, but real, believable relationships. Was this asking too much of personality animation?

Walt was not sure we were capable of animating this film quite yet, so while the rest of the staff moved on to *Fantasia*, two animators[2] were assigned to puzzle over the movements and drawing problems of deer and rabbits, and to search for a way of incorporating our tenets of communication into these foreign shapes. We knew we could make them real—that is, look like real deer—but we also knew that without establishing personality we could never make that type of deer carry a whole feature.

We studied film of deer, looked at pictures, talked to the sketch men who had been drawing deer for most of a year (while the story had been shaped and developed), and watched deer at the zoo. The two fawns kept at the studio had long since grown up and departed, so we got no help from them, but we did have film taken while they were young and frisky. However, nowhere could we see the leg squash as it took the weight of the body, and no cheeks fattened as the mouth closed. No eyes changed shape, no jaws dropped in a big yawn, no bodies bulged or stretched; they were annoyingly lithe and supple and strong and muscular. What were we going to draw, animate, move?

While studying live action film of rabbits, we noticed one white bunny hopping away in a very spirited manner. The action was faster than we would have thought, but it read well and had unusual life. A frame by frame check revealed that all detail on the rabbit's body disappeared with the first frame of action—all the camera recorded was a white shape that changed radically on each frame of the film. Each hop took only five frames, and while the direction often changed erratically, the positions in the action remained the same.

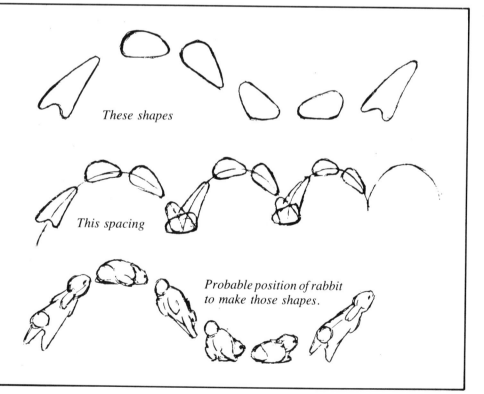

These shapes

This spacing

Probable position of rabbit to make those shapes.

It was in the tracing of the film that we found our answer. We did not have photostats on this footage, and the images were small and difficult to see, but once we discovered the secret of the animal's construction all the pieces fell into place. There was actually more squash and stretch than we could use, but it was not occurring where we had been looking. Instead of being out in the open, away from the body, the activity was at both ends of the legs, in the shoulders and haunches, and, again, in the fingers and toes. Here the action was as broad as any cartoon drawing, with great flexibility and spring in the tips, and massive swelling and thrusting up in the body.

It took some time to understand the deer's anatomy,

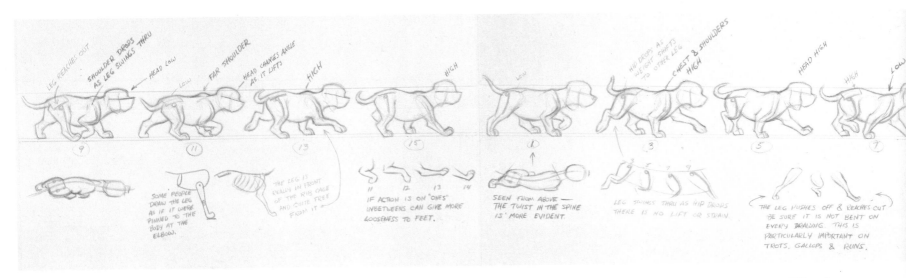

Basic animal walk on 10s, shown on a puppy because it is easier to see what is happening in his loose and floppy action. The principles are the same whatever the animal.

Animals seldom walk very far in the same gait. They speed up, slow down, vary the leg pattern, mainly concentrating on where they are going. Why they are going will also affect gait and stance. Their line of sight is usually the key to

ANIMATOR: *Frank Thomas*— The Fox and the Hound.

Cycle action of a puppy running on 10s.

to realize that the shoulders are nearly in front of the rib cage and that the rear end is practically all leg and haunch, but once this was understood our drawings of the animals began to have the fluid, loose feeling, combined with muscular power, that was so typical of deer. One day we were studying a strip of film showing an adult deer bounding across a small ravine. As the front legs took up the weight of the body and guided it into a turn, the elbow actually pushed up *above* the line of the back. After that, we believed anything was possible.

Our other big surprise came in the amount of movement in the deer's spine and pelvis. The twists and tilts and turns and flexibility were more than we knew how

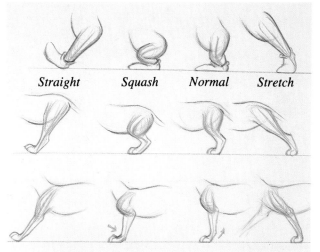

| Straight | Squash | Normal | Stretch |

Traditional squash and stretch on a walk in the thirties.

On a dog's rear leg, the squash is up in the haunch

—and in the shoulders and "fingers" of the front leg.

their action.
Once you understand the relationships, the drawing, and the character of the
animal, you can then add the personality traits to the walk: swagger, prance, caution, worry, confidence.
The head may be held higher, the feet may drag— changes in attitude and timing will change the character of the walk.
Study the animal—not the cartoon formula.

ANIMATOR: *Ollie Johnston— The Fox and the Hound.*
Cycle action of adult dog running on 8s.

Cinderella

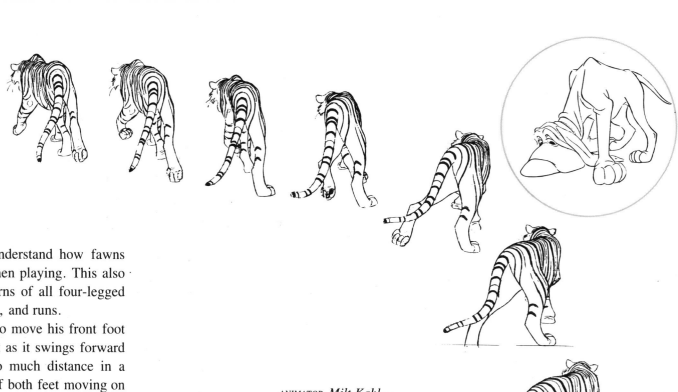
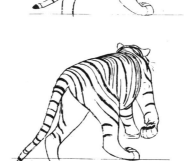

to draw, but they helped us understand how fawns achieved the frolicking look when playing. This also helped us learn the basic patterns of all four-legged animals in walks, trots, gallops, and runs.

A giraffe, for example, has to move his front foot out of the way of the back foot as it swings forward because his long legs cover so much distance in a stride. This gives the illusion of both feet moving on the same side at once, and in a sense they do for a few frames. But, essentially, all animals move their legs in a cross pattern of right fore followed by left rear. We got down on our hands and knees and tried it ourselves, and immediately discovered that it was the only natural way to progress and stay in balance. To move legs in any other pattern gives an awkward movement and a poor base for any kind of stability. While it is possible to train horses and some circus animals to special gaits, these are basically unnatural forms of locomotion. By studying the real animal instead of working over a cartoon formula, we had broken through to a new level of understanding that made other stories about ''real'' animals possible for the studio. More than that, once the physical relationships and character of any animal are understood, the way is open to portray its attitudes: belligerent, cocky, stealthy, nervous, worried, or timid. And if there is a scene that calls for a lack of coordination, the animator has only to break the animal's natural rhythm of movement, to mix up the leg pattern. His character immediately appears sleepy or drunk.

ANIMATOR: *Milt Kahl*—
The Jungle Book

The stripes on the tiger, which ordinarily would be time-consuming decoration, were used here to describe the form of Shere Khan. Because of years spent studying animal movement, the animator was able to do this scene without help from any live action film.

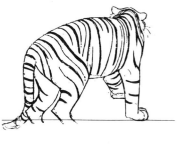

357

Walks ACTING AND ATTITUDES

Once the walks of the cartoon characters began to look real, the animators could experiment with characterization and attitudes. While pure inventiveness and imagination were still creating funny scrambles and semi-dog actions for Pluto, acting and emotions were capturing audiences in a new way. As the spectators watched Grumpy pull out of Snow White's embrace and stomp away defiantly, they were more concerned with his feelings than they were with the mechanics of his walk. Figaro, the cat in *Pinocchio*, was enor-

ANIMATOR: *Bill Tytla*—
Snow White.

Snow White tries to give Grumpy a parting kiss as he leaves for work.

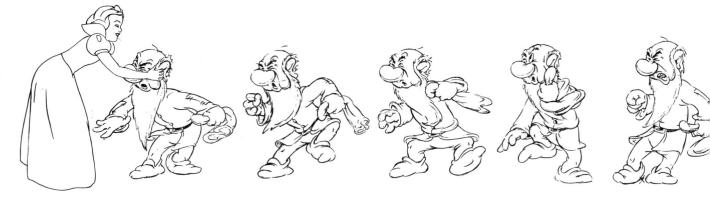

ANIMATOR: *Eric Larson*—
Pinocchio.

Figaro crosses the soft, down comforter on his way to bed.

ANIMATOR: *Eric Cleworth*—
The Jungle Book.

This walk was animated as a cycle; the drawings were later diminished in size step-by-step so the elephant would match the perspective of the layout as he walked away.

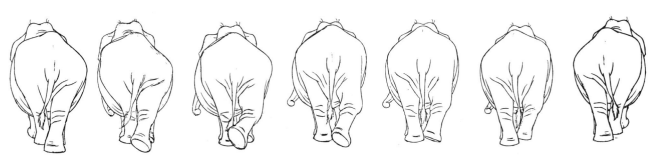

mously appealing as he walked across the bed, sinking deep into the soft covers, but it was his annoyance with the constant interruptions from Geppetto that made the scene come alive.

As a matter of fact, the animators found it easier to do a walking scene if the character had a strong attitude than if he was just moving from one place to another. There was nothing to caricature when nothing was happening; there should be some reason *why* the character is walking, and that is what you animate.

The acting possibilities in an action enable the animator to go beyond a mechanical performance.

ANIMATOR: *Ollie Johnston—* The Rescuers.

After a tender moment of affection between the girl Penny and the cat, she carries him out of the room in the loving but thoughtless and inept way that most young people carry their pets. It was just the right touch for this moment in the film.

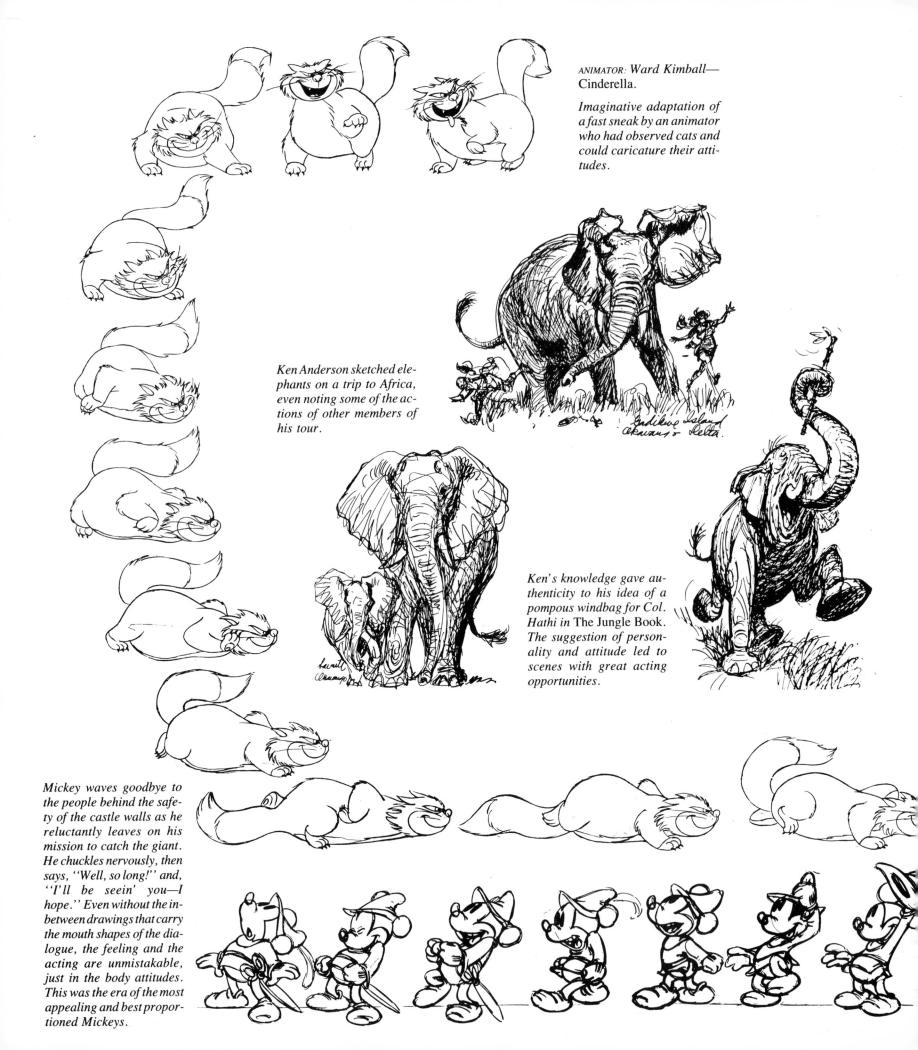

ANIMATOR: *Ward Kimball—* Cinderella.

Imaginative adaptation of a fast sneak by an animator who had observed cats and could caricature their attitudes.

Ken Anderson sketched elephants on a trip to Africa, even noting some of the actions of other members of his tour.

Ken's knowledge gave authenticity to his idea of a pompous windbag for Col. Hathi in The Jungle Book. *The suggestion of personality and attitude led to scenes with great acting opportunities.*

Mickey waves goodbye to the people behind the safety of the castle walls as he reluctantly leaves on his mission to catch the giant. He chuckles nervously, then says, ''Well, so long!'' and, ''I'll be seein' you—I hope.'' Even without the in-between drawings that carry the mouth shapes of the dialogue, the feeling and the acting are unmistakable, just in the body attitudes. This was the era of the most appealing and best proportioned Mickeys.

draws hands
up protectively

clears
throat

"COME --- COME TO   THINK   OF IT ____

leans out   pause -   then -   gradually straightens up.
slides foot back -

____ IF I WAS A PIRATE -

loose - expansive -

- I - -   WOULD. -   I - WOULDN'T - - -

loose points -   close eyes, start head shakes -

ANIMATOR: *Frank Thomas*—
The Rescuers.

Bernard tries to be nonchalant as he retreats from the chasm of the blow-hole. The action was worked out in thumbnails to match the dialogue and the gestures to the pattern of his steps.

The final drawings show how careful planning had solved the animator's acting problems.

Other Walks that Show Character Personality

ANIMATOR: *Milt Kahl—*
Robin Hood.

*Every drawing in this walk
is rich with the personality
of the callous Sheriff
of Nottingham. A model sheet
was made from the scene so
that the same walk could be
used throughout the picture.*

ANIMATOR: *Milt Kahl—*
"Pecos Bill,"
Melody Time.

This sassy walk with the
swinging hips has been
copied widely throughout
the animation industry. It
was created originally for
Sluefoot Sue, the girl who
captured Pecos Bill's heart.

ANIMATOR: *John Lounsbery—*
"Dance of the Hours,"
Fantasia.

*There was no chance for a
dramatic entrance for Ben
Ali, the leader of the alliga-
tors. A bright, little cocky
walk was used to make him
stand out from the others.*

ANIMATOR: *Eric Larson—*
Peter and the Wolf.

*Many duck waddles have
been animated, and it is a
challenge to find a pattern
of movement that is just
right for a new character,
matching both the person-
ality and the design.*

Group Movement

When more than one animal is walking or running in a scene, there is always a temptation to animate the same action for each figure. Once all the problems have been solved and legs are in the right place, the idea of doing a second set of drawings only slightly different seems like needless work. Still there is a special opportunity in the handling of groups that can make scenes of great impact. There is a feeling of elasticity as one figure pulls away from another, then closes in again, or passes someone up, or falls behind, that gives the charm and feeling of life to the group.

ANIMATOR: *Eric Larson—"Once Upon a Wintertime,"* Melody Time.

Eric Larson said, "The pattern of movement you get out of any group has always fascinated me." First, he drew the central figures, then started filling in with others, always searching for that flow and freedom that kept the group alive. The scene had a remarkable feel of the patterns of movement created by a group of skaters. Eric and Retta Scott followed the same procedure when animating the dogs chasing Faline in Bambi. *The lead dog was done first, then the others were filled in behind him, wherever they worked best.*

ANIMATOR: *Fred Moore—* Snow White.

Any group of characters should have careful thought given to their design and attitudes, whether they move together or individually. Fred Moore always made them interesting and pleasing.

ANIMATOR: *Bill Tytla—* Snow White.

Four of the dwarfs struggle as they take a furious Grumpy over to the tub to be washed and scrubbed. Bill Tytla's roughs show his thinking on this assignment and his feeling of how the thrusts and actions of one dwarf affected all the others. He could not animate any one of them singly, but had to consider the whole action of the group as the entertainment in the scene.

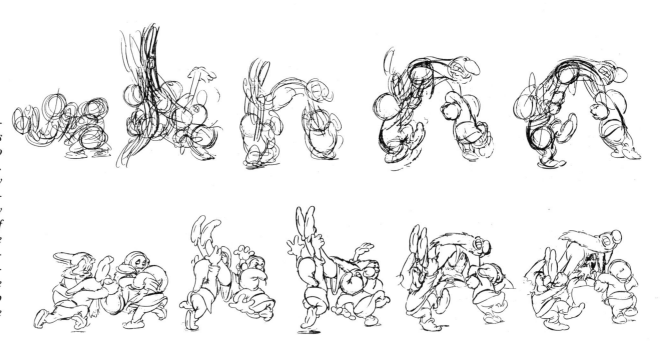

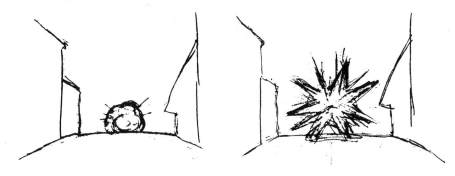

ANIMATOR: Frank Thomas—
Robin Hood.

This scene of kids going out to shoot the new bow and arrow that one of them had received was a happy occasion. Since the sequence immediately preceding had ended on a very quiet and somber note, it seemed best to start this section with a burst of laughter and music and running kids coming over a hill. The animator drew a set-up with a street coming straight into the camera. Then he animated a simple explosion, to match the spirit he wanted. Later he went back and determined which part would be somebody's arm and which a leg, or a head, a stick, or a ribbon. After the initial effect was over, the characters turned and ran down the street on a side pan, giving the audience a chance to see each of them individually.

ANIMATOR: Frank Thomas—
Snow White.

In Snow White *the dwarfs sneak into the bedroom with raised pickaxes, ready to kill the monster in their beds. It was important here that all the characters move together, look together, stop together, recoil together; so they were animated as one large mass doing the action. Afterward, this shape was broken down into the individual dwarfs, keeping all parts within the approved mass-shape. Even though Doc was in the lead, he was no more important than any of the others. The audience was intrigued by seven men reacting as one, with each still acting in his own way within the pattern.*

365

14. Story

"The story man must see clearly in his own mind how every piece of business in a story will be put over. He should feel every expression, every reaction. He should get far enough away from his story to take a second look at it . . . to see whether there is any dead phase . . . to see whether the personalities are going to be interesting and appealing to the audience. He should also try to see that the things that his characters are doing are of an interesting nature."

Walt Disney

ANIMATOR: **Art Babbitt—** The Country Cousin.

The unsophisticated country mouse, visiting the big city for the first time, inadvertently becomes drunk, and finds himself confronted with a difficult problem: how to get his umbrella out of the piece of toast.
STARTS ON PAGE 417

Preparing For Animation

A young high school filmmaker wrote us to ask "what makes a good story, great characters, good gags, good continuity, etc.?" Unfortunately, there is no closely guarded secret nor any simple answer, other than judgment, hard work, and talent. It begins, of course, with the idea for the whole picture. One storyman counseled, "Film, to me, is no different from creating a drawing, painting, song, play, or whatever. If you don't have a positive statement to make, you should never pick up the paintbrush or pencil."[1] More than a positive statement, it must have enough importance to be worth communicating—to be worth the work and the effort that will be required to put it on the screen. It must be interesting, provocative, spellbinding; it must

be a story. And, preferably, it should be a good one. One artist summed it up, "A good story cannot be ruined by poor animation, but neither can a poor story be saved by the very best animation."[2]

He could have gone on to say that a good story also can be ruined by poor development in the Story Department. Just because the story is great, there is no assurance that it will remain great after it has been worked over and over on the storyboards. Nothing is automatic in the animation business except the negative elements. How good a picture can become is much less certain.

First, there must be the big, simple idea: the story you can tell in two sentences. As you work on a picture it seems so complicated that even two paragraphs will not tell it all, but if it started out as a good idea,

FACING PAGE:
Lady and the Tramp.

— WHAT IN BLAZES!

MERLIN! MERLIN!

and you have been faithful to that concept, one day it will end up very simple again.

Alfred Hitchcock has recommended a similar approach.

> I always feel comfortable about a project when I can tell the story in a very simple way. . . . I like to imagine a young woman who has been to see the movie and goes home very satisfied with what she has seen.
>
> Her mother asks her, "What was it about?"
>
> And the girl replies, "Well, it was about a young woman who so and so and so. . . ."
>
> I feel that before undertaking to shoot a movie, one should be able to do just that, to satisfy oneself that it can be narrated just as clearly, the whole cycle.[3]

We have found that the story idea for an animated film must be even more direct:

> Jealousy leads a vain queen to threaten the life of a young princess, who flees into the woods where she is befriended by seven dwarfs. When the queen, in disguise, tricks her into eating a poisoned apple, the girl is thought dead and preserved in a glass coffin until a prince awakens her with love's first kiss.

> A baby elephant is considered a freak because of his enormous ears, until an enterprising mouse discovers a way to turn this liability into a startling asset.

> An orphan girl is held captive by an eccentric woman who is using the child to retrieve a large diamond held in a treacherous cave. Two mice from the Rescue Aid Society help the girl find the diamond; then, with the aid of some local animals, effect her escape.

Such a synopsis gives none of the flavor of the picture or the rich characters that motivate it, but it does reflect the basic drives that hold the picture together and make it work. If your idea is complicated in the beginning, there should be much more thought and discussion before even starting the picture. There are many temptations to overdevelop wonderful char-acters and put in lovable sequences and extra ideas you know will be great, but a hodgepodge can result unless there has been a clear, strong drive to the story from the very start.

Sequences

Our feature films always seemed to end up with about 14 sequences. No matter how each started out, whether with high adventure or complicated stories, by the time we developed and balanced and streamlined and edited we ended with little more than a dozen. At least two sequences would have been cut out after we started production, and something else would have grown to sequence length and been inserted even later. Still, we never had more than 15 nor fewer than 10 sequences.

This fact becomes quite important when a picture requiring many incidents in different locales is being considered. Constant action situations give no chance for the quiet sequences where audiences can fall in love with the characters. In our experience, a picture that attempted continuous excitement and dramatic tension never held the attention of the audience. It seemed to dull their senses. There could be a strong underlying theme, but the story had to be told with a balance of tempos and fresh ideas.

Snow White had these sequences:

1. Introduction: Queen and Mirror; Snow White in courtyard; arrival of Prince.
2. Queen orders Snow White's death; Snow White and Huntsman.
3. Panic in the woods; Snow White meets animals; they take her to dwarfs' cottage and help clean house.
4. Dwarfs in mine; march home and find something in their house.
5. Discover Snow White; agree to let her stay.
6. Dwarfs wash up for dinner; scrub Grumpy.
7. Queen turns into witch.
8. Dwarfs entertain Snow White; she sings for them; dwarfs give her their bedroom.
9. Witch prepares poisoned apple; leaves for cottage.

Peter Pan

10.	Dwarfs leave for work, after warning Snow White.
11. & 12.	Both sequences dropped.
13.	Snow White making pies; witch arrives and enters house.
14.	Animals warn dwarfs; they return too late; Snow White poisoned; witch falls off cliff.
15.	Dwarfs cry at Snow White's bier.
16.	Glass coffin; Prince comes; Snow White awakened and goes away with Prince.

The Rescuers had these sequences:

1.	Bottle found with call for help; Rescue Aid Society sends Bianca and Bernard.
2.	Mice learn about Penny from old cat at orphanage.
3.	At pawn shop, they learn where she is being held; Medusa leaves; mice left behind.
4.	Dropped.
5.	Albatross Air Service; mice take off, fly through clouds.
5.2	Devil's Bayou; Penny tries to escape, caught by crocodiles; mice arrive, meet Swamp Volunteers, ride with Evinrude.
6.	Medusa and Snoops plotting; mice chased by crocs into organ, shot at by Medusa.
7.	Medusa talks to Penny; sad song; mice arrive; escape plan.
8.	Evinrude sent for help, chased into bottle by bats.
9. & 10.	Dropped.
11.	Penny in Pirates Cave, finds diamond, barely gets out.
8.1.	Evinrude eludes bats; swamp animals to the rescue.
12.	The escape; diamond recovered; Penny rescued with aid of fireworks.
13.	Happy ending; mice sent on new mission.

Our goal must be to keep the audience pleased, but also excited, concerned, and, especially, wondering what is going to happen next. This will take place only if the audience is involved with the characters and what they are doing. In addition to an exciting visual presentation of the material, there should be a careful development of the drama inherent in each situation. A situation that is contrived simply will not hold up on the screen. Similarly, a situation that is ordinary or predictable quickly will become dull to your audience. It is vital that you have the viewers with you and carefully lead them through the story situations, but it is almost as important that they not get ahead of you. They can lose interest in even your best characters if everyone knows what to expect, or, worse, if things just seem to happen without regard for who the characters are or what is motivating them.

Often this situation cannot be uncovered until enough work has been completed to run the rough reels. It is not too late to correct, delete, or fortify, but it *is* crucial that the weakness be recognized and identified at this point. A criticism written about *The Fox and the Hound* after an early showing of approximately half the footage will illustrate the problems we incurred. (The basic story is that a young hunting dog plays happily with a kit fox when both are puppies, but as adults they live in different worlds. The fox has been raised by a kind widow living on a farm next to the hunter who is training his dog, and there is a mama owl who constantly is trying to help the little fox and explain the ways of the wild to him.) Our continuity was clear enough, but this was the reaction:

The biggest weakness is that there is no way the audience can relate to the characters. We don't know how the owl feels about the fox, really, or what she is trying to do—or why. Is she the same as the widow? And we don't see enough of the widow's feelings to justify the length of a whole sequence where she turns the fox loose in the woods. The pacing of the picture seems slow because we are not involved. More footage explaining these things will just make the picture even slower.

On an early showing of *Sleeping Beauty* we received a reaction that picks out the same type of weakness in our presentation:

There is no real conflict of Good and Evil. It is all about that, and it used all the symbols and it said it was about the age-old struggle, but because nothing came to life, no conflict really developed. The audience was never involved. The characters talked about the story they were in, but didn't live it—the audience never felt it—it was never real.

Every picture gets the same type of criticism at this stage, which brings up one of the more difficult challenges in the whole process of making the film. What should be done at this point, regardless of what was written in the script, to make this picture come to life? What will make the situations more believable? And, most important, how can we make the story seem to come from what the characters do?

Very often a few simple changes will bring dramatic results. After one of the sequences in *The Fox and the Hound* had been reworked, a young animator wrote this comment: ''All right! Now you feel that the story comes out of the personalities—it is not a plot you are trying to push the characters into—it doesn't even feel like a story! It's just something that happens when you get these personalities working against each other!''

Sometimes it is only a matter of a few new scenes; an establishing shot to clarify the location or the conditions surrounding the characters, or a new way of staging the original idea so that it has more strength. But occasionally the staff has to come up with a whole new compromise, or even a complete new sequence in order to make the continuity on the screen hold an audience.

Sometimes cutting out parts that have been overbuilt or become confusing (even though they might be entertaining) will simplify the story and make it clearer. Often, the enthusiasm for a rare bit of entertainment will have blinded everyone to the need for careful work in a story or layout before the scenes are passed on to the animator. Sometimes the animator himself can be so eager he does not wait for any more preparatory work before he begins. This became a real problem in the late thirties when it generally was felt that just about anything could be animated.

Veteran storyman Leo Salkin, speaking of those days, said that the story work was much more exciting and stimulating as the animators improved in their abilities to handle any kind of acting. But Ben Sharpsteen felt that now and then the storyman left his own work only half done. He wrote, ''I am inclined to think that too often people . . . grew accustomed to some of the great performances that animators gave, and they were continually relying on them in visualizing the making of a picture, instead of realizing that, frequently, simple story changes could produce even better results.''

To illustrate, he chose a section of *Dumbo* that shows Timothy Mouse becoming drunk. The clowns have been celebrating and dropped a bottle of liquor into a tub of water. Timothy and Dumbo come along, very disconsolate, and Dumbo begins to hiccup. Timothy suggests he drink some water, and soon the little elephant is behaving in a strange manner. Timothy wonders what kind of water is in that tub and takes a drink himself. This was the action the storyman left up to the animator.

The scene was given to Fred Moore, one of the top

ANIMATOR: Fred Moore—Dumbo.

Dumbo, the little circus elephant with enormous ears, has taken a drink from a water bucket containing spilled whiskey. He is acting strangely, so his friend Timothy Mouse looks into the bucket, loses his balance, and falls in. As the little elephant watches, we hear singing from the bottom of the bucket and see bubbles rising. Finally, a drunk Timothy emerges. This was an easier and funnier way of staging the business than trying to show Timothy gradually affected by the whiskey.

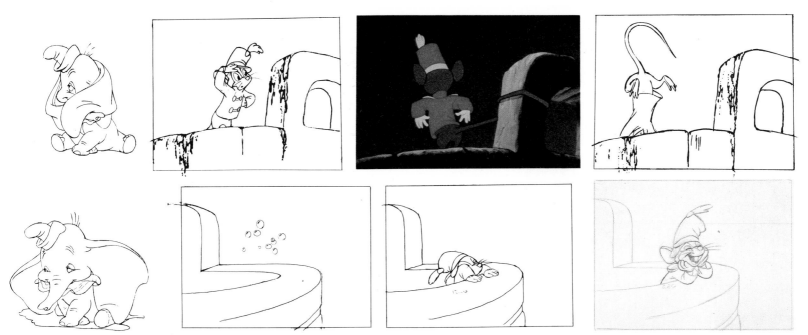

animators (with successes in *Pinocchio* on the characters of Geppetto, Lampwick, and Jiminy Cricket), but he had trouble with this assignment. Ben went on, "Moore was animating the scene, and we could not get the result that we had visualized. It was based on a very subtle and difficult piece of personality animation." Timothy, somehow, had to react in an appropriate and entertaining way, first, to the taste of the water, and, second, to the way it was beginning to make him feel. There was not enough time to have him complete the change to a funny drunk; the point of this scene was just to show his initial reactions to taking the drink. It *was* subtle—and questionable planning as well.

After Fred had sweated and squirmed through several tests, none of which felt right, the decision was made to change the story concept at that point. They went back to the storyboard, and after many discussions Ben recalled they came up with this idea:

When Dumbo showed signs of intoxication, Timothy remarked, "I wonder what kind of water this is anyhow." With that remark, he leaned over too far to look into the tub, fell in, and after a splash or two, the sound of his voice changed considerably. [In the final, they used a happy yodel.] This was done without showing animation of Timothy. The next time we saw him, he was resting on his elbows on the edge of the tub with a silly smile on his face.

This was a simple and easy way of putting the transition over. It was a far better means of doing it than to have squeezed everything we could have out of the animator in some subtle manner. In fact, the resulting animation could have been done by an animator of lesser abilities.

Another type of change to consider if the characters need strengthening might be a shift in character relationship. It could be the business itself that needs bolstering, but it also can be that the personalities do not have a chance to play properly and reveal just who they are. Adapting the personality traits more to the situations that are developing could be one answer, but occasionally a whole new relationship is needed.

When our production unit started *The Rescuers*, all of us thought we would make our team of mice detectives more interesting and a little different from other mice we had done by having them married. There had been several successful live-action shows using a husband and wife team, and the idea seemed to offer new situations that would be stimulating for all of us. We had moved the first sequences through the Story Department, even had our first recording session, and were well into experimental animation before it gradually became apparent that the responses of our mice to the various situations were too subtle for good communication in animation. In the live films, the fact that the characters are good-looking and involved in a predicament really was all that was needed. Any bits of dialogue between them could fortify the entertainment, but that was not vital. You either liked them, or you did not, and if you did like them you went along with what they were doing. In animation, that is not enough.

We had to have stronger reactions, more emotions, feelings the audience could recognize and understand. We tried bickering, affection, annoyance, dependence, but everything was too mild or slightly unpleasant. We finally realized that our biggest stumbling block was that there was nothing either mouse was trying to achieve in their relationship. Without the little bewildering moments of getting to know each other,

without the possibility of romance, without the excitement of a new companion, we were finding very few attitudes worth animating.

It has long been known in the theater that one of the best ways to get hold of any character is to find out what he is trying to do. If he is merely an observer, satisfied with his life, complacent, and only concerned intellectually in any situation, it will be difficult to make him either real or exciting. It is not until he begins to interrelate with other people or with human problems that he shows his array of unique traits. We needed to find interesting ways for our characters to react to anything they might encounter.

Instead of a professional team with the wisdom of experience, we changed our mice to amateurs who had only their pledge to the Rescue Aid Society to guide them. Immediately rich attitudes appeared, and storymen became eager to delve into the new possibilities of the situations. But even more helpful was to have the mice not even acquainted at the start, each seeing the other for the first time early in the picture. Now everything each of them did was colored by the presence of this new companion. Miss Bianca was very good-looking, with quite an appeal for Bernard, and, while his main duty was to the society and his desire to succeed at any cost, his predicaments were made much more interesting by having such an exciting female by his side. If he had to tell her that she was wrong, he had a problem that offered far more entertaining possibilities than if they had been married for twenty years. Now Bianca's lack of regard for logic created real situations, and any conflicts between the two offered unlimited possibilities to both the storymen and the animators. And all because we had changed their relationship to one that could grow and remain active. Certainly many good plays have been written with no change in the way the characters feel about each other from beginning to end, but, generally, the story will not progress as easily if the characters are not progressing too. Anytime there can be a development in their relationships, it will be easier to find business that will enrich their personalities and hold the interest of the audience.

We were so carried away by the potential of the changes we had made that we were inspired by Ken Anderson's sketches to build a whole sequence about the mice's preparations for the mission. They were told to check out the equipment needed from the sour old mouse down in the stockroom. While Bianca was selecting hats and outfits that would make them look debonair, Bernard was concerned with safety and ingenious inventions that a James Bond might have used. When asked by the clerk if he knew how to handle a special dart gun, he acted nonchalant and competent in order to impress Bianca. Naturally, he hit the release and nearly killed them all. His aplomb was further shaken when he was handed the survival kit with two pills to be taken in case of capture!

Ken made hundreds of drawings of the props that mice could make out of thimbles and erasers and things that humans had discarded, and we were all excited about the entertainment in both the locale and the situation. It was not until several weeks later, after we discovered that the plight of the little girl was the very backbone of our story, that we realized that we would have to give up all of the byplay of the mice getting ready to go on the mission. It just delayed our getting to the main part of the story. The picture became interesting when the mice had a real problem to solve, and all the talk before they actually started out became dull, and, worse, made later parts of the picture seem to be boring because they repeated attitudes we were using here. So the sequence had to be dropped. Of course, the big problem comes in recognizing that this should be done. Basically, it is built on a knowledge of what business is best suited to the animation medium. Every picture will have scenes that are difficult to draw and scenes that call for experience and talent, but the bulk of the film should be made up of scenes that are easy to do, should be effective and good-looking on the screen, and should make the best possible use of the animation potential.

Here are a few guidelines that can help anyone judge the material before the animation is started:

1. Avoid scenes or activities that are only continuity. This type of action is difficult to do convincingly and is always judged critically by an audience. If there is a mood to be established or scenic atmosphere is needed, as in the dwarfs marching home from the mine or the sequence in *The Rescuers* showing the mice flying on the back of the albatross, then the conti-

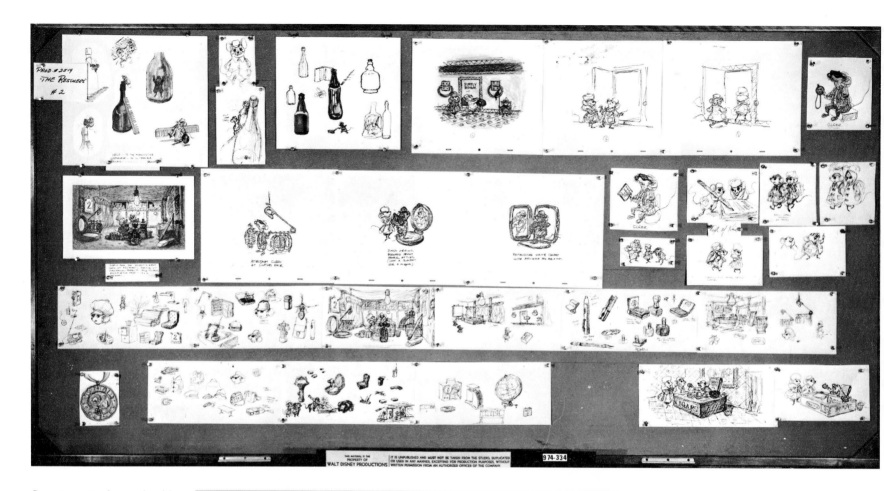

Secret agents always should be properly equipped before starting out. These drawings by Ken Anderson explore the idea of a stockroom where mice check out equipment needed for their missions. The many human props adapted to the needs of a mouse give charm and scale, keeping the characters small.

ARTIST: *Ralph Hulett*—The Rescuers.

Captain Orville gains flying altitude over Manhattan before heading south. This type of dramatic scenic shot adds excitement to a normally dull sequence of characters moving from one locale to another.

ANIMATOR: *Eric Larson*— Lady and the Tramp.

Peg, the faded star of the Dog and Pony Show; an example of a character that is believable but not realistic. The animator was not restricted in action or expressions by limitations of a real dog's anatomy.

nuity can be secondary to the pictorial effect. Otherwise, there is more interest in what happens once the characters get where they are going than there is in the laborious action of getting there.

2. Avoid scenes whose only function is to explain. Sequences where the characters have to stand around and talk are always difficult. Be sure there is a situation that gives the characters a definite attitude, or something to achieve, a disagreement, or a predicament to play out. Use a narrator or a title to set up the situation. Do not make the onstage actors do it.

3. Make sure the story incident or situation is really interesting. The actors must not be expected to carry the story just by their acting. They should motivate the story; their personalities and the decisions they make become the backbone of the whole structure, but there must be a strong situation that has enough interest in itself to hold the audience. Like the scene in *Dumbo* of Timothy taking the drink, it should not be left entirely to the animator to carry the story idea.

4. Be sure the characters have an opportunity to come to life. Walt always told us, "Find the entertainment in the situation and in your characters. Don't get bogged down in the story itself." Watch out for continuous activity or exposition. Back up immediately if you have both.

5. Look for places to show the characters thinking. Show them changing attitude, and look for ways to show more facets of their personalities; they should grow through the film. Consider this: a strong situation has been established. The character comes into it with a definite and interesting attitude. Confronted with the problem, he develops his own personality, grows a little, shows who he is, makes his decision for action, then does it in an entertaining way.

6. Ask yourself, "Can the story point be done in caricature?" Be sure the scenes call for action, or acting that can be caricatured if you are to make a clear statement. Just to imitate nature, illustrate reality, or duplicate live action not only wastes the medium of animation but puts an enormous burden on the animator. It should be believable, but not realistic.

7. Tell your story through the broad cartoon characters rather than the "straight" ones. There is no way to animate strong-enough attitudes, feelings, or expressions on realistic characters to get the communication you should have. The more real, the less latitude for clear communication. This is more easily done with the cartoon characters who can carry the story with more interest and spirit anyway. *Snow White* was told through the animals, the dwarfs, and the witch—not through the prince or the queen or the huntsman. They had vital roles, but their scenes were essentially situation. The girl herself was a real problem, but she was helped by always working to a sympathetic animal or a broad character. This is the old vaudeville trick of playing the pretty girl against the buffoon; it helps both characters.

Our own feelings were summed up very simply once in a story meeting: "Just be sure you give us something to animate. Don't give us a scene where nothing happens!"

Storyman Ed Penner had an unusual problem in *The Lady and the Tramp* with the sequence of the dogs in the city pound. The inescapable fact that the unwanted animals are put away at these places was a key part of the story and the thought had to be planted in this sequence. The pathos of melancholy dogs behind bars is one thing, but taking an animal to the gas chamber bordered on the morbid and overdramatic in our medium. How could it be presented so that it was unmistakable, yet done with a light touch?

Ed's solution: First, build a parallel with the live-action prison films that had been so popular just a few years earlier (*The Big House*, *The Last Mile*), making available clichés of dialogue and attitudes.

"Look, guys, they're takin' Jo-Jo."

"Yeah, he's taking the long walk."

"Oh, well, a short life and a merry one."

These were familiar terms the audience understood. Second, show the dog only in silhouette, as a shadow, to minimize identification. Third, change the dog's name to "Nutsy," and, fourth, give the animation to Cliff Nordberg with instructions, "Make it funny!"

Only Cliff could handle such an assignment. He had become known for his ability to create the unexpected, screwy actions where ordinary movements would have sufficed. His talents gave a zany quality to mundane situations and were just right for this delicate spot in the picture. No one doubted that Nutsy was indeed taking his last walk, but he was so comical about it that no one could become overly concerned.

Walt and the Storymen

Storymen are as diverse in their talents and interests as animators. They are not interchangeable and cannot be expected to do equally well on every assignment. When Walt wanted a certain result, he cast his storymen with the same perception and intuition he had displayed in casting his animators.

Ted Sears and Perce Pearce were strong on character development and personalities. Bill Cottrell added good taste, appropriateness, and judgment. Bill Peet could come up with a whole new visual concept. Erdman (Ed) Penner and Dick Creedon knew story structure and understood the mechanics of comedy. Otto Englander was a veritable librarian of Walt's discarded ideas that were too good to lose. The list continues on, with each storyman having his own individual strengths and talents.

Walt never was interested in story structure, relying instead on his almost infallible intuition for what was entertaining in any idea. He tore storyboards apart ruthlessly as he tried to find the spark that could be developed into an unusual and memorable sequence

Walt was not always available when a decision was needed, and storymen and directors often had to catch him on the run. Here, a simple question out in the hall from Joe Grant, center, and Jack Kinney has led to an impromptu story meeting.

on film. Prior to 1935, his storymen had been trained to look for the fresh, the unexpected, the different, and to think in terms of caricature and exaggeration—which they interpreted as meaning bizarre, wild, and impossible. The more outlandish, the better they liked it. To them, anything real or sincere meant "straight" and automatically would be dull. Now, since the animators could do so much more, Walt had to pull his storymen back and teach them new values of warmth and believability. He still wanted fresh situations and funny predicaments, but he also wanted his characters to achieve maximum identity with the audience.

This type of thinking is the ultimate in creativity. The challenge to the storyman plus the stimulation of Walt's constant pressure—not to deliver, but to search and probe and discover—kept an air of constant excitement in the Story Department. It is not too difficult to think of cute bits of business that dalmatian puppies might do, especially when there are fifteen of them in one family, but the big idea that has them all watching television like any family of kids is unique and comes from a rare talent. The idea goes further, for the program they are watching is a series featuring their idol Thunderbolt, the Wonder Dog. The audience has no trouble accepting this since they have seen it in their own homes night after night. It is completely believable and offers endless possibilities for business, personality touches, gags, and something entirely new on the screen. More than that, it is a warm, happy sequence that will play into the evil suspense of the puppies' all being kidnapped immediately following. Maybe it is not genius, but it certainly is creativity!

Many people contributed ideas to that sequence, with Walt leading the way, but the storyman on all of *101 Dalmatians* was the talented, pungent, irascible humorist from Indiana, Bill Peet. He shared some of Walt's feelings for farmlands, and his characters were always somehow real and down-to-earth, no matter how fantastic the concept. His amazing powers of observation enabled him to catch the essence of everything he drew, whether it was a boxcar on a freight train or a Bavarian dwarf living under a lily pad. Fellow storyman and sketch artist Ralph Wright, who was better known for his great gags in the Goofy pictures, once said that Bill was one of the few "who dreamed up real, live characters that lived and breathed and

thought and came from the heart of the story artist.''

Bill Peet always had a strong, overall concept of the story material that integrated the humor in both the characters and the situation. Rather than spot gags, his integrity drove him to search out an idea that lifted the situation out of the commonplace, and still left the door open to further development in this new direction. Yet after conceiving all this in his mind, he could reject the entire notion if it did not work with the other parts of the story.

One such invention that later had to be discarded was Ishtar, the buzzard, in the early versions of *The Jungle Book*. Bill needed some way that the beasts of prey could find out what was going on in other parts of the jungle, so they knew the movements of the hunter Buldeo and the boy Mowgli. He could have had them stalking about, peering through the tall grass constantly, or listening to the warning cries of some bird of the Indian jungles. But Bill found a more entertaining way of tying it all together. Since buzzards do not kill, he had Ishtar in the humiliating position of having to get his meals from the scraps left by the tiger and leopard and the wolves. Being enterprising as well as hungry, he promoted himself and his eventual meals by ex-

Bill Peet poses for a photo showing the storyman's life: too much coffee, crumpled drawings, and not even a place to sit. As both sketch artist and storyman, Bill had a unique talent for finding an entertaining way to tell a story in situations that could be well animated.

The family of dalmatians watch their favorite TV program together like any human family, in this imaginative and entertaining sequence in 101 Dalmatians.

Cinderella

(ROUGH CHARACTER SUGGESTIONS)

changing bits of information that these beasts might need or find interesting—especially information about the location of a prospective meal for everyone.

But all of these meat-eating animals moved by night, and the buzzard is not equipped for traveling in the dark. He was always suggesting, ''Perhaps we can go first thing in the morning . . .'' only to be cut off by a growling, ''Now!'' And as he ran off in pursuit of his benefactor, bumping into trees and stumbling, we heard his voice crying, whining, ''But why does it have to be now? It's dark and . . . Oof . . . maybe we could . . . glkk. . . . How about at the crack of dawn . . . Oooof! . . . ?''

None of these predators liked the buzzard, but they often liked the information he brought them, which presented a strong relationship on which to build their personalities. It is always good to know how one character feels about another. But Bill thought he was on the wrong track and tossed out both the character and the situation. Realizing it was more important to develop a very believable relationship between the panther and Mowgli, he found this weakened by the comic antics of other characters.

No one had an easy time with Walt or found him particularly comfortable to be around, and anyone as argumentative as Bill was bound to compound the problem. Still, he enjoyed a rare rapport with his boss that led Walt to relax more in Bill's room than in most others. This was not always to Bill's advantage. He told of one morning when Walt dropped in with a terrible cold and flopped in an easy chair in front of the boards. It was clear that he should be home in bed instead of roaming the halls with watery eyes and a stuffed-up nose. He admitted, ''My head feels like a block of cement,'' but quickly he set his jaw in a defiant attitude and continued, ''but I'm not giving in to it!'' Bill smiled weakly; then Walt, with a heavy sigh tinged with determination, went on, ''Well, what the hell ya got here, Bill?'' The boards were not approved, and that afternoon Bill started work on a new version of the material.

Walt's passing moods had a profound effect on both his judgment and his behavior, and on his dark days he was apt to rip a storyboard apart for no apparent reason. Bill always claimed that there were actually three different Walts: the dreamer, the realist, and the spoiler. You never knew which one was coming into your meeting. Bill quipped, ''You have to phone down to the front gate and ask the cop which Walt came in this morning.''

The biggest problem the storymen had with Walt was that he never would look where they were pointing when they explained the action on the boards. Usually he already had seen everything in the room a couple of nights before and was not even thinking about what was being said, but he also had the knack of listening with one ear while completely engrossed in something else. Nothing ever slipped by the man.

Webb Smith started off one meeting by asking Walt, ''Do you see this drawing up here?'' Walt assured him he did. Webb continued, ''And you see this drawing down here?'' Walt grunted a reply but his curiosity was piqued. Webb concluded, ''Well, when I'm talking about this sketch up here, I don't want you looking at this sketch down here.'' Walt laughed, but deliberately looked everywhere except where Webb was pointing from then on.

With Walt's policy of seldom using a single storyman working alone, there was always a temptation for each man to build his own private storyboard over in a corner instead of working together on a common effort. Ralph Wright insists that this is what happened on the short, *The Art Of Skiing*. One storyman had all his business going from right to left, while the other had his gags going left to right. When Walt tried to combine their efforts, the directions simply did not work. After an annoyed silence, someone suggested, "Why don't you use this stuff of the Goof going to the top of the hill and getting ready to make his descent down the steep slope facing him, then suddenly have him shoot backwards down the slope he has just climbed; that'll make him going the correct direction for the rest of the business." It also made the funniest gag in the picture.

To Ben Sharpsteen, Walt was the whole story department, no matter who was working for him. From the position of director and occasionally supervising director, Ben had a special view of what went on. He said, "Walt's acting and storytelling ability were an important feature in the success of the studio. He had a terrific personality for telling stories in such a way that the animators and directors were thoroughly confident and believed in them. He could tell a story so that you could see it as it would appear on the screen. I cannot give the man too much credit."

Ben went on to relate how Walt helped the director of the picture as well.

I was assigned to direct *On Ice*. As I began to plan its production, I naturally assumed that I would start at the beginning of the story on a sequence of Mickey Mouse showing off as an ice skater. Walt dropped in unannounced, sat down, and began looking at the story sketches. He said, "The picture, as it is, is too long." Then he pointed to two sequences that were pretty far down in the story. The first involved Donald Duck and Pluto. Donald strapped a pair of ice skates to Pluto's paws while Pluto was asleep. Donald then yowled like a cat, waking Pluto up in an agitated state. Pluto's first thought was to take off in pursuit of the sound. He hit the ice and skidded around badly, and so forth.

The second sequence presented Goofy as an ice fisherman on the same frozen pond. He had cut a hole in the ice, and then had dropped bits of chewing tobacco into it, with the intention of clubbing the fish as they came up to spit in the cuspidor he had provided. Being Goofy, however, he kept missing them. This sequence was a perfect companion for the Pluto sequence, because we could leave Pluto in a helpless situation and then cut back to Goofy and his troubles without wasting time on transitional footage.

Walt said, "Here you've got two great situations. It isn't important how we lead up to them. Now after you get them done and you know how much footage they use, then you can go back and build your beginning." Walt proceeded to describe the

Humbert, the faithful huntsman of the queen in Snow White, *was a menacing killer in these first sketches by Albert Hurter.*

This is the final continuity of the attempt to kill Snow White. The audience had never before been asked to believe that an actual murder could take place in a cartoon. Would they believe this?

various ways that Pluto would try to get up on his feet again, only to flop down. He went through the whole routine. He also described Goofy's fishing problems. He concluded by saying, ''Now when Goofy is completely outwitted by those fish, then they all come up as a group and spit in the cuspidor. And why don't you consider playing a little tune? Some sort of a little tune with the spit hitting the cuspidor.'' We ended up by using what musicians call a ''break.'' They were high spots in the finished picture. This experience was a valuable lesson for me.

A clear example of how Walt worked with the story material is found in the sequence in *Snow White* in which the Huntsman tries to kill the young girl. The original version of this classic fairy tale may say, ''So the queen ordered a faithful servant to kill the girl, but, instead, he told her to flee into the woods.'' The scene could have been played that way, with our artists illustrating the action in a few pictorial scenes, but that was not nearly enough for Walt. He felt there could be an exciting moment at this spot, and there had to be some way we could do it in cartoon. Could we possibly adapt any of the techniques of the current live-action cinema?

It was a time of stimulating advances and experiments as new areas of communication were being explored. Many exciting uses were being made of the montage, a collection of scenes cut together to give an overall mood rather than a specific continuity. *Dr. Jekyll and Mr. Hyde*, starring Fredric March, contained a gripping transformation from gentleman to beast right before our eyes. The film *Private Worlds* explored the minds of psychotic individuals in an institution, with one particular girl named Sally, who heard her name called over and over in a fading echo. The sound track was beginning to be used to interpret feelings and sensations in addition to just carrying the dialogue. Film had come of age as a medium of expression and Walt would not be left behind. He would find ways to adapt many of these ideas in an imaginative way to the limitations and strengths of the cartoon.

He wondered what he could do with his own sequence of an attempted murder, a burly killer who cannot carry out his mission. It all sounded so realistic, so straight, so emotional and dramatic, and none of those elements ever had been considered for animation before. More than once he asked, ''Can it be done? Can we find a way to bring it off?'' It was one thing to have the girl singing to a group of animals, and quite another to present two human characters gripped by intense emotions. How could he do it?

His first thought was to have the Huntsman a real villain, a heavy, with a ''voice that is rusty and cracked.'' He would have a name, Humbert, and would be a definite personality, like Wallace Beery, only meaner. His daily job was to kill, and perhaps he even

The Huntsman, faithful to the queen's orders, advances stealthily as the girl comforts a lost baby bird.

381

looked forward to this particular task. "When the Queen says, *'kill her,'* the Huntsman's face brightens up as though he wants to do it." Here was real menace.

The girl had been sent out to pick flowers, so the sequence should start on a happy note with no hint of trouble. Then gradually the suspense would start to build as Humbert sees his opportunity, draws his knife, and approaches cautiously. When something causes him to fail to carry out his bloody assignment, there is considerable dialogue explaining what he had been told to do, why he could not do it, and what Snow White should do now.

This first version told the story with melodramatic excitement, but, if it had been sent down to the animators at that point, it would have been difficult to do and undoubtedly very clumsy on the screen. It was a live-action situation with delicate acting. The animators would not be able to get hold of either character without endless study of film, and even then there was the danger that the result would be only a crude symbol, contorted by restricted movements and weightlessness. There had to be more thought, more refinement, more adaptation, before this would be right for animation.

More story meetings were held, and many more drawings were made and pinned on the boards. Instead of picking a bouquet of flowers, perhaps Snow White should be stretched out, reaching for a particular flower in the cranny of a rock. She would be more vulnerable and make a better target as the dagger was raised, and one lone flower would be more symbolic of the lonely girl.

Walt began to feel that even though the flowers represented innocence they lacked warmth, and maybe changing to an animal or a bird that could respond to Snow White would give a stronger situation. If she were helping an animal in trouble there would be great contrast to the evil approaching behind her, and it would help build her character as well. Immediately the ideas began pouring in.

"Should the bird be sick, or have a broken wing . . . ?"

"I don't see that it is sick, but just like a little kid who is lost and is frightened, crying. . . ."

"She asks, 'Are you an orphan?'"

". . . get a little baby bird idea there. . . . It is innocent, paralleling her own situation."

Looking over the sketches on the board, Walt could see that too much time was being spent on unimportant action. The preceding sequence had developed with a strong ending, and you knew of the consuming jealousy of the queen as she assigned the grim task to her faithful servant. This was no time to start a new idea. He commented, "The moment she tells the Huntsman

to kill Snow White we fade out and fade in on the thing being carried out—make it move faster.'' And the dialogue at the end had to be broken up with more action between the lines. ''That would be better than a long bunch of dialogue. She would ask short questions —and he would answer with short answers.''

There was a big discussion about how Humbert would weaken and when he should drop the knife.

''I think it would be a stronger picture if she just turns around and sees the knife over her. It would be more dramatic. . . .''

''I think it would be better if he dropped the knife when her back is turned.''

Walt stared at the board, his fingers drumming on the arm of the chair, one eyebrow down. There was a long silence, then unexpectedly, ''Maybe we could speed the whole thing up—or, maybe there is a better way we can do it. Maybe we don't need this situation with her at all!''

There was another silence as the fellows in the meeting tried to consider this proposal. Finally one suggested, ''A fellow like the Huntsman who is sent out on a job should do it. A fellow like that wouldn't confess that he couldn't do it.''

Another silence.

''You could have her escape. . . .''

More thought and more meetings and more sketches

on the board. Are we doing it the right way? Will it work? Maybe if we just kept it short and direct and stick right to the point, and do not develop the Huntsman as much; play out the situation, but do not get involved with him. Walt suggested that they work on the dramatics of the whole thing, keeping the Huntsman in shadow, showing only his feet as he comes forward, ''. . . and hear the crunching of the leaves and twigs.'' This would build it in the audience's imagination more. ''When you get close-ups of faces you have to tell them too much and you lose imagination.''

No one ever had done anything like this before, and it was imperative that the audience accept it the way it was intended. If they laughed at the Huntsman, it would mean that the audience had not been drawn into the situation and could not take his type of handling seriously in a cartoon. They must believe that this animated figure existed and really was going to kill the girl. There was good reason for Walt to wonder.

Still he kept coming back to the same ingredients as being the right way to go. In a story meeting in June he was able to outline what he thought were the best ideas, and though there were more refinements as the sequence went through the plant this is essentially the way it was done. Note the length of this meeting. Saturday, from 8:00 to 1:00, was a regular work period in those days.

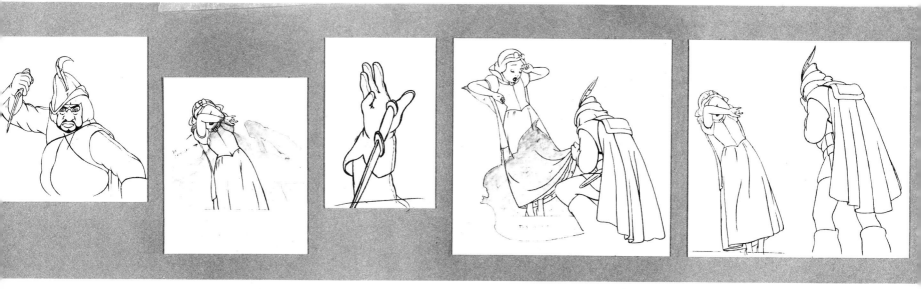

He raises his knife to strike, but cannot go through with the deed, and, dropping to his knees, urges the confused and frightened princess to flee into the woods.

SEQUENCE A—SNOW WHITE AND THE HUNTSMAN IN THE WOODS

Meeting held: Saturday, June 27, 1936—8:45 A.M. to 1:00 P.M.

Present were:

Walt   Joe Grant
Frank Churchill   Bill Cottrell
Charles Philippi   Larry Morey
Bob Kuwahara

Walt: Snow White is to be picking flowers—so that when you open up on the setup here there is a menace right off the bat—you just cut to a shot of the Huntsman there with just his eyes looking. What I see there—she is trying to help the little bird and then the Huntsman starts to come to her with the knife, and you cut to the Huntsman as he pulls the knife out and have a slow walk on him out of the scene—that is the last you see of the Huntsman, except his feet approaching. While she is talking to the little bird and saying things to cheer it up, here come the feet slow with a hesitating step—it could be the kind of a step that is trying to be light.

Larry: Would you see the shadows on the ground?

Walt: Yes, but the shadows are so that they carry through. She is there with the little bird and right behind comes the shadow—build up the shadow and the knife.

Joe: We just get a flash of the knife as it is being pulled.

Walt: We just flash on the shining article—cut to her and she kisses the little bird and it flies away —then we cut back to the knife over her and it begins to shake, hand opens and knife drops. Maybe he could drop down right in the scene, and she takes it as he says FORGIVE ME YOUR HIGH-NESS. Snow White is up there like she can't understand it—WHY, HUMBERT? WHAT IS IT? and

Even though both characters are limited in their actions by the extremely realistic handling, this sequence has great impact and was a milestone in proving that animation could present strong emotional situations convincingly.

Humbert could say, I COULDN'T DO IT YOUR HIGHNESS—Snow White says, WHAT?—Humbert: I CAN'T KILL YOU FOR HER—Snow White says, WHO? Humbert says, THE QUEEN, THE QUEEN. GO GO GO AND NEVER RETURN TO THE CASTLE FOR THE SAKE OF NOT ONLY YOURSELF, BUT FOR THOSE WHO LOVE YOU, DON'T RETURN. Maybe he could end up with GO GO GO. She is confused and runs off and maybe cut back to a shot of him in a breakdown quiver position at the last. Get a shot of the woods and she doesn't know what to do, but just goes on, hesitating at the beginning, but goes on deeper and deeper—maybe you could carry that "SALLY, SALLY" idea of KILL YOU—WHO?—THE QUEEN—building in the little things the Huntsman said to her. And always that GO GO GO when she stops.

Surprisingly, the next quote from Walt on those notes

is this: "Sizing the whole thing up—do you think that, generally, we are on the right track for a thing like this, or do you think it is too heavy?" There was no precedent to guide them and no way to test the sequence until it was completed in color. No one could say for sure, but Walt stuck by his intuition and decided to go ahead with it.

Today, we easily can see the ingredients that made it work so well. The crew concentrated on just the essence of the story situation, not letting any part become overdeveloped; they used carefully planned dramatic staging rather than explanatory scenes; and they underplayed the emotional aspects of the acting instead of calling for overwrought, tormented histrionics. As a result, the audiences were swept along, caught in a web of their own imagination, convinced of the intensity that never was actually shown. The less they were told, the more they filled in with their own thoughts; and the less that was said, the more they

seemed to understand. As little as was shown on the Huntsman, he probably ended up with more substance as a character than ever had been planned.

By March of the following year, the animation had been completed, and, as usual, several of the points so thoroughly discussed were not coming off. Alternative ways of doing some of the things would have to be found, and in this transcript of another meeting, Supervising Director Dave Hand explains the ideas they are considering as he listens to the reaction of the staff. Incidentally, the hours of 5 to 6:30 were not normal working hours, but reflect the overtime that already was expected of the personnel in order to complete the film.

SEQUENCE 3A—SNOW WHITE AND THE HUNTSMAN IN THE WOODS

Meeting held: March 17, 1937—5:00 P.M. to 6:30 P.M. Sweatbox 4

Present were:

Vern Papineau	Ford Beebe
Ted Baker	John Hubley
Jaxon	Ernest Nordli
Stuart Buchanan	Harold Miles
Ken Anderson	Charles Philippi
Terrell Stapp	Tom Codrick
George Goepper	Les Novros
Dick Creedon	Marc Davis
Hugh Hennesy	Dave Hand
Grim Natwick	Mike Holoboff

Grim: I didn't care for the shot of the Huntsman's feet very much—it didn't seem strong enough for the place it was in—it seemed a little clownish.

Dave: Yes, we are retiming it and possibly reshooting it.

Grim: the feet don't seem strong enough for the situation. I feel you want something big and dramatic. I think the shot doesn't even show the feet off to advantage. You're expecting something ominous and all you see is a pair of feet. A knife would represent what was going to happen better than a pair of feet.

Dave: A shadow comes in first, then the feet. We speak of having the feet step on her bouquet of flowers as he comes through the scene.

Tom: I think there ought to be a cut there to the Huntsman after Snow White screams—just a flash to a close-up front view of him.

Dave: We have discussed that to show his hand relaxing and the knife dropping, but it's a good point and I'm glad to have it. We are going to do it slower and have more furtiveness in his movements.

Creedon: He walks like he is going to meet something. He should be moving sideways or creeping back of something.

Dave: I recall a general reaction. People were agreeably surprised with the animation, it didn't look so bad.

Creedon: I was agreeably surprised. Hearing the voice alone, I thought it would be ham.

Dave: We still intend to get another character voice and do it over.

Buchanan: That's a pretty high cliff she falls over.

Dave: We have had a discussion of that, and we felt it should be a shorter drop—many of us.

Buchanan: It's too dangerous—it might kill her.

The scene of the feet was replaced by a shot of the Huntsman's face coming closer and closer, but with no change of expression. The menace of seeing the stealthy feet had sounded so good in the story meetings, but even Walt agreed that the replacement looked better. What is more interesting is the thought represented by the last three comments on the page. The cliff is too high . . . it might kill her! The girl had become as real to the crew of storymen as she did later to the audience. No one ever worried about Donald Duck falling too far!

This sequence has become a classic of communication with the audience. Everyone was drawn into the picture in a way that made the events that followed have a greater impact. It was melodramatic without becoming saccharine. Perhaps the sincerity of all who worked on it contributed the most to making it such a successful part of an outstanding film.

Dialogue

The easiest way to develop a story is to do it all with dialogue between the characters, explaining everything the audience needs to know. But, as Alfred Hitchcock said, "When we tell a story in cinema, we should resort to dialogue only when it's impossible to do otherwise."[4] The hardest way to develop a story is to do it all with pantomime. While it is true that a character seldom comes to life as a specific personality until the voice is added, there is also Dopey who made no sounds, Pluto who only howled and panted, and Donald Duck whose dialogue was fifty percent unintelligible. Still, most of the great characters owed much not only to the voice but to the carefully selected lines they said.

Walt usually left out the dialogue until a sequence had been developed to the point where he could see just how little was really needed. If the idea could be put over with an expression, an action or a sound effect, or with music, he would not use dialogue. The storyman had to think in visual terms first, and when he did write dialogue it had to tell something about the character and not be exposition. Walt insisted that no one wants to see a character chewing away on a bunch of words when a provocative situation is developing. The audience wants to see what is going to happen, and the storyman only wants the dialogue that will fortify and sharpen his story and the personalities.

Hitchcock also said, "To me one of the cardinal sins for a scriptwriter, when he runs into some difficulty, is to say, 'We can cover that by a line of dialogue.' Dialogue should be a sound among other sounds, just something that comes out of the mouths of people whose eyes tell the story in visual terms."[5] Perhaps that idea is too austere for the cartoon that has to rely on character and personality so heavily, but it is very true of words that try to carry the meaning of the scenes.

One producer at Disney's insisted that if a character said he felt a certain way, that was all that was needed. That would establish the fact and the audience would have to believe it. But it does not work like that. It is not enough simply to proclaim that a character is mad or worried or impatient. There must be business to support the statement and a situation in which he can demonstrate these emotions if the audience is to be convinced that it is so. Until the viewer feels the emotions, too, he is not impressed with the words.

The animators expressed it simply: "Anyone who merely states his feelings is not acting, and if a cartoon

character is not acting, he is not 'living.'" They had to know the feelings that go deeper than words before they could find the strong attitudes that would make the situation believable.

There were four major rules to writing dialogue:

Rule 1. Do not write dialogue that describes what you are seeing. If a character is panting and sweating from the heat, the last thing he needs is a line that states, "Boy, am I hot!" Or if he has started to leave, it is too late to comment, "Well, I guess I'll go now." His words should reflect his feelings *about* what is happening, and be written in a way that enriches his personality.

Rule 2. The words and the thought behind them should be special to this one character. No one else would say things quite this way. Look for unique wording, colloquial phrases, colorful expressions that are right for this one particular character.

Rule 3. Dialogue must be written so there is something to animate. It has to reflect an attitude that can be drawn or an emotion that can be shown. Exposition is deadly, and too many words water down strong attitudes. No one can keep any strength in a long line of dialogue.

Rule 4. Dialogue must be written so the actor doing the voice can contribute something. Without changing the meaning of the line, it is usually possible to give it more life by rephrasing or adding a touch that gives the actor a better chance. Often a chuckle, a sigh, a stutter, swallow, or gulp will reveal more of the personality than the words themselves. Other times, the actor may have an intimate knowledge of folk phrases from certain regions that will help build a more interesting character.

The voice talent usually is eager to help develop a unique character, especially one that is understood thoroughly, and this contribution should be encouraged. However, in the early days of wild chases and violent action, there was little opportunity for the nuances of an individual personality. As one actor admitted wryly, "It's a little difficult to build a strong

Storyman Larry Clemmons is caricatured just before his retirement by Ward Kimball.

Storyman Vance Gerry tries different costumes, expressions, and attitudes for Penny, the little star of The Rescuers.

character when all you say is 'Oof . . . ugh . . . yow . . . yip, and Wheee!' but it's still important to do what you can.''

Occasionally, the dialogue would be written before the sketches were made if an outline had been approved and the writer had a strong idea of how the sequences should play. Larry Clemmons, who had been in animation during the thirties, then left to write for radio before returning to the studio, had a talent for brisk dialogue that gave everyone a feeling for the characters and the entertainment potential in a situation. He always wrote scripts, then asked the story sketch man to follow them as closely as possible. If the sketch man was not alert, he would end up merely illustrating what was being said and not adding any new ideas or approaches to the problem from a visual standpoint. Woolie Reitherman directed these films, and, while he enjoyed the word-gags and the play between characters, he knew that there had to be a new ingredient added to make the sequence do its job. He would complain, ''There's nothing happening! I want a happening! I've heard enough words—I want something going on now. I want attitudes . . . you have to know how they're feeling, what they're thinking before you can tell if the words are right!'' Storymen must have the patience and energy to try many things before settling on a direction.

388

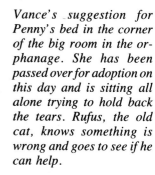

Vance Gerry, who did both story and story sketch, hit upon the best solution. He used Larry's script as a guide and a basis, but set it aside while he started making the drawings that seemed to fit the situation. One drawing led to another as he explored various ways of handling the characters as well as the whole mood of the sequence. Eventually, he was able to pin up a continuity that included actions that could be animated, business that developed the characters, and pantomime that strengthened the relationships. At that point he had a meeting, and all the ideas were presented. Following that, Larry would rewrite and Vance would redraw, but bit by bit they came together and the result was a unique, convincing sequence that probably could not have been achieved by any other process.

A good example of this cooperation is the introduction of the little girl Penny in *The Rescuers*. It had been assumed that the proper way to introduce her would be in a happy sequence where the audience could be taken by the appeal of a cheerful, spunky child. She was an orphan who wanted very much to be adopted, but it was felt that any sad scenes would have more impact if she were seen first in happier circumstances. A whole sequence was written, sketched, and partially animated of her on a visit to the zoo.

When it was discovered later on that the pathos of the little girl was the very heart of the picture, all of us decided her introduction should be in a situation with a strong heart-tug right from the start. We wanted the audience to become involved with Penny and her feelings as quickly and forcefully as possible, so our first sequence of her became the one in the orphanage right after she has been passed over for adoption.

In the story meetings, we had considered having Penny do a little act for the prospective parents, some little song or dance: something she thought she did well and on which she could pin her hopes for adoption—something she hoped would make a mother and father want her. If she did her best and failed, we knew there would be a strong empathy from the audience. But it also would necessitate showing the visitors watch her act and perhaps part of the act of the little red-haired girl who finally would be chosen. It had good pathos, but also problems with the added characters and more footage to put over the additional business.

Vance Gerry had been exploring the appearance of the bedroom in the orphanage for the next part of the sequence, and Larry Clemmons had written some poignant lines between the little girl and the orphanage cat Rufus, as he is trying to find out what had happened. Penny responds, "They looked at me, but they choosed a little red-headed girl—she was prettier than me."

Vance's suggestion for Penny's bed in the corner of the big room in the orphanage. She has been passed over for adoption on this day and is sitting all alone trying to hold back the tears. Rufus, the old cat, knows something is wrong and goes to see if he can help.

389

This sequence is the introduction of Penny, so the strongest statement possible must be made to establish the pathos of the situation and show the warmth of the friendship between the girl and the cat. Vance explores several ideas on this, showing front views, back views, side views, the position of the bed and how Penny will look sitting on it. What is the best way to reach out and touch the audience? At times, a simple attitude is all that is needed; if the animator tries to do too much, he will break the mood he is attempting to create.

Drawings from the actual scenes in the picture show how all of this planning and experimenting paid off. The moves are subtle, but the thinking is broad, and the impact of the scenes is powerful. If the animator had thought "subtle" in his planning, the scenes would not have communicated at all.

RUFUS: WHAT'S WRONG, PENNY HONEY?
PENNY: NOTHING.
RUFUS: COME ON, NOW, COME ON.

Between that line and Vance's drawings, there was no need for any other introduction. Her first scene in the picture showed her sitting on her bed, all alone, in the orphanage.

Now we had to concentrate on the strongest statement we could make for a sad, lonely girl. We had to have warmth, communication, and sincerity, and the girl had to be handled as a real girl in a real situation. There was no latitude for broad drawing or caricatured expressions. What had to be caricatured was the film approach to getting the audience to feel for this girl and her problems. It had to be immediate, succinct, and compelling. This was our heroine and she had to captivate the audience from the very first scene, with no false moves and no confusion. It was a delicate situation and required delicate handling. The moves would be subtle, but the planning had to be powerful.

Vance Gerry did charming drawings of the girl and the cat. He tried different uniforms for her and researched the kind of bed she would have, as well as the character of the room in which the orphans slept. The size of the room and the position of Penny's bed in it were both important. He tried various types of

RUFUS: NO SECRETS—YOU TELL OLD RUFUS--HUH

PENNY: WELL, IT WAS ADOPTION DAY AT THE ORPHANAGE

RUFUS: WHAT—

RUFUS: WHAT HAPPENED?
PENNY: A MAN AND A LADY CAME.

PENNY:...AND LOOKED AT ME, BUT THEY CHOOSED A LITTLE RED-HEADED GIRL.

staging, showing the girl from the front, the side, and the back. Each view offered something special, and the relationship to the cat varied with each angle, too. He could squeeze under her arm in the front view but not in the others—without an awkward move—and we were searching for the bold statements that would flow smoothly and naturally.

The animator who was given the responsibility for this crucial sequence decided that the rear view of the cat and girl was the best for the first scene.[6] Somehow, she looked more vulnerable with the sloping shoulders and little neck, and it allowed him to hold off the first actual view of the girl's face until later, when it would have more impact. The back view was also a good angle for the cat's action as he rubbed against her affectionately and tried to look up into her face. Many of the expressions were then played off the cat because his face was so much more pliable. His chin could tremble as he was on the verge of tears without being overly dramatic. It was hoped that the audience would have empathy for the girl through him. When she finally does turn so that her face can be seen, there is a tear rolling down her cheek, but no real dramatic expression—just a sad, little face. With the build-up preceding, it was all that was needed.

When the picture was released, we received a letter from a jaded critic with this comment: "That scene made me cry—which surprised me! From then on, I cared very much about what happened to Penny. Maybe it was the dialogue, or her expression, or the PERFECT voice . . . but something moved me as no other cartoon movie has before."

We always wonder if we are going too far, or shooting too high, in our attempts to get real feelings portrayed in our medium. We cannot be too dramatic with our characters, and if we start to copy real theater we look silly. Yet, within our limitations, we have found ways to develop emotions that have touched

audiences around the world and raised people's spirits, and that must be worthwhile.

William Faulkner said that the only subjects worth writing about were "the problems of the human heart in conflict with itself." He went on to say that it was the poet's and writer's duty and "privilege to help man endure by lifting his heart, by reminding him of the courage and honor and hope and pride and compassion and pity and sacrifice which have been the glory of his past."[7] Even the cartoon can try for such ideals.

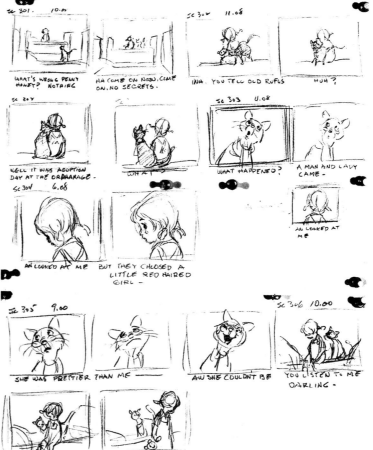

ANIMATOR: *Ollie Johnston—* The Rescuers.

The rough continuity put together by the animator from the staging that seems to work best in Vance's sketches. First, the audience will see only the back of the little figure with the thin neck and sloping shoulders while the cat rubs against her. Her face will not be seen until the crucial line, ". . . she was prettier than me." At that point, a sad little face with a single tear will have more appeal than any attempt at dramatic acting.

The strong expressions are used on the cat, who has a more pliable face. His reaction to the offstage dialogue tells more than would be possible using emotional expressions on the face of the little girl.

PENNY: SHE WAS PRETTIER THAN ME   RUFUS: AH, SHE   COULDN'T BE . .

15. Character Development

"I think you have to know these fellows definitely before you can draw them. When you start to caricature a person, you can't do it without knowing the person. Take Laurel and Hardy for example; everybody can see Laurel doing certain things because they know Laurel."

Walt Disney

Walt's development of a cartoon's characters was completely intuitive. He never had to analyze the ways he might establish them or find their personalities. He never worried about their motivations or searched for techniques to make them believable. There was no problem in how to integrate them into the story; they *were* the story. He could not conceive of business that did not relate to a specific personality. He had such a great feel for the entertainment in any situation that all of these considerations were automatic. From the beginning, these characters had been real to him; the task now was to make them as interesting as possible.

In November, 1936, we started having weekly meetings at night to talk of nothing but character development of the seven dwarfs: their relationships with each other, and how they would move and act in every situation. Many of the staff could not see beyond just finding something for seven characters to do while on the screen together, but Walt was looking for much more. He knew that the development of rich personalities would be crucial to this story, and it was a part of the picture-making that he particularly enjoyed. Walt was so immersed in these characters that at times, as he talked and acted out the roles as he saw them, he forgot that we were there. We loved to watch him; his feeling about the characters was contagious. Each succeeding week he refined and strengthened his conception, and ours, too. We would think to ourselves,

Walt's acting was spontaneous and rich with ideas that were special to him. He could act any type of character and give insights into the personality.

"Gee, if I could just get my hands on that scene of Doc and Grumpy the way he's talking about it. Boy, I can see it so clearly!"

Walt was saying, "Doc is upset by the least little thing, the least little annoyance. He doesn't know where he is; somebody has to help him out—that is, as far as mental reaction or personality is concerned. When Snow White says she is a princess, he becomes all flustered and gets his words mixed up; and, when he finally does get the word, he says the wrong one. For instance, when Doc says, 'WE ARE HONORED, WE ARE—' (he hesitates, he doesn't know what to say; Grumpy then comes in and feeds him the wrong word: 'MAD AS HORNETS,' and Doc immediately picks up what Grumpy says before he realizes what Grumpy says. I think Doc

is that way, in that when he becomes flustered, he stammers for words.

"He has this habit of getting mixed up, only when he is upset or when he is angered or when he meets Snow White. When he meets Snow White, he is like a fellow meeting a girl—gets awfully flustered—sort of an inferiority complex."

Another night, Walt was talking about Dopey. It was not just his personality but his physical appearance, too. As Walt described this little character, we could see how we should draw him, from his proportions down to how he would stand.

Dec. 9, 1936

Walt: Dopey isn't cute looking in these drawings. His body should be longer and his legs shorter. You should have the feeling about him that he is wearing somebody's cast-off coat, not as though he wore a big gown or something. He shows too much anatomy. I don't think you would see it in this little guy.

Babbitt: Do you see him quite erect most of the time?

Walt: Yes, alert. That would come right in with sprightliness. When anything happens, Dopey runs as fast as he can and gets ahead of the other dwarfs—turns around and looks back like a kid. Langdon had that kid action. He would hold on to his hat when running along with some fellows. In one of Langdon's pictures, in a factory sequence, Langdon was invited by some of the fellows to go along with them after work. The idea of his being taken along made him happy just to be with them. They ignored him and he would run ahead of them

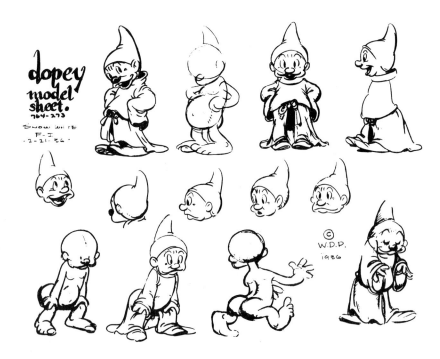

and look back like a kid. I feel that Dopey would be the same kind of guy—glad to be in on anything.

After the meeting, one of the men jotted down some notes: ''Walt is so aware of the fact that it would be easy to make Dopey imbecilic and he doesn't want that because it's not funny—he just wants him childish—appealing. It's elusive, but Walt always seems to have a way of seeing it so that it's right. Like the way he talks about when Doc goes into his thinking pose, and Dopey is trying to do the same thing. He has his fingers up to the side of his face, and his finger slips and goes in his eye. He is trying to imitate Doc there. But he has never spent any time thinking before and he

has to see somebody else do it before he can do it.''

The most stimulating part of all this to the animators was that everything Walt was suggesting could be animated. It was not awkward continuity or realistic illustrations but actions that were familiar to everyone. It would not be easy for the animators, but it would be fun. It seemed such a short time ago that they were animating spindly legged, weightless Mickeys and Minnies with their superficial little relationships. Occasionally there had been a glimmer of things to come in pictures like *Elmer Elephant* and *Country Cousin*, where there had been a special character who had strong feelings about what was happening, but for the most part this was all new, and it seemed as though it had blossomed overnight. Now we sat entranced as Walt talked about these seven little men who were becoming as much flesh and blood as the person sitting next to us; and while the problems they faced in their make-believe world were extraordinary, we could grasp them and could feel them ourselves.

These characters were dealing with life and death problems, sometimes in a humorous way, sometimes serious, but always sincere and believable, and each according to his own personality. This was real character acting, and it was all so easy when Walt explained how it should be. It could be funnier, or more serious, or more fanciful, but the crucial relationships had been

EARS CAN REACT TO MOODS LIKE (FIG ① + ②)

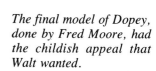

AND WILL ALSO BE USED IN ANIMATION GAGS

The final model of Dopey, done by Fred Moore, had the childish appeal that Walt wanted.

COAT CAN GROW A TRIPLE LONGER FOR ANIMATION

395

established and the criticisms now were all minor in
terms of character development. Without Walt's intuition, how do you build a character? How do you determine what is interesting? How do you know if it is
right for your story?

An article by drama critic Charles Champlin in the
Los Angeles Times tells how John Hurt went about
character development in his portrayal of Max in the
film *Midnight Express*. "In the superb way that actors
can, Hurt seemed to have built the character of Max
from the inside out, investing him with a past and a
persona only hinted at in the script." Champlin quotes
Hurt in some detail on his creative approach to building Max's character. "Without knowing," Hurt says,
"I imagined that he was of a very good family. Lots of
money. And that he had gone to a very good school.
Harrow, maybe, or Eton. And that he had started at
Oxford, probably, but dropped out as a lot did in the
'60s and hit the eastern trail that was popular then and

got into drugs."

We started on each of our characters in much the
same manner. Usually the storymen searched for the
broad type of person that would fit the story, concentrating on the general aspects rather than the refinements. One storyman enrolled in a writing class to
improve his skills and was surprised to find that the
same advice was part of the young writer's curricu-
lum. He reported, "You must develop character traits,
you must think out—what sort of person is this? What
kind of background does he come from? Is he an angry
character? A happy character? A foolish character—
how would he react? He might always carry a cane, he
might have a twitch when he moves, he might have a
habit of lighting his pipe. What sort of clothes would
he wear, how would he move? Well, this is what we
were doing [at the studio]. We were drawing the Goof
and having his pants hang down, and you have a vest
that doesn't fit. . . ."

*The imaginative humor that
is identified with the "How
To" Goofy shorts can be
largely attributed to the
enthusiasm of the crew and
the genuine fun they had
while making these films.*

When asked where we find our characters and our ideas, we point out that one of the biggest sources is the people right around us, wherever we may be. So, first, we say to train yourself to be constantly observant, to watch for the unusual and the entertaining. (Certainly that is what John Hurt did in his preparation for the role of Max.) If you see someone with a unique way of gesturing and talking, watch him and make a mental note—maybe draw him when you have a chance. A boy and his dog and the way they look at each other, or two lovers holding hands, someone waiting impatiently for another person, a salesman, a sports figure—they all hold the promise of inspiration for a potential character. But you must be thinking that way.

A baseball pitcher is constantly adjusting his cap and wiping his brow on his sleeve, taking his glove off or rubbing the ball. All pitchers do these things, but each one does it differently. Walt was continually taking his glasses off and on when talking over a script. Milt Kahl did not need his glasses for close work, so when looking at someone's drawing he would take the glasses off just one ear and let them dangle precariously throughout the whole conversation.

Once the general type of character has been found, work begins on finding the refinements, the details, the specifics that make him into an individual—unique and entertaining. This is more difficult to judge, but the animator will flounder with indecision unless he can get inside the character and know precisely what actions are right for that personality. As long as there is any confusion or lack of understanding, the drawings will be vague and indecisive. A good check on whether the character is really understood is this question: "Do you know how he feels about himself?" Without knowing his self-image, it will be difficult to know how he really feels about anyone else or what he

is trying to do or even what he wants to have happen in the story.

Obviously, this all will be easier and more interesting if the animator likes the character in the first place. We advised a group of young animators: "Look for things in your characters that make them so interesting that you end up loving them. They should be appealing to you; you are creating them. Endow them with all the great qualities you like that are consistent with their personalities, so that you will want to be around them. Like an actor getting a good solid role, you will look forward to each day, and at night you will think about your sequence and the characters in it and what you're going to do with it—and you just can't get it out of your mind. It's with you 24 hours a day."

Some of the funniest shorts the studio ever made came from the sheer enjoyment felt by animators working with a character they had come to know and understand extremely well. These were the "How To" Goofy pictures: *How to Play Baseball, How to Swim, How to Fish,* etc. Most of these were directed by Jack Kinney, with inspired work by animation supervisor Woolie Reitherman and zany touches from animator John Sibley. John, like Woolie, was especially good at funny, imaginative action and timing. They loved to talk about how funny the section they were working on was going to be.

ARTIST: *Ollie Johnston.*

Milt Kahl rarely used his glasses for close work and often let them hang in a disconcerting way from one ear while examining a drawing.

The more they would talk, the funnier it would become to them, and soon they were just killing themselves laughing at all the gags. So they would decide to go and tell "Ol' Kinney" about their new ideas, because he might think of something even funnier. Everyone could hear them going all the way up the stairs and down the hall, talking and laughing about this with an occasional pause while one of them showed the other how it was going to be; then the laughter

ARTIST: *Ken Anderson*—
Robin Hood.

A discarded sequence from
Robin Hood *showed a mes-*
senger pigeon so fat and
heavy he had to be shot into
the air. This gave us the
beginnings of The Alba-
tross Air Lines in The
Rescuers.

would get even louder. By the time they were at Jack Kinney's room they were both in tears, but Jack knew the material so well he could pick right up with them and very soon was in convulsions, too.

This love for the character is reflected in the finished pictures, for there is an inspired quality that never would exist if it had been put together mechanically from the storyboards. This clearly shows the importance of talking and talking and "kicking an idea around" and continually observing and thinking and watching each other act out the business. This is how great characters are developed.

In the early story conception of *The Rescuers*, Capt. Orville was just a bird—perhaps a pigeon—who would fly the mice agents to their destination. His most distinguishing business was that he would be catapulted off the ground instead of taking off under his own power. This was a novel idea, but it seemed to inhibit

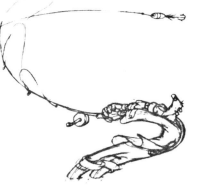

the development of the character. Things were happening *to* him rather than having him make anything happen.

On the strength of some of the studio's nature films, it was decided to base Capt. Orville's character on an albatross. Immediately this opened up all kinds of possibilities. An albatross in the air is a thing of beauty to behold, the ultimate in perfect coordination, but on the ground, either landing or taking off, it exhibits the height of incompetence. The albatross lands like a bowling ball, scattering companions around like ten-pins. His take-off, if possible, is even worse. Mother Nature had an off day when she devised this piece of clumsy uncoordinated action. He cannot even run well, taking a longer step with one leg than the other, which gives him a gimpy look and makes it doubly hard to acquire enough speed to get airborne (much of the time he does not succeed). After running what seems like miles, he will suddenly abort his flight as though

to say, "This can just as well wait till tomorrow."

Pilots say that the tough part of flying is landing and taking off. The albatross does not seem to recognize that he has a problem in either procedure, and this gave us our clue to his personality—the fact that when he landed on his face and then crashed into several of the other birds on the beach, nobody made a big deal out of it. They just shook the sand off and plopped down again as if nothing had happened. In our picture, the first time Capt. Orville landed, he plowed into the runway and slid to a stop on his face. Bernard came running out to see how badly the albatross had been hurt; his reply was, "One of my better landings, Bub!" And he meant it! This would be his personality throughout. He thought everything he did was the greatest, and the only way to do it.

His takeoff with the mice aboard became the funniest piece of business in the whole picture since it played into all three personalities. Bernard was afraid of flying,

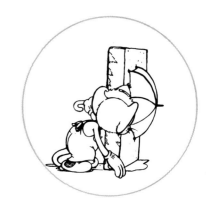

Captain Orville, the albatross in The Rescuers, *considered himself to be the perfect flyer. We conceived him as a crusty old World War I flying ace with puttees, scarf, and goggles and his own loading ramp. His role in the picture grew from a cameo part to that of a star. This was in large measure due to the fine dialogue performance done by Jim Jordan (Fibber McGee).*

The story must contain situations that allow each character to reveal the entertainment in his personality. The muskrat family in The Rescuers *consisted of Ellie Mae, the bossy, bustling wife, and Luke, her shiftless husband with his jug of "swamp juice." Jeanette Nolan, in contributing the voice of Ellie Mae, added more dimension by giving a delicate warmth to the bustling traits, and a shattering shriek to the aggressive side when the character was excited. Unfortunately, as the story evolved, there was no place to show these qualities and Ellie Mae ended up as a more conventional motherly type.*

and Bianca was looking forward to it with enthusiasm. This gave each of them definite attitudes that opened up new facets of their personalities.

Orville was sort of a crusty guy, but likeable. We thought of him as being a World War I ace with helmet, goggles, scarf, and puttees—the works. He tolerated Bernard, but warmed up to Bianca. The story could have been told without him. There was a time when we considered having the mice dart into a regular airliner, but how much better the sequence became through the development of Capt. Orville.

Difficult as it is to conjure up a successful character and to know him thoroughly, it is often surprisingly awkward to find the ways to tell the audience all about him. The opportunities to show all these delightful traits in a rich personality can slip away one by one as the sequences develop, leaving an interesting residue but none of the exciting moments that had been visualized. We had this distressing situation in *The Rescuers* in the very next sequence.

When the mice, flying with Capt. Orville, arrived at the bayou, they were forced to abandon ship and parachute to safety. Awaiting their arrival was a group of eager local animals organized into a home guard unit known as the Swamp Volunteers. When the parachute of the mice got tangled in a tree, the reception committee broke ranks and ran about like the Keystone Cops as they tried to rescue the suspended visitors. Throughout all these proceedings, the dominant character be-

came the muskrat Ellie Mae, wife of the shiftless Luke and self-appointed major domo of the area.

She had been thought of as a Germanic type of housewife, capable, energetic, strong, eager, and happy, with boundless energy, but now she had to become a specific individual within that category. A TV commercial showing about that time featured an actress who was extremely large, but very delicate and feminine in her gestures. To that "little girl" self-image we added the strength of a horse, and had the start of an interesting character. We did not know yet if she would be explosive, forgiving, self-centered, aggressive, or petulant, but we were finding out. Jeanette Nolan was chosen to do the voice, and she made a startling contribution that developed the idea further. She played the quiet lines with great sympathy and tenderness, supported by a slight lisp, then unexpectedly shrieked the excited lines in a voice that would shatter glass.

She helped Bianca from the mud with a warm, soft line, "Here, honey, let me he'p you." Then without even stopping to inhale, she bellowed, "You boys git over here right now!!" Then once again, all gentleness, "Oh dear, ain't that a shame." It was a fresh character and one that we all liked. The drawings of her showed strong arms, a stocky build, a defiant set to her head and a sweet little smile. She was the boss and could do anything, but she thought of herself only as sweet and delicate and very feminine. She did not need to be excitable because she was so competent, and she yelled only when she wanted someone else to do something—which was often. This supported the unpredictable changes in her delivery since it was not related to an emotional build-up, and it really was something she was not aware of doing.

Unfortunately, as the continuity developed and the sequence was refined, almost all of the business that made use of her outbursts was cut out, and we were left with a rich character who had only motherly lines. We searched through the rest of the picture but found no place to make use of the entertainment potential we had seen.

It brought home the point of how important it is to have business that gives your character a chance to show what he is. It is so easy to say that your character is great and that you know every angle of his personality and that he will be memorable and outstanding, but unless specific scenes are there in the film—integrated into the story—no one will ever know what was in your mind. It is not enough to say it is there; it must be shown. In our case, the work we had done made Ellie Mae a definite character, sincere and convincing, but without the fun we had anticipated.

All the while one character is being considered, close attention also must be given to the other players who work around him, for it is only their interaction that brings the scenes to life. It seems like a devastating assignment. When Ron Clements was new at the studio, he commented, ''The greatest challenge in animation is to create a relationship of characters through a picture that an audience believes in. To them, these characters exist—they're real. It's tough enough to create one character that lives, but to get two or more interrelating—that is the impossible dream.''

Actually there can be some advantage in working two characters together. If there can be some kind of tension between them, immediately there will be attitudes and drives and actions that reveal individual traits more clearly than would be brought out by passive agreement. This is something to consider when several of the characters work as a team with one unified purpose. The Swamp Volunteers all wanted the same thing and differed more in physical appearance than in either aims or personality. Without the conflict supplied by Ellie Mae's bossiness, their scenes had little vitality. The semicomic villains of *101 Dalmatians*, the Baduns, shared a common goal and a common personality as well. By having one more stupid than the other, and a little less aggressive, we were able to introduce some argument throughout the scenes.

Probably our most exasperating and elusive characters were the three Good Fairies in *Sleeping Beauty*, who were committed to doing only good; they had no apparent weaknesses or foibles at all to exploit. In the early stages, Walt actually toyed with the idea of their being all alike, but if they were there would have been nothing to animate—there was no play among them. They were like Donald Duck's nephews. This possibly would have been acceptable if they were to be just spectators commenting on what they saw.

But this was a story of how these three fairies tried to save a girl from the curse of the evil fairy Maleficent, and lost. For this role, they would need strength and purpose and a certain aggressiveness seldom seen in passive spectators. More than that, they were the rulers of their various domains, and while undoubtedly very gentle monarchs they should be more than just sweet and loving. There had to be more substance to them and to their relationship. The animators would need something positive they could caricature in order to make any kind of statement, but what should it be? What could be done with three seemingly vacuous ladies who agreed on nearly everything?

A few of the diverse ideas on the appearance of the three Good Fairies in Sleeping Beauty *in both their normal costumes and the peasant clothes they wore during their sixteen years in the woods.*

MERRYWEATHER   FAUNA   FLORA

As the supervising animators on these characters, we would be responsible for their personalities, and we spent many sessions with the story crew working out specific business for the first sequence. Even before the voices were recorded, we had tried ideas, discarded them, switched traits from one fairy to another, juggled and borrowed, built and appraised.

We had started out with Flora being bossy. To her it was more important that she be the boss than be right. So she would dominate and the other two would follow, but that did not make a good relationship. Then we thought, "What if she's the leader but not always right?" Merryweather would point out the error even though she was usually all wrapped up in herself and having fun. But this might make her too argumentative and that would not be desirable. And what do we do with Fauna? She is so wishy-washy—she always goes along with the last person talked to—and this leaves her too weak to be interesting.

Gradually we began to feel that Flora should not be bossy, but should dominate without realizing she is doing it. She would be just a more aggressive personality and full of ideas. It was not important that her idea be chosen, it was just that it was the *best* idea—the fact that it was *her* idea was immaterial. The important thing was that everyone start acting on it immediately. She felt the burden of any problems and thought of herself as having a sense of responsibility. Perhaps most important, she had a grasp of the big concept of what was going on.

Now we had to find the best way to play Merryweather against that character. What if she had better ideas than Flora, especially in times of crisis? Then the frustration of having to do it Flora's way would pay off. She could have a reason to argue with Flora, and this type of conflict would liven up their relationship. Also, maybe she is more impulsive and quick to act—more of a doer than the others but without an understanding of the big events around her. She would be interested in little things and how things looked and would volunteer to do the housework. We thought she would love to dance and to be happy and to express herself physically. Her feelings would be on the surface, and she would flare up in anger more readily than the others.

Now where in here could we fit another type? Fauna's character was the most difficult to find because we could not have another dominant personality; yet we did not want her simply to be battered between the other two. If we went too far that way, the whole

402

relationship became unpleasant. We had to remember that these ladies were ''good'' fairies, but that always led us into the saccharine.

Then, while on vacation in Colorado, one of us met a lady who was to have a profound influence on the character of Fauna. She could be described as wispy, constantly smiling, twinkling-eyed, and almost unaware of what might be going on about her. She loved everybody, thought beautiful thoughts, could scarcely conceive of wrongdoing, and delighted in spreading what she considered to be sunshine. Here was a positive character who saw only good in everything and still lacked nothing in personality. She was supposed to read an inspirational poem at each meeting of her women's club, but when she arrived and could not find her prepared selection—instead of being flustered, upset, embarrassed, or confused—she blithely pulled out something else, like a letter from her cousin in Indianapolis, and read it to the assembled ladies. She was always sweet and sparkling, and also a little infuriating, but as a model for a unique ''good'' character

who could move through any problem unscathed as well as unaware she was inspiring.

This opened up a whole new relationship and made us think a little of the great comedienne Billie Burke. At last we felt we had an understanding of the elusive Fauna. She still could be vague, in that she could lose track of what she was doing, but she did have ideas of her own—most of them little, feminine ideas. She was interested in small details. She liked the idea of baking a cake, but had trouble keeping her concentration throughout the process. Of the three fairies, she would worry the most and would be the one who would try to smooth over any conflict between the other two. This new slant had given Fauna an almost aggressive view of life.

About this same time, the multitalented Don DaGradi noticed that little old ladies tend to wear their hats flat on top of their heads. He made some drawings showing them as cuter, more winsome, more appealing. Our drawings had been too strong and heavy. Now Don suggested they could be filmier, more like maiden

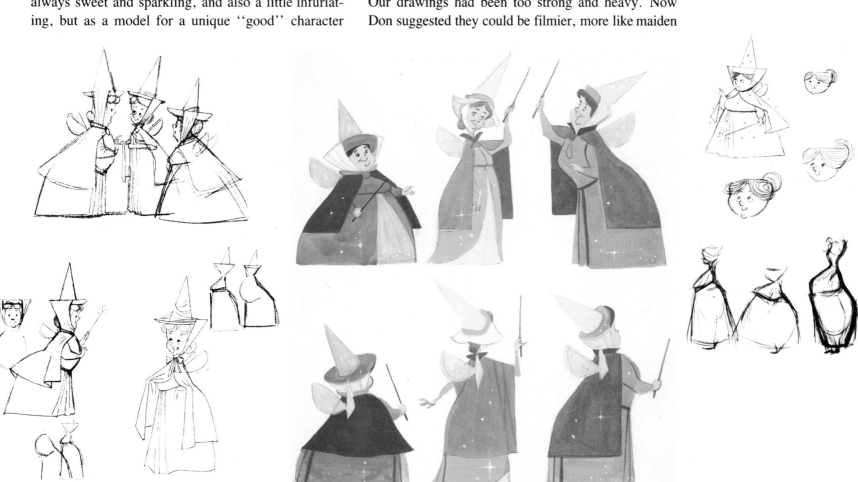

aunts, smelling of lavender. Suddenly it all fell together. These fairies were certainly no match for Maleficent, but still they felt they had to try. They were "good" all the way through, but entertainingly so.

They helped to tell the story in a fresh and surprising way, adding imagination and warmth. Until such characters have been "found," it is impossible to think of the story as anything but a collection of incidents. With them included, it becomes a personal account of something that happens to individuals people in the audience know. They are immediately concerned and interested and, suddenly, involved. As the concept of

ANIMATOR: *Frank Thomas.*

Hopping mad Merryweather shows squash and stretch even while she is airborne.

74

78

84

89

91

95

99

103

112

404

Merryweather and Flora battle each other with magic.

a character grows, inevitably it will influence the development of the story, and that in turn influences the character's relationship to others. The story is now becoming a tale about specific characters; what they think and decide to do determines what will happen and the way it will happen.

Character relationships must be built slowly and carefully through actions, expressions, and emotions. Occasionally there will be one key scene that clearly establishes all that is needed, but more often there will have to be many scenes, each contributing a tiny bit to the overall attitudes. An elusive sensation of warmth, of unspoken affection, of genuine concern between two characters may take more than one sequence before the audience shares the feelings. You cannot count on its coming off or being there, but you try and try and it is in all of your thinking; somehow, when you are done, the feeling is there.

This was particularly evident in the characters of Baloo and Mowgli in *The Jungle Book*, and many of the intangibles of accomplishing this kind of relationship become apparent as we look back on the dilemma. In the early stages, the story was all about the

*ARTIST: Bill Peet—
The Jungle Book.*

The story sketches suggest a serious minded Bagheera determined to see Mowgli returned safely to the man village. In contrast, the drawings of Baloo appear to be of a big, easy-going character—someone that could relate to the boy far better than the panther could.

A strong-willed and determined Mowgli registers displeasure at Bagheera's criticism.

panther Bagheera and the troubles he had getting the young boy Mowgli out of the jungle and back to the manvillage. Each of the animals they met along the way reflected a different philosophy, and Baloo, the easygoing bear, was there to show the slovenly lifestyle that is possible when one is strong and can eat anything.

Bagheera had to be very wise, orderly, and fastidious, which made him rather stuffy. Those traits are neither endearing nor interesting, and at this stage he was admittedly dull. His primary relationship was with Mowgli, whom we thought of as a tenacious kid of seven to twelve, confident but not smart-alecky—a young Tarzan who could turn out to be great, if he lived!

Mowgli had no intention of leaving the jungle and became obstinate. Bagheera's patience was at an end, so after one final disagreement he gave up and left. The boy, like any kid who has won an argument he did not want in the first place, was disconsolate, still a little annoyed, and very lonely. He had his independence, but no friends.

It was important at this point to build sympathy for Mowgli. He had been unreasonable, but he was young and inexperienced, and we needed audience identifica-

tion with his feelings of rejection. It seemed better if he did no strong acting or emoting. We felt we could portray his feelings better by using mostly long shots and featuring only kidlike actions such as kicking a rock, throwing a stick, climbing a boulder, sliding down a tree—all things he ordinarily would be doing playfully, but now is doing aimlessly. We felt that this approach portrayed a lonesome little boy on the screen better than any complex, close-up acting scenes would have done.

It was at this point that the big-hearted, slow-thinking Baloo entered the picture, singing "Doobey-do-doo, it's all so easy. . . ." He was a standard diamond-in-the-rough character, big and strong, and someone who could play right into the boy's predicament, being either comforting, threatening, silly, or friendly, depending on what worked best for us. It was time to start testing voices.

The panel that listened and judged consisted of the director, two storymen, and two supervising animators. With the very first actor we realized that our bear was too old-fashioned, too much like other bears we had done, too ordinary. We tried changing him to a sort of Ed Wynn—authority with a comic twist. We tested some exchange students from India to see if we could get a voice with a special quality indigenous to that area. None of these gave us any kind of character we could see when we closed our eyes and listened. Finally we found a funny voice that made a sort of bungling, confused bear out of Baloo, and we were trying to develop that thought when Walt suggested Phil Harris for the part.

Phil had been associated more with night clubs than the jungle, so we were surprised and he was stunned. He explained, "I don't do voices; I wasn't so good at reading to my two daughters when they were little." But we got him to come in and go through a few lines in spite of his obvious discomfort. Finally he backed up and said, "I can't act like a bear—and, besides, I

ANIMATOR: *Ollie Johnston.*

An argument with Bagheera leaves Mowgli upset. He shows his feelings with kid-like gestures rather than dramatic acting.

don't do that doobey-doo stuff.'' We asked how he would deliver the lines if he could do it his own way. He grinned at the script a moment, then threw back his head and shook the stage with an infectious, rhythmic chant. ''Well it's a doobey-do-doo; yes, it's a doobey-do-doo; I mean a. . . .'' Immediately we had a character.

As we warmed up to this new Baloo, Phil began to see more possibilities himself and became relaxed and excited by the end of the day. But before he left the recording session, he began to think that this new association with the Disney studio might be hard for his friends and family to understand. He asked, ''Can I have a copy of what I've recorded today? Otherwise Alice [his wife is Alice Faye] will never believe me.''

Once Baloo had become a definite individual, he was so entertaining it was impossible to keep him out of the rest of the picture. Instead of the little cameo part that had been planned, he was built into the story more and more until he was the main force that made it work. Phil Harris's performance added sincerity in a colorful character that gave new interest to everything he did, but, most important, this bear suddenly had great warmth, something the picture had needed. None of the other voices we tested or the personalities we considered would have done this. Baloo might have remained a cameo because he would not have been strong enough or important enough to use in more than one place, and the story would have been quite different.

While it may take a few minutes for an audience to disassociate the visual image of a well-known performer from his role in the film, the gain in character development is immeasurable. In the second and third releases, years later, to audiences who really had not known Phil Harris through radio or movie roles, *The Jungle Book* has proved to be increasingly popular. It is obvious that having established the character and used it in the best way is far more important than how well-known the voice talent might be at the time. In

ANIMATOR: *Ollie Johnston.*

Mowgli is not ready to make friends with the affable Baloo.

Pinocchio, we used Cliff Edwards, top recording star of the thirties, Walter Catlett, popular comedian of both stage and screen, as well as Christian Rub, Evelyn Venable, and Charles Judels—all well-known to movie patrons of that time. The type of talent that can give you the characterization you need almost always will be well-known in his own field, unless he is very young or, that extremely rare item, a natural.

When Walt heard Phil's test track he loved it, even to the point of starting to act out how the bear would first come dancing into Mowgli's scene. These new dimensions Walt was seeing because of Phil's voice naturally affected the appearance of Baloo. We began to draw an individual.

As we talked about this new character in our picture, we tried to get inside him, to know him better, to understand what he might do. If he were an animator, what kind of a guy would Baloo be? If you came into his room, what would it be like? He probably would be sitting there with his feet up on his desk and food all over the place, crumbs and coffee stains all over his drawings. Probably he would have his mouth full of food when he greets you: ''Come on in and sit down—take five.'' The trouble is, there is no place to sit. But somehow this disorder is not as bad as it first seemed, because you immediately like this individual and you feel good while you are around him. He is a free spirit, warm and friendly, and keeping everything in order is just not important to him. Life is simple and things are solved in a simple way. He would be rather easy to trick or deceive because we think of him as being gullible—gullible mainly because he likes people so much that it would not occur to him not to trust them. He would be impulsive. If something popped into his head that he would like to do, he would do it, never considering that it might not work out.

Most of all, he would love sensual pleasures—eating, or overeating, and singing. When you think of

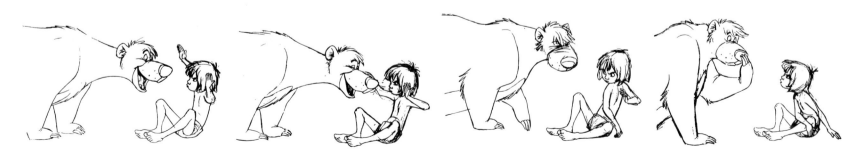

Phil Harris you think of rhythm and finger-snapping and moving to the beat, and that is the kind of thing Walt was looking for when he showed us how the bear would dance. Then scratching—that has got to be a big part of his life.

Soon we started seeing how this new Baloo would help us with Bagheera, too. What could work better with a free spirit than a stuffy, disapproving straight man? The looser the bear got the more entertaining the panther became. So we started building on Bagheera again and wondered what he would be like if he were an animator or perhaps a storyman. His room would be neat as a pin with every pencil sharpened and all laid out in nice rows according to color and length. Paper and pads would be neatly stacked, and there would be no food anywhere—just a bottle of antacid pills on the shelf. He would be friendly, but reserved.

When we were sure enough of our cast of characters, we came back to the scene where Baloo and Mowgli first meet and started creating the crucial relationship between them. How will they react to each other? Will the boy be afraid of this big guy? He is a courageous youngster, but he is still upset from his argument and still is trying to sort things out in his mind. When the bear talks to him, we decide Mowgli will take a swing at him. He is too naive to know any better, and at this point he wants to be left alone.

How does Baloo react to this little squirt hitting him? Is he sore about it? No. Instinctively he takes a completely opposite point of view. "This kid needs help. He'll get himself killed swinging at big guys like me if I don't help him." This isn't a mental problem; it is purely physical and right up the bear's alley.

We had animated about 35 or 40 feet of Mowgli and Baloo for a test when Walt saw it and said, "This bear is marvelous—we've got to keep him in the picture." Phil Harris came back for a second recording session, and we showed him this animation. He stared at it, unbelieving; finally he turned to us and said, "Gee, this will make me immortal. The way you guys animate me I can do no wrong." This picture was to bring him a whole different group of fans. When he walked down the street, kids would come up and grab his hands and run along beside him calling him, "Baloo." Everywhere they were reacting to his character just as Mowgli did. They loved him because he came across as a living character on the screen.

The relationship between these two began to have enormous possibilities for warmth, comedy, pathos, and suspense. They really needed each other. The bear never had a cub of his own and saw in Mowgli someone he could teach the things he thought were important. The story had been grim with everyone against the boy, and now he had a friend. But what a friend—irresponsible, impulsive, thoughtless. The audience knew the panther was right in his concern for Mowgli's survival, but they also could see the appeal of the bear to the boy. All the characters had clear drives; they were in conflict and they were enjoyable and provocative.

In the first sequence, where the two have met, the bear continues his lessons and tries to teach Mowgli to growl. Bagheera hears Baloo's roar, fears the worst is happening to Mowgli, and races back to help him. He is appalled to find that the boy has picked up with this "jungle bum." Baloo tells Bagheera that the kid is going to stay with him, and he will teach him all he knows. Bagheera's sarcastic response is, "That won't take long." The relationships among the three main characters are beginning to dictate the way the situations will play out and what the dialogue should be.

The second sequence has an entirely different flavor because it is all done to prescored music with the characters moving in sync to every beat, actually dancing their way through the song. Even the secondary actions are put on the beat as much as possible, since this always conveys a happy, exuberant feeling that can be achieved in no other way.

Through this sequence, Mowgli usually is trying to

ARTIST: *Frank Thomas.*

Mowgli and Baloo filled an empty place in each other's life. This helped produce one of the warmest relationships we have ever achieved.

ARTIST: *Ollie Johnston.*

Mowgli shows his affection for the bear by imitating him.

409

Thumbnails explore different ways Baloo might satisfy his insatiable urge to scratch.

back that sets him off, but whatever it is Baloo feels the urge to be scratched. ''Hey, Mowgli, how about scratchin' that old left shoulder?'' Mowgli does his best, scratching higher and lower and all over the place, but this is just a teaser for Baloo. ''This calls for some *real* scratchin'.'' He finds a very rough-looking palm tree and has at it. The more he scratches the more frantic he gets—his eyes become glazed—he no longer is in control of what he does. Finally he slides exhausted into the water, and he and Mowgli reprise the song together in a slow tempo as they drift downstream.

At one point during Baloo's scratching, he uproots the tree and scratches his back with it. The director decided we needed some music to make the track support this and add to the excitement of the picture. He called in four musicians—piano, drums, bass, and trumpet. While they were ad libbing to a section of ''The Bare Necessities,'' the trumpet player, Cappy Lewis, was asked to get more of what the bear was feeling—more frenzy—to get the feeling that the bear could not stop if he wanted to! Cappy finally got something we all liked, a really classic piece of imaginative trumpet playing. As a matter of fact it worked out so well that we decided to reprise it exactly at the end of the picture. This would send the audience out with a big lift. Danny Alguire, the assistant director, arranged to have a musician transcribe it note for note. Then musical director George Bruns inserted it into the final score.

The time came to do the final recording on this section, with the same trumpet player and the same ad lib solo all nicely written out for him. He looked at it—looked closer—blew a couple of notes—put down his horn and shook his head. The phrasing was beyond him. He looked up at Bruns and said, ''Nobody can play this!'' Of course, he did play it, and excellently,

mimic Baloo. This flatters the bear and gives the feeling that they are responding to the same vibrations, which adds to the closeness between them. They could not feel better about each other or themselves at this moment.

Baloo drops down on all fours as he finishes the lyrics and Mowgli hops up on his back. Perhaps Mowgli accidentally touches a sensitive spot on Baloo's

ANIMATOR: Ollie Johnston.

In his wild frenzy, Baloo actually uproots a tree, as suggested in the thumbnails.

410

giving a spirit of exuberance and vitality to the ending of the picture.

By this time the bear and the boy had developed a bond, something that grew out of all the things they had been doing together. Bit by bit they had opened their hearts to each other and there was a real feeling of trust between them. This was what we had hoped we were getting, because it was so vital to the next sequence where their friendship would be tested, in a different way, by each of them.

Mowgli is kidnapped by the monkeys, a big fight ensues, and Baloo and Bagheera get him back. Then comes a difficult all-dialogue section between the panther and the bear where Baloo is finally convinced that for the boy's own good he must go back to the man-village. But even though Baloo is convinced, he feels very unsure of himself. "Well, can't it wait till morning?" he pleads, but Bagheera answers, "It's morning now. . . ." Baloo starts toward the sleeping Mowgli, hesitates, and Bagheera has to urge him once more, ". . . go on, Baloo."

Before the animator started on this section he wrote down all his feelings about the situation and the characters, to clear it up in his own mind. It is easy to get lost in trying to do too many things when you are animating if you are not sure of what your main statement is going to be. By writing everything down first, your mind becomes organized, channeled into just what you want to do. You can always change your mind if this is not working, but it does give you a start and a direction.

Here is what the animator wrote:[1]

There should be an aimless feeling to Baloo's walk, and a huddled feeling, in contrast to his normal expansive, confident manner. He has nervous vague gestures as he searches for an idea. If he is too nervous, or has too many expressions, he becomes excited, or evasive, or even overly desperate. Our bear is desperate, but he is not excitable or evasive. He is a simple, direct character who meets everything head-on. He is used to settling his problems with physical force and this predicament is really beyond him. He is too honest to be evasive and too simple to have a complicated thought process. He should be desolate and lost, yet his love for the boy is so genuine that he cannot walk away from the problem.

So what does the bear do? What kind of acting will show these inner feelings in drawings? The best way to sort this out would be to make thumbnail drawings of different things he might do. They must be acting symbols that are in character and are easily identified by the audience. Baloo is in way over his head, but he is trying very hard to think of something he can say or

(Continued on page 414)

ARTIST: *Ken Anderson.*

Bagheera urges Baloo to wake Mowgli and tell him that for his own safety he must go to the man village. The sketch captures the attitudes of the characters and even the feeling of early morning.

ARTIST: *Frank Thomas*.

The animator searches for specific actions that will show Baloo's inner torment as he tries to tell Mowgli he must leave the jungle.

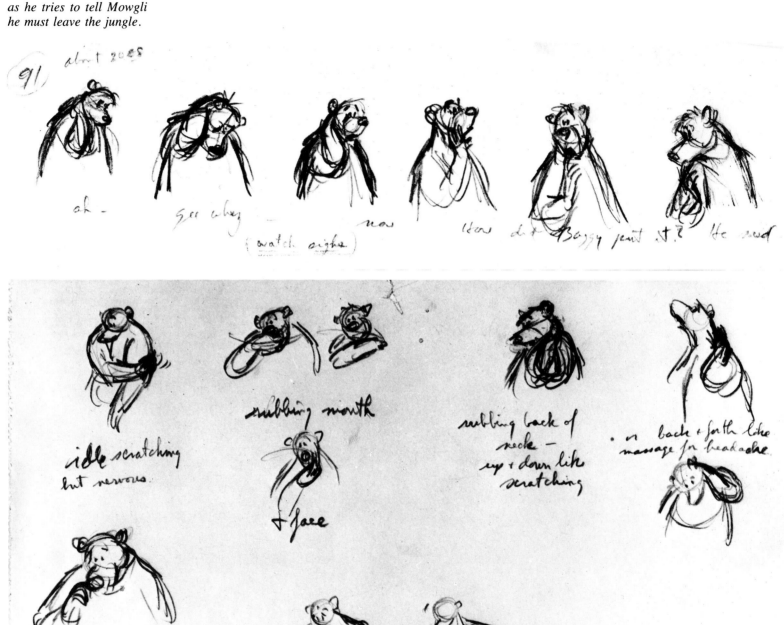

412

ANIMATOR: *Frank Thomas.*

The thumbnails become a scene that adds a new dimension to Baloo's character.

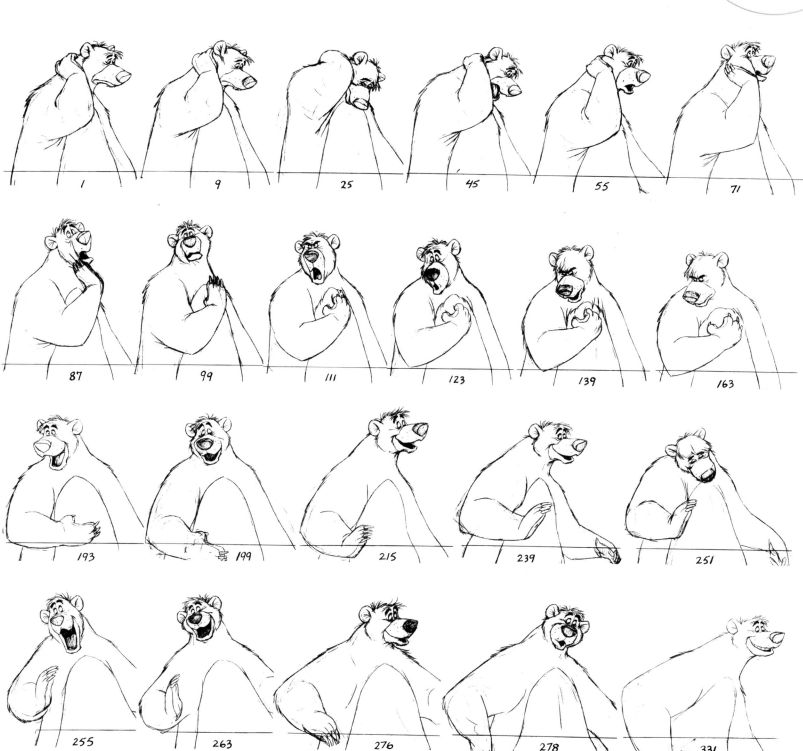

1   9   25   45   55   71

87   99   111   123   139   163

193   199   215   239   251

255   263   276   278   331

ARTIST: *Frank Thomas.*

Mowgli is horrified that his one true friend has turned against him and wants to get rid of him.

do. He can pull his ear, rub his arm, look around him for help, rub his nose or his jaw, sniff, scratch his neck, or roll his eyes. Any one of these is in character for him, but he cannot do them all. Does he move into this action or is he already in it at the start of the scene? How much movement will there be within this pose or attitude? How long will he rub his neck or how much time will it take to roll his eyes or do whatever action has been chosen?

As the bear agonizes over this problem, the acting of the boy becomes very crucial. With no idea that the bear even has a problem, he is running all over the place, happy and unable to settle down. If the boy would just stand still and listen to Baloo it would be difficult enough, but the fact that Mowgli is so excited about the day they are going to spend together just makes Baloo's problem impossible.

Baloo instinctively realizes that their relationship is different from anything he has had before. They have trusted each other, and he is afraid that this will end it all. But the right words just will not come to him. Finally he has to use force to make Mowgli listen. He grabs him and blurts out what he has to say: "I've got to take you back to the manvillage!"

Mowgli at first is unbelieving. Then, heartbroken, he pulls away and runs off into the woods. He has been betrayed by the one friend he loved the most.

These are the moments that live with an audience, making the film more than just a cartoon and the characters more than just drawings. They are also the moments that offer the greatest opportunities for memorable performances to actors, whether live or created

on paper. None of it is possible, however, if the crew has failed to develop the characters to the point where their thoughts and their actions seem natural and believable. It cannot be achieved mechanically, or by copying, or by wishful thinking, but only by careful build-up, understanding, and a love for the characters.

This powerful bond between Baloo and Mowgli was the ingredient that held the picture together and made the audience care. It also enabled us to build two special sequences at the end that never could have been sustained otherwise. Mowgli's emotions when he believes the bear is dead would otherwise have been maudlin, and the bittersweet farewell, when the lure of his own kind is greater than his love for his friend, would never have been convincing or satisfying as an ending. It was Walt who asked that the boy go into the village through his own choice rather than because the animals knew it was the right place for him. It gave the necessary light touch to end the picture on a happy note.

The Jungle Book was the first picture after *Snow White* to have the personalities and feelings of the characters so dominant. The audience understood the characters and identified with what each was trying to do. Every sequence gave new opportunities to see other facets of the personalities. And even though there was very little story as such, these character relationships and interesting personalities made this the most successful cartoon up to that time in our history.

Costumes

The value of the costume in creating a personality cannot be overestimated. In addition to the obvious eye appeal of the color and design, the specific articles that the character wears make him a specific individual. The animator can become excited by the possibilities for caricature and movement in the materials of a different kind of apparel, but, most of all, everyone is stimulated by the personality traits and cartoon business now that the character is becoming so definite.

When Charlie Chaplin first went to the Mack Sennett Studios, he was told to put on a comedy makeup. At the moment, he had no idea what he would put on.

"However, on the way to the wardrobe I thought I would dress in baggy pants, big shoes, a cane and a derby hat," he said. "I wanted everything a contradiction. Remembering Sennett had expected me to be a much older man, I added a small moustache which, I reasoned, would add age without hiding my expression.

"I had no idea of the character, but the moment I was dressed, the clothes and the makeup made me feel the person he was. I began to know him, and by the time I walked on the stage he was fully born. When I confronted Sennett I assumed the character and strutted about, swinging my cane and parading before him. Gags and comedy ideas went racing through my mind.[2]

Sketches for Cinderella's costumes for the ball and as a serving maid at home, by Mary Blair and Marc Davis. Many shapes and sizes, colors and designs were considered before the final selection was made.

Sketches by Marc Davis of typical medieval costumes for Sleeping Beauty.

415

Ken Anderson visualized a regal, Basil Rathbone-type Shere Khan who had only contempt for his victims.

The Appealing Villain

Villains are usually the most fun of all characters to develop, because they make everything else happen. They are the instigators, and, as Chaplin has pointed out, always more colorful than the hero. They may be dramatic, awesome, insidious, or semicomic, but inevitably they will be rich in unusual personality traits. Even before we know for sure how we want them to look, we know the role they are to play in the story and are fairly sure of the effect we want them to have on the audience. Which brings up the big question: just how scary should our villains be? Do we gain entertainment by scaring anyone here? Is it a quick, titillating scare that is soon over, or a deep, abiding fear? Almost any story becomes innocuous if all the evil is eliminated, but we do not necessarily gain strength merely by being frightening. We try to find a character that will hold an audience and entertain an audience, even if it is a chilling type of entertainment.

The tiger Shere Khan in *The Jungle Book* could have been a vicious, snarling, ill-tempered beast. The scenes could have been planned so they were terrifying; after all, he was out to kill the boy, and that was the motivation of the whole story. But Walt kept asking, "He's not going to be the same old slavering, growling guy like we've always done, is he?" We had not decided just how to handle this villain, but now we knew he was not going to be slavering and growling. The story called for Shere Khan to be the "heavy" of the jungle. He had to be powerful, extremely competent, and feared by everyone. But beyond that he could be sneaky or aggressive, scheming or direct, belligerent, unpredictable, bragging, or reserved. It depended on what worked best with our other characters, and what would give us the best opportunities for attitudes and actions in animation. As one of the crew suggested, "What if he's so confident and invincible that he doesn't have to prove anything to anybody? Like a really tough gangster who never has to shout or throw his weight around to show who he is—everyone knows!" However, we wanted more class and favored an aristocratic, regal monarch, so we made some drawings of a tiger reminiscent of Basil Rathbone. We were developing a villain who had only disdain for his victims and who was confident to the point of being arrogant. This was getting better! In fact, conceit would be a good trait, since he had to be defeated somehow by our hero, or combination of heroes. Nevertheless, by the time we were ready to record a voice, we felt that the intellectual refinement inherent in a voice like Rathbone's would no longer be quite right. We found the perfect combination of traits in the voice of George Sanders. He was the unquestioned king of the jungle,

Bill Peet's early drawings of Shere Khan show a surly, scheming tiger who is a real menace, in constant pursuit of Mowgli.

The queen from Snow White *had to be regal and beyond the reach of common people.*

a competent, intelligent, conceited killer who never had to slaver, or growl!

In *101 Dalmations*, the same type of decision was made in determining how broad the villain could be without upsetting the story concept. No one ever doubted that Cruella deVil actually would skin those puppies, yet this did not keep her from being a wild, fascinating figure who could get laughs. In contrast, the queen in *Snow White* had to be cold, ruthless, mean, and dramatic. Nothing would be gained by developing her personality any further or by letting the audience discover her weaknesses. Like a Shakespearean monarch, she had to be regal and beyond the reach of common people. The whole illusion would have been destroyed if she had slipped on the stairs as she swept down to her dungeon.

Captain Hook in *Peter Pan*, on the other hand, was his most entertaining when he lost all dignity and control, as he tried to get away from the crocodile. Yet this never weakened his relationship to Peter Pan, as either menace or adversary. Admittedly, Peter Pan was intrinsically invincible, and any foe was foredoomed to failure, so there was little point in restricting ourselves to personalities who were only threatening or villainous.

It is easy to see how a comic villain can be funny, and a dramatic one thrilling, but a more difficult challenge arises when the villainous character is somehow visually disturbing. In addition to the normal problems of making him or her convincing and theatrically sound, there is the increased burden of designing the appearance in a way not only acceptable but appealing. Without appeal, no one will respond enough to become involved with either the character or the story. With some creatures, this seems impossible. What if he is supposed to be revolting? Fearsome? Loathsome? What if he is a snake? Is it possible to make him appealing?

In the following pages we trace the development of two villains who started out physically handicapped, yet they grew to be among our most memorable (and lovable?) characters. This was accomplished by combining the elements and principles we have discussed: story, character development, expressions, acting, and emotions. There were dark days of doubt, and more disappointments than need be mentioned, but eventually a way was found to make them appealing. The creative mind always will find a way to do the most impossible assignments, given the opportunity and the stimulation.

Kaa

There is definitely something very disturbing and upsetting about seeing a snake. When the studio made *The Living Desert* with engrossing scenes of the sidewinder rattlesnake at work, an exhibitor in the east refused to release the picture. He claimed that every woman in the audience would leave the theater so fast that he would be out of business. Snakes may be fascinating creatures, but it is hard to love them or build much empathy for them. Bill Peet, one of our better storymen, had tried to sell Walt on a story with a snake as a main character for a propaganda film during the war, but even Walt had shied away from the idea.

Few artists had ever attempted to do a snake in animation, for how can you get any acting on a creature that has no shoulders, arms, or hands? Of course, there had been token snakes in a film like *Noah's Ark*, and there was a small sequence in *Birds in Spring*, made in 1933, where a sly, capricious snake tried to

PLAYS WITH RATTLE — SNAKE APPEARS

SNAKE RUNS FLAT-FOOTED

PART OF CHASE PAN

CHASES BIRD THRU HOLES IN LOG — TIES BODY IN KNOT

snake would establish the variety of dangers that lurk in the forest and enrich the picture with an exotic character, while showing that none of the animals had any respect or concern for the boy and that he had no friends to help him. Only Bagheera, the black panther, felt a responsibility to see Mowgli safely out of the jungle, and early in their journey the two had been forced to climb a tree to avoid the mad charges of a nearsighted rhino. Mowgli, laughing at the ineptness of the beast below, failed to notice anything strange about the vine upon which he was sitting. Bill Peet's script continues:

> It is a giant python and while they've been talking, the big snake has quietly arranged a few of his large coils around the boy until he is wrapped like a mummy, and Kaa is about to put on the big squeeze when the panther spots him. "Hold it, Kaa! Hold it!" And the python hesitates, "A friend of yours?" he asks politely. "Indeed no," replies Bagheera, "merely trying to save you from a very long case of indigestion. This miserable mancub is so spoiled he wouldn't be a fit meal for even Ishtar the buzzard." The python studies the boy with his hypnotic beady eyes for a moment, then draws back in disgust. "Ugh! I see what you mean!" and he makes a sour face. "I'll take toads and lizards any day," and he glides away, his endless body circling down the tree trunk to finally disappear in the dense growth far below.

The first story meeting brought out many new ideas. Walt felt there should be something more between the snake and the panther. He sensed that this unusual combination of characters offered more than we were getting, and he kept digging for more of a situation. "How about Bagheera hitting Kaa to stop him from eating the boy—what would that do?" Would Kaa resent it and start after the panther? One animal has attacked the other in defense of a small boy, and as a result becomes the potential victim himself. Does that not give us a real situation?

The best idea to come out of the meeting was that when Kaa was hit by the panther he would release his hold on Mowgli, who would then begin pushing the heavy body of the snake out of the tree while the head,

A snake character in Birds in the Spring *(1931) was outsmarted by a clever little bird who tricked him into tying himself into a knot. It was an effective gag but the snake was not a popular character with the audience. Many years later, the knot gag was used on snakes in both* The Jungle Book *and* Robin Hood.

Emerald Tree Boa— Jungle Cat.

capture a small bird that had been pecking at his rattles. This gave a flutter of excitement to the film and a couple of quick gags that proved this particular bird was bright and quick and a potential hero, but the snake got no raves from anybody.

When the decision was made to do *The Jungle Book*, it was obvious that the great snake Kaa should be one of the characters in the film, even though we had eliminated many sections of the original narrative. When the story work was begun, it was believed that the main potential for animation lay in the relationship of the boy Mowgli to the animals of the jungle. A

ARTIST: Bill Peet—
The Jungle Book.

Mowgli and Bagheera have escaped danger by climbing a tree, but at this point the boy encounters an even greater hazard, the giant python Kaa. In this first version of the introduction of the snake, there is very little personality on Kaa and no real development of the situation.

several feet away, was busily engaged in hypnotizing Bagheera. It was not an act of heroism to save Bagheera but an innocent act of selfish defiance; however, it worked very well, saving the panther from certain death and crippling the snake temporarily. That way, Mowgli would become confident, the panther frustrated, and Kaa completely humiliated. All three characters had definite business, clear motivations, and strong attitudes. We hoped the audience would be intrigued

with these characters and wonder what they would do next.

The revised storyboards, several meetings later, had the snake drop into the scene, unnoticed by Bagheera, look the boy over with considerable relish, and proceed to wrap him up for dining. When Bagheera saw what was happening, he hit Kaa full on the wide-open mouth, causing him to release the boy. Kaa's indignant response was, "Ooh, how dare you, Bagheera—

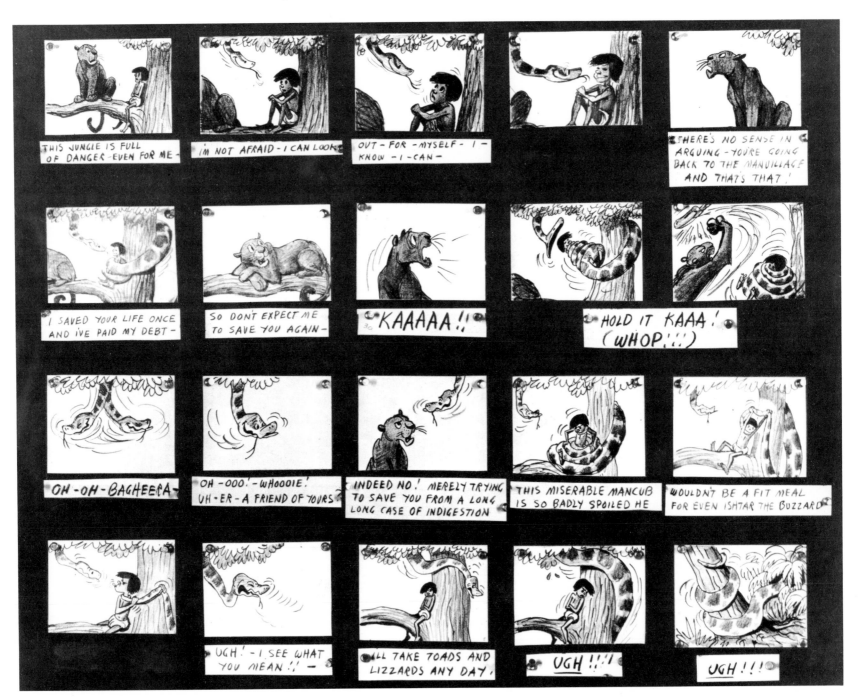

you should never have done that!'' and he started closing in on his adversary with hypnotic eyes. As Bagheera tried to keep from looking into those eyes, Mowgli pushed the snake off the limb, and the fall nearly snapped Kaa's head off. He landed in such a tangled mess of coils that he was unable to straighten himself out and had to crawl away with his whole body just one huge knot. A storyman suggested the line, ''O-o-o-o-oh, my crawler's broken!'' We laughed, but did not accept it.

Bill Peet's story sketches of Kaa showed a big, powerful python with a simplified drawing of the head, which alleviated some of the unpleasantness many people feel about reptiles, but he was still very much a real snake. Obviously, he had to be, or the story would fall apart. The audience had to believe that Kaa really would eat the boy unless something happened to stop him. Still, if we did our best to present a real snake at this point, we would get little more than shudders from a disturbed audience. The story situation would be no stronger, and it certainly would not be any more entertaining. We started wondering just how far we had to go to prove that Kaa was real, and that line of thinking led us to the big question, ''What is entertaining about a snake?'' We could not think of much.

While the story work continued to search for stronger character relationships, the rest of us started studying snakes and tried different ways of drawing them. From viewing our film of pythons, it was apparent that there are several objectionable features of a snake: (1) the head that is an extension of the body in one long thrust; (2) the beady, unblinking eyes; (3) the slithering movement, devoid of any apparent feelings; (4) the darting tongue. As soon as we bent the head at right angles to the body, we avoided the first problem. As soon as we gave him large eyes, even silly Ping-Pong ball eyes, we eliminated the beady look, and also gained an attitude that made him more interesting. Eyelids gave him a whole gamut of expressions unknown to regular snakes, but one animator insisted we were giving up too much of the real snake at this point. Kaa should not have eyelids, and always should maintain the glassy stare so distinctly reptilian. But the importance of expressions for his personality won out, and the eyelids came back.

The slithering movement became a matter of judg-ment on each individual scene; we tried to put over the business necessary to the scene, but in the least objectionable way. It would be wrong to give up the slithering completely, we all agreed. We also kept the darting tongue, since it did not seem to bother anyone once these other characteristics had been changed. There was even a small gag built around it. Kaa, in looking over the boy, seemed to express glee with his darting tongue. Mowgli, seeing this, stuck his tongue out at the snake to show his own feelings about this intruder. The final feature we emphasized was the big, blunt nose. For some reason, people and cartoon characters are never considered to be mean or really sinister if they have big noses. Comedians have big noses.

Real snakes do not have teeth and gums like a bear or a cat or a man. Some have teeth, but these are quite different from those of mammals, since they are not designed for chewing or tearing the food. The structure of the inside of the mouth is unique to reptiles, and the color of the flesh is apt to be a silky white. The jaw is hinged differently, too, which would make a difference in the way a snake would talk—if he could talk. However, we decided to treat the jaw like a normal cartoon jaw, the kind we knew how to handle when we were trying to draw convincing dialogue, but we wanted the inside of the mouth to be reptilian. That meant more study and more effort, but we felt the results would give strength to our character.

Somehow we failed to notify the color model people of our brilliant decisions regarding Kaa's mouth, so we felt completely betrayed when they suggested the pretty, pink mouth they put on all cartoon characters. We screamed that there never had been a python with a pink mouth. They asked why we had not said something before if it was so important, and then there were some accusations back and forth. Someone criticized the lack of communication between departments, and this was followed by the usual comments about animators who think they know everything. ''What's the big deal with the mouth? Show them some of our real problems!'' Eventually Kaa ended up with a slightly tinted, ivory-colored mouth, and a studio party at the completion of the picture, once again, smoothed the ruffled relations between at least two departments.

Some people wonder why we go to such lengths to keep something of the real animal in our presentation.

SIR HISS

ANIMATOR: *Ollie Johnston*—Robin Hood.

Sir Hiss's biggest weakness was that he loved to hear himself talk and constantly went too far with his flattery.

STARTS ON PAGE 461

There is certainly a temptation to forego the study and effort needed to incorporate the animal's anatomy and movements into our drawings. But if we were to throw out this special effort, we would soon have all the animals looking alike, and none of them looking like much of anything. As one animator said, ''Why do you try to make any drawing good? You do it because it looks better!''

While the changes we had made in the neck and eyes had rid us of the most objectionable features of a snake, we were tampering with the type of presentation that would make Kaa believable. Was he beginning to look too silly? Were we losing our menace? Had we given up so much of the actual snake that we no longer had the conviction the story needed? We felt the repulsive quality had been successfully eliminated, but he was far from appealing, and possibly too weak in appearance to put over the story points. We decided it was time to search for a voice, since the right contribution from an actor could give the needed direction to further refinements in our drawings.

We had dialogue written that seemed right for our particular snake, but there was still a wide range of interpretation possible when we began testing. As we explained the story situation to the voice talents, it became evident that Kaa was still rather ordinary and obvious. He had no personality quirks that made him unique or interesting, no mannerisms or ways of thinking that made him distinctive. Each actor would search to find some special quality, but for the most part all we got were a variety of hisses—sinister hisses, seductive hisses, hypnotic hisses, compelling hisses. Some asked if Kaa were a man or a woman, was he or she mean, conceited, playful, vindictive, autocratic? He could be any, or all, of these things without changing a line of dialogue or the appearance of a drawing. But none of these traits alone was entertaining enough, nor did any of them stimulate the animators to see expressions and attitudes for the character.

After eight attempts in different directions, it was Sterling Holloway who finally came up with the provocative voice and attitude that sparked us all. He not

Try different head shapes

— position of eyes.

Small noses?

only gave a reading that *was* the character, he was able to suggest lines that would fit better with this evolving personality. When Kaa hears Bagheera tell the boy to go to sleep, Sterling suggested, in a sing-songy voice, "Yes-s-s, mancub, go to s-s-sleep!" which led into his hypnotic stare. When Bagheera hit him in the mouth, instead of "Ooh, how dare you, Bagheera!" it became, "Ooh, my s-s-sinus-s-es-s-s!" followed by, "You have jus-s-st made a s-s-serious-s-s mis-s-stake, my friend, a very s-s-stupid mis-s-stake. . . ." Suddenly Kaa was alive! We could see him clearly, and he was funny. He was menacing enough, but he was also a living, breathing, entertaining creature. We could animate this guy! Everyone started suggesting lines that would fit. As Kaa backs Bagheera down the branch he says, "Look me in the eye when I'm s-s-speaking to you!" Ralph Wright added, "Both eyes, if you please," since the panther was squinting and trying to avoid looking into those deadly eyes.

As quickly as suggestions were made, Sterling was able to make the new words come alive by the way he read them. We wrote and rewrote and he made suggestions, and together we decided that this snake's weakness was that he could not keep his mouth shut when he was ahead. Just when he had everything he wanted, he had to overplay his hand and lose it all. When Bagheera told the boy, "Now no more talk till morn-

From left, writer Larry Clemmons, Sterling Holloway, the inspirational voice of Kaa, director Woolie Reitherman, and Sebastian Cabot, the fine voice of the fastidious Bagheera.

423

ing,'' Kaa could not keep quiet and simply take the boy away. He had to brag, ''He won't be here in the morning!'' which, of course, alerted Bagheera to the situation in time for him to take action. This was the line we had been looking for that would cause the panther to turn and see Mowgli about to be eaten. It not only gave us a richer character, but it solved a problem with the story structure. Now the whole scene played easily and naturally. What had begun as a bleak encounter with a minor character was beginning to be

more and more fun. It had seemed like such hard work at first, trying to build a situation and a character, and we were never sure if we were on the right track in the first place, but, finally, the doors seemed to open and we could now start experimental animation.

Suddenly, we had a new and unexpected problem. The girl who brought around the paychecks each Thursday was deathly afraid of snakes, and absolutely refused to come into our rooms to deliver our checks as long as we had any snake drawings in the room.

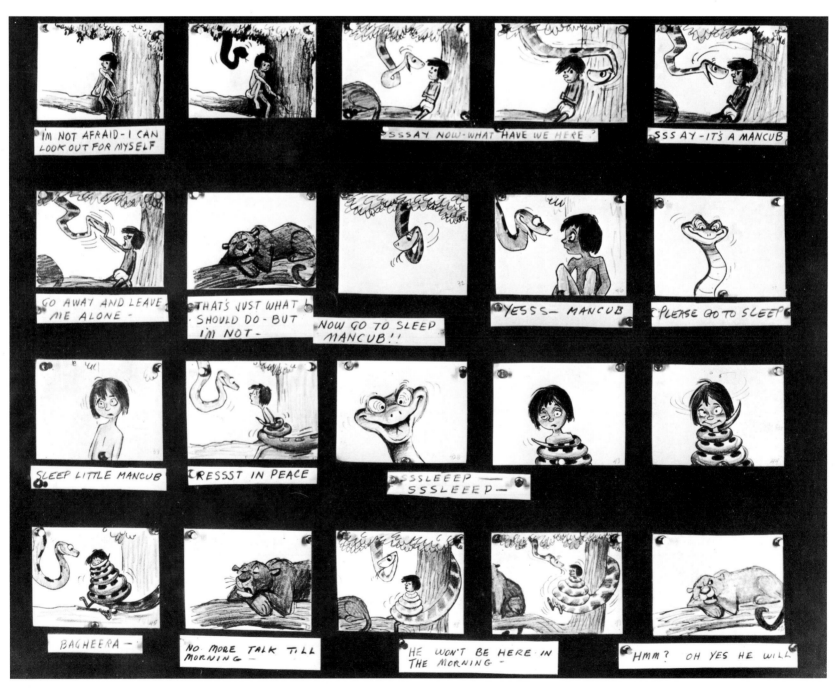

She would stand well out in the hall, bend over as far as she could toward the door, and then with a half-push and half-toss send the fluttering check on its way. This girl could not be coerced into coming even one step farther, and she warned us, repeatedly, that she would never, never go to see the film when it was finished! We tried to explain how great the character was, and how she would forget he was a snake. She would not even listen. We had thought she might be a good test audience when we had some footage done,

but since she absolutely refused to look at it we had a problem.

In the meantime, we worked, trying to draw a muscular body that stubbornly kept looking like a huge fire hose. A snake obviously is round, and yet really he is not. There are straight lines throughout his coils, but they have to come and go as he moves. And then we had those spots that seemed forever to animate backward on the screen. Should he have larger spots or slower moves? The answer seemed to be partly in

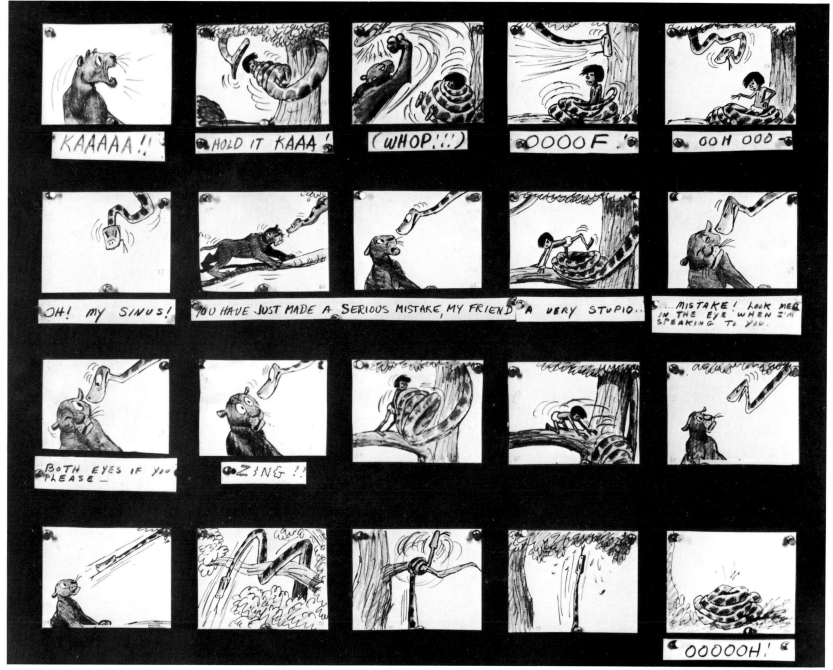

the design of the drawing, and in the way he twisted as he advanced, with the coils moving at different speeds. A more elaborate pattern of marking also would help, but that would add too much expense to the picture. How could we keep the design simple enough to be economically practical, yet detailed enough to be convincing and handsome?

Then, one day, Danny Alguire, the assistant director on the sequence, told us excitedly, "Hey, I have a friend in town from Texas who is terrified of snakes. What do you say I invite her in to see part of the picture and not tell her there's a snake in it, and we can see how she reacts. OK?" It was a mean scheme, but a necessary one, for we had to find out if we had gone too far, or if the snake should ever have been in the picture in the first place.

The showing was arranged, and the lady from Texas sat through the section of the film we had prepared, giggling and chuckling all the way. We were standing by with cups of water to revive her if she fainted, sedatives if she became distraught, and strong arms to catch her if she bolted for the outside without stopping for doors or stairways. But none of that was needed. She cooed, "Oh, he wasn't a sna-ake, he was cu-u-ute!!" We returned to our drawing boards with renewed enthusiasm.

Some ideas are funnier in a still drawing than they are in animation. That was the case with the tangled coils, after Kaa had fallen out of the tree. The drawing of the body as one gigantic knot was always funnier than it would have been in animation. There was so little body left over with which he could move, that he only could look gross, instead of funny, as he tried to limp off; but worse, it did not give our snake the proper attitude to support the expression he certainly would have had after such an indignity. He would be embarrassed and infuriated, and needed an action that would combine ruffled dignity, anger, and pain with, perhaps, a certain amount of flounce. He was not defeated, though he was badly beaten. As we argued over how to play the scene and how to make the drawings, we found that the knot was gradually getting smaller and smaller in our thinking, as our emphasis shifted to the manner in which he would move. Finally, the knot was no more than a simple configuration on the tip of his tail, and at that point we did not have enough of a picture to support either the gag or the attitude. The animator who finally did the scene decided to have an elaborate flopping and dragging action, as if the body had been broken into many segments that no longer worked together.[3] What had started out as a funny single drawing had now become a funny action that combined unexpected movement with the spirited acting we needed.

The end result of all this effort and fun was a highly successful sequence, and a villain who had become an entertaining personality in the picture. Walt liked Kaa so much that he suggested the character be brought in again later in the story. "If you've got some good entertainment working for you, use it!" One storyman felt that the snake should not be developed beyond the small role planned originally, since it would upset the balance of the story. The audience could easily grow tired of him. He thought we should quit while we had something good, and not take a chance of ruining it. Even though we had no idea at the time of how we could possibly work in another sequence with the snake—without completely destroying what little story we had—we voted to use him again.

We went to work prying and tugging on the story structure, rebuilding here and tearing out there, until we had a place to bring Kaa into the story in a very natural way. Mowgli had run away from Baloo, and was roaming about the jungle disconsolately. At the same time, his mortal enemy Shere Khan, the tiger, had heard that the mancub was around and unprotected. What if Kaa got the boy first, hypnotized him with a dreamy song, then played with him before consuming the delis-s-scious mors-s-sel?

The Sherman brothers, Bob and Dick, wrote a great little song called "Trust in Me," and everyone started contributing ideas on ways that Kaa could play with Mowgli. The boy would be rigid when hypnotized and could be tossed and turned, even made to flap his arms as if he were flying, or he could be a sleepwalker, with a silly grin on his face. This led to graphic ideas of the snake forming stairs for Mowgli to descend and a treadmill for him to walk on endlessly.

Soon we had far more material than we could possibly use, but we reveled in this luxury. Too often there is not enough business to support the dialogue or the story idea, and we are all scratching our heads trying

Walt liked the snake so much that he wanted him brought back into the picture again. In this new sequence, Kaa finally has captured Mowgli by hypnotizing him. The story sketch men suggested a variety of ways that the snake could play with his victim before consuming him.

to think of more material. The song could have been twice as long. We had another chorus planned that included some of the most imaginative business, but the director wisely felt that we were in danger of stalling our picture. Once we had made our statement of what

Kaa was doing, we should get on to the next incident; in this case, the introduction of the tiger.

Shere Khan, wandering by, had heard Kaa singing a "lullaby" to someone, and now he interrupted to find out who it might be. Kaa was in a fix. In one half of

ARTIST: *Frank Thomas*—
The Jungle Book.

Mowgli tries to avoid Kaa's hypnotic gaze, but the snake forces his head around so their eyes will meet. The markings give form to the body, suggesting a powerful, muscular snake with dimension.

ARTIST: *Frank Thomas*—
The Jungle Book.

Although he has no shoulders, Kaa laughs convincingly with this wiggly, jelly-like action.

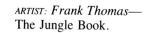

his body, up in a tree, he was holding the sleeping Mowgli, but down on the ground the tiger had a firm hold on Kaa's throat; he was not only asking embarrassing questions but wanted to see what the other half of the body was doing. It was a great situation for Kaa as an actor, and a juicy one for the men who would get to animate it.

We knew our character well by this time. The storymen knew how to write for him; we knew how to draw him; and Sterling knew how to play him. He was a formidable villain with strength and slyness, and he was all snake. He was heavy and convincing and real, yet he was not straight and he was not revolting. We hardly remembered those days, only a few months back, when we were wondering, "What's entertaining about a snake?

ARTIST: *Milt Kahl*—
The Jungle Book.

Shere Khan, the mighty tiger, wants to know who Kaa has been singing to up in the tree. Could it be young Mowgli?

Sir Hiss was first thought of as a powerful villain. Early sketch shows him as an evil character in the austere hooded garb.

Ken Anderson's other sketch of Sir Hiss, as an ineffective dandy.

Sir Hiss

Two pictures later we had another snake confronting us, but this one was of a very different kind. Partly because of knowledge we had gained by that time, and partly because *Robin Hood* was a much lighter story than *The Jungle Book*, we were able to handle Sir Hiss in a much broader fashion, making a character of him that simply could not have been imagined earlier. It had not been necessary to worry about how to make Kaa act when he had no arms or hands to use for gestures. Even with all of his expressions and activity, Kaa had very little need for shoulders or body language to support his dialogue. He was a big snake, and though his personality was whimsical he had a forthright manner of speaking, which fitted a snake's physical limitations ideally.

In contrast, Sir Hiss's dialogue and attitudes called for shoulders and shrugs and cringing and petulance, and even though he wore a small cape where his shoulders might have been, there was not the slightest vestige of anything with which to shrug. He, somehow, had to do all his acting with only his rather small and insignificant body, which was really little more than an extremely long neck. We could never have solved these problems at the time we were starting on Kaa.

The feature that followed *The Jungle Book* was *Aristocats* with the two giddy geese. Among other things, they had been an excellent proving ground for establishing attitudes with only a long neck beneath the head. Hands could be simulated by wing tips, but the shoulders were too far away to be used. There were not many ways to show an attitude, a pose, or even an expression, but with extreme care in the staging and considerable imagination in the approach to the problem, the results were successful. Sir Hiss benefited immensely from these experiences.

Since Kaa had been such a popular villain, Sir Hiss was at first conceived as being larger and more sinister than the model finally used. A drawing had been made of him wearing the type of hood popular in the eleventh century. He looked powerful and mean and a little ridiculous. This concept of a counselor snake, who actually wielded considerable influence with Prince John, was accepted for some time. Here was an evil character who could get into places where he would not be seen, through small openings where no other animal could go. He could slither up to his victims without making a sound. Those around him were in constant fear of being spied upon. He was a fearless villain who had power with the oppressor. What if he overheard what someone said? This Hiss liked the role of intimidating those around him.

The artist had made another drawing of a small snake posed on a cushion. He was wearing a short cape and a silly looking hat with a purple feather perched on top of his head. Instead of an active, physical type of villain who would enjoy getting out and searching for difficult information, this sketch suggested an ineffective, bright-eyed, nonphysical type. So, partly because we already had Prince John and the sheriff as villains who were capable of real harm, Hiss was cast as the fop who liked the soft life and protocol, his comfort and his importance. He liked clothes that suggested easy living—rather than the more austere hooded garb of the villain we first had considered.

This was an unexpected role for a snake, and a fresh character for the picture. We knew the audience would accept him, in spite of his reptilian heritage, as long as we gave him an intriguing personality, and that seemed like a certainty since he worked with the erratic Prince John. Sir Hiss was the counselor, with a sense of propriety and of villainy. Smarter than his prince, his world was the world of ideas. He was not a clown or a clod, as a despot's assistant usually is portrayed, but did his scheming in a gentle, intelligent way. He did not like violence.

Prince John enjoyed his relationship to Sir Hiss, since it gave him the opportunity to express his feelings in a flamboyant, Shakespearean manner that few others would have tolerated. But Hiss's weak character made him a perfect audience. If the prince became

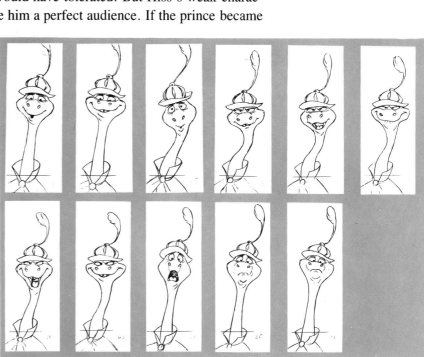

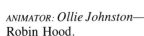

ANIMATOR: Ollie Johnston—
Robin Hood.

Prince John needed an underling he could dominate, and Sir Hiss wanted the job of counselor to the king so much that he was willing to put up with the constant indignities that went with it.

ANIMATOR: Ollie Johnston—
Robin Hood.

Dialogue: "You have a very loud thumb."
Prince John has a complex about his domineering mother. He comforts himself by sucking his thumb, much to the annoyance of his prissy counselor. Sir Hiss feels that hypnosis is the best way to cure him of this childish trait.

431

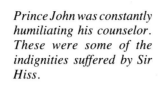

Story sketches of Hiss show an imaginative approach to aerial observation.

Prince John was constantly humiliating his counselor. These were some of the indignities suffered by Sir Hiss.

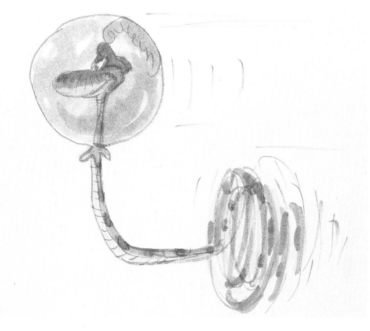

432

dissatisfied with the response he was getting, he could always hit his counselor on top of the head, which he did rather often. However, the prince was all that Hiss had, and his position gave him an importance he could get in no other way. Without this, he would have been nothing; even with it he commanded no respect. When the opportunity did present itself for him to be the representative of the crown, no one would listen to him. He could become haughty, but he was always ineffective.

During the tournament sequence, Hiss suffered the indignities of being sat upon, crumpled, dangled unceremoniously before Prince John, and, finally, dismissed from the royal box. Later, when he saw through Robin Hood's disguise, he felt that success was at last within his grasp. With this piece of news, he surely would be praised and respected. He could taste the thrill of victory. But, as usual, the highs in his life were measured only in seconds. He was intercepted by Friar Tuck and Alan a Dale and stuffed into a wine barrel.

If Hiss could have chosen his own role in the picture, he probably would have picked the one suggested by that first drawing, for as he played out the part the way we decided he was hit, beaten, criticized, accused in every way, and suffered great indignities throughout the picture. Through his gentleness and persistence, he did achieve a kind of pathos with humor. In spite of his pathetic, desolate existence, he was funny without trying to be funny. He never gave up; this was his life. The spectators had enjoyed seeing Kaa get physically beaten up because of his evil intent, but they almost felt pity for poor Hiss when he received repeated abuse.

Hiss and Kaa had one personality trait in common: when things were going well, they never knew when to stop talking. On occasions when Hiss was flattering Prince John, the words would pour out of him. He never seemed to realize that he was going too far, and ended up losing everything.

The interrelationships of these characters were of particular importance in *Robin Hood*, because the story was secondary to the characters. There was no real suspense in Prince John's many attempts to catch Robin. They are showcases for the histrionics of the two villainous actors who become richer and more enter-taining as the picture progresses. As we discovered new facets of their characters, we were able to write increasingly sharp dialogue for them.

The perfect voice for our neurotic monarch came from Peter Ustinov. His feeling that Prince John was obsessed with the idea of being king came across in the way trivial ideas were delivered in such a lofty manner. He would relish every word and dramatize each thought.

Terry Thomas, who became our snake, understood

Peter Ustinov, the voice of Prince John. His interpretation of the character helped the animator to capture the shallowness of the Prince's personality in an entertaining way.

The voice of Terry Thomas, as Sir Hiss, helped change the snake from a heavy villain to a funny, sympathetic rascal.

433

434

Prince John has just been robbed of everything but his underwear. An annoyed Hiss, who warned him that this was happening, runs over to him in a believable but nonreptilian fashion.

Sir Hiss just as well, and could capture the hurt feeling in his voice after cutting reprimands by his master. Drawings immediately came to mind—of this counselor sulking with a petulant expression. Perhaps the best thing Terry did was to fortify that nervous, ineffective quality that we wanted for contrast to the unpredictable prince.

The subtler shadings of this snake's personality were based on real experience. Occasionally, over the years, there had been men at the studio who in their determination to please Walt did a fair amount of bowing and scraping. In spite of our annoyance, we had to laugh at them. Suddenly there was a place to use these observations as our cartoon character matched the reality of human actions. "Now, what was so funny about the way those guys did it?" With this much depth to his personality, Sir Hiss was a very interesting snake.

Kaa moved and acted like a reptile, while Hiss, like his master, appeared to have enjoyed the soft life too much to have developed physically. Hiss did not slither in a reptilian way, but inched along or sort of crawled. If he was in a real hurry, as he was when Prince John was chasing him with the club, he would hop along on the end of his tail, pulling his coils up like a skirt. We

ANIMATOR: *Ollie Johnston—Robin Hood.*

Dialogue: "Another hiss out of you, . . uh, . . uh, . . Hiss, and you are walking to Nottingham."
Ustinov felt that the Prince was self-centered and forgetful and spoke the line with a preoccupied hesitation. This suggested to the animator that John was so engrossed in preening himself that he had difficulty remembering Hiss's name, and was even reluctant to leave his image in the mirror to turn to his counselor.

Hiss's reaction to another of Prince John's wild schemes is well summed up in this bleak look.

435

wanted him to move in a way that was special to him—not like Kaa.

We were no longer restricted by a real snake's anatomy or construction, because with this much character development we were caricaturing a personality more than a reptile. This always allows more freedom in the actions and movements, as long as they are in keeping with what the character would do. Ken Anderson had made a sketch of Hiss sulking in his basket, with his coils draped over the rim so they looked very much like two arms. It gave an attitude, an imaginative touch, and a funny picture.

Storymen Vance Gerry and Eric Cleworth went further in their thinking, coming up with all manner of activities based on the idea of a prehensile tail. He could hold his glasses, write a message, count money, even put the tip to his lips in a shushing action. His coils took the place of an arm as he cringed to ward off expected blows from Prince John.

He was given teeth because it helped in the type of

Prince John was too insecure to accept the blame when his plans went awry and always took out his frustrations on his counselor.

One of the best scenes in the picture sprang from this Ken Anderson sketch of Hiss sulking after Prince John has banished him to his basket.

ANIMATOR: *Ollie Johnston.*

Hiss had to escape the angry charges of his master any way he could.

436

ARTISTS: *Vance Gerry and Eric Cleworth—* Robin Hood.

Characters with physical limitation are often the most fun to work on. The story men found many ways to use Hiss's tail as a prehensile organ.

437

Inspirational Sketches for *Robin Hood*

expressions that were needed, and the animator decided to have fun by using the gap in Terry's teeth as a model, which gave an opening for Hiss's tongue to dart through. He even had hair in some cases to strengthen certain ideas. Whatever fit the situation and the personality was acceptable. What is entertaining about a snake? Everything!

There was one last ingredient that made this sinister reptile into an appealing villain. Just as important as all the story work and character development and relationships and acting was the feeling the animator had for this character. His understanding and affection imbued the little snake with a special quality that went beyond his personality. As the artist reflected back on the challenges of this assignment, he revealed these thoughts:

There is a moment at the start of a picture that I call the animator's moment. I sit at my board staring at a blank piece of paper. I have a sound track and endless ideas from everyone on how my characters should look and act. This moment is the heart and soul of the whole thing. I have thought a lot about what I will do with these two personalities, but putting the first lines down is still kind of awesome. I want to start out right. This is my chance to mold these characters and give them the relationship as I see it. I am eager to get it on film and see them come to life. I have thought about the expressions, and I know just how I want Hiss to look when he hears Prince John say, "Hang Friar Tuck." But first I have to build to that point. Now is the time to think of the things I have learned over the years. I want to be entertaining above all.

As I go along living with these guys over the years, I learn more about them, and the more I learn, the more exciting they are to me. I know what they like and what upsets them. They are real people to me—what they do comes from inside them, and from inside me. To me they exist, and I spend most of my waking hours with them.

I have to plan carefully so that every frame means something. I must make the audience feel what I feel. I may never have an opportunity like this again. It is not often that we have a sympathetic villain, like Hiss. This makes him a different and richer character. I like to think about how he feels about Prince John. I know he doesn't like him. Many times I think about this miserable existence we have forced upon Hiss and I feel sorry for him. I wonder if I should have Prince John hit him so hard. I also wonder if there isn't something I should do so that he could gain a little self-respect, but then I realize he is what he is, and I would be weakening his relationship with the prince if I made him a stronger personality. The best I could do for him was to let him have his fleeting moments of happiness, those moments when his world was right.

This is the part that makes animation like no other medium. To be able to play with the emotions of my characters, and know that I can make them laugh or cry or become very angry, is to experience animation at its best. It is difficult to explain the thrill I get out of seeing my drawings move through the changes in expressions and attitudes, in a way that gives them that mystical quality of life.[4]

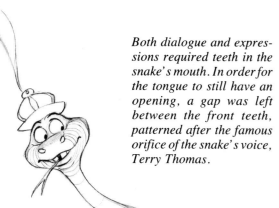

Both dialogue and expressions required teeth in the snake's mouth. In order for the tongue to still have an opening, a gap was left between the front teeth, patterned after the famous orifice of the snake's voice, Terry Thomas.

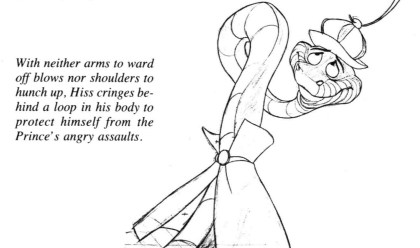

With neither arms to ward off blows nor shoulders to hunch up, Hiss cringes behind a loop in his body to protect himself from the Prince's angry assaults.

Lady and the Tramp

16. Animating Expressions and Dialogue

"After we have given the men all the suggestions we can that have to do with expressing ideas through the body, then we can come down to the value of the facial expression—the use of the eyes, eyebrows, the mouth—their relation to one another—how the eyes and the mouth have to work together (sometimes) for expression—how they work independently for expression at other times. In other words, then we would go into the combined use of expressive features and expressive actions of the body."

Walt Disney

One of our art teachers told us that the eyes in self-portraits reveal how an artist feels about himself. Every young painter stands in front of the mirror and finds that his true personality seems to be revealed as he lowers his chin and looks out from under his brows.

Later on, as he becomes more arrogant, he lifts his chin and looks defiantly at the world. Then, as he ages, he turns his head and looks with wisdom out of the corners of his eyes,[1] showing, as Coleridge said, "Common sense in an uncommon degree."

The artist's character emerges in a self-portrait.

ARTIST: Anselm Feuerbach. In youth the soulful eyes suggest deep thought.

ARTIST: Jean-Baptiste Corot. In maturity the head-on look of defiance.

ARTIST: Käthe Kollwitz. In age the appraising look of knowledge.

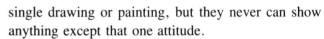

Eyes looking up have more appeal—a little guy with a big problem. From the left, Flower, the skunk in Bambi; *Dopey from* Snow White; *early model Bashful from* Snow White, *later model Bashful with long eyelashes; and Pluto the pup.*

Mickey believes he has shot Pluto instead of the moose, in The Moose Hunt *(1931). His feelings are shown in the crude, cartoon symbols of sorrow before the days of acting.*

There was warmth in The Ugly Duckling *(1931) even though the drawings were very simple and broad.*

The early Renaissance painters always had their main figures looking up. It is an accepted tradition for the innocent and the pure, but it does seem to be based on truth and reality. The artists at the studio have used this attitude repeatedly for cute characters. Somehow they look more wistful, more hopeful, more vulnerable. This was particularly important to Fred Moore, even though it was an instinctive thing with him. There was more appeal when the figure was drawn looking up at you out of the tops of the eyes. Somehow you cared more for the innocent, little character.

In each of our art teacher's examples there was an inner feeling the artist had about himself that caused him to choose the particular attitude he did. While these examples are all expressive ones, they are static. They may represent the best that can be shown in one single drawing or painting, but they never can show anything except that one attitude.

This brings us to the heart of what the animator or the actor can do. Imagine that while you are looking at one of these portraits, the subject gradually lowered his brows into a frown—paused—and then lifted one brow and glanced to the side. You immediately would sense a change from one thought to another. Something very important happened! *Through a change of expression the thought process was shown.* Since the first discovery of this principle back on the early Mickeys, the animator has found it to be his best method of showing his character's thoughts and feelings.

In those days there had been little need for any expressions beyond the crude portrayal of emotions suggested by the situations. A character was happy or he was sad; he was frightened or he was mad; he was worried or he was cocky—and it often was difficult to tell the differences among even those six basic reactions, unless something like tears, or trembling knees, or drops of perspiration were added. Then, as Walt's acting stimulated the drawing of body attitudes, it was discovered that there was better communication in the whole figure than in the face alone.

By the early thirties, the staff was able to do a version of *The Ugly Duckling* that was all feeling, and though it was drawn simply the audience believed it enough to enjoy the predicament of the lonely, dejected, baby swan. Soon after came *Playful Pluto* and the wonderful sequence of Pluto entangled with a sheet of

flypaper. Expressions played a very important part in the entertainment value of those scenes, and while everyone admitted that this was only a broad cartoon symbol for a dog and lacked any attempt at realism, it was still felt that the door had been opened for even greater achievements in animation.

In the next five years, everything possible was tried in the way of facial expressions—some so complicated they looked like road maps, others so simple they lacked interest. Refinements brought subtlety that, in turn, often brought vagueness. Some expressions just do not seem to work well in animation; they may be too obscure or too difficult to draw. In this case, the story situation should be checked to be sure it calls for a very specific attitude from the character. The artist also could try a simpler expression, something that offers more caricature. He should try it out in thumbnails, turning the head around, strengthening the lines of the face, searching for the best and clearest way to stage that particular expression. Often the animator may think of the right expression but becomes discouraged with it because his staging does not show it to good advantage. Only careful experimentation will reveal the best method of communicating an idea.

Tips for staging expressions:

(1) *Resist the temptation to try to tell too much in one drawing.* The important thing is that the drawing be quickly and simply read: no matter how beautifully it may be drawn, it should not be forced into a scene if

it does not animate properly. *Do not* be afraid to discard your best drawing if it does not fit your action. It is the idea that is important!

(2) *Do not let the expression conflict with the dialogue.* Nothing can be more distracting than this. Angna Enters, the American mime, told her class, "The most obvious problem was to avoid deflecting the meaning of the line [of dialogue] by erratic movements. The way a character walks, stands, sits, listens—all reveal the meaning of his words."[2] This rule would apply to pantomime as well, where it could be equally disturbing to have a character make an expression that does not fit the personality.

(3) *The expression must be captured throughout the whole body as well as in the face.* If the character is defiant, his eyes, brows, mouth, cheeks, and head attitude will be defiant. If any more of the figure is shown, it will be defiant too, with clenched fists, shoul-

ANIMATOR: *Ollie Johnston—* The Rescuers.

The animator must find the right angle to display the expression he wants on his character. This twisted smile only could be staged in a front or 3/4 view.

443

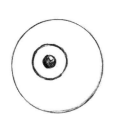

ders back, feet apart, and a belligerent thrust to all the related parts. Any expression will be weakened greatly if it is limited only to the face, and it can be completely nullified if the body or shoulder attitude is in any way contradictory.

We had learned what to draw and when to draw it, but we still had much to learn about *how* to draw it. We watched the best acting in the live action films of the time, but the expressions seemed to be far too subtle for us to attempt. The overacting of twenty years earlier would have been ideal for us, but a new school of realism and fine actors had taken over Hollywood. Eyes blazed with anger, or burned with passion; they snapped with jealousy, shone with happiness, twinkled with humor, sparkled with enchantment, darkened with suspicion, or were aglow with love. Some seemed to drill right through you. None of these eye expressions could be drawn no matter how we tried. We looked at our drawings of Mickey and Donald and Pluto and thought, "There's got to be another way."

The Eyes

As we always did when confronted with a new problem, we went to the real thing: the face, the eyes, and the brows, and tried to find out what made them work. The studying of photographs of real eyes revealed an obvious fact that was startling in its importance to us—the eye changes shape! We knew that the lid could half-close the eye, but there were other forces pushing up from below and tightening at the corners, causing

The eye is a three-dimensional ball, wrapped in lids that reveal only a small portion of its surface.

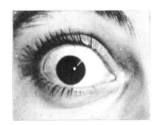
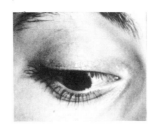

The forces that work on the eye: lower lid, upper lid, cheeks, and brows all change the shape of the exposed area of the eyeball. Photos show the changing shapes of the eye due to these forces.

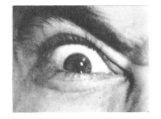
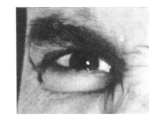

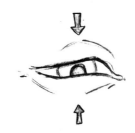

A great range of expressions is evident in just the eyes.

444

the eye to assume quite different shapes, from one expression to the next.

When an actor has to portray a robot or a sleepwalker, the first thing he does is to fix his eyes in a stare, a lifeless gaze with no movement. If he wants to portray an exuberance for living, the actor changes expressions constantly with darting looks, happy looks, and quick looks. Dancing eyes and sparkling eyes have a great deal of movement, ranging from wide with excitement to crinkled in laughter. The animated character somehow has to capture these same elements. If the eyes remain constant throughout a scene, the character will be consistent and look like the model sheet, but he also will look like a doll with painted eyes. This quality was used purposely in *Pinocchio*, first when the puppet was lifeless, and later when he was dancing with the marionettes in Stromboli's show. The eyes presented an interesting problem since Pinocchio was still a wooden puppet even though he had been brought to life, and part of the device that made him puppetlike was to keep his eyes as constant as possible, giving him a wide, innocent stare. Now he was working with real puppets whose eyes were only paint, and there was a fine line to be drawn between the lifeless and the living, while keeping both as puppets.

Cartoon eyes show squash and stretch from the same forces that work on real eyes. They also hint at the infinite number of expressions possible through opening more, closing more, or changing the direction of a look.

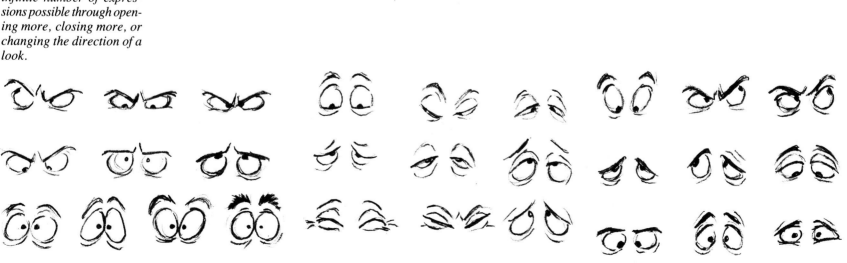

445

When Drawing Eyes . . .

The eyes are the most important part of an expression and must be drawn with extreme care. Any jitter or false move on an inbetween destroys both communication and believability.

Position of the Pupil Within the Eye.

Dwarfs with pupils floating in the white of the eye appear to be staring off into space, instead of at Snow White offstage.

1. *When there is too little of the pupil showing, it will be difficult to make a strong statement of either the expression or the direction in which the character is looking.*

2. *This pupil is clear and definite for a look to the side.*

Pupils not looking in the same direction make the expression lifeless.

3. *As the pupil moves away from the rim of the eye, the direction of the look changes.*

Three ways to animate a look to the right:

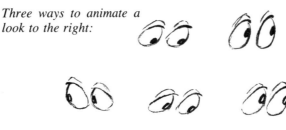

This is the weakest.

4. *As more and more white surrounds the pupil, there is an increased feeling of excitement and intensity.*

This is stronger.

5. *White all around the pupil gives a vagueness to the expression and makes the direction of the look uncertain.*

This is strongest.

The rising eyelids fortify the look, the change of direction emphasizes it, and the blink stages it by not only increasing the amount of the move, but by shutting out the white of the eye briefly, then adding it back on successive drawings. Blinks are good on any shift of eye direction as they call attention to the change, as well as allow the animator to make the expression stronger.

6. *A smaller than normal pupil gives a dazed look, a withdrawal from reality or lack of vision.*

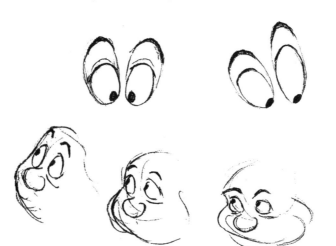

Fred Moore had a principle for drawing the pupils, eyelids, and brows as circles expanding from the same point. It kept a strong direction and relationship in the eyes.

7. *This cartoon symbol for a drunk or knocked-out character was used extensively in the early films, but generally was abandoned by the mid-thirties. A stock symbol can be useful, but always will destroy any feeling of realism.*

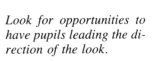

Look for opportunities to have pupils leading the direction of the look.

This placed a special burden on the clean-up man and inbetweener, who had been taught to emphasize the changing shapes of the eye to strengthen the feeling of life. Now, with less movement in those changes, there was an increased chance for wiggles and jitters on the screen, and the drawings had to be done very carefully, and thoughtfully, to keep them working smoothly. An inbetween out of place or poorly drawn may get by on an arm or a leg, but never on an eye. As Walt had said, the audience watches the eyes, and this is where the time and money must be spent if the character is to act convincingly.

For Disney cartoon characters, the basic shape chosen for the eye was the early formula of a circle. This is not the only way to draw an eye, but this shape has given us maximum expression. Walt would keep prodding us to come up with more realism, but we always came back to the circle. We have refined it but never found a better shape. Many artists tire of the old, round eye and want a more decorative design for some pictures, but often they lose more than they gain. Since the eye is the most eloquent tool of communication, added strengths must be provided in other areas to make up for any loss here, or the character is apt to end up with a lifeless, uninteresting personality that the audience never can quite believe. It is up to the animator to be sure he has not been lured into designing a tiny eye or one that cannot give the necessary expressions.

Mickey's eyes were a special problem. They had started as black pupils in large eyes that looked more like goggles than an eye shape. Since the whole figure was stock cartoon formula for the time, the eyes worked well, but when the animator started making the head bigger and rounder, and elevating the rims of the eyes to the status of eyebrows, a strange condition arose. The pupils were now considered to be the whole eye, a solid, black eye like that on a doll. It was cute and made a great design, but it created an almost impossible job for the animator who was trying to draw a look in any direction other than straight out in front.

Eyes wandering around the face tended to produce a queasy effect on the audience, so the animator had to curtail his attempts to make Mickey have that added touch of life. In most cases the restrictions were handled so adroitly that the audience never noticed, but

The earliest Mickey appeared to be wearing huge goggles with black pupils.

His head had to be raised to make him look up.

It was difficult to roll his eyes to the side and maintain a pleasing expression.

ARTIST: *Fred Moore.*

Mickey's new eyes used on The Pointer *(1939) opened up opportunities for more expressions.*

447

there were still times when the animator needed to roll Mickey's eyes in a special look without having to move his head. These restrictions were too limiting. What if Bashful had been drawn with a solid eye that had no pupil—or Dumbo? There would have been no way to get sparkle, excitement, and life—all of the variety needed.

So eventually Mickey's eyes were changed and pupils were added, opening up new acting possibilities. He could now look innocent or embarrassed out of the top of his eyes—or he could glance to the side without the expression falling apart.

On Winnie the Pooh, we had less of a problem than we had with Mickey, because he was a stuffed toy and was not expected to have eyes that wandered on his face. It seemed appropriate for him to turn his head in the direction of his "looks," and this actually gave him a less sophisticated feeling that was more in keeping with a "bear of very little brain." With this type of acting, we always could keep the eyes in a close relationship with the rest of the elements that gave expression. As the mouth and the cheeks animated, the shape of the little button eyes would be affected, and they would squash and stretch the amount needed to keep the particular action alive. Though many

subtleties had to be given up, the audience had no trouble in following how Pooh was feeling.

Piglet was more of a problem since he had the barest rudiments of a face. With only dots for eyes there was nothing to draw except the crudest expressions. We had to concentrate the acting in body attitudes and hand and head gestures to compensate for this loss.

Occasionally a question is raised whether button eyes should blink at all since there is so much charm in keeping the realism of the doll. Some artists feel they are losing their basic design if they alter the shape in any way, but they are throwing away their best symbol of life with this limitation. Ken Anderson expressed it well, "This creature has magically been imbued with life, and part of life is the ability to blink the eyes and get expressions. It has to pick up these accomplishments or else it would only be getting half-life."

Compared to Mickey or the dwarfs, the Bambi eyes appear to be very realistic. They are caricatures of a real deer's eyes rather than being cartoon eyes. We had the suggestion of a tear duct and had a carefully drawn upper eyelid with a thickness to it that fit over the eyeball. The pupil with the dark center and the highlight made the eye the most detailed we had ever drawn. Most audiences would have been hard pressed

Winnie the Pooh and Piglet had button eyes (which should not wander on the face), so they had to turn their heads when looking to the side. This actually enhanced the doll-like quality we wanted.

to tell that a real deer's eye was any different. In spite of all this detail, or disguise, it was still basically the cartoon formula, just more refined. We could not have squashed it so successfully otherwise.

In *101 Dalmatians*, Pongo's eyes had the dark center with a colored iris only in special closeups. There was no detail like the tear duct, but we did carry a carefully drawn upper lid that helped fit the eye on the head. Our problem on this character as well as on Bambi was not in animating the eye itself, but in trying to relate it to the other features that had to affect it for expressions.

To achieve dimension in this extreme close-up of Maid Marian in Robin Hood, *we used a shadow effect that set the pupil back under the lid.*

The little girl in The Jungle Book *has large pupils surrounded by a dark, dusky iris. We wanted to get the rich look of the East Indian eye and, hopefully, a seductive quality as well.*

The black eye of a real mouse has no white showing, and no expression either. For our mice in The Rescuers *the white was left off the eye, even though the shape was usually defined as in any cartoon character. It was a successful compromise, giving more feeling of a real mouse.*

Lucifer, the villainous cat in Cinderella, *had eyes with a colored iris, and a very small pupil. The shape was slanted and catlike, except in takes or surprised expressions.*

Faline's eyes were the most realistic we ever had done. When details like the tear duct, lashes, and two-toned pupils were used, great accuracy was required in the drawing.

449

A cat's eyes are extremely expressive and change shape radically as they convey different emotions. At times they are mere slits, lost in a puff of cheeks and brows, or they are half closed in complete contentment, or wide with curiosity. The dog can convey some of this, but he reveals his feelings more with his body, general attitude, cocked head, and his particularly expressive ears and brows. In contrast, the horse has only two expressions, bland or excited. With wrinkled brow and ears and head positions other emotions are clear, but it is not often in the eyes. The pig has a limited range, but it is difficult to distinguish whether he is satisfied or merely sleepy.

Eye Blinks

Blinks may at first seem like the more mechanical side of animation, but they do many things to keep a character alive. If there is an intensity in a look that does not allow changing the shape of the eye itself, a blink will keep it from going dead. If the eye starts to look like a tennis ball or has the lifeless stare of a doll, the blink will make it real again.

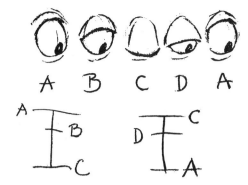

In blinks there should be a feeling of flesh and thickness to the eyelids. Where there is only one inbetween, "slow out" of each extreme (see chart). If the inbetween is drawn in the middle, there will be more pictures on the screen of a half-open eye than of either extreme position.

Inbetweens should animate smoothly and not change angle or wobble.

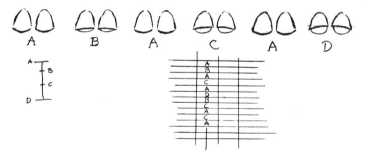

Blinks of disbelief, puzzlement, or wonder usually are shown with a slight squint. In the closed eye, the top and bottom lid meet across the center of the pupil.

In the flutter blink of a stunned or half-conscious look, the inbetweens are done as indicated in the chart at the left and then exposed in the stagger timing shown on the exposure chart. Only the white of the eye—not the pupil—is exposed as the lid gradually opens.

Blinks are a useful device to ease the shock of going into a held drawing. There is always a visual jar when the drawing suddenly stops moving, and the illusion of roundness and dimension quickly fades as it is held immovable. In most cases, 2 feet 8 frames (less than 2 seconds) is the maximum time a drawing can remain on the screen without movement. However, the simple addition of a blink during the hold recaptures the living quality, keeping the spectators from realizing it is only a drawing after all.

Blinks will make a big visual change just by the color alone, especially if the pupil is enclosed in a white eye. The dramatic change from light to dark eyelid to light again can be very startling and undoubtedly will attract the audience's gaze. The eye, the lid, and the blink must be carefully drawn and timed to convey the precise attitude of the character when they have become so important.

The Face

We have found over the years that certain relationships make an expression read. No one part of the expression, the eye, or any other part by itself, is going to communicate if the expression does not work as a unit. To get this unity, there must be a close relationship between the crucial parts. If the features are spread too far apart it is harder to read them and more difficult to make one part react to another. This is, of course, because most of our experience with expressions has been on the human face. An animal such as an anteater, which has its mouth so far from the eye, is a tougher problem than one whose features relate in a pattern closer to a human's. If the line of the mouth has a close relationship with the eye, it can push the cheeks up against the bottom eyelid in a smile, thereby relating all the key parts of the face.

The human face shows a strong relationship between the eyes and the shapes of the cheeks and the mouth in any expression.

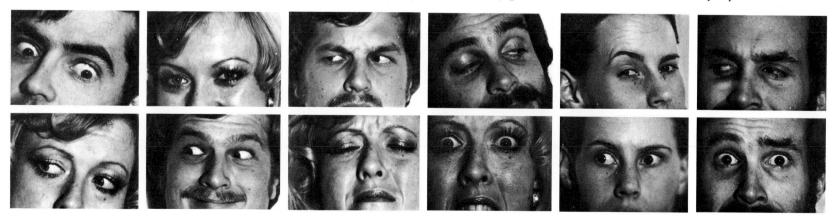

Dumbo

The animator must be very aware that he is working with forms—not lines. The mouth, the cheek, the lids, the eyeball, the nose, the forehead, the brows are all made up of cartoon flesh that is being moved about with a definite plan. The cheek must be regarded as a solid mass that retains a certain volume whether it is stretched to accommodate a wide-open mouth or pushed into a new shape by pressure from the corner of a closed mouth. In an extreme smile, the cheek even may be forced across the bottom part of the eyeball itself. Now everything is squeezed up together.

When the smile is relaxed, these forms all will separate. This gives dimension to the forms as they change in relationship to each other, squashing up or stretching out—and it is the use of this fundamental principle that gives life to the face. As the cheeks drop away from the eyes, the nose will drop slightly, the mouth will make a larger move, and the whole head will elongate vertically to help accentuate the change.

When the brows are raised high and the eyes are wide open on a character like Mr. Smee in *Peter Pan*, or one of the dwarfs, there will be wrinkles above the brows. In the normal position, the forehead may be just the space between the brows and the cap. Now, the forehead being pushed up and squashed by the brows will be full of wrinkles that may even extend up past the edge of the cap. Still, this is not nearly as strong as Norm Ferguson's early drawing of Pluto with the brows sticking up above the head circle. If Smee were to go into a frown from this position, he probably would have a move forward and downward on the head, but this would be much less than the action of the brows, for they define the expression that must be seen.

As the brows descend, the flesh that has piled up behind them flattens out. When they contact the circle of the eye, they begin to push it down and change its shape. As the frown becomes more intense the pupils will be partially covered by these rolls of flesh. There is a thickness to these brows, more refined now than the roll of flesh on Pluto, but still representing the same principle.

It takes more than mere lines gliding back and forth over the face to register emotions—the face must seem like flesh—and the movement must be timed to have the feeling of weight. Naturally, in a take the expres-

It is extremely difficult to animate human expressions on a face that has the mouth too far from the cheeks and eyes. An anteater is a real challenge.

Fortunately the flying horses in Fantasia *did not have to act.*

The grown deer in Bambi *presented a special problem since these animals have no cheeks, only a thin lower jaw, and virtually no chin. Human expressions were difficult to adapt to these restrictions. The lower lip seemed to flop up and down in dialogue as the mouth shapes defied the animal construction. The solution was not so much a matter of logic as good judgment in where the liberties were taken.*

These crocodiles from The Rescuers *had no dialogue, and few of their expressions demanded complete distortion of the reptilian shapes.*

453

In these Bill Tytla drawings the whole face shows what the character is feeling. The mouth and cheek cause the eye to squint, and even the nose is affected too, either flattening out or pushing up, depending on the action of the face. Underneath all this, the shape of the head changes to fit the new design created by the expression.

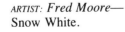

ARTIST: *Fred Moore—* Snow White.

On each drawing of Sleepy, one eye is open wider than the other or one cheek is squashed more than the other, to give life to the expression. The bags under the eyes create a puffy, sleepy look.

sion change can be as fast as the animator wants to make it; certainly Bill Tytla made lightning changes with Stromboli in dialogue. But in each case there is a reaction afterward—a settling or follow through; otherwise the flesh will lack weight and not be convincing.

The expression changes on Walt's face were particularly stimulating as he described something for us. His acting showed the basic humor in the situation, but the activity in his face inspired every animator. His brows would rise high in one attitude, then suddenly plunge down into a deep frown, with the cheek pushing against the eye, giving an intense, piercing quality to his look. Then one brow would shoot up in a flowing shape across his forehead. This was truly squash and stretch used at its best to communicate with an audience.

Dialogue

When dialogue was added to the stories, animators suddenly were faced with a whole new problem. What does the character do while he is talking? There had been single words and exclamations and short phrases before, but now the speeches were longer and demanded some kind of acting. Walt previously had created a mood with music or imaginative use of effects or occasional pantomime; now he was unsure of the type of acting a cartoon character would use to support and fortify the lines he was saying. As long as the dialogue only sprang from embarrassment in front of Minnie, or from a boy scolding his dog for doing something stupid, Walt knew how the character should look and act, but as soon as the words became part of the story the animators were expected to find the solution.

"Hi, Minnie" and "Watch out!" had been done with only the mouth opening and closing, but when a pig had to say, ". . . I'll be safe and you'll be sorry when the wolf comes to your door," flapping the lower lip (there were very few lower jaws at that time) did not do the job. The animators tried nodding the head up and down, but still there was no feeling that the voice was coming from the character. Something had to be found that would give the impression the character was saying the line. The animators searched for key words that seemed to be said with more emphasis than the others and then put in an accent, a gesture, a bounce,

or a dip at that point. There was very little attempt to choose the most appropriate action while everyone was so desperate about getting anything to work.

In many pictures the character sang the lines. No one remembers whether this was an attempt to make necessary exposition more palatable or whether it was just a way to avoid bad, amateurish acting during a long speech. Walt felt that a singer with a pleasant voice established an immediate rapport with the audience, "If you like his voice, you like him." (After one unsuccessful meeting, John Hench quipped, "I'm gonna start taking voice lessons!") But, actually, it was one way of drawing viewers into the film with a positive attitude right from the start. There were many scenes of questionable acting that were carried by an appealing voice.

If the character had no reason to sing, he would speak his lines in rhyme, which was not as easy for the animator as the singing, but this was better than realistic acting. In *Santa's Workshop* the clerk tells Santa that "Willy Brown for seven years / hasn't washed behind his ears." Both the drawing and the action were crude but the combination was successful in the theater. Even if the character did not quite look as if he were doing the talking, the spectators were not too critical because they were enjoying what they were doing.

The big problem was to find a way to accent the dialogue, or to match the accents already there in the

delivery. These were marked on the exposure sheet, so the animator knew where they came. He had a copy of the track and could listen to the lines over and over, but for him to capture the same feelings in his drawings and timing was a real problem. Heads wobbled from side to side, hands were placed on hips, arms were folded—but by far the most popular solution was to have the index finger point either up in the air or at another character. It was not really acting, but it was an easy way to get the necessary accents to match the feeling of the dialogue.

Some animators varied this a little by using a clenched fist instead of a finger exended, but it was still the arm accenting the words, and, usually, every word that was said. Walt inadvertently curtailed that approach by planning stories that demanded a more convincing type of acting—not all the way through, but in key spots. *The Flying Mouse*, released in 1934, showed a new concept of a cartoon character saying a line of dialogue, and while the animator saw it only as a tougher variation of the same old problem, it was actually another step forward. The whole story was built on the feelings of the characters and the changes that occurred as the situations developed. The characters were thinking, and making decisions, and revealing new emotions, and, most of all, interacting with other characters in the story. The pointing finger was too limited for this kind of acting.

The following year brought a success and a disaster. *The Tortoise and the Hare* contained the sharpest character development, the clearest personality expressions, and the best sync with dialogue yet achieved. In con-

By 1934, in The Flying Mouse, *subtle emotions were requiring acting rather than mere gestures.*

ARTIST: *Ham Luske*—
The Tortoise and the Hare.

The animation of gullible Toby Tortoise and cocky Max Hare set a new standard for acting to dialogue.

trast, *The Golden Touch* failed all the way around. Everyone was puzzled. What went wrong? Why did it not work? Everything done had worked before: singing some lines, speaking in rhyme, pointing a finger for accents, wobbling the head on the dialogue. It had been a wonderful acting opportunity, too, for this King Midas was no miserly monarch, mean and thin, a skinflint hoarding his gold and hating the world. He was a happy man and enjoyed his wealth and his life.

He loved his flowers and his fountain and his food almost as much as his gold.

Then after getting his wish that everything he touched would turn to gold, he gradually realized that he was losing everything he loved and was faced with starvation and a slow death. What a situation for an actor: the thought processes, the concern, the despair, the mounting panic. There was a wealth of possibilities, but somehow the cartoon did not come off. More was

457

needed than mere gestures, happy smiles, worried looks, and a king running around the courtyard for the audience to relate to the character.

That was 1935 and work already was starting on *Snow White*, a picture that demanded far more in convincing characterization and believable acting than anything done before. Both the tortoise and the hare had been broad comic characters shown in strong situations that had insured their success, but *The Golden Touch* was more like the feature being started. How could *Snow White* be successful if King Midas could not be made convincing? There would be no problem with the dwarfs, stumbling around, bumping into each other as they try to discover who is in their house, and only minor problems with the queen consulting her mirror, since that could be carried with the strong dramatics of the situation. But the dwarfs arguing about whether the young girl should stay and where she should sleep and, especially, crying sincerely when they think she is dead—how could we ever succeed in making the audience believe?

As the animators studied the problem, they began to see that meaningless, unrelated movements of characters during dialogue destroyed what little personality they may have attained in earlier scenes. They already knew that a mouth flopping about like that of a ventriloquist's dummy lacked conviction and a head bobbing back and forth did nothing to develop the character. They also realized that too much movement on the character made it impossible for the audience to see the expression on his face. In looking back at scenes that had been successful before, the animators got the idea of phrasing the action in terms of the phrases of dialogue. When the fairy in *The Flying Mouse* had said, "Brave little mouse, you've been kind to me, I'll grant one wish, what shall it be?" the

animator had used a different body attitude on each phrase with appropriate gestures. There had been a slight pause at the end of each phrase, which gave a chance to display the expression while the body was quiet. The next phrase had a new attitude with a new gesture, and perhaps a variation of the expression. This simplified the whole problem of dialogue by eliminating all the extraneous moves that had kept the character moving without meaning.

This began to focus the animator's attention on a relationship of attitude, gesture, and expression, and without realizing the advance being made, he started asking questions as he studied each new scene. "What should this character do on this line—lean forward? Lean back? What is the point here; why is he doing anything in this scene? Do I want to show this silly grin on his face, or just put over that he is happy and not worried about anything? Can I do it better in a close-up or in a full-figure shot?" As he asked these questions, he was thinking of acting and personality, and this would soon lead to a new kind of believability in the animation.

Of course, phrasing a line of dialogue did not answer all the problems. In *Pluto's Judgment Day* there were several scenes of the cats in Pluto's dream testifying about all the awful things he had done to cats. One very round cat had been chased into the path of a steamroller and been flattened wafer-thin. The gag was that on the last line of his testimony, he would turn sideways and walk off, showing his predicament and making a funny contrast to his appearance in the three opening lines. To aid in this visual contrast, he carried a balloon that somehow had become just as thin without popping. It was a cute gag with a surprise twist, and every effort had to be made to support the illusion that he was really a very fat cat at the start.

Ham Luske was given the scene, and he talked it over with his young assistant Ward Kimball. The first line, "That great big bully picked on me," seemed fairly easy, and they agreed that the cat would point toward the offstage Pluto while he was leaning forward, with a petulant wiggle. Now he could draw back and stick out his stomach on the next line, ". . . because I was so fat," and either pat his tummy, or make a sweeping gesture with his hand. But the third line, "He chased me under a steamroller . . ." stopped

both of these creative minds. They thought of his running in place, turning in fear, doing a take at an imaginary steamroller, but nothing was imaginative enough, nor seemed to fortify the line of dialogue. Finally Ward suggested, "We're supposed to do something different aren't we? Well—how about having steam come out of his ears when he says 'steamroller'?"

Ham thought it was just crazy enough to be worth a try, but when Walt saw it in the sweatbox a week later he stopped the film with a long, slow, "What in the hell was that?" To him, it kidded the character and the situation and lacked the sincerity he wanted in his pictures. Many times he would laugh at a suggestion or a bit of animation but still discard it because it destroyed the believability of the situation, and Walt believed in his pictures and in his men and in his audience and would do nothing to break that bond.

Gradually the extraneous or arbitrary actions began to disappear and a type of acting was seen that seemed so natural and so right for the character that no one could question the believability. There were still some animators who felt they were not doing anything unless they had an arm waving or the head flip-flopping throughout the scene, but eventually they learned that these actions drew the audience's attention away from the expression and contradicted the attitude.

The successful scenes were the ones where the animator had felt the right expression, had understood the personality of his character, and knew how he would react to every situation in his own particular way. And, further, he had avoided making drawings that were just drawings, but worked to capture the feeling of life. As Liv Ullman, the great actress, has said, "It is what is behind the smile that matters."

ANIMATOR: *Milt Kahl—* The Rescuers.

Dialogue: "Of course you have, but we must try harder, mustn't we?"
At the start of this scene, Medusa looks briefly offstage toward the little girl Penny, then turns away to look at herself in the mirror. The mouths are clearly staged with accurate sync, but the focus, once she turns to the mirror, is on the eyes, which have nothing to do with what she is saying. She is totally preoccupied with removing her false eyelashes, making her contempt and coldness for Penny more obvious.

If this action had come on a different line of dialogue, it might have been distracting, but the spot was well-chosen since it did not matter if the line was lost under laughter or if the audience became so engrossed in this performance that they did not listen. The squash and stretch went beyond real flesh and showed great skill in this sophisticated use of fundamentals.

ANIMATOR: *Ollie Johnston—* Robin Hood.

Dialogue: "Poppycock, female bandits, rubbish, ha ha hah." This dialogue was delivered by Prince John with an air of bored arrogance, calling for a drifting type of action with minor head accents. The nearly closed eyes with the lids in a down curve helped the feeling of contempt. On the word, "rubbish," he turns away, rolling his eyes upward in a gesture of impatience. The same expression has been carried throughout the scene but with varying degrees of intensity. The one thought has been, "You, Hiss, are stupid! I am clever."

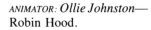

460

How Do I Make It Sync?

Even though the animators on those early pictures with sound made a strong accent in the drawing that matched the frame where the beat was marked, something seemed to be wrong with the sync. "I put the squash drawing right where you marked the X," the animator claimed. The director answered, "Yeah, but he seems to be late; I hear the sound before I see him do it." On the Moviola the sound head is separate from the picture screen, so the film with the animation was advanced while the sound was left in the same place. At first it was advanced just one frame, but that did not help very much. Then two frames, and finally three. When the whole action was exposed three frames ahead of the actual beat, the character appeared to be moving exactly on the beat! Mysterious illusion!

The word went around the animator's rooms, "Hit the accents three frames ahead of the beat!" No one knew why it should work, but somehow it did. Then somebody had a scene in a tempo of eights (a beat coming every eight frames), and when he shifted his action by three frames he found he actually hit the half-beat and got no sync at all. For a jump, a land, a

ANIMATOR: *John Lounsbery*
—101 Dalmatians.

Dialogue: "You mean the old DeVil place?"
Sometimes the limitations of a characer bring out the best in an animator. The eyes of the sheepdog are partially or completely covered through most of the scenes, so the animator focused his attention on the mouth. The mouth positions and changes in shape are excellent, but what makes the scene unusual is the extensive use of the tongue and the teeth. At the end of the phrase of dialogue, the mouth retains the feeling of the last word rather than relaxing into a nondescript position. It took thoughtful analysis by the animator to pick these elements out of his sound track and figure a way to handle this special problem.

461

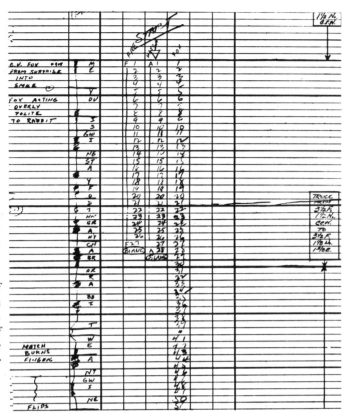

The accent marked on the exposure sheet is ''leading'' the sound; in this case by three frames.

James Baskett, the voice of Brer Fox, in Song of the South, rattled off this dialogue in one and a half seconds—which averages about 1/8 of a second per word.

ANIMATOR: Ollie Johnston— Song of the South.

The mouth shapes for the high speed dialogue shown on the exposure sheet. The only possible way to achieve mouth sync with this rapid delivery is to put the action on ''ones.''

hit, a take, three frames nearly always gave a better illusion than having the extreme drawing right on the beat. Yet, in this case, it did not work at all. There seems to be no hard and fast rule on sync, whether it is on dialogue or a musical beat. One scene in *Pinocchio* had to be shifted a full eight frames ahead of the actual sound before the character seemed to be saying the line. It consisted of only two words, which might have been part of the problem, but no one ever has been able to say precisely why any of this is so. The animators have become pragmatic: If it works, they do it; if it does not, they experiment. The best suggestion is to be alert to the possibilities of shifting any action against the sound track until it appears that the character is matching the sound. (Of course, an honest attempt must be made to animate the feeling of the sound in the first place, or no sync ever will be possible.)

These general rules on approaching mouth action in dialogue are based on, and refined from, the principles that Ham Luske developed:

1. Anticipate dialogue with head, body, or gestures

462

three to four frames ahead of the heavy modulation, but mouth sync should be right on the modulation. If it is a closed mouth, it will be on the consonant, and, if possible, remain closed for two frames in order to be seen. If you are using "twos" and the mouth action falls a frame ahead, that is okay.

2. You need interesting mouth shapes that reflect the personality of the voice. Look for shapes that give you an extra touch of character and are peculiar to this one personality. You have a different voice for each character, and you should have a different mouth action for each voice.

3. Try to show enough time on the important shapes so that the viewer will be aware that he has seen a picture of the word.

4. On holds at the end of a phrase or a line of dialogue, try to retain a mouth expression that reflects the character of the last word. Do not change the mouth shape just because you are through with the word or phrase. Retain the character of the shape in the hold or pause with a softening action to keep it alive.

5. There are not too many straight inbetweens in dialogue. You may want to retain one mouth a little longer and then move quickly into the next one, or vice versa. Either way you will favor one extreme over the other—both in timing and the shapes you draw.

6. If you have a word that has been stretched out fairly long, treat it like a moving hold. Make an extreme which shows the shape you want, then make a second one that is even stronger and "slow into" it. If the sound is diminishing rather than growing, then your second extreme will not be as strong. Either way, you will keep the feeling of flesh and life in the mouth.

7. When using the eyes only for sync in an extreme closeup, start the eyes into the move at least three frames ahead of the accent. If it is a mushy, soft line, then the action does not need to lead the sound by more than a frame or two. If the accents are strong, then you may want to lead by four to five frames. By "lead," we mean to have the big move that far ahead of the heavy modulation of the word.

The same problems occur in drawing mouths in dialogue whether they belong to a bird with a rigid beak, a bloodhound with loose jowls, or a pretty little girl.

Shown here are three basic mouth shapes: the closed mouth, which could be a "B" or "M" or "P"; the open mouth, which could be most any vowel; and the puckered "U" or "O" mouth.

463

8. When using a blink to help get sync, the eyes should close ahead of the accent by three to four frames.

9. If you are going to start your dialogue on a drifting or slow move without an anticipation, it helps to start this move anywhere from three to eight frames ahead of the accent.

10. There are times when all your dialogue will have to be on "ones." When working with Brer Fox's voice in *Song of the South*, we found that the actor talked so fast we could not possibly hit the accents without animating all the dialogue on "ones." Some of the words were as short as two exposures and not many were over four.

11. The vowel sounds, A, E, I, O, U, always will require some opening. O and U are actually complete word sounds at times. The actors each will have their own way of saying these sounds. Some will draw them out and some will clip them off.

12. The consonant sounds, M, P, B, are all closed mouths. Keep in mind that the mood of the character will determine the shape of the mouth. If he is grinning while talking, his closed mouth will be wide. If he is pouting, it can be a very "pooched-up" closed mouth. Say the rest of the consonants over to yourself, always remembering that in sequence you do not hear them the way you do individually. But in saying them you will get a feel for them—where the tongue is and how much the teeth show on certain sounds. All these things give a color texture to the mouth as the sounds are made. Generally, the ones that have the E sound show teeth. T and G also can pucker like a U, and Y and W can go into a very small O or U shape. V and F are often best shown with the under lip tucked under the upper teeth. But listen carefully to your track and draw little thumbnail mouths till you have a series that works together and is entertaining.

13. Be sure the teeth are not painted *white* or they will flash. This can be especially annoying if the mouth is overarticulated.

Other Ways of Syncing

Because of the limitations in design imposed on us in many pictures, we had to find other ways besides the mouth to get good sync and make the lines of dialogue convincing. Here are some of the methods we used:

1. Rely more on head moves.
If the head moves are properly conceived in relation to the dialogue, the expression on the face and the mouth shapes become far less critical.

2. Character rear view, in shadow or silhouette. Sync will come from head and body moves as well as good gestures. This type of staging gives variety and often makes a very dramatic scene.

3. Offstage dialogue. (Character talking is not shown.)
The camera might be on a scenic shot, some effects animation, rain, a panorama, or some objects in a room that have a special meaning.

4. Camera "on" a character other than the speaker. In showing one character listening to another character's lines, you often expose the feelings of both of them at the same time—one through his dialogue and the other through his reactions. This is a good idea to consider at any time.

Listen to Your Track

Careful study of the sound track will reveal two very important things. First, the overall phrasing and timing of the line, the accents, the fast moves, drifting moves, the pauses. And, second, the personality touches of the character shown in the specific way a word is said that will be different from the way anyone else would do it. Neither of these things should be overlooked, for between them they offer the key to how the character is feeling.

The expression chosen is *illustrating the thoughts* of the character and *not the words* he is saying; therefore it will remain constant no matter how many words are said. For each single thought, there is one key expression, and while it can change in intensity it will not change in feeling. When the character gets a new thought or has a realization about something during the scene, he will change from one key expression to another, with the timing of the change reflecting what he is thinking.

If the thought process is a sudden realization, then it will be a quick change. If it involves a scheming action,

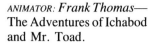

ANIMATOR: *Frank Thomas*—The Adventures of Ichabod and Mr. Toad.

With his fears mounting as he rides deeper into the glen, Ichabod tries to whistle to keep up his courage, but his mouth is too dry.
STARTS ON PAGE 521

ANIMATOR: *Frank Thomas*—Alice in Wonderland.

Dialogue: ''No, impassable. Nothing's impossible!''

Can a doorknob be animated so that it appears to be thinking about what it is saying? The knob is a simple piece of machinery, and had to be drawn with great care. Sizes that changed or jitters would have been more noticeable in this case because the character is anchored in one place. The outside edge stays constant except for a slight move at the top in reaction to the brows lifting. The knob itself moves but never changes shape, so it retains its metallic quality. The keyhole mouth gives the feeling of enunciating the words very carefully, which fits the stuffiness of the voice.

ANIMATOR: *Bill Tytla*—Snow White.

Dialogue: ''She'll be tying your beards up in pink ribbons and smelling you up with that stuff called—par-foom.''

Grumpy is fuming about the fact that the other dwarfs are all so eager to please Snow White. His first major expression change comes as he moves from his annoyed hunched-over attitude into, ''She'll be tying your beards up in pink ribbons . . .'' The animator has captured the wonderful sarcasm of the line as Gumpy daintily pretends to make little ribbons out of his beard.

As he says, ''and smelling you up with that stuff called—par-foom!'' he drops his act and goes back to being mad. He momentarily has trouble thinking of the word ''parfoom'' and puts his hand on the back of his head as though that would help him remember. Tytla, even with his great acting ability, used the finger point twice here, but on both occasions it seemed like the natural thing for Grumpy to do.

465

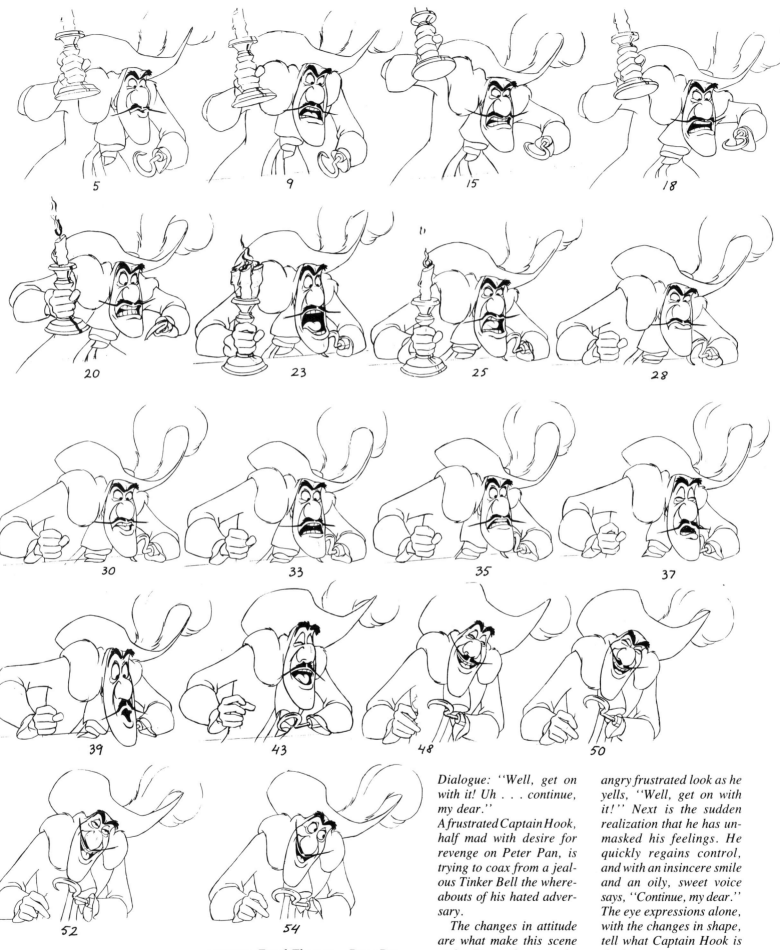

5   9   15   18

20   23   25   28

30   33   35   37

39   43   48   50

52   54

Dialogue: "Well, get on with it! Uh . . . continue, my dear."

A frustrated Captain Hook, half mad with desire for revenge on Peter Pan, is trying to coax from a jealous Tinker Bell the whereabouts of his hated adversary.

The changes in attitude are what make this scene rich. First, there is the angry frustrated look as he yells, "Well, get on with it!" Next is the sudden realization that he has unmasked his feelings. He quickly regains control, and with an insincere smile and an oily, sweet voice says, "Continue, my dear." The eye expressions alone, with the changes in shape, tell what Captain Hook is thinking.

ANIMATOR: *Frank Thomas*— Peter Pan.

the movement will be slower. The stepmother in *Cinderella*, Prince John in *Robin Hood*, and Captain Hook in *Peter Pan* were all schemers who took time to show their evil thoughts. A change to a smile or a puzzled look may also take time because all of these thought processes are of a more deliberate nature; the expression moves more gradually across the face and is likely to remain there longer. In pantomime, the only key the animator will have to the timing of these changes will be the particular personality of his characters. With the addition of dialogue, much of the texture in the moves in his scene will come from the little nuances and shadings in the sound track, which will suggest the speed of his actions as well as how broad or restrained they might be. They will affect whether he moves continuously or pauses and then continues. Listen to dialogue carefully; *listen to the thoughts and ideas*—they are your character's. He is thinking them, and you must capture them.

Perhaps there is a mannerism that will fit and add life. It could be a thoughtful move of the eyes, a special glance, the tongue moving across the lips, the character pulling on his chin, or pushing the hair out of his eyes. Any of these and other similar actions can become part of the expression if chosen carefully. If the actor doing the voice has delivered the lines as though he was thinking them for the first time, they will suggest expressions. As has been mentioned before, it is absolutely essential that the actor give a spontaneous performance. If he suggests taking his lines home to practice, it is a good tip-off that we may not have the right actor. He is almost sure to give a polished performance instead of uttering the unusual little sounds that make it possible for the animator to visualize expressions.

Above all the voice must be believable and it must communicate. Our standard for a sincere voice speaking with spontaneity and reflecting a thought process was set early when Lucille LaVerne was recording the lines for the witch in *Snow White*. Bill Cottrell, storyman and director, was in charge of the session and said Miss LaVerne was so convincing that when she read from the script, "A glass of water—please!—a glass of water!" the assistant director leaped to his feet and dashed out on the stage with a brimming cup before she could get to the next line.

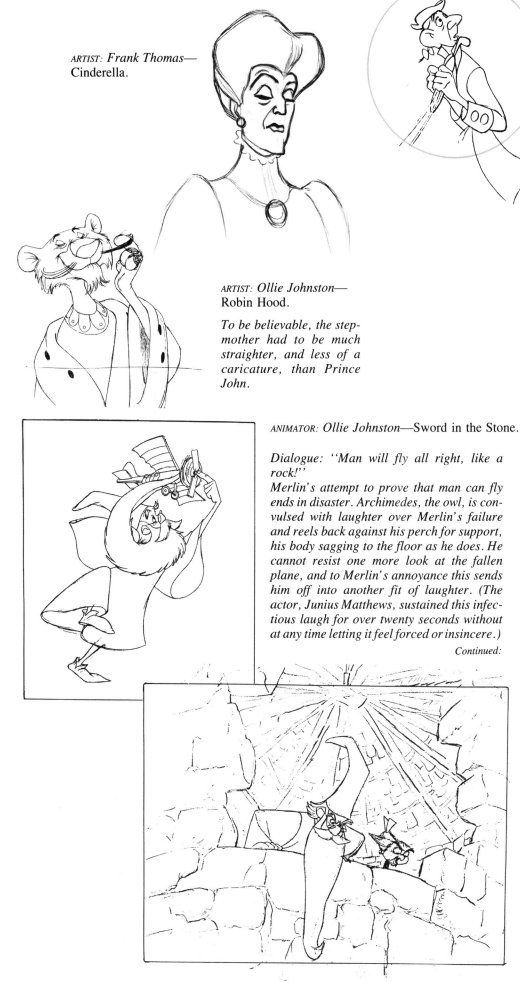

ARTIST: *Frank Thomas*—Cinderella.

ARTIST: *Ollie Johnston*—Robin Hood.

To be believable, the stepmother had to be much straighter, and less of a caricature, than Prince John.

ANIMATOR: *Ollie Johnston*—Sword in the Stone.

Dialogue: "Man will fly all right, like a rock!"
Merlin's attempt to prove that man can fly ends in disaster. Archimedes, the owl, is convulsed with laughter over Merlin's failure and reels back against his perch for support, his body sagging to the floor as he does. He cannot resist one more look at the fallen plane, and to Merlin's annoyance this sends him off into another fit of laughter. (The actor, Junius Matthews, sustained this infectious laugh for over twenty seconds without at any time letting it feel forced or insincere.)

Continued:

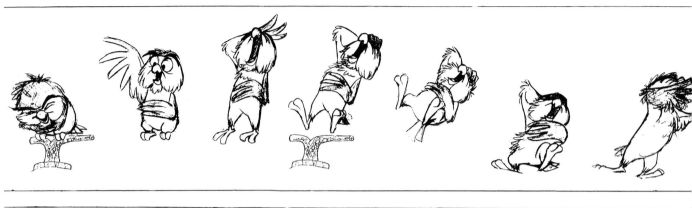

By the final scene, both the actor and the owl were completely exhausted, and Archimedes only could point feebly at Merlin and finally slide to the floor where he rolled and kicked and gasped for air. Merlin, who had bickered with the owl throughout the picture, could think of no way to retaliate other than to puff on his pipe and look very irritated.

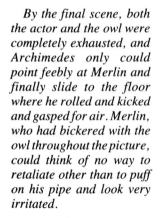

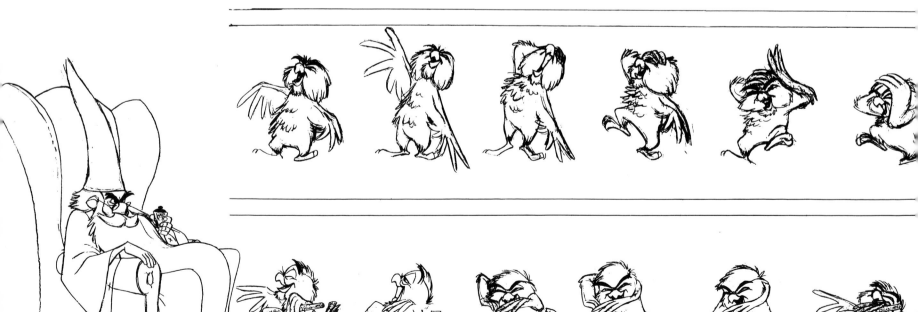

The Total Expression

Trying to think of everything at once can be very confusing. While worrying about the shape of the mouth or syncing the action to the dialogue, it is easy to forget the attitude or the essential expression for the whole scene. To overcome these obstacles is the daily challenge animators must face.

All of our rules, lists, and suggestions have come from trying to unify our message into one statement that has impact. Someday, animators may be able to advance into the areas of hidden meanings, sly suggestion, even double entendre. A quote from Alfred Hitchcock reminds us that there are still some exciting types of communication to be considered. "People don't always express their inner thoughts to one an-

Another Fred Moore principle for relating the whole head to the facial expression. A frown compresses all the parts, a "take" opens them up.

other; a conversation may be quite trivial, but often the eyes will reveal what a person really thinks or feels."[3]

A sequence overloaded with dialogue can become very disturbing to the viewer, but hopefully this can be

ANIMATOR: *Eric Larson*— Pinocchio.

Figaro throws a tantrum in this beautifully conceived bit of pantomime. What could dialogue possibly have added to the scene? The violent, petulant flurry at the start, the strong anticipation, and the angry slump into the final attitude show Figaro's feelings far better than if he had said what he was thinking.

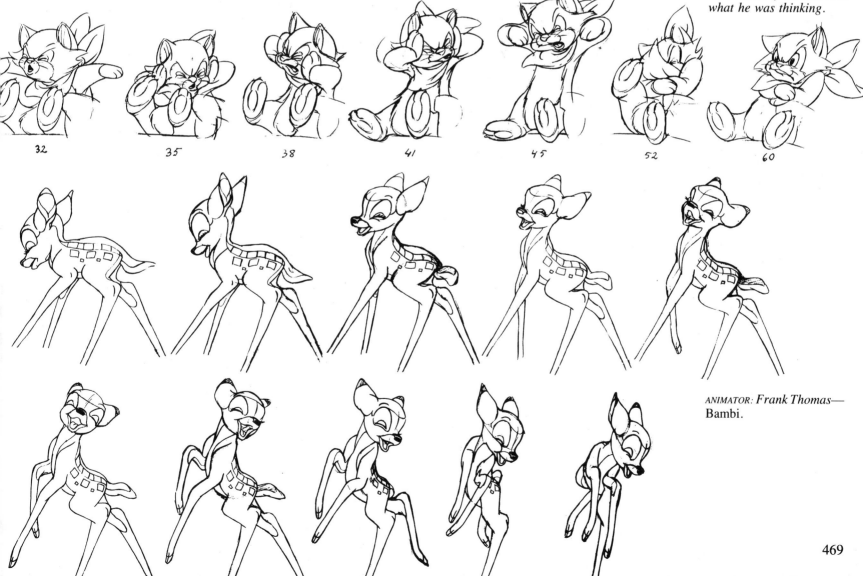

ANIMATOR: *Frank Thomas*— Bambi.

469

Aristocats

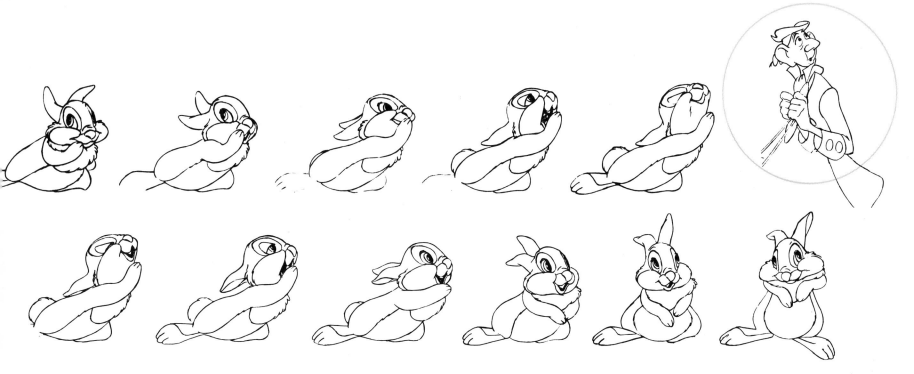

discovered before too much of it is animated. On more than one occasion we have tried running a sequence without the dialogue track and have been surprised to find it played beautifully with just the right pantomime and the music. A key line may be needed here and there for explanation, but the idea of the sequence actually is communicated better.

"There is nothing wrong with dialogue," T. Hee once said. "You and I are using it right now. Hundreds of plays have been written based entirely on it!" But somehow the cartoon communicates better through expression than words.

If the line of dialogue does not require a strong, definite physical expression, it might be a warning that the scene should be handled differently. It should be reappraised both for the writing and the actor's delivery, and steps must be taken to improve any weakness before more time is spent.

Many of the scenes will be entirely pantomime, which gives the animator a chance to build the emotions of his character in his own way. This is more challenging, but when done well these moments can be the most rewarding to the audience. This point is nicely illustrated by the story of a famous Greek actor who lost his voice on the day of a performance. He went on anyway, but acted only with gestures. People liked it so much that they said, "Don't talk anymore!"[4]

In summing up, here are some of the rules we have learned over the years:

1. Show the expression change!
   a. Avoid making a fast move while changing the expression.
   b. Change your expression before the move, or at the end, when the character is moving slowly enough for it to be seen.
   c. Do not lose the expression change in an active secondary action—such as a hand waving, a big arm action, or follow through on clothes.
2. Avoid looking up for a frown, unless it is a sinister, domineering one.
3. Do not hide a smile with the head tilted down too far or behind a big nose or moustache.
4. Be sure you have the right staging to show *all* the expressions in your scene to best advantage.
5. Have you the right expression for what your character is thinking? Are all parts of the head and face related to this one idea?
   a. Do not change shapes too much all over the face.
   b. At times, hold down activity on the face so that just the mouth is moving.
6. As we were told so many times before we learned: It is the change of shape that shows the character is thinking. It is the thinking that gives the illusion of life. It is the life that gives meaning to the expression.

Saint-Exupéry put it so beautifully in his classic line, "It's not the eyes, but the glance—not the lips, but the smile. . . ."[5]

ANIMATOR: *Ollie Johnston*—Bambi.

The ideal facial relationships are found in characters like Thumper. He is realistic enough in design to be compatible with the deer, yet he has none of the same restrictions. Rabbits are soft and furry, revealing very little bony structure, and they appear to be even softer when their faces move with squash and stretch. In contrast, the deer has a hard, smooth surface that reveals many bones. Softness here would give a rubbery effect.

Alice in Wonderland

17. Acting and Emotions

"In our animation we must show not only the actions or reactions of a character, but we must picture also with the action . . . the feeling of those characters."

Walt Disney

Leopold Stokowski recognized Walt's truly unique talent when he commented, "Walt had the imagination, insight, humor, and sense of design to enter into the feeling of life of any man, animal, tree, or stone and make us feel with him."[1] From the very beginning, it was obvious that these feelings of the characters would be the heart and soul of the Disney pictures. The stories, which at first had been told through bits of business and incidents, were told more and more through the reactions of the characters to those incidents. The incidents themselves remained vital to the story, but how the characters felt about what was happening became more important.

In every art form it is the emotional content that makes the difference between mere technical skill and true art. The poet, sculptor, dancer, painter, singer, actor—all eventually can become proficient in their crafts, achieving dazzling mechanical perfection, but their work will be empty and meaningless unless the personal perceptions of the artist are communicated as well. This thought was stated most simply by one studio artist when he noted that many of the young men "could animate beautifully, but that isn't what makes you laugh and that isn't what makes the tears come."

In the animated film there is actually a double potential for this type of personal expression; first, in the emotions of the characters in the film that arouse additional responses in the audience, and, second, in the artistry of the work itself. It will show in the writing and the choice of the material, in the design and presentation, the staging, the picture-making, the voice talents, the color, the music—and especially in the animation. There are the individual drawings with their elusive sensation of life, and there are the relationships of all the drawings in movement and time.

In this book we have outlined the basic skills that must be mastered if strong, clear communication is to be achieved. We also have pointed out many examples of fine animation that became memorable because of feelings the artist had about the character and the situation. There was more than just frowning in anger, more than a single expression, or even one lone convincing scene. There was real drama with the full range of emotions.

Too often there does not seem to be any real reason to probe this deeply into a character, but any omission here is soon noticed. One critic complained that a certain animated film had nothing more than a gallery of passions, as the character's "face twitched through

    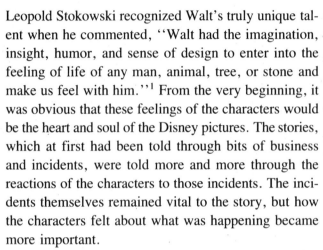

473

its limited repertoire of grimaces over and over.'' Great scenes were never built that way.

Is there a magic formula we have learned for building scenes of great emotion into our pictures, of making drawings with personal feeling that can transmit the same emotion to an audience? An astonishing number of people in the field are not aware of the potential, nor, actually, understand how animation works. Even Walt never realized what made some scenes more successful than others, but he was such an outstanding storyteller that he knew what should be shown, what would hold an audience, what would get a certain reaction, and he could afford to pay for the fumbling errors of his artists as they learned.

It was the supervising animators who had to find the more effective uses of the artists' limited abilities. Working with their crews, they searched for easier ways, simpler ways, stronger ways, trying to find the essence of the entertainment in the scenes they were doing. And here they discovered that increasingly their problems were in the field of acting.

Several people at the studio enrolled in acting classes, seeking a greater understanding of the disciplines of the theater. Leo Salkin, from the Story Department, reported his experience:

I began to sense why certain people, good actors, communicate and make a character believable. I've sat and watched young student actors . . . and they're saying the lines the way they were written, and they're trying to be angry, or trying to be sad, or trying to be humiliated, trying to be aggressive, and they're doing all these things . . . and it's lousy! And it lies there hour after hour—and you know it's not working and you think, ''How can you get it? How can you make that contact?''

And then right out of nowhere, somebody will be doing a scene, and for a brief, maybe, 30 seconds that damn thing comes to life! Suddenly that woman is a woman in trouble, and this guy is being mean and you're reacting, and your whole being is suddenly focused on that, and then suddenly it dissipates. I mean, one wrong word, one wrong emphasis, and the thing is gone! I think, ''What made that work? Why did that happen at that moment?''

That golden moment is our goal. That is what we must understand and recreate in our own medium. Is it possible? As the animator sits at his desk flipping the drawings and throwing them away and making new ones, he probably should wonder at the audacity of anyone proposing to duplicate an actor's artistic and moving performance with only a collection of drawings.

The actor and the animator share many interests; they both use symbols to build a character in the spectator's mind. Certain gestures, attitudes, expressions, and timing have come to connote specific personalities and emotions, some regional, others universal. By using the right combination of these in the proper sequence, the actor builds a bond with the people in the audience, and they are with him, they understand

Early attempts to portray emotions were limited by the drawing ability and acting knowledge of the animators, as well as the lack of support in story development. Albert Hurter's suggestions for attitudes on the grasshopper and the devil were based mainly on the broad acting of the turn of the century.

him; and if they like him they will be concerned about what happens to him. These are the animator's tools as well, but while the actor can rely on his inner feelings to build his portrayal, the animator must be objectively analytical if he is to reach out and touch the audience.

Katharine Ommanney, in her book on acting for students, has defined the rules and the exercises that are the steps for the beginner.[2] She asks the performer to consider these questions as he tries to communicate with an audience:

Are the characters interesting, lifelike, and vivid?

Do you become emotionally involved with them?

Do the gestures and movements seem sincere, convincing, clear and properly motivated?

Does all of the action help to delineate the characters and their situation for you?

Is the action clear-cut, realistic, prolonged sufficiently, and exaggerated enough to be seen by the whole audience?

Undeniably, these are the criteria for judging any performance, animated or live. They sound so simple, written this way, and are easy to pin up on one's desk—but so difficult to achieve.

The demands were quite simple in the early films, limited mainly to gestures of annoyance that tried to be "anger" and a kind of fright that wished it could be "fear." Gradually a kind of formula developed for making "pathos" the prime ingredient in a film, such as *The Ugly Duckling*: an appealing little character wants very much to achieve something and fails in a way that hurts him; the other characters ridicule him; he tries again, fails again; the audience feels the hurt and starts to pull for the little guy; when he finally succeeds in a unique and heartwarming way, everyone feels like cheering.

It is an old formula and the acting choices are elemental. As long as the central figure is sincere, his actions can be broad and touched with humor without upsetting the pathos. The ugly duckling's mournful cry of rejection was a ludicrous honk, which only increased the awareness in the audience that this poor little outcast did, indeed, have a real problem. Laughter and sympathy were combined in a way that offered a high potential for entertainment and for personality development, but there were no great demands in acting.

By the time the studio began *Snow White*, the animators were being asked to depict much more than just happiness and sadness. Now, they were faced with the task of communicating such subtle emotions as love, dejection, hate, jealousy, concern, and fear. The first real example of an entire sequence based on pure emotion showed the dwarfs crying beside Snow White's bier; it was a critical decision even to attempt this type of sequence. The supervising director was concerned "that the audience would not react as we hoped it would. It was not a matter of what field size we used, or panning, or what character we cut to—it was the mood in which we wanted our audience at the time."[3] It was important that the viewers be involved

ANIMATOR: *Frank Thomas*— Snow White.

When the dwarfs showed their grief over Snow White's death, we were asking the audience to share the emotions of the cartoon characters.

This action of Dopey breaking down was cut after the preview when it was misinterpreted by the audience. Now the scene starts with him sobbing on Doc's shoulder. This sequence was a new challenge to animation. Could mere pencil drawings make an audience cry?

Grumpy, the last of the seven dwarfs to succumb to Snow White's charms, turns away to cry alone.

completely in the feelings of the dwarfs, and no one knew how this could be done with moving drawings. There were two enormous problems.

First, the animators knew of only one way to communicate any emotion: show the change of expression that would reveal the character's thought process. He had to move to stay alive, and a series of drawings moving from one attitude to another was the only way known to establish the emotion. If he were seen to change from a portrayal of concern or worry to one of despair, or from despair to fighting back the tears, it might be possible to make him believable. But that would make too much movement for this sequence. Obviously all the dwarfs should be overcome with grief from the beginning to the end, with no change of attitude and as little movement as possible. There would be good impact on the initial picture, but what would keep the dwarfs from going flat and lifeless after that?

The other problem lay in the fact that the audience had become conditioned to laugh at the dwarfs whenever they came on the screen. Now, the spectators were being asked to respond to these cartoon figures in a new way and to share their feelings of desolation. A laugh at this point would have destroyed the whole concept. In the original version of this sequence, the audience had laughed at a crucial scene of Doc and Dopey. At that time, Dopey began the scene staring bleakly with misty eyes at the offstage Snow White, before turning away to bury his face in Doc's shoulder. It was a touching moment; however, the viewers' response to this shot of the usually jolly Dopey was an anticipatory laugh, one that quickly turned to confusion and then embarrassment, but by then the spell had been broken. Fortunately, this was easy to correct by cutting off the first part of the scene. How could anyone have known ahead of time? You cannot always do it right the first time; many things do not work the way they are "talked."

There was an unexpected bonus from this cut, because now Grumpy was the only dwarf with a major body move. He had been the last to give in to the girl, but he may have had the deepest feelings for her. Who

476

but Grumpy would be the one to sob openly at her bier? He could not have put his head on someone's shoulder like Dopey. True to his personality, he must turn away and cry alone.

The animator whose assignment was to make this all come to life said:

It just felt like they should all move as little as possible. These guys were consumed with grief and wouldn't be moving around. They'd have strong body attitudes that could be held for the most part, and maybe a sagging move on the head here and there, just enough to keep it alive. Even a sniff seemed too much action for the mood. Frank Churchill had written a great melody that really carried the sequence, and my problem was more of not breaking the spell than establishing how badly anyone felt. Sad eyes, slow blinks, and a few tears were all that was needed.

So we drew very carefully and packed in as many inbetweens as we possibly could—we didn't want any jitters, but we didn't want any short, jerky moves either—and we matched the timing of the tears to the contours of the faces. Unfortunately, my first tears were so well liked that more tears were asked for, and then even some on all the characters. Soon it looked like the worst hay fever epidemic of the century, which was not helped much by the eager Effects Department adding highlights and reflections and glistening effects, until each drop looked more like a marble than a tear. At this point, we backed up and eliminated a few. To me, there was more value in a tear-stained face than in all these rivulets soaking their collars, but no one could devise a way to create that effect. We settled for moist eyes, which they could do very effectively, and lots of lovely, shining tears running down the cheeks."[4]

These decisions proved to be right for the sequence, especially the decision to keep the dwarfs in nearly "held" positions. Their subdued attitudes contributed more to the working of the sequence than we realized

New techniques by the Effects Department and the Inkers and Painters created moist eyes and realistic tears to help the sincerity of the scenes.

at the time. Undoubtedly, Walt was a big influence in this also, for he had written in his famous memo to Don Graham in 1935,[5] "The animators don't make the held positions and the relaxed positions express anything. They try to do all the expression with the parts that are moving—whereas the body should enter into it." But the dwarfs did not let Walt down by making any false moves. The audience cried for the first time during an animated cartoon.

The film *Bambi* contained another reaction to death —this time very real—as the young fawn lost his mother to a hunter's bullet. A scene was animated of the doe actually being shot in the middle of a leap, throwing back her head and crashing to the ground where she lay collapsed in the snow, but it was cut out when we found that the sequence played better in the imagination. Everyone sensed the danger, knowing the hunters were near; and when the shot was heard it did not matter whether you knew the mother was dead or whether you were as innocent as Bambi, returning to search for her. It was powerful either way. The tiny figure in the midst of the huge trees helped the feeling of overpowering loss, and the quiet of the forest at this point contributed to the sensation of loneliness. The best idea, however, came about by accident. When the stag appeared, he was too much of a shock, visually. We wanted him to be impressive with a feeling of wisdom and compassion. Instead, he somehow looked ominous and threatening. He had to be in the sequence in some form, so the decision was made to cover him partially with falling snow, lightly at first, then heavier and heavier, so that in the final scene the stag would be only half visible. The snow also added an immense emotional dimension to the whole sequence. We looked at each other and said, "Why didn't we think of that in the first place?"

Twenty years later there was another sequence of characters crying over the apparent death of a young girl as the three Good Fairies bade a tearful farewell to Aurora, the sleeping beauty. Here, however, the story structure lacked the ingredients that would have allowed this to be a scene of strong emotion. The character relationships were not as important, and there was little concern over the fairies' attempts to thwart the evil prophecy. That point was not felt to be the important one in this later film. The animation was as well done as in the dwarfs' sequence, but, since it only illustrated what happened, it could not involve the audience. This is a vivid example of the importance of story structure in communicating an emotion.

These crucial feelings of the characters can be portrayed in many different ways. Besides using the structure of the story elements, there is the graphic presentation: the layouts, the settings, the cutting, the staging; and there are all the facets of the animation: the acting, the expressions, the dialogue, the attitudes. Story, graphic presentation, and animation are important enough to be considered separately.

Story—Structure

When the story is well designed, the emotions of the characters will be so logical and natural that little else should be needed to make them work with an audience. The wise storyman, however, also will learn how to use animation more effectively, and provide opportunities for dramatic graphics in the presentation.

The best example of a great sequence created entirely by story is found in *Cinderella*, as the Fairy Godmother appears. The girl has run into the garden in a dramatic long shot and is now sobbing with her head in her arms; her friends, the mice, are staring dumbly, along with the horse and the dog, and the only animation is found in the tiny sparkles of fairy dust gradually convening on the spot where the Godmother will appear. Yet, everyone in the audience has a lump in his throat, and it gets bigger and bigger as the scene progresses. This is all due to the careful story work that has preceded this point in the picture. The people in the audience know this girl, and what she wanted, and how she feels at this time. They also know her friends and what they were trying to do, and when this moment comes there is nothing more to be said. A simple scene of a girl sobbing, the helplessness in the faces of her friends, and the magical answer to all the problems quietly forming before us are all that is needed, or wanted. Anything more would be an intrusion.

Another sequence that relies more on story than animation is the one of Snow White running in panic through the woods after she has left the Huntsman. This reveals more of Walt's sense of how a thing should play and includes a very dramatic presentation

throughout, but it asks little of the animator. It is an effective sequence, arousing great emotion in the viewer by thrusting him into the situation along with the girl. It is the events that occur rather than the acting that involve him in this activity, but the considerations are just as detailed and complicated.

How long does it take to build Snow White's terror? How many incidents do we need to shock and scare? Do we lose or gain by showing, in her mind, the logs in the water that appear to become crocodiles with wide-open mouths? The faces in the trees are terrifying to both the audience and the girl, but how long should this be allowed to go on, beyond making the point of what she is seeing? How long should she be on the ground, sobbing, after the terror and panic in the woods, before she sees the eyes in the dark—eyes that gradually become innocent little animals? The audience is more than ready for the humor that comes as a release when the animals are curious about Snow White, and even a little frightened of her. This is an example of leading the audience through contrasting emotions, and giving just enough time to each, without moving too fast or becoming redundant.

There are many ways a character may be handled in a film, and it is largely the responsibility of the storyman to determine the most effective use of the role. If a story calls for the main character to be threatened by death some kind of killer must be introduced, but what type of person he is will depend upon the way the scenes are conceived. The Huntsman in *Snow White* became more real by having a suggestion of personality. His assignment was more than he could do, as it turned out, and there was more drama in his inner

In a strong story situation, very little movement is needed to sustain the mood. Cinderella's friends watch helplessly as the broken-hearted girl buries her head in her arms. The main action consists of the magic sparkles slowly gathering to form the Fairy Godmother.

turmoil than there would have been if he were only a visual symbol of a killer. The executioner in *Robin Hood* had no such role to play, so he was more ominous by being completely impersonal. His judgment was not involved in the decision to chop off Robin's head or to let him go, and the more he was presented as only a professional, with no emotions, and not even a face showing behind his mask, the greater the emotional impact he had on everybody. Once again, the sequence had not been built for melodrama up to this point, since this lighthearted version of the popular

OVERLEAF:

Snow White flees through the forest in panic after leaving the Huntsman. The planning of this very successful sequence is found in the storyboards. Dramatic staging and exciting images combine with the attitudes on the girl to involve the audience in her terror.

479

SEQ. 3A

SEQ-3B

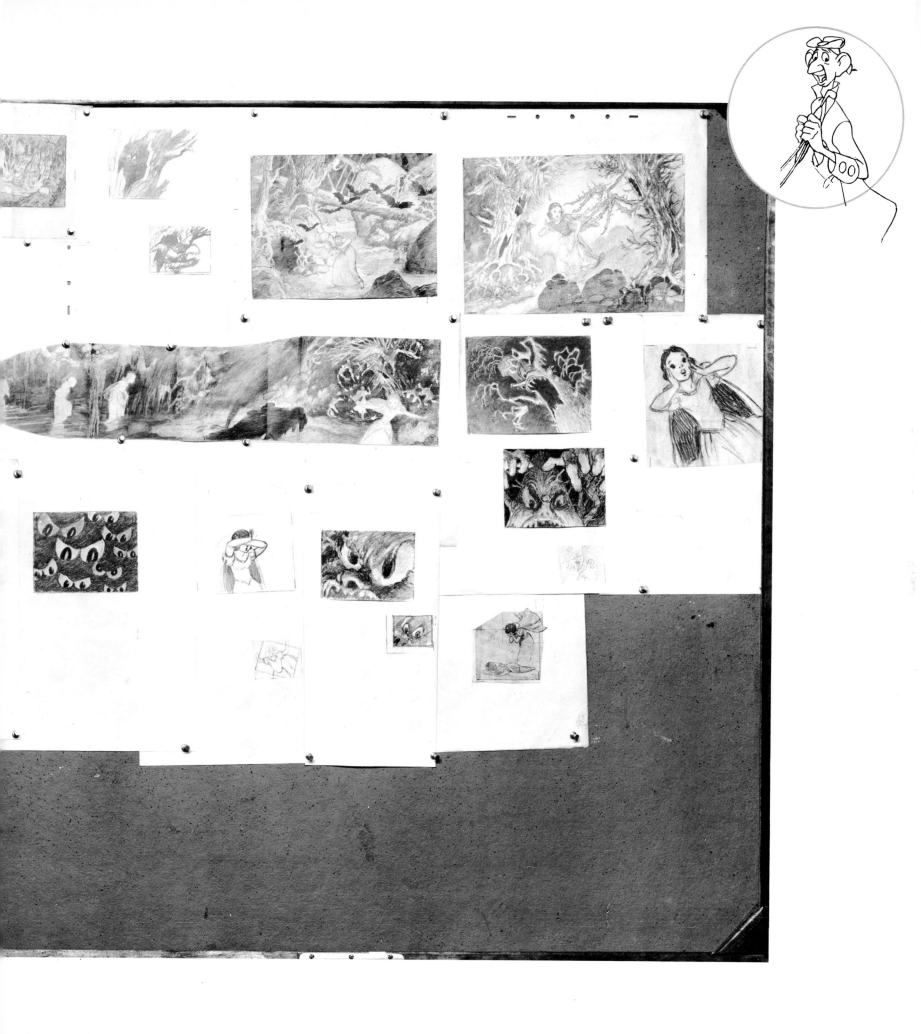

legend required only a momentary situation with the hero as a captive. However, the sinister feelings that the sequence did have were almost solely dependent upon this characterization of the executioner.

Killers can be presented in many other ways, each contributing its own values to the story. If the scene is shown entirely through the killer's eyes, revealing even more of his own feelings (or lack of feelings), there is still another dimension to the sequence. This perspective is often used, especially in live action, because it can show how cold-blooded, how methodical or diabolical the killer actually is; which, in turn, builds more concern for the intended victim. One approach is no better than another, since the key factor is what works best for the specific situation and what reaction is wanted from the audience.

If a scene calls for showing tense emotions such as anguish, scorn, bitterness, or envy with only facial expression, the animator will be quite limited. But if the story is built so that the character reveals these feelings in what he does and how he does it—reserving the close-ups only for emphasis—the scenes can be gripping and entertaining.

There is an inherent danger in animating scenes of inner struggle, because most attempts to achieve clear, concise communication cause the character to overact badly and lose credibility. More than beautiful drawing and expert analysis often is needed to keep the feeling of sincerity. A special effort on everyone's part is required to find just the right scenes to display the needed emotions, but it is worth the effort. The queen in *Snow White* was handled very realistically, as was the stepmother in *Cinderella*, and they communicated well. Both depended on careful drawing, exacting animation, and flawless scene planning to make them convincing; but with the story constructed so that

ARTIST: Marc Davis—
Sleeping Beauty.

482

ANIMATOR: *Ollie Johnston*—Robin Hood.

Prince John, in Robin Hood, *based on a traditional type of design, offered flexibility in the ways his personality could be defined. The evil fairy Maleficent, in* Sleeping Beauty, *had an aloof, ominous quality to her design; if she had been animated with the normal changes in these shapes her dramatic impact would have been lost.*

it depended on this meticulous type of work, there was no other way to do it. As the animators said, ''No fun to do, but needed for the picture!''

Maleficent, the evil fairy in *Sleeping Beauty*, showed her feelings in a more dramatic and flamboyant way, because the style of the whole presentation relied on design, color, and pageantry. This was reflected in her movements, which gave the animator slightly more latitude and freedom, but it was still an equally demanding drawing assignment. The scenes were impressive without losing believability. Just as much intensity of emotion was shown by Prince John in *Robin Hood*, but this sequence was structured for humor, so the animator could concentrate on the expressions and attitudes more than intricate drawing. As a result, it was more fun for the animator.

These characters showed hatred and scorn in their own way, but in a convincing manner. They were equally entertaining, but they were in no way interchangeable, which points up the importance of the storyman's knowing his characters and building his situations through them.

Graphic Presentation

Most of the examples we have discussed so far have not mentioned that each required an excellence in the presentation of the idea in addition to the story work. Seldom is emotion established on the screen only through story, graphic art, or animation by itself. Here we are separating them in an attempt to understand the extent of the contribution from each. ''Graphic presentation'' covers the cutting and staging, the planning, the design, the settings, the color—all of the pictorial components. Their goal is to build a make-believe world around the viewer, making him feel a certain way about what he sees. Every scene must say its message clearly with no confusion and no contradictions, but it must leave something to be imagined.

In *Bambi*, there is a stirring fight between two male deer. Beautiful animation was done of the battle, perfect in drawing and movement, but somehow it was not exciting. The plan had been to draw the audience into the fight by showing close-ups of horns and hooves and straining muscles, yet seeing all this tended to make it matter-of-fact. Walt had the answer: create a mood, make the scenes dark and dramatic, let everything go black, lose the little parts, and define the characters only by ''rim lighting.'' Use the music and sound effects instead of all that drawing. Immediately the sequence became tense and thrilling.

Dark figures of the fighting deer are made more intense and dramatic through the use of silhouettes with only streaks of ''rim lighting'' to define the forms. The less the audience sees, the more will be imagined.

483

Nine Economical Ways
that Animation Can Build Emotions
in the Imaginations of the Audience

Resist the temptation to make everything bigger and more gorgeous when you need strong communication.

1. REAR VIEW   Sleeping Beauty.

The two lovers look off into the distance and dream their private dreams. Since their feelings are better imagined than they could ever be shown in detail, the audience dreams along with them.

4. OVERLAYS   The Jungle Book.

Baloo is desperately searching for Mowgli who has just run away. Having Baloo partially covered by the branches in the background makes a more rewarding scene than trying to draw his distraught face.

5. DRAMATIC LAYOUT   The Ugly Duckling.

Overpowering shapes and a path of action going down the hill both add to the feeling of depression as the Ugly Duckling slowly walks away. The portrayal of his feelings relies on the layout that makes him look small and desolate.

8. HELD DRAWING
WITH CAMERA MOVES   101 Dalmatians.

Some expressions cannot be strengthened by movement. Instead of moving the character, a simulated feeling of activity was achieved by slowly moving the camera—in this case, trucking into a closer shot of the dog's eyes.

2. SHADOWS   Snow White.

Shadows are usually associated with suspense and drama. They can add interest and variety to a continuity while saving the time needed to draw all the detail on each character.

3. SHADOWS OVER THE CHARACTER   Bambi.

Faline watches transfixed as Bambi fights off the intruder. The excitement of the situation is better conveyed by her whole attitude, with the shadows of the action passing over her, than it could have been by just the concerned expression on her face.

6. PICTORIAL SHOT   Cinderella

Cinderella had been prevented from going to the royal ball. Her keen disappointment is best communicated by the romanticized view of the castle where she wants to be. A background with a strong mood can save difficult animation.

7. EFFECTS ANIMATION   Bambi.

Fine animation of forms from nature can establish a mood either by symbolism or showing what the character sees. Falling rain, a storm, approaching fire will quickly create strong feelings. The stark colors of these autumn leaves foretell the harshness of the approaching winter.

9. OFFSTAGE SOUNDS   Lady and the Tramp.

No animation is needed on a comprehensive shot of the locale if appropriate sounds can build images in the imagination. The entrance to the dog pound in Lady and the Tramp *looks forlorn and mournful enough, but it was hearing the howling and the barking and whining of the dogs inside that really told the story.*

485

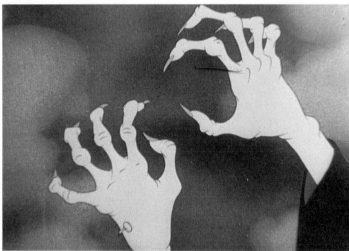

Some situations become more powerful by showing all the realistic detail. This is particularly true where magic or fantasy is involved. We were spellbound seeing the queen gradually become an old, withered witch.

In *The Rescuers*, there is a very important scene on the riverboat of the little girl leaving the cabin of the villainess Medusa and slowly walking up the stairs to the deck. She has just been badly hurt by Medusa's callous remark, ''Who would want a homely little girl like you?'' and is fighting back the tears as she walks out into the night. It was decided that the most effective way to play the scene would be from a rear view on the dimly lit stairs, featuring her very young age and her helplessness. Once on deck, she is bathed in soft moonlight.

When the picture was completed we wondered if we had made the best choices. Would it have been better if the stairwell had been completely dark, just a trickle of light coming down from above, with the girl's action shown only in silhouette? The situation called for the strongest mood we could create. When we saw these scenes completed in color and in continuity, they did not have the visual impact they could have had. They were dark and gloomy, but not dramatic. Perhaps this was not a place to be more dramatic, and maybe the silhouette treatment would not have been the best way either, but we still wonder.

In contrast to the benefits of not letting the spectators see everything, there are other times when forcing them to look at certain elements might create more visual excitement. When the queen in *Snow White* drank the potions that changed her into an old hag, there was emotional involvement because of the fear of the unknown. Watching this dramatic change before your very eyes held you spellbound and a little apprehensive of what you might see next. What will she turn into? Will it be something hideous? Will I want to look at it? This section was cut out of the picture in Sweden as being too frightening for children, which proves that, right or wrong, there was a strong emotional experience in the presentation of the material.

Another frightening series of scenes is found in *Pinocchio* in the sequence on Pleasure Island where unsuspecting boys are changed into donkeys in payment for a night of fun. This is a case where excellent animation added even more than had been expected, but it was the combination of the staging and planning that made this impossible situation so believable and so scary. The mood had been started with the scenes of the almost shapeless, all black, faceless workers who

We watched Pinocchio's friend Lampwick turn into a donkey right before our eyes.

In contrast, the faceless workers on Pleasure Island were more frightening because we could not see who they were.

were closing the gates and crating the donkeys, and then a great voice track, along with the realistic handling of the backgrounds, the effects, the shadows, and all the details, kept the audience so involved that their eyes never left the screen. The whole film would have been so much weaker and flaccid without this emotional surge to give it the necessary importance and to make the fantasy so stirring.

Animation—Acting

The storyman can develop the right business for the character to perform, and the director and layout man can stage it and make the presentation graphically satisfying, but it is the animator who must think deeply into the personality of the cartoon actors. Each must be handled differently, because each individual will express his emotions in his own way.

The self-appointed leader of the dwarfs, Doc, would show defiance in a way different from that of Grumpy. He would have blustery, nervous movements, and take shorter steps. He never would swing his arms as Grumpy did in his defiant walk after Snow White had kissed him. That walk, and the gradual stop as he smiled, showing his true feelings, were part of the artful delineation of a personality in both story and animation. The conception was thorough in all respects: the staging of the expressions, the use of fundamental principles like squash and stretch, the amount of time used to show each emotion before moving on to the next one—these show animation at its best.

The audience became involved in these scenes because of its understanding of the characters and the feelings that were so familiar to everyone. But there are other ways of involving the viewers besides getting them to identify with sympathetic characters. The devil in *Fantasia*'s "Night on Bald Mountain" was anything but sympathetic, and his feelings were beyond our comprehension, yet the scenes involved the audiences, drew them in, caused them to react to what they were seeing. To point up the difference, one has only to imagine the sensations that would have been aroused if, during this awesome ritual, a young boy and girl had been seen as two tiny figures trying to climb the inner walls of that volcanic mountain without being discovered, or perhaps progressing deeper into that fiery cauldron on some important quest. Your heart would be in your mouth as you tried to scale those stones with them, and you would jump at each sign of possible detection. You react *to* the evil characters, but *with* the sympathetic characters.

The same is true of Cruella deVil in *101 Dalmatians*, and she is a comic villain. Few of us could share her compulsion to skin puppies to make a fur coat, yet we were completely involved in her sequences. Because of our fascination with her explosive personality and our enjoyment of her outlandish behavior, appearance, and actions, she was funny without losing either her menacing quality or her audience. Whether people thought she was horrid, ridiculous, or wonderful, they all sat enraptured.

In the next example, we are involved through our

487

Story sketches for Ichabod Crane *(1949) by Joe Rinaldi. Joe had a flair for bold, dramatic staging and could make cartoon characters fit into awesome environments quite naturally.*

appreciation of a situation and share the sensations of the character, but without any sense of identification with him. This is the case with the rather unsavory Ichabod Crane as he rides the old plowhorse into the terrors of Sleepy Hollow. That sequence made animator Blaine Gibson decide to leave the Effects Department for the dramatic challenges of character animation. The superstitious Ichabod gets increasingly agitated the farther he progresses into the hollow, but his sleepy steed is barely alert enough to stay awake. It reminded Blaine of his own experience as a boy in eastern Colorado. ''Ichabod, and this horse, and the guy whistling—this is a cartoon, but I can empathize with this guy because I've been on a horse out on the farm at night when I wanted to whistle, because I'd heard some noise and I wouldn't know what it was— and, also, the way the horse went! Somebody took the trouble to analyze . . . what horses look like. It *looked* like a horse. These are the things that, to me, made the difference between good and bad animation. It's taking the trouble to put that little thing in there.'' The animator on that particular section had indeed known horses, and he had suffered more than his share of miserable experiences in trying to get unresponsive nags to behave like the wonder horse of the cowboy movies.

This point in the picture certainly had been well structured in the story development, and the presentation was well suited to the situation, but it was the animation itself that carried audiences along. They saw the fear in Ichabod's eyes and in his whole attitude, and, as he licked his lips and swallowed, they could feel the sensation of the dry mouth from his extreme apprehension. The musician Ollie Wallace made an enormous contribution when he recorded his own whistling for Ichabod's feeble attempts to keep up his courage as he came closer and closer to panic, and the story sketch man Joe Rinaldi had done a masterful

ANIMATOR: *Frank Thomas*—
Ichabod Crane *(later combined with* Mr. Toad.*)*

The animator carries the ideas a step further with more care given to size relationships and specific business.

series of drawings exploring every possible position for a tall, skinny man trying to hide on top of a horse. So the animator had great help in getting started, but the burden of the development and the entertainment in the acting rested on his shoulders alone.

Once the Headless Horseman appeared, the whole mood changed to wild, tumbling, comic panic, with both Ichabod and his horse frantically defying all the natural laws of weight and gravity—in a very believable way. The screen fairly exploded with their feelings of desperation as they slithered and scrambled on their bellies, the horse so low that the rider was half-riding and half-running himself. The viewers did not really care whether Ichabod got away or not, but they were completely caught up in the excitement of the chase

Joe Rinaldi suggests an outlandish gag for the wild chase by the Headless Horseman. By this time, Ichabod's panic was so intense the audience could almost believe his legs could hold a horse during a turn.

ANIMATOR: *John Sibley—* The Adventures of Ichabod and Mr. Toad.

Consumed with fear, both horse and rider scramble on their bellies to elude the slashing sword of the Headless Horseman. Animator John Sibley could make any action funny as well as believable.

and were thoroughly involved in the whole situation.

Such sequences are particularly tricky to do because of the need for the tempo to be maintained and the action to become more and more tense, so the scenes will build continuously to an ever-greater pitch of excitement. An action that is just too slow, or a choice of business that is too ordinary, can kill the overall effect. Story structure cannot do much to help in this case. The layouts and settings and the cutting play a more important part, along with the constant experimentation, correction, and revision of the animation. The sequence must be kept loose until it really works.

In *Cinderella*, there was the classic sequence of two mice trying to carry a large and heavy key up two long flights of stairs in order to free Cinderella from her room before the Grand Duke had left with the glass slipper. The characters had been well established so that their determination and emotions were quite clear, but the tension of their tremendous effort, which exhausted the audience almost as much as the mice, was all in the animation. No one could deny that the spectators shared the sentiments of the cartoon characters completely.

Back in 1935, Walt had asked some provocative questions about just this type of action. "When someone is lifting a heavy weight, what do you feel? Do you feel that something is liable to crack any minute and drop down? Do you feel that because of the pressure he's got, he's going to blow up, that his face is going to turn purple, that his eyes are going to bulge out of their sockets, that the tension in the arm is so terrific that he's going to snap?"

Fifteen years later, these questions were well answered by Woolie Reitherman as he animated this sequence. There is no doubt that the key was too heavy for the two little mice, that the pressure on them, mentally and physically, was tremendous, that at any minute Gus's eyes could bulge out of their sockets or that Jaq's face could turn purple. The timing of these actions gave the frantic quality, and the strength of the extreme drawings gave the impression of effort and exhaustion.

The most important element in making the sequence so outstanding, however, was the fact that these little mice were doing all of this because they cared very much about the girl's happiness. Usually, this feeling of warmth cannot be structured in the Story Department and must depend entirely on the animator for its portrayal, but it remains a very mercurial sensation. A note cannot be pinned to the storyboard saying, "Get warmth through here," nor can it be written as an action on the exposure sheet, "Animate 3 feet of warmth." It cannot be analyzed, or acted out, or represented in the same way as an expression or a passing thought, since it is more of a sentiment that grows within the viewer from the special way the business has been animated; actually, it grows from the sensitivity of the animator who makes the drawings. It is undoubtedly one of the most important factors in bringing the audience close to the characters.

Desperation will not be displayed always through frantic action or panic. At times, it is numbing despair, and that presents an even greater challenge to the animator. In *101 Dalmations*, it became necessary to have a very delicate, sincere, and convincing sequence showing the expectant female dalmatian Perdita reacting to the news that Cruella deVil is planning to take all of her puppies as soon as they are born. The storyman had felt that a dog's normal reaction would be to hide somewhere in the house, in some location that offered a tiny sense of protection. He made a drawing of her under the kitchen stove, way back in the corner. This was Perdita's emotional response to the near-panic she felt at the thought of losing her puppies to this horrible

woman. She could do nothing but remain passive. The mice in *Cinderella* at least could temper their panic by doing something. In their desperate plight there was still a chance to reverse the situation if they just could get the key there in time. For Perdita, there was no such chance. On the storyboard, the drawings were impressive and gave a good, subdued feeling to the touching situation. The voices were recorded, and they, too, were effective, adding sincerity and concern. But they were "straight." The characters themselves were "straight."

At the story meeting, there was apprehension expressed about the difficulty of animating such a sequence. There was nothing to get hold of to caricature. The voice talent had given a beautiful, dramatic reading of the lines, charged with emotion, but that type of tension is difficult to represent. Even the voice of Pongo, the male dog, though soothing and comforting, could give no emphasis or strong attitude to suggest an action that could be animated. And, to top it all off, the scene was set beneath a stove, in an area so restricted that the characters could not even raise their heads or shift position to accent the words in the dialogue. How could we possibly make the audience believe the dogs were talking if we could not move them, and how could we make the sequence convincing if the animation did not hold up? It was all too subtle and delicate.

There is always this problem with the "straight" characters who lack the flexibility in design and personality to allow much more than a rigid illustration. Thinking back on *The Ugly Duckling*, we recalled wistfully how that character did not have to be "straight" and that his mournful honking brought laughs along with the tears. Now, the story material was of a different sort. For this picture to be successful, there had to be extremely convincing, heroic action, not from a

queen or an evil devil but from four-legged creatures with animal faces that were not designed, even by nature, to communicate delicate expressions. Perdita was not flamboyant enough to have feelings other than motherly concern, anxiety, and occasional hope, while Pongo was simply Mr. Average Nice Guy, trying to get along in a difficult situation. Their roles were basically designed to hold the story together so that the broad characters surrounding them could work. These two characters had to be convincing for the rest of the cast to be entertaining. A stern assignment. But if no one believed the sincerity of the dogs' concern, no one

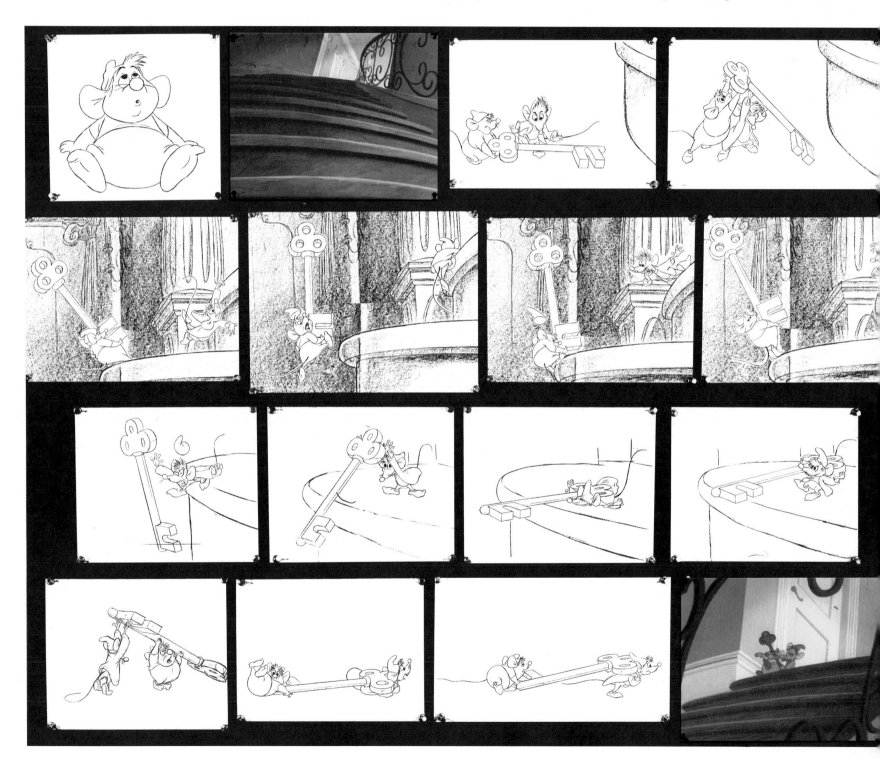

would believe Cruella. And if no one took her seriously, she would not be a villain. The sequence had to be in the picture. Finally, one animator thought he could see a way to do it.[6] Immediately, it was dumped in his lap.

In the first two scenes, the animator featured the pictorial value of the hiding place, with only such action as was needed to get the dogs in position. He chose an angle on the stove so that the leg visually would separate the hiding Perdita from Pongo, who wanted to help but did not know how. The presentation was simple and underplayed, letting the picture of

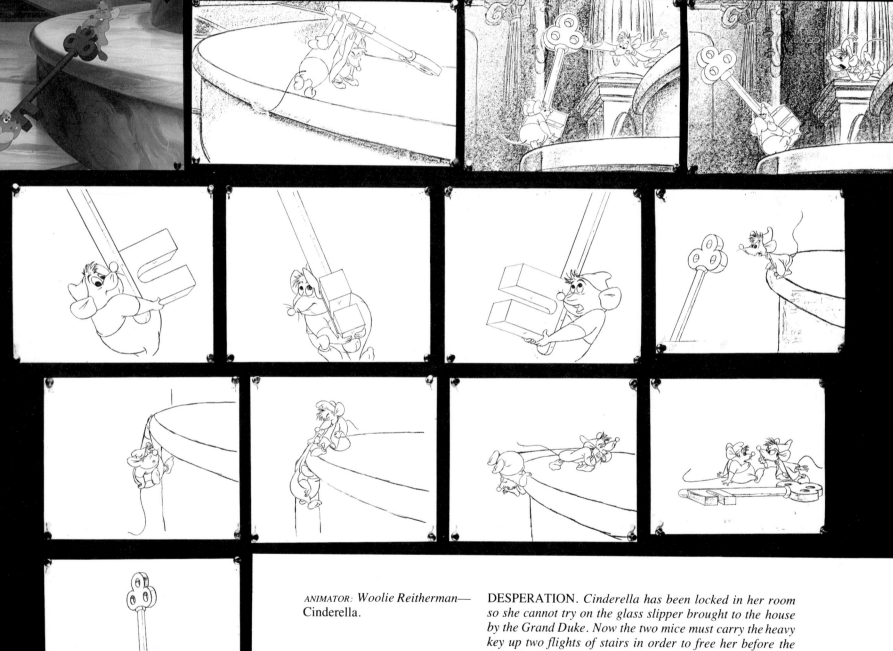

ANIMATOR: *Woolie Reitherman*— Cinderella.

DESPERATION. *Cinderella has been locked in her room so she cannot try on the glass slipper brought to the house by the Grand Duke. Now the two mice must carry the heavy key up two flights of stairs in order to free her before the Grand Duke leaves.*

The animator's assignment. *Get a frantic feeling of tense activity, suspense, effort, and determination in the scenes individually and in sequence.*

493

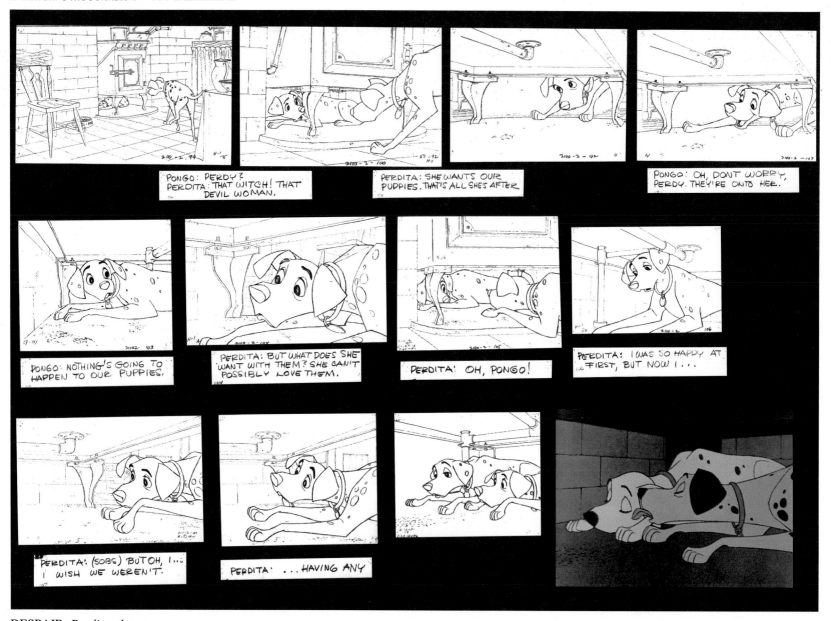

PONGO: PERDY?
PERDITA: THAT WITCH! THAT DEVIL WOMAN.

PERDITA: SHE WANTS OUR PUPPIES. THAT'S ALL SHE'S AFTER.

PONGO: OH, DON'T WORRY, PERDY. THEY'RE ONTO HER.

PONGO: NOTHING'S GOING TO HAPPEN TO OUR PUPPIES.

PERDITA: BUT WHAT DOES SHE WANT WITH THEM? SHE CAN'T POSSIBLY LOVE THEM.

PERDITA: OH, PONGO!

PERDITA: I WAS SO HAPPY AT FIRST, BUT NOW I...

PERDITA: (SOBS) BUT OH, I... I WISH WE WEREN'T.

PERDITA: ...HAVING ANY

DESPAIR. *Perdita, the expectant mother, has just learned that the evil Cruella deVil plans to take all of the puppies shortly after they are born. The unhappy dog hides under the kitchen stove while her mate Pongo tries to comfort her.*

The animator's assignment. *Get a feeling of helplessness and apprehension on the mother dog, but keep her in a very confined area. Pongo's attempt to console Perdita must be restrained and gentle, but sincere.*

the dog under the stove tell the story. The next scenes featured Pongo's difficulty in getting under the stove, which forced him into interesting and different actions. The audience became more aware of his attempts to get near his mate than of his mouth movements in phrasing the dialogue. It never occurred to anyone that this was a restricted or subtle scene. The concern of the dogs for each other, and for their unborn pups, was all anyone saw. Once the camera was under the stove, it was possible to have a little more movement on Perdita since the new angle was not so restrictive. She lifted her head to inhale, looked away, and sank down in a defeated sigh. Pongo reached out and licked her

gently on the cheek. The audience believed them both and felt the warmth of their relationship, as well as their concern for what the future might bring.

Depicting love between two cartoon characters is even more difficult than warmth; it is possibly the most elusive emotion to portray. Like the sensation of warmth, love is built almost solely through the animator's personal feelings about the drawings he is making. No one can say exactly which drawing, or which scene, or which action has sold the idea because they are so subtly related; it is only the sum total of the ingredients that creates the illusion.

There is one particular component in our pictures,

The sincere handling of the deer in Bambi made any expression of love very elusive. Instead of subtle acting, fantasy was used with a romantic setting, soaring music, and the glow of moonlight.

Bongo was the little circus bear who had to learn the ways of the wilds. For his romance with a helpful girl bear, a much lighter handling was appropriate, with an imaginative use of valentines and other symbols of sweethearts.

quietly enriching our emotional and dramatic movements, that has gone by nearly unnoticed. This is the delicate contact between our characters—the touching. This always has been a big part of the theater and of live action films, usually affecting the spectators emotionally. Two lovers hold hands for the first time, or there is an unexpected coming together in a tense situation—the contact breathes a special excitement. There must be a subconscious reason for this response, going back to earliest man, since it is observed today

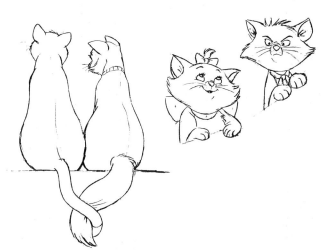

Two characters touch in an unexpected way and a special sensation is transmitted to the audience. In Aristocats, instead of holding hands, Duchess and O'Malley hold tails, which is anatomically impossible, but helped the audience understand the cats' emotions. The romance was further fortified by showing the reactions of the young kittens to their mother's love affair.

495

Once again story sketches by Marc Davis influence the final handling of the scenes.

Another act of touching with a comic result. When the adult Thumper met a gorgeous female rabbit, his reaction was an uncontrollable thumping of his hind leg. Only a soothing touch on the nose could calm him down.

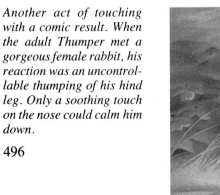

as a prime factor in the communication between chimpanzees in the wild.[7] It seems to be vital to the emotional stability of the individual, having more importance than we understand. We know only that there can be intense drama in this simple act of touching.

Actually, physical contact was at the center of most of the early shorts, with kicking, biting, hitting, and every type of violent contact imaginable the basis for most gags. But it was not until we had the believable characters in *Snow White* that anyone realized how provocative the act of touching could be. No one could

When Merlin, the wizard in The Sword in the Stone, *changed himself into a squirrel, he had no idea he would be so attractive to a gushy, old female. This action went beyond mere touching.*

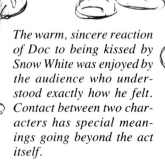

The warm, sincere reaction of Doc to being kissed by Snow White was enjoyed by the audience who understood exactly how he felt. Contact between two characters has special meanings going beyond the act itself.

have guessed how much the audience would be moved by mere drawings of the girl kissing the dwarfs.

A few years later, this touching between two cartoon characters had a special impact far beyond anything the story crew had imagined. The film was *Dumbo*, the story of the unfortunate baby elephant with the enormous ears. When his mother had tried to defend him from the torments of a group of boys, she had been labeled a "Mad Elephant" and chained inside the battered old wagon that served as a jail for recalcitrant animals.

ANIMATOR: Bill Tytla— Dumbo.

LOVE BETWEEN MOTHER AND CHILD. *Timothy Mouse takes the forlorn Dumbo to visit his mother who is kept chained inside a wagon. The two elephants cannot see each other and can touch only with their trunks.*
The animator's assignment. *Get a tender, poignant series of scenes that show how much Dumbo and his mother miss each other, and how much even this limited contact with her means to him.*

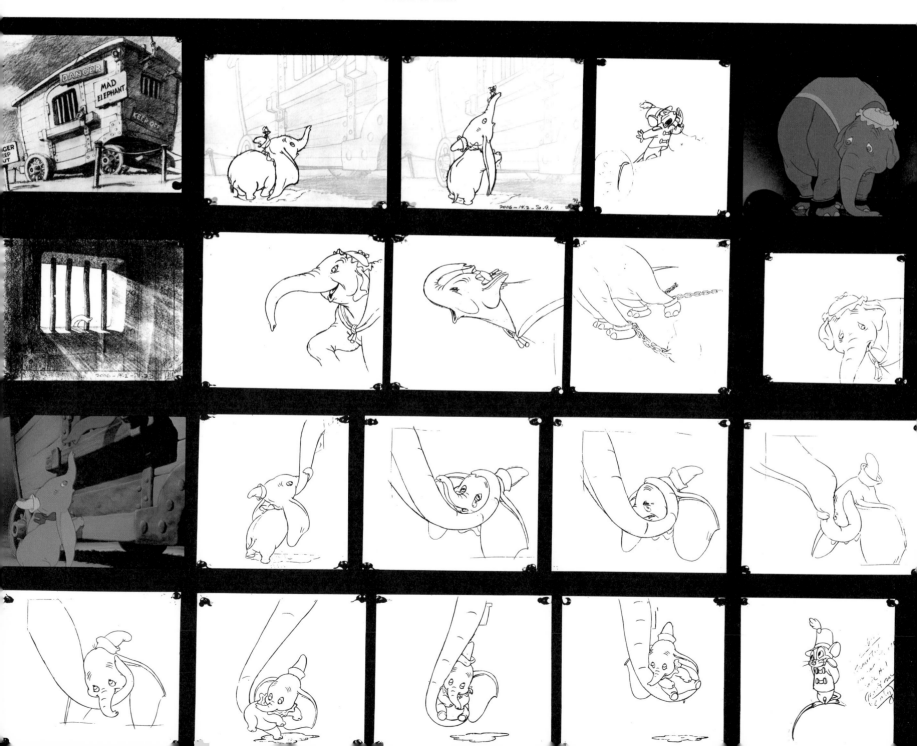

ANIMATORS: *Frank Thomas, Tramp and Lady; John Lounsbery, Tony and Joe—* Lady and the Tramp.

FALLING IN LOVE. *The dog of the world, Tramp, has taken a young lady from a sheltered background to his favorite dining place behind a restaurant. Instead of the handouts he expects, the romantic proprietor and his cook serve them the specialty of the house complete with musical accompaniment.*

The animator's assignment. Two dogs are to fall in love while eating a plate of spaghetti (in a refined manner). Make the audience believe that this really could happen.

Without his mother, Dumbo's problems had increased, and he was soon in deep despair. His friend Timothy Mouse suggested that they pay her a visit in the quiet of the night, when everyone else was asleep. Dumbo stood on tiptoe to try to see his mother, but he was too small to reach up to the one window in the wagon, and she was chained so that she could not come any closer to him. Only their trunks could reach far enough to touch and caress. It remains one of the most tender sequences ever animated, yet one of the most unlikely. With nothing to draw but a couple of wormlike trunks groping about, it would seem that the animator would have been completely defeated before he began, but Bill Tytla had this assignment and he felt the emotions very strongly. His handling of Dumbo tearfully hugging his mother's trunk and then gently swinging on it made this sequence outstanding for sensitivity, delicacy, and good judgment. Every move is so full of love and the artist's feelings are so genuine that nobody laughs, nobody questions.

Lady and the Tramp was another picture with a strange set of ingredients that had to be brought together in a way that said "Love." Two dogs eating spaghetti while being serenaded by a couple of romantic chefs with mandolin and accordion did not seem like the most appealing situation for a romance. Besides, the comedy implicit in the whole broad story concept, the very thought of dogs digging into a plate of pasta, sounded unattractive and crude. Even Walt was not sure this would not defeat the main story point here—that the dogs were falling in love.

The rear of the restaurant where Tramp usually got a bone or two was not a romantic setting, but it did fit the realism of the dogs looking for a handout. The surprise began when Tony, the owner, saw that the second dog was a lady of class and deserved something better than a bone. He ordered his assistant to serve them "the best in the house," complete with tablecloth and dishes. Next came the music, and with it the challenge to the animators. Could the human characters convince the audience that this was a real situation? Could the actual eating be entertaining? Could Lady be made appealing and attractive and dainty while consuming long strands of spaghetti?

Lady and the Tramp

499

Backgrounds for *Lady and the Tramp*

ANIMATOR: *Milt Kahl*—
The Sword in the Stone.

Even teapots have feelings in the world of fantasy. This one was belligerent and needed constant correcting from Merlin.

Nothing was inanimate to Albert Hurter. He could find a face and a personality in everything around him.

Tramp's gift of the last meatball, animated the way it was, is a charming indication of his love for her. It is not a sure-fire message of affection, but the gentle way he pushed it toward her and his expression as he looked at her left no doubt about his feelings. This demonstration of his love was set up by the unexpected contact as they chewed their way to each other on a single strand of spaghetti. The excitement of that moment demanded a reaction on his part. It relied on the build-up in the preceding scenes, and on the fact that the dogs believed it all themselves. This was actually a big evening to them and not a farce or a gag. Once that point was established, everything else in the rest of the picture followed naturally. If we had failed to make this relationship believable for the main characters, none of their later actions would have had the ring of sincerity needed for this type of story.

Sincerity is the key word when conveying emotions through characters that must be believable. More than one animator has had imaginative suggestions for business and actions that fit the personalities and the situa-

tion superbly, but their animation has lacked the sincerity to give these ideas the impact they should have on the screen. They might have been intellectually perfect—but emotionally barren.

The animator has three very special problems in the field of acting, and they cannot be ignored. First, he must know what the character should do in a particular circumstance. Second, he must be skillful enough as a craftsman to capture in drawings what he knows in his head. Third, he must be able to retain the fleeting, delicate thought of the moment over the several days it may take to animate the scene. When the actor on the stage feels right about an attitude or an action, he does it and the moment passes. Somehow, the animator has to stop time while he captures that elusive moment, dissects it, recreates it, and gets it all down on paper. The live actor does not have an easy time, but at least he can walk through a part, test ideas, try different approaches, stronger attitudes, bits of business, and make his changes all at the same time. When an animator "walks through a scene," it will be two weeks before he can see a test; and when the director says, "No-o-o, it's not working," it is much more difficult and expensive to try the scene another way.

All of the animator's skills are brought to play in creating true emotions: his knowledge of the fundamentals, of story, character development, action analysis, acting; this is the highest form of the art.

It makes little difference whether the characters who have these feelings are humans, animals, make-believe creatures, or even inanimate objects given a personality. In each case, the procedures of establishing audience identification through a special type of communication are the same, although there is admittedly more of a problem in getting people to care about an old shoe or a garbage can. To get individuals concerned about the emotions of a fantasy character is also somewhat of a challenge.

Most people have feelings of some sort about a living creature like a dog or a bear or even a mouse, because these animals do possess definite personalities of their own. But outside of a very personal experience or two, most people do not have the same feelings about a hat (*Johnny Fedora and Alice Bluebonnet*), or a tugboat (*Little Toot*), or a car (*Susie, the Little Blue Coupe*). In some cases, such as the brooms in

502

When animator Hardie Gramatky left the Studio and moved to New York, his apartment window looked out on the tugboats on the East River. Almost immediately he found a character like those he had animated. He called it Little Toot, sold the story to Walt, then went on to write book after popular book about the adventures of the youthful tugboat.

A steam shovel entertains the spectators.

Bill Peet found faces and attitudes in the parts of the object he was drawing when he did the various cars for Susie, the Little Blue Coupe. *The broom from "Sorcerer's Apprentice" in* Fantasia *needed neither face nor character development. The boy and girl in* Musicland *had faces superimposed on their bodies with no attempt to make the design come from the instrument itself.*

503

ANIMATOR: *Bob Wickersham*
—Thru the Mirror.

A happy-go-lucky tele-phone answers his own ring, then talks to himself.

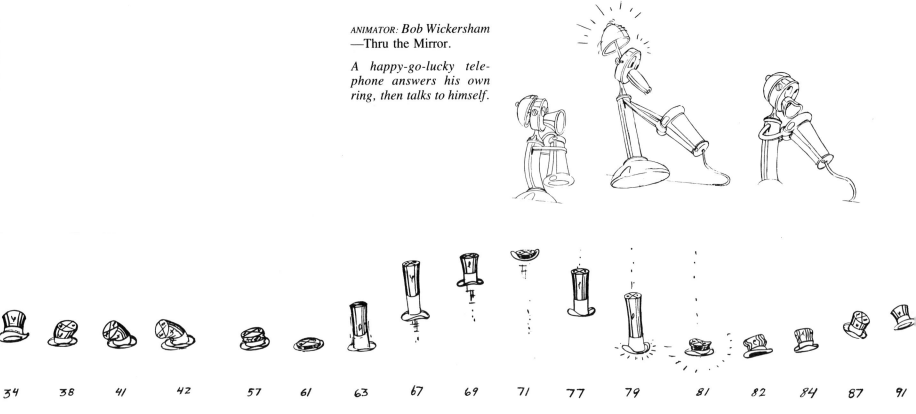

34   38   41   42   57   61   63   67   69   71   77   79   81   82   84   87   91

ANIMATOR: *Norm Ferguson*

Fantasia's ''Sorcerer's Apprentice,'' it was important that they be living and active, but have no feelings and no means of communication. In others, such as the doorknob in *Alice in Wonderland*, the specific personality and suggestions of the friendly but unhelpful doorknob were very necessary to the situation.

In many cases, the personality will be suggested by the job the object normally performs. A steamboat whistle is big and authoritative. It is almost impossible to think of a shy one. A rocking chair is matronly, or gossipy, and a bench would be robust and healthy, unless it is an old, decrepit one outdoors in a park.

Some objects have potential faces in their basic design, as in cars, with either the headlights or a divided windshield being the eyes, while on others there must be a face created and superimposed (*Musicland*). There is much more charm and conviction in a character if the eyes and mouth can grow out of the natural appearance, such as the telephone in *Thru the Mirror*, but when this is not possible great care should be taken to make the additions as believable as possible. Sometimes the character is more provocative without a face at all, if his whole being can convey the pantomime to show his attitudes. The magician's hat that Pluto encounters in *Mickey's Grand Opera* needs nothing more to show its reaction to this big dog intruding in such an offensive way. A face would have been wrong, because it would have destroyed the elements of fantasy that made the hat so entertaining.

Many people insist that most of the machines in their lives have personalities that are clearly apparent: the elevator that works only when it wants to (and goes particularly slow when its occupant is in a hurry); the car that will not start (or seems to sulk when not treated just right); the door that always sticks when it can cause the most trouble; the typewriter that continually reverses letters in the words—we are surrounded by objects that do seem to have minds of their own. To find the face in the design of these objects, and one that expresses the feelings that we already have sensed, is the problem for the artist. To move the parts of this design so that it has a suitable personality and seems believable is the problem of the animator.

The Illusion of Life

In the final sequence of *The Rescuers*, the villainess Medusa is being pulled behind the swampmobile by a rope. She is bouncing and splashing around as she is

504

dragged along and takes quite a beating. We all suggested additional gags that would make the situation even funnier, but the director hesitated: ''I don't want more gags; I want to know how she is feeling about this. Let's put in a close-up of her face as she comes up out of the water—the action is funnier if we've seen what she's thinking!''

This incident illustrates the drive that has run through all the Disney films, the way of thinking about entertainment that led to such a high degree of art in the animation. An interviewer asks:

''What's funny about a hat sneaking up on a dog?''

''It depends on the hat's personality—what kind of a guy he is.''

''Then how do you make a hat into a believable character?''

''The same way you made a crude cartoon dog into Pluto. By showing the emotions. How else do you get life into anything?''

Veteran artist Mel Shaw added a thought, ''It is a personal thing. You're taking the whole personality and character and making that person believable in motion and E-motion. That's the art of animation for me.''

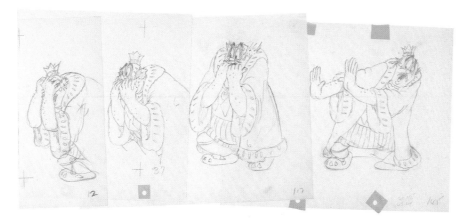

From the earliest days, it has been the portrayal of emotions that has given the Disney characters the illusion of life.

505

Cruella deVil rivaled Donald Duck for emotional outbursts and temperamental tantrums.

With all of the forms of outstanding entertainment devised by Walt Disney, the most original and unusual contribution is still this quality of life with which he endowed all of his characters. From the first bashful Mickey, hoping for a kiss from Minnie, down through the growing fear and panic that King Midas felt as he realized he was going to starve to death because of his greed, to the dramatic richness of seven bachelor miners falling in love with an innocent young girl, it has been the characters' emotions that have made the Disney films great.

The animators at the Disney studio have created many great characters over some fifty years of picture-

making, characters that have motivated stories, brought sequences to life, and endeared themselves to audiences around the world. There is something of magic in the whole process that comes from the very act of creativity, individually and collectively, that transcends the single steps of production. It is more than a drawing and more than an idea. Possibly it is the love we feel for characters so heroic, so tender and funny and exciting—all of them entertaining, yet each different, each thinking his own thoughts, and experiencing his own emotions. That is what makes them so real, and that is what makes them so memorable. It is also what gives them the astounding illusion of life.

Lady and the Tramp

Points to Remember When Animating Emotions

1. Make sure the emotional state of the character is clearly defined.
2. The thought process reveals the feeling. Sometimes it can be shown with a single, held drawing or a simple move. Other times there should be gestures, body moves, or full action. Determine which is best in each case.
3. Be alert to use of cutting and camera in helping to accentuate the emotion.
4. Ask yourself constantly:
   What am I trying to say here?
   What do I really want to show?
   How do I want the audience to react?
5. Use the element of *time* wisely:
   to establish the emotion of the character,
   to convey it to the viewers,
   to let them savor the situation.
   Don't be ponderous, but don't take it away from them just as they start to enjoy it.

18. Other Types of Animation —and the Future

"We're searching here, trying to get away from the cut and dried handling of things all the way through— everything—and the only way to do it is to leave things open until we have completely explored every bit of it."

Walt Disney

Not all the Disney films depended on the illusion of life for their success. Walt was interested in entertainment, and that broad field included more than stories told through believable characters. He loved to see actions that moved in perfect sync with music, flowing or accenting or surging, wherever the sound led. He sought beauty, not only as a background for a storytelling episode but for itself, in design and colors and mood. He enjoyed making the comedies full of gags, and he liked to create new characters, but he also wanted to try films where the story was subordinate to the graphics, pictures without gags, with just the good feeling he got out of seeing great artwork. He told his crew at an early meeting on the "Nutcracker Suite" sequence in *Fantasia*, "It should be something beautiful and something fantastic—a will-o'-the-wisp feeling."

It was the audiences who selected the cute, round, anthropomorphic animals with rich personalities as the type of characters they liked best. This may have represented the most difficult and highest form of our art, but it was by no means the only product of either the studio or Walt's fertile imagination.

The notes from the story meetings on *Fantasia* reveal the way he went about trying to capture a new and illusive concept. "If we don't attempt to weave story here, it will be more enjoyable. . . . Our overall effect is the most important thing." In the "Nutcracker Suite," Walt did not want to waste footage on showing the Nutcracker and the girl watching this series of dances (as was done in the original ballet), but, instead, he was looking for something in each section interesting in itself. "It's the fairyland thing we are picturing."

He had thought of the Chinese dance as something with a group of lizards wearing flowers in the shape of coolie hats, and the Russian dance as more comic, using turtles with their heads going in and out. Several of our finest artists were working on this and were, daily, presenting ideas and drawings, everything from the characters' appearance to the whole visual concept. Although Walt liked many of their suggestions, there was still something missing; just handsome artwork was not enough.

He had often said, "When I'm interested in something, I want to see what's going on," and that ex-

FACING PAGE:
101 Dalmations

Sketch for Mushroom Dance—"*Nutcracker Suite*," Fantasia.

One of the hundreds of mushroom sketches that helped a tiny idea grow into one of the great moments in the Disney films.

pressed as well as anything his dissatisfaction with these early drawings. There was not enough "going on." There was not enough of an idea, yet, for a picture to be started.

Then, one day he saw a drawing of a mushroom that Elmer Plummer had made. Walt immediately saw a potential that far surpassed anything that could have been done with the lizards. He started talking of how a mushroom even looked Chinese, how it could do a certain type of dance, and soon he had added another mushroom who was always out of step and causing trouble for the whole group. This did not happen in a day, or all in one meeting, but it did become a solid, unified idea that even without a story would hold anyone's interest. Walt said, ". . . people will remember it—every time they look at a mushroom after that they'll try to see those Chinese."

At the same time, he was developing his thoughts on the other dances, searching for ideas that matched the music. He liked the tiny fairies moving from plant to plant making everything sparkle and glisten as they waved their wands: first the dewdrop fairies "make the spider web look like it's made of pearls—their

own light follows these fairies around—all that lights it up is the fairies."

Then Walt began to wonder if they could represent the seasons and group certain effects together on that basis. "That's where we bring in Fall—and bring in the wind and the seed pods—but don't try to tell a story—just the three seasons. . . . Those big brown leaves drop down and whirl around making patterns of movement against the wind from the sky." Rather than a story, it was a progression of ideas that built to pictures and movements, which were increasingly more interesting.

The music was helping the idea more than anyone realized, by giving a structure and a development of thematic material that, in itself, carried the audience along. Possibly lesser music would have lacked the strength to sustain so much picture footage; certainly when *Fantasia* is run without sound it seems vague and lacking in purpose or direction.

When all the right ingredients had been found, there was an amazingly complete unit of entertainment. Music, design, action, and color all worked together, reflecting a unity of thought that combined authority with beauty. It was not shallow or merely "pretty," and the ideas were not scattered in a hodgepodge presentation. It was exciting.

Even more adventurous was the visual interpretation of Bach's "Toccata and Fugue," which had no representation of real forms, only colors and shapes and movement that matched the feeling of the music. Walt had stated, "We don't want to follow what anyone else has done in the abstract. We have never dealt in the abstract; we have given things a reason for existing, and tried to convince the audience that it could happen, or was possible."[1] Now he had to feel his own way into this new area and find pictures that would do more than just dazzle or stimulate; they would have to reach an audience and hold its interest.

As all the parts began to relate, Walt became more enthusiastic over the possibilities in these experimental ideas, which were far ahead of anyone's thinking. The artists had created startling new visual effects, the technicians were putting things on film that scarcely could be believed, the music tracks were exciting, and Fantasound, the new sound system developed especially for this show, was a whole experience in itself. Walt was fascinated: "... if we can get what we're after here, on the screen, with that music put over the way we can put it over—I believe it's going to knock everybody out; they just won't believe it. It's an entirely new field opened up for our medium."

But *Fantasia* had no chance to knock everybody out. Even though it ran for a record-breaking fifty-one weeks in New York, and thirty-nine in Los Angeles, the special sound equipment required limited it to only a few theaters across the country, and most of the regular theater patrons had no opportunity to see it. The opening, late in 1940, coincided with the escalation of the war in Europe. Growing tension in this country, along with the studio's losing its foreign markets, made it impossible to expand the production ideas Walt was so eager to try. *Fantasia #2*, which was well past the planning stage, was abandoned, and the two segments already in work, "Clair de Lune" and "Peter and the Wolf," were reworked and used in later pictures. This was a disappointment to Walt and to the staff of 1200 employees, all of whom had been excited about the intriguing future of animation. We still wonder what we would be working on today if *Fantasia* had been as popular as *Snow White*.

Fantasia had given our artists the best opportunity to use both their imaginations and different kinds of graphics, but even more was attempted over the next ten years. The showcase for most of this experimentation was the "package pictures," *The Three Caballeros*, *Make Mine Music*, and *Melody Time*, which combined several delightful themes into one feature film, like a variety show. They gave the staff a chance to try out intriguing ideas that were not strong enough to sustain more than ten or fifteen minutes. Many of these ideas introduced a new style of drawing and design that was an important part of the whole concept.

Choosing the style for a picture follows the same guidelines as choosing the design of the characters. The style must emphasize the elements that tell the story best, create the moods, and establish the degree of sincerity for the complete idea. A somber topic will be handled quite differently from a frivolous one, in all graphic aspects, and the choice of what is best for the subject matter is one that must be considered carefully.

Walt wanted each of our features to have an individual style that would be different from any of the others. *Snow White* was done with soft watercolor washes so reminiscent of old book illustrations; *Alice in Wonderland* combined a more modern design with unique color combinations, to make it look slightly weird and zany; *Lady and the Tramp* was made of nostalgia, like an old postcard, with bright, sunny colors and soft edges. *101 Dalmatians* used a strong linear treatment, with flat swatches of color in the backgrounds to match the handling of the characters.

For *Sleeping Beauty*, the opposite was tried: the design of the characters was altered to fit the overall design of the backgrounds. Stylist Eyvind Earle had done the inspirational sketches that caught Walt's eye, and now the sparkling results that came from the flat colors used in two-dimensional patterns was calling for a new type of drawing in the animation. Even though four and five hours were required to make some of the drawings, the end result was a gorgeous tapestry of colors and pleasing shapes—cold and ponderous, but startling. The pageantry of the Middle Ages was captured with a magnificence that never will be duplicated again in this form; and when viewed on the wide screen required by the 70mm film used for this one production, it is extremely impressive.

To make the most effective use of this visual material, storyman Ed Penner worked out an involved sce-

ARTIST: Martin Provensen— Peter and the Wolf.

First suggestions for Proko- fieff's musical story had a strong feeling of Russian folk art.

511

nario that relied not so much on character identification as a busy sequence of events that romped along with good pacing and surprising twists. The story, being highly romantic, called for warmth and humor and dramatic moments more than austere design, and unquestionably we surrendered some audience involvement to this strong style. Still, we have not made a comparable feature with so much beauty in both appearance and color and such consistent treatment from start to finish—which was just what Walt wanted for the picture.

Careful attention always should be given to the value of the graphics in any film, for the whole product rapidly can become barren and dull and earthbound without some excellence in drawing, design, and color. This is easy to forget under the pressure to put a story on the screen that will live and build and captivate.

Good design, in itself, will make the drawings clearer and the ideas behind them easier to see and understand; the style will strengthen the communication, because it has been chosen, in the first place, as the best way of presenting the idea. It is a difficult point to put into words, since it is made up of taste and judgment and talent and sensitivity. While the audiences may not seem to notice, they sense the difference, and they are drawn to the object with the better design. It is one of the differences between Disneyland and the average amusement park.

Walt's search for the solid, unified idea that made the graphics hold an audience is probably the closest we can get to an explanation of what constitutes successful visual communication. Today, most people refer to that kind of an idea as "story." Bruno Bozzetto, the Italian animator, designer, and producer, stressed this on a visit to the studio. "The first thing is always the story—not a drawing or a background—but a story I want to tell. Then I choose the medium." He went on to emphasize the importance of making that story as strong and as rich as possible. "Disney was a fantastic storyteller," he said. "There's never a moment in his films in which you relax; the story is always moving."

Whatever the idea, it will be told better and in a more interesting way with a style that is supportive and compatible. Like a good caricature, it will help to achieve the essence of a particular idea that makes

ARTIST: Richmond (Dick) Kelsey—Trees.

good work so memorable. All of the elements being presented—story, character, animation, color, music, design—must contribute to the one statement, the overall concept.

Still Pictures and Limited Animation

A picture that has no movement will go "dead" on the screen in only a few seconds, no matter how compelling its elements. Moving the camera about will help, but only two factors really can keep the footage

"alive": a story idea that moves the audience, or a sound track that has meaning of its own.

If Walt saw a sketch or painting that he particularly liked, he would look for a way to get it on the screen just the way it was, and then figure out how to keep it there long enough for the audience to enjoy it, too.

In *The Three Caballeros*, Mary Blair's charming paintings of the Mexican children acting out Las Posadas had only the movement of the flames on the candles, but they held the audience's interest because they illustrated a story. In another place in the same picture, more of Mary's paintings were used with no story or continuity; however, a song, telling of the wonders of

Mexico, made an appealing sound track that supported the fine artwork.

Joyce Kilmer's poem *Trees* set to music by Oscar Rasbach provided the sound track for a film with no animation that made extensive use of camera movement, gently probing and searching, moving in and out and examining the details of paintings. Dick Kelsey, stylist and painter, had a remarkable talent for drawing trees that had strength and beauty and a unique design, combined with a color sense that was extremely personal and exciting. The sound track (in *Melody Time*) offered little variety in either mood or tempo, so the camera moves were restricted in the textures that might otherwise have been more interesting, but this is still an excellent example of what can be done with only still paintings and imagination.

The titles for *The Rescuers* were done in much the same way, using Mel Shaw's pastel renderings as illustrations of the journey of a lonely bottle, from the swamps along the Gulf of Mexico to New York harbor. It was felt that full animation of this subject matter would not be as effective as the glowing colors and rich detail in the pastels. The orchestral treatment of the song, "The Journey," allowed a greater variety of camera moves here, some even suggesting movement in Mel's superb drawings.

"Baby Weems," a short film from *The Reluctant Dragon* (1941), was presented the way a storyman might tell his narrative from the sketches on the storyboards. Since it was made up of separate sketches, there was neither reason nor justification for any movement. Still, to make the picture clear and more interesting, limited movements were added here and there, just an arm, or a leg, or a simulated walk, or perhaps a moving jaw during dialogue. It was effective, economical, and soon picked up by other studios searching for a cheaper way to fill the Saturday morning TV demands. It became known as "limited animation."

Animated Designs

Most of the scenes of "The Nutcracker Suite" in *Fantasia* had little more than the animation of designed shapes of flowers and frost and snowflakes, or the changing light in this special wonderland as a fairy

darted by. Even these fully animated characters were subordinated to the pictorial effects of the scenes, yet this was enough to sustain nearly fifteen minutes of film.

"Toccata and Fugue," also from *Fantasia*, probed in another direction, combining abstract designs and undefined shapes with pure music. Once again, top quality effects animation was needed to match the mood of the track, in both sync and feeling. All of the technical advancements were called upon to create visual images that carried the same depth and power as the music. *The Three Caballeros* contained more experimentation with the animation of designs, but due to budget restrictions during the war it is less pretentious though just as imaginative and revolutionary, with more emphasis on the changing of shapes as they animated. Because of the Mexican background in this part of the film, the designs were based on Mexican and Indian

motifs, and, in some cases, Donald Duck was introduced working through the evolving patterns. While he added little to the artistic merit of the sequence, he brought the audience into the film in a way that the geometric designs never could have by themselves.

An intriguing idea that never reached completion was Salvador Dali's visualization of a song, "Destino," written by Armando Dominquez. Working with John Hench, Dali had put together a whole storyboard of the surrealistic drawings that had made him famous, but, unfortunately, the project was cancelled with only one scene ever put on film. As a short interlude in the feature film it would have been provocative, whether people followed the ideas or understood any of it or not. Dali and Walt got along very well, but the picture was not becoming quite what either of them had hoped when they started, so it was abandoned, by mutual agreement.

Probably the most charming of the films that were essentially the animation of design elements was found in the introduction to "Baia" in *The Three Caballe-*

ARTIST: *J. Gordon Legg*— *"Toccata and Fugue,"* Fantasia.

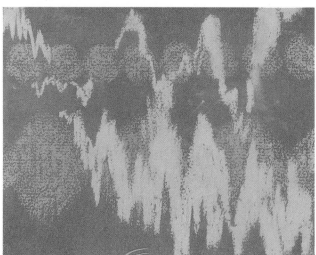

ARTIST: *Cornett Wood*— *"Toccata and Fugue,"* Fantasia.

ARTIST: *Salvador Dali*— Destino.

515

◁ ARTIST: *Mel Shaw*—The Rescuers.

Strong Design
With Animated Characters

ros. Mary Blair had made a dazzling sketch of the Brazilian jungle with a tiny, colorful train jogging along to a samba beat. Les Clark animated the train, keeping the drawing so that it matched perfectly to Mary's overall picture. There were no demands on the animation, other than to keep the design elements in the movements, while the little locomotive chugged along the track to the station at the end of the line. It met several problems along the way, which kept the idea alive and added interest to the progression through the jungle, but the outstanding design in the original concept contributed the most to making the sequence memorable.

Usually the animator must give up his best tools of communication if he limits his drawing to the restrictions of a strong design, but in "Once Upon a Wintertime," in the feature *Melody Time*, Eric Larson, working with director Ham Luske, animated Mary Blair's stylized ideas with great success. He bordered on limited animation where he could, moving the whole character stiffly, but timed it so convincingly that everything worked. It was impossible ever to become really concerned or involved with either the characters or the story, but it was entertaining and delightful, and showed that designs could be animated successfully when the whole idea was properly unified. There was a nostalgic song setting the mood, and a simple story that called for a quaint, unreal quality, so the special kind of animation fit in perfectly, without losing life or warmth or the needed communication.

Melody Time offered another venture into pure design animation, with a popular rendition of "Flight of the Bumble Bee" done in Boogie Woogie rhythm. Called "Bumble Boogie," it featured musical symbols mov-

516

ANIMATORS: *Characters,*
Fred Moore. Paint brush,
Josh Meador—
"Aquarela do Brasil,"
Saludos Amigos.

ANIMATOR: *Fred Moore—*
"All the Cats Join In,"
Make Mine Music.

ing in a wild turmoil to match the excitement of the score. There was little story, other than the plight of the bee trying to escape this mad world of sharps and flats and staff signs and notes all dashing about in a dizzy abstraction.

A particularly fascinating device was to paint or draw the pictures as needed, just ahead of the action—a sort of "Draw as you go." Sometimes the main character would be in the scene, progressing down the street, or climbing stairs, or viewing the scenery, with all of this background material being added just at the last moment. At other times, the entire screen would be empty, and a brush would paint the picture as you watched. The whole scene could be floated on from

one magic brush filled with watercolor, or the brush actually could paint each detail while you watched. It was always surprising and often exciting.

Imaginative use of this technique was combined with an extremely simple style of drawing in "All the Cats Join In," done for *Make Mine Music*. The story line was simply that a group of teenagers got together at the local drugstore to dance to the juke box, but with Fred Moore's animation it set a style that has influenced other filmmakers ever since. The clean, simple design of the characters, the appeal of the drawings, the strong outline, the directness of approach combined with the sync to the music and the crispness of the timing were worth copying.

517

Styled Animation

Ward Kimball found an excellent medium for his brand of humor in the styled animation of *Toot, Whistle, Plunk, and Boom* and the later TV specials he directed about man and his varied activities in space. The term "styled" means that the whole idea has been conceived with a dominant design that will influence both the appearance and the action of the characters.

Not everyone can adapt his work to this kind of thinking. Art Stevens, key animator on these films, said, "Give some guys a styled character and they don't know how to move it—you can't make it move realistically." If the story concept is realistic, then the animation must be realistic, too. But if it is a styled concept, then the character must move in a special way that is compatible with that style. The two do not seem to mix.

This type of animation is only illustrating rather than sustaining the story, so you are free to engage in a completely different form of caricature. Both Art and Julius Svendsen became adept at animating movements that fit this type of design.

The chief reason for selecting a strongly designed style is to use a stronger type of caricature, which is particularly well suited to satire and commentary on the world we live in. These characters are created to do a different type of job and are not interchangeable with those from other styles of animation. The cavemen in *Toot, Whistle* . . . could never play the role of the puppeteer in *Pinocchio*, and Stromboli would be just as wrong plucking a harp string or blowing on a raspy reed. The design of each was determined by the needs of the story and developed through the requirements of

the role. It is unique to that one particular show. Art Stevens concluded with this thought: "The characters in *Toot, Whistle* . . . aren't flesh and blood. They move in a more abstract way—but you aren't saying that one isn't as entertaining as the other."

Victory Through Air Power began with a short history of aviation done in an engaging style created by T. Hee. By removing the realism of aerial warfare, he removed the horror and was able to bring about a humorous treatment of the subject. When the design is this dominant, limited animation will support it better than other types of styled animation. As is often the case in these films the basic humor is in the drawing itself, and the animator must be careful that his additions do not weaken the communication already there.

Imagination Unlimited

Man and the Moon, directed by Ward Kimball, featured a simulated flight to the moon long before NASA was sure anyone really would be going there. Sets were built and costumes created, but for the rockets and the big events, only drawings could give the illusion, and to be convincing they had to be very special. Ken O'Connor, a top layout man, was given the assignment. His experiences with background, color, and the labs, dating back through *Snow White*, made him well suited for this exacting job. With technical assistance from rocket expert Wernher von Braun, the whole procedure from launch to circling the moon was so well conceived that when the actual flight was made more than twelve years later, many of the details were just as they had been shown in the film.

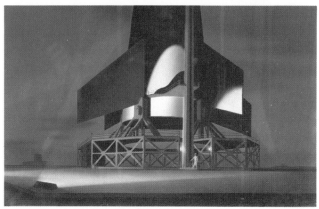

Noah's Ark, released in 1959, was made by Bill Justice and Xavier Atencio and featured the astounding caricatures of animals done by T. Hee. Bill did the stop motion work under the camera, moving the little figures in special ways, and T. created a whole jungle of improbable animals from the simple items found in any variety store.

Bill Justice teamed up with X. Atencio again, to design, construct, and move the colored paper characters used in several TV shows. Movement by stop motion has been a favorite of filmmakers for many years, because it saves the time of making extra drawings and fully utilizes the appeal of one good-looking design. There is a fascination to the movement when the viewer can recognize and identify the elements being used, whether they are made of paper, sand, nuts, or whatever.

The three films about *Winnie the Pooh* made constant reference to the book from which the episodes were animated, and, to keep this idea alive, shots of the book itself and the printed letters on the page were used repeatedly. When the wind was blowing in *Blustery Day*, it blew the type right off the page. When the flood came later, the water dissolved the type and washed it away. Often the scenes were designed as illustrations in the book, and the figures moved about within those limitations, or hopped across the page to a new location. It was only an inventive device, but it fit the mood of the films, keeping some of the whimsy of the original stories.

STYLING AND LAYOUT:
Ken O'Connor—
Man in Space *and* Man and the Moon.

Winnie the Pooh

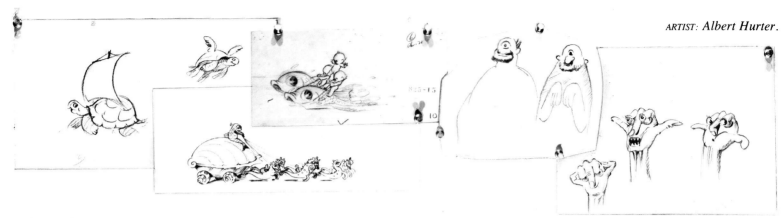

ARTIST: *Albert Hurter.*

ARTISTS: *Children of schools in Inverness—* The Loch Ness Monster. ▷

ARTIST: *Mel Shaw—* *The Black Cauldron.*

Everyone has looked into the top of the whirlpool, but what does the bottom look like? This one is the secret entrance to an underground world, and Mel's drawing makes it all seem very plausible.

ARTIST: *Mary Blair—* Alice in Wonderland.

Mary's drawings had a special appeal for Walt. Here, she shows her unique approach to the introduction of the famed Tulgey Woods. Who else would have conceived of the entrance to a forest as a doorway? Such drawings opened up our thinking and started a more imaginative approach to our own work.

Before the days of space exploration, our artists wondered what we might find on other planets.

(At top and below.)

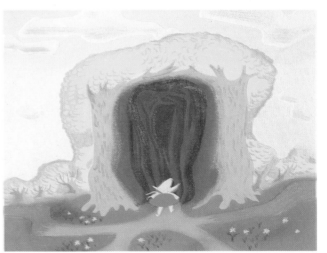

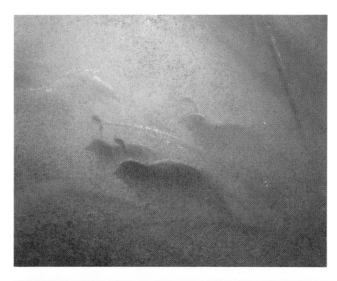

When a film was being made about the Loch Ness monster, school children were asked to draw their ideas of how ''Nessie'' should look. These delightful drawings were incorporated into the style of one section of the film, with certain of the drawings going into movement. Considerable inventiveness was needed to animate suggestions from the schoolroom, but it made a charming bit of entertainment.

Strong Personalities with a Different Type of Life

While Mickey Mouse was giving up his formerly preposterous antics to become more of a human hero, his pals Donald and Goofy were developing a wilder, broader type of comedy, where the incident was more believable than the character. Both types of animation relied primarily on personality, but where Mickey supported his sincerity with believable actions his buddies engaged in the most improbable activities.

They could fall 2000 feet, be electrocuted, blown up, cut into sections, burned, flattened, drowned, even frozen in a cake of ice, yet be right back in fighting shape in a matter of seconds. The only thing that could not be destroyed was the personality.

In *How To Ride A Horse*, the first of the long series of pseudo-instructional films starring Goofy, a format was established that opened another door for the animators. Any device that a teacher might use to demonstrate a point was used with Goofy as the subject. He was drawn as a chart in white lines, used as a diagram, shown in simulated slow motion, run backward and forward, and through it all he could still react to what was being done.

Even the role of the narrator[2] was caricatured to be an integral part of the comedy. He would speak about

Goofy, commenting on his actions ("You will notice that the subject raises his leg high . . .") or correcting his performance ("No, no, not that way!") or thoughtlessly leaving him in an awkward predicament while expounding the philosophy of the whole subject. This idea of putting the star of the picture through such rigorous treatment led to the development of new techniques in the use of held drawings, limited animation, and limited life, unified only by Goofy's indomitable personality. The films were highly entertaining and, since they had practically no story, relied on strong gags, clear staging, brisk timing, surprising actions, and a fast tempo.

All manner of camera tricks were used to heighten the effects. When the first combat film footage came back from the war zones in the early forties, it revealed that the camera itself was jarred by the force of nearby explosions. Practically the next day, the cartoon camera would be jarred when Goofy walked into a wall (actually, the jar was simulated by moving the pegs back and forth a brief moment). Vibration gags and animated effects had been used for several years, but the crew was looking for new tricks that would give more impact. When the Goof hit that wall, they wanted the audience to feel it! It was not necessary that anyone believe in the character as a sincere entity, only that the beating he took was real.

The Pink Elephants sequence in *Dumbo* called for much inventiveness from the animators. No matter how peculiar or impossible the picture on the screen, it had to move convincingly and in keeping with the whole weird dream the little elephant was having. Instead of moving the characters in terms of a believable personality, the emphasis was put on the animator's ability to surprise the audience with actions that are completely beyond anyone's experience.

Ward Kimball was a master of this type of invention, astounding the industry, first, with his handling of the title song from *The Three Caballeros*, and continuing that special type of madness through "Pecos Bill" in *Melody Time*. Ward had a way of disregarding logic when it suited him and of getting right to the heart of the matter. He was caricaturing the whole idea of his sequence, not just the action or the character, which enabled him to make a very direct and pure statement of what he considered funny. His scenes

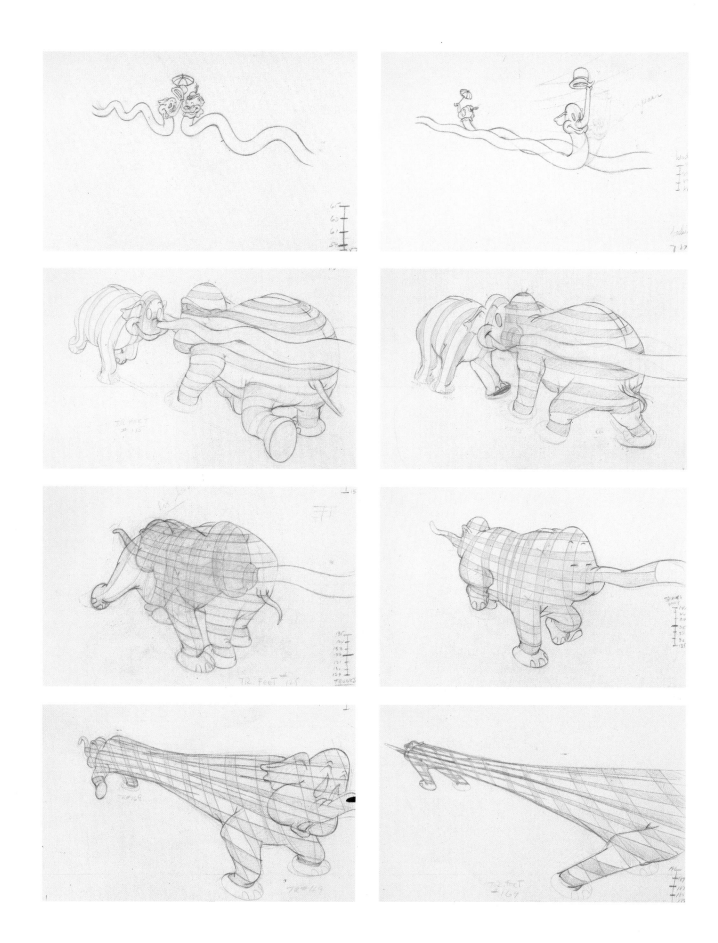

523

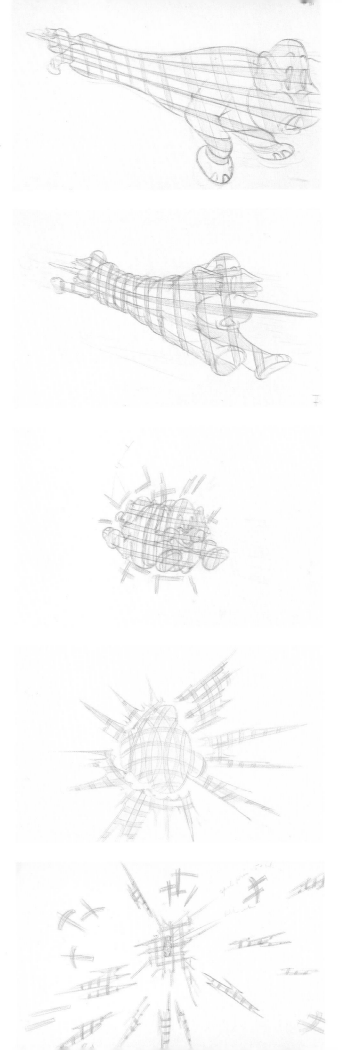

spawned a whole wave of preposterous actions and brittle timing throughout the industry.

The Brazilians have a bird that is considered completely crazy and apt to do just about anything—the Aracuan bird. To animate him was a special challenge to Eric Larson, for if the bird will do anything what is left for the artist to contribute or caricature? Eric found a way that was light and zany and so unexpected that Walt later had a whole short built around the character, *Clown of the Jungle*. Part of the craziness was the fact that the bird did not even follow the rules of picture making, defying perspective, cutting, and scene planning. He would walk anywhere, around the frame borders, in and out of scenes—all the things that normally confuse an audience—but Eric set this up so adroitly that the audiences merely gasped, and laughed. They probably would not have been surprised if the Aracuan bird had walked right out of the screen and into the theater beside them. It was a singularly inventive use of full personality animation.

Combination Live Action and Cartoon

Walt always had felt there was a special fascination in combining live action with the cartoon, as he had done in his very first shorts back in 1923 with the Alice pictures. Together, the two mediums create a different kind of fantasy with a potential far beyond what anyone has done. New restrictions are placed on all the participants, because they are not simply adding another dimension to the familiar product; they are now working in what is actually a third medium. It must be planned more carefully, conceived with even more imagination, and budgeted realistically, but the results can be pure magic.

In *The Three Caballeros*, there was an elaborate display of talents and technical proficiency in the section titled "Baia." The Brazilian singer and entertainer Aurora Miranda, with a chorus of musicians and dancers, worked on a stage set that combined animated buildings with real streets, drawn props with real structures, painted illusions with reality. It worked particularly well because the "real" parts were only theatrical sets in the first place, and had been designed with flat

ANIMATOR: *Eric Larson—*
The Three Caballeros.

surfaces and simple shapes so they would match the drawings that had to be part of the whole composition.

Working in and out of this maze of actors and props and backgrounds was Donald Duck, with his newfound friend José Carioca. In some cases the animation was done first, and the live actors had to react to the timing and action set by the cartoon characters. In other scenes, Aurora and her companions were photographed first and the animators had to match their drawings to the live characters. In the first case, the animation was projected onto the back of a translucent screen, which became the background behind the actors. In the second, the artists matched their drawings to photostats of the actors, and the two pieces of film were combined later in the optical printer.

In either case, it is difficult to know how the final pieces will all fit together and to judge how anyone should act (whether human or cartoon) in any particular scene, since half the scene is still in the creative minds of many other people. The audiences are never aware of the problems or difficulties, or the discussions that have brought this all to a magical conclusion, for if it has been done well they are enthralled, believing that somehow, all of it is real and happening right before their eyes.

ARTIST: *Mary Blair—*
"Baia,"
The Three Caballeros.

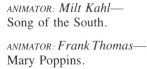

ANIMATOR: *Milt Kahl—*
Song of the South.

ANIMATOR: *Frank Thomas—*
Mary Poppins.

Song of the South, produced in 1946, kept the cartoon segments separate and complete for the most part, but integrated them so well with the few connecting scenes and careful story work that the result was one of the studio's most successful. It was also one of the favorite films of the animators who worked on the sequences, for it combined broad characters with strong situations, in a setting that was pure fantasy. Part of this came from Bill Peet's excellent story work in adapting the Joel Chandler Harris classics about Uncle Remus, part of it was the design of the characters, which offered maximum communication tools to the artists, and a very large part was the marvelous voice tracks, contributed primarily by the wonderful, multi-talented James Baskett. The fact that all of the action actually was taking place inside a young boy's mind, as he was being told the story, added an extra touch of life to the whole concept.

Mary Poppins, produced eighteen years later, in 1964, once again placed the live actors in a cartoon world, combining backgrounds that were partly real and partly drawn, with story situations that put all the actors together. No rear projection was used this time, however, so all the humans were photographed before any animation was begun. Since no one was a secondary character, the normal problems of getting a scene

to "play" took precedence over planning for the total effect of the scene in its eventual form. The live action director had his hands full just staging the action properly and getting the characters to come to life. The idea of making any allowances for some little drawings that would be added later was the last thing he wanted to hear about.

In fact, Walt encouraged this attitude by telling the director: "Don't worry about what the animators are going to do; just make your own stuff as good as you can, because those guys will top you!" As a result, there was never enough room in the scene for four penguins, the camera was never at the right angle to show them off to the best advantage, and the action was never staged so they would fit into the picture. Nor was there ever the right amount of time left to do everything called for in the script. Penguins have very short legs and cannot fly, so it is almost impossible for them to keep up with a long-legged dancer like Dick Van Dyke; putting four of them in each scene really compounded the problem.

Of course, Walt knew exactly what would happen. The animator would fuss and complain and call a few names, but in the end he would become more inventive and more entertaining than he would have been if everything had been made easy for him. No animator ever would back away from such a challenge. He might scream and rave a bit, but he never would give up and admit defeat! And Walt knew that, too.

While there might have been more invention in doing the scene Walt's way, a better result overall will be obtained if the animator and the live action crew can cooperate. Without advance planning the animator is apt to be left with long continuity scenes to animate simply because it was comfortable cutting for the live action. He is faced with the awkward job of trying to stretch his action, keep his characters alive, and invent appropriate bits of useless business, just to fill out the footage given to him.

In the animation itself, there are many new problems that arise when the drawings are seen, side by side, with a real person on film. The cel animation always looks flat and shapeless by comparison. It is not economically practical to make the perspective absolutely accurate in both drawing and action, and it is completely impossible to match the lighting on the live action figure. If a broad action is used on the cartoon character, it will seem out of place and unnatural, while a more subdued version may go by almost unnoticed. The characters come from different worlds, and need special consideration to make them compatible.

Worst of all, there will be a lack of weight, no matter how carefully the action is timed. The subtleties of the human form in movement cannot be matched, and the caricatured actions that seem so real when viewed in an animated film rapidly lose credibility alongside the real thing. Such handicaps rather easily can be overcome or minimized by careful organization of the material—so that the audience's attention is led off into other areas. However, rather than waste the skill and talent of good animators in doing this, the money is better spent planning just how each thing should be presented.

Technically, there are a number of ways of combining the live actors with their cartoon counterparts, and the choice depends on the result desired. Essentially, what is needed is two sections of film, each with its own separate image, but so arranged that the two pieces fit together precisely. If you have that, the wizardry of the process lab can combine the two into one impeccable print. Fortunately, that technical aspect is not the problem facing the animator, or the layout man, or the color consultant, or the background painter. All of these people must search for a way to produce a series of drawings on the screen that will match in weight, texture, shading, color, and perspective the live characters who are sharing the bit of film with them.

The color almost always comes out too bright, too flat, too intense, even if the live background has been painted in gaudy colors and lit with a very flat lighting to burn out all shadows. In addition, there is texture to almost everything in the real world, and the flat, shiny paint on the sheet of celluloid never quite fits in.

There was a scene in *Song of the South* that showed Uncle Remus fishing beside an old bullfrog, and, for a brief moment, everything was perfect in the matching of the two mediums. The frog was small, but with enough detail so that texture was not a problem, the perspective of the drawing was identical to that of the live background, and the choice of color was just right for everything else. The whole crew had worked just as hard on each scene in the sequence, but fortune smiled on their efforts a little more warmly on this one scene, and it always has been held up as the example of what is possible in combination footage.

Educational Films

During the second World War, the studio had used its animation skills to make training films, educational films, scientific films, and health films for various government agencies. When peace returned, Walt continued to probe into other uses of the medium, even having a special unit make commercials for the emerging TV market, and industrial films for a few corporations. Of all these, only the educationals became an important division of the company.

Animation is particularly well suited for teaching, because of its ability to get inside the mind of the viewer, as well as inside any object or subject it is covering. Whether it is a philosophic concept, a natural phenomenon, or a complex machine, animation can make it all come alive in the viewer's imagination. The series of weather films that explained the anatomy of clouds and storms to Navy pilots showed the powerful elements that scientists knew were there, which no one ever will see.

In a series of films on behavioral alternatives, and again in *The Story of Menstruation*, use was made of animation's competence in handling highly personal subjects in a very impersonal way. The use of real people in either of these sensitive subjects would have had the "kids reacting to other kids" as actors, whereas drawing the figures allowed the audience to see only the idea that was being presented.

Walt shied away from trying to tell too much in a film, saying, "We are not trying to lecture and let them think we know a lot and have discovered something—it's all in a light mood." This philosophy kept him from the usual pitfalls found in educational films, of merely illustrating a dull lecture, or using only diagrams to explain the point. *Donald in Mathmagic Land* had begun as an attempt to explain arithmetic to the beginner, but it changed to a more general introduction and orientation, which would remove any concern or worry about the subject while arousing curiosity and creating a base for future understanding. Educators have acclaimed it as one of the most successful films on the subject.

The field of educational films has an almost unlimited future with very little of its potential explored.

Audio-Animatronics

One last use of the animation principles to achieve communication and entertainment might be mentioned, even though it went far beyond just the drawings. Walt always had been fascinated with mechanical devices and enjoyed doing fine model work himself, so it was only natural that his interest would be aroused by the automated whistling bird he saw in Europe in 1948. He bought it immediately and brought it back to his machine shop at the studio, giving it to Roger Broggie, the talented head of the shop. Roger had a way of making things work, no matter what they were or what they were supposed to do, and he had grown accustomed to Walt's requests not only for the impossible but the unthinkable. Now, Walt asked him to tear apart the little bird and find out how it worked.

Before long, other engineers were adapting the principles Roger uncovered to other mechanical figures: old Granny Kincaid in her rocking chair, a soft shoe dancer, a barbershop quartet, a Chinese head with eyes that blinked and a mouth that talked and lips that formed letters. These were impressive additions to the workshop, and an intriguing hobby for a creative man.

A head of Abraham Lincoln was built with eyes that moved, and teeth behind the lips, and suddenly Walt was talking about building a whole figure that would walk up and down and duplicate the famous gestures of our sixteenth president and sit in a chair and be just like the man himself. Technical and mechanical problems forced him to curtail some of these ideas, but to everyone's amazement he did construct a replica of Lincoln that has awed millions of people in repeated performances. That was only the beginning. Show after show was built around the improved figure, now dubbed Audio-Animatronics, to fill the Disney theme parks and amaze the crowds.

The early experiments had been programmed by the technicians who knew how to make a figure perform, but they lacked the knowledge of what it should do to be entertaining. For this, Walt took the men from his animation staff, who could adapt their experience with drawings to this startling new medium. These mechanisms moved in a completely different way, but the same principles of communicating with an audience did apply, and the highly specialized training these men had received on the cartoons made them uniquely suited for this assignment.

Marc Davis had the rare ability to make drawings of characters in situations that captured a living predicament and stimulated endless ideas of what might happen next. He could capture a moment in time, just when a relationship of characters was reaching a peak, and present it in a clear and appealing way. This talent had given the start to many great story sequences in the past, so he was an obvious choice for this new medium.

As Marc summed up his assignment, "We actually try to create a situation and make it believable. I'm working in a field with tremendous limitations on what you can do with action, so the whole thing hinges on a picture, and it has to be the moment when things happen. Otherwise, you don't have anything." Walt called Marc's drawing a "story-telling tableau," which is really just another way of describing a good story sketch.

When the initial drawings for the animatronic figures were approved, a sculptor was needed to carry these plans into three-dimensional form, and who would be better for this than a sculptor with a background in animation? The man selected was Blaine Gibson, whose hobby was sculpture and who already had won several prizes.

Blaine was puzzled about designing one shape that

would work for a whole line of dialogue; for even though the figure would move, it could not change its attitude extensively. Walt told him, "A good cartoon can tell its story without the line of dialogue, and a figure with the right expression and attitude requires little animation to tell its story." It seemed that Walt had been telling his staff that same thing for many years, and it was still the right advice.

Claude Coats was moved from doing inspirational sketches, color keys, and painting backgrounds to helping design the areas where the animatronic figures would be working. He compared the new problems to the backgrounds he had painted: "Before the time of *The Old Mill*, the backgrounds had been washed out, flat. . . . Now there was a kind of space for the character to act in, not quite reality but believable space. We're still doing that on these rides; we consider the space the people move through." He went on to say that today the public is so used to seeing things on a TV screen that when suddenly they are thrust into a designed area that totally surrounds them and become participants in a space, they are overwhelmed.

If planning actions and designing figures were familiar jobs to the men from animation, they were in for a shock when they began constructing these figures. Plastic skin had to be created that would survive almost continuous stretching and pulling, and eyebrows and beards had to be built up by inserting one hair at a time. At least the eyes were something that could be bought outright, since the manufacture of glass eyes had long achieved very high standards.

The studio wrote to American Optical Company in Boston, requesting a catalogue and some samples. Roger Broggie tells what happened. "We received a case of some 70 different eyes, which was the method used by ophthalmologists to match a patient's eye for color. Blaine Gibson selected eyes from these samples, but when we ordered 37 *pairs* of artificial eyes, we received several phone calls from Boston asking if we were really serious." It seems that no one ever had asked for a *pair* of eyes before, since the whole point was to match the patient's good eye.

They ran into more trouble when they asked for heavy veining in several sets of eyes. As Roger explained, "This was for the Pirate Ride, and Marc and Blaine wanted bloodshot eyes in the drunken pirates."

The manufacturers eventually understood what was behind the strange requests and produced a new line to the studio's specifications. Roger concluded, "We became American Optical Company's largest customer."

These mechanical figures, carefully designed and programmed to communicate and to involve the audience, were more successful than anyone could have anticipated. John Hench said of them, "People get more out of it than if there were a real actor there. For some reason, those things project—they actually do a better job—there's something *super* human about them." Like the cartoons, they touched that special world of magic that was the real secret at Disney's. When Dick Huemer asked his famous question in the early thirties, "What's the secret over at Disney's?" the answer should not have been "timing," or "analysis," —it was, in fact, that, somehow, the characters were made to live in the audience's imagination.

ARTIST: *Claude Coats—* Pinocchio.

One of the backgrounds that had a feeling of atmosphere and believable space.

The Future

Today, the future of animation looks more exciting than at any time in the last forty years. Around the world, young artists have been experimenting with animation, studying animation, dreaming animation. Where the Disney artists had to pioneer and discover—and then gradually build up a credibility with the audience—today there exists a sophistication and understanding that allows ventures into many new fields. In addition to the long list of cartoon features the Disney studio has created, the small commercial studios for years have been producing creative animation for TV. That medium, in itself, has trained viewers to accept and expect quick communication, brisk cutting, short scenes, and clear pictures. The world is familiar with animation in many forms and ready for great films.

As the audience has been maturing, the space age has created many new materials and fantastic tools for artists to use. The video camera, converted to run at 24 frames a second, made a major change in work habits, since a scene could be viewed and corrected while it was being animated. New types of computers appear on the market almost daily; some claim only to replace the more tedious functions of getting the animator's drawings on the screen, but others have a much more stimulating potential. E. Cardon Walker, who rose from traffic boy to president of Walt Disney Productions, in looking at the variety of electronic devices offered the studio, commented that these devices ". . . will never take the place of . . . the great creativity or the artistic ability. Whatever form it's photographed in . . . it's still going to require the originality, the imagination, and the newness of what you do to make it real, to make it last."

Just as important are the markets opening up on many fronts, from the home entertainment centers to new uses of TV itself. For years, the filmmaker has been restricted to the ten-minute short, the hour-and-ten-minute feature, or the half-hour TV special. Many wonderful stories are ideal for a twenty-minute film, and almost unlimited ideas exist for very short subjects of less than six minutes. A concentrated message can have impact, as well as a great capability to delight, to charm, inform, provoke—to entertain. Once a market has been found that will make different lengths of pictures profitable, whole new areas of exploration will be open to fertile minds. And as the sophistication of the audience grows, a greater range of subject matter will become acceptable. Who can predict what will be next?

Walt was always way ahead of any of us, searching for new procedures, new forms of entertainment, and we never can think of the future without remembering how he turned ideas over in his mind. One theme that kept haunting him was the story of Hiawatha. He kept bringing it up over the years, trying to find the right way to do something with it. He said to us, "There's something there, y'know? Something we could do—something that's right for us. I don't know what it is or how we'd do it. Don't think of a film, don't even think of a show—don't limit your thinking to a regular theater. Maybe it's something out in the woods, or on a mountain, maybe the people are brought in—or—I don't know—but there's something there!" That is the way we view the future today.

In the late thirties, Alexander Woollcott, author and critic, visited the studio and was greatly impressed with the appearance of the rough pencil tests he was shown. All the extra lines that helped construct the characters and search out the movement were little more than cobwebs on the screen, yet, somehow, they seemed to coalesce into a character, causing Woollcott to state that there was more creativity in this form than in any finished animation. Walt always liked the vitality of the rough animation, but he never found a way to use it properly in a picture. Could it be combined with live action to suggest the inner ideas or dreams of some character? Could it represent a fantasy of wandering thoughts, of visions, of only half-formed notions? Could it be a mystical character that was not earthbound and only partially formed most of the time? In one discussion, Mel Shaw commented, "It just seems to me that there's even more of an art form in an impressionistic medium out there, somewhere. We haven't experimented."

In addition to the excitement of experimenting with

untried uses of animation, there is always the challenge of trying to achieve audience identification through other means. How much sympathy can you build for a shapeless glob? What technique would you use to create memorable personalities out of three swatches of color? How can you make the audience care about a spot of light? The great Russian animator and director Fedor Hitruk has had considerable success in building warmth in a situation and a strong feeling for his characters, using limited animation, or cut-outs, or hinged figures, and stylized designs. How much further anyone could go in these directions is not known. It would require a special kind of story and an inspiring type of design to conjure up a completely unique world, but who knows if there are any limits to fantasy and imagination?

Of course, there are some critics who prophesy that animation will not survive the present era. Skyrocketing costs have put pictures like *Pinocchio* and *Fantasia* far beyond anyone's means, but fortunately there is no reason to duplicate either of these classics. They have been done, and now it is time to look forward to the challenges that await us, ahead. Cost always has been a prime factor; Walt consistently looked for a cheaper way to get the same result, or a less expensive result that would still do what was needed. The notes of the old story meetings are full of his admonitions to hold the cost down and to keep production moving. Even on the most elaborate parts of *Fantasia*, he was cutting out "extras" that did not add enough to the scene to be worth the expense. No, it is not the cost that will hold back the great pictures of tomorrow; it will be lack of creative ability or foresight or planning.

When the uncertainty of the future for animation was being discussed, one alarmed student exclaimed, "It's too good a medium to let slip away! It can go where nothing else can go—it can show things that can't be seen! It can show things that exist only in the animator's mind!"

The art of animation does indeed wield magic powers, but competition is coming from two unexpected quarters. First, there are the inroads from imaginative live-action cameramen. With filters, special lenses, exotic printing techniques, multiple exposures, intricate models, trick lighting, and even the pushing of a filmed image through a computer, the cameramen are daily eroding the private fantasy-world of the animator and his hand-drawn craft. To the alert artist, these incursions do not rob him of anything as much as they show him a way to free himself from antiquated procedures—so that he may extend his own reach.

The second and more startling invasion comes from advanced equipment used in scientific discoveries that gradually are revealing the true nature of our world and our universe. It is becoming harder and harder to tell the difference between reality and fantasy. From unbelievable organisms revealed by electron microscopy, to shapes and colors in the undersea world, to

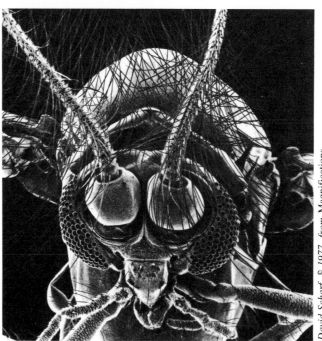

These are not the wild creations of an imaginative artist but photographs of real creatures in the world and of a planet in the space around us.

astounding photos from space, we are seeing things beyond man's dreams. From diaphanous, filmy shrouds to knobby, armored animals, we are discovering that our own world has more beauty, and more awesome beings, than anyone ever had envisioned. Just the infinite variety of the shapes in a spoonful of plankton would put any designer to shame.

If photography now can show us a real world of fantasy, as well as a fantasy world that appears to be real, what is left for animation to do? The answer, of course, lies in the area of personal interpretation, as it does with any art form. It may be hard to find things that do not really exist anywhere, but how they are used in a film, what is said about them, and how they relate to other phenomena are jobs for the artist. In this area, animation will be around for a long time because of its unique ability to communicate. What is needed are artists who have something entertaining to say, and the training to say it in a way that involves the

audience.[3] The ancient counsel "Know thyself" is full of wisdom, but, for the entertainer, it is possibly just as wise to suggest, "Know your audience."

When Rodney Rice, the Irish radio personality, was interviewing people at the studio, he asked one of the Nine Old Men,[4] "Does the animator feel isolated from society, living in a dream world?" The answer was, "No, he has to be part of the community, part of the human experience, to know what to communicate, and how to do it. He would be both out of date and out of touch if he isolated himself." Mr. Rice was surprised. "But don't you have to be wacky to get inside the skull of a ducky or a Goofy?" Instead of the lively answer he had anticipated, he got the straight, bare truth. "No, the things the audience likes about these characters are the human characeristics. They can say, 'That's just like Uncle Joe,' or 'That's the way I felt in school,' or 'Some kids did that to me once!'"

That person waiting in the theater has paid his money, and is now waiting to be entertained. He is not anxious to help you with your job. As Marcel Marceau told his students, "Don't expect the audience to use its energy to come to you—the energy should come from the performer . . . you must reach out and touch them." Other greats of the entertainment world have agreed with this analysis of the audience. The late Jean Renoir, outstanding film director, wrote in his memoirs, "The spectator is a human being, capable of reflection and, therefore, of imagination. Being human, he is attracted by the least effort; but also, being human, he is devoured with curiosity."[5] If M. Renoir is correct, the best way to involve the spectator in a film is by playing on that curiosity with the big idea that has a progression, leading the spectator in deeper and deeper.

The graphic form used to present this idea can be as varied as the concepts of the artists, but the same age-old principles of communication still will apply, as they have for the last two thousand years. They will not change until man's experiences and deductions have elevated him to a new state of understanding. The advertising agencies, who have enlivened the TV screens with all kinds of visual stimuli created with the aid of electronic technology, still revert to symbols the world understands for their subject matter: the cute baby, the grandparents, family get-togethers, sunsets, a full moon, a miserable, rainy night, the boy-girl

The characters in Snow White *became so real and so well known throughout the world that in 1938 they could be used in a political cartoon depicting the sorrow of the small nations of Europe over losing their collective security as the power of the Nazis was growing.*

romance. They may have trained the public to accept cutting and camera work and technical ideas that would have been completely confusing twenty years earlier, but they can communicate their message only through symbols that have a broad appeal.

The popularity of the Disney films around the world is proof that entertainment values are similar everywhere, in spite of geography and cultural differences. People are people, wherever they live, and while they may be attracted to a broad variety of activities and subjects, the one thing that always interests them the most is themselves. Regardless of techniques, to be successful the idea for a film must be presented in terms of universal understanding directly related to a person's experiences; for the most important experiences are the individual's own.

This incident was observed one noon hour, on the steps of a building across the way. A girl was waiting impatiently for someone. She obviously was annoyed and restless. She was not settling down for a long wait but changed her position constantly, and the positions were all unusual: crouched and leaning against the wall, then leaning against the balustrade, first facing it, then with her back to it, waiting—waiting.

Finally the young man came up happily, unsuspecting. She was accusing; he was unprepared, baffled. Her frustration broke out in tears, her head was dropped. She pointed to her watch, he pointed to his—but he had to bend down, and twist to see into her face. He was concerned, loving, but confused. She turned away; he followed, pleading. She accepted the situation at last, but she could not forget. They walked off together, but when he tried to take her hand she pulled it back and thrust her chin up in the air.

This situation could be presented in almost any graphic form without altering its basic strength. You feel for both characters, you understand, you identify. They can be young, ageless, ugly, anatomical, shapeless, styled, or only torn pieces of paper—it would not matter. The wristwatches are the only props, and they are not necessary; they merely are conveniences that simplify the communication for anyone who is familiar with watches.

All the ingredients are there to reach almost anyone, and this is still without introducing any personalities. That addition would refine the situation to make it

funny or sad, ridiculous or poignant.

As the audience's sophistication grows, there is an increasing burden on the young animator or filmmaker. Finding an idea worth putting on film, presenting it with enough imagination to capture fleeting interests, and involving the audience emotionally is a big assignment. It is also the very soul of entertainment. Yet, to Walt, there was one more component of his films that cannot be quite classified under just entertainment. That was the uplifting feeling that pervades audiences as they watch Disney pictures.

John Hench said of Walt's philosophy, "I know he looked at entertainment as something more than escape. There was a kind of reassurance—he always made people feel good." There was no one scene, or one action, or one background that created this sensation, but the special feeling stayed with people for days. It was the final bit of magic.

We hope that the great pictures of the future will have some of this same aura, regardless of the graphic forms they take. This feeling is needed in our world, and the potential is there, as it is in no other art form. Marc Davis summed it up very well: "Animation is just an incredible medium, and . . . it's just waiting for another great leader . . . and it will be equally great. And yet, there's something that came out of the Disney point of view, this business of bringing things to life. . . ."

Randy Cartwright stares at the blank paper, and like many other young animators, ponders the infinite opportunities in animation.

NOTES

Notes *(Dates after names represent time spent at Disney Studio.)*

Chapter 1

1. Vladimir Tytla (1934–1943), supervising animator.

2. Baroness Jane van Lawick-Goodall, *My Friends the Wild Chimpanzees* (Washington: National Geographic Society Special Publication, 1967), pp. 134, 135, 136, 138, 139, 140.

3. Jane Goodall, lecture at Caltech, L. S. B. Leakey Series, 1974.

4. Charlie Chaplin, *My Autobiography* (London: Penguin Books, 1966), p. 143.

5. Angna Enters, *On Mime* (Middletown: Wesleyan University Press, 1968), p. 46.

6. Roy O. Disney (1923–1971), business manager, president of Walt Disney Productions, chairman of the board.

7. John Hench (1939–   ), background artist and designer. Moved to WED (subsidiary that designs displays and rides for Disneyland and Walt Disney World) in 1955. On board of directors at WED, 1966, and vice president. Chief operations officer, 1972, and senior vice president, 1980.

8. Consensus quote from many interviews.

Chapter 2

1. Ben Sharpsteen (1929–1959), animator. Director of cartoon shorts starting in 1934. Among those were *Mickey's Service Station, Moving Day,* and *Donald and Pluto.* Supervising director on *Pinocchio,* production supervisor on *Fantasia* and *Dumbo.* Producer of live-action nature films, 1948–1959.

2. Ub Iwerks (1924–1930 and 1940–1971). Walt was more fortunate than he realized in having his old friend Ub Iwerks working with him and doing the animation on those early films. He had been lured from Kansas City on the promise of a partnership, but as Dave Hand, who later became a top director, put it, "They were partners, but Walt was the boss." Ub was not a great draftsman, but he was amazingly facile and had an outstanding feeling for that first type of animation. He would have laughed in later years about the crudeness of their early work, but anyone who can turn out 600 drawings a day, stage a whole picture for both layout and attitude, contribute gags, train the new help, and keep the company car running is an asset to any studio!

Possibly the greatest part of his talent at that particular time was his ability to capture in drawings the actions that Walt was asking everyone to get. Ub had not been trained by any experienced animator. He just picked up what he needed to know as he went along, which was his way with most of the things he did. Yet he was able, and willing, too, to help the young fellows who came in knowing absolutely nothing about the business. Two of the men he trained, Les Clark and Jack Cutting, both say that Ub was very patient and helpful in getting them started, and, usually, was the only animator who would stop his own work to encourage others. He was gentle and gentlemanly, and always absorbed with what he was doing or with some idea that was bouncing around in his head.

He was later to be an outstanding inventor at the studio, creating projection machines that ran continuously, the sodium vapor screen that was used for combination live-action and cartoon productions, and adapting the Xerox process to the studio's needs, to name a few contributions. He had always had an interest in mechanical gadgets and used to putter endlessly with his auto, even while turning out so many drawings.

Dave Hand tells the story of how annoyed Walt would be as he watched through the window while Ub happily fussed with the engine of his car. "Look at that!" Walt would mutter. "Wasting his time out there. He could get a mechanic for 65 cents an hour to do that kind of work!" But in later years, Walt was extremely grateful that Ub had this interest and made him head of the machine shop, so he could putter continuously.

3. Walter Kerr, *The Silent Clowns* (New York: Alfred A. Knopf, Inc., 1975), p. 77.

4. Wilfred Jackson (1928–1961), first director after Walt. Among the cartoon shorts he directed were *Ugly Duckling,* 1931 (first Disney cartoon to communicate pathos and warmth), *Santa's Workshop, The Grasshopper and the Ants, The Band Concert, The Tortoise and the Hare, Mickey's Grand Opera,* and *The Country Cousin.* He was also a sequence director on features.

5. Les Clark (1927–1975), animator, supervising animator, later director and producer.

6. Dave Hand (1930–1944), animator from New York. Shorts cartoon director, 1932; among his best were *Pluto's Judgment Day, Alpine Climbers,* and *Little Hiawatha.* Supervising director on *Snow White* and *Bambi,* animation supervisor on *Victory Through Air Power.*

7. Dick Huemer (1933–1948), animator from New York. Started in 1916 at Raoul Barré Studio; later, director and story director. Returned to Disney's, 1951–1973, to work in comic strip department.

8. Excerpt from interviews recorded by Joe Adamson in 1968 and 1969 as part of the American Film Institute University of California at Los Angeles Oral History Program. Reprinted in part in *Funny World,* No. 17, Fall 1977.

Chapter 3

1. Most of the animators who came out from the East knew only Straight Ahead animation. Les Clark felt that Pose to Pose, as we knew it, was developed at the Disney studio.

2. Marc Davis (1935–1978), animator, storyman, supervising animator, and designer at WED from 1961 to 1978.

3. Vladimir (Bill) Tytla.

4. John Hench.

5. Grim Natwick (1934–1938), animator. Worked at Hearst International Studio in 1916. Did *Flip the Frog* for Ub Iwerks' Studio in 1931. Animator on *Snow White* and *Fantasia* ("Sorcerer's Apprentice").

Chapter 4

1. Donald W. Graham (1932–1941), art teacher for Disney personnel. While studying engineering at Stanford University, Don became interested in art. He attended Chouinard's Art Institute in Los Angeles (now absorbed into the Disney-founded California Institute of the Arts) and later became a member of the faculty. In 1932 he was hired by Walt Disney as a drawing instructor, and for the next nine years he conducted classes specializing in line drawing, composition, and action analysis. Don was an exceptionally fine teacher. Instead of criticizing your drawing, he made you think about why you were drawing it that way,

stimulating a whole new way of thinking about art. He continued as a consultant until the time of his death in 1976. Author of *Composing* Pictures (New York: Van Nostrand Reinhold Co., 1970).

2. Ken Anderson (1934–1978). In 1930, while attending architectural school at the University of Washington, Ken won the highly competitive Fontainbleau Traveling Scholarship. After two years abroad, he returned to Washington and was graduated in 1933. Worked at MGM before coming to Disney's. Layout, story, story sketch, styling, and character design were his specialties; he was also instrumental in designing Disneyland attractions for WED.

3. Milt Schaffer (1933–1954), animator, cartoon shorts director, and storyman.

4. Norm Ferguson (1929–1953), animator from New York, supervising animator, director, and production supervisor.

5. Clarence Nash (1933–   ), voice talent. The first picture with Donald Duck's voice was the *Wise Little Hen*, released, June, 1934.

6. Hamilton Luske (1934–1973), animator, supervising animator on *Snow White*, supervising director on *Fantasia*, cartoon sequence director on *Mary Poppins*. Other credits under cartoon features.

7. Ward Kimball (1934–1973), animator, supervising animator, and director.

8. Roy Disney, by his own admission, was always holding back, reluctant to spend more money on new developments—often the very things that made the studio what it is today—like switching over to color. But, still, he was the one who had the headaches with the bankers, had to face the day-to-day trials, and always had to have enough money for the payroll. After the war it was not until Disneyland opened that the company really became solvent again. But Roy, for a long time, was opposed to that project, and even was against calling it Disneyland. In a light mood, he said, "I was against everything that Walt ever tried, but he made me do it." When the time came for financing Walt Disney World, Roy believed in it, and he carried out what many consider a remarkable piece of textbook financing.

He had a friendly easy-going relationship with the animation personnel, but was not above needling us about the cost of our cartoon features. He thought of these pictures as being like precious stones, and that the fewer of them there were the more valuable each one

would be—that the company actually would be better off to stop making them and just pay us to sit home.

At the time of Walt's death, the only property that had been discussed for animation was *Aristocats*. According to producer Bill Anderson, Roy said, "Bill, I'd just as soon not make it." But six months later, *The Jungle Book* was completed and was a smashing success; after that Roy supported us and even backed the idea of rebuilding the animation department. On both *The Jungle Book* and *Aristocats*, Roy okayed bonuses for the animation department—the first in over thirty years—and this may have been his way of admitting he had misjudged the continuing value of the cartoon features.

On more than one occasion, rumors circulated through the studio that Walt and Roy had had a serious falling out. This caused considerable apprehension and uneasiness among all of us, not only because we were fond of both of them but because it was unthinkable that they would ever be anything but a team; they needed each other. Fortunately, our concerns were always unwarranted, for, as Walt said, he and Roy must have had a guardian angel and that they could never split up because "Roy doesn't know whether it's my guardian angel, and I don't know whether it's his."

Chapter 5

1. Jack Cutting (1929–1975), animator, assistant director to Dave Hand, director, head of Foreign Department.

2. Arthur Rackham, noted English illustrator. Born 1867, died 1939. Illustrated Kenneth Grahame's *Wind in the Willows*, which was later used as a basis for Disney's *Mr. Toad*.

3. Albert J. Guerard, *The Triumph of the Novel, Dickens, Dostoevsky, Faulkner* (New York and London: Oxford University Press, 1976). Professor of literature, Stanford University, since 1961. Distinguished critic and novelist.

4. The term "sequence" refers to a group of scenes all related to a single idea that make up a section of the story. They are like the divisions of an act in a play, in that the action usually occurs in one locale and has one overall mood. There can be an exciting sequence, a sad one, a musical one, a funny one; each is built to exploit the entertainment potential in the idea, and to give texture and a contrast to the other sequences around it.

Chapter 6

1. From an interview with Steve Hulett.

2. George Stallings (1935–1963), story director until 1946. Worked in comic strip department until 1963.

3. Thornton Hee (1938–1946 and 1958–1960 and six months in 1961), storyman, director, teacher, and outstanding caricaturist. Worked intermittently on many projects at WED.

4. Don Graham was particularly impressed with Bill's work because it reflected a solid art background. Don was also constantly alert to tangible examples of principles, rules, and devices that he could explain and pass on to his students. Often the animator was nonplussed by the academic accomplishments that were being seen in his work, but it made the classes more exciting and stimulating than continued action analysis. When Don fully understood that much of the strength in Bill's animation came from the thrust in the moving parts, he thought he had found a whole new principle that would revolutionize animation forever. He called it Forces and Forms and built a complete approach to movement through isolating the leading edge of any movement and drawing only that part that represented the thrust of the action. In his mind, the balance of the drawing could easily be filled in by a lesser man once this essence of movement had been captured. Bill was not too sure about all of this, but had to admit that he did indeed consider the strength of the movement in all the related parts very carefully in any animation that he did. As a principle, Forces and Forms talked well, was an intriguing proposal to contemplate, led to many heated class discussions, but produced no great animators. Animation like Bill's was far too complex ever to be covered by a single concept.

Don reluctantly learned that animation is a matter of feeling, and no one can do successful work if he is trying to draw like someone else or change his own style to that of another. It must be felt deeply by the individual artist in order for it to be a personal expression.

Chapter 7

1. C. Northcote Parkinson, *Parkinson's Law* (Boston: Houghton Mifflin Co., 1957), p. 61.

2. Mel Shaw (1938–1941 and 1974–   ), storyman and stylist.

3. King Features, the same syndicate that handled the Disney comic strips.

4. Claude Coats (1935–), background artist and stylist. Moved to WED in 1961.

5. Interview by A. Eisen in *The Harvard Journal of Pictorial Fiction*, Winter, 1975.

6. J. R. Kist, *Daumier, Eyewitness of an Epoch* (Uxbridge: printed in England for Her Majesty's Stationery Office by Hillington Press), pp. 3, 4.

7. Ken Peterson (1936–1974), assistant animator, casting director, and animation department manager in 1945. Production supervisor in 1966 and producer in 1970.

8. Richard Merryman, "Andrew Wyeth: An Interview," *Life*, May 14, 1965. From *The Art of Andrew Wyeth* (Boston: Little, Brown and Company, 1973), p. 72.

9. William Garity (1929–1942), engineer. Responsible for the development of the multiplane camera and for the first use of stereo sound with a major motion picture. The latter was called Fantasound and was one of the major promotional ingredients used in advertising *Fantasia*. The first person to hold the position of studio manager.

10. Ollie Johnston (1935–1978), supervising animator.

11. C. Northcote Parkinson, *Parkinson's Law* (Boston: Houghton Mifflin Co., 1957), p. 4.

12. Ken Peterson.

13. 3C–11 and 3C–12 were later changed to 3E–11 and 3E–12.

14. Cornett Wood (1935–1941), effects animator.

Chapter 8

1. One might think this would have been an area where money could be saved after Walt died, but, instead, one morning when Donn Tatum, then chairman of the board and now chairman of the executive committee, came in to work he noticed that there were no flower beds—only green shrubs, trees, and lawn. So he had the landscape designers brought up from Disneyland to reorganize the grounds with flowers brightening every vista; these were replaced continuously the year round as each blooming season ended. Other areas retreated from Walt's idealism, but not the landscaping.

2. In order of seniority with starting dates: Les Clark, 1927; Woolie Reitherman, 1933; Eric Larson, 1933; Ward Kimball, 1934; Milt Kahl, 1934; Frank Thomas, 1934; Ollie Johnston, 1935; John Lounsbery, 1935; and Marc Davis, 1935.

3. Recognition came to the Nine Old Men on April 9, 1978, in the form of the "Pioneer in Film" award from the University of Southern California chapter of Delta Kappa Alpha National Honorary Cinema Fraternity, but by that time there were only eight left, since John Lounsbery had died two years earlier. Further honors came from the American Film Institute at the Kennedy Center in Washington, D. C., on June 19, 1978.

4. Marc Davis.

5. John Culhane, "The Old Disney Magic," *New York Times*, August 1, 1976.

6. John Culhane, "The Last of the Nine Old Men," *American Film*, June, 1977, p. 15. Referring to Frank Thomas.

7. *Ibid.*

8. *Ibid.* Referring to Ollie Johnston.

9. John Canemaker (author, historian, animator), "Sincerely Yours, Frank Thomas," *Millimeter*, January, 1975.

10. Ken Peterson, producer of all TV and educational films directed by Les Clark.

11. John Culhane, *loc. cit.*

12. *Ibid.*

13. John Canemaker.

14. Interview by A. Eisen in *The Harvard Journal of Pictorial Fiction*, Winter, 1975.

15. An old-timer recalls: "One time when Marc was down the hall visiting, Milt Kahl quietly slipped into Marc's room next door and moved the furniture—not much, but just enough to barricade the normal path across the room to the phone. Then, back in his own room, Milt dialed Marc's number, and somehow Marc could always recognize his ring and he jumps up and says, 'Jeeze, there's my phone again' and takes off down the hall, turns the corner and goes barging into all that furniture that's not quite where he remembered it. Marc got terribly mad at the furniture, but finally after bruising his knees and shins he managed to reach the phone—only to hear the click of someone hanging up.

"I don't know whether he ever did realize all that stuff had been moved around—Milt did it so subtly."

Chapter 9

1. Ollie Johnston.

2. Bill Peet (1937–1964), story, story sketch, and character design.

3. Woolie Reitherman (1933–1980), animator, supervising animator, director, and producer.

4. James Thurber, *The Years with Ross* (Boston: Atlantic Monthly Press, Little, Brown and Co., 1957), p. 174.

5. Don Duckwall (1939–1980), assistant director, production manager.

6. Douglas Slocombe, BSC, was director of photography for *Jesus Christ Superstar, The Great Gatsby, Travels with My Aunt, Rollerball,* and *The Lion in Winter.* Quoted by David W. Samuelson in *American Cinematographer,* March, 1978:

"In the short time that a scene is on the screen, the eye can take in only a few things. I found actually that you've only got time to see one really definite thing and one subsidiary thing. Therefore, I find that the secret of any composition and the secret of any lighting approach is really to try to keep those things as simple as possible. I've noticed, in studying the paintings of the great masters, that even though their audiences have much more time to stand in front of a work and examine every detail of it, the greatest paintings are still the ones that catch you with just one or two very strong elements. I've always tried to keep to this—call it a form of journalism, if you like. I just try to tell the story terribly simply, and every time I forget that rule I regret it."

7. Ron Clements (1974–), animator.

8. Frank Thomas (1934–1978), supervising animator, storyman.

9. Blake Edwards, quoted in interview with Peter Stamelman, *Millimeter*, January, 1977.

10. Munro Leaf, "The Adventures of Snow White and the Seven Dwarfs," *Stage*, February, 1938.

Chapter 10

1. Our paint is especially ground and mixed in our own paint lab and cannot be purchased on the market. It is a form of gouache in that it is an opaque watercolor paint but more finely ground than most paints of this type. It was called simply "tempera" or "poster paint" by the people who used it, even though those terms are not really correct. Also a special formula of our own was the Aqua-fix, which kept the colors from picking up on subsequent levels of paint, as details were put in or values accented.

2. Jim Algar (1934–1977), animator, sequence director on cartoon features, producer and director on nature films.

3. Jack Boyd (1939–1973), effects animator.

4. *Ibid.*

5. If this had been a normal composite of sound and picture, they could not have cut in the scene without destroying the balance of the sound; however, for Fantasound to work, the track was separate.

Interestingly enough, the whole last reel of sound track was on the same plane with the precious film, since Walt had left instructions for some important changes before he left for New York. As Herb Taylor tells it, "We had a motorcycle waiting right there by the door to rush the track to the airport just as soon as it was all put together. I went home at eight in the morning while everyone else was coming to work." Herb was later head of the sound department.

6. Fred C. Kelly, *The Wright Brothers* (New York: Harcourt, Brace and Co., 1943). John E. Walsh, *One Day at Kitty Hawk* (New York: Thomas Y. Crowell Co., 1975).

7. Ann Lloyd (1936–   ), painter, color models.

8. Lillian Bounds and Hazel (Bounds) Sewell, who later married Bill Cottrell, then a storyman. Roy Disney's wife Edna even was brought in for a while. Everyone had to help complete the pictures.

9. There were no screen credits given on Disney cartoon short subjects until 1944. Many of the animators who helped build the studio, for one reason or another, did not work on the features, or, if they did, were below the allotted footage that would entitle them to receive screen credit. Among those were Johnny Cannon, Walter Clinton, Chester Cobb, Chuck Couch, Rex Cox, Nick de Tolly, Giles de Trémaudan, Nick George, Hardie Gramatky, Jack Hannah, Emory Hawkins, Volus Jones, I. Klien, Lee Morehouse, Ken Muse, Charles Nichols, Frank Oreb, C. F. Otterstrom, Tom Palmer, Harry Reeves, Archie Robin, Leonard Sebring, and Rudy Zamora.

Chapter 11

1. Charlie Chaplin, *My Autobiography* (London: Penguin Books, 1966), p. 324.

2. Ub Iwerks reasoned with Carl Stalling that the speed of the film running through the projection machine was the only constant factor to which any sync could be related. Ninety feet a minute was broken down to 24 frames a second, and the metronome became the device for giving that tempo to the director and the musician as they planned their picture.

3. Jerome Kern, as quoted by Christopher Finch, *The Art of Walt Disney* (New York: Harry N. Abrams, Inc., 1973), p. 124.

4. Jim Algar, letter of September, 1979.

5. Frank Thomas.

6. Charlie Chaplin, *op. cit.*, p. 209.

7. Frank Thomas.

Chapter 12

1. Card Walker (1938–   ) worked in the camera department prior to moving into the area of management. A vice president in 1956, in 1971 he was elected president of Walt Disney Productions, and in 1980 moved up to chairman of the board.

Chapter 13

1. Eadweard Muybridge, *Animals in Motion*, ed. Lewis S. Brown (New York: Dover Publications, Inc.)

2. Milt Kahl (1934–1977) and Frank Thomas, supervising animators.

Chapter 14

1. Leo Salkin (1937–1953), animator, storyman.

2. Ted Berman (1940–   ), animator, storyman, director.

3. François Truffaut, *Hitchcock*, collab. Helen G. Scott (New York: Simon and Schuster, 1967), p. 237.

4. *Ibid.*, pp. 42, 43.

5. *Ibid.*, p. 163

6. Ollie Johnston.

7. Nobel Prize for Literature acceptance address, 1949.

Chapter 15

1. Frank Thomas.

2. Charlie Chaplin, *My Autobiography* (London: Penguin Books).

3. Milt Kahl.

4. Ollie Johnston.

Chapter 16

1. Edward M. Farmer, distinguished painter and art teacher at Stanford, 1923–1964. Both Frank Thomas and Ollie Johnston studied with him while at Stanford.

2. Angna Enters, *On Mime* (Middletown: Wesleyan University Press, 1968), p. 42.

3. François Truffaut, *Hitchcock*, collab. Helen G. Scott (New York: Simon and Schuster, 1967), p. 152.

4. Marcel Marceau, seminar, May, 1973, at the Actor's and Director's Lab., Beverly Hills. (Notes by Ollie Johnston.)

5. Antoine de Saint-Exupéry, *Wind, Sand and Stars* (New York: Harcourt, Brace and Co., 1932), p. 177.

Chapter 17

1. *Fantasia* (New York: Simon and Schuster, 1940), p. 6.

2. Ommanney and Schanker, *The Stage and the School* (New York: McGraw-Hill Book Co., 1972), p. 151.

3. Dave Hand, lecture on staging, October 13, 1938.

4. Frank Thomas.

5. On December 23, 1935, Walt dictated an eight-page memo to Don Graham that outlined his plans for the training of the new men and gave a complete summation of his approach to the uses of animation. Over the years, this detailed statement has become the guide for animators at the studio. Most of our chapter headings use quotes from this memo.

6. Ollie Johnston.

7. Baroness Jane van Lawick-Goodall, *My Friends the Wild Chimpanzees* (Washington: National Geographic Society Special Publication, 1967), p. 138.

Chapter 18

1. German filmmaker Oskar Fischinger, who had pioneered films of abstract art moving in sync with a sound track, was hired at the studio late in 1938. Walt had hoped that this addition to the staff would stimulate the other creative people to new ideas, but, unfortunately, it was not a happy or productive relationship for either party and Oskar left in less than a year.

2. John Ployart McLeish (1939–1941), story sketch man.

3. Eric Sevareid, noted newscaster, made this comment at the time of Walt's death in 1966:

"By the conventional wisdom, mighty mice, flying elephants, Snow White and Happy, Grumpy, Sneezy, and Dopey—all these were fantasy, escapism from reality. It's a question of whether they are any less real, any more fantastic than intercontinental missiles, poisoned air, defoliated forests, and scrap iron on the moon. This is the age of fantasy, however you look at it, but Disney's fantasy wasn't lethal. People are saying we'll never see his like again."

4. Frank Thomas, November 23, 1976.

5. Jean Renoir, *My Life and My Films* (New York: Atheneum, 1974), p. 141.

APPENDICES

General Outline of Animation Theory and Practice
by Hamilton Luske, December 31, 1935

Class on Action Analysis
by Vladimir (Bill) Tytla, June 8, 1937

Character Handling
by Hamilton Luske, September 30, 1938

Analysis of Mickey Mouse
by Fred Moore

Analysis of Donald Duck
by Fred Spencer

Analysis of Pluto
by Norman Ferguson

Analysis of the Goof
by Art Babbitt

General Outline of Animation Theory and Practice

I. Benefit of exchange of ideas

  A. Spirit that exists here of co-operation and exchange of ideas should be encouraged, as it enables beginners in animation to get a head start, pick up methods in use and improve on them instead of starting at the beginning and attempting to produce their own working rules. It gives the entire animation staff the opportunity to take advantage of every new method of achievement.

  B. Sources of information on animation methods and procedures:

    1. Specialists among studio men
    2. Library of scenes
    3. Exposure sheets
    4. Old pictures

  C. Main considerations in story animation:

    1. Simplicity and Clarity
    2. Caricature: We should make action stronger than it would be in human life. Otherwise, we are not taking advantage of our medium.

  D. There are no hard and fast rules in the studio—exceptions to everything.

II. Methods of animation

  A. Old Method:
  Working from pose to pose. Holding one pose, called a hold or an extreme, as long as possible, then inbetweening to the next one.
  Advantages: Quick way to work. Generally told a good, clear story if the holds were expressive.
  Disadvantages: unnatural action. Jerky.

  B. Second Method:
  Working straight ahead. Rather than drawing poses, as before, we'd take each part of the action as it came along, limiting ourselves only by exposure sheet timing.
  Advantages: Gave an overlapping action that was smooth and showed an even timing. More natural action.
  Disadvantages: Might be aiming wrong. Might get to main points in wrong positions. Development of idea that holds were not wanted, and a consequent skipping over of vital spots.

  C. Present Method:
  Combination of advantages of two previous methods. Putting in the extremes and then working straight ahead with the extremes as guides for the in-betweens. Elaborating or simplifying resulting drawings for caricatured action.

    1. General Primary Routine

      a. "Set-up" drawings (ones that tell the story)
      b. "Result" drawings from those, and all "anticipation" drawings, keeping in line with others.
      c. There is no action in the scene at that point but its essential parts are there, and the rest of the work is comparatively simple.

III. Scene Planning—General routine. Scenes are planned from start to finish before animation is begun. The drawings are the expression of your thoughts. Timing, exposing, etc. all follow later.

  A. Know the story and how your scene fits in it

    1. Study connecting scenes

    2. Character must not do anything that does not apply to the story.
      a. Simple walk across the floor should be done characteristically, as that particular character would do it, should be as direct as possible unless funny business is specifically called for.
      b. Audience should not be made to laugh in the wrong place, killing the buildup of a later gag.

  B. Know your character

    1. Method of developing a new character (Mortimer in *Mickey's Rival*, for example)
      a. Classification of general type: Collegiate mouse, very cocky.
      b. Study of same type as shown in previous picture: Hare in *Tortoise and the Hare*

        1. Chesty, fanny out, comparatively small body with S-curve
        2. Swagger walk—arms out, back stiff
        3. Quick movements into poses
        4. Self assurance expressed by continuous smile.
      c. Comparison of fictitious cartoon character with real person: Jimmy Cagney
      d. Study of model drawing: small sweater, voluminous pants with very definite crease and bell-bottomed, small hat on side of head, buck teeth

    2. Examples of analyses of other characters

      a. BULL: Massive shoulders, small rear end—all crowded up in front. High neck in back. Lowered head.
      b. BULLDOG: (Dirty Bill) Bull neck, underslung jaw, accented by pointed top with head coming down so he was built out. Big shoulders and bowlegs.
      c. KITTENS AND ELMER ELEPHANT: very young, cramping eyes in lower part of head, softness, large heads.

  C. Know the kind of action your character would have. Walks (as example)

    1. JENNY WREN—floats through her walk. Picks up foot daintily, transfers weight, sways over before putting foot down.
    2. PIED PIPER—young—spring in his stride. Old man would show lack of spring—walk bent-legged.
    3. HARE—fast, swagger
    4. DIRTY BILL—Rotating motion because of large body and bow-legs. Carrying body to keep balance. Slow.

  D. Putting over the gag—directness

    1. Plan to keep the main action out in the clear, not necessarily profile, although this angle is clearest.
    2. Look at drawings made by layout men to see whether they express strong poses. If they aren't clear, re-arrange them.

E. Anticipation

1. Anticipate the action with on-a-line motion (See IV) Audience must be ready for what is going to happen.
2. Kinds of anticipation
    a. Picking a flower: Looking, coming up and going down into the pick
    b. Jump: squat
    c. Running through a door: coming back on a line with the door
    d. General: Always an up before a down, a back before a front, a look before a grab. Do the motion that leads into the action.
    e. Anticipation done in overlapping previous action when scene is not very important.

F. Exaggeration—Caricature

1. Enlarge on drawings and tell the story just as clearly as possible with that drawing. Examples:

    Man looking in a vase. He should be up above, looming over it—no doubt he is looking in it

    Man hitting something with a hammer. Anticipation: arms back, body high and arched, on toes. Where he has hit the object, he is down extremely low—object is squashed. Likely no drawings from place where hammer starts to come down and squashed object. Maybe a blur. Then a rebound in man from force of hit. That's the result—a moving hold of six to ten. Then react into straight drawing.

    Mickey's head into Pete's stomach. A bump in Pete's back to show effect of force.

2. Assistant must not just clean up. He is not working over the same ground, but is exaggerating what you have.
3. Enlarge the equipment used by the character. Example: Hero with big tennis racket, glove, bat. He is small in comparison.
4. Uses in place of speed lines
    a. Stretching is better than speed lines. Example: Hare with racket arm pulling through. Brought arm down and pulled it through. It moved a great distance.

G. Holds

1. Old Way of looking at a hold—as a number on an exposure sheet—something stiff and frozen.
2. New Way of looking at holds—as moving all the time (Telling the story with a drawing or a group of drawings, yet having the hold alive all the time)

    Example: JENNY WREN as based on Mae West (Who Killed Cock Robin?)

    a. Characteristics of Mae West
        1. Always moving, swaying, weaving in typical poses (hand on hip or arranging hair) Rotation of body not like hula dance, but from the front.
        2. Walk: Plants foot, shifts weight. Longer time on shifting than planting.
        3. Talks: Drops eyes, comes up with them half-closed. Talks out of side of mouth. Little lip movement. Sideward glances—looks away disinterestedly. Starts conversation and walks away. Elusive.
        4. Arms and shoulders—overlapping with body. Leave body rather than being right with it.
    b. Characteristics of Jenny Wren
        1. Caricature of Mae West: Movements in coming out door, talking to Robin expressed in groups of holds, yet no full stops.
        2. Rotation of body shown in wide tail movement.
3. Methods of drawing holds
    a. Put in everything that is not an inbetween. Anticipations and all extremes.
    b. More drawings used up to the point where you are halfway into the hold than rest of way in. After the eye is started, action can be faster.
    c. Coming out of a hold is generally slow. Use more frames.
    d. Accent—down with few drawings
    e. Settling in—a lot of drawings. (Going slowly into a hold)
    f. IT IS THE RESULT THAT IS HELD. In exposing, you start the eye of the audience in one direction with one or two drawings. Then you show the result. Enough exposures must be put in to show the result. That is called a hold. Not one drawing, but a group of drawings.

H. On-a-Line Action

1. Hat spinning over head of tortoise, Toby spinning on ground. Hat could have been directly over head and Toby could have been pulled right up into it for more force on the action.
2. On hitting mallet—line directly down for height.
3. On kick—head reacting in line with arc of foot. Feeling of foot going through.
4. Pulling a cow's tail and ringing bell around his neck. Backbone on line with tail, neck on line with backbone. Gives reality to ringing of bell.
5. Elmer squirting water from his trunk, around a post, to hit a flame. Had to anticipate with trunk—shoot on a line with the curve.

IV. Timing

A. Work with director in acting things out and timing them.

B. Examples:

    Walk: Take a basis. Soldiers march about 120 steps to the minute or two to the second. That is twelve frames to the step. (24 frames a second)

    Run: On above basis, about twice as fast as walk,

    Walk of Jenny Wren: Out of doorway in about three twelves. Each step thirty-six frames. Three times as slow as a soldier. Later changes tempo for musical beat.

    Tennis serve (Hare): Three poses to serve a tennis ball. Divide the time into thirds for timing each part of action.

    GENERAL PROCEDURE: Figure on 24 frames a second. You know how fast he moves. You have acted it out in front of a mirror and timed yourself on it. You find out how long it takes to do it as the character would do it naturally, and how long it would take if you caricatured him, and figure how you can save space. Then you start working and put your punch in the strong points of action, conserving time on the unimportant points.

C. Let the audience see what you want them to see. Make the rest fast.

1. When the scene is finished, if you have placed too much stress on unimportant things or not enough on important things, you have not planned the scene correctly.

V. Exposing

A. General rule: Fill in numbers on exposure sheets. Follow up with notes on drawings to show where to speed in and out of poses. (Number of exposures on each drawing and directions about speed.)

1. Start out of a hold with two exposures is a good rule. Slow way of going out. Then another two exposures and then go into ones on a line. Then two to go in again.

2. Three exposures for a contact in a running action. For faster action, blur when foot hits or after it has left.

B. Two exposure action used most of the time. Saves inbetweens and gives smooth action.

VI. Takes—a feeling of *lift*

A. Sudden surprise—two or three holds:

1. Sees it
2. Registers
3. Sudden reaction or stiffening up

B. All clothing, etc. follows the line in which the original take took place.

C. Hardly any in-betweens. One or two to start, then the result and a hold of eight to sixteen frames.

VII. Dialogue

A. Phrase expressions to suit dialogue. Body position for the phrase, head action to catch words.

B. On lips, the main thing is to catch the close mouth (b's, p's, m's) Lip accent the last thing you work on.

VIII. Sparks:

Should no longer be used. If it's the spot for an effect, put in the effect. A character is not surprised by sparks, but actually surprised in eyebrows, general facial expressions, etc. Thinking was once shown by a question mark over the character's head.

Dec.31,1935
ET
Ham Luske

Class on Action Analysis

Date held: Monday, June 8, 1937
Conducted by: Don Graham
Speaker: Bill Tytla

I don't mean to discourage you by saying a man either has a feeling for the work, or hasn't. You fellows have been selected out of literally thousands of applicants. Your work, after a period of training, shows you have been able to survive a lot of picking; and no doubt the majority of you will eventually come out as animators. But all this training which you are going through which is absolutely essential, is not just merely being done to make it possible for you to draw another little duck or something. The work now being planned, and the work they will continue to do here, will call for men who can draw to beat hell, not just in the conventional sense, but men who have absolute control over what they are trying to do. The men who are surviving realize this. There are some of the old-timers who are good because they have developed with the industry; but that doesn't mean all the old-timers will. Even around here there are men who can't stand the gaff—men who in their time were considered sensational, but who can't do things you fellows take for granted today. You don't realize the progress in the field, not only artistically, but technically as well.

Yesterday, I started to paint again, and I found that anything I learned in animation I could apply in painting. The stuff Don has mentioned in action analysis classes—balance, counter balance, weight—apply to everything.

Just for the fun of it, it would be very interesting if you fellows would take a little human character of any kind and make him do a walk—any kind of walk—a gimpy walk, if you preferred that; then you would know what you have to know about drawing before you can really animate. Dress the character very simply—just a simple jacket and pants, and perhaps a pair of Dutch wooden shoes. Then not only rough in the action, but clean it up—then you will realize how much you men need to know drawing.

I consider a walk to be one of the toughest things to do in animation. For the problem I suggest to you, evolve your own little character. If you are still not satisfied and really want to know what I mean when I say how much you must know about drawing, have your character go through pantomime as Chaplin does it. You don't need dialogue there—just try to get some of that stuff into animation—then I won't have to tell you how important drawing is—you will have proved its importance to yourself.

So if you fellows hope to animate, you must realize in your rough drawings you have to know the stuff is really there. You all know how nicely a quick sketch comes up, and you are apt to fool yourselves regarding the effectiveness of a rough by making allowances for the flickering of roughs—but in finishing up, you really come up against the weakness or strength of the rough drawing.

Here's another interesting thing I'd like to stress. You fellows possibly may think that just because you are doing a bunch of Ducks and Mickeys, that all you must do is learn how to draw well enough to draw a Duck and a Mickey. But the funny thing is that the more you know about drawing, the more ably you will handle the Duck and other characters. And besides, five years from now you won't be doing Ducks anyway.

The type of stuff we have been doing here the last few years has been a change from what preceded it, and will be different from what is about to follow. You men who have animated before, will agree there has been quite a bit of change since you started to animate. In those days we never had a problem of animating characters that were similar and yet markedly different. Today we are really on the verge of something that is new. It will take a lot of real drawing—not clever, slick, superficial, fine looking stuff—but real solid, fine drawing to achieve those results, and those results will have to be achieved by the fellows who have absolute control of what they are trying to do. These animators will have to be able to not only draw, but to take a figure, and no matter how they twist, distort, slap [squash] or extend the figure, that will still have weight—it will still weigh 100 pounds.

Those animators will have to be able to put across a certain sensation or emotion . . . for that is all we are trying to do in animation. Remember your animation must get over—whether you have sound effects to help it or not. You have to get in picture form the same effect that sound and dialogue can give you. You must learn how to draw and control your drawing to the nth degree.

We are getting away gradually from the limitations of cute little business. At times you will want to animate stuff where you just can't be cute or coy. Those are the times when you will have to know something about drawing—whether it is called form, force or vitality, you must get it in your work, for that will be what you feel, and drawing is your means of expressing it. In order to get a certain sensation over, it means you must have perfect control of your timing too—over the way you accent something. It is these little accents too, that will give you sensations and effects. Accenting in animation might be compared in a way to a person sitting at a piano who keeps on playing without any definition. In drawing it is the same thing, whether you call it phrasing or force—it is the way you accent the drawing that gives you the result.

Every time you start a scene, it is the same heartache of trying to analyze the work; you have the situation, the exposure sheet, dialogue track, sound effects; you try to break that down to what you think should be done, and you keep on breaking the whole thing down to the single drawing, and you break a single drawing down to accent whatever you want to put across in that single drawing, because you are leading up to it and away from it to another thing. In phrasing a scene, you must consider that something happens—there is a pause—you want to put that thing across—the way you work up to the point and anticipate into the next thing, will be important. Then you go about your business again till you hit into the next pose or situation—and you keep on breaking the scene down to the single drawing again and break that down to the expression or mood you are trying to project. Really the thing is as simple as that.

Whatever I have to say about breaking a scene down applies to the bigger division of a sequence. You break a whole sequence down into scenes, subdivide the scenes, break the whole scene down to one or two characters—perhaps one character in a group of 3 or 5 talks, another answers. Therefore, you try to plot an emphasis on a certain character—have a bit of anticipation by the way you pose him, break it down so the eye will always go to the character you want the audience to follow. One of the characters will start talking—you must switch the audience to that particular character.

In that event you won't have all your characters come out one by one and give their lines—like the Happy Hooligan kids in the old cartoons with the tin cans on their heads, when each would give his line, "I" "love" "Uncle" "Happy." We can't go back to that sort of system.

Whether you handle 1, 2, 3 or 7 characters you must phrase or force or define so that the eye always follows. Very often you must do things you might call bad drawing in order to accent or force. We all realize that in animation one drawing is just a part of 100 or 300 drawings. In itself it is nothing—just a continuation of a vast whole. If you always try to keep perfect form, you will not get the feeling across—it will be just something that continues without any flavor.

You can give a drawing an accent—you can twist an eyebrow or a mouth—you can force or accent it—you can do something to the little character's shoulder or chest; but it is a continuous flow, and it always comes back to its original shape.

We have an interesting problem in the 7 little dwarfs. They all have a slightly different way of doing things, even down to their individual dialogue. The animation, spacing, timing—everything was done to interpret those little characters so that when the audience finally hears the voice coupled with the animation, there is a feeling of completeness and rightness to it all. This was achieved through interpretation of the individual characters—not through a stock way of doing anything.

Instead of all reacting at the same time,

Sleepy is the last one to do what they are supposed to be doing. Then naturally he does it in a Sleepy way. Happy responds in a very vivacious way. He is quick moving. He is the most alive after Grumpy, who is angular in everything he does. Grumpy always acts the way he does because he is sore as hell. Happy is vivacious and bubbling over with life, and all these quick little movements. Sneezy, too, is a bit more alive than Sleepy in reaction. A problem presented itself in the third scene around the tub, where one says, "IT'S WET," another "IT'S COLD," not everyone reacts to the same thing at the same time. The "looks" will be the only thing that represents each as there are no particular mannerisms. The hands are on the side of the tub. The only thing you can rely on is their reaction, not their mannerisms—only how they would react to a sentence—how fast they would do it. This is merely in the timing. Each one has his own way of reacting at a different time.

This handling gave the scene a soft kind of feeling and not a mechanical one as if a company of infantry were present and on the order, "Eyes right" all eyes went right. But our work here is different—these characters animate according to their mental reactions. You cannot expect a fellow like Sleepy to be vivacious and to react as quickly and forcefully as the other characters do. Therefore, the accent or forces or lack of it is all in what you are trying to do.

Sometimes the layout man does not digest the piece of business as the animator will see it. This is no criticism of the layout man, but most of the time I refer to their sketch to see how many figures they have and what the dialogue and story call for; and then I reorganize the thing myself to put across a certain thing as I would like to see it, which means the animator must practically stage and do everything else besides drawing, accenting, etc. You take a group of figures and do it as you would a single figure—you draw the arms, hands, eyes, twist the bodies in a way to have interest. It is the individual animator's artistic taste and reactions that help, and besides the animator has a story to tell. When you are animating you have various things to do—you are acting, directing, a cartoonist mimicking all sorts of things.

We can't be mystical about our work—we cannot turn out the lights and have confessions. This is a business. In comparison with other places, we have more time, more means for doing things at our disposal, whether technical or artistic. But you do have a time limit. You have to have a time limit whether you are drawing, painting, loving or fighting—you just can't keep on forever. You can go into a beautiful trance contemplating what you want to do, then exhaust yourself thinking about it. You have a unit director to contend with, a director in charge of all the directors—then Walt.

Character Handling

Ham Luske—September 30, 1938

We have learned to maintain the illusion of life in our characters by the following methods:

1. By drawing simple characters that can be duplicated by any of the many artists that have to handle them.
2. By making every part of their bodies round and animatable, so that they can be squashed and stretched and turned softly and without flaws.
3. By using our own cutting technique of short scenes, clipped speeches and offstage dialogue.
4. Our fourth method of making our character life-like is the invention of moving holds, which are a substitute for the necessary pauses in good acting.

The advantages and disadvantages of our medium are fairly obvious. The advantages:

1. A newer field
2. An open field of fantasy and fairy tales never successfully invaded by the regular movies.
3. We can make the impossible seem possible and exaggerate to our hearts' content.
4. We can rework and simplify scenes until perfection is reached.
5. Absolute synchronization to music.
6. An appreciation by the public for our efforts.

Our disadvantages are stories that are out of our reach—there are more of these than there are of the others.

Another disadvantage is the human element.... we have a variety of animators—some of them are good artists and bad actors, some are good actors and bad artists—yet they all have their hands in working on our characters.

Our production takes a long time. It is hard to keep feeling and enthusiasm and consistency for that long a time.

We can't manage slow movements, and it's hard for us to handle long speeches. Long holds are necessary but tough. Trick camera angles and perspective problems are difficult to combine with drawn acting. Long shots are a problem. It's hard to make our transitions of thought subtle.

Then there are the little problems, hair, noses, thin faces, graduated shadows, normal human beings, characterless girls, muscles— it seems wise to acknowledge these difficulties and avoid them when possible.

When we are casting a character, the first thing we must do is pick the type that will be convincing and alive in animation.

Type of Character

It is advisable to select an actor whose natural voice and mannerisms are caricatures of a normal person's.

Type of Business

In choosing business for our picture or individual scenes, it is well to remember that this is a *moving* picture business and animation means movement, and animation is at its best dealing with movement.

—Broad pantomime is better than subtle speech.
—Old school acting is better than the modern reserved school.
—Dialogue spoken during action is better than dialogue followed by action. (Snow White saying, "It's covered with dust" while touching the mantel with her fingers was more convincing and moved the picture better than if she had touched the mantel and then said the line.)

We often have to invent to move our picture interestingly and to give the animator opportunities. (The idea of Figaro opening the window while Geppetto mused about his Pinocchio offstage gave interest to a difficult sequence.)

Analysis of Mickey Mouse

I. Character and Personality

Mickey seems to be the average young boy of no particular age; living in a small town, clean living, fun loving, bashful around girls, polite and as clever as he must be for the particular story.

In some pictures he has a touch of Fred Astaire; in others of Charlie Chaplin, and some of Douglas Fairbanks, but in all of these there should be some of the young boy.

II. Construction

A. Mickey's head is drawn as a circle; or better as a ball—with the features placed on this ball. The eyes and the blacks and whites, as well as the mouth, are drawn to fit the ball. The snout protruding out from the ball, and the ears to be drawn as two "not quite" circles, overlapping slightly into the ball. It is nice to keep the black and whites fairly well distributed—so to not have too much white or vice-versa.

See illustration (27)-also 4-4a-4b-4c.

B. The body to be drawn as somewhat pear-shape, fairly short and plump.

(See figure 1a–some poses following that.)

This is a new procedure on Mickey and is not meant to change him so much as to improve him. Notice on (1) and (1a) the change is small but makes the body pliable.

The body should be pliable at all times, depending on pose desired on extremity of action.
(See figures 6–7–8–13.)

If Mickey were taking a deep breath we would give him a chest. If he were sad we would loosen chest and droop shoulders, etc.

The body could be thought of as having a certain volume, so when it is stretched it should grow thinner or plumper as it is squashed.

If the body is stretched out to an extreme for anything, do *not* leave it stretched out long enough to see.

The body can assume anatomy as it is needed; such as a chest, stomach, fanny—according to pose.

In distorting Mickey's body—it is always a good idea to compare this new body with the old one, (Fig. 1), to keep it from getting too long.
For distorting Mickey's body, see figures (20–20a–20b–also 21–21a–21b)

By that I mean if you have Mickey in a scene with lots of wild action, he is likely to grow tall unconsciously, even when you come to a pause. So it is good to compare your drawing to the old Mickey just for height.
For suggestions of poses (with "anatomy") see figures (8–11–13–also 22 to 26 inclusive.)

These drawings do not cover nearly as many poses as there can be on Mickey, but are there to suggest ways of getting poses—or maybe a way of putting anatomy on Mickey for a pose.

Mickey is approximately 3 heads high—so from the bottom of feet to body—it should equal a head.

The shoes (see figures) are fairly large and bulky—a medium between hard and soft—flexible enough to help animation, but stiff enough to be shoes. For instance, do not have them too floppy on a walk. But that doesn't mean they can't be distorted in an action.

The legs are better drawn tapering from the pant leg to the shoe, that is, larger at the shoe with the knee coming low on the leg. This also applies to the arms; the hands being fairly large.

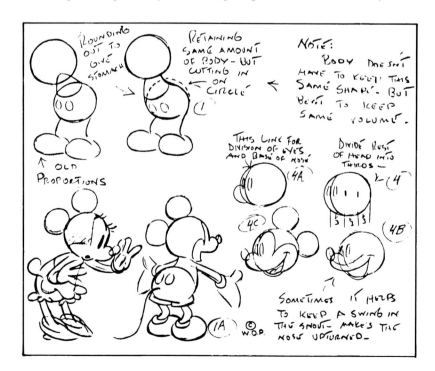

NARROW
SHOULDERS
MAKE HIM
LOOK
PATHETIC
→

SUGGESTING A
SWING IN BODY—
LIFTING HIPS ETC

(15) W.D.P.

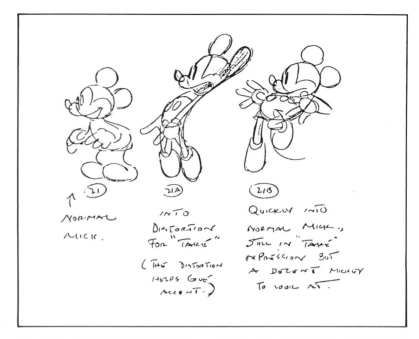

↑
NORMAL
MICK.

INTO
DISTORTION
FOR "TAKE"

(THE DISTORTION
HELPS GIVE
ACCENT.)

QUICKLY INTO
NORMAL MICK.,
STILL IN "TAKE"
EXPRESSION BUT
A DECENT MICKEY
TO LOOK AT.

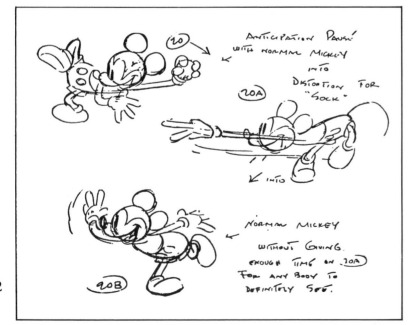

ANTICIPATION PAUSE
WITH NORMAL MICKEY
INTO
DISTORTION FOR
"SOCK"

← INTO

NORMAL MICKEY
WITHOUT GIVING
ENOUGH TIME ON 20A
FOR ANY BODY TO
DEFINITELY SEE.

III. Handling of Mickey in Animation

Mickey has already been compared to a young boy, so, of course, he should be handled as that. His poses, not only hold poses, but positions of body while walking, running, talking, etc., should contain the young boy feeling.

Mickey is cuter when drawn with small shoulders, with a suggestion of stomach and fanny—and, I like him pigeon-toed. The pigeon-toes are more of a suggestion because I like to think of him that way. There are many times when his feet would be pointed, toes out, and in those cases, pigeon-toes would be bad.

The small shoulder effect can be had by starting the arms further down on body. Don't let this keep you from using the shoulders when needed for a pose, take, or any kind of action. See Fig. (7–13–16.) Ordinarily shoulders are hard to make and are better left off. They can be used to best advantage if their use is reserved for emphasis in expressions, poses and takes.

The suggestion of stomach and fanny can be had easily with his back arched.

See Fig. (1a–6–8–9)

About the handling of Mickey's head—we know it is good to keep the blacks and whites well balanced so when Mickey has a smile, there is very little black, but when he changes to an expression with the mouth small, there would be too much black if we followed the mouth with the black the same distance away as on the smile. So it is better to cheat and not bring the black down so far. The mouth, as a rule is better kept inside circle of head; this doesn't mean it has to always be drawn that way—especially not in dialogue or big take, etc.

The ears are better kept far back on the head and often act as a balance for the figure. However, *do not* shift them around on the head just to balance.

Mickey's pants are to be handled as pants and not as made of metal. By that, I mean the pant-legs should drape over the legs and the pants between the legs should stretch as his legs part and react to the movement of body as all pants do. With a straight leg they would hang—with the knee lifted they would wrinkle and drape over leg, etc.

IV. Minnie Mouse

Drawn same as Mickey, substituting a skirt and lace pants for his pants, and high-heeled slippers in place of his shoes with addition of a small hat and eye-lids and lashes.

Minnie's poses and mannerisms should be definitely feminine. This means, too, her expressions, reactions, etc.

Minnie seems cuter with the skirts high on her body—showing a large expanse of her lace panties. This skirt should be starched and not hang limp.

Her feet and hands are large but not clumsy.

In order to make Minnie as feminine as possible, we should use everything in her make-up to achieve this end. Her mouth could be smaller than Mickey's and maybe never open into so wide a smile, take, expression, etc. Her eyelids and eyelashes could help very much in keeping her feminine as well as the skirt swaying from the body on different poses, displaying pants. Carrying the little finger in an extended position also helps.

SHORT LEGS - UP INTO THE BODY - WITH BODY SAGGING - HELPS TO KEEP THE WEIGHT IN DONALD -

PEAR SHAPED BODY - IS EAISER TO HANDLE FOR SMOOTH ACTION -

WALKS 'N RUNS

IN A WALK - GET THE TWIST IN THE BODY TO MAKE IT WADDLE

STOCK FIGHTING POSE - WITH ARM SWINGING LIKE A PENDULUM -

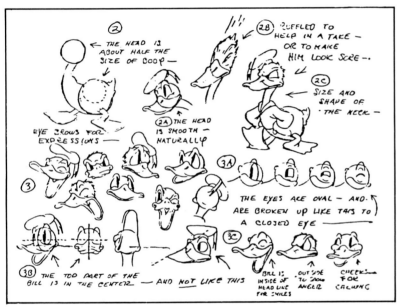

THE HEAD IS ABOUT HALF THE SIZE OF BODY -

RUFFLED TO HELP IN A TAKE - OR TO MAKE HIM LOOK SORE -

THE HEAD IS SMOOTH NATURALLY

SIZE AND SHAPE OF THE NECK -

EYE BROWS FOR EXPRESSIONS

THE EYES ARE OVAL - AND - ARE BROKEN UP LIKE THIS TO A CLOSED EYE

THE TOP PART OF THE BILL IS IN THE CENTER - AND NOT LIKE THIS

BILL IS INSIDE OF HEAD LINE FOR SMILES

OUT SIDE TO SHOW ANGER

CHEEKS FOR CALLING

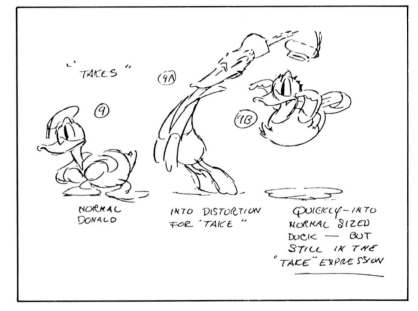

"TAKES"

NORMAL DONALD

INTO DISTORTION FOR "TAKE"

QUICKLY - INTO NORMAL SIZED DUCK - BUT STILL IN THE "TAKE" EXPRESSION

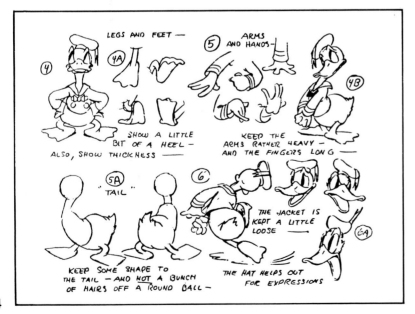

LEGS AND FEET -

SHOW A LITTLE BIT OF A HEEL -
ALSO, SHOW THICKNESS -

ARMS AND HANDS -

KEEP THE ARMS RATHER HEAVY - AND THE FINGERS LONG

"TAIL"

KEEP SOME SHAPE TO THE TAIL - AND NOT A BUNCH OF HAIRS OFF A ROUND BALL -

THE JACKET IS KEPT A LITTLE LOOSE

THE HAT HELPS OUT FOR EXPRESSIONS

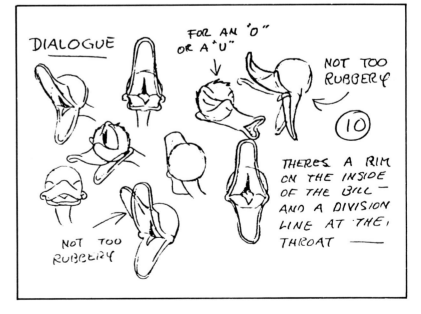

DIALOGUE

FOR AN "O" OR A "U"

NOT TOO RUBBERY

NOT TOO RUBBERY

THERE'S A RIM ON THE INSIDE OF THE BILL - AND A DIVISION LINE AT THE THROAT -

Analysis of Donald Duck

I. Character and Personality

Donald has developed into one of the most interesting screen comics. The audience always likes him, provided he plays true to his own character. His best features are his cocky, show-off, boastful attitude that turns to anger as soon as he is crossed; his typical angry gestures with which the audience is familiar, especially his fighting pose and his peculiar quacking voice and threats when angry.

The Duck gets a big kick out of imposing on other people or annoying them; but immediately loses his temper when the tables are turned. In other words, he can "dish it out" but he can't "take it".

The Duck takes himself very seriously. He has a high opinion of himself, and as soon as anything goes wrong, he immediately wants to fight. When he is pleased with himself, or happy about something he has done, we show his nervous character by wiggling his tail. I don't think it wise to use the tail wiggle when he is angry.

He has a very suspicious nature; is quick-tempered but is just dumb enough to be trapped repeatedly into losing his temper. However, he is not as dumb as Pluto or the Goof. Donald cannot be funny if the situation does not fit his peculiar mannerisms.

II. General Construction

A. Body

Donald is drawn as Fred Moore draws Mickey. He is one piece rather than two parts; has a pear-shaped body; is short, squatty, and is drawn to show weight in the body. Keep as much weight in him as possible, that is, feel that he is hugging the ground. To attain the best results, one leg is bent and the other kept straight. The straight leg is as short as possible, keeping the bulky mass down close to the ground. Keeping the leg up into the body and showing a sag underneath will help to get a feeling of weight.

B. Size of head and neck

The size of the head is supposed to be half the size of the lower part of the body, and is kept round.

To show anger, give a ruffled effect on the head; but otherwise keep the head smooth.

The neck is thicker at the head than it is at the body end and is to be kept weighty, but not too long.

C. Eyes, Bill, and Cheeks

The most important thing about Donald is his expressions. A lot can be done in this connection with the eyes and the eyebrows. We also find that the hat and the position of the bill help the expression of the eyes.

The eyebrows are used in the same way that Pluto's eyebrows are used. Sometimes they protrude above the top circle of the head.

The eyes are not round as in previous pictures. They are more oval in shape and are kept to the side of the head. In this way more black can be used in the eyes for the expressions. When the eyes are closed, we break up the circle and animate it into a roundness.

The eyes are kept wide apart to give better expression and on a 3/4 view the eye on the opposite side is lost.

The top part of the bill fits into the center of the head. Instead of there being a straight line from the top of the head down to the end of the bill, the corner of the bill curves into the inside of the head when he smiles or is happy; when Donald frowns or is angry, it protrudes on the outside of the circle of the head with a down-in-the-mouth feeling.

We use cheeks on Donald only when we indicate chewing or blowing.

D. Legs and Feet

The legs are supposed to be short and squatty and the feet kept large to give more of a comedy effect.

The feet have three toes and they are neither pointed nor long, but a happy medium between the two. He usually plops them down on a walk or run.

The foot is drawn with a thickness so that in a 3/4 back view half raised, we show an under side which can be painted to, as the "sole" is painted a darker shade.

Where the leg fits into the foot, it does not come right at the back end of the foot, but leaves a knob or a bit of heel.

E. Arms, Hands and Tail

The arms are kept thick to help in the weight, and the hands are made more like real hands—rather long, with three fingers and a thumb. In the first drawings the hands were simply the ends of the wings with wing feathers.

The tail is supposed to be like a regular duck's tail. There is a little fleshy part before the feathers start on the tail, and they are kept curled whenever possible.

F. Hat and Jacket

The jacket is to be rather loose, but not so loose that it is floppy—loose enough to help in the flow of animation.

The sleeves are a little loose around the wrist and the collar has a stripe around the outer edge.

The hat can be used effectively to help expressions and takes. When Donald is meek or when he is thinking, the hat can sit straight on top of his head with the ribbon flowing in back; but to show anger it is good to have the hat down over his eyes and the ribbon falling down in front.

Another established characteristic of Donald's is that when his hat flies off on a take or in anger and lands on the ground, he absent-mindedly reaches down for it without looking at it, picks it up, and slams it on his head before going into the next action.

III. Line of Action

When drawing Donald for a line of action, try to make the whole thing curl in one line to give directness.

A. Walks and Runs

In walks to show cuteness, it is best to have him walk pigeon-toed, and to draw the leg back and forth with the action of the body so it will make it look like a waddle. This can also be used in the run.

B. Takes

On takes, Donald is more active and more versatile than any of our characters. To show his nature, Donald's takes are almost to the extreme. That is, he jumps up in the air, turns fast whirls, gets himself all out of shape, and in general is fast and furious to show his excitable nature. All his clothing, including hat and jacket, point in the direction of the take.

The hat can be used to advantage by keeping it fastened to his head and pulled out of shape. Or it can also fly off into the air, circle several times and land back on his head.

IV. Dialogue

The upper bill is to be kept more stationary than the lower one, but not to the point of rigidity. The lower bill should be flexible, but not to the point of being rubbery.

To get the desired effect on "o" and "u" or on a blowing action, we distort the bill.

When the bill is open wide and shows the inside of the upper bill, there is to be a black shadow effect above the tongue to give depth. There is a line around the inside of the bill and also a throat line to give the painters a place for change of color, as the inside of the upper bill is a darker shade than the inside of the lower bill.

V. Fighting Pose

One of the characteristics the Duck had to start out with and one we have tried to keep, is his fighting pose. It was established by Dick Lundy in ORPHANS' BENEFIT, and we try to use it in every picture where he gets mad and wants to fight. It is an up and down movement of the whole body and one arm is held straight out with the fist up. The other arm moves as a pendulum. The timing of this action is that the body moves twice as fast as the arm that swings. Donald is usually in dialogue in this action, and his straight-out arm doesn't interfere with the action of the mouth.

Refer to illustrations on all points covered.

Fred Spencer

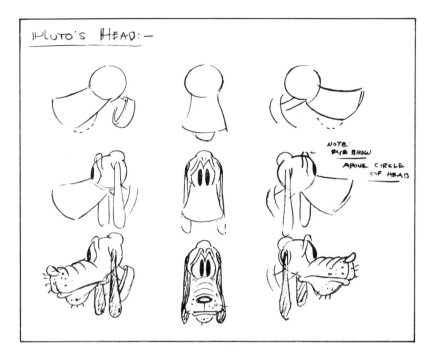

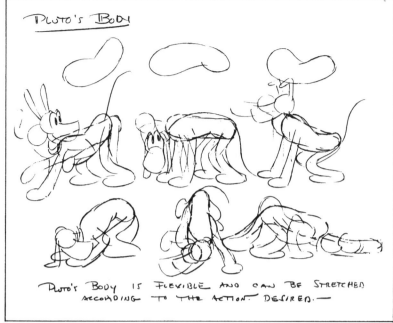

Analysis of Pluto

I. Construction

A. Body

1. In the rough—shaped like a jelly bean
2. In cleanup—put in shoulders and shape it out for a feeling of bones under the skin.
3. General conception: Heavy dog. When he starts into action, there is lots of anticipation.

   Example:
   Pluto sitting down, moves over to sniff something. Before he gets up, anticipation of a sag with head out and body coming up before he attempts to get out of sitting position. Head moves over to new position.

B. Eyes

1. General Expression: Dumb and sad-eyed
2. Nobs over eyes like prominent eyebrows or furrows: always there.

   Example: ON ICE. Pluto slips, falls, Duck laughs offstage and Pluto looks back at tail, eyebrows down, conveying thought: "There's something wrong here."

Shifts eyes from tail to audience to make expression definite. Before shifting one eyebrow goes up, the other down. Eyes and eyebrows straighten out, then eyes go from side to side. Head kept still during expression.

When Pluto pauses for expression or thought in a situation like trying to get on his feet in ON ICE, in shifting the eyes, definite pauses should be made at each end of the expression, with a definite move of the eyes from extreme to extreme. This helps to convey clearly the idea that Pluto is thinking.

C. Ears: Handling for weight

1. Pluto jumping up in air. Instead of having the ears carry through the same distance as the head, the first two or three drawings of the ears are slower to start. When he lands, the same holds good. The ears are still quite long and they come down with a sweep. In the extreme down there is a stretch and then they go up into a normal resting position.
2. In a fast surprised take the ears shoot up faster, but settle the same way.

3. In the case of a mild take with a dumb look in the eyes, ears go up in three or four drawings. When they reach the extreme up, they might go additional distance for accent then settle into curved position at the tips. (Sometimes the head will look with the ears and settle back, but usually the ears are more noticeable in action than the head.)

D. Jowls: When Pluto is sniffing the ground, the jowls are brought back so they drag.

E. Nose Wrinkles: Flexible, but usually four in number.

II. Handling of Pluto for Action

A. Pluto was originally a bloodhound, but has developed into just a big dog. In some instances he has been animated too much like a small dog without any weight to him. Pluto's comedy value lies in using him as a heavy, cumbersome, awkward dog, and to avoid the effect of lightness, whenever he is used running, jumping or falling, it is well to bear in mind the fact that a

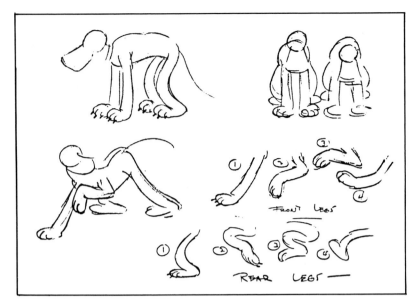

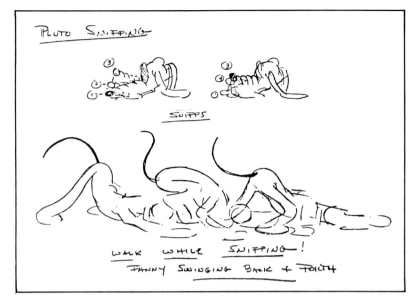

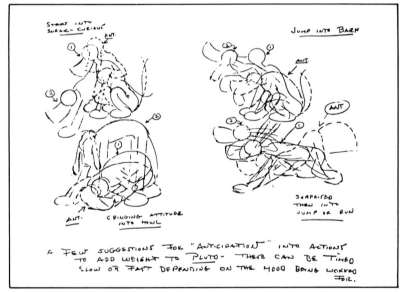

heavy dog would naturally need more anticipation to his run or jump, and in the case of a fall his land would take more stretching and recovery than that of a lighter dog. In the case of a *run* Pluto would take half again the timing of a light weight dog in the same kind of run.

Of course, there might be situations where it would be too straight for Pluto to anticipate slowly. For example, if Pluto were to react very fast to something that happens, the action following his reaction could be handled in an awkward or slow effect to give Pluto his weight, as in his jump out onto the ice in ON ICE. His slip was very fast but his turn over in the air gave the necessary weight for the land following.

In a *jump* where a small or light dog might take off quicker, in Pluto's case a good anticipation will give you the weight feeling and at the finish or land, a good sag to the body and legs to a stop position up, or follow take to another action, is helpful.

B. *Slip Effect:* (ON ICE) In all slips with his head, two drawings were used going up. When his foot slipped, his body sagged, at the same time. The head shot up and after he collapsed, the body landed very quickly, but the head came around in an arc and then snapped through. When he hit, two drawings were squashed, then he came slowly out of it into a hold. He did not stop when he hit the ice.

C. *Rebounds:* When Pluto leaps and lands, he lands front feet first and then back feet. The whole body sags and in coming up, if he is still to remain in a crouch position, a drawing halfway between a first land position and the extreme sag position can be used as a final position for a hold. But in bringing him out of his lowest sag position, enough drawings are used to bring him up slowly into it so as to take up just a slight rebound. Possibly even in the case of him continuing the leap you could use the same rebound and then continue with him leaping forward into the air again. This is a

good example of giving the feeling that Pluto is a heavy dog. (See 1–A–3)

D. *Sniff Action:* Usually done in two drawings of two exposures each. One extreme down on the ground, with nose touching ground, another extreme is the nose up and wrinkled. It also can be handled on one exposure with four drawings with extremes up and down using in-betweens—close to the extreme up on starting down and close to the extreme down on the start up.

F. *Snort Action:* Anticipate back with Pluto's head and keep nose in normal position. In shooting head forward the nose wrinkles and the bulb increases in size, showing the nostrils in the extreme position which is the accent of the snort.

For a definite accent on the snort, draw back slowly with a swelling up of Pluto's body, together with a drawback of the head and then shooting into an extreme position with the nose wrinkled, mouth closed, teeth showing disgusted expression, and bulb showing nostrils, using one in-between with a pause settling back slowly from the extreme position but still in an attitude of having snorted.

G. *Sneeze:* Same as the snort except an open mouth is used.

H. *Barks:* In a bark the teeth show a little with the upper lip curving over and the gum showing. In short barks which are done in 6's, 3's and 4's, a turned up effect is used on the jowls at the extreme position, giving the feeling of flesh in an extreme wide open mouth.

III. Handling of Pluto for Expressions

A. In the laying out of Pluto's action on exposure sheets before animating, it is hard to anticipate the necessary feeling in certain spots where expressions

will be used. This sometimes means it will be necessary to add footage when such spots are reached in animation. For example, in the flypaper sequence (PLAYFUL PLUTO) as well as Pluto on ice skates (ON ICE), so much depended on the building up of the situation and the pauses for Pluto to think about different ways of getting rid of the flypaper or getting up on his feet on the ice. Good expressions were necessary in these spots to build the gag or situation to a climax. To arrive at the footage needed for such spots, as well as the follow up in action, the animator has to feel the situation himself. Of course, there can be too much time or stalling at certain points, although it has been found easier to cut down stalling in the rough test than to build up undertimed situations later on. The reason for this is that the animator works spontaneously when he feels the situation, and trying to crowd things into a given footage handicaps him to the extent of breaking the spontaneity of his work. This applies to any situation in cartoons, regardless of character. Of course, in building up a situation or gag, the value of each piece of business should be determined as to the amount of footage it can stand.

IV. General Working Method:

In roughing out action in a scene a good method to follow is to work from extreme to extreme as the action is visualized. This helps to hold the spontaneity of the situation or gag and prevents the animator from dwelling too much on an unimportant spot in the action. In going back over those drawings, extremes can be exaggerated when necessary, or a new slant may be had on different points throughout.

Jan.4,1936
E.T.   Norm Ferguson

The "GOOF."

Analysis of the Goof

It is difficult to classify the characteristics of the Goof into columns of the physical and mental, because they interweave, reflect and enhance one another. Therefore, it will probably be best to mention everything all at once.

Think of the Goof as a composite of an everlasting optimist, a gullible Good Samaritan, a half-wit, a shiftless, good-natured hick. he is loose-jointed and gangly, but not rubbery. He can move fast if he has to, but would rather avoid any over-exertion, so he takes what seems the easiest way. He is a philosopher of the barber shop variety. No matter what happens, he accepts it finally as being for the best or at least amusing. He is willing to help anyone and offers his assistance even where he is not needed and just creates confusion. He very seldom, if ever, reaches his objective or completes what he has started. His brain being rather vapory, it is difficult for him to concentrate on any one subject. Any little distraction can throw him off his train of thought and it is extremely difficult for the Goof to keep to his purpose.

Yet the Goof is not the type of half-wit that is to be pitied. He doesn't dribble, drool or shriek. He has music in his heart even though it be the same tune forever and I see him humming to himself while working or thinking. He talks to himself because it is easier for him to know what he is thinking if he hears it first.

His posture is nil. His back arches the wrong way and his little stomach protrudes. His head, stomach and knees lead his body. His neck is quite long and scrawny. His knees sag and his feet are large and flat. He walks on his heels and his toes turn up. His shoulders are narrow and slope rapidly, giving the upper part of his body a thinness and making his arms seem long and heavy, though actually not drawn that way. His hands are very sensitive and expressive and though his gestures are broad, they should still reflect the gentleman.

Never think of the Goof as a sausage with rubber hose attachments. Though he is very flexible and floppy, his body still has a solidity and weight. The looseness in his arms and legs should be achieved through a succession of breaks in the joints rather than through what seems like the waving of so much rope. He is not muscular and yet he has the strength and stamina of a very wiry person. His clothes are misfits, his trousers are baggy at the knees and the pant legs strive vainly to touch his shoe tops, but never do. His pants droop at the seat and stretch tighly across some distance below the crotch. His sweater fits him snugly except for the neck and his vest is much too small. His hat is of a soft material and animates a little bit.

The Goof's head can be thought of in terms of a caricature of a person with a pointed dome—large, dreamy eyes, buck teeth and a weak chin, a large mouth, a thick lower lip, a fat tongue and a bulbous nose that grows larger on its way out and turns up. His eyes should remain partly closed to help give him a stupid, sleepy appearance, as though he were constantly straining to remain awake, but of course they can open wide for expressions or accents. He blinks quite a bit.

He is very bashful, yet when something very stupid has befallen him, he mugs the camera like an amateur actor with relatives in the audience, trying to cover up his embarrassment by making faces and signalling to them.

He is in close contact with sprites, goblins, fairies and other such fantasia. Each object or piece of mechanism which to us is lifeless, has a soul and personality in the mind of the Goof. The improbable becomes real where the Goof is concerned.

He has marvelous muscular control of his fanny. He can do numerous little flourishes with it and his fanny should be used whenever there is an opportunity to emphasize a funny position.

This little analysis has covered the Goof from top to toes, and having come to his end, I end.

Art Babbitt

561

INDEX

Index

(Page numbers in italics refer to illustrations. Numbers in parentheses following film titles are dates of release.)

Aardel, Ed, 256–58

Abner Mouse *(The Country Cousin)*, 48

Academy Award, won by *The Old Mill* (1937), 78

Acting: animated film and, 23, 77, 99, 100–101, 165, 223, 332, *341*, 380, 393; emotions and, 473–505; rules for, 475; styles of, 13, 18, 223, 459, 471, 482

Action: analysis of, studied at Walt Disney Productions, 30, 72, 135, 320; real, lack in early animated films of, 30; types widely used in early animated film of, 42–45 *(see also under* specific terms of, e.g. Cycle action, Repeat action, Ripple action); types used in later animated film of, 133, 164; Walt Disney quoted on, 93, 441, 473

Actor, role of, in animated film, 18, 66, 167, 323, 474

Adventures of Ichabod and Mr. Toad, 73, 165, 490–91

Adventures of Mr. Toad, 79, 343

Aiming, 52. *(See also under* Animation, principles of, 47–69, 71)

Airbrush, use of, 258, 271–72, 279

Albatross *(The Rescuers)*, 206

Algar, Jim, *188, 332*

Alguire, Danny, 410, 426

Alice in Wonderland (7-28-51), *255, 300*, 301, *316, 465, 472*, 511

"Alice" shorts, 524

Alice the Beach Nut, 29

Alice's Wonderland, 29

"All the Cats Join In" *(Make Mine Music)*, 517

Analysis, importance as technique in animation at Walt Disney Productions, 47, 62, 80, 90 133, 530

Anatomy, study at Walt Disney Productions of, 333–36, 341–42, 254–56

Anderson, Ken, 167, *188, 191*, 215, *331, 360, 373–74, 398, 411, 416, 430, 437*; his career at Walt Disney Productions, 244, 246, 281; his ideas on planning and making layout, *218–19; quoted,* on Mary Blair's style of drawing, 192; on importance of eye blinking, 449;

on Don Graham's explanation of live action film of horse, 72; on Bill Tytla's high standards for layouts, 135

Anita, characterization of *(101 Dalmatians)*, 329

Animals, in animated films: live action films used for drawing of (at Walt Disney Productions), 331–65, *354–55;* acting and emotions of, 473–74, 475, 492–99, 504–07; character development of, 398–401, 405–14, 416–39; dialogue of, 455–71; expressions of, 442–54; story development and, 370–75, 379–80, 387, 389–91

Animation: definition of, 146–47; Walt Disney quoted on role of, 13, 243; fundamentals of, 174; future of, 27, 511, 531–35; history of, during birth and early days of, 13–27; during coming of age of, 74, 93–117; during period of greatest discovery in (1934–36), 71–91; during explosion of (at Hyperion Avenue Studios, 1931–39), 141–57 *(see also under* Walt Disney Productions, history of); during Golden Age of, 97, 135, 165; during period of Burbank and the Nine Old Men (1940–78), 159–83; during World War II, 159, 211, 266, 280, 511, 527; from 1946–present, 527–30 *(see also* Walt Disney Productions, history of); illusion of life as goal in, 13, 37, 146–47, 153, 164, 225, 473, 504–07; use of live action as reference for animators in, 319–65; general aspects as medium of, 15, 18, 69, 72, 75, 225, 235, 532, 535; twelve principles of, 47–69, 71 *(see also under* specific terms, e.g. Anticipation, Squash and stretch); procedures of, 185, 241 *(see also under* specific procedures, e.g. Clean-up; Handout; Pose test); styles of, other than believable, 204, 221–23, 311, 510–21, 528–31; terminology and jargon of, 47

Animation Board, 159–60, 167; second and final photograph of, *161*.

(See also under Nine Old Men)

Animation effects, role in Walt Disney Productions of, 251–59

Animator(s): as artists, 16; art classes and (Chouinard's Art Institute, and Walt Disney Productions), 30, 35, 71, 104, 107, 120, 142, 177; development of role at Walt Disney Productions of, 71–91, 93–139, 141–57, 159–83, 223, 225, 226–28, 439, 473, 491, 535; *photographs of:* Churchill, Jackson, Tytla, *81;* three directors, 1934 (Hand, Jackson, Sharpsteen), *84;* caricatured, as Captain Hook, (Davis, Johnston, Kahl, Kimball, Mallery, Thomas), *171;* first Moviola and, *82;* first New York animators at Walt Disney Productions, *31;* staff of Walt Disney Productions in 1927, *30;* staff in 1932, *80;* new team, trained by Ub Iwerks, *31;* "The Team," *188 (see also under* specific names of animators, e.g. Clark, Les; Reitherman, Woolie); Sweatbox 4 and, 157; role of young animators at Walt Disney Productions, 15–16, *67, 72,* 83–84, 146, 222, 397, 473, *535*

Anthony, Richard, *250*

Anticipation, as principle of animation: aiming and, *52;* audience need for, in animated film, 51–52; Les Clark quoted on innovative quality compared to present common usage of, 53; Walt Disney's interesting demonstration of, 53; Donald Duck as illustration of, *52;* role leading to "punch line" and to follow-through of, 61

Appeal, as principle of animation: importance in characterization of, 68–69; illustrations of, *68 (Sleeping Beauty, Lady and the Tramp);* compared to weak drawing, 68

"Aquarela do Brasil" *(Saludos Amigos)*, 517

"Arabian Dance" sequence *(Fantasia)*, 273–74, *274*, 278

Aracuan bird *(The Three Cabal-*

leros), 169, 524, *525*

Archimedes *(The Sword in the Stone)*, 467, 468

Arcs, as principle of animation: 47, 62–63, 229; illustrations of, *346, 348–49*

Aristocats, The (12-24-70), *187, 204,* 234, 298–99, *335, 342,* 343, 430, *470*, 495

Art, role of, shared with animation, 13, 15, 323, 531

Art of Skiing, The, 380

Art Students League, 134

Assistant Director: role at Walt Disney Productions of, 200, 207, 229, 232, 275–76, 299, 312–13

Astaire, Fred, 120

Atencio, Xavier, 519

Audience response to animation, as important goal of animated film, 15, 18–19, 22, 74, 250, 293, 297, 484–87, 507, 509, 512, 530, 532, 535

Audley, Eleanor, 321

"Ave Maria" sequence *(Fantasia)*, 264–66, *521*

Babbitt, Art, *54–55, 376, 394; quoted,* on animation testing at Hyperion Avenue Studio, 142

Babes in the Woods (11-19-32), 75

"Baby Weems" *(The Reluctant Dragon)*, 513

Background(s), role of, in getting animated drawings on the screen, *246–47,* 250; and emotion, 487; styles of (specific films), *246–48, 250;* role of, realized by background man (background painter), 215, 232, 244–45, 248–51, 232, 244–45, 248–51, 269

Baduns *(101 Dalmatians)*, 326, 329, 401, 419, *420*, 421

Bagheera *(The Jungle Book)*, 205, *405, 420, 424–25*

"Baia" *(The Three Caballeros)*, 515, *516*, 524, *525*

Baker, Buddy, 286

Baker, Ted, 386

"Ballerina Blossom" sequence *(Fantasia)*, 272–73